The American

This is a definitive history of the American Army's role and performance during the First World War. Drawing from a rich pool of archival sources, David Woodward sheds new light on key themes such as the mobilization of US forces, the interdependence of military diplomacy, coalition war-making, the combat effectiveness of the AEF and the leadership of its commander John J. Pershing. He shows us how, in spite of a flawed combat doctrine, logistical breakdowns and the American industry's failure to provide modern weaponry, the doughboys were nonetheless able to wage a costly battle at Meuse-Argonne and play a decisive role in ending the war. The book gives voice to the common soldier through first-hand war diaries, letters and memoirs, allowing us to reimagine their first encounters with regimented military life, their transport across the sub-infested Atlantic to Europe, and their experiences both in and behind the trenches.

DAVID R. WOODWARD is Emeritus Professor of History at Marshall University, Huntington, West Virginia

Armies of the Great War

This is a major new series of studies of the armies of the major combatants in the First World War for publication during the war's centenary. The books are written by leading military historians and set operations and strategy within the broader context of foreign policy aims and allied strategic relations, national mobilisation and domestic social, political and economic effects.

Titles in the series include:

The American Army and the First World War

David R. Woodward

CAMBRIDGE
UNIVERSITY PRESS

CAMBRIDGE
UNIVERSITY PRESS

University Printing House, Cambridge CB2 8BS, United Kingdom

Cambridge University Press is part of the University of Cambridge.

It furthers the University's mission by disseminating knowledge in the pursuit of education, learning and research at the highest international levels of excellence.

www.cambridge.org
Information on this title: www.cambridge.org/9781107011441

© David R. Woodward 2014

First published 2014

Printed in the United Kingdom by Clays, St Ives plc

A catalogue record for this publication is available from the British Library

Library of Congress Cataloguing in Publication data
Woodward, David R., 1939–
The American army and the First World War / David R. Woodward.
    pages cm. – (Armies of the Great War)
Includes bibliographical references.
ISBN 978-1-107-01144-1 (Hardback) – ISBN 978-1-107-64886-9 (pbk.)
1. United States. Army. American Expeditionary Forces.   2. World War, 1914–1918–United States.   3. World War, 1914–1918–Campaigns.   I. Title.
D570.W57 2014
940.4'0973–dc23   2013050333

ISBN 978-1-107-01144-1 Hardback
ISBN 978-1-107-64886-9 Paperback

To Frank Buckles
The last American veteran of
World War I who died on his farm in
West Virginia at age 110 in 2011.

Contents

Figures

Maps

All maps are adapted from *American Armies and Battlefields in Europe* (Washington, DC: Government Printing Office, 1995)

Tables

Preface

My commander-in-chief, Michael Watson, the capable and patient military history editor for Cambridge University Press, presented me with a formidable objective in late 2010: write a holistic history of the US Army's role in World War I that examined diverse social, political, diplomatic, and military themes. At times during the past two years I have felt as if I were one of Pershing's Doughboys attempting to navigate the unfamiliar and intricate German defenses at Meuse-Argonne. Indeed, their persistence was required to achieve my assigned mission.

Once the United States becomes a belligerent I address multiple themes, including the raising, training, transporting, and logistical support of a diverse force which included African and Native Americans as well as many other hyphenated Americans, coalition warfare (a new experience for the US military and political leadership), failures in war production, the interdependence of armed force and diplomacy, armed intervention in Russia, and the creation of an independent US force with its own strategical objectives. Although this narrative with its emphasis on leaders such as Pershing and Wilson generally embraces a top-down rather than a bottom-up approach, ordinary American soldiers are given their due by including their voices through the use of letters, memoirs, and other personal accounts. Finally, by placing the American Expeditionary Force's role within the larger war, I avoid examining American participation exclusively from a US perspective.

This account is much indebted to recent scholarship on America's involvement in World War I but it will stand on its own because of its holistic approach. I wish to recognize and express my considerable debt to the scholarship of the older generation of Great War historians, which includes Edward Coffman, Robert Doughty, David Trask, Robert Ferrell, Allan Millett, John Milton Cooper, Timothy Nenninger, Donald Smythe, Daniel Beaver, Holger Herwig, Russell Weigley, and Arthur Link, as well as the rapidly expanding new generation of scholars with their original insights, which includes David Stevenson, Mark

Grotelueschen, Richard Faulkner, Robert Bruce, Elizabeth Greenhalgh, Douglas Johnson, Jennifer Keene, and Michael Neiberg.

I am also exceedingly grateful for the support of the Marshall University history department, especially its chair Daniel Holbrook and its administrative secretary Teresa Bailey, the latter having assisted, really mothered, the history faculty for almost two decades. The university library staff, especially members of Special Collections and Government Documents, generously gave of their time and the university administration provided me with office space following my retirement to work on this and other manuscripts. The West Virginia Humanities Council awarded me with a fellowship that supported archival research at the United States Army Military History Institute at Carlisle, Pennsylvania and elsewhere. I remain most appreciative of the advice and assistance that I received from staff members at Carlisle and elsewhere in both the United States and Great Britain. I owe a special debt to Edward Coffman, "Mac" to his friends, who reviewed the entire manuscript with his always astute and knowledgeable eye, sharing valuable insights with me. Any errors in fact or interpretation, of course, are my responsibility. Facets of this manuscript have previously been published in my *Trial by Friendship: Anglo-American Relations, 1917–1918.*

Finally and most importantly I express my appreciation to my wife and closest friend of over four decades, Martha Cobb Woodward, whose encouragement and sharp proof reading skills played a major part in bringing this manuscript to fruition.

Abbreviations

AEF	American Expeditionary Force
AFG	American Forces in Germany
AHEC	Army Heritage and Education Center, Carlisle, Pa.
AUAM	American Union Against Militarism
AWOL	absent without leave
BEF	British Expeditionary Force
BL	British Library, London
CAB	Cabinet Papers, The National Archives, Kew, United Kingdom
CCC	Civilian Conservation Corps
CIGS	Chief of the Imperial (British) General Staff
CPI	Committee on Public Information (United States)
CTCA	Commission on Training Camp Activities
DAN	*Détachement d'Armée du nord* (Northern Army Detachment)
DMO	Director of Military Operations
Doughboys	nickname for US soldiers in Europe; also called "Sammies"
FO	Foreign Office (British)
GHQ	General Headquarters
GOC	General Officer Commanding
GQG	*Grand Quartier Général* (Supreme Headquarters of French Army)
IWC	Imperial War Cabinet (British)
IWM	Imperial War Museum, London
LHCMA	Liddell Hart Centre for Military Archives, King's College London
LOC	Library of Congress, Washington, DC; also Line of Communications
MID	Military Intelligence Division (United States)

NA	National Archives, Washington, DC; also The National Archives (formerly Public Record Office), Kew, United Kingdom
NAM	National Army Museum, London
NCO	non-commissioned officer
NLS	National Library of Scotland, Edinburgh
OHL	*Oberste Heeresleitung* (Supreme Army Command)
OTC	Officer's Training Corps (United States)
poilus	nickname for French soldiers ("hairy ones")
POW	prisoner of war
PWW	*The Papers of Woodrow Wilson*, ed. Arthur Link, 69 vols. (Princeton, NJ: Princeton University Press, 1966–94)
RG	Record Group, National Archives, Washington, DC
ROTC	Reserve Officers' Training Corps
SOR	Services of the Rear
SOS	Services of Supply
SWC	Supreme War Council (inter-Allied body created late 1917)
Tommy	nickname for British soldier (from "Tommy Atkins")
U-boat	*Unterseeboot* (German submarine)
USAWW	Department of the Army, Historical Division, *United States Army in the World War, 1917–1918*, 17 vols. (Washington, DC: Government Printing Office, 1948)
USMC	United States Marine Corps
WC	War Cabinet (British)
WIB	War Industries Board
WO	War Office records, The National Archives, Kew, United Kingdom
WP	War Cabinet papers, The National Archives, Kew, United Kingdom
WPC	War Policy Committee (British)
WWIS	*World War I Survey* (US Army Military History Institute)

Introduction

Despite its expanding population and booming economy, the United States had the smallest armed force of any major power prior to World War I, essentially an Indian constabulary. It is true that prewar reforms had federalized the National Guard, providing for a more ready and better-trained reserve, created a General Staff, and established an enhanced system of officer education that included the War College. This provided the framework for a modern military force, but the American public continued to associate universal military service and large and well-armed forces with militarism. With an authorized strength of only 3,820 officers and 84,799 men, the volunteer US Army consequently did not possess either the manpower or the modern weaponry to conduct a campaign in Europe, much less against a great power such as Germany, when the United States entered the war in April 1917.

Many Americans initially hoped to wage war against Berlin with the country's navy, finances, and industrial, agricultural, and natural resources such as oil. But it soon became obvious that soldiers must be dispatched to European battlefields.

Two men in particular are destined to dominate America's role in the war: President Woodrow Wilson, the son of a Presbyterian minister, and General John J. Pershing, a Missourian country boy of Alsatian ancestry. Wilson made a critical and war-winning decision when he abandoned the American tradition of voluntary military service and embraced conscription, which made possible an American force of some 2 million men in Europe by the Armistice of November 11, 1918. Never before had the United States fought a war without an army recruited by the states. At the same time conscription also required new and enlightened approaches by the army's leadership in dealing with the rank and file. The Progressive movement played an important role in this but pressure from citizen soldiers also created a new relationship between the leaders and the led.

After choosing Pershing as commander-in-chief of the American Expeditionary Force (AEF) Wilson gave him virtual control over America's military role in Europe. Although the United States was involved in a coalition war no American field commander has before or since been given a freer hand to conduct military operations. Convinced of the superiority of the American people and their traditions, Pershing planned to show the British and the French how to defeat the Germans. He and his staff subsequently developed plans for what they expected to be a war-winning American offensive against Metz in 1919, an objective destined to play a critical role in America's relationship with its war partners in 1918.

Pershing's vast powers created a dysfunctional chain of command between the War Department and GHQ which hampered the war effort. On the other hand, it can be argued that Pershing was right in both his determination to create an independent US Army in Europe and his opposition to amalgamating US troops with under-strength French or British divisions. Without question the British and French faced a perilous military situation during the spring of 1918 and feared that they would be overwhelmed by the series of powerful German offensives without the United States feeding troops into their battle-depleted divisions. At the same time the British and French frequently had ulterior motives. For example, the British sought to substitute US manpower on the British front for troops to be employed in the outer theaters to protect or expand the British Empire. Moreover, when Americans were placed under foreign command as was the case in the undeclared war in north Russia, the experience was not a happy one for the Americans. An independent US Army playing a key role in Germany's defeat also seemed essential if Wilson were to succeed in imposing a liberal peace settlement on both the enemy and America's coalition partners. Although the US Army's leadership did not have the benefit of a Joint Chiefs of Staff or a National Security Council to integrate political, economic, and strategic planning it embraced military policies generally in harmony with Wilson's political objectives.

Some readers may be disappointed that this is not triumphal or celebratory history. This wide-ranging account of the creation of a modern US Army and its role in World War I also does not examine American participation exclusively from a US perspective. Rather it places the role of the American Expeditionary Force within the larger war and examines the tactical and operational successes and failures of the opposing forces. Particular attention is paid to AEF doctrine that emphasized self-reliant infantry armed with rifles and bayonets. Although this doctrine may well have made US soldiers more aggressive than their European counterparts it contributed to unnecessarily high casualties. The rapid and unprecedented expansion of the US Army and the haste in which Doughboys were deployed on European battlefields also negatively affected combat readiness and increased casualties. Some soldiers were actually sent into battle without having previously fired the rifle they carried. Many junior officers were also almost as inexperienced as the men they led. This, however, was not Pershing's fault. He fought with the troops that the War Department sent him, and the American leadership believed that it had no choice but to send every available man to Europe to avoid a German victory during the first half of 1918.

Breakdowns in logistics (or Services of Supply (SOS)) and the inability of US industry to provide the AEF with modern weaponry also undermined the American war effort. During the last months of the war the AEF found itself desperately short of the supplies and the SOS personnel it required to sustain American forces in the field. US industry had been capable of building great warships with powerful guns but failed to provide Doughboys with the required equipment to fight a modern war. As the war abruptly and surprisingly ended in November, the AEF remained a "beggar" army, dependent upon its allies, especially the French, for tanks, aircraft, and artillery.

Although many obstacles had to be overcome, the AEF eventually proved itself on the battlefield and played a decisive role in Germany's defeat. The French and the British were quick to criticize (belittle is not too strong a word) the AEF's performance at Meuse-Argonne (the costliest battle in American history), but Doughboys learned to fight as they fought. Faced with certain defeat, especially after the American First Army's breakthrough and rapid advance at the beginning of November, the German high command felt that it had no choice but to accept an armistice despite Allied terms that amounted to unconditional surrender.

For many Americans World War I remains the forgotten war. This may change with the 100th anniversary of the Great War in 2014. And it should. The United States mobilized some 4 million men in 1917–18 and sent half that number to Europe. Although involved in intense combat for only some 110 days, the AEF played an essential role in preventing the Second Reich from establishing hegemonic control of Europe. That US forces would have to return to European battlefields some two decades later to assist the Russians and British in destroying Hitler's Third Reich should in no way diminish this achievement.

1 Birth of a modern army

On the evening of February 15, 1898, Captain Charles D. Sigsbee, the commander of the second-class battleship USS *Maine*, dispatched a shocking report to the Secretary of the Navy. His modern warship had been ordered earlier from Key West to Havana to protect US citizens from the turbulence of an insurgency against Spanish rule in Cuba. At 9:40 p.m. a tremendous explosion in the stern had rocked his warship which quickly sank to the bottom. This explosion killed 266 members of his crew.

What had happened? "The loss of this magnificent battleship is the most remarkable known to naval history," editorialized the Milwaukee *Journal*. "Ships have floundered, burned, been wrecked, and in many ways destroyed; but it remained for a vessel of the best type to be blown up and burned in a peaceful harbor. It is difficult to imagine, in the absence of full information, how the accident occurred."[1] A US Naval enquiry concluded that the explosion had been caused by a mine but did not attempt to fix blame. (Careful enquiries following the Spanish–American War suggested that the explosion had been caused by a spontaneous combustion in one of the *Maine*'s coal bunkers which ignited the forward magazines.)

Encouraged by an overheated popular press, many Americans concluded that Spain was responsible for the sinking of the *Maine*. Patriotic fervor swept the country. The war cry was sounded: "Remember the Maine! To hell with Spain!" On April 19, 1898, Congress authorized the President to employ force to secure the independence of Cuba. In response to the subsequent US naval blockade of Cuba, Spain declared war on the United States on April 23, 1898.

As Allan Millett has noted, the United States became involved in a "conflict that should not have been fought and could not have been lost."[2] Nonetheless the US Army was not prepared to fight overseas. With five battleships to Spain's one, the US Navy was ready for war. The same could not be said of the Regular Army, which existed as a small constabulary force designed to police Indians. The threat of Indian

4

uprisings was now more imagined than real. The last major encounter with Indians had been the Massacre of Wounded Knee in South Dakota in 1890 when approximately 500 troopers from the 7th Cavalry had killed perhaps as many as 300 men, women, and children of the Lakota Sioux. The Army also manned the powerful 8-, 10-, and 12-inch guns of the coastal batteries mounted on both disappearing and barbette carriages. As tension had developed between Spain and the United States, Congress had authorized $50 million to the Army and Navy for national defense. Secretary of War Russell A. Alger subsequently took his share of these Congressional funds and spent almost all of it on strengthening coastal defenses rather than modernizing the Regular Army, which had an authorized strength of only 28,747 officers and men at the outbreak of the Spanish–American War. By contrast, Spain had as many as 80,000 troops in Cuba.

Once at war Congress quickly raised the authorized size of the Regular Army to 64,719 officers and men. Granted the authority by Congress, President William McKinley also asked for 125,000 volunteers. Many of these volunteers came from state militias. The courts had not determined that the President had the authority to order militiamen (or National Guardsmen) to serve outside the country so they volunteered individually for federal service. Later, in May, the President issued a second call for 75,000 volunteers. Manpower, however, did not prove to be a problem as many young Americans flocked to the colors. When the war ended in August 1898, the nation had 263,609 enlisted men and 11,108 officers under arms.[3]

Equipping, training, supplying, and transporting these eager recruits to foreign battlefields, however, initially had seemed beyond the War Department's capabilities. Many American soldiers marched off to war carrying single-shot, breech loading, black-powder .45–70 Springfields. The allegedly backward Spanish soldiers were equipped with smokeless Mausers with twice the range of the .45–70 Springfield. Spanish artillery also outgunned American artillery with its smoke powder and limited range. The Chief of Ordnance, General Daniel Flagler, later offered the following justification for his department's failure to provide the Army with modern weapons. "A nation that does not keep a standing army ready equipped is still less likely to undergo the great cost of changing arms in store in order to be always ready to furnish the latest and most improved patterns immediately."[4] Flagler, of course, was correct that money could be saved by not adopting the most current advances in weaponry and standardizing the production of them. This pleased Congress which controlled the purse strings but it meant that the US Army would always be at a disadvantage if forced into a war with another great power. Doughboys, for example, needed the superior American-made Browning machine guns and automatic weapons in 1917–18, not during the final weeks of the war when they at last began to arrive on the battlefield.

As a constabulary force, the Regular Army began the war with no unit larger than a regiment and tactics and weapons more suited to fighting Apaches than Europeans.[5] The press had a field day with the confusion, congestion, and delay at Port Tampa that characterized the War Department's efforts to load men and supplies on transport ships destined for Santiago. Tampa was the closest US port to Cuba but it lacked the necessary rail and port facilities. Rations, critical to the morale of any army, also proved to be a serious problem. The Commissary Department supplied troops with tasteless canned boiled beef which was never intended to be eaten uncooked and unseasoned. During the siege of Santiago, "the very sight of canned beef began to nauseate the men, and fewer and fewer of them could keep it down if they could manage to eat it at all."[6] There had been no up-to-date information on Spanish forces or accurate maps of either Cuba or the Philippines. Medical services for the sick and wounded had also been deplorable.

America's most spectacular victory in the Spanish–American War came at sea. On May 1, Commodore George Dewey's ships destroyed an entire Spanish fleet at Manila Harbor. "The guns of Dewey at Manila have changed the destiny of the United States," trumpeted the *Washington Post*. "We are face to face with a strange destiny and must accept its responsibilities."[7] And indeed the United States emerged from the war as a world power with an overseas empire that included the Hawaiian Islands, Guam, the Philippines, and Puerto Rico.

American forces were now deployed well beyond North America and would continue to remain there until the present day. But at the turn of the century this had been done almost unconsciously. Unlike other world powers, most Americans did not associate their new global position with military strength. They continued to believe that they should base their country's diplomacy on a superior morality rather than on armies or even navies. Entangling alliances should be avoided at all cost. "Blinding themselves to the inescapable obligations of their new world role," Foster Rhea Dulles has written, "they somehow thought they could avoid responsibility – in Asia and in Europe – by merely declaring their right to go their own way. Had isolationism really been abandoned in realistic acceptance of the twentieth-century world, history would have followed a quite different course."[8]

Protected by two great oceans, weak neighbors, an established balance of power on the European continent, and a benevolent domination of the high seas by the British navy, Americans had reason to feel secure from foreign threats at the beginning of the twentieth century. This was not true of European great powers with the possible exception of Great Britain. Although the English Channel did not provide the British with the same sense of security that the Pacific and Atlantic afforded Americans, a successful cross-channel invasion still seemed unlikely as long as the British maintained their naval supremacy and the Low Countries remained independent. This largely explains why, among the world's great powers, only the United States and Great Britain, which shared a historical aversion to large standing armies, had small volunteer forces. As for the Continental powers, their insecure borders and powerful neighbors encouraged them to train a majority of their able-bodied young men for war. When war erupted in August 1914 anywhere between 15 million and 19 million men were quickly mobilized.[9]

The creation of mass conscript armies coincided with a revolution in military technology that dramatically altered the face of war. The industrial revolution brought forth advanced weapons of unprecedented killing power, and the emergence of two rival blocs, the Triple Entente (France, Russia, and Great Britain) and the Triple Alliance (Germany, Austria–Hungary, and Italy), served as the catalyst for an unprecedented arms race.

Although the American people could conceive of no necessity that would require embracing the European military model of mass armies based on universal service, the perceived mismanagement of the war with Spain revealed command-and-control weaknesses that Army reformers exploited to effect change. America's chaotic mobilization was blamed on the absence of prewar planning and a lack of professionalism. The left hand frequently did not know what the right hand was doing.

Technical advances and the existence of armies of unprecedented size certainly made military campaigns more complicated. Warfare now required more than just a "great captain" of war such as Napoleon Bonaparte. The Prussians, with their efficient and complete victories over the Austrians in 1866 and the French in 1870, had apparently mastered the complex problem of mobilizing, transporting, deploying, and supplying mass armies. Rather than relying on a single "genius," the Prussians waged war with a committee composed of technicians and highly trained officers who served as the "brain" of the army and taught a philosophy (or doctrine) of war. Located in a red brick building (the Red House) on Königsplatz opposite from the Reichstag, the German General Staff had been widely copied by other great powers.[10]

Secretary of War Elihu Root, a prominent corporation lawyer, emerged as the champion of the Army's modernization. In 1899, when

President McKinley had asked him to replace Secretary of War Alger, whose competence was widely being questioned, Root's response had been: "I know nothing about war. I know nothing about the army."[11] Nonetheless, he proved to be the right man for the job. He understood that the existing Army establishment was unsuited to America's new role as a world power and he had political skills to gain Congressional support. He was soon telling Congress that America's military system had no "directing brain which every army must have to work successfully. Common experience has shown that this cannot be furnished by any single man without assistants, and that it requires a body of officers working together under the direction of a chief and entirely separate and independent from the administrative staff of an army."[12]

Ironically, some of the strongest opposition to reform, especially the creation of a general staff, came from within the War Department, especially from the Commanding General of the Army, Nelson Appleton Miles, who had risen through the ranks. Headstrong, ambitious, and egotistical, Miles had presidential aspirations. Teddy Roosevelt famously called him a "brave peacock." A self-educated soldier, he had won promotion on the battlefield and held officers who had attended West Point in contempt. He strongly opposed the creation of a committee of "educated soldiers" modeled after the German General Staff that would supplant the Commanding General of the Army, who in reality received his authority from the Secretary of War and was not truly a "commanding" general in anything but name. Miles was joined in his opposition by many other senior officers who "having learned by practice, discounted the power of study, soft officers weakened by swivel chairs, lazy officers who wanted no post-commission education, and political officers with friends in Congress."[13] The bureau chiefs, who controlled armaments, the flow of information, and logistics, proved to be especially formidable opponents. Because of their long tenure in the War Department, the bureau chiefs were embedded in the Washington establishment and had powerful friends on Capitol Hill because of their power to award lucrative army contracts.

Moving cautiously, Root first concentrated on broadening military education beyond the military academy at West Point. He reorganized the Infantry and Cavalry School at Fort Leavenworth, Kansas and opened it to officers who had been commissioned from the ranks as well as to West Pointers. From 1902 to 1904, a one-year course, named the General Service and Staff College, served largely as a remedial program for junior officers, most of whom had never attended college. In 1904, a second-year and more rigorous program of study was established. The first-year program, renamed the School of the Line in 1907, emphasized tactics. The second and more selective year of study, called the Staff College, focused on war games and military history with little attention being given to strategic planning and administration.[14] After gaining an appropriation of $20,000 from Congress, Root by a general order in November 1901 also established the War College Board (the forerunner of both the Army War College and the General Staff), which he envisaged as a war planning agency in association with a future general staff.[15]

Gaining Congressional approval for a general staff, however, proved much more difficult. General Miles fired the first broadside, telling the Senate Committee on Military Affairs that the establishment of a general staff represented a threat to American principles and democratic values. Root fought back by taking his case to the press and enlisting the support of prominent military leaders. Root won in the end. The General Staff Act in 1903 created a Chief of Staff, two other general officers, and forty-two junior officers. These officers, assigned to one of three divisions, dealt separately with the following areas: administrative matters, military intelligence, and military education and technical questions such as mobilization. The last of these divisions, the 3rd Division, was later renamed the War College Division because of its close relationship with the Army War College.

The creation of the General Staff also led to abolishing the office of General Commanding the Army, which traditionally went to the senior officer in the Army. After the Civil War this approach had resulted in the leadership of the Army by experienced and middle-aged officers such as Grant, Sherman, and Sheridan. This distinguished line of proven soldiers, however, had run its course leaving the position to the longest living major-general.

One problem in replacing the ranking line officer in the Army by a chief of the General Staff was that his role appeared to be that of another bureau chief. Root got around this difficulty by using the title "chief of staff" instead of "chief of *the* general staff" which indicated that the head of the general staff supervised line officers as well as staff officers.[16] Although the chief of staff now coordinated the work of the War Department he still, of course, did not have commanding authority. That authority came from the Secretary of War who got his authority from the President. Another important change rotated staff officers between their desk jobs in the War Department and the line.[17]

Root's emphasis on professional training for officers proved critical to the Army's modernization. The War Department dispatched some American officers abroad to further their understanding of the armies of other great powers. In 1912, some Leavenworth graduates visited and observed the French, British, and German armies. Captain Fox Conner, who later became John J. Pershing's Chief of Operations, and some other junior officers actually served in French units. Earlier, Pershing, Peyton C. March, and Douglas MacArthur had been American military observers during the Russo-Japanese War, 1904–05. As Coffman has noted, "These officers in 1918 represented the harvest of the Root education system."[18] But the impact of his reforms on the efficiency and professionalism of the Army prior to America's entry into World War I should not be exaggerated. Less than 10 percent of the small officer corps in 1916 had actually graduated from either the Staff College at Fort Leavenworth or the War College in Washington, DC. Moreover, less than one-half of the officers selected to serve on the supposedly elite General Staff had actually received postgraduate military education.[19] Nonetheless, Leavenworth men dominated Pershing's staff in France, and of the twenty-nine US divisions that experienced combat on the Western Front only three did not have Leavenworth men as their chiefs of staff.[20]

As the "brain" of the army, the General Staff focused on the planning and directing of military operations rather than on day-to-day administration of the War Department. Yet General Staff members frequently found themselves dealing with trivial matters, which ranged from whether or not to issue toilet paper to determining the color of the stripes on army trousers.[21] The first Chiefs of Staff were also confused about their responsibilities. The bureau chiefs, who dominated the Army's logistics, filled this vacuum. As Russell Weigley has astutely noted: "The bureaus administered the Army *now*; the General Staff Corps, like the commanding general before it, was important for a war that only *might* happen."[22]

Having increased the authorized size of the Regular Army (the Army Reorganization Act of 1901), Root addressed the role played by the National Guard, the country's only reserve force in time of war. Indifferently trained and equipped and with questionable leadership, the National Guard operated on the basis of the Militia Act of 1792 which did not define the militia's relationship with the Regular Army. Root sent Colonel William Gary Sanger, the Inspector of the New York National Guard, to Europe to study how other great powers organized their reserve forces. Sanger found the British military organization with its volunteer army backed up by a reserve of militia and yeomanry cavalry to be most congenial with the American system.[23]

Not surprisingly Regular Army officers wanted a federal reserve that would be under its direction. Acutely conscious of the strong public support for the traditional militia, Root was not prepared to go that far. Convinced, however, that it was vital to have a better-trained militia closely aligned with the Regular Army, he pressed Congress to pass the so-called Dick Militia Bill (named after Congressmen Charles W. Dick of Ohio). "I earnestly urge that this measure be made a law," he wrote in his Annual Report for 1902.

> It is really absurd that a nation which maintains but a small Regular Army and depends upon unprofessional citizen soldiery for its defense should run along as we have done for one hundred and ten years under a militia law which never worked satisfactorily in the beginning, and which was perfectly obsolete before any man now fit for military duty was born.[24]

When passed, the Dick Militia Act provided for a much closer relationship between the traditional militia and the Regular Army. National Guard units, now equipped by the government, became the designated reserves of the Regular Army whose officers participated in the training of National Guard units. National Guard officers were also encouraged to attend Army postgraduate schools. Each year National Guard members now attended twenty-four local drills and spent an additional five days in the field, including joint maneuvers with the Regular Army.[25] Members of the militia were also admitted to the army schools but the results proved disappointing. Only three guardsmen graduated from the School of the Line from 1904 through 1916.[26]

Root's reforms created a framework for a modern fighting force but the Army still faced a basic dilemma: it remained too small to provide the necessary muscle to support the political or security concerns that would inevitably confront the United States in its new position as a great power. Although the United States had a population of approximately 100 million people by 1914, only a tiny percentage of its population actually served in the military. From 1910 to 1917, the Army enlisted as many as 30,000 men only nine times. Twice during this same time period, the number of recruits fell below 20,000. The actual number willing to enlist, however, was actually higher than these numbers suggest. Army recruiters and doctors rejected between 70 percent and 81 percent of those who tried to volunteer. Physical condition alone did not explain the high rejection rate. The Army rejected many young men because of illiteracy or their alien status.[27]

Racial prejudice, which was on the rise during the prewar years, also prevented some blacks from being accepted. Although never voted on, a proposal in Congress to prevent blacks from joining the military was presented each year from 1906 to 1916.[28] The Army actually needed little encouragement to limit black participation in the infantry and cavalry. Two of the fifteen cavalry regiments, the 9th and 10th Cavalry, were black. And out of thirty infantry regiments, only the 24th and 25th Infantry were black. On August 13, 1906, following a number of incidents including the pistol whipping of a black soldier in Brownsville, Texas, where a black battalion from the 25th Infantry was stationed, a small number of blacks went on a rampage that resulted in the death of a bartender and the wounding of a policeman. Although the local grand jury issued no indictments, the Army dishonorably discharged 167 black soldiers, in effect wiping out the battalion. This blanket punishment was clearly an injustice. A court inquiry in 1910 allowed fourteen men to reenlist (thirteen did so). But the remaining 153 had to wait until 1972 when they (there were only two survivors, one of whom had been allowed to reenlist) or surviving family members received some redemption. Under Congressional pressure, the Army upgraded their "dishonorable" discharge to "honorable."[29]

Infighting within the War Department threatened further significant Army reform prior to World War I. The chief protagonists were two major generals, Leonard Wood and Fred C. Ainsworth, both of whom had begun their military careers as army contract surgeons. Although Wood's command experience was negligible (he had participated in the campaign against Geronimo in 1886, almost dying from a tarantula bite), Secretary of War Alger appointed him colonel in command of the famous volunteer unit, the Rough Riders. It no doubt helped that Wood served as Alger's family physician.

In 1910, President Taft promoted the dynamic and strong-willed Wood to Chief of Staff to the initial dismay of some senior officers because of the latter's unconventional military background. Junior officers, who appreciated his managerial skills and professionalism, proved more forgiving of the apparent favoritism that led to his selection. Wood's most recent biographer portrays him as a product of the Progressive Era.

Just as individualistic captains of industry gave way to the more institutionally oriented corporate executives, so the "heroic officer" was supplanted by "military managers." In this era of mass armies when management techniques seemed as essential as tactics and strategy, officers with managerial capacities and perspectives appeared more valuable than traditional warriors.[30]

Ainsworth, who had introduced a successful card-index system for Civil War veterans in the Records and Pensions Office, had achieved fame because of his bureaucratic skills. (His popularity had also been enhanced with Congressmen because he made it a point never personally to turn down a request for a pension from a Civil War veteran.)[31] Skillful political infighters Woods and Ainsworth had the support of powerful political friends. Accustomed to getting their way, as one historian suggests, they "both loved to command but hated to be commanded."[32]

Ainsworth had become the Military Secretary (formerly Adjutant General) shortly after the General Staff had been created and a rivalry soon developed between the Adjutant General Department and the new General Staff. When the then Secretary of War Taft and his assistant secretary had been away from Washington, Taft had unwisely chosen Ainsworth to act as Secretary of War rather than the Chief of Staff. This encouraged Ainsworth to believe that he was the superior of the Chief of Staff.[33]

This "battle of the doctors" came to a head when army commanders supported the consolidation of the muster roles which currently required considerable busy work on their part. Ainsworth opposed this change and his anger grew when the General Staff took up the issue and began to interfere in other questions that Ainsworth believed to be the prerogatives of the Adjutant General. Ainsworth turned to a political ally, the new chairman of the House Military Committee, James Hay of Virginia. Hay obligingly drew up a bill to merge the General Staff with the Adjutant General's and Inspector General's Departments. Hay also intended that Ainsworth would replace Wood as Chief of Staff. Fortunately for Wood, Henry L. Stimson, a partner in Root's law firm who had volunteered during the Spanish–American War, became Secretary of War at this juncture. As tension escalated between Wood and Ainsworth, Stimson defended his Chief of Staff before Hay's Military Committee and implied to Ainsworth that he supported the General Staff's position on the muster roles. In his 4,000-word response Ainsworth let himself go, acidly commenting on the folly of "allowing young inexperienced officers to draft plans." This act of insubordination sealed Ainsworth's fate. When Stimson began court-martial proceedings and relieved Ainsworth from duty, the Adjutant General asked to be allowed to retire.[34]

Ainsworth, however, did not go quietly. A man of considerable means, he took up swanky quarters at the Concord Hotel in Washington, DC and nurtured his contacts within the Army and in Congress. In 1912, his supporters succeeded in reducing the number of officers on the General Staff to thirty-six in the Army Appropriation Act.[35] In 1913, he encouraged Congressman Hay, no friend of the General Staff, to attach riders to military appropriation bills that would have forced Wood out and given the Adjutant General's Department considerable influence over the General Staff by appointing thirteen of its members to that body.[36] If President Taft had not exercised his veto powers, Ainsworth and his supporters might have succeeded in fatally compromising the proper role of the General Staff.

As war clouds gathered over Europe, the General Staff turned its attention to assembling a mobile force to defend the country from foreign attack. Army units remained scattered across the United States in small "hitching post" forts that Congress refused to close. Few of these posts had more than 1,000 men. It had taken an embarrassing three months to assemble an under-strength "maneuver division" of 13,000 men in San Antonio in 1911 following an armed uprising in Mexico. A more critical question was how to expand the small professional army with trained soldiers in an emergency. The 1912 Report on the Organization of the Land Forces, initiated by Stimson and Wood, recommended that the United States model itself after the British professional army of volunteers backed up by the Territorials (a home defense force established in 1907 that in some respects was similar to the American militia). In contrast to Great Britain, the other great European powers had created mass armies through conscription.

The War College Division accepted that the creation of a large standing army was unacceptable to the public. But if the Regular Army could only serve as "the peace nucleus of the greater war army,"[37] how was it possible to create an effective reserve? In the view of professional officers, the existing militias with their short-term training seemed quite inadequate. Wood's solution had been to propose a system that encouraged new recruits to serve three years on active duty and then serve an additional three years in the reserve where they could be called to arms in an emergency. To improve the battle readiness of citizen soldiers Wood also wanted to enhance their training through the creation of a "national militia" – as opposed to the state militias – whose members would be subject to being drafted into the Regular Army. To secure officers for the national militia, the report suggested that West Point increase the number of its graduates and that colleges be encouraged to expand their military training. If Congress accepted the recommendations in the "Report on the Organization of the Land Forces of the United States, 1912," the General Staff anticipated that the United States could field a mobile force of 460,000 men.

An army of this size, however, did not seem possible when Congress continued to favor existing state militias over Wood's proposed national militia. Congress authorized an Army reserve, but not the one favored by Wood and Stimson where enlisted men served three years on active duty before being furloughed into a reserve for an additional four years. The 1912 Army Appropriations Bill gave the recruits a choice. They could sign up for a straight four years or they could commit to three years on active duty and then serve in an unpaid reserve for four years. This approach offered little or no incentive to become an unpaid reservist. When World War I began only sixteen reservists were ready to serve.[38]

Since the destruction of the USS *Maine*, Wood, Root, and other army reformers had laid the foundation stones for a modern professional army. A new relationship with the militia had been forged and a laudable system of army education established. Major General Robert Alexander, who had entered the Army as a private, gave credit to the reformed service schools and staff college at Fort Leavenworth for his successful command of the 77th Division during World War I. "That asset," he later wrote, "is, in my opinion, of such professional value that an officer can scarcely hope, without it, for fully successful command of troops in battle."[39]

But army reformers had been unable to build a fighting force commensurate with America's new status as a world power, and its "brain," the General Staff, remained a work in progress with its numbers severely restricted by Congress. Between 1903 and 1917 seven officers served as Chief of Staff. Only two of them, J. Franklin Bell and Wood, effected significant change. Bell remains the forgotten man. Three officers had already preceded him when he became Chief of Staff in 1906. Wood is given credit for taking on the bureau chiefs, but Bell confronted them first in an attempt to establish the General Staff's administrative authority. At the same time, Bell recognized that the General Staff's priority should be planning and intelligence. To accomplish this goal, he divided the General Staff into two sections in 1908, one in the War Department that coordinated the work of the bureaus, and another at the Army War College (the Second Section) which concerned itself with planning, intelligence, and education.[40]

When Lieutenant Colonel John A. Lejeune, a graduate of the Naval Academy and future Commandant of the Marine Corps, reported for duty at the War College in 1909 along with Fox Conner, Hunter Liggett, and some other officers who were destined to serve in Europe during World War I, he found that he had "a hard grind ahead" of him. For the first six weeks he frequently studied until two o'clock in the morning. Previously students had studied the Franco-Prussian War, 1870–71, working with maps of Germany and France, but a new President of the War College, Major General William W. Wotherspoon, insisted that they conduct war games where, according to Lejeune, he thought that "it was at least possible we might some day be called on to serve." Students now generally ignored Europe in their war gaming and concentrated on Hawaii, the Philippines, and the North America continent. "Eight years later," Lejeune writes,

I stood on the very ground the study of which had been discarded, and gazed at the distant spires of Metz ... it was beyond the powers of any man then living to foresee that in December, 1918 ... an American Army, victorious in many pitched battles on the frontiers of France, would march in triumph to the Rhine, cross that historic river where Caesar did, and occupy a bridgehead on its eastern bank.[41]

The American Civil War received the most attention during the fourteen-month curriculum. Lejeune in April and June 1910 toured Civil War battlefields on horseback. Later students made even more extensive horseback excursions. Students in 1913, for example, spent forty-seven days covering 637 miles on horseback as they toured the battlefields of Virginia, Maryland, and Pennsylvania. Tours of such battlefields as Antietam, Gettysburg, and Chancellorsville provided them with models for wars of maneuver. Unfortunately, as Coffman suggests, "apparently they paid little attention to the siege of Petersburg which would have offered them the closest model to the trench war which they were to face in France."[42] Nor did they apparently spend much time studying the more recent Russo-Japanese War which demonstrated the destructive power of modern weaponry.

According to Liggett, there was "nothing of the old-time Fourth of July sham battle" about his study. While at the War College the future commander of the US First Army remembered studying warfare in all of its aspects, including "supply, equipment, transport, mobilization of troops and industries, recruiting, training, replacements and disposition of the rapidly expanding army."[43]

Although the Army made important strides during the prewar years, important questions remained unresolved when general war erupted in Europe. Did the commanding authority of a Chief of Staff, for example, extend beyond the General Staff to the entire Army, especially one fighting abroad? Or was his primary role that of administrating the General Staff and when called upon serving as an adviser to the President and Secretary of War on military matters? And then there was the matter of the Army's manpower and armaments. A closer relationship had been established between the Army and the traditional militia by the Dick Act. But an effective national reserve remained to be created, and Congress showed no inclination to equip American soldiers to fight a modern war. Military aviation had its roots on February 10, 1908, when the US Army Signal Corps purchased an aircraft from the Wright brothers and had them provide flight instructions for two officers. Later that year Oliver Wright performed flying demonstrations for the French. The result: in 1913 Congress appropriated $125,000 for the new flying machines while the French appropriated $7,400,000.[44]

2   World war and American preparedness

Shortly before Woodrow Wilson took the oath of office as President, on March 3, 1913, he remarked to a friend that "it would be the irony of fate if my administration had to deal chiefly with foreign affairs."[1] Wilson had run on a campaign slogan of "New Freedom" by which he meant freedom of opportunity for all Americans and freedom from the domination of the great trusts. Yet his administration was soon to be confronted with the most precarious global situation for the United States since the War of 1812. As Europe moved closer to general war, Colonel Edward M. House, President Wilson's closest confidant, toured European capitals in May 1914. The report to the President that he filed from Berlin was ominous: "The situation is extraordinary. It is jingoism run stark mad."[2]

Within weeks House's prophecy became a reality. On June 28, a young Serb assassin gunned down Archduke Ferdinand, the heir to the Austrian throne, in the streets of Sarajevo, setting off a chain of events that led to general war. The American public generally looked on in horror as conscript European armies, equipped with weapons of unprecedented lethality, clashed. French losses, for example, were double the size of the US Army during the first twelve days of fighting. At the same time, the savage war being waged in Europe strengthened Americans' belief in American exceptionalism. That European powers in 1914 seemed bent on destroying each other with their mass armies demonstrated to many Americans the superiority of their system and its ideals which included an aversion to large standing armies or resorting to military force to achieve political objectives. The historical record might be at variance with the view that Americans were reluctant to bear arms.[3] But most Americans in 1914 had grown up in a time when wars, especially wars between "civilized" nations, were viewed as anachronistic.

In messages to Wilson, Walter H. Page, the US Ambassador in Great Britain, "thank[ed] 'Heaven for the Atlantic Ocean' and emphasized the 'deplorable medievalism of a large part of Europe' which prevented many of its leaders from appreciating the 'criminal folly and the economic suicide of war.'"[4] The popular maxim, "if you wish for peace, prepare for war," now seemed to be a dangerous fallacy. Americans hence took comfort in their country's isolated position and freedom from entangling alliances as well as the avoidance of universal military service which many Americans believed fostered militarism.

President Wilson responded to the outbreak of war in Europe by issuing an official proclamation of neutrality. Two weeks later he formally appealed to the American people to conduct themselves in a manner that would "best safeguard the nation against distress and disaster." Americans, he proclaimed, should "be impartial in thought as well as in action."[5]

Earlier Wilson had made a point of muzzling America's military leadership. On August 6, he had instructed his Secretary of War Lindley Miller Garrison to order all army officers, whether active or retired, to refrain from any comments "of any kind upon the military or political situation on the other side of the water."[6]

Clearly uncomfortable in his constitutional role as commander-in-chief of the armed forces, Wilson reacted angrily when someone sent him an etching that depicted him in military dress. Suspicious of the motives of men in uniform, he fiercely defended civilian supremacy over the military. According to Arthur Link,

he had no interest in military and naval strategy, little understanding of the role that force plays in the relations of great powers, and a near contempt of *Realpolitik* and the men who made it. Military men, he thought, should speak only when they were spoken to; and the suggestion that his military advisers might know more about important strategic matters than he was enough to evoke suspicions of a sinister attempt to undermine civilian control.[7]

Consequently, his administration initially made no effort to harmonize the country's military policy with its foreign policy objectives. Wilson's approach to preparedness in 1915–16, for example, had almost no connection to the global crisis that threatened to involve America in the war.

On February 4, 1915, the German Admiralty announced a submarine blockade of the British Isles, a decision certain to create greater tension between Washington and Berlin. On May 7, a German U-boat torpedoed and sank the British passenger liner *Lusitania* as it steamed through the Irish Sea on its way to Liverpool (1,198 of the 1,959 people aboard died, including 128 Americans). The *New York Times* expressed outrage: "From our Department of State there must go to the Imperial government at Berlin a demand that the Germans shall no longer make war like savages drunk with blood, that they shall cease to seek the attainment of their ends by the assassination of non-combatants and neutrals." In contrast to these fighting words, Wilson's initial response was passive. "There is such a thing as a man being too proud to fight," he proclaimed on May 10. "There is such a thing as a nation being so right that it does not need to convince others by force that it is right."

The President's response to the sinking of the *Lusitania* infuriated the future commander-in-chief of the AEF. "What do you suppose a weak, chicken-hearted, white-livered lot as we have in Washington are going to do?" John J. Pershing had earlier asked his wife after the sinking of the *Lusitania*. Wilson thus didn't surprise him with his "too proud to fight" statement. "Isn't that the damnedest rot you ever heard a sane person get off," he snorted.[8] Wilson quickly regretted his choice of words and his rhetoric grew stronger in the days ahead. In his third note to Berlin, he firmly said that any future sinking of passenger liners would be considered a deliberate and unfriendly act.

Growing tension between Berlin and Washington focused attention on the country's ability to back its diplomacy with force. James W. Gerard, the US Ambassador in Berlin, warned Wilson that "the Germans fear only *war* with us – but state frankly that they do not believe we dare to declare it, call us cowardly bluffers and say our notes are worse than waste paper."[9]

Despite the strain between Berlin and Washington, Wilson remained determined to keep the US Army small and professional soldiers in the background. Early in the autumn of 1915, the President abruptly summoned Henry Breckinridge, the acting Secretary of War, to his office. Breckinridge "found him holding a copy of the *Baltimore Sun* in his hand, 'trembling and white with passion.'" He angrily pointed to a paragraph that suggested that the General Staff was planning war with Germany and demanded that he conduct an investigation. If the allegations were proven true, Wilson wanted "to relieve at once every officer of the General Staff and order him out of Washington." Tasker H. Bliss, the President of the War College and acting Chief of the General Staff, attempted to reassure Breckinridge that there was nothing sinister about the War College's "war gaming." Since its inception, it had made a practice of studying the possibility of war with other countries, including Mexico, France, Japan, and Great Britain. This apparently satisfied Breckinridge who told Bliss that in future the War College should "camouflage" its studies.[10] The matter did not end there. When Wilson learned in 1916 that the War College had continued playing its war games, he once again raised questions, this time with his new Secretary of War, Newton D. Baker. "Mr. President," Baker responded, "they have made war at the War College with every country in the world."

The way they do it is to propose a problem. For example, 'Suppose we had a war with France.' Then a war is fought with France on paper, and the paper folded up and put away." Wilson was unconvinced. "That seems to me a very dangerous occupation," he told Baker. "I think you had better stop it." But in the days that followed Wilson decided to allow the War College to continue its studies but warned them through Bliss "to be on guard against receiving any publicity."[11]

Although Washington seemed determined to defend the nation's rights as a neutral, the size and organization of the Army remained unaffected by the war. The United States might have a male population of 54 million but few Americans had any military experience. With only 4,948 officers and 101,806 men,[12] the Regular Army in 1915 was ranked seventeenth in the world. Organized in small units, the Regular Army had no field armies, army corps, combat divisions, or brigades. It remained a constabulary force with added responsibilities because of the overseas expansion that had followed the Spanish–American War. In addition to being attached to coastal defenses in the United States, Regulars were scattered throughout the Caribbean and Pacific to police America's new colonial empire. Indicative of the nation's insularity the only branch of the Army prepared for a major conflict was the Coast Artillery Corps which numbered almost 20,000 officers and men.[13] In an emergency, the War Department believed that it had the resources to form a meager mobile force of only about 24,000 soldiers. Given time, the War Department hoped to field a force of 500,000 through volunteers and by mobilizing the anticipated 112,000 "ready reserves" of the militia. Despite prewar reforms, however, many professional soldiers continued to believe with some justification that these citizen soldiers were indifferently trained and poorly led.

It was also one thing to raise an army, quite another matter to equip one to fight an industrialized war against nations equipped with modern weapons. The War Department had adopted the 1903 model Springfield rifle, but it only had on hand enough of these excellent rifles to equip a force of half a million men and wars could no longer be won with rifles and bayonets. Automatic weapons and especially heavy artillery were proving to be the most deadly weapons available to the European powers. Congress in 1912 had funded only four machine guns per regiment, a tiny fraction of what modern warfare required. Moreover, the War Department had not even selected a standard machine gun to manufacture and would not do so until after the United States entered the war when it adopted the Browning water-cooled heavy machine gun and the Browning automatic rifle, both superior automatic weapons. American artillery was equally inadequate. As late as April 1917, the US Army had only 900 artillery pieces, most of which were light rather than heavy (the army, for example, possessed only a handful of 4.7-inch howitzers). Approximately 60 percent were old model 3-inch fieldpieces which were better suited to a war of movement than the prevailing trench warfare in Europe. Among other modern weapons, the US Army in 1915–16 lacked poison gas, flame throwers, mortars, and hand and rifle grenades. The Air Service Section of the Signal Corps possessed fifty-five obsolete aircraft, suitable for intelligence gathering but not for combat.[14] With almost no motorized transport the Regular Army depended upon horses and mules to transport its supplies. Given the size, organization, and killing power of the armies of America's possible European adversaries, the United States was less prepared to wage war than at any previous time in its history.

During the last half of 1915, the heightened debate over "preparedness" began to influence both American politics and army policy. Advocates of "preparedness" predated the sinking of the *Lusitania*. Theodore Roosevelt and Leonard Wood vigorously supported preparedness, and organizations such as the Army League, the Navy League, and the Security League argued that the United States lacked the force necessary to protect or further its national interests. With the exception of the US Navy, ranked fourth in the world, the country's first and really only line of defense, the United States appeared defense-less in a world increasingly dominated by force rather than reason.

Although "preparedness" advocates remained in the minority, their voices began to be heard, especially after German submarines threatened American commerce and lives on the high seas in 1915. Suggestions ranged from the reasonable to the ridiculous. In May the *New York Times* published an interview with one of America's most famous inventors, Thomas Edison. To defend the country from invasion and yet preserve its tradition of citizen soldiers and no large standing army in peacetime, Edison suggested that 40,000 men be trained as drill instructors. These men would then resume their civilian careers. If an invasion seemed imminent these drill instructors could quickly train volunteers who would then be rushed to the coastline in vast convoys of Model Ts. Meanwhile, giant machines would construct multiple lines of trenches for them to man. They would fight with modern weapons and munitions which had been produced and stockpiled. Declared Edison, "with our unlimited supply of the most intelligent and independently thinking individual fighters in the world we would be invincible."[15]

On July 21, 1915, Wilson asked Lindley M. Garrison, his Secretary of War, to advise him on "a proper training of our citizens to arms." On August 12, Garrison sent him a brief appreciation, "An Outline of

Military Policy," that rejected America's traditional dependence on state militias for its primary defense. Garrison bluntly informed the President that the National Guard as constituted was inadequate and should be superseded by a trained reserve, a "citizen force" of 400,000 men. He also urged Wilson to engage the public in a debate over the training and organization of America's land forces. Sensing a political bombshell, Wilson disagreed. He told his Secretary of War that "the method of preparedness is something which the country is not prepared to discuss."[16]

Meanwhile, a secret and thoroughgoing examination was already underway. Prior to Wilson's request in July, Garrison had instructed the General Staff in March "to make a complete and exhaustive study of a proper military policy for the United States."[17] Responsibility for this appreciation fell to the General Staff's planning unit, the War College Division, located outside of the War Department at Washington Barracks, which also housed the Army War College. Brigadier General Montgomery M. Macomb headed the War College Division, which worked closely with the Army War College. The War College Division's distant location at Greenleaf Point, however, meant that there was often little communication with their superiors Scott, the Chief of Staff, and Bliss, the Assistant Chief, who had their offices in the grand old State, War, and Navy Building with its mansard roof. The 1912 Report on the Organization of the Land Forces, initiated by Secretary of War Stimson and Chief of the General Staff Wood, served as the starting point for Macomb's review.[18]

In the event of an attack on the United States, the War College Division wanted the ability to expand quickly the armed forces. It recommended that "500,000 fully trained mobile troops" and "at least 500,000 more – a total of 1 million men – should be prepared to take the field immediately in the event of war and should have had sufficient previous military training to enable them to meet a trained enemy within three months. (Twelve months of intensive training was considered the minimum to prepare troops, whether militia or regular, for war service.)[19] The War College Division's recommendations, however, had no connection to the possibility that the current war being fought primarily on European soil might spill over to North America.

The War College Division's approach to reorganizing the armed forces mirrored in important respects the ideas of a reform-minded Civil War veteran, General Emory Upton. One of the army's more profound thinkers, General Emory Upton had campaigned for the creation of a European-style army following the Civil War. A protégé of General Sherman, Upton had been sent on a tour of Europe and Asia following the Franco-Prussian War, 1870–71, to study military organizations. Especially impressed with Germany's military organization, Upton worked for years on a manuscript on military policy which he had not quite finished when he committed suicide in 1884.

Widely circulated within the officer corps and studied at West Point, Upton's manuscript was eventually published in 1904 as "The Military Policy of the United States from 1775." Upton argued in favor of making the Regular Army the core around which any wartime force might be created. In the event of war "national volunteers" would be called upon to swell the ranks of the Regular Army. State militias, their role confined to maintaining public order in their areas, would only be used as a "last resort." Although left unsaid Upton implied that compulsory service might be necessary.

Upton understood that his system favored the central government over states' rights and might result in a stronger government. But it was his view that "no soldier in battle ever witnessed the flight of an undisciplined army without wishing for a strong government, but a government no stronger than was designed by the fathers of the Republic." Upton also warned that "battles are not lost alone on the field; they may be lost beneath the Dome of the Capitol, they may be lost in the private office of the Secretary of War. Wherever they may be lost, it is the people who suffer and the soldiers who die."[20]

Upton was not the first and would certainly not be the last soldier to argue that military policy was best left to the professionals and kept from the meddling hands of civilians. The fierce civil-military strife in most European countries during the Great War is a testament to this inevitable conflict. A cautionary note, however, is sounded by one of the most authoritative students of the US Army, Russell Weigley, who argues that Upton did "lasting harm" by encouraging military leaders to abandon "inherited institutions" and demanding "that national institutions be adjusted to purely military expediency."[21] In his defense David Fitzpatrick argues that Upton "was not an anti-democratic militarist, and that he believed his reforms would defend democracy, not destroy it."[22]

When submitted on September 11, 1915, the War College Division's "Statement of a Proper Military Policy for the United States" received an icy reception from Garrison, who had asked for such an appreciation but was unimpressed. When the War College Division stood behind its recommendations despite his strong objections, the plain-speaking Garrison did not mince words when he forwarded their statement to Wilson. After explaining the role of a general staff to the President, he emphasized that the War College Division's personnel did not compare favorably with European general staffs. Dominated by "officers of junior grades," it possessed the expertise to assess "technical matters of military science" but it should not be relied upon to formulate or justify "a military policy for the Nation."[23]

Their proposed expansion of the armed forces was also bound to be costly and unpopular with Congress. The Army's budget in fiscal year 1914/15 had been $116,127,753,[24] or about $2.5 billion in today's money.[25] In the first year of expansion, the War College Division estimated that it would quintuple the Army budget (figured to the last penny the estimate was $506,136,100.95),[26] a shocking and unprecedented increase for an American peacetime budget. On the other hand, John D. Rockefeller, whose personal wealth on the eve of World War I was approximately $900 million, could have personally funded this expanded army budget for almost two years.

Garrison subsequently ignored the War College Division's analysis and returned to his "An Outline of Military Policy" which he had earlier submitted to the President. Noting that he had the backing of both Scott and Bliss, the Assistant Chief of Staff, Garrison advocated a modest increase in the Regular Army and a trained reserve or "citizen" force of 400,000 men.

Garrison had an uneasy relationship with the President. The latter, supremely confident in his own judgment, did not welcome dissent. Garrison, who dared to interrupt him at Cabinet meetings, infuriated him. He believed that his Secretary for War focused "his entire attention on his own opinions and does not listen to mine." In a letter to Edith Bolling Galt, he dismissed this "self-opinionated politician" as "a solemn, conceited ass!"[27] Garrison held an equally jaundiced view of the President. Wilson's "over powering self esteem left no place for common counsel of which he talked so much and in which he did not indulge at all," he once noted.[28]

Wilson much preferred the elderly Scott, who was prone to fall asleep at his desk in the War Department, to Garrison. General Scott's brother, William B. "Wick" Scott, a senior faculty member at Princeton, had earlier supported Wilson in his rancorous disputes with faculty members over such issues as the graduate faculty. This perhaps led Wilson, after entering the White House, to promote Scott to major general. In Wilson's view he could not have been served by a better Chief of General Staff. Scott listened and did not disagree, perhaps because he had difficulty getting his points across in conversation. Dennis E. Nolan, who later headed the AEF's Intelligence Section, believed that "Scott was an inarticulate sort of a man and it was very difficult for him to express himself on something he knew perfectly well. He could read it but in a casual conversation and cross-questioning he was not quick. He would know it but he would have trouble answering it, and give the impression he didn't know, when he did know it."[29] Scott was clearly the opposite of the aggressive and opinionated Leonard Wood, who had been Chief of General Staff, 1910–14. Scott "entirely understood [his opinions] and entirely and intellectually obeyed," Wilson approvingly noted.[30] On this occasion, however, Wilson needed no prodding from Garrison to reject the ambitious and expensive preparedness program advocated by the War College Division. But the political dangers of altering America's traditional military system which relied upon the state militia greatly concerned him. And he had reasons to be apprehensive.

The War Department formally submitted its revised appreciation to the President on October 28. This plan recommended a modest increase in the Regular Army from 108,008 men and officers to 141,797.[31] But the heart of the "Garrison Plan" – a federal force of national volunteers called the Continental Army – "threatened to divide the country as had no other political issue since the Civil War."[32] Under federal control as opposed to the militia, the War Department planned to form a reserve force of 400,000 men, to be recruited over the next three years in annual contingents of 133,000 men. Recruits served two months a year for three years on active duty and then an additional three years as part of a "ready reserve." Acutely aware of the public's support of volunteer forces, Garrison cautioned the General Staff not to advocate compulsory military training. He also wanted it emphasized that the proposed Continental Army's role was strictly defensive.[33] In retrospect, what is striking about the War Department's consideration of a proper military policy for the United States was its isolationist stance. The United States would soon be forced into the war, but America's civil and military leadership emphasis remained firmly fixed on defending the country from some undetermined threat *after* the conclusion of the present global conflict.

Wilson launched his effort to gain Congressional support on November 4 at the Manhattan Club in the Biltmore Hotel. He made no attempt to connect the success of his diplomatic efforts to keep the United States out of the war with the country's military strength. Instead he proclaimed that "the mission of America in the world is essentially a mission of good will among men," and emphasized that war preparations were only being advocated for "defense."[34] Wilson's platitudes had little effect. National sentiment remained hostile to any strengthening of the armed forces either through the reform of the militia or through compulsory training. Prior to Wilson's speech, William Jennings Bryan, Wilson's great pacifist rival in the Democratic Party and his former Secretary of State, had proclaimed in his monthly magazine, the *Commoner*, that citizens should tell Congress "that this nation does not need burglars' tools unless it intends to make burglary its business; it should not be a pistol-toting nation unless it is going to adopt pistol-toters' ideas."[35]

Bryan and Wilson were both prominent members of the Progressive movement which included leaders from both parties. As social activists, Progressives focused on domestic reform and saw little or no connection between the European war and America's ability to defend itself or further its national interests through warlike means. When Progressives thought of world affairs, Link has suggested, most of them "believed that America's unique mission was to purify herself in order to provide an example of democracy triumphant over social and economic injustice and a model of peaceful behavior." Baker, who was as close to Wilson as any other member of his administration, notes:

From the time I went to Washington until we were nearly in the War, the President gave me the idea – although I could not quote anything he said – that to him the function of the United States was to be the peacemaker, and that the idea of intervening in the war was the last thought he had in the world. It was just not in the range of his mind. The President thought the War had made him an instrument of Providence, but he thought it humbly.[36]

As European rivalries intensified and as an arms race of unprecedented magnitude took place, Wilson apparently saw virtue in his country's military weakness. By occupying the high moral ground, the United States could provide enlightened and disinterested guidance to the other great powers. "A second major progressive conviction," according to Link, "was the belief that wars in the modern world were mainly imperialistic and economic in origin and, perforce, evil."[37]

Wilson would later understand that his country had to employ military force to make a liberal peace. But prior to America's forced entry into the war, he initially rejected the views of the Prussian officer Carl von Clausewitz. More philosopher than soldier, Clausewitz argued that war was a rational instrument of national policy. His famous dictum that "war is not merely a political act, but also a political instrument, a continuation of political relations or carrying out of the same by other means," did not ring true to Wilson and most of his countrymen at the beginning of the twentieth century.

The world in 1916, of course, looked quite different from the one that confronted Americans during and after World War II. Following the most destructive war in history, the two super powers which emerged after 1945, the United States and Soviet Russia, with polar opposite political and economic systems, competed for global domination. Fearing the spread of Communism, the United States signed entangling alliances, intervened militarily throughout the world, fighting undeclared wars in Korea and Viet Nam, built weapons of mass destruction, maintained a permanent and powerful army, air force, and navy, and developed a military-industrial complex of staggering dimension and expense.

With supporters of the National Guard up in arms, Congress actually needed very little encouragement from the press to oppose the "Garrison Plan," especially after Scott testified before the House Committee on Military Affairs on January 10. The Chief of Staff took an extreme position, suggesting that compulsory military training for all young men between the ages of 18 to 21 years might be necessary. "I feel that the Armies of all civilized countries of great size, or countries that are in danger of being invaded, have been obliged to come to that," he noted, "and I see that while England stood out until now she is coming to it now, although they are late about it."[38] A disappointed Scott later claimed that Congress received his request for increasing the army's size through conscription "with great hilarity. I was asked, 'What do you want with a million men? The United States will never be at war with anybody. Do you want them to eat? You certainly cannot have any other use for them.'"[39]

Not a single Democrat on the House Military Affairs Committee supported the creation of a Continental Army. Its chair, James Hay, an arch opponent of the General Staff and a strong states' rights advocate from Virginia, informed Wilson that "many southern members fear it because they believe it will be the means of enlisting large numbers of negroes."[40]

Although he did not have the votes in Congress, Garrison refused to compromise on a Continental Army. He wrote Wilson on January 12, bluntly stating that the nation could not rely on an army "that it does not raise, that it does not officer, that it does not train, and that it does not control."[41] Initially Wilson supported his Secretary of War. Throughout January and into early February he campaigned in the East and Midwest for modification of America's military system. In a speech at Chicago on January 31, he proudly proclaimed that the United States had always fought its war with citizen soldiers from the state militias, and it "had never been disappointed." But "warfare has changed," he cautioned, "so within the span of a single life that it is nothing less than brutal to send raw recruits into the trenches and into the field."[42] (Little did Wilson suspect that he would do exactly that in 1918.) By this time, however, Wilson no longer had his heart in the fight. As the New York *Press* noted: "He still hates the sword; he can not warm to this subject because his heart is not in it."[43]

Without the President's support for a Continental Army, Garrison resigned on February 10, and he was soon followed by his Assistant Secretary Henry Breckinridge of Kentucky. Wilson replaced Garrison with Newton D. Baker, the former mayor of Cleveland and one of his former students at Johns Hopkins, who had once shared meals with him at the same boarding house in Baltimore. Baker had no military experience (he had not even played with lead soldiers as a child) and was a self-professed pacifist, referring to himself as a "peace-at-almost-any-price man."[44] On the other hand, he certainly had not demonstrated pacifistic tendencies following the sinking of the USS *Maine*, for he attempted to volunteer but was rejected because of defective eyesight.[45]

As Secretary of War, Baker was immediately confronted with an attack against the United States. In October 1915, Wilson had recognized Venustiano Carranza's Constitutionalist Party as the de facto government of Mexico. Wilson's actions infuriated Carranza's arch rival Francisco (Pancho) Villa, who apparently believed (incorrectly) that Wilson had struck a deal with Carranza to make Mexico "a virtual protectorate of the United States."[46] On March 9, 1916, at 4:15 a.m., Villa's force attacked Columbus, New Mexico, and the adjacent camp of the 13th US Cavalry. Villa led the way as his men shouted "Viva Villa" and "Viva Mexico." Shooting wildly they killed American troopers and civilians. Washington responded immediately. Within a week, the first elements of the Punitive Expeditionary Force crossed the border in pursuit of Villa's force. The future commander-in-chief of the AEF, John J. Pershing, led this essentially cavalry campaign (although it did include infantry regiments), the last ever waged by the US Army.

Villa's raid reinvigorated the debate in Congress over preparedness. His attack both enraged and alarmed the American public. "Suppose a first-class Power, instead of a Mexican bandit, had struck at the United States!" warned the *Kansas City Star*. It seemed obvious that the Regular Army, though much improved by recent reforms, was incapable of waging a major conflict. It could only be a nucleus around which a larger force could be raised by calling up the state militias. But the US Constitution limited the powers of Congress by limiting state militias to "executing the laws of the Union, suppressing insurrections, and repelling invasions." Nothing was said about deploying state militias beyond the borders of the United States, or even outside the state of their origin.[47] (During the Spanish–American War, members of the militia had enlisted as volunteers in the Regular Army before being dispatched to Cuba and the Philippines.)

On March 23, the Military Affairs Committee passed, by a vote of 402 to 2, a bill that incorporated Hay's ideas on federalizing the National

Guard by bringing it under the control of the War Department and increased the authorized strength of the Regular Army from approximately 100,000 men and officers to 140,000.[48]

Wilson, as he wrote Hay, considered the passage of this bill "a first step towards adequate preparation for national defense."[49] Led by George E. Chamberlain, who had once served in the militia (the Linn County Rifles in Eastern Oregon), the Senate Military Affairs Committee dissented and looked more favorably upon the War Department's more ambitious proposals. With Wilson threatening to break off relations with Germany over the sinking of another passenger ship, the *Sussex*, which resulted in the injury of four Americans, the Senate in a voice vote passed the Chamberlain bill that increased the authorized strength of the Regular Army to 250,000 men and federalized the National Guard (raising its authorized strength to 280,000 men). It also retained the concept of the Continental Army or national reserve force, but lowered its authorized strength to 261,000 men. A conference committee, however, failed to reconcile the considerable differences between the House and Senate.[50]

Wilson intervened to break the impasse and after delicate negotiations the Senate passed the National Defense Act on May 17 and the House on May 20. On June 3, Wilson signed the bill into law as the Army Reorganization Act. During the first three years of the war the Regular Army had grown from 98,544 officers and men to only 108,399.[51] Congress now increased its authorized peacetime strength to 175,000 through five annual increments. The size of the Regular Army, however, was subject to debate because noncombatant troops in administration, supply, etc. were not included in this total. Senator Chamberlain and Congressman Hay actually differed in the tens of thousands as to the eventual strength of the new Regular Army after five years, especially if the United States were at war. Estimates for a peacetime army ranged as high as 211,000 officers and men when noncombatants were included. If at war, the strength of the army might increase to 236,500 officers and men to which staff troops, scouts, and unassigned recruits (at least 25,000) would be added.[52] The term of enlistment for volunteers was seven years. A typical soldier served three years on active duty and four years in the Enlisted Reserve Corps.

Given time to develop, the new Enlisted Reserve Corps appeared to give the War Department the ability to expand the Regular Army in a crisis.[53] An expandable armed force, of course, required additional officers; so Congress created the Officers' Reserve Corps, a corps of reserve officers available to serve as temporary officers, and the Reserve Officers' Training Corps (ROTC) which brought commissioned and noncommissioned officers to campuses throughout the United States to supervise officer training programs.

A striking and permanent feature of the reorganization of the Army was the federalization of the militia, making it a true *National* Guard. National Guardsmen took a dual oath to both their state and to the national government. Congress gave the President the authority to call the National Guard into federal service in the event of a war or national emergency. This bill also forbade states from maintaining any troops other than National Guardsmen.[54]

The term for enlistment for the National Guard was six years, the first three years "in an active organization" and the "remaining three years in the National Guard Reserve." Discipline and training conformed to that of the Regular Army, with Regulars conducting inspections and supervising training. "The militiamen will have a chance to learn the soldier's art under good masters," the *New York Times* approvingly noted. "They will be closely watched; they may be sure of that."[55] Each detachment now assembled for at least forty-eight days annually at local armories for drill and instruction. In addition, National Guardsmen spent a minimum of fifteen days on maneuvers, in encampments, or participating in other exercises such as target shooting outside.[56]

Curiously, Congressional representation determined the authorized peacetime strength of the now federalized National Guard.

The number of enlisted men of the National Guard to be organized under this Act within one year from its passage shall be for each State in the proportion of two hundred such men for each Senator and Representative in Congress from such State, and a number to be determined by the President for each Territory and the District of Columbia, and shall be increased each year thereafter in the proportion of not less than fifty per centum until a total peace strength of not less than eight hundred enlisted men for each Senator and Representative in Congress shall have been reached.[57]

Many politicians apparently viewed the militia payroll as patronage and, according to the New York *Evening Sun*, wanted their "proportionate share of the military pork."[58] This convoluted system of determining the limits of the incremental expansion of the National Guard led to confusion over its maximum authorized expansion, with estimates ranging from a low of 425,000 to a high of 457,000 officers and men.[59]

America's defense required armaments as well as manpower, and Congress wisely addressed the question of industrial mobilization by granting the President and the War Department extraordinary economic powers during war or when war appeared imminent. Congress also authorized the Secretary of War to compile a list of all arms and munitions plants and to determine a "reasonable price" for armaments.

If plants capable of manufacturing military supplies refused to cooperate, the President had the authority to take "immediate possession of any such plant or plants" and place them under the control of the Ordnance Department of the US Army.[60]

Congress also granted the President the authority to create a Board on Mobilization of Industries Essential for Military Preparedness. Congress subsequently created a Council of National Defense, with an advisory board of seven civilians, when it attached a rider to the Army Appropriations Act of August 29, 1916. The President then appointed six Cabinet members (War, Navy, Interior, Agriculture, Commerce, and Labor) to this body. Wilson charged this council, chaired by the Secretary of War, with the responsibility of coordinating the economic mobilization of the country in the event of war, or in effect to act as a general staff for civil life.

Prior to America's entry into the war, however, the Council of National Defense proceeded deliberately, taking its time in selecting experts for the advisory commission. Even after Germany resumed unrestricted U-boat warfare in early 1917, President Wilson told them on February 12 that he "was not in sympathy with any great preparation." Major-General Hugh L. Scott, the Chief of Staff who occupied the chairman's seat in the interim between Garrison's resignation and Baker's arrival at the War Department, certainly did not provide the civilians with a sense of urgency. Franklin K. Lane, the head of the Interior Department, noted in his diary on February 16 that the "Chief of Staff fell asleep at our meeting today."[61]

The Army Reorganization Bill, which called for the greatest peacetime expansion of American military power in the nation's history, has been described as "the most comprehensive military legislation the American Congress had yet passed."[62] Yet the Army leadership understandably received it coolly. The outspoken Leonard Wood, the former Chief of Staff and a key leader of the preparedness movement, characterized the bill as "a menace to public safety in that it purports to provide a military force of value ... It has not the support of the members of the General Staff of the Army or of the Army as a whole. It would be far better to have no Army legislation than to have this measure put through."[63]

Many army officers had reasons to despair. As America's neutral rights and honor were being threatened, Congress's reorganization of the US Army had almost no connection to the war that America was most likely to fight. The leisurely buildup of land forces designed by Congress left the country woefully unprepared when it went to war a year later. Congress had authorized an expanded armed force but it had not created one. Without compulsion there was no guarantee that either the Regular

Army or National Guard could get enough volunteers to achieve their authorized strength. What happened during the first ten days after America declared war on Germany in April 1917 was a striking example of this. William Jennings Bryan had predicted that "a million men would spring to arms over night."[64] Despite the surge of patriotism after America's declaration of war against Germany, only 4,355 men had volunteered for the Regular Army after ten days, an average of 435 a day. The National Guard did little better. The numbers did improve: after three weeks 32,000 men had enlisted, but this larger figure did not come close to raising the number of men required.[65] Never before had the United States made such a poor showing after becoming a belligerent.

Fearing that a large army would make military intervention abroad more likely, many Congressmen did not want or expect the Regular Army and National Guard to attain their maximum authorized strength after five years of incremental growth. As Hay noted at the time, once the war ended and sanity returned to the American people, "there is no reason why Congress should not repeal these provisions of increase and bring the Army back to its usual strength."[66]

The future commander-in-chief of the AEF certainly belonged to the group that believed that both the President and Congress had failed to create a credible fighting force. "It is almost inconceivable that there could have been such an apparent lack of foresight in administration circles regarding the probable necessity for an increase of our military forces and so little appreciation of the time and effort which would be required to prepare them for effective service," Pershing later concluded in his memoirs. If the country had possessed the military muscle to back up its diplomacy he argued that it was "not improbable" that "our rights would have been respected and we would not have been forced into the war." Conversely, once forced into the war, Pershing believed that the "war was prolonged another year and the cost in human life tremendously increased" because of America's lack of preparation.[67]

An unexpected and damaging consequence when Congress passed the National Defense Act was its attempt to cripple the General Staff. Ainsworth supporters such as Congressman Hay seized the opportunity to undermine a military entity which they associated with creeping militarism. The National Defense Act had actually authorized a gradual increase of the General Staff to a Chief of Staff, two general officers of the line, ten colonels, ten lieutenant colonels, fifteen majors, and seventeen captains (a total of fifty-five officers). But Hay and others remained determined to limit the General Staff's influence in the nation's political center. Hence the Act allowed no more than one-half of its junior officers to serve in or near the District of Columbia at any one time,[68] leaving the "brain" of the Army critically shorthanded when the United States declared war with only nineteen General Staff officers available, eleven of whom were assigned to the War College Division. Scott, however, found a way to get around these Congressional restrictions by including the faculty and students of the War College, approximately seventy-five officers, as unofficial members of the General Staff. By the war's end the number of officers on the General Staff in Washington had grown to 1,072.[69]

Another restriction on the Army's war planners was that both Congress and the President discouraged the War Department from dispatching high-ranking officers to visit European battlefields,[70] thus keeping the Army's leadership in general ignorance about the course of the war and the dramatic advances in warfare taking place across the Atlantic. As the future commander of the First Army Hunter Liggett later lamented: "The fundamentals of warfare remain the same, but the application changes constantly, and under the forced pressure of three years of desperate fighting, human ingenuity had devised many new aids to killing and perfected old ones, a great deal of it known to the American Army only by hearsay."[71] Those generally ignorant of European battlefields included General Scott. The Chief of Staff once questioned a member of his staff, Colonel Robert E. Lee Michie, about the First Battle of the Marne, which had prevented the German Army from overwhelming France in 1914. "Michie," he said, "everybody's talking about the Battle of the Marne. What happened at the Battle of the Marne anyway?"[72]

3   Coercive power and Wilsonian diplomacy

Despite public displays of outrage over the loss of American lives to German torpedoes, the great majority of Americans continued to oppose going to war to protect their country's neutral rights. So did Wilson, although he continued to warn Berlin that he was prepared to hold Germany to strict accountability. At the same time, he refused to equate the defense of American national interests with an interventionist military policy. When he talked of strengthening America's army and navy in November 1915, he stressed that he was thinking only of defense. He had a very practical reason for holding an olive branch rather than sword. As he told Edward House on December 15, 1915, "if the Allies were not able to defeat Germany alone, they could scarcely do so with the help of the United States because it would take too long for us to get in a state of preparedness. It would therefore be a useless sacrifice on our part to go in."[1]

House offered a policy that was amenable to Wilson's idealism: an interventionist political policy as the mediator of a compromise peace between the belligerents. Encouraged by both House and the British Foreign Secretary Sir Edward Grey, Wilson hoped to exploit what he assumed was America's superior moral position to achieve a negotiated peace followed by general disarmament and a league of nations.

But what if Germany, with its ambitious war objectives and its armies considerably beyond its own borders in both Eastern and Western Europe, refused to accept a negotiated peace? As early as September 9, 1914, Theobald von Bethmann Hollweg, the German Chancellor, had embraced the so-called September Program which called for a German-dominated Central European economic bloc and the "security for the German Reich in west and east for all imaginable time." Germany wanted France to pay a war indemnity and be weakened "to make her revival as a great power impossible for all time." The Russian Empire was to "be thrust back as far as possible from Germany's eastern frontier and her domination over the non-Russian vassal peoples broken." Luxembourg was to be annexed and Belgium made a "vassal state."[2]

The September Program remained the basis of German war objectives until Russia's defeat opened up even greater opportunities for German hegemonic control of Europe. British and French leaders, convinced that their future security depended upon the destruction of German militarism, might be equally opposed to a compromise peace.

As Wilson's peace emissary, House proved to be a poor conduit between European war leaders and the White House. Misrepresenting the President's views House told them what they wanted to hear and then misled Wilson about their views. On December 28, 1915, House departed for Europe on his peace mission. On February 17, he and Sir Edward Grey, the British Foreign Secretary, drafted what became known as the House–Grey Memorandum. It read as follows:

Colonel House told me that President Wilson was ready, on hearing from France and England that the moment was opportune, to propose that a Conference should be summoned to put an end to the war. Should the Allies accept this proposal, and should Germany refuse it, the United States would probably enter the war against Germany.

This memorandum also stated that if Germany accepted a proposal to negotiate but proved unreasonable "the United States would leave the Conference as a belligerent on the side of the Allies."[3]

Five days later, February 22nd, the German Fifth Army, commanded by the Kaiser's son, Crown Prince Wilhelm, unleashed a nine-hour bombardment against French fortifications around Verdun. At Bois des Caures, in an area 500 yards by 1,000 yards square, as many as 80,000 shells exploded. Erich von Falkenhayn, the German chief of the general staff, planned to "bleed the French Army white" through a gigantic battle of attrition.

On the day that the Battle of Verdun got underway, Grey brought the House–Grey Memorandum before the British War Committee, a small war council made up of Cabinet members. Contrary to many accounts, Grey took American mediation quite seriously. He told Paul Cambon, the French Ambassador in London, that he "was convinced that President Wilson really was prepared, if the Allies desired it, to take the action that Colonel House stated."[4] Grey's colleagues, however, were skeptical of Wilson's peace efforts even though he now suggested that he was prepared to back up his diplomacy with force. Grey sought to defend Wilson's motives, but he had no response when Asquith questioned the "coercive power of the United States." Lloyd George, the Minister of Munitions, agreed with Asquith and noted that the United States would "possess no coercive power this year."[5]

Wilson's suggestion that his country would probably enter the war if Germany refused to relinquish its conquests during peace negotiations thus carried little weight with the Allies. Moral force did not serve as a substitute for military power in the hard coin of diplomacy. Wilson's tepid support of preparedness, which was isolationist in nature and directed at some unknown future threat, strongly suggested that he had no intention of becoming a belligerent.

The War Department's response to Villa's raid across the border also underscored America's military weakness to the rest of the world. With no motorized transport, the War Department had to purchase trucks to pursue Villa. The weapons of Pershing's expeditionary force were antique when compared to the weaponry being deployed on European battlefields. "Broadly speaking," harrumphed the Boston *Transcript*, "it is like what we should have done if we had attempted to fight the Civil War with flintlock muskets."

Professional soldiers were just as blunt. Colonel Edwin F. Glenn, the Chief of Staff of the Eastern Division of the Army, noted that "the cold fact is that the American Army to-day is the most pathetic thing any nation ever knew or contemplated, and other nations know it very well, I assure you."[6] Even Colonel House joined the chorus, writing in his diary: "I have urged him [Wilson] ever since the war began to make ready, and we are no more ready today than we were two years ago ... we have no army worth speaking of."[7]

An overriding consideration for Wilson in his peace efforts was his fear that at any time his hand might be forced by the actions of a single U-boat commander. On March 24, a German U-boat torpedoed but did not sink the *Sussex*, a French passenger ferry, in the English Channel. Four Americans were injured. After waiting until he was certain that it was a German torpedo rather than a mine that had damaged the ship, Wilson on April 18 threatened to break off diplomatic relations with Berlin.

Momentarily, the British dared to hope that the United States would be forced into the war. On April 27, Lord Kitchener entertained the American military attaché, Lieutenant Colonel George O. Squier, who was paying his respects to the Secretary of State for War before returning to the United States. Kitchener enthusiastically talked of the "two English-speaking" nations achieving a "lasting peace." "Tell your Secretary of War, if he will merely send me a wire for any assistance that I can give, it will be given immediately without the necessity of regular diplomatic channels." Aware that an American army capable of fighting in Europe had to be raised from scratch and as a precursor to later British efforts, Kitchener suggested to Squier that American soldiers should complete their training in France, enabling them to enter the trenches "in the shortest possible time."[8] British hopes that the United States might be forced into the war, however, were dashed on May 4 when

Berlin issued the so-called *"Sussex"* pledge not to attack passenger or merchant ships without warning.

There was, however, no guarantee that Berlin might not resume unrestricted U-boat warfare. Wilson may not have recalled Napoleon Bonaparte's dismissive remark about moral force ("How many divisions does the Pope have?") but he began to understand the relationship between his liberal agenda and his country's military weakness. In a meeting with the American Union Against Militarism (AUAM), Wilson emphasized that "a nation which, by the standards of other nations, however mistaken those standards may be, is regarded as helpless, is apt in general counsel to be regarded as negligible."[9]

Without a credible army to support his diplomacy Wilson began to speak of the prospect of *future* US military support for peace. In a speech to the League to Enforce Peace at the New Willard Hotel on May 27, 1916 he committed the United States to a

universal association of the nations to maintain the inviolate security of the highway of the seas for the common and unhindered use of all the nations of the world, and to prevent any war begun either contrary to treaty covenants or without warning and full submission of the causes to the opinion of the world – a virtual guarantee of territorial integrity and political independence.[10]

That Wilson would ever support the building of an American army equivalent to the other world powers, however, is open to question. A few weeks earlier he had tried to reassure members of AUAM that America's future contribution to world peace might be quite small if the world "ever comes to combine its force for the purpose of maintaining peace."[11]

One did not have to question Wilson's sincerity to doubt that the American people were ready to accept such a global role. As Cecil Spring Rice, the British Ambassador in Washington, later warned Arthur Balfour, Grey's successor as Foreign Secretary: the Americans

will have to abandon the Monroe doctrine and the Washingtonian tradition against entangling alliances. They will also have to have an army and a fleet ready on an instant and distant call for foreign service. The people who could not spare one word to Belgium are now to engage to send their armies and navies to the defence of threatened right. This is a big change.[12]

The isolationist nature and the inadequacy of the preparedness movement certainly did nothing to encourage the Entente to believe that Wilson would back up his words. Nor did the rhetorical gymnastics he employed after he was attacked by isolationists for his speech to the League to Enforce Peace. At a Memorial Day address at Arlington National Cemetery, May 30, he emphasized that he would "never consent to an entangling alliance." He only favored a "disentangling" alliance to dismantle the old power blocs based on narrow self-interest rather than on "common right and justice."[13]

Frustrated with the Allies for not embracing America's mediation efforts, House was brutally correct when he told the President on May 24: "It is evident that unless the United States is willing to sacrifice hundreds of thousands of lives and billions of treasure we are not to be on good terms with the Allies."[14]

As diplomatic notes flew back and forth between Washington and the warring capitals the war continued unabated. Entente generals had agreed that their armies would establish a ring of fire around the Central Powers by launching simultaneous attacks. The Italian Army in March attacked first, initially on the Isonzo Front and then later on the Trentino Front as well, gaining little ground but inflicting heavy losses on the Austro-Hungarian Army. On June 4, the Russian Eighth Army, led by General Aleksei Brusilov, attacked the Austrian Fourth and Seventh Armies on the Russian Southwest front. This offensive, the Entente's greatest success yet in the war, brought Romania into the war on the Allied side, overran some 15,000 square miles, and inflicted 1.5 million casualties on the Austro-Hungarians. Fearing collapse on the Eastern Front, the German high command eventually transferred fifteen divisions from the Western front to the East. On July 1, a powerful Anglo-French offensive began along a twenty-five-mile front on the Somme. This Entente offensive, which lasted until November 19, 1916, did not result in the anticipated breakthrough. But it inflicted heavy losses on the Germans and forced them to suspend their offensive at Verdun. In the outer theaters, the British on August 4 almost annihilated at Romani a Turkish force sent to threaten the Suez Canal.

Wilson won reelection in November in one of the closest elections in American history, in part because of the Democratic slogan, "he kept us out of the war." Theodore Roosevelt had been his most severe critic on military issues. The former president's Progressive Party's platform had included universal service and a considerable increase in the size of the Regular Army and the budget of the War Department.[15]

With another four years in the White House, Wilson redoubled his efforts to force peace negotiations on the belligerents. Given the balance of forces on the European fronts, however, his chances of brokering a peace were not good. The Entente's success on the battlefields in the summer had actually led to the further militarization of German society and even more grandiose national war objectives, which, if achieved, would make Germany the dominant power in Europe as well as a world power that might in future threaten American interests.[16] In late August

Kaiser William II had removed Falkenhayn from supreme command, replacing him with Paul von Hindenburg, who became Chief of the General Staff, and Erich Ludendorff, who took the position of Chief Quartermaster-General. The famous Hindenburg and Ludendorff combination, which had come to prominence because of an overwhelming victory over the Tsarist Army in 1914 at Tannenberg, soon established what amounted to a military dictatorship. "Ludendorff," writes Holger H. Herwig,

with Hindenburg in tow, sought through a "strategy of annihilations" to bring the war to a victorious end and to force his adversaries to sign a peace that included monetary indemnities and vast territorial annexations. Assured of almost universal popular support, the military duumvirate could dictate policy to the government, knowing that neither the Chancellor nor the Kaiser could afford to arouse their ire.[17]

By fall, the Entente's military situation no longer seemed as favorable as it had been in August. Although the Entente still held the strategical initiative on the Western Front with approximately 4 million French, British, and Belgian soldiers facing 2.5 million Germans, the British and French armies had suffered enormous losses in attritional battles at Verdun and on the Somme. As for Italy, its repeated attacks on the Isonzo had achieved nothing of strategical value. On the Russian front, the Germans had regained the initiative, overrunning Romania and rescuing the Austro-Hungarian Army from collapse. Brusilov's army was now back on its heels with ominous signs of unrest emerging among his war-weary peasant soldiers.

On December 22, 1916, Admiral von Holtzendorff, the Chief of the German Admiralty Staff, submitted a memorandum for the eyes of the General Staff and the Chancellor that changed the course of the war. Identifying Great Britain as the most important member of the anti-German coalition, Holtzendorff argued that "if we can break England's backbone, the war is at once decided in our favour." In Holtzendorff's view Britain's "backbone" was its shipping tonnage. Germany had held its hand because of American opposition to unrestricted U-boat warfare. But Germany's military and naval leadership now discounted the military or naval role that the United States could play in what was largely a Continental war.

On January 9, 1917, at a meeting at Pless Castle in Silesia, Germany's war leaders considered Holtzendorff's proposal. Admiral Eduard von Capelle, who had succeeded Tirpitz at the Naval Office, had previously informed Reichstag leaders that the military threat posed by the United States "was zero." Hindenburg on the day before Germany's leaders met at Pless had insisted: "It has to be. We expect war with America and have made all preparations [for it]. Things cannot get worse." Germany's two leading generals are in agreement, with Ludendorff asserting at Pless, "I don't give a damn about America."

Chancellor Bethmann Hollweg, who had previously resisted the military and naval leaders who advocated unrestricted U-boat warfare because he believed that it would force President Wilson's hand, now, reluctantly, fell in with the majority. He believed that "America's assistance, in case she enters the war, will consist in the delivery of food supplies to England, financial support, delivery of airplanes and the dispatching of corps of volunteers."[18] In sum, the Second Reich's leadership expressed confidence that the United States was incapable of preventing a German victory.

On January 31, General Leonard Wood, the former Chief of Staff, gave alarming testimony in the House of Representatives which supported Germany's view of American weakness. Wood had previously angered the White House as one of the nation's most prominent preparedness advocates. Neither Wilson nor Baker had been able to muzzle him. He now spoke his mind again, this time before the House Military Affairs Committee. The Regular Army, he asserted, did not possess the modern weaponry deemed "vitally essential in modern war." Nor had the War Department taken the necessary steps to expand production of military equipment in an emergency.

Our arsenals for small arms have been working only to a small extent of their capacity. We are without reserves of clothing, shoes, or other equipment necessary for war. We have not taken the necessary steps to establish plants for the manufacturing of our military rifle at the great arms factories in various parts of the country. This is absolutely necessary in order to permit that expansion which will be necessary in order to meet the demands of modern war.[19]

Wood could also have added that the Regular Army was currently 20,000 under its authorized strength.

The War College Division, now under the direction of Brigadier General Joseph E. Kuhn, had just submitted a "Plan for a National Army" to General Scott. But the General Staff's proposal was unrelated to the current crisis with Germany because it looked to the future. If implemented immediately it would still be 1922 before the new National Army had 310,000 men on active duty backed up by 2.5 million reservists (trained by Regular Army officers and organized into reserve units).[20] The anticipated strength of this reserve was problematic because the Army's plan relied upon the willingness of enough citizens to volunteer.

On the same day that Wood emphasized the weakness of the US military, Lansing received a visitor at the Department of State, Count Johann von Bernstorff. After shaking hands, the German Ambassador presented the American Secretary of State with a note that announced that Germany would resume unlimited U-boat warfare on February 1. With a fleet of 111 U-boats, Germany planned to attack all sea traffic in the blockade zones around Great Britain, France, Italy, and in the eastern Mediterranean. Having marked large blockade zones on the map in international waters the Germans then announced that American ships entering these zones, including those carrying passengers, would be sunk on sight.

With Germany allowing the United States to send only one passenger steamer a week in each direction to Britain the President had little room to maneuver. Yet he remained determined to keep America on the sidelines. As he told House, it would be a "crime" if America became involved "in the war to such an extent as to make it impossible to save Europe afterward." He later expressed similar sentiments on the eve of America's declaration of war. On March 19, he told Frank Cobb, editor of the New York *World*, that "a declaration of war would mean that Germany would be beaten and so badly beaten that there would be a dictated peace, a victorious peace."[21]

On February 3, President Wilson recalled the American Ambassador from Berlin and severed diplomatic relations with Germany. Although he had been quick to break off relations with Berlin, he still hoped that America might remain neutral. He emphasized in a speech to Congress that the United States did "not desire any hostile conflict with the Imperial German Government. We are the sincere friends of the German people and earnestly desire to remain at peace with the Government which speaks for them."[22] Wilson's only warlike action was quietly to ask Baker to have the general staff prepare a plan to raise and train a *volunteer* force of 500,000 men to reinforce the Regular Army and National Guard.[23] At the same time, he ordered the War Department not to take any public actions which might suggest that the country was contemplating war.

Baker subsequently went out of his way to make sure that the irrepressible General Wood, the Commander of the Eastern Department, did not take any provocative steps such as deploying Federal troops in the District of Columbia.[24] Congress followed the President's lead. In mid-February the House Military Affairs Committee without a dissenting vote decided to make no substantial changes in the nation's military policy.[25]

Wilson had been a small boy in Augusta, Georgia when General Sherman left a path of destruction across the state as he marched from

Atlanta to the sea. Although Sherman's army did not burn Augusta to the ground, Wilson witnessed wounded Confederate soldiers and heard their cries as they were being treated in his father's Presbyterian Church. The President had not closely followed the war in Europe but he clearly understood how warfare had changed since the Civil War which many of his countrymen were now inclined to romanticize.

In late November 1916, he had recorded his thoughts on the industrialized semi-siege warfare being waged in the trenches of the Western Front. "Never before in the world's history," he wrote,

have two great armies been in effect so equally matched; never before have the losses and the slaughter been so great with as little gain in military advantage ... The mechanical game of slaughter of today has not the same fascination as the zest of intimate combat of former days; and the trench warfare and poisonous gases are elements which detract alike from the excitement and the tolerance of modern conflict. With maneuver almost a thing of the past, any given point can admittedly be carried by the sacrifice of enough men and ammunition. Where is any longer the glory commensurate with the sacrifice of the millions of men required in modern warfare to carry and defend Verdun?[26]

As Wilson struggled to keep the United States out of the war, the only appreciation he apparently read concerning the military consequences of America's entry into the war came from a civilian, Herbert Hoover, who had played a central role in organizing the Commission for Relief in Belgium, which was feeding civilians in Belgian and French territories occupied by the German Army. Hoover sent a letter to House who forwarded it to the President on February 14. In his letter, Hoover warned against any political alignment with the Allies if America became a belligerent. He also suggested that cooperation on the European battlefields should be limited to a narrow military role. An expeditionary force, Hoover stressed, would be expensive and would require extensive transport, training, and equipment. Hence the United States should allow the French and British to recruit and train American manpower to keep their armies up to strength. Meanwhile, the United States should build a formidable army on its own soil to give "weight" to Wilson's influence on the peace settlement.[27] Hoover's comment on the connection between America's military strength and the success of Wilson's liberal diplomacy apparently resonated with the President. Several weeks later, he told a delegation from the Emergency Peace Federation that visited him in the White House that "as head of a nation participating in the war, the President of the United States would have a seat at the Peace Table, but that if he remained the representative of a neutral country he could at best only 'call through a crack in the door.'"[28]

On February 25, the same day that a German submarine sank the British liner, *Laconia*, with the loss of two American lives, Wilson was handed a copy of an intercepted cable from the German Foreign Secretary Zimmermann to the German Minister in Mexico, Heinrich von Eckhardt. The so-called Zimmermann Telegram contained the shocking news that Germany wanted an alliance with Mexico if the United States abandoned its neutrality. In return for Mexico's support, Germany promised financial aid and support for Mexico's "conquest [of] the territory lost by her at a prior period in Texas, New Mexico, and Arizona." Zimmermann also suggested that Japan be invited to join this anti-American alignment. On March 1, the White House released the Zimmermann Note to the press. Mexico and Japan immediately denied complicity, but two days later, when asked at a Berlin press conference by a Hearst reporter if his alleged note to Mexico were genuine, Zimmermann replied: "I cannot deny it. It is true."[29] Wilson now lost all faith in the German leadership.

The U-boat campaign combined with the notorious Zimmermann Note led to a clamor for war in the press. On March 20, Wilson played a round of golf with his physician friend Dr. Cary Grayson and then met with his Cabinet at 2:30 p.m. to consider the question of ending American neutrality. The atmosphere was electric, with reporters packing the corridors of the Executive Office and State Department. Lansing and other Cabinet members had to push their way into the small Cabinet room. Wilson, calm and collected, entered last and took his usual place at the head of the table. He told his Cabinet that he wanted it to address two questions. First, should he summon Congress to meet at an earlier date than planned? And, second, "what should he lay before Congress when it did assemble?"

In their remarks Cabinet members reflected their country's anger. The United States was one of the world's great powers. Yet its honor and self-respect had been trampled upon by German warlords who plotted with Mexicans and unleashed their submarines against American vessels. Albert S. Burleson, the Texan who headed the post office, wanted to demonstrate to the Germans that they had "woke up a giant." Confusion, however, existed over what an awakened America should or could do to assist the Allies. William McAdoo, the Secretary of Treasury who had married the President's youngest daughter, spoke first and said that war was "inevitable" but that he "doubted whether we could furnish men." Rather than armed assistance he suggested that the United States could best serve the Allies "by underwriting their loans." David F. Houston, whom Wilson had earlier considered as a possible successor to Secretary of War Garrison, spoke next. The Secretary of Agriculture said that he doubted whether we should plan to do more than to use our navy and to give financial aid to the Allies; that to equip an army of any size would divert the production of our industrial plans and so cut off from the Allies much needed supplies; and he thought that we ought to be very careful about interfering with their efficiency.

With no military advisers present to offer their professional advice, Baker spoke for the Army. He strongly recommended "preparing an army at once" to dispatch to Europe "in case the Allies became straitened in the number of their men." But he also expressed the view that such an army might never have to be sent to Europe because "the very knowledge of our preparations would force the Central Powers to realize that their cause was hopeless." Secretary of Navy Josephus Daniels, with his eyes brimming with tears and his voice trembling with emotion, spoke in favor of summoning Congress and getting its support for "active measures" against Germany.[30]

In the view of a majority of the Cabinet members, "active measures" did not include sending an army to Europe. Secretary of War Baker wishfully suggested that it might only be necessary to raise an army to frighten the Germans into submission. It was obvious that the United States did not presently have the required soldiers or equipment. At best the Army might organize a mobile force of some 24,000 men.[31]

As the United States edged towards war, the British Chief of the Imperial General Staff, Sir William Robertson, had offered his professional assessment of the military impact of America's entry into the war: "I do not think that it will make much difference whether America comes in or not," he wrote a fellow general. "What we want to do is to beat the German Armies, until we do that we shall not win the war. America will not help us much in that respect."[32] American Assistant Chief of Staff Tasker H. Bliss, who was destined to play an essential role in the American war effort, could not have agreed more with Robertson. On March 31, he wrote that "the war must last practically two years longer before we can have other than naval and economic participation."[33]

Cabinet ministers had realistically focused on supplies, ships, and money to assist the Allies. And indeed the Allies, especially the British, desperately needed American credit to continue fighting. Warfare had become ruinously expensive. Burleson urged his colleagues to "authorize the issue of five billions in bonds and go to the limit." (One billion dollars was an immense sum in 1917. According to the *Literary Digest* it took 31,500 tons of silver to coin that many dollars and would require 2,083 freight-cars, drawn by 104 locomotives, to haul that amount to the mint.) The direct cost of the war for the United States actually turned out to be $35.5 billion when over $11 billion loaned to other countries during and immediately after the war are included.[34] (Most of this money was borrowed and the rest raised through taxation.) The President thanked the Cabinet and on the following day issued a call for Congress to meet in special session on April 2.

While soldiers guarded the Capitol, Wilson played golf with his wife on the morning of April 2. Following dinner with Colonel House and members of his family, he left the White House, accompanied by a troop of cavalry, and drove up the hill to the Capitol. At 8:32 p.m. he made his way to the rostrum of the House chamber. To thunderous applause, he asked Congress "to exert all its power and employ all its resources to bring the Government of the German Empire to terms and end the war." Wilson listed what would be required: financial credits, materials of war, the "full equipment" of the navy, and "the immediate addition to the armed forces of the United States already provided for by law in case of war at least five hundred thousand men ... and also the authorization of subsequent additional increments of equal force so soon as they are needed and can be handled in training."[35]

Wilson warned that there might be "many months of fiery trial and sacrifice ahead" for American soldiers. But, in what is often regarded as his greatest speech, he did not employ a warrior's language. Instead he assured Americans that they would be putting their lives at risk for a higher purpose, that of making the world "safe for democracy." He also expressed confidence that American fighting men would conduct their "operations as belligerents without passion and ourselves observe with proud punctilio the principles of right and of fair play we profess to be fighting for."[36] Americans, he emphasized, were at war with the German government rather than the German people. This was a distinction that a diplomat might understand but it would be lost on many Doughboys who, with bayonets fixed, later advanced across fields strewn with their dead and wounded into the firestorm of German defenses at Meuse-Argonne.

Wilson concluded his thirty-six-minute speech to wild cheering and flag waving. Both the House and the Senate introduced the war resolution the next day and it was ready for the President's signature by April 6. At 1:18 p.m., in a private ceremony with no reporters present, Wilson penned the following: "Approved 6 April, 1917. Woodrow Wilson." News of the signing was telephoned to the Executive Office where Lieutenant Byron McCandless, an aid to the Secretary of Navy, waited. McCandless then rushed to the Executive Avenue entrance to the White House grounds and signaled a naval officer standing in the window of the Navy Department to release wireless and cable messages to the Navy announcing that the United States was at war.[37]

Although the nation was now at war, the public's enthusiasm was quite muted in contrast with America's later declaration of war against Japan in 1941. "The national mood reflected more resignation than eagerness, insofar as it is possible to measure such an elusive phenomenon," writes Justus D. Doenecke. "Most people believed that the nation sought to vindicate its rights, honor, and self-respect, not to advance the cause of humanity, preserve the balance of power, foster the aims of the Allies, or establish self-government."[38]

Despite Wilson's talk of "many months of fiery trial and sacrifice ahead," it remained unclear what form American belligerency might take either to his government or to the American people. Although the war resolution voted on in both the House and Senate instructed the President "to employ the entire naval and military forces of the United States and the resources of the Government to carry on war against the Imperial German government," it has been suggested that a majority of the Senators and Representatives who voted for war actually did not expect American troops to fight on European battlefields. Fiorello La Guardia, a Republican from New York, later wrote that at least 60 percent of those who voted for war did not expect American soldiers to be dispatched abroad.[39]

The American press was also divided on the role that the United States should play as a belligerent. "No ladies' war," proclaimed the *Chicago Tribune*, and demanded three "mandatory policies": universal military service, the dispatch of troops to Europe, and an agreement with Great Britain, France, Russia, and Japan for no separate peace. An opposing view was that the United States could best assist the Allies with money and supplies. According to the New York *Morning Telegraph*, the Allies did not "need more warriors; they want money and food, and munitions of war." One writer even suggested that "the greatest contribution America can make to the success of the common cause is a bumper wheat-crop."[40]

The immediate and most critical question for the Wilson administration was raising an army. The heated national debate in 1916 over the proposed Continental Army had divided the country. The resulting compromise, the National Defense Act, had not provided an armed force capable of influencing the outcome of the present war. The US Army in April consisted of 127,588 men in the Regular Army and 66,594 Guardsmen in federal service. In the words of a future Chief of Staff, Peyton C. March, this was "scarcely enough to form a police force for emergencies within the territorial limits of the United States."[41] Moreover, two out of every five men in uniform had learned their warrior trade in the National Guard.

Just prior to his war speech, Wilson made one of the most critical decisions of his wartime presidency. In a dramatic reversal of his previous position, he abandoned the volunteer system for a selective national draft. The US government had attempted conscription only once in the past. The introduction of draft lotteries during the summer of 1863 as Lee's army advanced on Gettysburg had sparked some of the worst riots in American history. Armed anti-draft resistance in New York, Boston, and other cities and towns led to many deaths, including thirty-eight enrolling officers. Troops had to be called in to restore order.

It has been suggested that Wilson made this decision in large part so that the economy might be mobilized more efficiently if skilled workers were deferred and left in their jobs. Without question industrial mobilization proceeded more smoothly because of the selective draft. But the economy was not Wilson's primary concern in his decision to abandon the traditional volunteer system and embrace the draft. John Whiteclay Chambers II has convincingly argued that Wilson was responding to a threat posed by his old rival Theodore Roosevelt. The former president, who agreed with Allied leaders that a good peace could only come through Germany's decisive defeat and derided those who desired a "limited liability" war, was the most admired American political figure in London and Paris. In a personal note to the President, Georges Clemenceau suggested that "at the present moment there is in France one name which sums up the beauty of American intervention – Roosevelt . . . Our poilus ask, 'Where is Roosevelt?' Send them Roosevelt – it will gladden their hearts."[42]

Although fifty-eight years old, blind in one eye, and possessing limited military experience, Roosevelt wanted to raise and lead an all-volunteer division – largely commanded by Ivy Leaguers and including a black regiment and a German-American regiment – to fight alongside the French and British. Roosevelt might confide in a friend that "I will promise Wilson that if he will send me to France, I will not come home alive,"[43] but the President obviously feared the potential threat he posed. If the old Rough Rider succeeded in commanding the so-called Roosevelt volunteers on the Western Front, he almost certainly would become the focus of America's war effort and a formidable threat to Wilson's control of his country's role in the war.[44]

Opponents of conscription had their say in Congress. A congressman from Georgia who had volunteered to fight in the Spanish–American War argued that "ten thousand volunteers patriotic enough to bare their breasts in battle are worth one hundred thousand conscripted men."[45] Robert M. Lafollette, a Progressive senator from Wisconsin, made an especially powerful speech against the draft in the Senate on April 27.

He accused the government of seeking the authority "to enter at will every home in our country, at any hour of the day or night, using all the force necessary to effect the entry" in order "violently [to] lay hold" of "our finest and healthiest and strongest boys" in order to send them "across the seas to a foreign land three thousand and more miles away, and to require them, under penalty of death if they refuse, to wound and kill other young boys just like themselves and toward whom they feel no hostility and have cause to feel none." He went on to argue that "the draft is the corollary of militarism and militarism spells death to democracy . . . There is not the shadow of an excuse for pressing men into involuntary military servitude for the conduct of this war."[46]

By large majorities Congress abandoned America's tradition of voluntary enlistment and passed the Selective Service Act. For the first time in its history the United States would fight a war without depending upon an army recruited by the states.

State soldiery in future wars would be dominated by professionals, an arrangement that would not be without friction. It has been noted that the National Guard mobilizations in 1916 and 1917 had "promised eager recruits, capable officers, and a fighting spirit," but had "too frequently delivered raw amateurs, gross inefficiency, and appalling ignorance. Conversely, the Regulars offered rationality, efficiency, and professional expertise that too often proved to be institutional snobbery and bureaucratic myopia . . . The echoes of that clash have reverberated throughout the twentieth century."[47]

The President signed the Selective Service Bill on May 18. Over 24 million men, or nearly one-half of the male population, eventually registered for the draft when the act was amended to increase those eligible for induction from eighteen to forty-five, inclusive. Most of these draftees came from the first and second registrations when almost all of those eligible for induction were in their twenties.[48] The percentage of eligible Americans who actually served was quite small when compared with the European powers which had been at war since August 1914 and had been forced to mobilize a much greater proportion of their young men to fight the monster battles of attrition that characterized the conflict. Nonetheless, what America's war leaders achieved in only eighteen months after passing the Selective Service Bill was quite unprecedented in American history. They built the country's largest army, and did it primarily through a draft. Without selective service there would not have been the sizable American force in Europe that guaranteed an Allied victory, if not in 1918, then in 1919 or 1920.

4 "You're in the army now"

Prior to Congressional approval of selective service, Baker had ordered the printing of some 10 million registration forms, hiding them in the basement of a post office in the capital, stacked from floor to ceiling. He now secretly shipped them to some 40,000 sheriffs, who served ex-officio as representatives of the national government in conducting the registration and subsequent drafting of young men into the armed services. The government avoided the word "conscript," using "selective service" instead because draftees were chosen through a selective system administered by the local draft boards. As opposed to the existing Regular Army and National Guard, both composed of volunteers, the government euphemistically called this new army raised by selective "coercion" the "National Army."

The Wilson administration also sought to soften the reality of forcing almost 10 million young American males to register as a preliminary step toward possible induction into the armed forces. Using the Committee on Public Information (CPI), which had been created by an executive order on April 13, 1917, Wilson attempted to mobilize the nation through an extensive and unprecedented government propaganda campaign.[1] "Carried in all our hearts as a great day of patriotic devotion and obligation," he proclaimed, "when the duty shall lie upon every man to see to it that the name of every male person of the designated ages is written on these lists of honor."[2] He then published this "Call to Arms" throughout the United States. Threats accompanied the President's appeals to patriotism. On the eve of registration the US attorney general, Thomas Watt Gregory, instructed all US attorneys and marshals to arrest anyone attempting to disrupt the registration drive. Within the next few days, the government arrested twenty-one people and threatened them with imprisonment.[3]

President Wilson characterized American participation as a great "crusade." On the day that Americans registered he told an assembly of Confederate veterans that these registrants were doing God's work. "They are crusaders," he proclaimed, "fighting for no selfish advantage for their Nation." The Committee on Public Information later produced a film, *Pershing's Crusaders*, which was shown in nearly 4,500 US theaters.[4]

Registering where they had previously voted, with family and neighbors looking on, fully one-tenth of the US population answered the call on June 5 between 7 a.m. and 7 p.m. (The Army continued to administer the draft through local polling places until the draft was abandoned in 1973.) Despite its scope and the haste with which it had been organized, registration went remarkably well. After completing their registration forms, each man received a green card with his name and number on it. "Ten million actors called at once to possible appearance on the most amazing of stages," trumpeted the *Chicago Tribune*. "It staggers the imagination. A nation, the freest of all democracies, after less than two months of hesitation, calls by law to the most rigid of all employments one-tenth of her population. What body so huge ever before moved psychologically so quickly to such tremendous action?"[5]

The government next selected from Wilson's "lists of honor" the men to be inducted. A draft lottery took place on the morning of July 20 in the public hearing room of the Senate Office Building. Wearing a blindfold, Baker stood before a large black board filled with rows of numbers from 1 to 10,500 (the latter number reflected the largest number of registrants in any single draft board). On a table in front of him sat a large glass bowl filled with 10,500 black capsules containing numbered slips of paper (Fig. 1). The first capsule Baker removed contained the number 258. The 258th man who had registered in each local board was now in the armed forces unless he could show cause why he should be exempted. The drawing continued for another 16 hours and 46 minutes until all 10,500 numbers had been recorded. This gave local draft boards a pool of over three million men from which to conscript the number of men required by the War Department. Those selected had only one week to apply for an exemption.

The hoopla associated with the registration drive and the draft lottery tended to exaggerate popular support for forced service. Draft boards published in their local newspapers lists of those who registered, an obvious attempt to shame those who had not. During this and subsequent registration drives it appears that from 2 million to 3 million failed to register. In a few localities, locals took up arms to resist the draft and a few pitched battles were fought with the authorities, resulting in perhaps fifteen to twenty deaths.[6] Others sought means to fail their physicals. One Kentuckian actually poured carbolic acid over his face. Still others bought drugs or defective eyeglasses which were supposed to enable one to fail one's physical examination.[7] Some young men fled to Mexico

Fig. 1 Second draft. The first number drawn was 246, and was picked
from the urn by Secretary of War Baker

or Canada. The great majority of those who sought to avoid military
service, however, remained in the United States, falling into three categories: "slackers" (those who failed to register), "delinquents" (those
who failed to report for physicals or accept the jurisdiction of the local
boards), and "deserters" (those who refused to report for military duty).
The total number of "deserters" reported from June 5, 1917 to
September 11, 1918 was 474,861. These deserters, however, were passive rather than active. In other words, they did not desert after being
inducted and trained. Also, the failure of 111,839 men to report was later
found to be explainable. Some, for example, were enemy aliens and
others had already enlisted in the armed services.[8]

The total number of registrants on June 5 was 9,586,508. Local draft
boards subsequently called 3,082,949 of this total. Of these fully one-half
filed for exemptions and 77.86 percent were granted, primarily on the
grounds of dependence. Draft boards certified 1,057,363 men for service. Forty percent of those so designated subsequently filed for exemption.[9] Among those seeking an exemption was Alvin Cullum York from
Fentress County, Tennessee. The deeply religious York, who became
America's most acclaimed enlisted man on the battlefield, had his appeal

Fig. 2 Secretary Baker and first recruit in army

as a conscientious objector denied by his local county board. Other young men attempted to escape military service by getting married. When a record number of young men, 527 in all, took their vows on July 31 in the city of New York, General Crowder threatened to prosecute anyone seeking to avoid service through marriage. Selective Service regulations were later amended to return men to Class I status if they had married after America became a belligerent. (Nine out of ten husbands initially drafted still received an exemption.)[10]

If exempted you received a white postcard; if not you received a green one. This would be followed by a pink postcard informing you to report to your local train or bus station for transportation to a training camp. On September 18, flags flew, bands played, and loved ones, some cheering while others wept, bid farewell to the new recruits as the largest troop movement in US history began; 250,000 draftees departed New York for training camps across the United States (Fig. 2). This extraordinary mobilization continued on the next day when draftees at more than 4,000 other locations entrained for military service. Receiving badges to attach to their lapels, draftees were assigned to a leader who held their train and meal tickets as well as their mobilization papers. These leaders had been instructed to prevent any man under his supervision from purchasing alcohol (drunkenness proved to be a major problem on the trains) and to hand his group over to an officer or non-commissioned officer at their destination.

National Guardsmen belonged to another category (Fig. 3). Approximately 80,000 Guardsmen were already in federal service. They either had been on active duty because of the Mexican crisis or had just recently been called up to protect potential targets such as bridges and the water supply of New York City from sabotage. The President ordered the rest into federal service in July. Many of these 433,478 Guardsmen spent their first days on active duty being trained at their local armories prior to being sent to National Guard training camps being constructed.[11]

Selective Service proved to be a war winner for the United States, providing the US Army with the necessary manpower (two of every three members of the armed forces were draftees) to wage a successful campaign on the European Continent. Its success almost certainly could not have been replicated in an earlier era. Russell Weigley has astutely noted that its acceptance was in large part due "to the discipline implicit in industrial society, to the consequent immense power of the modern state, and to modern mass media of communication and publicity, on which neither George Washington nor Abraham Lincoln had been able to draw."[12]

What is surprising in retrospect is that those who volunteered apparently did not believe that Germany represented a direct present or future threat to the United States. The most comprehensive survey of American veterans is the *World War I Survey* conducted by the US Army Military History Institute, Carlisle Barracks, Pennsylvania. Thousands of surviving veterans responded. Those who volunteered in 1916 often mentioned the threat posed by Pancho Villa as a reason for enlisting but neither Germany nor Kaiser Wilhelm is mentioned by those who followed in 1917–18. Instead their responses usually referred to their patriotism; they wrote: "My country needed me" or "I was about to be drafted." Educational levels appear to have influenced their enthusiasm for donning a uniform. Having made an extensive study of veteran responses in the *Survey*, Mark Meigs concludes that "more than half (56 percent) of the better educated group remembered enlisting enthusiastically, while less than half (41 percent) of farmers and laborers remembered that spirit."[13]

An extraordinary construction program preceded the training of these volunteers and enlisted men. Existing American military installations

Fig. 3 Private T. P. Loughlin of the 69th Regiment, New York National
Guard (165th Infantry) bidding his family farewell

could not possibly train a mass fighting force, so training facilities had to be provided for an anticipated 900,000 men during the last half of 1917.[14] Over 300,000 men had volunteered for the Regular Army or the National Guard during the first three months following the declaration of war. The first draft was expected to provide an additional 687,000 men by September 1917. (By January 1918, however, only 516,000 draftees had actually been certified and sent to camps for training.)[15]

Sites for training camps had been selected on May 7; on June 15 building began. Approximately 50,000 carpenters and 150,000 other workers raced to complete 32 cantonments, 16 camps with wooden barracks for the National Army, and an additional 16 tent camps for the National Guard. Thirteen officer training camps and special army schools in artillery, aviation, chemical warfare, engineering, and the tank corps also had to be built. Workers hammered nails, shoveled dirt, and sawed lumber in a race to finish the training camps and army schools before the new draftees and volunteers arrived. Erected throughout the country, these training camps had the capacity to house the combined populations of Arizona, Nevada, Delaware, and Alaska. A standard army barrack was 43 feet wide, 40 feet long, and 2 stories high. A typical wooden cantonment of between 40,000 and 50,000 men contained hundreds of these barracks in addition to numerous other buildings such as hospitals and mess halls. A single wooden cantonment required 4,500,000 board feet of lumber, and thousands of doors, toilet bowls, and cots. Workers also prepared drill grounds and rifle ranges, paved roads, and laid water and sewer lines.

A decision by the AEF's leadership in July 1917 to adopt a division roughly twice the size of European divisions further complicated the building of these cantonments. Rather than the anticipated 150 men to a company, for example, the builders discovered that they must provide space for 250 men. The effect, according to Frederick Palmer, was "much the same as if, after all plans had been made and material ordered for constructing a high office building, the owner had suddenly decided to add ten stories, put the elevators in different places, and reduce the height of the ceiling by a foot."[16]

The Council of National Defense, created by Congress prior to the war to assist economic mobilization, sought to limit costs by committing private contractors to cost-plus contracts which allowed contractors a profit of 7 percent, but not more than $250,000 for any one camp. Nonetheless costs remained high. Each cantonment cost an average of $8 million, each tent camp $1.9 million. War-related construction also took place overseas to provide logistical support for US forces in France.

Not surprisingly, this gigantic construction program did not always live up to expectations. The tent camps, although not always complete, were generally usable for the National Guard by August. Many of the initial draftees and volunteers, however, arrived at partially finished wooden training camps in September and were put to work to complete construction. Corporal Paul Murphy, Company H, 309th Infantry Regiment, 78th Division, found Camp Dix in New Jersey "a marvel of construction, having been erected during the previous three months, upon what up until that time was nothing but farm land, woods and a few scattered farm buildings." But "construction was still going on and we were training in the midst of dust[,] dirt and the apparent confusion of a large construction job. The grounds were littered with scrap lumber, nails, nail kegs, saw horse and various other building materials." During his spare time and on Saturdays, Murphy was put to work cleaning up some of this mess. Among other tasks, he and other enlisted men "piled huge mounds of scrap lumber on what was later to be the parade grounds, to be carted away by horses and wagons."[17] Construction continued into 1918 as the War Department attempted to meet Pershing's expanding demands for more men in Europe. By the end of the war the training camps were capable of training 1.5 million men.[18]

Young Americans arriving at the training camps entered a world unlike anything in their past experiences. Private Henry L. Henderson, Company K, 358th Infantry Regiment, 90th Division, describes his first day at Camp Dodge, Iowa on May 1, 1918:

They herded us like a bunch of cattle ready for the market, first in one barrack door, down the aisle, sign your name, a preference for any branch of the service, what you were working at, and so on down the line, out the door for another tramp down the line first this way then that, finally we wended up at another barrack where they slung a straw tick, 2 blankets, mess kit, knife, fork, and spoon, also canteen, and cup.[19]

Military authorities also gave soldiers a thorough physical examination, especially during the severe winter of 1917–18 when disease disrupted training. "We were immediately subjected [to] a physical examination[,] the examiners using flash lights to peer at our most intimate parts and woe to him who showed any indication of vermin or disease," writes Corporal Murphy. He was also "isolated[,] deprived of his clothing and given only a blanket to cover his nakedness, like an Indian, which he had to wear for several days until his clothing had been sterilized and eventually returned to him."[20]

Fig. 4 A corner of Pennsylvania Ave, 112th–111th US Infantry, National Guard Battalions, and Signal Corps, Camp Hancock, Augusta, Ga., February 1918

Exchanging civilian attire for either winter olive drab or cotton khaki (the quartermasters had abandoned the traditional blue after campaigns in Cuba and the Philippines), the volunteer or enlisted man (the War Department refused to refer to him as a draftee) entered a regimented and demanding environment with strict discipline and onerous and unfamiliar regulations. Not surprisingly, many did not immediately adjust to military life. Private Oscar C. Heig, a farmer from Worthington, Minnesota, who served in a machine gun battalion in the 86th Division, had a rude awakening after being issued a uniform from Army supply which "fit like the skin on an elephant's rear." Attired in his uniform Heig next encountered an officer. "We were green and dumb," he wrote on his *World War I Survey* form, "and only stared at him admiring his well pressed uniform and polished boots and did not salute. He immediately lectured us in very strong Army language which I can believe none of us ever forgot."[21]

At Camp Hancock, Georgia (Fig. 4), Howard Munder, a bugler in the 109th Infantry Regiment, 28th Division, witnessed a more extreme form of Army discipline when a soldier in his company refused to shower. "They gave him warning and he paid no attention to it," he wrote his parents on October 29, 1917, "so they tied him hand and foot[,] put him on a stretcher with all his clothes on and shoved him under the shower. They then stripped him and made him wash from head to foot with sand and scrubbing brush. Some bath. That is what they do to anybody who persists in being dirty."[22]

A serious and common offense was leaving camp without a pass – "absence without leave." Private John J. Blaser, Company B, 47th Infantry Regiment, 47th Division, guarded prisoners in the stockade, mostly Southern enlisted men, at Camp Pike, Arkansas. "Some tough nuts in there," he wrote his brother in ungrammatical English.

10 or 12 of them got chanes on there legs so they can only take a short step. Them chanes are'nt only locked on. Thay take them to the "Blacksmith" and have them "welded" right on to stay. Them are fellows that have been getting away from the

guard house. But thay don't care. Thay have one hell of a time in there. Them chanes would rattle in there[,] it sounded like a cage of wild animals. Around the guard house they got a high barbd wire neeting fince about 15 feet high ... The most of them left camp with out pass. They would get them back. And the first chanch thay got thay went again.[23]

As infractions increased, the War College Division's training committee concluded that many citizen-soldiers intentionally committed military crimes to escape their military obligation. The Judge Advocate consequently suspended sentences of dishonorable discharge for the duration of the conflict. A National Guard Commander offered an alternative explanation for the failure of some enlisted men to live up to the Army's expectations: "These young men are wholly unaccustomed to the exactions, restrictions and discipline of camp and field life," he informed the General Staff. It was his view that "during the early months of training, they will commit many offenses against military law, such as desertion, absence without leave, disobedience of orders, sleeping on post, various disorders and neglects and other offenses which are peculiar to the military establishment."[24]

For the first time in its history the US Army sought to establish a uniform program of training for all combat troops. A typical day in the camps might go as follows. Buglers sounded reveille around six o'clock in the morning, earlier in the summer, later during the winter. A popular song composed by Irving Berlin captured how many recruits reacted to the bugler:

> Oh! How I hate to get up in the morning,
> Oh! How I'd love to remain in bed;
>> For the hardest blow of all
>> Is to hear the bugler call –
>> "You've got to get up,
>> You've got to get up this morning!"
> Some day I'm going to murder the bugler,
> Some day they're going to find him dead;
>> I'll amputate his reveille
>> And step upon it heavily,
> And spend the rest of my life in bed!

Private Henry Henderson described his first morning at Camp Dodge. Deciding that reveille might be "pretty music, but not at that time of the morn," he scribbled the following in his diary:

They told us to get outside and "fall in," very simple after you learn the "how of it" but not that morning, finally they got us into two ranks and then a bunch of officers came out to give us the "once over." Had roll call, when our name was called we say present very faintly as we were all a little bashful. And then they would proceed to burn our ears with a hard boiled language, as we had it all wrong, we should have said "here" at the top of our voice, the one can holler the loudest is the best soldier ... then came "Attention," and they told us what we could do and what we couldn't do. I know I forgot it as soon as they said it. At last we were "Dismissed" by that time it was breakfast, grab your messkit, make run for the table.[25]

Following nourishment, recruits policed their quarters and stood inspection. Recruits often spent the rest of the morning in "close order" drills where they were taught to march in formation for parades and ceremonies or route marches, which were longer and conditioned soldiers for physical endurance. Some recruits also trained in "extended order," operating in small units maneuvering on the battlefield.

Weighed down with full equipment, these young soldiers initially marched from two to three miles on their route marches. Officers gradually extended these daily route marches to full day marches, again with full equipment. According to the US Army's *Infantry Drill Regulations*, soldiers received fifteen minutes of required rest after marching one-half or three-quarters of a mile and then ten minutes' rest after every hour of marching. The pace was brisk, from two to three miles an hour. Water consumption was confined to "gargling the mouth and throat or to an occasional small drink at most."[26]

Although the US Army's *Infantry Drill Regulations* stressed that the "hardening" of men in daily route marches should be gradual, some officers pushed their men too hard. At Camp Dix, New Jersey, Corporal Murphy's company received a blistering reprimand after returning from its route march and lining up in company formation to be inspected by their commanding officer. "When it became our turn," Murphy remembered, "he asked the Captain the usual question, did any of your men fall out? The Captain answered no/sir and the general was about to ride on, when one of our Lieutenants spoke up to the Captain and said one of our men did fall out on account of blisters on his feet." Hearing this, the general

whirled his horse around and said – "you let a man fall out for blisters on his feet? absurd, preposterous – young man do you know that it is a tradition in the regular army that they haven't had a man fall out in forty years, when a man couldn't walk any more he got down on his belly and crawled and when he couldn't do that any more, the last man in line kicked him off to the side of the road, so he wouldn't be run over by the following units of horses and guns." The general then demanded an investigation and a court martial if justified for the soldier who had fallen out.[27]

Recruits usually ate their biggest meal of the day at noon. Each cantonment had around 350 kitchens using high-pressure steam for cooking vegetables. Thirty-five gallons could be prepared in fifteen minutes. The following is a sample menu from Camp Dix:

BREAKFAST: boiled rice and milk, fried bacon, fried potatoes, hot muffins, bread and butter, coffee or milk

DINNER: puree of bean soup, croutons, roast beef, sweet potatoes, stewed kidney beans, tapioca pudding, bread and butter, coffee or milk

SUPPER: meat and potato pie, hot biscuits, fresh apple-sauce, bread and butter, coffee or milk[.][28]

Not surprisingly, many soldiers gained weight while in training. It cost roughly 40 cents a day to feed a man. Soldiers were inclined to complain about the quality if not the quantity of army chow. Many who did so surely had reason to regret their words if they were later given British rations overseas. Doughboys found the British Expeditionary Force (BEF)'s grub such as Maconochie stew, a tinned mixture of meat (largely gravy) and vegetables (mostly carrots and turnips), noxious and believed that they were slowly being starved to death.

During the afternoon there were more drills which might include musketry training on the range. Doughboys especially liked the Army's standard-issue Springfield model 1903/06 with a 30-caliber magazine. This superb bolt-action rifle, however, was difficult to mass produce. Hence Secretary of War Baker decided to equip the Army with a modified version of the British Lee Enfield .303 rifle, which was manufactured in the United States and used American ammunition.[29] "We boys from the country, who had been shooting squirrels from the tallest trees of the forest, did not expect to learn much that we did not know," writes Private Herbert L. McHenry, who trained at Camp Lee, Virginia, "but we found that there were plenty of things about putting bullets where we wanted them to that we had not learned while squirrel hunting. Among those useful things we learned was the 'trigger-squeeze.'"[30]

Recruits also experienced the terrors of chemical warfare after donning gas masks and being subjected to non-lethal gas in chambers. Malcolm Aitken, a young Marine private who trained at Quantico, Virginia, described his training in a gas chamber in a letter to his mother. We "go into an air tight room containing gas, I don't know what kind but it smarts like wood smoke, makes you weep gallons [and] also makes your nose feel funny. Outside of that there is no effect. We only stay in 5 min without the masks – 15 min with them."[31]

Infantry drill regulations stressed bayonet training. As raw recruits practiced against dummies stuffed with hay straw or shavings, instructors emphasized that the force of their bayonet thrusts should be "delivered principally with the right arm, the left being used to direct the bayonet. The points at which the attack should be directed are, in order of their importance, stomach, chest, head, neck, and limbs." Corporal Carl Klaesi, a noncombatant who was initially attached to the 311th Engineers at Camp Grant, Illinois, received little training before being dispatched to Europe and assigned to the 4th Ammunition Train, 4th Division. But he was given bayonet training and told by his instructor that after bayoneting the enemy he should "kick him in the face[;] that what you got those hob nail shoes for." Corporal Klaesi notes on his *World War I Survey* form: "After going thru this I had enough and wanted to [go] home."[32] Not many Germans were actually to be killed by thrusting American bayonets. In fact, little face-to-face encounters with the bayonet took place on the Western Front. But the Army's leadership wanted American soldiers to be aggressive, to close with the enemy as opposed to seeking cover under fire. Cold steel seemed to be the best available tool to teach this aggressiveness.

Training normally ended at 5 o'clock with the retreat ceremony, an army tradition that dated back to the Civil War. A band played the national anthem while soldiers and officers, standing at attention, faced the American flag while it was slowly lowered. Supper followed with a time for rest until taps sounded at 10 o'clock and soldiers retired to their bunks: no sheets and mattresses stuffed with straw.

Opinions differed on the length of training necessary to turn raw recruits into soldiers capable of taking on the formidable German Army, which was arguably the best fighting force in the world. Major General Leonard Wood, the Army Chief of Staff prior to the war, believed that it could be done in six months. But Wood was in a minority. Most officers believed that it would take at least a year.[33] The schedule adopted was sixteen weeks of basic training, with an additional two months' training before being shipped to Europe where ideally soldiers received another two months' training before spending another month in a quiet sector of the front lines. The Army then deemed him fit for heavy fighting.[34]

Unfortunately the German high command did not allow either Pershing or the War Department to follow this schedule. A series of powerful German offensives, which began on March 21, 1918, forced the War Department to ship divisions to Europe without regard to their training schedules. Also, many untrained soldiers crossed the Atlantic as shipping was made available as replacements to keep AEF divisions at full strength. One of Lieutenant Hugh McPhail's responsibilities at Camp Custer, Michigan, was to select these replacements. "As the men poured into Camp Custer," he recalls, we would get orders from headquarters to send various numbers of men down to headquarters fully equipped and ready for overseas duty. Of course the orders always read to send the best-qualified and trained men. As I seemed to get in most of the drilling, I knew the men better and was given the job of selecting the quota. On consulting with the other shavetails of the regiment, I found that we all did the same thing. Instead of sending the best-qualified men we kept those men longest in the company and sent the newest recruits down to headquarters. Sometimes the poor lads hadn't even been taught squads left and squads right yet.[35]

The harsh reality is that many of Pershing's soldiers, replacements or otherwise, had been given little or insufficient training when committed to combat during the last months of the war.

The unusually severe winter of 1917–18 also hampered training (Fig. 5). Corporal Murphy provides a graphic example of training at Fort Dix, New Jersey, during the winter. His 78th Division had been cannibalized for special services or as replacements to fill up depleted divisions overseas. Companies had been reduced to forty or fifty men from the normal 250.

Digging trenches at that time seemed to be a total loss because the temperature was 16 below zero and the ground was frozen so hard that you could spend hours trying to drive an iron stake into it . . . It was so cold that they established a system where by each man would work for fifteen minutes then stand by the fire for the same length of time, you couldn't stand it any longer and even then some ears, toes or fingers were frozen.

There was no respite from the cold when the troops returned to their barracks with snow blowing through the windows. "Our beds were covered with snow and the only way you could keep warm, was to make a sort of sleeping bag out of all the blankets we had, pile your over coat and rain coat on top, then crawl in, that way we could manage, all except our heads, which got a freezing."[36]

The unusually severe weather in December and January hampered training in southern as well as northern camps. Hale W. Hunt, a native of Wisconsin and no stranger to cold weather, trained at Camp McArthur, Texas. On January 11, he recorded the following in his diary. "The blizzard is raging. Snow is on the ground. Sleighing in the morning. A heck of a storm . . . got up at six and went out to toilet through snowdrifts two feet deep. Snow sifted through the tent on all sides . . . Felt like ten below zero in Wisconsin. Nearly froze my toes."[37] Hunt, as well as many others, got sick.

The United States had no experience fighting a war with an army made up largely of draftees. During the American Civil War, draftees made up only about 6 percent of the Union Army.[38] With fewer men to

Fig. 5 Wall scaling at Camp Wadsworth, South Carolina, c.1918

draw upon, the Confederacy had been forced to conscript a higher percentage of its armies (estimates range from 10 percent to 21 percent).[39] Over time these newly conscripted soldiers imposed a new relationship between the rank and file and the military establishment, with authorities accepting greater responsibility for soldiers' well-being and morale. In October the War Department began giving every draftee a *Home Reading Course for Citizen Soldiers*, which, among other subjects, instructed him how to brush his teeth, chew his food, and empty his bowels. This pamphlet also emphasized that the United States fought its wars for freedom and justice and had "no taste for warfare and no lust for territory or power," and suggested that the Army was not "a big soulless machine that moved with mechanical precision" but a "team" that treated each soldier as being intelligent and self-reliant.[40]

In troop training the General Staff embraced the school of scientific management which was being preached by both government and business leaders. The War Plans Division distributed Major General David C. Shanks' *The Management of the American Soldier*, which included "valuable suggestions ... of assistance to those who have charge of education, recreation and character building of the Army."[41] Shanks suggested that troop morale would be improved if soldiers' names were learned and they were treated with respect. In June 1918 the War Department further emphasized building morale with the establishment of the Military Morale Section, which was "charged with the 'psychological stimulation of troops to promote fighting efficiency.'"[42]

The nearly half million immigrants and thousands of second-generation immigrants drafted into service represented an unprecedented situation for army authorities. The brass responded by altering some of its traditional training policies. Their new approach, as in the case of scientific management, owed much to Progressivism. In fact, Baker referred to the officers involved as "Progressive officers."[43] Working with ethnic leaders, military authorities sought to meet the cultural and social needs of their foreign-born soldiers, including a goodly number from Germany and Austria–Hungary, in an attempt to socialize and Americanize them.

With immigrant draftees speaking forty-six different tongues, the language barrier represented a potential threat to unit combat efficiency. The War Department consequently established English language schools in the camps. As part of their regular training, immigrants who could not read, write, or speak English spent three hours in daily mandatory English classes, usually for a period of four months. Instructors, many of whom spoke the language of their students, drilled them on useful military terms such as "tent," "guard," "drill," "march," "shoot," "bayonet," and "run."[44] Foreign-speaking draftees also frequently served in ethnic units commanded by officers who spoke their language.

These multinational US units surprised many foreign leaders when they arrived in Europe. After his first encounter with rank-and-file American troops, a surprised Sir Douglas Haig, the British commander-in-chief, exclaimed to a fellow officer: "The Americans are not trained at all and talk all manner of languages."[45] The War Department's response to the unprecedented influx of immigrants into the Army, however, proved generally successful, as reflected by a French soldier's comment when he came face to face with American soldiers:

You could not imagine a more extraordinary gathering than this American army, there is a bit of everything, Greeks, Italians, Turks, Indians, Spanish, also a sizable number of boches. Truthfully, almost half of the officers have German origins. This doesn't seem to bother them ... Among the Americans are sons of emigrated Frenchmen and sons of emigrated boche. I asked one son of a Frenchman if these Germans were coming willingly to fight their brothers and cousins, he squarely answered me: yes![46]

Not surprisingly, the General Staff had been concerned about Austrians and especially Germans, who constituted the country's largest immigrant group at the beginning of the twentieth century. Joseph E. Kuhn, the head of the War College Division, assessed the potential danger as follows in June 1917, the month that Congress passed the Espionage Act: "We know that [the Germans] have already established here a very complete and efficient espionage service ... Agents are found all over the country in every walk of life of our population. They are also to be found not only in the ranks of the Army, but in our offices, arsenals and munitions plants."[47] To confront this potential threat to the Army, the War Department created within the War College Division the Military Intelligence Division (MID), headed by Major (soon to be Colonel) Ralph H. Van Deman. The MID quickly established an intelligence presence in all US military camps. This network of intelligence officers paid particular attention to the Lutheran Church, concerned that its chaplains would collect information from individual soldiers about their movements, enabling Berlin to determine when units were being shipped to France. These intelligence officers never discovered any evidence to support the Army's suspicions about the Lutheran Church. In fact, the MID, despite its at times overzealous activities, failed to uncover any German network of spies in the Army.[48]

After being called up, Edward A. Schaffer, a member of the National Guard, visited his local tavern, run by an elderly German and frequented by Germans. He was asked if he "really was going to fight the Fatherland." He (as did other German immigrants in the Army) answered in the affirmative by their actions.[49] It is noteworthy that when German-surnamed veterans responded to the *World War I Survey*, 66 percent recalled that they had enthusiastically enlisted. The most popular other responses were simply "drafted" or "conscripted." Few if any veteran with a German surname expressed concern about marching off to war against his ethnic relatives.[50]

Unfortunately, many Americans with German surnames suffered discrimination, including Schaffer's mother, who was mistreated by a local merchant. Government officials on the local, state, and national levels by their actions sometimes encouraged these nativist reactions. An incident on April 3–4, 1918, which shocked the nation, revealed the consequences of viewing ethnic Germans as potential traitors. Robert Paul Präger, a German-American who had been rejected when he attempted to enlist because he was blind in one eye, took a temporary job in a coal mine in Maryville, Illinois. Accused by miners of being a German spy, he was paraded through town. The next day a mob seized him and forced him to sing patriotic songs and kiss the American flag. Before being hanged, he told his killers: "All right boys, go ahead and kill me, but wrap me in the flag when you bury me."[51]

A moral booster for both volunteers and draftees was that the government made them the best paid American soldiers in history. Before America's entry into the war, the Army Reorganization Bill, June 3, 1916, had set a private's monthly pay at $18 a month. Once at war the government dramatically increased a private's pay to that of an unskilled worker's pay, $30 a month, with an extra $3 for serving overseas. A first sergeant made $60 a month if serving abroad. This made American soldiers much better paid than their European counterparts. For example, a German private received the equivalent of $3.21 a month, a French private $1.70.[52] Although some foreign soldiers called the US Army the "Millionaire's Army," many Doughboys overseas often felt short of cash, especially after their pay was reduced by the Liberty Bonds they purchased, their allotments for dependents, and by war insurance. A lack of skill at craps and poker also left many soldiers feeling poor while serving in France.

If an enlisted man had dependents, half of his pay had to be allocated to his wife and children. (The only other country that paid its soldiers enough to require mandatory allotments to his dependents was Canada.) The government also recognized its responsibility to the soldiers' dependent family, paying an additional $15 for a wife, $10 for the first child, $7.50 for the second child, and $5 for each additional child up to a total of $50. Some 1.7 million men with eligible dependents submitted applications for allotments and allowances. And this was just the beginning of the American government's support for its citizen soldiers and their dependents. If a soldier or sailor paid the ultimate price or was disabled his dependents were also generously treated. "For the first time in the history of American wars, the families of soldiers became charges of the national state," proclaims K. Walter Hickel.[53]

With its allotments and allowances, compensation for death or disability, and government insurance policies administered by the Bureau of

War Risk Insurance under the direction of Secretary of Treasury William G. McAdoo, Congress's War Risk Insurance Act foreshadowed the New Deal with its comprehensive government programs to assist ordinary people. Significantly, the government provided equal benefits for both blacks and whites. An Army pamphlet, *Valuable Information: For Discharged Soldiers of the United States Army* (1919), compiled under the direction of Major General W. A. Holbrook, proudly proclaimed: "This is the greatest measure of protection ever offered to its fighting forces by any nation in the history of the world."[54]

In case of death in the line of duty, compensation, ranging from $20 to $70 a month, was paid to the soldier's widow, children, and dependent father or mother. Compensation to a widow continued until she remarried, and to a child until the age of eighteen, or until marriage. The government also assumed an obligation for its wounded warriors. In the event of total disability, the amount of compensation varied from $30 to $95 per month, according to the size of the man's family. ($10 in 1918 equaled approximately $150 in 2011.)

The government also offered inexpensive insurance policies which were separate and distinct from these programs. Unsurprisingly, private insurance companies when approached by McAdoo had been uninterested in selling insurance to men about to engage the formidable German Army in battle. With the government bearing all overhead expenses, McAdoo was able to provide soldiers with inexpensive term life insurance. All enlisted personnel were eligible on the basis that they had been deemed fit for service when inducted. Policies ranged from $1,000 to $10,000. A twenty-one-year-old soldier, for example, could purchase a $1,000 policy for only 65 cents a month that paid $5.75 a month for twenty years. The cost of the full $10,000 policy averaged between $6 and $7 a month and paid $57.50 a month for twenty years to the "permitted" class, which was namely spouse, child, grandchild, parent, brother, or sister. With interest, the payout for twenty years was $13,800 (or more than $200,000 in 2014 money). By 1919, 4,561,974 individual policies had been written, or approximately 38 billion dollars in policies.[55]

Mental testing by the newly created Psychological Division also represented an innovation by the US Army. Beginning in the spring of 1918, psychologists tested more than 1.5 million men. Most enlisted men were poorly educated by the standards of today. The median number of years of education was 6.9 for Indians, 4.7 for immigrants, and 2.6 for Southern blacks. The psychologists deemed as many as one out of every three recruits illiterate. They gave two tests, "alpha" tests for those who could read and write and "beta" tests for the illiterate. These

Table 1 *Intelligence tests for army recruits prepared by college graduates*

Question	A	B	C	D
The Overland car is made in:	Buffalo	Detroit	Flint	Toledo
Mauve is the name of a:	drink	color	fabric	food
Scrooge appears in:	*Vanity Fair*	*A Christmas Carol*	*Romola*	*Henry IV*

"mental meddlers," as one officer called them, used the soldier's mental age as a score. They concluded that "a moron has been defined as any one with a mental age from 7 to 12 years." Of those tested, "47.3 percent of the white draft had an average mental age of 13.15 years; while the average mental age of the black draft was 10.1." Although perhaps useful in assigning men to army responsibilities according to their tested intelligence, the tests were slanted against recruits from city slums and rural areas, especially if they were recent immigrants or African-Americans from the South. Over half of the Russian, Polish, and Italian draftees tested, for example, were shown to be "inferior."[56] It is not surprising that many were perplexed by questions such as the ones in Table 1, which were prepared by college graduates. As Coffman has suggested, "either this pioneering testing venture was invalid or most American men in their twenties were very stupid."[57] The former apparently was much closer to the truth. Keene suggests that both the content and protocol of these intelligence tests were faulty.[58] Moreover, one's education was not necessarily a good measure of how someone might perform in combat. As one young 2nd Lieutenant in the 4th Division who trained at Camp Greene in North Carolina noted: "Some of the men from rural Arkansas & Texas could not read or write but they could shoot. Later replacements from New York and the East could read and write but could not shoot."[59]

The unhealthy influences that young men might encounter in the military represented a major concern for the War Department. Secretary of War Baker wrote the President:

My experience with the Mexican mobilization (when the National Guard had been mobilized) was that our young soldiers had a good deal of time hanging rather heavily on their hands with two unfortunate results. 1. They became homesick. 2. They were easily led aside into unwholesome diversions and recreations, patronizing cheap picture shows, saloons, dance halls and houses of prostitution.[60]

This was more than a moral issue. The new National Army's effectiveness was at stake. Alcoholism and venereal disease had constituted serious threats to the well-being of the old Regular Army. The Army's admission rates to hospitals due to excessive drinking had been twenty-two times higher than the British Army's, which was also composed of volunteers. Venereal disease, however, constituted the greater health risk. Secretary of War Henry L. Stimson admitted in 1912 that "the high percentage of venereal disease continues to be the reproach of the American Army, and the daily average number of those sick from that cause during the past calendar year was larger than the daily average number of those sick from all other of the more important diseases combined."[61]

Baker assigned troop morale to Raymond B. Fosdick. While serving as mayor of Cleveland, Baker had been impressed with Fosdick's investigation of New York City's departments and his study of police methods in Europe. Concerned about conditions in the camps and towns along the Mexican border in 1916 where units from the Regular Army and the National Guard had been assembled, Baker had sent Fosdick to assess the situation. Fosdick visited the "red light" districts of Columbus and other border towns and witnessed thousands of soldiers on the prowl. No prude, Fosdick recognized that "men would be men." He understood that many soldiers, tired of the regimentation of their military routine and their loss of individuality, sought an outlet. "There was absolutely nothing in that town [Columbus] that could in any way legitimately interest them," he reported. "There were no moving-picture shows and no pool tables, no place where they could write letters or read, no place where they could purchase a newspaper or magazine."[62] After his appointment as head of the new Commission on Training Camp Activities (CTCA), Fosdick told the *New York Times*:

Our boys are to be drafted into service. We cannot afford to draft them into a demoralizing environment. The responsibility of the Government is doubly obvious in view of the measure of conscription. A man might volunteer for service and ruin his chance with vicious surroundings. When conscription comes into play, however, the Government must assume the responsibility for eliminating these evils.[63]

Under Fosdick's leadership the CTCA launched a vigorous campaign against the sale of liquor and the presence of prostitutes within the vicinity of its camps. "A German Bullet is Cleaner than a Whore," one CTCA poster proclaimed. Another announced: "You wouldn't use another man's toothbrush. Why use his whore?" The CTCA largely won its battle against venereal disease on the home front, with Fosdick claiming that by the end of the war he had successfully closed every red light district in the country.[64] Army physicals had revealed that

259,612 men had contracted venereal disease *before* becoming soldiers. A study after the war of five large cantonments revealed that of 48,167 cases treated only 4 percent had contracted the disease *after* entering the service.[65]

Overseas Pershing also enthusiastically waged a thoroughgoing war to keep his soldiers clean. On his way to France aboard the *Baltic* he had suggested to the War Department that part of a soldier's pay should be withheld to discourage him from spending money on prostitutes. In France, he constantly questioned his generals about the condition of their men when he inspected their divisions; his first question usually concerned the division's number of reported cases of venereal disease. Among other measures, the US Army made prophylactics readily available in every billeted town, and medics in some divisions examined both officers and men twice weekly. As a result, according to Smythe, "Pershing returned to America the cleanest army in the history of the world."[66]

Although sports had been popular in the prewar army, Fosdick gave added emphasis to them. He especially emphasized the manly and violent sports of football and boxing (Gene Tunney, a private in the Marine Corps, later became heavyweight champion), but he also encouraged baseball and track (Fig. 6). Most colleges had discontinued football during the war but many college athletes continued to play in the armed services. In 1918, with President Wilson's approval, the Marines from Mare Island, California, took on the Army from Camp Lewis, Washington, in the Rose Bowl. Before a capacity crowd of 25,000, the Marines triumphed 19 to 7. Within a few months most of these Army and Marine players had exchanged their leather helmets for steel ones and were waging war against the Germans on the Western Front.

The CTCA did more than focus on physical activities. It constructed "Liberty Theaters" in the training camps. Vaudeville shows, concerts, and amateur theatricals entertained soldiers, along with movies. The CTCA also worked with benevolent associations, such as the YMCA, Red Cross, Salvation Army, YWCA, Knights of Columbus, and the Jewish Welfare Board, among others, who played an active role in moderating the tedium of military life. Private donations as well as the government financed the CTCA's activities. Books of coupons, called "Smileage" books, were also sold, many being purchased by patriotic citizens who gave them to soldiers so they could gain free admission to the "Liberty Theaters."[67]

The YMCA, which offered a place to relax and provided writing materials, also had a positive effect on many young men. Howard W. Munder, a bugler with Company G, 109th Infantry Regiment, the

Fig. 6 Baseball in the army

28th Division, wrote the following to his mother and father while training at Camp Hancock, Georgia:

Last night I was over to the YMCA building to listen to a retired Capt. from the French Army speak ... His speech was wonderful and I learned a lesson, which I hope I never will forget. It was a picture he drew before us in our minds of men who were terribly wounded. Not by shells or bayonets but by the young man's greatest sin, disease. He pictured how these men wanted to die, couldn't face home, with a body wrecked of manhood and his own lusts satisfied to this end. Then the picture of the wounded and crippled who were proud of their bullet wounds. Why? Because they were inflicted in honorable battle.[68]

American soldiers serving in an army largely made up of draftees had never been treated better as individuals by their government or by the military authorities. From afar, the first American officers to arrive in Europe, the Regulars of the 1st Division, looked on in wonderment as young Americans at home prepared to be soldiers. "We learned of new organizations and new officials," writes George C. Marshall, who was destined to become the US Army's Chief of Staff during World War II. "In the midst of our labors on the new American front and in the gloom of the winter, we heard tales of instructors in singing and boxing, of psychiatric experts, and of many other strange additions to Army life."[69]

But the soldiers in these cantonments when dispatched across the Atlantic, although generally physically fit and disciplined, remained largely unprepared for industrialized warfare. Even their training under generally good conditions frequently amounted to little more than close order drill and extended marches. Pershing's insistence on "open warfare" training also proved disruptive because few trainers stateside really understood this concept and adopted "the linear formations of an age gone by."[70]

America's allies looked on with mounting alarm. The following comments were made in a report prepared by the French General Staff that was circulated in the British War Cabinet on January 25, 1918:

Training in the United States is at present hardly organized. The Infantry are still engaged on individual training, and the training of the Artillery has practically not begun. The Experience of British Divisions proves that 6 months divisional training and holding quiet sectors is only just enough to break in the officers and staffs of large units to cope with the difficulties of modern warfare; a fortiori, the barely organized American Divisions which are expected in France during the first 3 months of 1918 will require 6 months war training.[71]

Unfortunately, the Germans were not prepared to allow American divisions arriving in France an additional six months' training.

5   US army doctrine and industrialized trench warfare

With only some 6,000 officers in the Regular Army when the United States became a belligerent, the army did not have nearly enough officers or non-commissioned officers (even when National Guard officers were included) to train the masses of men arriving at training camps. An army of 1 million men needed at least 50,000 officers. To meet this need, the War Department established officer training camps. The originally required four months of training was quickly reduced to three months, resulting in "ninety-day wonders," as some lieutenants were called. Officer training camp graduates, however, learned little of modern warfare, especially as it was being waged in the trenches in France with machine guns, grenades, automatic weapons, chemical warfare, and mortars as well as aircraft and tanks.[1]

France and Great Britain sought to educate Americans about modern warfare by dispatching experienced soldiers to assist in specialist training. The French dispatched 286 officers; and the British sent over a further 261 officers and 226 non-commissioned officers.[2] Although these officers were veterans there were not nearly enough of them to prepare adequately America's youth for what lay ahead. When these foreign officers began arriving at US training camps many of them were shocked by what they encountered. Lieutenant-Colonel Gilbert W. Hall, a machine gun specialist, had been sent over from Britain in October 1917. He served as an instructor with the 89th Infantry Division, composed of draftees from Arizona, Colorado, Kansas, Missouri, New Mexico, Nebraska, and South Dakota, at Camp Funston, Kansas. "We could see almost at a glance that after having been at war for nine months, the men were poorly clothed and very poorly equipped, if it could be said that they were equipped at all," he noted. "No rifles had been issued, Wooden guns were being used, making the instruction of an infantryman in musketry almost impossible. For drill purposes the men wore blue overalls, all had hats, poor boots, good underwear. The machine gunners had old and obsolete Colt guns which could never be used with ammunition with any degree of safety."[3]

This lack of modern weapons and communication systems proved to be a serious handicap for American soldiers being trained. The absence of grenades, trench mortars, flame throwers, automatic rifles, artillery, and communications equipment also made it difficult if not impossible for foreign officers to train draftees about the "intimate coordination of the use of the different weaponry."[4] To be blunt, inadequate equipment limited training to fighting basically a nineteenth-century war with rifles, pistols, and bayonets. Conditions improved little in the months ahead. His superiors had assigned Corporal Harold C. Vaux, a dairy farmer from Minnesota, to a machine gun company at Camp Travis, Texas in April 1917, but he never saw a machine gun until a few weeks before he went into action at Saint-Mihiel, in September.[5]

Nor was the emphasis of these foreign officers on trench warfare appreciated by many officers serving in the AEF. "Unfortunately, the groups of instructors sent to America by our Allies brought with them the tactical theory that there was nothing left in warfare but the trench, that there was no further possibility of maneuver," writes Alexander, who commanded the 77th Division at Meuse-Argonne. "The yielding of our then chief of staff and his principal advisers to the heresy of the trench warfare cult merely meant that invaluable time was wasted in non-essentials."[6]

It was one thing to conscript, feed, and house soldiers and teach them how to dress, march, and salute, quite another matter to provide them with an effective combat doctrine and modern weaponry to fight in what quickly had become the world's most deadly conflagration. Leaders of peacetime armies are expected to prepare for future wars. This had certainly been true of the European general staffs prior to the Great War. The French had moved from an emphasis on the defense to an extreme position on the superiority of the offense. Influenced by the Napoleonic Wars and the wars of German unification, other European general staffs as well expected that the armies under their direction would engage in a war of movement. Modern weaponry, which dramatically increased an army's killing power, did not alter their thinking. To the contrary, writes David Herrmann, "tacticians realized that firepower was deadlier than ever, but they often expected that this would, if anything, make attacks more effective and place a premium on rapid, decisive movements."[7]

Charles Ardant du Picq, an influential French military theorist, argued that an army with a superior spirit and aggressiveness would prevail over an opposing force even if its firepower were inferior. This emphasis on "moral superiority" inspired the military philosophy of the *offensive à outrance* or "offensive to excess." Joseph Joffre, Chief of the French

Fig. 7 Training camp activities. Bayonet-fighting instruction by an English Sergeant Major, Camp Dick, Texas, *c*.1917–*c*.1918

General Staff, embraced this philosophy before the war and replaced defensive-minded generals. In October 1913, the French established new regulations for large units which stressed: "Battles are above all moral contests. Defeat is inevitable when hope for victory ceases. Success will come, not to the one who has suffered the least losses, but to the one whose will is the steadiest and whose morale is the most highly tempered."[8] The French embrace of the do-or-die offense led to a lesser role for artillery and an emphasis on bayonets, which French infantry regulations of April 1914 described as the infantry's "supreme weapon."[9]

British official doctrine in 1914 differed little from the French with its emphasis on the bayonet but was more cautious in the attack (Fig. 7). British soldiers were trained to advance using cover, extended formations, and short rushes to establish a firing line some 200 yards from the enemy. Suppressive fire from rifles (also artillery if present) would then be laid down; after which the enemy would be finished off with a bayonet charge.[10] Despite the enormous casualty rates, many European officers continued to emphasize the rifle and especially the bayonet to encourage their men to close with the enemy. If infantry went to ground and relied upon its rifles or bombs (grenades) to dislodge the enemy, attacks frequently became bogged down. On the other hand, it soon became obvious that if your opponent's firepower had not been suppressed a frontal assault either by a single line of packed infantry or by a succession of waves of infantry was costly and had little chance of success.[11]

In 1905, the new American General Staff had produced the first edition of the *Field Service Regulations*, which mirrored the German General Staff's attempts to regulate tactics and operation of their army. Revised American editions followed. That the US Army's approach to tactics and operations had much in common with the European armies prior to 1914 is reflected in both its 1911 *Infantry Drill Regulations* and its 1914 *Field Service Regulations*. Because of the Spanish–American and Philippine Wars, many of America's military leaders had experienced war first hand. But these colonial wars did not prepare them for the industrialized and semi-siege warfare being waged on the Western Front. (The same could be said of the European powers prior to World War I.) The war as it evolved on the Western Front required an engineer's meticulous attention to detail and his methodical approach rather than a cavalryman's elan. The US Army's *Field Service Regulations* focused on the unlikely event of armies encountering each other on the march. In that event, "boldness in decision and in action is usually the best line of conduct." If the enemy were close enough to attack, "recourse to the bayonet must be unhesitating." American war planners also emphasized open warfare with "turning movements" and "enveloping attacks" rather than static trench warfare. With no existing field armies, army corps, combat divisions, or brigades, the military's leadership naturally had difficulty envisaging a stalemated war between vast armies equipped with weapons of unprecedented lethality.

Firepower, especially heavy artillery and machine guns, determined success or failure in the trenches of the Western Front (Fig. 8). Although it has been calculated that artillery was responsible for the majority of all casualties during World War I,[12] the US Army leadership assigned it a secondary role. This is not to say that the Army did not take note of the artillery's role in conducting successful attacks. The *Field Service Regulations* noted that "the greater the difficulties of the infantry the more powerful must be the artillery support."[13] The *Infantry Drill Regulations* recognized that "as a rule one's artillery is the best weapon against hostile artillery."[14] But it rejected the dictum of many European generals after they experienced trench warfare: "Artillery conquers, infantry occupies." At best the Army considered artillery as the infantryman's "close supporting arm." But at the same time it emphasized in its *Provisional Drill*

Fig. 8 Greatest French gun [320-mm] at moment of firing during a night bombardment

and Service Regulations for Field Artillery (Horse and Light) that artillery-men should be economical in their use of the shell. Mark Grotelueschen has noted that "while in Europe the artillery forces were expending millions of shells in support of single offensives," it is significant that "US Army regulations treated the economic use of ammunition as among the most important concepts to be mastered by American gunners."[15] In defense of the Army, artillery had not played a dominant role in recent wars. American officers studied the Franco-Prussian War, 1870–71, in which it has been calculated that only 8.4 percent of casual-ties were caused by artillery, and they had been observers during the Russo-Japanese War in which it has been calculated that 10 percent of the casualties were caused by artillery.[16] It was the reverse of this in 1918, with the Medical Department of the US Army calculating that "87 percent of all AEF combat casualties were caused by artillery fire of one form or another."[17]

The Army also generally failed to recognize the importance of machine guns. At 400–600 rounds per minute cyclic rate, one machine gun had the potential to equal the firepower of as many as eighty riflemen and might cover an area approximately 500 yards wide. Both the *Field Service Regulations* and the *Infantry Drill Regulations*, however, looked upon these rapid-firing guns as "emergency weapons." In 1911, the War Depart-ment had replaced the Vikers-Maxim, a heavy, water-cooled, belt-fed gun that weighed more than 100 pounds, with the Benet-Mercie, a light, water-cooled, clip-fed machine rifle that was approximately 75 percent lighter than its predecessor. This light machine rifle, called the "Benny-Mercy" by the troops, was not really suitable for either cavalry or infan-try. The cavalry liked its portability but it frequently jammed in the field. The infantry rejected it because it was incapable of sustained fire and ineffective as a defensive weapon. Moreover, its ammunition clips had to be loaded "upside down."[18] The flawed automatic weapons possessed by the US Army no doubt contributed to this deadly weapon being under-appreciated by its leadership. Each German infantry battalion had an allocation of at least thirty-six modern machine guns,[19] and the Germans appeared to substitute machine guns for rifles in their defensive positions in 1918 when full-strength US divisions faced depleted German divisions.

Despite dramatic advances in firepower, the US Army thus made it clear as the country entered the war that it expected infantry, armed with rifles and bayonets, to dominate the battlefield.[20] The *Field Service Regulations* emphasized that "the infantry is the principal and most important arm, which is charged with the main work on the field of battle and decides the final issue of combat." It also stressed that "in doubtful cases aggressiveness and initiative will usually win."[21] In sum, discipline and morale would triumph over firepower. This belief was actually not surprising and dominated the views of many European general staffs as well when war first erupted in 1914. With Wilson and the Congress both determined to keep the United States out of the war, the US General Staff did not follow the evolution of tactics on foreign battlefields or explore a combat doctrine or tactics designed for an American force fighting on French soil against the powerful German Army. What is indefensible, however, is that Pershing and most other officers in the AEF continued, as we will see, to give priority to the American infantryman, armed with a rifle and bayonet, on battlefields dominated by automatic weapons, strong defenses, chemical warfare, and exploding shells. Although their learning curves had been agonizingly slow, his European counterparts had discovered that such a combat doctrine was a prescription for disaster.

Mobilization plans, with their meticulous railway timetables for troop movement, served as the hair trigger that ignited general war in 1914. Following Russia's mobilization in response to Austria–Hungary's declaration of war on Serbia, Germany began general mobilization. Russia's mobilization jeopardized Germany's prewar plan to win a two-front war against Russia and France. Every hour counted. The German General Staff had given itself only six weeks to defeat or cripple the French Army before the Russian "steam roller" began to press forward from the East. As the German Army began a great wheeling movement through Belgium and Luxembourg, the French Army launched an all-out offensive in Alsace-Lorraine. Generals, expecting a short war, focused on flanks, envelopments, and annihilations. They believed that their large conscript armies might defeat their opponents with a single decisive blow.

The French were the first to be disabused of this view. In Alsace-Lorraine, the 1st and 2nd French Armies attacked the Germans in waves. Bugles blared and long bayonets glittered under the hot August sun as French soldiers, wearing their traditional blue coats and red trousers, advanced with reckless abandon. Their massed formations and brightly colored uniforms were characteristic of nineteenth- and even eighteenth-century warfare. French elan proved no match for German artillery, magazine rifles, and machine guns. With little or no artillery to suppress enemy firepower, the advancing French were stopped in their tracks. In some twelve days the French lost an extraordinary 4,478 officers and 206,515 other ranks.[22]

German hopes of a quick victory soon faded, however. In September an Anglo-French counterattack stopped the German Army after its distant advance across Belgium and into Northern France at the First Battle of the Marne. Following this German setback both sides attempted to outflank the other. This so-called "race to the sea" came to an end when a Belgian force took up a position on the Channel. Soldiers now began to dig in. Over the next months opposing armies constructed an almost continuous defensive system from the Belgian coast to the Swiss Alps. The immense size of the armies had not, as many assumed, contributed to a quick and decisive end of the conflict. Quite the contrary. For the first time since the days of the Roman Empire, an army could strongly defend an almost continuous front of great length. Unprecedented manpower (which could be quickly moved by rail to a threatened sector), modern weapons with their dramatically increased firepower, and a cratered battlefield crisscrossed with barbed wire strung on trestles and stakes to a height of from three to five feet combined to give the advantage to the defense.[23]

Machine-tooling and an abundance of cheap high-quality steel provided European armies with unprecedented firepower. With no flanks to turn, a frontal assault was the only option, but it was certain to be costly, even suicidal, for the attacker if he advanced in close order without suppressing the enemy's firepower and cutting his wire. An especially egregious example of this occurred during the Allied autumn campaign (Loos, Artois, and Champagne) in 1915. At Loos, Sir Douglas Haig, the commander of the British First Army, mistakenly believed that the German front was about to be broken. On September 26, he sent forward two reserve divisions, the 21st and 24th, both New Army, composed of volunteers who had no previous combat experience. Without significant or accurate artillery support and with no covering smoke, they formed up in columns, each numbering about 1,000 men, and advanced up a gentle slope with bayonets fixed, against strong German defenses bristling with machine guns and protected by barbed wire (Fig. 9). The results, as described by a German regimental diary, were as predictable as they were catastrophic. "Ten columns of extended lines could clearly be discerned ... offering a target as had never been seen before, or thought possible. Never had the machine gunners such straightforward work to do nor done it so effectively. They traversed to and fro among the enemy's ranks unceasingly." Some German infantrymen were so sickened by the sight of the wounded and dead that they held their rifle fire as British wounded dragged themselves or staggered from the battlefield. Germans later described the battlefield as the *Der Leichenfeld von Loos* (or "Field of Corpses of Loos"). Of the some 10,000 British soldiers involved, 385 officers and 7,861 men were killed or wounded or missing in a little over an hour. The German units facing them reported no losses.[24]

Fig. 9 German machine gunners in a trench

While the British in 1915 expanded their munitions industry and raised an army from scratch capable of taking on the German Army, the French largely sustained the Allied position on the Western Front. Determined to drive the Germans from their soil, they launched a series of costly offensives with the British playing a limited supporting role. With the exception of a single offensive at Ypres, Germany concentrated on the Russian Army. Although these Allied offensives on the Western Front offered indirect assistance to beleaguered Russia, they are remembered more for their cost than their results. At no point did these large-scale attacks alter the Western Front more than three miles in any one direction.

Many senior officers had difficulty adjusting to the new realities of stalemated, industrialized warfare.[25] They continued to rely on acquiring more men and munitions to break the stalemate and return to a war of movement. By the end of 1915, however, some senior officers adopted a more cautious (and less optimistic) policy. Rather than seek a return to a war of movement by breaking the enemy's front they adopted attritional warfare. This was true of General Joffre, who served as the de facto Allied commander-in-chief. Earlier he had been a leading disciple of the *offensive à outrance*. His "Plan of Action" for 1916, however, emphasized wearing down the enemy through coordinated and simultaneous offensives against the Central Powers on the Western, Eastern, and Italian fronts.[26] Success would come when the enemy could no longer either replace or endure his losses and his front collapsed, which in reality was exactly what happened to the German Army in late 1918.

A variation of Joffre's emphasis on waging a war of attrition was the growing emphasis on "bite and hold" operations, or the launching of deliberate, step-by-step attacks that focused on inflicting heavy losses on the enemy rather than a single-blow strategic breakthrough. Conflict between these two approaches (enemy losses v. ground gained) helps explain the confused planning that preceded the Battle of the Somme and led to a compromise that limited the effectiveness of British artillery. Haig, who had replaced Sir John French as the commander-in-chief, believed that his force would achieve a breakthrough which would enable him to deploy his cavalry against the fleeing Germans. Sir Henry Rawlinson, who commanded the new Fourth Army, was not as optimistic and favored a more cautious step-by-step approach.[27]

The first day of the Battle of the Somme in July 1916 was Loos writ large for the BEF. The temporary British commander of the 94th Infantry Brigade, 31st Division, Brigadier-General H. C. Rees, watched his men leave their trenches and advance across no-man's-land against strong German defenses. Young British subalterns with their swagger sticks and polished Sam Browne belts led the way. "They advanced in line after line, dressed as if on parade, and not a man shirked going through the extremely heavy barrage, or facing the machine gun and rifle fire that finally wiped them out," Rees later reported to his superiors. "He saw the lines which advanced in such admirable order melting away under the fire. Yet not a man wavered, broke the ranks, or attempted to come back. He has never seen, indeed could never have imagined, such a magnificent display of gallantry, discipline and determination . . . hardly a man of ours got to the German Front Line."[28] British courage and tenacity no doubt motivated these young men to leave their trenches and advance into the teeth of German artillery and machine guns. But compulsion also played a role. Armies employed military police to prevent stragglers from remaining in the relative safety of their own trench systems.[29]

By any standard the British Army's attack on July 1 was an unmitigated disaster. The British suffered 57,470 casualties, of which more than 19,000 were killed or later died from their wounds. British dead actually exceeded the number of Germans defending the trenches being assaulted. Many British soldiers never reached their first day's objective. The primary reason for the worst day in British military history was the failure of the BEF's big guns to dominate the battlefield by smashing German defenses and neutralizing the enemy's artillery through counter-battery work.[30] The French Sixth Army, which supported the British attack on July 1, enjoyed greater success on its front with many fewer casualties, in large part because of its overwhelming artillery superiority, in both weight of fire and experienced gunners. In contrast to the British, the French also employed their infantry in depth and in small groups rather than in waves or extended lines of massed infantry. French staff officers of the Sixth Army were shocked at British tactics and complained that they were participating in an offensive prepared "for amateurs by amateurs."[31]

What is often overlooked is that senior officers learned from their mistakes and warfare on the Western Front continued to evolve during the four-and-a-half-month Somme campaign. The BEF's artillery improved and soon matched the French in leveling German trenches and other obstacles. German soldiers often found shell holes a more secure refuge than their carefully constructed trench systems. Entente forces also made great strides in fighting an all-arms battle as their aircraft attacked German ground forces and pinpointed German artillery positions for counter-battery fire. The machine gun, which was deployed in depth and often placed in shell holes as well as trenches, proved to be the most effective German defensive weapon. As one German analysis noted: "The infantry battle was always supported by our machineguns. As long as the machineguns and their crews were intact, every English attack was bound to be beaten back."[32]

With artillery and machine guns dominating the battlefield during the monster battles of Somme and Verdun, a strategy of attrition prevailed by default. Optimistic generals such as Sir Douglas Haig continued to believe in a strategic breakthrough and a war-winning advance. But the reality was that the war of maneuver which had characterized the first months of the war in the West was no longer possible. "Creeping barrages" escorted infantry across no-man's-land and suppressed the enemy's artillery and machine guns. Tanks also appeared on the battlefield for the first time. Improved military technology made possible a break-*in* against the multi-layered defenses that existed from late 1914 onward. But these break-*ins* never truly converted into breakthrough*s* that led to the war of maneuver that had characterized the first months of the war.

It is true that German and Allied attacks in 1918 succeeded in breaking the enemy defenses and returning to a limited war of movement before they inevitably ground to a halt. A decisive breakthrough and a fluid battlefield still remained beyond the capabilities of either opposing force.[33] Slow-moving and unreliable tanks – and certainly not horse soldiers – did not have the capacity to maintain the momentum of the offensive. Chewed-up battlefields also made it difficult for artillery and vital supplies to keep up with advancing infantry. Trench warfare thus resumed once reinforcements were brought up by rail or trucks to plug any holes in the front.

What remains surprising until the present day is that Pershing and many other AEF officers had what Chief of Staff Peyton C. March has described as a "profound ignorance"[34] of both British and French offensive doctrine that predated the Great War and continued to influence the thinking of leading Allied generals such as Haig and Foch who had been forced to adopt a defensive strategy on the Western Front at the beginning of 1918 following the collapse of the Russian Army and the near collapse of the Italian Army. The AEF leadership was also too ready to accept the outdated *Infantry Drill Regulations* and the *Field Service Regulations* as being adequate to provide American soldiers with the basics. "If all that was required of those regulations providing instruction in the basic 'School of the Soldier' – that is, how to dress, march, and salute – they would have been fine," note Johnson and Hillman.[35] But that most definitely was not the case as was quickly demonstrated on the modern battlefield.

6   Over where?

Shortly after America entered the war Major Palmer E. Pierce, one of Baker's aides, appeared before the Senate Finance Committee to give the War Department's estimated cost of maintaining and equipping an army of 1 million men. His list was long and included "clothing, cots, camps, food, pay, medical supplies, haversacks, blankets, slickers, cooking outfits, horses, mules, motor trucks, gun carriages, all forms of transportation, airplanes, balloons, marching equipment, guns, rifles, pistols, tanks, gasmasks . . ." The anticipated cost, $3 billion, was equally astonishing to the Senators. "Why so much?" asked Chairman Thomas S. Martin of Virginia. When Pierce responded by suggesting that the United States might have to maintain an army in Europe, Martin was stunned. "Good Lord!" he sputtered. "You're not going to send soldiers over there, are you?" Major Pierce responded by telling members of the Senate Finance Committee that sending a US force to Europe might "be the only way to win the War."[1] This, however, was a decision not yet made by the government. Nor had any decision been made over the theater in which an American force might fight if dispatched across the Atlantic.

Prior to Germany's resumption of its all-out U-boat campaign, the General Staff's war planning had focused entirely on the defense of American soil, with one exception. Captain Edward Davis, an American military attaché in Greece, had sent a series of reports to the War Department in November and December 1916 advocating the dispatch of an American expeditionary force of 500,000 men to the Balkans. Captain Davis did more than share his strategical views with the War Department. He approached General Maurice Sarrail, the Allied commander-in-chief on the Balkan Front. Not surprisingly, Sarrail enthusiastically endorsed a proposal that might strengthen his front with 500,000 fresh American soldiers.[2]

In the aftermath of the failure of their Gallipoli and Dardanelles campaigns in 1915 the British and French had opened a new front in the Balkans by landing troops at Salonika, Greece. Directed initially at keeping Serbia from being overrun, this Allied intervention soon focused on Bulgaria after that country joined the Central Powers in October and assisted the Austrians in crushing Serbia. During the following months the Allies assembled an international force of Italian, Greek, Russian, Serbian, Indian, Indo-Chinese, French, and British soldiers. The British military leadership in particular opposed opening this new theater, arguing that it diverted men and supplies from the Western Front where the Allies were at death grips with the main body of the German Army. They had a point. Allied forces suffered heavy losses on this malaria-ridden Macedonian front and achieved no significant military success until the last weeks of the war. Germans were soon referring to this theater as an "internment camp" for Allied forces.

In his reports to the War Department, Davis made misleading though appealing arguments. He suggested that a US force operating in Macedonia could maintain both its political and military independence. American forces in this theater would also "be employed in striking hardest, and in the softest part, that antagonist who will quit the easiest." Davis actually took his optimistic forecast a step further by suggesting that America's "fair diplomacy" in combination with its military presence might encourage the Bulgarians to drop out of the war without putting up a fight. In arguing that Bulgaria's defeat would lead to the collapse of Austria–Hungary and Turkey, Davis echoed a popular myth that German allies such as Turkey and Austria–Hungary were "props" holding up the Second Reich. Knock away those props and Germany's defeat would quickly follow. In truth, Germany propped up its allies – not the other way around. Moreover, Sarrail's forces soon discovered that Bulgaria's defenses proved just as difficult to break through as German defenses on the Western Front.[3] In his analysis Davis did not explain how the United States could find the necessary sea transport to get its soldiers across the sub-infested waters of the Atlantic and Mediterranean. Nor did he suggest how the United States, which would be dependent upon Allied logistical support and weaponry, could possibly maintain its independence while operating with an international force commanded by a French general.

Despite the daft quality of Davis's proposal, it apparently found some support within the War College Division and prompted concern that it might become public knowledge. Major General Joseph E. Kuhn, the president of the War College, who had earlier served as the American military attaché with the German armies in the field, warned Davis that both Scott and Baker were "somewhat apprehensive that reports of this character are fraught with possibilities of harm, in the event that their contents become known to others than the authorities of the War Department."[4]

As the United States edged closer to war after Germany's resumption of unrestricted submarine warfare, Scott sent Davis's report to the War College Division and asked it to "submit without delay a statement of a plan of action that should be followed by the United States in case hostilities with Germany occur in the near future." On February 2, Kuhn, who headed the War College Division, subsequently asked his colleagues to examine Davis's proposal for a Balkan campaign.

Acutely aware of America's military weakness, the War College Division cautioned the government against making a precipitous decision. It recommended the raising through conscription of a force of 1.5 million men. But until this force had been organized, equipped, and trained, Kuhn "earnestly" advised against sending it across the Atlantic. He also emphasized that the success of any foreign military venture depended upon a "definite understanding between ourselves and other belligerents engaged in seeking a common end." The War College Division believed that America's best option was to limit its support to naval and economic support, although "ultimately it may include joint military operations in some theater of war to be determined by agreement with other nations."[5] If this approach had been adopted, and it had much to recommend it on practical grounds, it is very unlikely that the United States could have raised, equipped, and shipped an army to Europe in time to prevent a German victory in 1918.

In February the War Department now had before it two possible European theaters for the US Army: Macedonia and Holland. The first theater, the Balkan Front, was unrealistic for US operations. The second, Holland, even more so. Neither proposal had originated within the War College Division. Captain Davis, a military attaché, had been responsible for the proposal to send a US force to the Balkans and Major General Scott had suggested a campaign in Holland. Believing that the Dutch might be drawn into the war by German attacks on their shipping, the Chief of Staff requested an evaluation of a surprise attack against the German Army via Holland by 1 million American troops. Kuhn had emphasized that it would be impossible for the United States to establish its own front in Macedonia and wage an independent war against Bulgaria. Cooperation with the Allies would be just as imperative if the United States attempted to attack by way of Holland against the German Belgian flank. A large US force would have to be assembled in Britain prior to crossing the Channel. This would eliminate the possibility of surprise. Kuhn sensibly concluded that it was "impossible" for the United States to wage a private war with Germany. Any land campaign by necessity had to be conducted "in cooperation with the Entente powers." To do otherwise "might aid Germany by embarrassing the armies now operating against her."[6]

Allied leaders in France and Britain also pondered the military role that the United States might play in the months ahead. In mid-March the German Army had begun a step-by-step retreat to new defensive positions which the German high command had begun building in September to shorten and strengthen the German front. The construction of the sophisticated defensive system, popularly known as the Hindenburg Line, involved as many as 370,000 workers and represented the greatest construction project of the war. This German withdrawal, especially from the Noyon salient, which shortened the German front and eliminated vulnerable flanks, threatened to undermine Allied plans for a spring offensive.

General Robert Nivelle, the new commander-in-chief of the French Army, had won the support of the French and British political leaders by promising to achieve a breakthrough on the Aisne in twenty-four to forty-eight hours. His method at Verdun had been to concentrate his artillery and fire in depth throughout a narrow zone to clear a path for the rapid advance of his infantry. This had worked at Verdun and had resulted in the recapture of Fort Douaumont. Some French generals, however, believed that his method would not work on a broad front. As Henri-Philippe Pétain told the French War Minister Paul Painlevé, "even the waters of Lake Geneva would have but little effect if dispersed over the length and breadth of the Sahara Desert."[7]

The BEF, to the consternation of its commander-in-chief Haig, had been assigned a supporting role to draw down German reserves before Nivelle launched his breakthrough attempt. On April 9, the BEF's diversionary attack got off to a splendid start with the capture of Vimy Ridge, one of its greatest achievements of the war. The Battle of Arras, which officially ended on May 17, however, soon degenerated into another battle of attrition. Judged exclusively by its average daily casualty rate (4,076 a day), this battle proved to be Haig's most costly offensive of the entire war.[8] Meanwhile, on April 16, Nivelle launched his offensive. Measured by the standards of his grandiose expectations, the results are bitterly disappointing. When Nivelle continued his offensive after failing to achieve a breakthrough, incidents of mutiny emerged and continued into early June, when it peaked. French soldiers refused to leave their trenches and at times assaulted their officers. There was talk of revolution. The headlong decline of the Russian Army following the overthrow of the Romanov dynasty in March also gravely concerned the British and French leadership.

The costly Anglo-French offensives emphasized the brewing manpower crisis for both countries, especially if Russia could not be counted upon to tie down German divisions on the Eastern Front. While Britain

raised a large army in 1914–15, the French had borne the primary
burden of fighting the main body of the German Army. Beginning with
the Battle of the Somme, however, the BEF began to suffer casualties
commensurate with their allies. Lord Rhondda, who chaired a committee concerned with keeping the BEF up to strength, warned the British
government in March "that the strain on the man-power of the country is
becoming acute, especially in view of the heavy industrial and financial
responsibilities which have to be borne by this country."[9] The French,
who had already suffered some 2 million casualties, also looked to the
United States for manpower assistance.

Both the French and British military understood how long it would
take the United States to raise an expeditionary force capable of helping
them defeat Germany. The British General Staff, for example, predicted
that "not more than 250,000 men could be put into the field" within a
year. And this was based on the assumption that an American force
would by that time have the required weapons, equipment, and shipping.[10] Lord Eustace Percy, a junior member of the Foreign Office who
specialized in American affairs, mirrored this assessment when he
warned his government that "the only sound war policy the United States
can pursue is to encourage enlistment in the British and French
Armies."[11] Minister of War Painlevé was of a like mind and urged the
French military attaché in Washington to encourage Wilson to dispatch
"with little delay, small units, companies or battalions of volunteers" to
serve in the French Army.[12]

Although amalgamation with existing British and French units was
surely the quickest and most practical means of getting Americans to
the front line it was asking much from a great power. Britain's
leading military war correspondent, Charles à Court Repington, wrote
Robertson that it would be a great mistake to include Americans in
British units and pointed out many of the practical difficulties. "You
would be faced with difficult questions of pay," he noted, "and you
would have endless trouble about discipline. The Yankee would bring
disturbance into our ranks and would upset our men. If you shot him for
disobedience of orders, as of course you would, our enemies in America,
who are many, would exploit it against us. Take my advice and keep off
this lay and keep others off it."[13]

President Wilson suspected the motives of the British and French
when they suggested sending joint political/military missions to
Washington to coordinate America's war efforts with their own. When
he received London's request to send a mission to Washington, headed
by the British Foreign Secretary Arthur Balfour, he hesitated. "The plan
has its manifest dangers," he wrote House on April 6. "A great many will

look upon the mission as an attempt to in some degree take charge of us as an assistant to Great Britain."[14] Although Wilson was right to suspect Allied intentions he had little choice but to welcome British and French missions.

The British mission by way of Nova Scotia arrived in Washington on April 22. Balfour had been handed an urgent message when he had arrived in Canada from Spring Rice. The British Ambassador warned him about the American fear that their country was "relapsing into the condition of a colony." Spring Rice emphasized that "there would be the very greatest reluctance to taking part in the war under British control or as part of a British campaign."[15] This information made Balfour's job doubly difficult because he had been instructed by the War Cabinet to explore the recruiting of Americans for service in either the British or French armies. The War Cabinet also hoped that Wilson would immediately send at least one American battalion to France to be followed by partially trained soldiers to complete their training there and then fight in British divisions. General Robertson had a pragmatic though bloody-minded reason for wanting a few Americans in the trenches as soon as possible. As he expressed it to Haig on April 10: "It would be a good thing to get some Americans killed and so get the country to take a real interest in the war."[16]

A wounded veteran, Lieutenant General Tom Bridges, headed the military contingent on Balfour's mission. He wasted little time in antagonizing both President Wilson and the War Department. He wrote Chief of Staff Scott: "If you ask me how your force could most quickly make itself felt in Europe, I would say by sending 500,000 untrained men at once to our depots in England to be trained there, and drafted into our armies in France."[17] He also made the preposterous claim that it would take only nine weeks' training in England and nine additional days in France to turn these raw recruits into soldiers. Robertson had expressed confidence that Americans could "be made into soldiers much quicker than men of most communities,"[18] but Bridges' proposal was tantamount to a murder sentence for many American recruits. To make his extraordinary proposal more palatable, Bridges suggested that the immediate dispatch of recruits to Europe would not prevent the later creation of a US Army in France. "The drafts sent to us," he explained, "could eventually be drafted back into the US Army and would be a good leavening of seasoned men."[19]

Not surprisingly, Bridges discovered that "he was on the wrong path" and he abandoned his outrageous proposal "like a hot potato." Bridges, however, continued to work closely with Marshal Joffre, the leading soldier on the French mission which had arrived in Washington on

April 25 to persuade Wilson to commit immediately troops to the European theater. The President had been willing to commit the US Navy to joint anti-submarine operations with the Royal Navy but he initially hesitated in making any commitment about the US Army's role. Joffre and Bridges wanted him to send a division to Europe at once with a second one to follow. In his discussions with Bridges, Joffre made it clear that he wanted any US troops to be placed in the French sector. "I indicated to Marshal Joffre that it was a matter of indifference to us where they went as long as they come over soon," Bridges wrote Robertson. "We cannot well press for them as we have had so far a complete success with the naval questions, and the French are a little touchy."[20]

Although the British appeared willing to allow the French to monopolize US forces coming to Europe, this was misleading. Many different ideas percolated within the British leadership for the future deployment of US manpower, which included using American forces to prop up Russia on the Eastern Front, a suggestion quickly vetoed by Robertson. "First because America has not moved a single inch yet with respect to raising troops and secondly because it would be futile for the United States to enter into any communications with Russia on the subject in these chaotic times," he wrote Maurice Hankey, the secretary of the War Cabinet.[21] Despite Spring Rice's warning to Balfour, many British leaders remained confident that Americans would eventually fight alongside the British rather than the French. As Bridges suggested to Robertson, "I believe finally the armament [British Enfield and 18-pounder as opposed to French Lebel rifle and 75 mm field guns] and linguistic factors will force the Americans to come to us, and also we find, in spite of what we were told that popular sentiment leads that way."[22]

Lord Percy, thought to be an "expert" on American affairs, went even further when he suggested that Americans understood "little or nothing of the way in which a war is conducted. The first and main point is that for this reason the administration in Washington will be very ready to follow our lead."[23]

When Bridges finally met Wilson, he found the President prepared to talk about his favorite recreational activity, golf, "but of war, not a word, and the hundred and one questions to which I had prepared answers remained unasked."[24] Marshal Joffre had much better success in dealing with the White House and War Department because he made it clear that although the French should assist in the training of American soldiers and provide them with modern arms American units would be kept together as a first step toward building a powerful US force in Europe.[25]

As Joffre later wrote: "No great nation having a proper consciousness of its own dignity – and America perhaps less than any other – would allow its citizens to be incorporated like poor relations in the ranks of some other army and fight under a foreign flag."[26]

Sending troops piecemeal to France, however, remained anathema to the War Department and this included sending either a brigade or a division to give a psychological lift to the war-weary French and British people. Earlier, when asked by Baker what he thought of Roosevelt's proposal to send an all-volunteer division to Europe, Bliss, the Assistant Chief of Staff, had condemned the idea because any small American unit sent into combat would have to be "accompanied by two or three times its strength in order to promptly meet the excessive losses that an insufficiently trained force will incur. We will have to feed in raw troops to take the place of raw troops." This reckless slaughter of young Americans would hardly aid the Allied cause. If America had no choice but to commit untrained troops to save the Allies from defeat, Bliss believed that it should be a large force which had the potential to have an impact.[27]

When Joffre met with officers at the Army War College on April 27, he suggested that a division be sent to Europe as soon as possible. The War College Division, however, continued to oppose this idea. One of Kuhn's subordinates, Colonel W. H. Johnston, warned that the presence of an American force on the Western Front, no matter what its size, was certain to undermine efforts to build a powerful, independent US Army in the United States. Also, if many veteran officers were sent abroad, who would train and lead the large army being proposed?[28]

On May 2, Wilson asserted his authority as commander-in-chief, informing Marshal Joffre "to take for granted" that the United States would send an expeditionary force to France "just as soon as we could send it." On May 14, Secretary of War Baker and Joffre formalized an agreement to send an expeditionary force "equivalent to a division" which would be trained by the French and deployed on their front.[29] The French thus won the first round in their competition with the British for American manpower. Bridges, however, remained confident that this arrangement would only hasten the day when the Americans chose to fight alongside the British. "There will be friction and difficulties but the French will be saddled with them," he suggested to Robertson.[30]

The new commander-in-chief of the French Army, General Philippe Pétain, who had replaced the now disgraced Nivelle, greeted Joffre's agreement to establish an autonomous American force on the Western Front with dismay. Pétain wanted immediate relief which could only be gained if American soldiers were amalgamated with existing

French units. Probably Joffre's most telling rejoinder was that if the French reneged on their May 14 agreement with Baker, the Americans might choose the British over the French as war partners.[31]

At this point it must be noted that there was no guarantee that Wilson was prepared to accept more than a symbolic force in France. Baker's May 14 agreement with Joffre did include the sentence, "The secretary gives me to understand that, from now on, the efforts of the United States will be restricted only by transportation difficulties." This apparently open-ended commitment of American manpower was not what it seemed. Not only did the United States not have adequate sea transport, it did not have an existing force capable of influencing the outcome of the war. Wilson had just signed the Selective Service Act, so it would be at least a year before it did, whether that force was primarily trained in Europe or in the United States. In his correspondence with Baker, Wilson had only agreed to send one division to France while another was being formed in the United States – "ready to follow fairly shortly, so as to get the advantage of the training received by the first division and be able to supplement it should battle losses or sickness diminish its numbers."[32]

Uncomfortable in the presence of professional soldiers, Wilson at this time did not look to them for advice on military matters. He, for example, initially ignored Tasker H. Bliss, a scholarly soldier, who served as acting Chief of Staff after Scott was appointed to the Root mission to Russia which Wilson announced in April. The President had just received from House an appreciation written by an amateur strategist, George G. Moore, a retired New York businessman who had recently visited the Western Front as a guest of the former British commander-in-chief, Sir John French. Impressed by the strong defenses he inspected and horrified by the massive losses experienced by the French and British in their spring offensives, Moore stressed the "impossibility" of breaking through the German trenches in 1917. He accused the Allied generals of causing "a hideous wastage of the man-power of England and France in attacks from which there was no intelligent hope of success." Rather than "rush troops" to the bloody battlefields of France, Moore wanted to delay an expeditionary force until the United States had created a well-equipped, 2 million-man force. Wilson was drawn to Moore's proposal. He wrote Baker, the self-professed pacifist and former mayor of Cleveland who served as his primary adviser on military questions, that Moore's views had made "a considerable impression on me and I should very much like to discuss it with you when we have the next opportunity."[33]

From a purely military perspective Moore was correct and his views resonated with the President and mirrored the War College Division's position of sending a large, independent force to Europe rather than dispatching troops across the Atlantic in driblets to be trained and deployed by the French. In any military emergency, the Allies were also almost certain to renew pressure for amalgamating American units with the existing French and British armies.

It is likely that Wilson believed that there was no pressing need to rush untrained and unorganized troops to Europe. Preparation for rather than actual participation in the costly trench warfare might be enough to maintain America's moral position and encourage Germany to seek a compromise peace. Wilson certainly did not believe that total victory served his plans for world peace. This, however, was not the position of the individual who now had the greatest influence on the President's war policy, Secretary of War Baker. Wilson resisted being pushed, but Baker did so. In an unusually strong letter on May 27 he warned the President that the United States might not have any Allies left if it waited until it could conduct largely independent military operations on the Western Front. Moreover, there might be serious political consequences if the United States did not provide substantial military support as soon as feasible. The Entente nations would be discouraged and Wilson's war administration would be criticized at home. Wilson's claim that he wanted to "make the world safe for democracy" might become a source of ridicule.[34]

Baker's intervention proved to be a critical moment for American participation in the war. On June 14, as the first American units embarked for Europe, Wilson proclaimed: "We are about to bid thousands, hundreds of thousands, it may be millions, of our men, the young, the strong, the capable men of the nation, to go forth and die beneath [the flag] on fields of blood far away – for what?" He answered his own question by emphasizing Germany's expansion, both in Europe and Asia, which posed a threat to American security. "America will fall within the menace," he warned. "We and all the rest of the world must remain armed, as they will remain, and must make ready for the next step in their aggression."[35]

The White House and the Army's leadership now seemed on the same page. The War College Division appreciated that American assistance might arrive too late if it waited until a large American army was organized in the United States. Beginning in August, the War Department planned to ship "approximately 120,000 men with their equipment and paraphernalia per month." To relieve the "critical situation now existing in France," the War College Division also suggested expanding the existing army to 1 million men within the next four months. "Manifestly," the War College Division asserted, "this force is being raised for the purpose of placing it, at the earliest practicable date, alongside the forces of other nations at war with Germany."[36]

As noted above, the War College Division expected American soldiers to fight "alongside" and not within foreign armies as amalgamated units. Just prior to Baker's intervention, Bliss had written an alarmist memorandum that underscored the threat of amalgamation. "It seems to most of us that what both the English and French really wanted from us was not a large well-trained army but a large number of smaller *units* which they could feed promptly into their line as parts of their own organizations in order to maintain their man power at full strength." If Entente demands were not resisted, Bliss suggested that 1 million Americans might go into combat "as parts of battalions and regiments of the Entente Allies" with "no American army and no American commander." If its soldiers served as cannon fodder for the French and British, America's role in achieving victory would be diminished along with Wilson's ability to influence the peace settlement. Bliss wanted Wilson to urge the Allies to "stand fast" until a powerful American force could be created to deliver "the final, shattering blow."[37]

Whether by accident or design Baker selected as commander-in-chief of the AEF an officer who would fiercely and successfully support the creation of an independent American force fighting under its own flag no matter what the consequences for Allied military fortunes. Few World War I generals had greater presence, stubborn determination, or driving ambition. He stood only five feet and nine inches tall, yet his erect posture and formidable presence made him appear to be over six feet. One famous British military historian, Captain B. Liddell Hart, later referred to him as the "THE ONE HUNDRED-PER-CENT AMERICAN."[38] That soldier was Pershing. Born in Laclede in north-central Missouri, John was the eldest of nine children sired by John Fletcher Pershing, the great-grandson of an Alsatian immigrant who had come to America as an indentured servant named Frederick Poersching (or Pförschin) in the fall of 1749. The depression of 1873 brought hard times to his family. Young John farmed his father's land and worked as a janitor in Laclede's public schools before becoming an elementary teacher in a neighboring school at Prairie Mound. After several years of teaching, Pershing attended a normal school at Kirksville and acquired a Bachelor of Elementary Didactics. He aspired, however, to be a lawyer rather than a teacher. To advance his education and prepare himself for the law, he next applied for and got an appointment to the US Military Academy in 1882. Five years older than the youngest of his fellow plebes, Pershing made up for any academic deficiencies he may have had by being a leader of men. He held the office of class president for four years and in his last year attained the rank of First Captain, the highest military rank for a fourth-year cadet.

After serving with the 6th Cavalry in New Mexico and Arizona, Pershing became a Professor of Military Science at Nebraska where he earned his law degree. After a brief tour of duty with the 10th Cavalry, Pershing served on the staff of General Nelson A. Miles in Washington and taught tactics at West Point, before returning to the 10th Cavalry to fight in Cuba during the Spanish–American War and later in the Philippines against the Moros. While a student at the Army War College in 1905 he married Helen Frances Warren, the Daughter of Senator Warren, chairman of the Senate Military Affairs Committee. The following year, while serving as an observer in Manchuria during the Russo-Japanese War, President Roosevelt promoted him from captain to brigadier-general, a promotion that elevated him over 257 captains, 364 majors, 131 lieutenant colonels, and 110 colonels, all of whom were senior to him. It was immediately and widely noted in the press that his father-in-law chaired the Senate Military Affairs Committee. In his defense it must be noted that Pershing had been recommended by all but one general officer in the Army.[39] Roosevelt's response was: "To promote a man because he married a senator's daughter would be an infamy; and to refuse him promotion for the same reason would be an equal infamy."[40]

In 1914 Pershing returned to the United States from the Philippines, where he had most recently been serving as governor of the Moro Province, to assume command of the 8th Brigade which had its head-quarters at the Presidio in San Francisco. With Mexico being destabil-ized by revolution, he and his brigade were dispatched to Fort Bliss near El Paso. Pershing was thus in the right spot when President Wilson decided to retaliate for Pancho Villa's raid on Columbus. As head of the Punitive Expedition, although Villa was never brought to justice, he became the leading candidate to lead an expeditionary force to Europe. None of his contemporaries had ever commanded a force as large as the Punitive Expedition.

His role in Mexico had been both military and political, and he had been generally successful in both areas. Villa remained on the loose. But as a fellow West Pointer noted, "all military men know that under the orders he received he had as much chance to get Villa as to find a needle in a haystack."[41] Pershing's force had advanced some 300 miles into northern Mexico and he had done so without involving the United States in a serious military confrontation with Carranza's government despite several skirmishes with Mexican troops. In the words of his confidant and friend James G. Harbord, "If his judgment did not endorse the policy under which his command operated, or failed to operate, his loyalty and discretion left nothing to be desired."[42] Nonetheless, rumors had been circulating in Washington that he resented the tight restrictions that Washington had placed upon him. In a letter to Scott, Pershing strongly denied these accusations and insisted that he sympathized with Wilson's Mexican policy, which he described as being "prompted by the very highest of motives." He wanted the Chief of Staff to assure both Baker and Wilson that he could be counted upon "to the last extremity, both as to word and deed, for loyalty and fidelity, in any task that may be given me to perform."[43]

Although Pershing, a Republican, had once thought Wilson a weak president his forceful actions against Germany had apparently altered his views. Prior to his appointment as commander-in-chief, he wrote that Wilson "is going down in history as one of the three greatest presidents, if not the greatest ... It is also gratifying to a soldier to have such confidence in his leader."[44] After Wilson's war message he sent the President a personal message that his "soul-stirring patriotic address" had aroused "in the breast of every soldier feelings of the deepest admiration for their leader."[45] Wilson and Baker were going to place similar confidence in Pershing once he became commander-in-chief. There really was never a chance that Wilson would accept General Wood, the other leading candidate. Wood was neither loyal to the President nor discreet. He especially angered the President by his involvement in politics. He had been a vocal critic of the President's military policies and had flirted with a presidential bid as a Republican candidate in 1916. "I have had a great deal of experience with General Wood," Wilson later wrote. "He is a man of unusual ability, but apparently absolutely unable to submit his judgment to those who are superior to him in command."[46]

Pershing met Wilson only once prior to his departure for France, when he and Baker visited the White House on May 24. At their meeting Wilson quizzed Pershing about his knowledge of France and discussed the transport of American troops to Europe. But he said nothing about cooperation with America's allies or the extent of America's commitment to the Western Front, almost certainly because he himself had not yet decided.[47]

Pershing was later given a copy of Bliss's alarmist memorandum along with two sets of instructions. When he made his last visit to the War Department before sailing for the Western Front, Baker told him, "Here are your orders, General. The President has just approved them." This was not the only letter of instruction he received, however, a state of affairs that mystified Pershing then and historians later. What apparently happened was that Bliss signed one letter which had been prepared by

Pershing and his Chief of Staff, Major James G. Harbord. But Bliss's concern that Allied demands for American manpower would obscure American contributions to final victory and undermine the country's diplomatic leverage struck a sensitive nerve with Baker and Wilson. Baker subsequently had Colonel Francis E. Kernan, the acting Assistant Chief of Staff, prepare a second letter. The precise language in this letter concerning the protection of the "identity" of the AEF in all likelihood was added at Wilson's and Baker's insistence. This second letter begins with the following words: "The President directs me to communicate to you the following." Similar to the first letter, Pershing was instructed to cooperate in the joint military effort against Imperial Germany and was given total control over the extent and timing of this military cooperation. Unlike the instructions over Bliss's signature, however, these orders used very direct language to insist that "the underlying idea must be kept in view that the forces of the United States are a separate and distinct component of the combined forces, the identity of which must be preserved."[48]

Pershing was destined to be the most independent of the Allied commanders-in-chief. Entente generals, close to their capitals, were in close proximity with their political superiors. This civil–military relationship was frequently contentious and not without intrigue. No commander-in-chief other than Pershing succeeded in retaining his position from the beginning of his country's participation in the war until the Armistice. And no commander-in-chief exercised greater freedom from civilian interference. Given Wilson's distrust of soldiers and his country's traditional fear of militarism this is all the more remarkable. "Pershing was to be no less of an autocrat in France," writes an early biographer, Frederick Palmer, "than the commander of a western post under Indian attack in the old army in the west. He was to build his own kingdom in France as an absolute monarch."[49]

Before he departed for Europe, Baker gave Pershing only two verbal orders, "one to go to France and the other to come home, but that in the meantime his authority in France would be supreme." But Baker added a caveat: "If you make good, the people will forgive almost any mistake. If you do not make good, they will probably hang us both on the first lamp-post they can find."[50]

The remarkable independence that Baker gave Pershing was not out of character. Unlike President Wilson, who instinctively distrusted the military, the civilian head of the War Department deferred to men in uniform. Baker's father, who had served for four years with Jeb Stuart's cavalry, had earlier regaled his son with Civil War stories. "I think that the thing he more often said to me than anything else," Baker later told his first biographer, Frederick Palmer, was that the reason the South seemed to prevail for so long from a military point of view was that President Davis let Lee alone, while Stanton and Lincoln constantly interfered with Federal commanders. Only once did President Davis give General Lee a military order, Father told me, and Lee's answer was to unbuckle his sword and hand it to Davis. Davis handed it back, tore up the order, and from that time on never interfered.

Baker had concluded from this that "the military man is commander-in-chief and that civilian interference with commanders in the field is dangerous."[51]

On May 28 Pershing and his hastily assembled staff boarded the S.S. *Baltic* of the White Star Line for a voyage across the submarine-infested waters of the Atlantic. "None of the original fifty-plus officers who sailed on the Baltic had any practical experience at all in higher staff functions," notes James Cooke. "What they did possess, however, was a high level of intelligence, a willingness to work extraordinary hours, and best of all, the confidence of Pershing."[52] His most important selection had been his choice of James G. Harbord as his Chief of Staff. After graduating from Kansas State Agricultural College (1886), Harbord had been unable to gain an appointment to West Point. He joined the army as a private and worked his way up through the ranks. In 1917, he was fifty-one years old, a Major of Cavalry, and a student at the War College.

Much discussion had taken place over how officers should dress prior to departure. Many dressed as civilians, in part to mask the purpose of their voyage, but also because of the fear that German submarine commanders would open fire on lifeboats if they were filled with men in uniform. And indeed the chances of being torpedoed were great. As the *Baltic* crossed the Atlantic between Halifax and Liverpool, German torpedoes sank no fewer than fifteen ships in British waters. Some men slept in their life jackets while others did not sleep as they sailed through the "danger zone." In Harbord's view, there was little chance of survival in the event of a U-boat assault. "It is inconceivable that a German submarine knowing that General Pershing's Headquarters were aboard would permit them to get off in open boats and possibly escape to lead troops against Germans. Solution: Shoot 'em up."[53]

Pershing's party had much to occupy its attention other than the submarine threat. As some brushed up on their French, Pershing had his staff examine a multitude of critical questions concerning the AEF's role in the war once it became a reality. AEF planners faced enormous obstacles, first and foremost being the German Army, which was renowned for its professionalism and fielded on multiple fronts 241 divisions (or approximately 6 million men) in 1917. General Robert Bullard, after listening in on a conversation between two staff members who had been instructors at Leavenworth, concluded that "the impression the average man derives from hearing them is the hopelessness, the utter folly of our resisting or fighting the Germans at all."[54]

Plans made for the AEF, however, strongly suggest that most American officers were not intimidated by the German Army. Their planning aboard the *Baltic* began with the creation of boards to examine such topics as the size of the AEF, its transport to Europe, and its supply lines. Although the first American had yet to be drafted and the Army had not formed a single division, Pershing and his enthusiastic but inexperienced staff did not think small.

Getting divisions once formed to Europe represented a considerable obstacle. When the United States entered the war the Army had available to it only one unseaworthy transport and the USS *Henderson*, which had not yet been commissioned. Additional tonnage had been found by commandeering Austrian and German ships which had been marooned in American ports when war erupted in Europe in 1914. Joseph E. Kuhn, who headed the War College Division, had optimistically predicted that 500,000 American soldiers could be transported to Europe over a period of seven months.[55] But first an army had to be raised and training camps built. It would be September before enlisted men began arriving at these camps, many only partially completed. Kuhn's estimate generally mirrored the views of General Bridges when he returned to London in June. "It seems probable that America can have an army of 120–150,000 men in France by 1st January 1918, and of 500,000 by the end of 1918," he informed the War Cabinet.[56]

Despite what appeared to be overwhelming obstacles to deploying a credible American force on the Western Front, Pershing and his staff assumed that the United States would play a decisive role in Germany's ultimate defeat. While aboard the *Baltic*, Pershing's staff initiated planning to create an independent US force with its own front and supply lines where, in Pershing's words, it would be possible "to strike the enemy where a definite military decision could be forced."[57] In choosing a front and operational objectives for the AEF, Pershing and his staff operated independently from the theoretical "brain" of the Army, the General Staff located in Washington. This was in sharp contrast to the role played by some general staffs of the Entente powers. Sir William Robertson, the Chief of the Imperial General Staff, for example, was in almost daily contact with the British political leadership as their designated adviser. His position as the government's supreme military adviser was given the full force of law by an order in council issued by the King in January 1916.

The AEF's location in France represented a critical question for both the British and French and both had been keen to make suggestions.

As early as April, Haig's Chief of Intelligence General John Charteris suggested to Lieutenant Colonel Stephen Slocum, the American military attaché in London, that the Americans should replace an isolated French division on the northern end of the British–Belgian front.[58] When it became obvious that American forces were going to be trained by the French, Bridges while in Washington had suggested to Scott that American troops might be located at the juncture of the Anglo-French forces where they could be supplied by the British and trained by the French. When Bridges learned that the French wanted to position American forces in the south, far removed from the BEF and the Channel ports, he cautioned Pershing "not to get jammed up against the Swiss frontier," where American forces might be trapped if the French front collapsed.[59]

Not understanding the fragile nature of the French Army following Nivelle's failed offensive, Pershing found little merit in Bridges' alarmist views. He believed that Lorraine, the area between the Argonne Forest and Vosges Mountains, offered distinct advantages. Having studied military operations during the Franco-Prussian War, 1870–71, at Fort Leavenworth, many of his staff members were familiar with the landscape around Metz. Relatively inactive since the disastrous French offensive in 1914 this portion of the front also promised to provide a reasonably secure training area. But these factors were secondary to Pershing's thinking. He expected to launch an American offensive that achieved decisive results. When asked by a reporter at a press conference if he thought a breakthrough possible on the Western Front after so many costly failures by both the German and Entente forces, he replied: "Of course the western front can be broken. What are we here for?"[60]

Pershing was not acting alone when he sought to deploy his forces in a manner that would make possible the creation of a uniquely American force with its own tactics and strategic objectives. "The GHQ staff," writes Allan R. Millett, "which included many personalities as strong as Pershing's, planned the AEF's employment with the full knowledge that its planning would ultimately shape every phase of the AEF's organization from troop strength and shipping schedules to training and tactics."[61]

In early September Pershing ordered his Operations Section, headed by Colonel Fox Conner, to prepare a strategical appreciation that concentrated on German defenses running from Verdun to the Swiss frontier.[62] The resulting memorandum, dated September 25, 1917, and titled "A Strategical Study on the Employment of the AEF against the Imperial German Government," decisively shaped the American role in the land war for the remainder of the conflict.

If shipping were made available, the Operations Section estimated that by April 1918 Pershing would have at his disposal "the equivalent of 7 combat and 3 replacement divisions and 163,000 L[ine]. of C[ommunication]. troops." By February 1919 the AEF would have "the equivalent of 17 combat and 8 replacement divisions and 329,000 L. of C. troops."[63]

American officers echoed Wilson's view that American operations, unlike those of their European partners, were not directed toward "territorial or economic aggression or indemnity." Contrary to what some shell-shocked German soldiers might later think, the AEF war planners echoed Wilson's position that the United States had no quarrel with the German people. They took the position that the AEF's primary objective was the "displacement" of the Imperial German government.[64]

This apparent harmony between the AEF leadership and the White House concealed one basic difference. Wilson still hoped that "peace elements" would triumph in Germany and make possible a peace of reconciliation rather than a victor's peace. The AEF's military leadership, seeking the decisive defeat of German arms, sought "peace through victory" as opposed to Wilson's "peace without victory."

Cooperation with the British in either 1918 or 1919, even if the BEF found itself in dire straits, was firmly and specifically rejected, with the possible exception of naval assistance along the Belgian coast. It was emphasized that it was "out of the question for us to take over any section in the British line. If the British cannot hold, etc., their own line, certainly our entrance therein cannot produce any decisive results." Equally unattractive was placing American forces at the juncture of the British and French trenches, for this would also assign American arms "an indecisive part." The AEF planners also argued that assistance to the French in 1918 should be withheld except for "minor operations" to boost morale in war-weary France and Britain as well as on the home front in America. These "minor offensive operations" should be directed against the south flank of the Saint-Mihiel salient as a prelude for a major American offensive in 1919. In sum the AEF leadership planned on husbanding American military resources until 1919 when an independent American force might be strong enough to achieve decisive results. "Piecemeal waste of our forces will result from any other action and we will never have in France the power to accomplish our objective," this strategical appreciation emphasized.[65]

As they looked at their maps of Lorraine, AEF planners focused on the fortified city of Metz where they saw important strategic opportunities. Its capture, or so they thought, would sever German railway lines running laterally between the German right and left wings. By rupturing

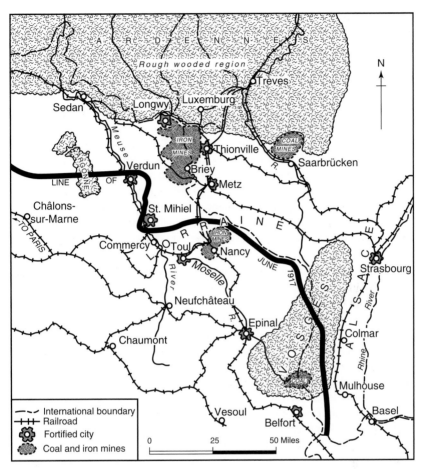

1. Strategical features influencing selection of the Lorraine Front for the American army

these vital communications they hoped to collapse the German southern defenses and force the enemy to withdraw beyond the Rhine or "at least to the eastern part of Belgium." As US forces advanced beyond Metz, they might also overrun the Saar basin with its coal and iron deposits which AEF planners deemed essential to the German war economy.[66]

Unfortunately, there was much that Pershing's staff got wrong in developing their ambitious plan (Map 1). Allan Millett has demonstrated that

the Germans had never intended that Lorraine would be a major theater of operations, and their railroad system had been developed accordingly. Capturing Metz would have given the AEF little, for the critical lateral railroad that Pershing stressed in his planning did not run directly from Metz to Sedan as the maps in Pershing's memoirs indicate. Instead, it turned west at Thionville (well north of Metz) and ran northwest through Longuyon and Montmedy until it reached the Meuse River at Sedan; the line then followed the Meuse to Mézières and turned north into German-occupied Belgium. To break this line would require an AEF offensive that advanced well past Metz.

Moreover, the coveted iron and coal resources of the Saar basin amounted to only around 10 percent of Germany's raw materials.[67]

The first phase of the September 1917 plan, viewed as a minor operation in 1918, was the elimination of the pronounced salient of Saint-Mihiel, southwest of Metz, with the assistance of the French. With the AEF's line straitened at Saint-Mihiel and the threat of a German counterthrust from Metz neutralized, the AEF's war-winning offensive would be launched in 1919 to the east of that fortress city in conjunction with other Allied attacks against the German defenses on the French and British fronts.

Much had to be done before Pershing commanded a force capable of taking on the German Army. On June 28, 1917, 14,000 US soldiers of the 1st Division had begun disembarking at Saint-Nazaire, France.[68] Technically they were Regular Army. But this was misleading. The War Department had hastily assembled the 1st Division by collecting the 16th, 18th, 26th, and 28th Infantry Regiments from the Mexican border and shipping them to France. Raw recruits and soldiers from other divisions had been added to bring these regiments up to strength. Over half of the soldiers in the division had just recently exchanged civilian dress for khaki. These raw recruits had received little or no training and were often unfamiliar with their weapons. "They did not know how to keep step and which is the business end of a rifle and that when you march in a column of fours this does not mean threes and two. Many were as they had come to the recruiting station, plus a certain amount of drill at home, and all stiff-legged, pasty and somewhat unkempt," writes Frederick Palmer.[69] Most of their officers below the grade of Captain were almost as inexperienced because most seasoned Regular Army officers had been retained in America to assist in training the anticipated hordes of draftees and volunteers.[70]

As the first American soldiers walked down the gangways at Saint-Nazaire and strolled through the town they seemed more like tourists than France's future saviors. As George C. Marshall, the future Chief of Staff of the US Army in World War II, writes: "Most of them were ignorant of the first rudiments of march discipline and were busy looking in the shop windows and observing the French crowd."[71]

Military discipline as well as France was thus foreign to many soldiers in the 1st Division. A French general was stunned when he approached an American sentry. Rather than standing at attention the American handed him his rifle to free his hands to roll himself a cigarette. "This was not an army. This was a rabble," writes Donald Smythe.[72]

Nonetheless, Pershing's arrival in France, which was soon followed by elements of the 1st Division, had the desired effect on French public opinion. Parisians gave Pershing and his staff a tremendous reception. Huge crowds lined the streets, shouting "*Vive l'Amérique*" and showering them with roses. Several weeks later, on July 4, a battalion of the 16th Infantry, 1st Division, paraded through Paris and received an equally enthusiastic welcome. Many women forced

their way into the ranks and swinging along arm in arm with the men. With wreaths about their necks and bouquets in their hats, the column looked like a moving flower garden. With only a semblance of military formation, the animated throng pushed its way through avenues of people to the martial strains of the French band and the still more thrilling music of cheering voices,[73]

Pershing later recalled in his memoirs.

Their broad-brimmed hats, designed for Indian campaigns in the American west, especially delighted the French – "les homes au chapeau de cow-boy." The hats as well as the men who wore them, however, were unsuited for modern warfare. Steel helmets might be purchased from their allies but an army that could offer real assistance to the British and French on the Western Front was in the distant future. If Pershing's plan were followed, it would be 1919 before Americans began appearing in substantial numbers on the battlefield. As GHQ's Operations Section succinctly stated: "The part the United States plays in 1918 should be no more than is necessary to satisfy public opinion and to prepare for 1919 offensive."[74] Harbord, who accompanied Pershing to Paris, was surely correct when he later wrote: "The acclaim with which our party had been received seemed a little like something obtained under false pretense."[75]

7 American Expeditionary Force organization, overseas training, and deployment

The US Army could not have been less prepared to wage war abroad when Wilson decided to send an expeditionary force to Europe. As Pershing recalled later in his memoirs:

Figuratively speaking, then, when the Acting Chief of Staff went to look in the secret files, where the plans to meet the situation that confronted us should have been found, the pigeonhole was empty. In other words, the War Department was faced with the question of sending an army to Europe and found that the General Staff had never considered such a thing. No one in authority had any definite idea how many men might be needed, how they should be organized and equipped, or where the tonnage to transport and supply them was to come from.[1]

On the voyage to Europe, the decisions made by Pershing and his staff had serious implications for their European partners. Only in Lorraine did Pershing and his staff believe that an American campaign could play a decisive role in ending the war. Desperate to acquire American assistance for their war-weary army, the French welcomed, even encouraged, the positioning of US forces in the Lorraine sector between the Argonne Forest and the Vosges Mountains.[2] But the French to their dismay soon came to understand how much GHQ's plan to capture Metz dominated Pershing's expectations of the role US forces would play in 1918.

Pershing's first order of business was to organize his staff. In General Order No. 8, issued on July 5, 1917, he and Harbord created a General Staff of three sections: Administration, Intelligence, and Operations (later amended by a further order on August 11, 1917, that added two more sections: Training Policy and Coordination).[3] The five main sections of the General Staff, headed by assistant chiefs of staff, were later renamed G-1 under Avery D. Andrews; G-2 under Dennis E. Nolan; G-3 under Fox Conner; G-4 under George Van Horn Mosley; and G-5 under Harold B. Fiske. An assistant chief of staff headed each of these divisions. With some modification this organization continues to the present day. Many of Pershing's junior staff officers were young and inexperienced and it showed. To further their instruction Pershing established an Army General Staff College at Langres.

Immediately after organizing his staff, Pershing cabled the War Department that he needed "at least one million men by next May," of which 40 percent would be noncombatants in the zone of interior. Pershing's insistence on an independent army with its own SOS required tens of thousands of noncombatants, both skilled and unskilled. By the end of the war, roughly 33 percent of Pershing's force consisted of skilled noncombatants, ranging from clerical staff to mechanics to craftsmen. Another 27 percent performed unskilled or semi-skilled labor in vital areas such as unloading ships or building roads. Much of the heavy lifting and shoveling was done by black soldiers. Ninety percent of the black enlisted men in fact were assigned to the SOS. These non-combatants, comprising 60 percent of the AEF's ration strength by the Armistice, received little or no military training prior to being dispatched to Europe.[4]

Pershing's Operations Staff soon followed this cable with a daunting request for "at least 3,000,000 men" along with their equipment over the next two years.[5] President Wilson, who considered alternate theaters to the killing fields of the Western Front as late as November 1917, was surely shocked by the enormity of the AEF's requests. The expeditionary force of some 14,000 men that he had originally dispatched to France had within a few months grown to expectations by his commander-in-chief that as many as 3 million Americans would be required on European battlefields by 1919.

In determining the AEF's organization and equipment, Pershing's Operations Section worked with a group of American officers, the Baker Mission, so named after its head, Colonel Chauncey B. Baker, which the War Department had dispatched to make its own independent report. As Harbord later noted, "it was a situation that called for extreme tact. The Mission had to be lined up and the two recommendations must agree."[6] Baker, a friend of Pershing's and a former West Point classmate, under-stood the delicacy of the situation and suggested that he meet with Pershing before he returned to the United States.[7] In two days of at times vigorous discussion, Pershing and his Operations Section generally prevailed.[8] Their agreement, achieved on July 11, became known as the General Organization Project.[9] The American Army's combat divisions and their commanders in future were organized as in Table 2. Although the United States had no complete or permanent organization larger than a regiment in its prewar army, the General Organization Project now recommended creating divisions of approximately 28,000 combatants, or approximately twice as many riflemen as full-strength Allied and

Table 2 *The American army's combat divisions and their commanders*

Combat division	Division commanders
Squad	normally consisting of seven privates and a corporal
Platoon	the basic fighting unit, 50 men, led by either a 2nd or 1st lieutenant
Company	6 officers and 250 men led by a captain. 200 of these men were classified as riflemen and organized in 8 squads. A US company's armament consisted of 235 rifles and 16 automatic rifles ("hand bombers" armed with grenades and rifle grenadiers armed with rifle grenades were later added without reducing the number of rifles). In sharp contrast, a French company consisted of 68 primarily riflemen out of a complement of 172 soldiers.[a] The difference between the number of riflemen and weaponry of French and US companies reflected the AEF's continued emphasis on the rifle (musketry) and bayonet.
Battalion	4 companies, led by a major
Regiment	3 battalions and a machine gun company, 112 officers and 3,720 men, led by a colonel
Brigade	2 regiments and a machine gun battalion, 258 officers and 8,211 men, led by a brigadier general with a brigade headquarters of 25 soldiers
Division	2 infantry and 1 field artillery brigades, 1 engineer regiment, 1 machine gun battalion, 1 signal battalion, and trains (mule and horse transportation); 72 guns and 260 machine guns, 17,666 rifles; 979 officers, 27,082 men; led by a major general. Regular Army divisions in 1917 were numbered 1 to 8, National Guard divisions from 26 to 42, and National Army divisions from 76 to 93. 13 of the 42 divisions (the 93rd was not counted as a division because it was never organized to its full strength) were designated as either "depot" divisions or "replacement" divisions. "Depot" divisions consisted of pools of replacements to keep combat divisions up to strength. As losses mounted once the AEF entered heavy combat, these "replacement" divisions by necessity became combat divisions with the exception of the 41st Division which served as a "depot" division for the entire army. A 6-week program of additional training for replacement soldiers before they entered combat was established but almost never completed as American casualties mounted during the last months of the war.[b]
Corps	2–6 divisions, led by a major general
Army	3–5 corps, led by a lieutenant general or major general
Group of Armies	2 or 3 armies, led by a general, lieutenant general, or major general[c]

[a] Allan Millett, "Cantigny, 28–31 May 1918," in Charles Heller and William Stofft (eds.), *America's First Battles, 1776–1965* (Lawrence: University Press of Kansas, 1986), p. 160.
[b] Robert Alexander, *Memories of the World War, 1917–1918* (New York: The Macmillan Company, 1931), pp. 20–26.
[c] John Pershing, *My Experiences in the World War*, 2 vols. (New York: Frederick A. Stokes, 1931), vol. 1, p. 101; see also "Memorandum of a Conference on Organization and Equipment," *USAWW*, vol. 1, pp. 73–75.

German divisions.[10] When SOS personnel are included the division ration strength rose to approximately 40,000 men.[11] These super-sized divisions were called "square divisions" because they had two infantry brigades with two regiments in each brigade.

Numerous explanations have been given for this decision. It is true that both the British and French, emphasizing the availability of an apparently unlimited supply of American manpower, recommended large divisions. But American officers had their own reasons. With only a small cadre of experienced officers available they apparently believed that super-sized divisions provided better command and staff leadership at the top. Additionally, they contended that larger divisions might stay in the line longer before being relieved.

Some of their reasons do not stand up to close scrutiny. The United States did not need to increase the size of its divisions to position more men on the front lines. Additional although smaller divisions could accomplish the same goal. Moreover, smaller divisions were more mobile and presented fewer logistical problems. A full-strength German division in 1917, for example, consisted of approximately 12,000 men (8,500 of which were infantry) for greater mobility. Firepower and maneuver rather than manpower often determined the outcome of an attack.

Accompanied by its guns and transport, the American super-sized divisions occupied between thirty and forty miles of road on the march. This was certain to contribute to command and maneuver difficulties. The American divisions also proved difficult to supply, especially after being introduced into combat.[12] Moreover, the intensity and duration of combat rather than its size largely determined a division's staying power. In the view of John Votaw, the super-sized divisions decided upon by Pershing and his staff proved to be "the very antithesis of General Pershing's concept of 'open' warfare where maneuver and rifle fire, supported by artillery, was the formula for success in battle."[13]

Perhaps the best explanation for Pershing and his staff's support of super-sized units can be found in Harbord's account. Harbord, who initially served as Pershing's Chief of Staff, writes the following in his *American Army in France*:

With the deep and very powerful defense developed in the World War, no decisive stroke could be secured in battle without a penetration necessitating several days of steady fighting. It was thus reasoned that the infantry of the division must be of such strength as to permit it to continue in combat for such a number of days that the continuity of battle would not be interrupted before decision was reached.[14]

In sum, Pershing and his staff believed that their oversized divisions (with companies that increased from their authorized peacetime strength of fifty-eight to a wartime strength of 150 men and then to 250 men) conformed to the AEF's combat doctrine and methods which were designed to transition from the methodical "set piece" battles that characterized static trench warfare to "open warfare" or a war of maneuver. Given the strength of the German defenses that the AEF encountered, especially at Meuse-Argonne, however, these large divisions seemed more designed for attritional than open warfare. Even then firepower, including the sophisticated use of combined arms, more than quantity of manpower, proved to be the decisive factor in the battles ahead.

It has also been argued that the AEF's oversized companies, given the shortage of experienced officers and NCOs, often proved detrimental to battlefield effectiveness. Johnson and Hillman argue that "chaos was induced from the bottom up"[15] by the unexpected wartime expansion from 150 men to 250 men. Faulkner agrees, arguing that "overnight Pershing presented his half-trained junior leaders with monumental problems in maneuver, supply, combat, and command by saddling them with these cumbersome units."[16]

Major General Robert Alexander, the commander of the 77th Division who during the Meuse-Argonne offensive joined other commanders in reducing the size of their companies because of heavy losses, ultimately did not view this as a disadvantage. "The larger company almost invariably resulted in placing too many men in the front line," he writes. "If that line is to advance at all the men composing it must be so disposed as to give the line great flexibility. Each small group must have ample space in which to seek cover and covered ways of advance."[17]

What has been called a "storm of steel" had become the crucial element for a successful offensive on the Western Front. Rifles and bayonets and even automatic weapons had become very much secondary weapons when compared to artillery shells, including those that delivered poison gas. Unlike small arms the artillery cut wire, demolished defensive positions, demoralized defenders, and – unless suppressed – stopped any attack across no-man's-land in its tracks. The British historian Paddy Griffith offers the following interesting "profit and loss" comparison:

> – The Infantry lost one casualty (i.e. all types, not just dead) for every 0.5 it caused, with an average loss during the war of 200 per cent of each division's starting strength, including perhaps 600 per cent in "élite" battalions (assuming losses were always replaced).

- The Artillery lost one casualty for every 10 it caused, with an average loss of forty per cent of each unit's starting strength.
- The Special Gas Brigade lost one casualty for every 40 it caused, with a turnover of 100 per cent of its starting strength during the war.[18]

Pershing and his officers sought to rebut this argument by arguing as follows. "The infantry soldier, using intelligently the fire power of his rifle," writes Alexander, the commander of the 77th Division at Meuse-Argonne, "is still as always since the introduction of firearms, the dominant factor of victory." It was Alexander's view that "machine guns, trench mortars, hand and rifle grenades, gas and all the rest are valuable, sometimes indispensable, auxiliaries but they are only auxiliaries and their value is measured by the degree in which they assist the infantry to close with the enemy."[19]

It is significant that the major disagreement between Pershing's Operations Section and the Baker Mission concerned the proportion of infantry to artillery. Colonel Charles P. Summerall, the senior artillery officer on Baker's mission, and Colonel Fox Conner, were at sixes and sevens. Conner, who earlier had been attached to a French artillery regiment in 1913 and had also served as an American military observer on the Western Front in 1916, argued against what the Operations Section deemed a "disproportionately large amount of artillery."[20] Although outvoted, Summerall stood his ground in demanding double the number of guns that the Operations Section thought necessary. He insisted that an AEF division needed 259 dedicated artillery pieces for an assault against German defenses rather than the 122 guns the Operations Section thought necessary. He later included his reasoning in the report that the Baker Mission submitted to the War Department. Summerall contended that previous offensives on the Western Front failed to force a distant withdrawal by their enemy because they lacked "a sufficient number of guns." The reason for this was that

it has been necessary in all cases to withdraw artillery from other parts of the line to reinforce the section attacked, thus enabling the enemy to assume the offensive against the section so denuded and to conduct bombardments to which no adequate reply could be made. It, therefore, becomes a question as to whether victory should be obtained through a long and exhaustive period, after great losses of men and money, or whether success should be sought through the use of a maximum of gun fire over a shorter period and with a minimum cost in lives. It may fairly be stated that losses in war today are inversely proportional to the volume and the efficiency of friendly artillery fire.[21]

To justify its position, the Operations Section provided charts demonstrating that its recommendations were in line with the weight of artillery employed by the British at Messines Ridge, a recent and successful "set piece" offensive with limited objectives launched in June 1917.[22] (It should be noted, however, that this British attack had been assisted by the detonation of explosives packed in mines dug by sappers beneath the German defenses.) Although his arguments for a greater concentration of artillery were initially rejected, Summerall's firepower-based approach as opposed to the Operations Section's infantry-based approach represented the first serious challenge to the US Army's prewar doctrine.[23]

The US Army during the first months of the war had been radically reshaped, both in the way it was raised and the manner in which it was organized. On May 18 Congress had abandoned America's tradition of voluntary enlistment with the passage of the Selective Service Act. The Pershing–Baker Program now changed the structure of the existing Army from small, mobile units well suited to fighting on the frontier to large and generally cumbersome formations.

This restructuring also eventually led to the breakup or elimination of National Guard units. On August 7, 1918 Chief of Staff Peyton March issued an order consolidating all divisions, Regular (composed of professional soldiers), National (made up largely of enlisted men), and National Guard (which incorporated the state militias), into one army, the US Army.[24] In his haste to get as many full-strength divisions to Europe as possible, March thus ended the at times divisive system of dividing the Army into three components which had become meaningless as units from different categories were being combined to form divisions to ship to Europe. The War Department announced that in future all personnel would be interchangeable.[25] This resulted in the cannibalization of National Guard divisions training in the United States, with many of their men and officers being reassigned to divisions about to embark for France. The consequent gaps were then filled with recent conscripts. Unit cohesion suffered as a result and there was little conformity in the level of training.[26]

Having made essential decisions about the AEF's organization and deployment, and establishing his headquarters in a large house on the edge of Chaumont, a city of some 15,000 on the upper Marne, Pershing turned his attention to the training of American soldiers. By the end of 1917 Pershing had three complete divisions and a fourth in the process of being brought up to strength. Elements of the First Division had arrived in late June. The 26th "Yankee" Division, which had been formed in the United States in August, followed this division. Although its first units were shipped to Europe in September it would be the end of October before its last elements arrived. The first units of the 42nd "Rainbow" Division, a composite division of National Guard units formed in August from National Guardsmen from twenty-six states, arrived in France on

November 1 with its last elements arriving on December 3, 1917. A fourth division, the 2nd Division, was formed in France, with its last elements arriving on March 15, 1918.

Extremely conscious of the impression that his citizen-soldiers made on European officers, Pershing demanded that his men look and act like soldiers. An important principle in their training was that "the standards of the American Army will be those of West Point," which included "uncomplaining obedience to instructions."[27] Broad-shouldered and ramrod straight, Pershing himself projected a powerful physical presence. His tailored uniforms (he never put anything in his pockets) fitted him perfectly. As one member of the AEF once opined: "Pershing was all soldier – right-side-up – upside down, inside, outside, dead or alive – every day in the week and twice on Sunday."[28]

When Pershing visited the 1st Division in August he was appalled by what he witnessed. Enlisted men frequently failed to snap to attention and salute their officers. Many officers also did not live up to Pershing's standards of military etiquette. The sloppiness that Pershing witnessed when he inspected the 1st Division should not have surprised him. "Over fifty percent of the soldiers in the division are recruits almost entirely without training. Practically all of the officers below the grade of captain have been appointed less than six months," their commander general, William L. Sibert, reported to the French who were helping to train the Doughboys. Sibert went on to say that he thought it "essential that the training of the troops should be limited for the next four weeks, at least, to elementary work and the development of a proper military disciplinary spirit."[29]

Looking smart on the parade ground and obeying orders, of course, play an important role in good soldiering, but was Pershing's emphasis on "spit and polish" really essential to battlefield performance? Australian soldiers, for example, were often nonchalant and improperly dressed. As a result of their hell-raising behind the front, there were more Australians in military prison than any other nationality in the BEF. In 1915 they had also been responsible for a serious riot in the brothel district of Wasser in Cairo. But at Gallipoli, in Palestine, and on the Western Front they proved to be some of the war's best soldiers.

In making citizen soldiers into warriors the Army soon discovered that it had to make accommodations both at home and abroad. According to Keene, "to protect their credibility, army officials began either accommodating behavior that the troops themselves refused to modify or abandoning policies deemed unenforceable."[30] The AEF's principles for the training of US troops, for example, included the following instructions for officers: "Officers will not lose sight of their personal obligation to provide for the comfort of their men ... [to] create a spirit of contentment and confidence in the future ... small derelictions of duty will be disposed of so far as practicable by immediate commanders. Confinement in the guard house will be resorted to only in case of incorrigibles."[31]

The civilian leadership also made it clear that the ultimate disciplinary weapon, death by a court-martial, could only be used in extreme cases (rape, murder, mutiny, desertion, or espionage), and then only after Baker and Wilson had reviewed each individual case.

In November 1917, the first American soldier was court-martialed and executed. Earle R. Poorbaugh, Company L, 26th Infantry Regiment, 1st Division, served as Sergeant of the Guard. "Most unpleasant – man hanged was a Cherokee Indian, who raped and killed a small girl. Entire Division witnessed execution. Very sobering effect," Poorbaugh later wrote.[32] The Army hanged nine more Americans before the war's end for murder or rape but none for cowardice or desertion. By contrast, according to official records, the British executed 361 men, 321 for military offenses and 40 for murder between September 1914 and November 1920.[33]

Pershing, of course, understood that a smart-looking soldier who conformed to military etiquette was not necessarily a warrior. But, convinced that Americans were the best soldiers in the world, he wanted them to look like it. Nevertheless, his highest priority remained training them to take on the German Army. "The most important question that confronted us in the preparation of our forces of citizen soldiery for efficient service was training," he later wrote in his memoirs. "It was one thing to call one or two million men to the colors, and quite another thing to transform them into an organized, instructed army capable of meeting and holding its own in the battle against the best trained force in Europe with three years of actual war experience to its credit."[34]

With many untrained or inadequately trained men and officers being sent across the Atlantic, Pershing established a wide-ranging system of AEF schools under the supervision of the Operations and Training Section of his General Staff. Experienced French and British officers initially played an essential role in their training. Much of what they learned was eye-opening and unlike anything they expected or had earlier experienced. Lieutenant K. E. Walser, 101st Field Artillery, 26th Division, who had received his first training at Plattsburg, was greatly impressed with his schooling at Saumur Field Artillery School. At Plattsburg, New York, he had "learned little because the instructors themselves knew little of modern warfare."[35] But his French instructors at Saumur carried out their instruction "so scientifically and exactly and they know so much about the whole thing, that it is almost discouraging. They are without exception the finest bunch of men I ever came into contact with."[36]

Charles Edward Frampton's diary offers further insight into this tutelage by foreign officers. A member of the West Virginia National Guard, Frampton served on the Mexican border in 1916 where he rose through the ranks from private to sergeant-major. Mustered out in March he was immediately reactivated when the United States declared war on Germany. Commissioned Second Lieutenant after attending an officer training camp at Fort Benjamin Harrison in Indianapolis, he departed for France along with many other newly minted lieutenants as replacement officers to take the place of the lieutenants in the first units arriving in Europe who had been promptly promoted to captain because of the shortage of officers. Officer training camp graduates eventually comprised 74 percent of officers commissioned. Never before had American volunteer officers received as much training before being commissioned but what they learned often had little in common with what they encountered on European battlefields. In September Frampton arrived in France to complete his training under foreign tutelage.[37]

He spent all of October and the first nine days of November at one of the AEF's infantry schools for officers at Valreas, a small town in the foothills of the Alps. On October 2, their French instructors introduced him and his fellow American officers to trench warfare when they observed a mock attack by French soldiers with smoke bombs and grenades. None of Lieutenant Frampton's previous limited military experience on the Mexican border prepared him for what he witnessed. The "battle scene was wrapped in a blanket of thick suffocating smoke," he recorded in his diary. "The din was awful & we could imagine how hellish the real thing must be." There was more of the same with additional firepower on the following day: "Spent morning watching a French Company storm entrenched position on hill – artillery – machine guns, bombs, grenades & rockets made it sound life like. An example of what might happen was seen when a hapless dog ran into the barrage fire & was blown to pieces by a bursting grenade."[38]

During the following days, Frampton and his fellow officers occupied trenches and the French subjected them to mock attacks with "real grenades – auto-rifles [signal rockets]." They also learned how to take and entrench positions. An entirely new technology of warfare had to be mastered. As Robert Lee Bullard, who had been assigned the task of establishing American infantry schools under French instruction in the Gondrecourt area, writes in his reminiscences:

We had trained infantrymen with the rifle, and now we found that the infantryman was not only a rifleman but a rifle-grenade man, a hand-grenade man, a light-machine gunner, a heavy-machine gunner, a Stokes-mortar man, a gas specialist, sometimes a signal man and sometimes half artilleryman for the accompanying gun. Soldiers of other arms of the service, artillery, engineers, signal men, and even labour troops, were similarly required to be all sorts of specialists.[39]

Frampton took lessons in or attended demonstrations about liaison at night, the use of Morse flasher signals, Stokes mortars, machine guns, and flares. Live ammunition placed him in some danger and he was twice slightly wounded by shell fragments in grenade drills. In addition to training for trench warfare, the young American officers exercised and participated in bayonet drills. The climax of their training came on November 8 when they defended their trenches against a mock French attack.[40]

After he completed his training at Valreas, the Army assigned him to Company E, 9th Infantry, 2nd Division. He found quarters along with other soldiers among the families of the village. Officers usually stayed in farmhouses, the men often in barns. Tent camps did not seem tenable because the intensively cultivated fields surrounding the villages left little space for hundreds of officers and men to pitch tents. Authorities also feared that rows of tents would make inviting targets for German aviators.

Pershing wanted his own SOS, but he did not have the necessary auxiliary troops to construct his lines of communication. Hence he at times employed combat troops in hard labor. Frampton spent most of November and all of December supervising men building a railroad cut for a large supply depot near Is-sur-Tille. Some 600 men worked with inadequate tools and explosives to make a cut of sixteen feet in "almost solid limestone." This work proved dangerous as well as difficult, and some soldiers were killed and others injured.

On January 4, Frampton began instruction at the First Corps Center of Instruction at Gondrecourt, one of four training camps where American divisions trained alongside French divisions billeted in the same locality. Once again Frampton's training proved realistic. As part of a two-week specialist course in grenades, he practiced a trench raid on January 15. "About 60 of us – armed to teeth – crossed no-man's-land – penetrated the enemies wire & raided the trenches. Mortars – 37 m/m & rockets & lights made it seem real life like," he wrote in his diary. Too real for a young lieutenant next to Frampton who lost his life when he accidentally exploded one of his grenades.

Following the successful completion of his grenade course, Frampton began studies in handling troops in tactical situations and learned more about the new military technology. He spent most of his time in the field but he also attended lectures given by foreign officers. These lectures included sniping, aerial photography, wave formations, care of troops on the march and in camp, map reading, sending and receiving messages, finding one's way through darkness by compass, and conducting trench raids. In the field he experienced the terror of chemical warfare, exploding shells, and machine gun fire. "I got my eyes full [of tear gas] as well as my clothes were saturated as result," he recorded in his diary. "I have wept copiously all day." Allied instructors also introduced him to creeping or rolling barrages (he described it as a "wall of fire"). In the first wave he "advanced under creeping barrage – at zero line the wave of this line left trenches & started forward. The barrage creeping along in front. A riot of sound – like all hell had broken loose. Over the inferno hovered the aeroplanes – directing artillery. The whole was big success."[41] Frampton also participated in an attack in three waves against trenches under a machine gun barrage.

Foreign instruction had properly trained him to come to grips with the Germans when his platoon took its place in the trenches alongside French units on March 20, 1918. Little time had been allocated to musketry, bayonet drills, or long-distance marches. Instead he had received realistic and intensive training that focused on modern weaponry and included creeping barrages, chemical warfare, and grenades.

If many US officers had their way, however, their men would not come under the influence of foreign instructors. On March 6, 1918, on the eve of the series of German offensives in 1918 designed to win a victor's peace, General Ragueneau, the Chief of the French Military Mission with the American Army, forwarded the following warning to his superiors:

In the first place, the title of "instructor" (Tantamount to "teacher"), given to the French officers assigned to American troop units, did not strike Americans right. Perhaps the terms "consulting expert" or "technical advisor" would have answered, but the term "instructor" insofar as it meant a "teacher or preceptor" did not fit. The term "instructor," implied the adoption, bag and baggage, of a foreign theory of warfare, and foreign military methods. Now both theory and methods had to be American to the core, and neither French nor British.[42]

To diminish foreign influence, GHQ issued "Principles Governing the Training of Units of the American Expeditionary Forces," dated April 9, 1918, which Pershing and his staff insisted must be followed to the letter. "Strict compliance with those principles will be exacted and nothing contrary thereto will be taught" in order to prepare the AEF for "the assumption of vigorous offensive." GHQ insisted that "the rifle and the bayonet are the principal weapons of the infantry soldier. He will be trained to a high degree of skill as a marksman both on the target range and in field firing. An aggressive spirit must be developed until the soldier feels himself, as a bayonet fighter, invincible in battle."[43]

The AEF's official training plan proscribed three additional months of training after a division had been dispatched to France, one month of training behind the lines, another month in a quiet sector of the front lines with seasoned Allied divisions, and a third month devoted to "open warfare." Henri-Philippe Pétain, the commander-in-chief of the French Army, however, made an obvious point, correctly observing that American infantry needed not just additional training but the right training. He noted that their

instruction was approximately limited, during their stay in camp, in the United States, to gymnastic exercises, close order drill, rifle fire and drill in field warfare, which consisted too much of small operations, having but little relation to actual warfare, such as attack and defense of convoys, requisitions, etc. They have but slight knowledge of specialties (grenades, F.M., machine guns, etc.).[44]

The AEF's leadership, however, continued to demonstrate that they could not have disagreed more with Pétain. They increasingly deplored the influence that French training was having on American troops. Colonel Harold B. Fiske, prior to his appointment as head of the AEF training section, summarized the general view of the detrimental effect of foreign training in a memorandum for the AEF Chief of Staff.

Our young officers and men are prone to take the tone and tactics of those with who they are associated, and whatever they are now learning that is false or unsuited for us will be hard to eradicate later. In many respects, the tactics and technique of our Allies are not suited to American characteristics or the American mission in this war. The French do not like the rifle, do not know how to use it, and their infantry is consequently too entirely dependent upon a powerful artillery support. Their infantry lacks aggressiveness and discipline.[45]

Many Doughboys later came to disagree with Fiske. In his response to the *World War I Survey* question, "Did your training prepare you adequately for your service abroad?," corporal Frederick Shaw, Headquarters Company, 18th Infantry Regiment, 1st Division, wrote: "I feel our Division was fortunate in that we received bulk of our training overseas, enabling us to become acclimated ... also more instruction by [foreign] veterans in various areas of combat."[46] This was not an isolated view.

As noted previously, France's military leadership had entered the war committed to the *offensive à outrance*, a military philosophy that emphasized the individual soldier's courage and stressed that his bayonet was his "supreme weapon." Following unprecedented casualties with little or no gain of ground this philosophy had been replaced by the belief that firepower rather than the aggressiveness and morale of individual soldiers won the day. "Americans dream of operating in open country, after having broken through the front," Pétain lamented. "This results in too much attention being devoted to this form of operations, which the Americans consider as superior, and in which, our Allies sometimes seem to think, we are incapable of offering them the same assistance which they expect from us in trench warfare."[47]

The French commander-in-chief was genuinely puzzled why Pershing believed that the AEF's doctrine, which was described as "open warfare," offered a better chance of defeating the Germans. In fact, it was not clear to him and many other Allied leaders exactly what the Americans meant when they spoke of "open warfare." Both the French and British had launched one offensive after another against heavily entrenched positions in an attempt to return to a war of maneuver and drive the Germans out of France. Yet Pershing seemed to equate this structured and deliberative form of offensive warfare with defensive warfare.

Harbord, Pershing's first Chief of Staff, is not very helpful when he attempts to distinguish between the American version of "open warfare" and the prevailing "trench warfare." "The French officers," he writes in his account of the war, "were products of the trench warfare that had so long prevailed. Such trained officers as we had were imbued with the teachings of the Leavenworth Schools, where Minor Tactics, involving security and information, patrolling, advance and rear guards, protection of flanks and rear, were of the essence of the training."[48] But the minor tactics described by Harbord had little relevance to the siege warfare prevailing on the Western Front despite repeated and ever more sophisticated attempts to achieve a breakthrough.

Harbord's next comment, which appears to overlook the many Allied attempts to achieve a breakthrough, is puzzling to say the least. French and British soldiers had most certainly not spent 1917 crouched behind earthen walls waiting for the Germans to attack. To the contrary, Nivelle, the French commander-in-chief, had spectacularly failed in 1917 to live up to his promise to rupture the German front in twenty-four or forty-eight hours. Haig, the British commander-in-chief, had then spent the last half of 1917 in an overly ambitious campaign to capture the Belgian coast and drive the Germans out of Belgium. The French Army had mutinied after their offensive failed, and the cost for the BEF in maintaining the strategic initiative for the Allies throughout 1917 on the Western Front had been more than 800,000 casualties.[49]

In sum, both Allied commanders-in-chief had attempted to end the war of attrition with war-winning drives. Yet Pershing's Chief of Staff writes:

Our Commander-in-Chief believed, and time confirmed his judgment, that the War would never be won by troops of both sides remaining in parallel trenches separated by a few hundred yards. Some day someone somewhere would come out of his trenches and start forward, and thus a stalemate would be broken and the war would eventually be won. When even one soldier climbed out and moved to the front, the adventure for him became open warfare, a war of movement, and the essentials of minor tactics were then in play. His flanks and rear must be protected as his maneuvers began. Mere training in trench warfare would not be enough for our officers when this event happened.[50]

"Combat Instructions," dated September 5, 1918, issued by GHQ, is no more helpful when it attempts to contrast "trench warfare" with the American doctrine of "open warfare." "Trench warfare," it asserted, "is marked by uniform formations, the regulation of space and time by higher command down to the smallest details, absence of scouts preceding the first wave, fixed distance and intervals between units and individuals, voluminous orders, careful rehearsal, little initiative upon the part of the individual soldiers." By contrast, GHQ argued that open warfare was

marked by scouts who precede the first wave, irregularity of formation, comparatively little regulation of space and time by the higher command, the greatest possible use of the infantry's own fire power to enable it to get forward, variable distances and intervals between the units and individuals, use of every form of cover and accident of ground during the advance, brief orders, and the greatest possible use of individual initiative by all troops engaged in the action.[51]

Without a doubt infantry continued to play a vital role on the European battlefields despite the dramatic increase in firepower. Artillery might pulverize the enemy's defenses and suppress its artillery, but foot soldiers still had to occupy and hold surviving strong points. Over time tactics had evolved through trial and error on both sides of the trenches. Trench raids – which required meticulous planning, improved communications, grenades, artillery box barrages, and support from machine guns and trench mortars – "amounted to dress rehearsals in miniature" for further major offensives.[52]

But the infantryman's success more than ever depended upon his supporting arms which now included an increasing number of tanks and aircraft on the Allied side. The "tactics of infiltration" practiced by German "storm troopers" represented the culmination of these tactical advances which emphasized concentrated artillery firepower with combined-arms assaults by the infantry. In 1918, every German officer down to and including battalion commanders had a copy of *The Attack in Position Warfare* which had been authored by a Bavarian officer, Captain Hermann Geyer. This manual emphasized the "speed and decisiveness" of attacking infantry to achieve operational maneuver. Equipped with enhanced firepower (which included flamethrowers) German soldiers were trained to "penetrate quickly and deeply," bypassing strong positions, in an uninterrupted advance.[53] Attention was also given to supporting arms such as low-flying aircraft, light trench mortars, and heavy machine guns. Firepower was further enhanced by substituting light machine guns and rifle grenades for rifles. "The fact that the light machine gun was now the true 'infantryman' while the 'infantryman' of yesterday was nothing more than a 'rifle-carrier'" is the way that Ludendorff puts it in his memoirs.[54]

What were the consequences of the AEF's doctrine of "open warfare"? Grotelueschen provides the most scholarly and comprehensive answer to this question. He argues that GHQ's reliance on the "anachronistic and obsolete ideas" of the Army's prewar doctrine minimized the importance of artillery and failed to understand the limitations placed on the infantry. "Infantry needed to use new formations and tactics on the Western Front, not mimic the old prewar guidance," he contends. Moreover, the AEF's frequently limited and inadequate training, which focused on marksmanship and the bayonet, did not prepare most American soldiers to fight in the open if a war of movement actually became a reality. Too much was being asked of inexperienced Americans, the great majority undergoing combat for the first time. GHQ "also underestimated the importance of control, communication, and coordination, especially regarding infantry–artillery cooperation, a factor essential under nearly all battlefield conditions." General attacks were launched "without either sufficient tanks or enough preliminary artillery bombardment to take strong defensive positions held by defenders fully expecting an attack." Finally, AEF doctrine encouraged unrealistic expectations. At Saint-Mihiel, and especially during the first stages of the Meuse-Argonne offensive, GHQ "established such ambitious – indeed, essentially unlimited – objectives that they were completely unattainable by the forces employed."[55]

Johnson's conclusion is equally damning in his characterization of the consequences of the AEF's outdated doctrine.

It produced infantry that attacked in linear formations of the decades gone by. It produced infantry that only knew how to attack straight ahead. It produced infantry unfamiliar with its normal supporting arms. It produced infantry willing to be killed in straight-ahead attacks because it knew no better. Because of their aggressiveness, impatience, and faith in their cause, they paid the price of improper and inadequate training in blood.[56]

It remains difficult to comprehend why Pershing and his staff believed so strongly in the superiority of AEF doctrine. Pershing may have been overly influenced by his last command in Mexico where his cavalrymen fought small-unit actions and where individual initiative, marksmanship, and reconnaissance played a key role. It is more likely, however, that psychological and political considerations largely motivated him. Emphasis on the Doughboy's rifle and bayonet represented an attempt to make American soldiers think that they were invincible on the battlefield. Colonel Harold B. Fiske, the acting and later head of the AEF Training Section, summarized the prevailing American view of the French and British armies in 1917:

The offensive spirit of the French and British Armies has largely disappeared as a result of their severe losses. Close association with beaten forces lowers the morale of the best troops . . . The French do not like the rifle, do not know how to use it, and their infantry is consequently too entirely dependent upon a powerful artillery support. Their infantry lacks aggressiveness and discipline . . . Berlin can not be taken by the French or the British Armies or by both of them. It can only be taken by a thoroughly trained, entirely homogeneous American Army, in which the sense of initiative and self reliance upon the part of all officers and men has been developed to the very highest degree. An American Army can not be made by Frenchmen or by Englishmen.[57]

Allied pressure to amalgamate American forces with their own armies also encouraged Pershing and his staff to develop a distinctly American doctrine. By arguing that French (and British) doctrine differed from the AEF's, and was essentially defensive in nature, they believed that they had a strong case for creating an independent army with its own strategic objectives. When Colonel House questioned the American Secretary of War about the AEF's doctrine, Baker told him that "it has seemed to me from the beginning, better for us to have our own doctrine, and be soon in a position to occupy an independent place on the line." This would enable the United States to be "a great power conducting *pro tanto* a war of our own, rather than having our forces merged with that of one of the other combatants and losing its identity."[58]

8 Will the Americans arrive in time?

As Pershing and his staff planned and prepared for a war-winning offensive in 1919, British and French war leaders by necessity focused on the present. Increasingly it became apparent to them that the flow of American reinforcements across the Atlantic would determine the war's outcome. Russia's headlong decline especially weighed on their minds. The overthrow of the Romanov dynasty in March had not revitalized the Russian Army. Outnumbering the Habsburg forces by a ratio of three to one, and supplied with British and French artillery, the so-called Kerensky offensive had been launched on July 1 towards Lemberg (or Lvov). Berlin responded by transferring eight German divisions to the Eastern Front and launching a counteroffensive on July 19. The plain-speaking "Wully" Robertson described the result: "The Russians broke, with the result that three Russian armies comprising some 60 to 70 divisions, well equipped with guns and ammunition, are now running away from some 18 Austrian and German divisions."[1] General Mikhail Vasilevich Alekseev, the Russian commander-in-chief who had resigned in protest against the Kerensky offensive, now proclaimed that the Russian Army "remained nothing but human dust."[2] If the Russian Army's collapse portended Russia's withdrawal from the war the strategic landscape would be dramatically altered in Germany's favor. By transferring German divisions from the East, Berlin might be able to launch a war-winning offensive on the Western Front.

The encouraging arrival of the first American troops in June had coincided with a serious breakdown in discipline in the French Army that occurred in the wake of Nivelle's failed offensive in April 1917. At its peak the mutiny affected fifty-four French divisions. Some soldiers refused orders to enter the trenches. Others were willing to defend their positions, but refused to take the offensive.[3] Pétain's appointment as commander-in-chief gradually contributed to a restoration of discipline, but under his leadership it soon became apparent to the British that they could count on the French for only limited support for the remainder of 1917.

France's new commander-in-chief now accepted that the war would not be decided by a single great battle. He predicted that victory could only come after a number of limited, set-piece battles that exhausted the reserves of Germany.

In the actual state of equilibrium existing between the [opposing] forces, [a breakthrough] is not possible. Experience – and reason – prove this. The capacity of resistance provided by modern fire permits personnel already in place to hold a continuous front between the sea and Switzerland. Railways facilitate the convergence of reserves on any point in minimum time (seven days to go from the Russian front to the French front). A breach can be envisaged only when successful pushes or attrition have created intervals in the enemy's line or have diminished German reserves considerably.[4]

At an Allied military conference attended by Pershing on July 26 to consider the effect of Russia being forced out of the war, Allied leaders raised the doomsday prospect of Germany concentrating as many as 273 divisions on the Western Front by June 1918. (This was clearly an exaggeration and assumed that Germany might be able to utilize many Austro-Hungarian divisions; a more reasoned analysis anticipated that Germany might have 217 divisions in the west by early spring to 167 Allied divisions.)[5] Pershing suggested that he might have twenty divisions in France by that time if shipping were made available. Thereafter an additional twenty-five or thirty divisions might be forthcoming.[6] A skeptical Robertson reported to the War Cabinet that Pershing was being overly optimistic about the AEF's future strength.[7]

Acutely aware of the looming British manpower crisis, Lloyd George had reluctantly sanctioned a long-planned offensive to liberate the Belgian coastline from German control. He would have preferred a standstill strategy on the Western Front until American forces arrived in appreciable numbers but this now seemed months if not years away. But with Britain's European allies wavering the British high command and a majority of his colleagues believed that Britain had little choice but to assume the primary burden of keeping pressure on the German Army. On July 20, the War Cabinet, after days of agonizing deliberation, sanctioned Haig's offensive.

Lloyd George now believed that the United States offered Britain its best hope of surviving the war as a great power. As the Third Battle of Ypres (popularly known as "Passchendaele") got underway on July 31, Lloyd George talked with some of his colleagues about getting Wilson "to come over and swear to support us."[8] But Wilson could not be summoned to London for discussions as if he were a Dominion prime minister. To forge a special relationship between London and Washington, Lloyd George considered visiting the United States, something that no previous prime minister had ever done before. No invitation, however, was forthcoming from the White House.

Wilson wanted to make the world safe for democracy – not for the British Empire. Both men believed that German militarism must be eliminated. But in opposition to Lloyd George, who spoke of delivering a "knock-out" blow against Germany, Wilson still hoped that liberal elements in that country might triumph over the autocratic and military clique, making it possible for him to act as the honest broker between the Allies and a new, liberal Germany. He earlier had made it clear that America was entering the war as an "associate" and not as an "ally." Just as Pershing and his staff wanted an independent army with its own doctrine and strategical objectives, Wilson sought to pursue an independent course in diplomacy, to fight and negotiate at the same time.

As British casualties mounted during the Third Battle of Ypres, Lloyd George's attention turned once again to military ventures away from the Western Front, especially against Austria–Hungary or the Ottoman Empire. More than ever, he believed that the road to redirecting Allied strategy was through Washington. On September 20, Lord Reading, who had just arrived in the United States to discuss financial questions, hand delivered a letter from the Prime Minister to Wilson. In this private and personal communication, Lloyd George suggested that if one of Germany's allies could be forced out of the war the "whole enemy military edifice might fall rapidly in ruins." The Prime Minister suggested working with Wilson to give a new direction to the anti-German coalition's military and political efforts. He insisted that he had not "the slightest desire that the United States should surrender the freedom of action which she possesses at present." But in his view it was now clear that the destruction of the "German military oligarchy" and the making of "a just, liberal and lasting peace" depended "more and more upon the British Commonwealth and the United States."[9]

Robertson learned of Lloyd George's secret efforts to recruit Wilson as an ally when Bliss told the French military attaché in Washington that efforts were being made to employ American forces in theaters other than the Western Front. Robertson immediately attempted to quiet French fears. He informed the French War Ministry that "no pressure of any kind has been brought to bear on America by Chief of the Imperial General Staff to send troops elsewhere than to France."[10]

Wilson distrusted Lloyd George and the right-wing Tories in the War Cabinet and was not about to act as the Welshman's point man in Allied conferences to further his "eastern" strategy, which really amounted to any front but the Western Front. Nevertheless, Lloyd George's belief that it was futile to seek victory on the Western Front seemed confirmed by a paper, "Memorandum on the General Strategy of the Present War between the Allies and the Central Powers," that Wilson had just received from Major Herbert H. Sargent, who had briefly served in the War College Division before becoming a professor of military science and tactics at Princeton University. Given the strength of Germany's defenses, Sargent argued that American military power would be "bottled up" in Western Europe. Hence the United States should deploy its main force elsewhere: either in the Balkans to "cut the Central Powers in two, much as Grant cut the Confederacy in two," or in cooperation with the British in Mesopotamia.[11]

There is no evidence that Wilson was sympathetic with Sargent's hare-brained strategic musings. He obviously had no desire to expand the British Empire in the Persian Gulf. Nor were the proposed Balkan operations, with their inevitable political complications, likely to appeal to him. The United States was not even at war with either Bulgaria or Turkey. At the same time, siege warfare had prevailed on the Western Front for three years. The prospect of massive American casualties without a decisive outcome clearly alarmed him. As he told House at this time, "The American people would not be willing to continue indefinite trench warfare."[12] Tens of thousands of young Americans were currently being transported to camps to be trained and dispatched to Europe, and Pershing's Operations Section was putting the finishing touches on what it hoped would be a war-winning campaign against Metz in 1919. Yet at this very moment Wilson ordered the General Staff to initiate an inquiry into "the strategic considerations" that had led to choosing France as "the theater of operations of our army."[13] This speaks volumes about the lack of coordination between the military authorities and the executive office during the formative period of America's commitment to a land war in Western Europe.

Prompted by the President, the War College Division considered all possible theaters for American forces, not just those proposed by Major Sargent. Logistics, especially shipping, the advantage of interior lines possessed by the Central Powers, and the fundamental military principle of concentrating forces against the enemy's main army were all employed to debunk Sargent's peripheral strategy. One appreciation warned: "Let Germany once get the upper hand of or defeat France, or even let England and France get the idea that the United States proposes to embark on questionable, though highly desired operations elsewhere, and the war is won – by Germany."[14]

The General Staff made no effort to soft pedal the cost of defeating Germany and advanced no cheap or easy way to achieve victory. Weight of men and material would ultimately determine the victor. Once the

United States had concentrated its forces in France, Germany would be forced to do the same. "The contest will then narrow down to a tug of war like Grant had against Lee until, by means of our unlimited resources, we are enabled to force a favorable conclusion." The AEF's numerical superiority compensated for its inexperience. "We must make our superiority in men and material so great that we can be certain of crushing the enemy in spite of misfortune and errors," Colonel F. S. Young asserted.[15] Young spoke the language of a strategy of annihilation rather than a more limited or indirect strategy to gain a favorable peace. His arguments reinforce the thesis of Russell Weigley who writes that "the Civil War tended to fix the American image of war from the 1860s into America's rise to world power at the turn of the century, and it also suggested that the complete overthrow of the enemy, the destruction of his military power, is the object of war."[16]

Wilson appeared curiously detached from this critical strategical debate which could determine the fate of tens of thousands of young American men. Before receiving the General Staff's response to Sargent's musings on strategy, he had perused another General Staff defense of its western strategy prepared for but never sent to Senator George E. Chamberlain, the Chair of the Military Affairs Committee. His comment had been: "I have been able to give it only a cursory reading but I am glad to keep in touch with these things."[17]

The General Staff's extensive rebuttal of Sargent that he received on October 11 apparently made no impression on him because a month later he was once again quizzing Baker about the validity of Sargent's views. When Baker responded by sending him once again the General Staff's strong defense of the American commitment to the Western Front Wilson's response was: "I am glad to feel that all suggestions, good and bad, are being seriously studied."[18] But not by the President apparently!

A cablegram arrived at the War Department several weeks later that brought home the consequences of America's commitment to the war in Europe to the President. Fresh from a conference that included Pershing, Robertson, and Ferdinand Foch, the Chief of the General Staff of the French Army, Bliss forwarded an Allied request for a minimum of twenty-four trained US divisions in France by June 1918. By the end of the summer the American contribution in manpower should rise to thirty divisions or five complete corps – a figure which, not by chance, was precisely what Pershing's Operations Staff had deemed necessary for a successful offensive against Metz.[19] Pershing, in fact, had been the catalyst for this request. The Allied generals, dubious that the United States was capable of providing that many trained divisions, had played along. At this time the United States had four under-strength divisions in

France, the 1st, 2nd, 26th, and 42nd, and only the 1st Division was thought ready to receive additional training by entering the trenches alongside French troops in a quiet sector of the front.[20] A stunned Wilson responded: "Is such a programme *possible?*"[21]

Robertson certainly did not think so. In late October he had attempted to debunk the view held by some British leaders, most notably Lloyd George, that Britain should adopt a standstill policy on the Western Front until the United States had formed a well-trained army in France. "If by some miracle," he reported to the War Cabinet,

we could suddenly pass over the next 18 months and in 1919 resume the war under present conditions, plus the reinforcement in France of, say, a million well-trained American troops, there would be no question as to the best policy. But unfortunately we cannot perform miracles, and therefore we have to consider whether, *all* things considered, the Entente may not, despite American assistance, be much weaker, and not stronger, in 1919 than in 1918.[22]

Robertson's memorandum coincided with a turn for the worse for Allied fortunes. Haig's offensive concluded in early November with the capture of the village of Passchendaele, but the Belgian ports remained firmly in German hands, as did some of the original object-ives of his first drive on July 31. Haig's losses had been heavy, and there were reports of an alarming rise in drunkenness, desertions, and psychological disorders among his troops. Haig himself characterized his army as "much exhausted and much reduced in strength. Many divisions in the line urgently require relief, while the great majority of those for the first time being in reserve are neither sufficiently rested to relieve them nor really fit to be thrown into a fight to meet an emergency."[23] On the Italian front on October 24 a surprise Austro-German attack had ripped a fifteen-mile gap in the Italian front at Caporetto. The withdrawal ordered by the Italian commander-in-chief Count Luigi Cadorna quickly become a rout, with 1 million Italian soldiers fleeing the mountains in panic. In Petrograd, the Bolsheviks committed to getting Russia out of the war on November 7 had stormed the Winter Palace and overthrown the Provisional Government. Although it was by no means certain that the Bolsheviks could retain power it was "quite clear," as Robertson informed the War Cabinet, that "whatever happened politically in Russia, the bulk of the Russian Army refused to continue the war."[24] Russia's subse-quent defection undermined the Allied blockade and threatened Britain's Asian flank. Only in France was there some cause for opti-mism on the European fronts. Clemenceau, the "Tiger," had become premier on November 16. When questioned about his policy in Parliament, he had thundered: "I make war!" His words carried some

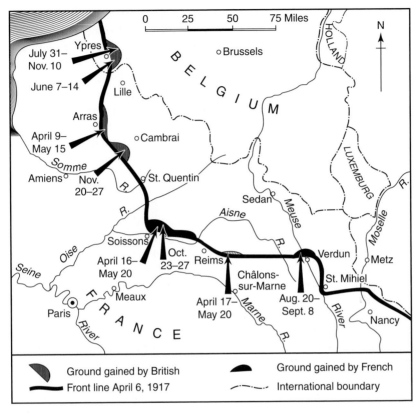

0   25   50   75 Miles

July 31–
Nov. 10
Ypres
June 7–14
Lille
o Brussels
B E L G I U M
Arras
April 9–
May 15
o Cambrai
Somme
Amiens° Nov.
20–27
o St. Quentin
Sedan
Aisne
Soissons
April 16–
May 20
Oct.
23–27
Reims
Verdun
Metz
Meaux
Châlons-
sur-Marne
St. Mihiel
Paris
April 17–
May 20
Aug. 20–
Sept. 8
Nancy
F R A N C E
Seine
Oise
Meuse
Moselle
LUXEMBURG
HOLLAND

N

Ground gained by British   Ground gained by French
Front line April 6, 1917   International boundary

2. Allied attacks on the Western Front in 1917

weight because of the recent success of a limited French offensive
on the Aisne (Map 2).

On November 24, Hankey, the War Cabinet's secretary and Lloyd
George's confidant, described the situation as he saw it:

Russia has collapsed under the strain; Italy is near collapse; France's arms are
held up until the hour of sunset by Britain and America; Austria and Turkey are
exhausted. Germany, Great Britain, and the USA are still stalwart. The contest
has become one of endurance, and on the whole the balance of advantage lies
with us, provided we do not deliberately exhaust ourselves prematurely.[25]

To the British it seemed more important than ever to forge a close
relationship with the United States. Wilson had rebuffed a state visit from
the Prime Minister, and there was no chance that he would personally

participate in any inter-Allied conference in Europe. But he did decide to send House as the head of a mission to England and France. The so-called House Mission departed for Europe on October 29 with the outcome of the war now very much in doubt. To represent the War Department, Wilson chose Bliss, who had officially become Chief of Staff in September. This artillery officer had never held a combat command but was recognized for his scholarly pursuits. He had earlier gotten the President's attention when he expressed alarmist views about Allied intentions to diminish the AEF's influence through amalgamation. The Chief of Naval Operations, Admiral Benson, an Anglophobe, represented the Navy Department.

The House Mission arrived in London in the midst of a full-blown political crisis over the powers of the new Supreme War Council which had been created in the wake of the collapse of the Italian Front. At Rapallo, Italy, on November 7, Lloyd George had played the leading role in creating an Allied body to coordinate war policy. But his critics with justification believed that he was primarily interested in undermining Sir William Robertson, the government's adviser on strategy and Haig's staunch ally. Robertson's and Haig's supporters in the press asserted that the Prime Minister's concept of unity of command should not be confused with support for civilian meddling in military strategy. When asked for his opinion, Wilson threw his support to Lloyd George: "Please take the position that we not only accede to the plan for a single war council but insist on it, but think it does not go far enough."[26] Wilson's later actions did not live up to these words. Despite his unequivocal support for unity of command, he continued to assert America's political and military independence. An important consideration for the President in November may have been his belief that this new inter-Allied body might facilitate a clear statement of the Entente's war objectives, for which he was then pressing.

Meanwhile, in London, members of the House Mission pored over confidential materials and talked with Britain's war leaders. Repeatedly it was impressed upon them that the war might be lost, and soon, if the United States did not do more. One British General Staff memorandum, "American Assistance to the Allies," dated November 17, 1917, painted an especially alarming picture. According to this memorandum, the Anglo-French reinforcements either sent to or contemplated for Italy and the planned cannibalization of French divisions on the Western Front to keep other divisions up to strength might mean a total reduction of Allied strength in the west by from twenty-four to thirty divisions. With Germany able to transfer its divisions from the Eastern Front, the balance of strength on the Western Front in 1918 might be altered "in favour of the enemy by as many as 60 divisions."[27] The message was clear: only American manpower could enable the French and British to hold their own. But Bliss was all too well aware of the snail-like pace of mobilizing America's resources, both material and manpower. As he had written his wife when he first arrived in London, "It is pitiful to see the undercurrent of feeling that the hopes of Europe have in the United States, pitiful because it will be so long before we can really do anything, although the very crisis seems to be at hand."[28]

When Bliss asked the British for estimates of the tonnage required for Pershing's program of four complete army corps of six divisions each by May 1, 1918, he was staggered by the response of the Director-General of Movements and Railways, who gave him a conservative estimate of an additional 2,740,700 gross tons to convey twenty-four divisions, with auxiliaries and reserves, to France by that date. Presently the United States had only twenty-four ships with a gross tonnage of 338,000 allocated to transporting troops to Europe.[29] Statisticians on the Council of National Defense provided an even more alarming report. They projected that the transport and supply of twenty-four divisions would require the United States to suspend all of its foreign trade for the duration of the war.[30] When he later made inquiries, Bliss also discovered to his amazement that "of more than fifty ships that have been commandeered on completion by the Government, only one has been placed available for the transportation of troops and equipment."[31]

When Bliss returned to Washington he did not mince words with his colleagues in the War Department. Unless the War Department could find the means to expand and hasten the transport of soldiers to Europe, the United States would "be responsible for continued enormous destruction of wealth and of life and, to crown all, will have maintained an idle Army at home at a cost of billions of dollars for mere maintenance," he told Baker.[32]

Bliss proved equally frank in the final report that he submitted after the House Mission returned to the United States. "There may be no campaign of 1919," Bliss warned, "unless we do our best to make the campaign of 1918 the last."[33] If the United States continued its leisurely pace of expanding the AEF and accepted Pershing's plan of concentrating his forces in Lorraine, withholding them from major combat, and waiting until 1919 to launch a war-winning offensive against Metz, it might guarantee a German victory.

To prevent a catastrophe, Bliss suggested a major realignment of US strategy. After Nivelle's failed spring offensive, the British had assumed the primary burden of fighting the main body of the German Army. It thus seemed likely that decisive blows against Germany in the future would be delivered by British and American arms. If the French could be persuaded to accept a new arrangement, Bliss wanted the AEF to join forces with the British at once. In his words, "every purely military consideration points to our joining them now."[34]

In his final report Admiral Benson agreed with Bliss that there was a strong possibility "of the burden of the entire war sooner or later devolving upon the United States and Great Britain." He then offered a *realpolitik* rationale for greater American sacrifices. "Every day that we can keep any of the European Allies in the war, just so much of the burden is being borne by that ally which otherwise would have to be borne by ourselves."[35]

On December 18, Wilson held a critical council of war in the White House with House, Baker, and Bliss. Bliss, who did most of the talking, had only been included after House suggested to Wilson that the Chief of Staff should also attend. American leaders now found the military situation dramatically different from when the United States entered the war. In April, American credit had rescued the Entente from bankruptcy. Now some eight months later it appeared imperative that the United States play a military role commensurate with its population and industrial power to prevent Germany's military masters from dominating the Continent.

An obvious predicament for American leadership was that although amalgamation offered the surest and quickest way of getting Americans on the battlefield it would dramatically diminish American contributions to victory. "If once we merge with them," House had earlier warned in his final report,

we will probably never emerge. The companies and battalions placed with them will soon be mere fragments ... and will never get credit for the sacrifices they make. It can, I think, be taken for granted that this plan would be the most effective immediate help we could give the French and England, but it would be at great cost to us.[36]

At the conclusion of this meeting it was decided that Baker should send Pershing a cable reflecting the tenor of their deliberations. Pershing had to be concerned by what Baker relayed to him. The Secretary of War suggested that he should consider positioning his forces "nearer the junction of the British and French lines which would enable you to throw your strength in whichever direction seemed most necessary." This, of course, would negate GHQ's plan to capture Metz in 1919. What was surely even more alarming to Pershing and his Operations Section was Baker's suggestion that maintaining the "identity" of American forces in France was "secondary to the meeting of any critical situation by the most helpful use possible of the troops at your command," which was an indirect way of saying that some form of amalgamation might have to be accepted.[37]

Pershing gave Baker's cable to Harbord, who passed it on to Fox Conner with instructions to "examine the best place to employ the AEF on the Western front." Both Harbord and Pershing surely knew what the Operations Section's response would be, for Conner's staff had already chosen Lorraine where it believed a war-winning American offensive could be launched against Metz in 1919. To parcel out troops to the French and British in 1918, Conner argued, would "use them up prematurely in piecemeal" and prevent the United States from launching an offensive in Lorraine. Conner admitted that the presence of US troops on the British front would raise British morale. But that might be counterproductive. French morale would just as surely plummet if American soldiers were withdrawn from their front and sent to the British. And placing them at the juncture between the British and French armies was not a workable compromise. "It is difficult for us to avoid friction now and to place our forces between those of our Allies would increase our difficulties."[38]

The only concession that the Operations Section was prepared to make was placing some American divisions behind the British front for training purposes only. As far as GHQ was concerned any amalgamation of American battalions or brigades with either French or British divisions was out of the question. For the moment then the establishment of an independent US Army on European soil remained official American policy. But British and French pressure for amalgamation intensified during the following weeks.

9 Failed expectations: "the military establishment of the United States has fallen down"

The war as December began looked quite different from what it had been when the United States had first taken up the sword eight months earlier. With their armies exhausted and demoralized, the French and British leadership by necessity adopted a defensive strategy. As early as October 1917, Pétain had told his British counterpart Haig that he had no future plans for a major offensive.[1] During the following months, the French Army participated only in limited local attacks with battalions rather than divisions. Haig had been reluctant to abandon the offensive, but he had little choice, especially after the Permanent Military Representatives on the Supreme War Council recommended a defensive stance. On December 19, 1917 Robertson assured the War Cabinet that it was "fully realised by Sir Douglas Haig that we must act on the defence for some time to come," and that he had "no offensive plans in mind at present."[2]

With the Allies embracing a defensive strategy in the west, two critical questions were: Would the Germans seek victory in 1918 with an all-out offensive in France? And, if they did, could American reinforcements arrive in time to avert disaster? French and British intelligence made generally accurate forecasts about the large number of enemy divisions being transferred from the Eastern Front and predicted a German offensive as early as March 1918.[3] But many doubted that Germany would deplete its manpower in an all-out effort given the failure of either side to breach the other's strong defenses on the Western Front during the previous three years. Lloyd George, for example, wrote on one of Sir William Robertson's appreciations predicting a powerful German offensive in 1918: "By all means. Nothing would suit us better – but unfortunately he has learnt his lesson."[4]

If Lloyd George's government had its way, Britain would limit its casualties in France in 1918, shift military resources to the outer theaters, and leave the burden of killing Germans to the Americans. When the United States had been forced into the war, Lord Milner, a key member of the War Cabinet and future Secretary of State for War, had put the following questions before the War Cabinet: "The entrance of America

134

into the war has introduced a new factor, of great ultimate promise but small immediate value. What are we going to do to fill up the time before the weight of America can be thrown into the scale? How do we hope to get the greatest benefit from her assistance in the long run?"[5]

Several months later Milner had his answer. He and his War Cabinet colleagues were confronted with the frightening prospect that the Entente might not be able to deliver a knockout blow to the German Empire and that Russia's demise opened the door to Turko-German expansion against Britain's Asiatic Empire. On November 3, 1917 Milner wrote the Prime Minister and suggested that prudence dictated that the British adopt a defensive posture on the Western Front, withdrawing as many troops from the British sector as possible to create "*the mobile force of the alliance* wh[ich] we have never had & without wh[ich] we can never win."[6] Success on Turkish battlefields might secure the British Empire against the emerging Turko-German force in addition to giving the British bargaining chips in any general peace negotiations. "We might find it possible if Damascus were in our possession," Lloyd George told the War Cabinet on February 21, "to persuade the French to be content with something less than the whole of Alsace-Lorraine in return for compensation in Syria."[7]

In sum, the ominous global strategic landscape and the deterioration of Britain's army on the Western Front (which forced Haig to reduce his battalions per division from twelve to nine) served as a powerful impetus once again to press Washington and Pershing on the amalgamation question. A British scholar has harshly characterized this approach as follows: "In 1914 the British had intended to fight to the last Frenchman and the last Russian. By late 1917 they had nearly done so ... in the Prime Minister's opinion it was the turn of the Americans to die for Britain and its empire."[8]

The war-weary French were equally determined to wait for the Americans. On December 19, Clemenceau told French Chamber members that "the German interest is to make peace in 1918, while ours is to make peace in 1919, when we will have an indisputable victory."[9] When Pétain, who had replaced Nivelle as commander-in-chief, told the French War Committee that he would resign if his policy of limited attacks were challenged, he was strongly defended by Clemenceau. The Tiger said that he also thought it was "necessary to endure ... I do not want to risk today the outcome of the war on an offensive. General Pétain is under my orders; I support him entirely."[10]

Pétain's pessimism ran deep. Determined to limit France's offensive role in the future, he feared that France would still exhaust its reserves if the Germans launched a major offensive that lasted longer than one month. "There is only one remedy: the rapid arrival of the Americans and amalgamation," he told the French President Raymond Poincaré.[11] During the following weeks both the British and French pressed Washington to speed up its delivery of troops to Europe, even suggesting that Pershing integrate American regiments and companies into their armies.

After Wilson discussed the question of amalgamation with Baker, House, and Bliss on December 18 following the return of the House Mission from Europe, Baker sent the following ambiguous message to Pershing. "We do not desire loss of identity of our forces but regard that as secondary to the meeting of any critical situation by the most helpful use possible of the troops at your command." On the other hand, Wilson and Baker left total control to Pershing and made clear their preference. "This suggestion is not, however, pressed beyond whatever merit it has in your judgment, the President's sole purpose being to acquaint you with the representations made here and to authorize you to act with entire freedom in making the best disposition and use of your forces possible to accomplish the main purposes in view."[12]

Wilson then decided that this letter to Pershing should serve as America's official response to British and French requests for increased American military support. It was read to all Allied ambassadors simultaneously in Washington. It is surely extraordinary that the President conferred so much power on his field commander in Europe. As the constitutional leader of both the military and government he should have either accepted or rejected Pershing's advice and then given his response to the Allies. But he did not. In the nation's first major overseas war, he turned over a decision with important political and military implications to one of his generals. At the same time, and he surely saw this as an advantage, he created a formidable shield between himself and foreign leaders. No American proved to be a more formidable opponent of amalgamation than Pershing.

Pétain had already made entreaties to Pershing, asking him to abandon his step-by-step approach in building an American Army on European soil. A "quicker method," he suggested, was to "have each of the four infantry regiments of each of our divisions, together with the proportion of the artillery, engineers and other troops, assigned to a French division at once."[13] After Pershing rejected Pétain's proposal, Clemenceau appealed directly to Baker. In a note to Wilson, the Secretary of War made clear his own objections to amalgamation.

It seems to me entirely clear that if our regiments are integrated with either French or British Divisions the great difficulty of getting them back when we want them would be very great, and that the ultimate effect of such a course would be practically to put our troops here and there in French and British divisions under the command of French and British Commanders, with a corresponding weakening of the forces under General Pershing's command for independent operations.[14]

And Wilson's influence over any peace settlement, he might have added.

On January 9, it was Robertson's turn to take on Pershing. Facing a grave manpower crisis, Britain's need for American troops was now greater than ever. In competition with the French for American manpower, Robertson had an advantage: British ships to carry American soldiers across the Atlantic. Because of the destructions of Union ships by Confederate raiders in the Civil War and the increasing uncompetitiveness of US ship construction because of cheaper labor, capital, and materials in foreign countries, only about 10 percent of the country's exports were being carried in ships flying the American flag.[15] German and Austro-Hungarian ships, which had been interned in American ports, had been confiscated by the government, but this still left the country critically short of shipping.

Attempts to accelerate shipbuilding had not filled this void and were unlikely to do so in the near future. In fact, the British to their dismay discovered in December that the United States planned to reduce its industrial target of constructing 6 million tons dead weight to 2 million. This meant, according to Lloyd George, that the United States would be unable to "get the American troops over in American ships at the rate we had thought possible a short time ago."[16]

US shipbuilding eventually hit its stride, but not in time to alleviate the shipping crisis which faced the United States when it appeared that the German Army might triumph in Europe. Clearly the only way that the United States could develop a substantial American force in Europe in 1918 was to expand dramatically the number of men being shipped in British vessels, currently about 12,000 men a month. This the British were unwilling to do so long as American soldiers were being located exclusively on or near the French front lines. The British merchant marine, with some 16 million gross tons at the beginning of 1917, remained by far the largest in the world. Serving as the merchant marine for the Entente, the British shipped cereals to France and Italy in addition to supplying their own needs, both civilian and military. British finance also depended upon maintaining the country's export industries. Britain had survived the resumption of German unrestricted U-boat warfare by adopting the convoy system. Although German mines and torpedoes continued to sink Allied ships, the number steadily declined. Excluding the Mediterranean, some 49,000 merchant ships sailed in convoy from February to October 1918. Only 120 of them were sunk. The toll was about three times greater for unescorted ships.[17]

Unable to keep its divisions up to strength, the War Office had been forced to reduce its infantry divisions from twelve battalions to nine. Overnight this effectively eliminated 134 British battalions, either through disbandment or integration into other divisions. The Supreme War Council's recent decision to extend the BEF's front from ninety-five miles to 123 miles created another problem for Haig. As a consequence, the British now defended a longer front with slimmed-down divisions. Not surprisingly the British increasingly viewed American soldiers as a solution to their deteriorating manpower situation. The War Office suggested that the BEF could absorb three US battalions per division or approximately 150,000 riflemen. If reinforcements were included the number would rise to 200,000. The temporary loss of 450,000 tons of imports that would be required would be worth the sacrifice. But only if Pershing agreed to amalgamation. Otherwise it appeared that it would be months, if not years, before the independent army demanded by the Americans played a meaningful role. A French General Staff memorandum circulated within the British War Cabinet even suggested that an independent US force by mid-1919 would still be unable to undertake and carry out "offensive action on a large scale."[18]

Robertson, accompanied by the British Shipping Controller, began negotiations with Pershing on January 9. A sticking point was that Pershing wanted to transport entire divisions, which included cooks, typists, supply clerks, and other non-combat personnel. The British estimated that the Americans had only succeeded in transporting 58,000 infantry and machine gunners to France in 1917.[19] Robertson wanted only riflemen and machine gunners shipped, arguing that it required as much merchant ship tonnage to ship three divisions (with its thirty-six battalions, artillery, and transport) as would be required for 150 infantry battalions.[20]

The initial negotiations did not go well for Robertson. Pershing expressed doubts that the British really feared an impending crisis on the Western Front, especially when Lloyd George's government contemplated an offensive in Palestine in 1918 to knock Turkey out of the war. Robertson, whose opposition to this offensive was one of the primary reasons for his removal as CIGS a few weeks later, could not disagree.[21] Pershing made a counter proposal: why not withdraw all combat units from a British division and replace them with Americans? Robertson rejected this proposal, noting that it would necessitate withdrawing these divisions from the line while they were being reconstructed. Moreover, the divisions would still be partly American and partly British.[22]

On the following day Pershing bent a little and agreed to forward Robertson's so-called 150-battalion program to the War Department with his recommendation "to the effect that as this scheme was only proposed as a help to win the war, it should be given consideration if other schemes do not appear suitable."[23]

Despite Pershing's willingness to forward the British 150-battalion program to the War Department, Robertson remained hugely disappointed with the American commander-in-chief. He informed Lloyd George that "America's power to help us to win the war – that is to help us to defeat the Germans in battle – is a very weak reed to lean upon at present, and will continue to be so for a very long time to come unless she follows up her words with actions much more practical and energetic than she has yet taken."[24] The CIGS was just as blunt when he wrote Haig on January 12:

> He [Pershing] seems to have no grasp of the task in front of him and to have far too much administrative work to do. Further he is certainly in no hurry to get his divisions in front of the Germans. His one idea seems to be to amass an enormous Army before doing anything. It is necessary that he should be convinced that he must hurry up, and he must give us some idea as to what assistance he hopes to be able to afford in the near future.[25]

British pressure to integrate American battalions into their divisions could not have come at a worse time for the Wilson administration, with a storm brewing in Congress over the snail-like pace of American mobilization. The War Department exacerbated the situation by making extravagant claims and issuing optimistic press releases which the press trumpeted.

Airplanes appeared to be the quickest and most dramatic contribution that the world's leading industrial power might make to the war effort (Fig. 10). There was wild talk of producing a vast armada of aircraft based on the misconception that American industry could churn out aircraft almost as quickly as it produced autos. An enthusiastic Congress appropriated the enormous sum of $600 million, and the War Department began issuing optimistic official statements. On October 6, *The Times* correspondent in Washington reported that

> more than 20,000 aeroplanes are now in course of construction in the United States, and this country will soon send the first all-American battleplane to Europe ... It is not possible to make public all the details of the work accomplished, but the War Department can only say that the earlier expectations and hopes for the consummation of an extensive aircraft programme have been more than realised.[26]

The reality was that Pershing continued to depend upon the French for most of his equipment. A disgusted Bullard noted that the AEF's requests for supplies and equipment were always answered thusly by the

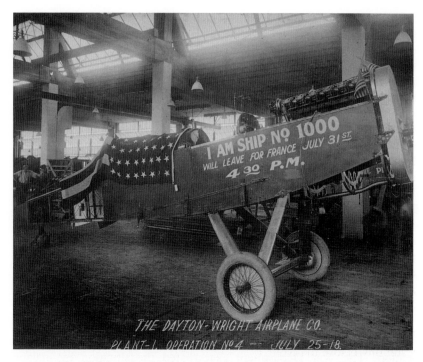

Fig. 10 Manufacturing airplanes for the government by Dayton-Wright Airplane Company. Completed plane on exhibition

War Department: "We cannot get it sent from home; it has been asked for repeatedly and long ago but not yet sent; no answer or promises … Never, it seemed to Americans in Europe was American brag so great, and never was our actual accomplishment so small in proportion to the brag."[27]

Clearly America's industrial war engine was sputtering (munitions production fell and steel production was down by two-thirds in February).[28] And a harsh winter, exacerbated by coal shortages and breakdowns in rail transportation, made the situation appear even worse than it actually was. Many New York apartment buildings went without coal as temperatures fell to thirteen below zero. A severe blizzard paralyzed rail transport in the western and central states, with temperatures in Chicago, Detroit, and St. Louis registering from fourteen to nineteen degrees below zero.

The coal shortage became so severe that Harry Garfield, the Fuel Administrator responsible for coal and oil supplies, announced on

January 16 that all industries east of the Mississippi would be shut down for five days, beginning on January 18. The so-called "Garfield holidays" created havoc. Meanwhile, especially in unseasonably cold weather in the southern tent camps, many enlisted men shivered in their summer uniforms and attempted to sleep without blankets. Some caught pneumonia and died.

When Congress resumed its work in early December, Senator George Chamberlain, the chairman of the Senate Military Affairs Committee, announced that his committee would conduct an investigation of alleged breakdowns in mobilizing the country for war. Baker responded by dismissing the mounting criticism and emphasizing what the War Department had accomplished. As he told the annual meeting of the New York Southern Society on December 12: "People are sometimes disposed to adopt a complaining tone about our efforts – not many, but here and there one. There are two ways of looking at this war and our preparations for it. One is to look at what we have done, and one is to look at what we have not done ... You will soon see we have accomplished great things."[29] During the following weeks, however, the Senate Military Affairs Committee began to examine "what had not been done."

Major General William Crozier, who had just been reappointed by the President as Chief of Ordnance of the Army, gave especially damaging testimony before the Military Affairs Committee. In his prepared statement he admitted that Pershing's forces would not have their own artillery until next summer and then only guns of 6-inch caliber or less. Nor did the War Department have enough rifles for men training in the cantonments. A minimum of 17,000 rifles was required for each camp but only 10,000 had yet been supplied, many of which were unsuitable for target practice. He then startled the committee by admitting that the War Department had been unable to deliver a single machine gun to American forces abroad although the War Department had placed orders with the Colt Company in May for the superior Browning water-cooled heavy machine gun and the Browning automatic rifle.[30]

Crozier placed the blame for the War Department's inability to provide adequate arms for the US Army squarely on Baker's shoulders. In truth, however, the inability of America to wage modern war in 1917 was more a result of the unrealistic nature of the Army Reorganization Bill, signed into law by the President on July 3, 1916, which provided for a leisurely modernization of the army over a five-year period and was unrelated to the war waging in Europe.

Further damaging revelations were made as the Military Affairs Committee continued its inquiry. Complaints ranged from the serious to the ridiculous. One officer, Major General Edwin Greble, the commander of

Camp Bowie, Texas, complained that the War Department had been unable to fulfill his request for a flagpole. (A local electric light company finally donated one.) Senators were up in arms, with Senator Frelinghuysen of New Jersey charging the War Department with "innumerable delays and almost inconceivable blunders" in equipping the country's soldiers.[31]

Clothing and food should not have been difficult for the War Department to supply. And indeed soldiers could expect three square meals a day in the cantonments. Clothing, however, proved to be another matter. The Military Affairs Committee discovered that at Camp Custer, Battle Creek, Michigan, there was a shortage of shoes, or at least shoes that fit. "As a result," the Senators were told, "it was necessary for half of the soldiers to remain in barracks until the others returned from drill or target practice so that the second detail might use the shoes that had been worn by their comrades."[32]

Many soldiers had also not been provided with uniforms, or if they had the uniforms furnished did not fit them. The Quartermaster General's attempt to explain clothing shortages was not well received by the press. The *Literary Digest* noted that some editors believed that General Henry G. Sharpe was "saying in substance that there was not enough clothing because the Army for which he had to provide was larger than he expected and that the clothing did not fit the soldiers because the men, like the Army, were too large."[33] There may have been truth to what Sharpe said. The average weight and height of Army recruits just prior to the war had been 144 pounds and five feet seven inches.[34] Selective Service apparently produced more physically impressive soldiers.

Sharpe had equally alarming revelations for the Senators when he discussed how overwhelmed his department was by the required paper trail for requests from commanders in the field. "As I understand the course of that telegram," one Senator queried,

it comes from the officer in the field to the Adjutant-General. Then it comes to the Quartermaster-General. Then from the Quartermaster-General back to the Adjutant-General; then from the Adjutant-General to the Assistant Chief of Staff, and from the Assistant Chief of Staff back to the Adjutant-General and the Quartermaster-General combined; then from the Adjutant-General back to the officer, and the Quartermaster-General then acts upon it.

If approved, the Senator continued, it then had "to go through that entire course in order to get back to the officer in the field and to get action." "Yes," Sharpe meekly responded, but this practice "is a thing that always has been done, and army regulations require."[35]

On January 10, a combative Baker appeared before the Senate Military Affairs Committee and testified for six hours. He began by reading a

Table 3 *Equipment furnished to the American Expeditionary Force, April 6, 1917–November 11, 1918*

Equipment	France	Britain
field artillery	3,532	160
railroad artillery	140	0
caissons	2,658	0
trench mortars	237	1,427
automatic weapons	40,884	0
tanks	227	26
aircraft	4,874	258

Source: Robert Bruce, *A Fraternity of Arms: America and France in the Great War* (Lawrence: University Press of Kansas, 2003), pp. 104–05; see also Department of the Army, Historical Division, *United States Army in the World War, 1917–1918*, 17 vols. (Washington, DC: Government Printing Office, 1948), vol. 14, p. 8.

formal statement in which he insisted that "arms of the most modern and effective kind, including artillery, machine guns, automatic rifles, and small arms, have been provided by manufacture or purchase for every soldier in France, and are available for every soldier who can be got to France in the year 1918." He concluded by declaring that "no army of similar size in the history of the world has ever been raised, equipped, or trained so quickly."[36]

The reality, however, was that the United States would have been forced to dispatch virtually unarmed men to fight in Europe in 1917–18 if not for British and especially French assistance. A compromise was struck: the United States would send men and the mature defense industries in France and Britain would provide artillery, horses and mules, airplanes, automatic weapons, tanks, etc. in exchange for raw materials such as steel and oil. When the first US troops arrived in France in June, the French immediately supplied them with 168 excellent Hotchkiss machine guns and the less reliable 444 Chauchat automatic rifles. This was just the beginning of the essential foreign equipment provided to the AEF. As Pershing ruefully admitted, "We were literally beggars as to every important weapon, except the rifle."[37] And even the Doughboy's rifle, although manufactured in the United States, was based on a British model, the Lee Enfield .303, which was easier to mass produce than the Springfield model 1903/06. Table 3 illustrates how dependent American soldiers were on foreign equipment.

Explanations for the delays in manufacturing modern American weaponry, some of them valid, abounded. For example, manufacturing artillery, some of which were of a foreign design with metric measurements, caused many technical difficulties since machine tools and standard gages were in short supply.[38] As a result, the AEF employed virtually no American-made artillery pieces and with the exception of shrapnel almost no American-made shells reached the AEF's front lines. Aircraft production proved to be America's greatest industrial fiasco in providing the AEF with the means to defeat the German Army.

In two further days of testimony Baker stood his ground, insisting that nothing was wrong with the existing supply system. On January 13, however, his position became increasingly untenable when David Willard, the President of the Baltimore and Ohio Railroad who headed the War Industries Board and had a son fighting in France, and Bernard Baruch, a wealthy Wall Street investor, testified. Willard and Baruch joined other prominent businessmen in condemning the War Department's red tape and demanded a shakeup.

The climax of this mounting Congressional criticism came on January 19 when Senator Chamberlain spoke at a luncheon at Hotel Astor in New York under the auspices of the National Security League attended by over 1,900 men and women. He did not mince words. "The military establishment of America has fallen down; there is no use to be optimistic about a thing that does not exist; it has almost stopped functioning, my friends. Why? Because of inefficiency in every Department of the Government of the United States."[39] Roosevelt, who was also scheduled to speak, jumped to his feet and led the prolonged applause that followed Chamberlain's brief remarks.

Just prior to his speech, Chamberlain and other members of the Senate Military Affairs Committee had reported a bill to create a munitions director similar to what both the French and British had done to increase their supply of munitions. Senators also worked on a bill to create a "super-cabinet" or war cabinet which reported directly to the President.[40] On January 21, Chamberlain introduced this bill to establish a war cabinet of three "distinguished citizens of demonstrated executive ability" which pointedly excluded members of Wilson's cabinet, including the Secretary of Navy and Secretary of War.

On this same day, Wilson, who according to Daniels had "his blood up,"[41] issued a press release that called Chamberlain's accusations against his government's direction of the war "an astonishing and absolutely unjustifiable distortion of the truth." In the President's view, "the War Department has performed a task of unparalleled magnitude and difficulty with extraordinary promptness and efficiency."[42] Wilson clearly gave Baker and the War Department more credit than they deserved. But he was on solid ground in disputing the authority of

Congress to appoint a war cabinet. This would subvert the constitution which made the President commander-in-chief. Wilson alone had the constitutional right to select and designate a committee as his "war cabinet."

As Wilson squelched attempts by Congress to appoint a "war cabinet," elements of Pershing's 1st Division adjusted to trench life in a quiet sector of the French front which they had occupied on January 18. This token force represented America's only concrete contribution to the fighting on the Western Front thus far. To Pershing, "it was depressing to think that ten months had elapsed since our entry into the war and we were just barely ready with one division of 25,000 men."[43]

Amalgamation, of course, remained the quickest way to introduce Americans to combat. As Pétain argued in late January:

The American army will be no help if it wants to conserve its autonomy in 1918; even if its soldiers and lower ranks are excellent, it will not have commanders and staffs this year ... The Americans cannot participate in battle [as an autonomous force] until 1919. While waiting, amalgamation is imperative; if we do not take these measures, the war will enter an extremely critical period.[44]

Unlike the French, the British had shipping as a bargaining chip. Wilson and the War Department now had before it the British promise to ship 150 battalions. If accepted, it would give the lie to the President's response to Chamberlain. One can only imagine the national outrage if Wilson had accepted the British proposal to integrate American battalions into British divisions at the very moment that he was touting the "extraordinary promptness and efficiency" of American mobilization.

For his part Pershing continued to have serious reservations about any proposal that threatened GHQ's plans to create an independent army. Once amalgamated, it would be almost impossible for him to retrieve his soldiers from British divisions for his own use. Yet there seemed no better way to speed the flow of American troops to Europe. He had made the following point to Baker on January 17 when he forwarded the Robertson proposal to the War Department: "Can we afford not to send over extra men to help our allies in what may be an emergency and when the necessary extra sea transportation is offered and we have the spare men?"[45]

Time, however, might be running out for creating an independent American force in France. Four days after Pershing suggested to Baker that America should consider the British plan, General Erich Ludendorff, determined to achieve a victor's peace before the United States could "throw strong forces into the scale," issued orders for a major German offensive in March against what he called the "center" of the

Allied front.[46] The German high command chose "Michael" as the code name for its offensive but not until March 10 did Ludendorff set the date, March 21, for launching his attack.

As Ludendorff planned a war-winning offensive to establish Germany as the hegemonic power in Europe, Pershing continued to navigate the treacherous shoals created by French and British desire for American manpower. This Anglo-French rivalry over strengthening their respective fronts with American soldiers actually proved to be an advantage for him. On January 25, Pershing stunned the British by telling them that he now opposed their 150-battalion program. Instead he demanded that the British transport six complete American divisions to train with the British prior to the creation of an independent American force in Europe. Robertson protested. This would mean that only seventy-two battalions of riflemen and machine gunners could be shipped because of the support troops required for full divisions.

A showdown occurred at the Supreme War Council on January 29. Pershing and Bliss, America's two four-star generals in Europe, faced a phalanx of British leaders which included Lloyd George, Lord Milner, Robertson, Haig, and Sir Henry Wilson, the British Permanent Military Representative on the SWC. Bliss had been openly sympathetic to strengthening British forces with American manpower. But he now stood firmly with Pershing. "Pershing will speak for us and whatever he says with regard to the disposition of the American forces will have my approval."[47]

Faced with a unified American command the British capitulated. Pershing's six-division plan replaced Robertson's 150-battalion program. In an attempt to mollify both the British and French, Bliss assured them on January 31 during a meeting of the Supreme War Council that US battalions and regiments might be *temporarily* attached to French and British divisions for the purpose of training. But as soon as it was practicable these units would be withdrawn and placed in US divisions under their own officers with the goal of forming an autonomous US force.[48]

Haig suspected political motives, recording in his diary that Americans "were criticizing their Government because there seemed to be no results to show for the money which America has been spending! No troops in the field, no aeroplanes, no guns, no nothing yet in fact."[49]

President Wilson went out of his way several days later to reassure the British, whose merchant marine eventually transported half of Pershing's army to Europe. Over lunch with William Wiseman, a British intelligence officer who was close to House, Wilson confessed that domestic politics had influenced his position on brigading American soldiers with the BEF. "The placing of American troops in small bodies under foreign leaders," he said, "would be taken as a proof that the recent criticism of the War Department was justified and that the American military machine had broken down." At the same time he promised Wiseman that public pressure would not prevent him from accepting the coordination of Anglo-American arms in an emergency. But he emphasized that the British must not use shipping to pressure the Americans to accept anything but the temporary training of American soldiers alongside British divisions.[50] In a letter to Baker on the following day, Wilson stressed that only a "sudden and manifest emergency" should be allowed to "interfere with the building up of a great distinct American force at the front, acting under its own flag and its own officers."[51]

While negotiating with the British over shipping, Pershing tried not to ruffle the feathers of the French who expected Washington to adhere to its original agreement to station all American troops on the French front. He made a point of telling Pétain that his nation's lack of shipping left him no other choice but to negotiate with the British. Pétain made no objection but noted that he wished that Pershing would also consider integrating American troops with French forces. In response, Pershing agreed "to send temporarily to the French four colored Infantry regiments of the 93rd Division."[52] Pershing, however, rejected future French requests for additional black infantry as well as all future requests for integrating US battalions with French or British divisions.

If Pershing needed additional reasons for opposing amalgamation he had gotten them on January 26 from an unexpected source: Marshal Joffre, who had arranged the original special relationship with the Wilson administration that placed all American troops in or near the French front. Speaking as a fellow officer and off the record, Joffre played down the seriousness of the German threat in 1918. He also stressed the many disadvantages of integrating American soldiers with either French or British divisions. Division cohesion and effectiveness would be weakened by mixing American soldiers with foreign soldiers, especially under any arrangement where Doughboys took their orders from foreign officers. "You must consider the American people at home and their interest in and their support of the war, which could be adversely affected by amalgamation," Joffre cautioned Pershing.[53] Joffre, however, was dead wrong about the German threat in 1918. And the Allies quickly revived the question of amalgamation when the German Army resumed the offensive on March 21, 1918.

The unwelcome presence of General Wood, who had earlier been Pershing's chief competitor for the command of the AEF, served to complicate Pershing's negotiations with the French and British. To familiarize

commanders of divisions being trained in the United States with conditions in Europe, Baker dispatched them to France. As the commander of
the 89th Division, Wood had arrived in Europe on December 28 to begin
his inspection tour. As usual the former Chief of Staff proved temperamentally unable to keep his mouth shut, especially when it involved taking on
old rivals. He quickly became embroiled in the amalgamation question by
openly criticizing breakdowns in America's mobilization. Bliss was soon
reporting to the War Department: "It is going to make it much more
difficult for us to negotiate about getting aid in shipping if people here
believe that whatever sacrifices they make to give us additional tonnage is
only for the purpose of bringing over an unorganized and undisciplined
mob."[54] Pershing himself wrote March that "It seems high time that
meddling, political generals be put where they can do no harm."[55] After
Wood returned to the United States, Baker removed him from command.
When the former Chief of Staff insisted on meeting with the President their
interview did not go well. Wood later wrote in his characteristically bombastic style that it was "extremely disagreeable for him [Wilson] to meet
anyone who does not approach him as an Oriental approaches his master."
The only way one could get the support of the President, he went on, was
"by stimulating an already over-stimulated egoism."[56]

   Critics of Baker and Wilson, of course, had no idea that an all-out
German offensive to win the war in 1918 was just weeks away. But they
sensed that indecisive leadership in both the White House and War
Department might portend disaster. A common theme in the press was
that it was incongruous to put a "pacifist" in charge of the War Department. *Harvey's Weekly* harrumphed that "the chattering ex-Pacifist" was
sitting "on top of a pyramid of confusion which he had jumbled together
and called a war machine."[57] Declared the *Milwaukee Sentinel*: "If
experience in the War Department has not cured Mr. Baker of his
pacifism, the War Department should be cured of Mr. Baker."[58] This
newspaper also suggested that Wilson was temperamentally unsuited to
be a commander-in-chief. The normally pro-Wilson *New York Times*
agreed and editorialized:

There is universal satisfaction with the President as an interpreter of the people's
will and as a prophet of democracy. But as the ancient Israelites tired of their
prophets and called for a king to lead them forth against their enemies, we note a
growing insistence that the President should delegate some "strong man" to
prepare us for battle or that he should apply his own energies more directly to
that task.

In *The New Republic*, William Hard suggested that Wilson become the
country's "'war-lord,' the strong man to lead us to battle." Although

Wilson had succeeded as the "interpreter of America's conscience," Hard argued that he had not "kept his hand on the administration of the war."[59]

Wilson had his defenders and partisan politics clearly played a role in some of the attacks against his administration. At the same time the record suggests that much of this criticism was justified, at least until the series of massive German offensives that began on March 21 and continued into July raised the specter of Allied defeat and encouraged the President to take a more active involvement in military questions.[60]

An instructive example of the manner in which the President and his War Secretary at times mishandled the war economy was their vendetta against Pierre S. DuPont whose business had grown rapidly during the war through the purchase of smaller powder firms and the construction of new plants paid for in advance by Allied contracts. When the War Department approached DuPont, he insisted that for him to invest in plants which would be of little value when the war ended his construction costs must be amortized by the government. Major General William Crozier, the Chief of the Ordnance bureau, subsequently signed a contract with DuPont in October 1917 for $250 million which included $90 million for the expansion of smokeless powder plants. When this contract reached Baker's desk for his signature, the Secretary of War refused to sign it. Baker, supported by Wilson, was upset by what he considered obscene war profits for DuPont that would result. Although Pierre DuPont was prepared to compromise and no other American firm was capable of producing high-quality smokeless powder, Baker and Wilson decided that they were "going to win this war without DuPont."[61] But they could not as they soon discovered. Baker did sign a contract with the Thomas-Starrett Company. But this construction firm had no experience with producing smokeless powder and insisted that DuPont's assistance was required. The War Department (while Baker was in Europe) finally signed a "cost plus one dollar" contract on March 23. The government agreed to pay all construction costs while DuPont received one dollar for building the Old Hickory Plant near Nashville, Tennessee. But valuable time had been lost which would have been critical to America's war effort if the mature British and French munitions industries had not been able to supply the AEF's requirements in 1918. The Old Hickory Plant began producing smokeless powder in July and the Thomas-Starrett factory in St. Albans, West Virginia, began production on the last day of the war.

Wilson remained uncomfortable in his role as commander-in-chief. Unlike contemporary war leaders such as Lloyd George and Clemenceau, his inclination was to leave the details of military decisions without clear political ramifications to others, allowing Baker free rein in the War Department. He also allowed Pershing to act as America's proconsul in Europe. In Palmer's words, "A dictatorship had been created for Pershing the day that he sailed. In our world in France his nod was law. No American in all history had ever been delegated so much power."[62]

Beaver contends that Wilson's "apparent disinterest in the actual battle stemmed not only from his concentration on high policy, but also, as he said later, from his fear that awareness of the human costs of the war would reduce his effectiveness and interfere with the detachment he felt necessary to pursue his greater purposes."[63] For his part, Baker believed that he and Pershing were given such latitude because Wilson believed "that his health was very infirm and that he had a limited amount of strength. By the most rigid self-discipline he determined to spend it only on things worth while."[64] Which to Wilson was a liberal peace settlement.

Although Wilson had grown to appreciate the Clausewitzian relationship between employing armed force and achieving political objectives, strictly military questions remained secondary to him. Instead he focused on defining and achieving America's war objectives. Several weeks before Chamberlain's frontal assault on his war leadership, he had delivered his widely acclaimed "Fourteen Points" address to a joint session of Congress in which he had presented his program for a just and liberal peace settlement.

Facing the most serious political crisis of his wartime presidency, Wilson went on the offensive against his critics. In an effort to undercut the Senate's proposal for a war cabinet that excluded his secretaries of war and navy and would only answer to him, he announced the creation of his own war cabinet which met for the first time on March 20. It included Baruch – whom Wilson had given extraordinary power over the war economy as Willard's successor as chairman of the War Industries Board – McAdoo, Daniels, Baker, Garfield, Edward Hurley, the Shipping Board chairman, Vance G. McCormick, War Trade Board chairman and chairman of the Democratic National Committee, and Herbert Hoover, the Food Administrator. Hoover and Garfield were the only Republicans. No minutes were taken and circulated of its meetings which were held in the Cabinet Room of the White House. Military authorities, including the Chief of Staff, were not invited to attend.[65] According to one Wilson biographer, the President's meetings with these like-minded progressives served to refine "his emerging conception of a society and a world in which voluntary cooperation could replace competition and conflict."[66] As a means to coordinate and provide central direction for the nation's first major war overseas it proved to be a very poor imitation of the British War Cabinet.

As Wilson successfully thwarted efforts by Congressional critics to limit his authority, Baker tacitly recognized the validity of some of their criticisms by shaking up the War Department. When the United States entered the war, the War Department, especially the General Staff, had been short handed. As the "brain" of the Army the General Staff officially had only sixty-four officers as late as July 1, 1917 and was drowning in a sea of paperwork. This was especially true for the Bureau Chiefs, who operated independently of each other and frequently stepped on each other's toes in their frantic and uncoordinated efforts to supply the Army.

Colonel Robert Lee Bullard had passed through Washington in June on his way to France and found both the Chief of Staff and War Department overwhelmed by events. He concluded that if "we really have a great war, our War Department will quickly break down. To me it appeared fearfully weak and complicated and centralized." Especially troubling was the failure of the General Staff and bureaus of the War Department to work "well together." He departed Washington "frightened . . . as to our prospects for the war."[67]

To his credit Baker chose two subordinates of great ability, George Washington Goethals and Peyton Conroy March, who together organized the War Department for victory. March had been recognized for his administrative abilities as Commissary General of the Prisoners in the Philippines. He was Pershing's artillery chief when Baker brought him to Washington as Acting Chief of Staff. He arrived in New York on March 1 to replace General John Biddle, the current Acting Chief of Staff. (Bliss had retired as Chief of Staff on December 31, his 64th birthday.) When the two men met in the War Department the next day, Biddle informed March of his practice of leaving his office at 5 p.m. and not returning unless an urgent cable required his personal attention. Biddle's subordinates followed their chief's lead. When March later returned to the War Department that evening, he found the corridors of the department deserted; unopened mail sacks were stacked in front of the Adjutant General's office. The only officer he found on duty was in charge of the code room. The Acting Chief of Staff – he would not become Chief of Staff until May – was not pleased.[68] "Symbolically," Coffman writes, "the lights came on in the staff offices the night after his arrival and stayed on until the war was won."[69] The piles of unopened mail quickly disappeared and officers stayed at their desks long into the night seven days a week.

March's two greatest accomplishments were getting American troops to Europe in time to prevent disaster on the Western Front and

reorganizing the War Department. Believing that the British would provide the necessary shipping, he immediately telegraphed Bliss at the
Supreme War Council after arriving in Washington that, beginning in
April, a minimum of two divisions a month would be shipped to Europe.
Reorganizing the War Department represented a different set of problems because Baker was part of the problem. The Secretary of War did
not believe in "top down" management and kept his door open equally to
the Chief of Staff and the Bureau Chiefs. There were simply too many
decision makers at work. The machinery of the War Department seized
up in a morass of red tape and lack of central direction.

Earlier, when he relinquished his position as Chief of Staff, Scott had
proposed a solution. In his final report he had suggested that there

should be one and only one organ through which the Secretary of War commands
the Army – the Chief of Staff. In all that concerns discipline, recruiting,
instruction, intelligence, training, arming, equipping, mobilization,
transportation, education, movement of troops, the appointment, promotion,
detail, and selection of officers, the Chief of Staff should be the medium of
recommendation to the Secretary and of execution for his orders.[70]

March's arrival in the War Department ended the incredible merry-go-
round between Scott, Bliss, and Major General John Biddle as they
rotated in and out of the War Department. They had not been effective.
"Scott was out of the country most of the time, Bliss had his problems,
and Biddle couldn't make decisions," concludes Donald Smythe.[71]
March's forceful and steady leadership soon "transformed the general
staff from a planning and coordinating agency to a command center."[72]
He united supply (Purchase and Supply) with transportation (Storage
and Traffic) into a single Purchase, Storage and Traffic Division located
in the General Staff. He then chose Goethals to manage the flow of war
materials from the factory floor to France.

Goethals, who had graduated second in his class at West Point, had
become a national figure as chief engineer of the Panama Canal, which
had been completed two years ahead of schedule. His leadership style,
authoritarian rather than consultative, was the opposite of Baker's. At the
same time he did not hesitate to delegate authority. In December Baker
had brought him to the War Department as Quartermaster General and
Director of Storage and Warehousing. Goethals and March were in
strong agreement that the supply of the army required central direction.
"You are given complete charge of all matters of supply," March told
him. "I hold you responsible for results, and I will take all the responsibility for anything you have to do to get them." Goethals did his job well,
deserving March's apt description of him as "virtual Chief of Supply of

Fig. 11 General Paul von Hindenburg, Kaiser Wilhelm II, and
General Erich Ludendorff standing at a table, examining
large maps

the Army."[73] "By war's end," notes Beaver, Goethals "had begun
the most far-reaching reorganization of military supply in American
history."[74]

But would American assistance arrive in time? March's arrival in the
War Department coincided with a massive German offensive that began
on March 21 (Fig. 11). The War Department now found itself in a
momentous race with Ludendorff. Russia's demise enabled the Germans
to reinforce the Western Front with forty-four divisions from the moribund Russian front. Between February 15 and March 20, 10,400 packed
German trains had run day and night transporting men and material to
the section of the British front defended by Julian Byng's Third Army
and General Hubert Gough's Fifth Army.[75] Beginning on March 16,
German troops had been concentrated on the front in night marches. As
they marched, bands played and the troops sang: "*Muss I denn, muss
I denn*" ("There's a time, there's a time").

Prior to this concentration of 1 million German troops, British and
French intelligence gathering suggested that the Germans were planning

a powerful offensive. French intelligence took note of new codes being established for the enemy's encrypting wireless transmissions. Previously the Germans changed the codes prior to an offensive. On March 11, Sir Henry Wilson, who had replaced Robertson as CIGS, informed the War Cabinet that while civilian traffic behind the German lines on the French front remained normal it had been suspended in Belgium. Moreover, civilians were being moved out of Lille and La Bassée while heavy artillery movements were being made in the direction of the British front. Wilson concluded that "the situation looked very much as if the Germans meant to attack the British line, as they were concentrating on our front and had 92 divisions opposed to our 57." (The authorized strength of a German division in 1918 was nine battalions of 850 men, or slightly smaller than a British division.) Sir Henry Wilson, however, was by no means confident that the Germans would attack. It all depended, he opined, on "whether or not the Germans felt confident of their ability to defeat us in the field."[76]

On March 20, Ludendorff had seventy-six German divisions available, including fifty-two attack divisions supported by eleven *Stellungsdivisionen* (or regular divisions which were not as well equipped or trained)[77] to attack twenty-six British divisions of the British Fifth and Third Armies along a fifty-mile front. On the juncture between the British and French armies, defended by the Fifth Army, the Germans outnumbered the British eight to one. This offensive by three German armies, General Otto von Below's Seventeenth Army, von der Marwitz's Second Army, and General Oskar von Hutier's Eighteenth Army, would not be equaled in scale until May 20, 1940, when Hitler's legions struck at France, Belgium, and Holland.

For this offensive the Germans deployed one-half of all of their guns on the Western Front. At approximately 4:45 a.m. on March 21 the massed German artillery, with 6,608 guns, some 2,598 being either heavy or super-heavy, unleashed a five-and-a-half-hour bombardment. This gave the Germans a tube superiority over the British of 2.5 to 1.[78] A mixture of gas and exploding shells, this bombardment was state of the art as it moved from zone to zone and then back again. The magnitude of this bombardment, some 3.2 million shells, stunned British defenders. Major General Oliver Nugent, who commanded the Ulster Division, penned the following words to his wife: "The German bombardment began at ¼ to 5 this morning and is still going on. In all my experience out here I have never known anything more terrific. It isn't a series of reports, but it is just one long roar."[79]

Initially trench mortars concentrated on the British forward positions while the larger guns shelled the main British defenses. After roughly fifty minutes the artillery joined the mortars in blasting forward positions. The artillery with its high-explosive shells then returned to the main defenses before moving back to the forward positions. Then followed the familiar rolling barrage designed to shepherd groups of German assault troops across no-man's-land. These "storm troopers" embraced new tactics. Instead of acting as "a battering-ram, pounding head-on against a wall," they advanced "rather like a flood of water, flowing around obstacles, isolating them, and following the path of least resistance deep into the enemy's territory."[80]

In a single day, the Germans overran 98.5 square miles. Since the emergence of static trench warfare, no army had previously achieved such success on the Western Front. Many anxious days lay ahead for the Allies. What did this German offensive portend for America's future role in the war, especially Pershing's determination to form an independent army with its own front, strategic objectives, lines of supply, and a combat doctrine that emphasized the rifleman and his bayonet?

10   Atlantic ferry

As the outcome of the war hung in the balance following the first of five German offensives, the War Department and Chaumont confronted critical decisions that might well determine the success or failure of Berlin's attempt to become the dominant European power. By default the United States had become the manpower reserve for the Entente. Approximately one-half of America's male population by war's end had either registered for the draft or was serving in the armed forces. This vast untapped reserve of manpower seemed to represent the Entente's best hope of thwarting German expansionism.

A credible American force in Europe, however, seemed in the distant future after Ludendorff virtually destroyed the British 5th Army. On April 10, Major General Whigham, the deputy CIGS, informed the British War Cabinet that the United States had only 319,000 men in France and most of these soldiers were not riflemen. Pershing had insisted upon shipping many noncombatants, including many black soldiers who were provided with shovels rather than rifles, to give him the necessary logistical support for an independent force. Of this number only 70,000 US troops were thought ready to enter the fighting line. An additional 10,000 troops were in the United Kingdom.[1] But questions quickly emerged about the combat readiness of even this small number of riflemen. On April 24, the War Cabinet learned that American soldiers "with six months' training were to be found side by side with raw recruits." Pershing himself had confirmed that this was true and "expressed surprise at the occurrence, which he supposed was due to the haste with which the orders to push forward troops had been carried out."[2]

After being at war for one year the United States did not have a single division on an active front. In effect the United States had a "non-existent" army in Europe after a year of belligerency which seemed to justify the French jibe that the AEF stood for "After Everything's Finished." Certainly American assistance on the battlefield had thus far been "non-existent." The War Department released a list of casualties to March 15, 1918 (see Table 4). By contrast, the British had been forced to

Table 4 *War Department list of casualties to March 15, 1918*

Killed in action	136
Killed by accident	134
Died from disease	641
Lost at sea	237
Died of wounds	26
Died, various reasons	38
TOTAL DEATHS	1,212
Wounded	475
Captured	21
Missing	14
TOTAL CASUALTIES	1,722

Source: Shipley Thomas, *The History of the AEF* (New York: George H. Doran, 1920), p. 66.

assume the costly task of killing Germans after Nivelle's failed 1917 spring offensive and the subsequent mutiny of his army. As a consequence, the British had suffered approximately 790,000 casualties between January and November.[3] Lloyd George, believing that the war could not be fought to a conclusion before 1919, feared that Britain would have little influence at any peace conference if its army had been reduced to a shell on the battlefields of France and Flanders. These fears were not unfounded. On July 19, 1918 the Minister of National Service reported to the War Cabinet that the available number of men in 1914 up to the age of forty-three had been 9,500,000 "and of these 6,100,000 had been recruited."[4] With a total population of only 38 million, France mobilized 8,500,000, of which 5,300,000 were killed, mutilated, or wounded by war's end.[5] By contrast, the United States, with a male population of 54 million, inducted 2,810,296 men during the three stages of the draft out of the 24,234,021 who had registered, the great majority between the ages of twenty-one and thirty-one.[6]

British comparisons of British and American mobilizations, of course, overlooked the formidable obstacles facing an independent US force waging a campaign in Western Europe, including transporting the required men and their supplies and providing them with their own lines of supply. On December 28, Colonel William J. Wilgus completed a study of the logistical side of Pershing's request for twenty-four divisions in France by July 1, 1918. When required, support troops (estimated at one-third of the AEF's ration strength, an additional 710,000 men), along with their animal and mechanical transport and supplies, would have to be transported to France over the next six months to fulfill

Pershing's requirements. Colonel Wilgus, who had been Vice President and Chief Engineer of the New York Central Railroad, certainly did not underestimate the difficulties. His report stressed that American soldiers would have to be transported

from various points in the United States to the seaboard, an average distance of say 1,200 miles; thence across the Atlantic Ocean, a distance of say 3,200 miles, and thence from various ports in England and France, by rail and water, to the battle line, a further distance of say 600 miles and upwards, the aggregate distance being in excess of 5,000 miles.

This expeditionary force also had to be supplied – Wilgus's estimate being fifty pounds per man per day (which included twenty pounds a day for coal and construction materials for the AEF's lines of communication).[7]

Shipping rather than rail transportation presented the greatest logistical obstacle to forming a formidable fighting force on European soil. Colonel Wilgus determined that the Army Transport Service required 2,580,000 ship tonnage (1,430,000 for troop and animal and mechanical transport and 1,150,000 for cargo vessels) in January to begin supplying Pershing with the men and supplies he requested. But it had available only 780,000 tons.[8] Although some of Colonel Wilgus's estimates were wide of the mark,[9] shipping remained the greatest obstacle for the United States to overcome in forming an independent army in Europe.

The first contingent of American troops sent to Europe actually averaged 2,392 land miles in the United States per man as trains transported them to embarkation camps prior to their sailing from the two designated ports of embarkation, New York Harbor (or Hoboken, NJ) and Hampton Roads (or Newport News), Virginia, which were supervised by a section of the General Staff, the Embarkation Service.[10]

Overloaded rail lines, poor management, and extreme weather initially led to a national railroad logjam. In December 1917 the government took control of the railroads. Although a Director of Inland Transportation assumed authority the following month it was not until June that an efficient system began to emerge. The transport of the 8th Division, 18,819 men, from Camp Fremont, California to Camp Mills, Long Island in October 1918, a distance of 3,444 miles, reflected the rail transport of troops to embarkation camps at its best. Six empty trains, averaging fourteen cars a train, arrived at Camp Fremont each day and were loaded in minutes, thirty-two men to a car. For seven days, trains were loaded and departed Camp Fremont at ninety-minute intervals. Two trains barely missed their target by either four or five minutes; the other forty trains met their schedule, traveling at an average rate of

twenty miles per hour and reaching their embarkation camp in an average time of seven days and three hours.[11]

Earlier rail transportation of troops had frequently not gone as
smoothly. The first troops to go overseas were the 16th, 18th, 26th,
and 28th Infantry Regiments, stationed along the Mexican border.
Packed into trains, with "Bound for Berlin," "Can the Kaiser," and other
warlike slogans written on their cars, they had been transported in June to
Hoboken to be shipped to France where they formed the 1st Division.

Approximately 2 million men followed them to the embarkation ports.
Private Henry Henderson had enlisted on April 29, 1918, been trained
for a couple of weeks at Camp Dodge, and then transferred to Camp
Travis along with other replacements for the 90th Division. After some
drilling and a week of musketry training, he boarded a train for Camp
Mills, Long Island, one of the embarkation camps. On the second day of
his journey, Henderson's troop train stopped at the outskirts of a town

where we were forced to take a plunge in a dirty pond, a bunch of women around
us but they beat a hasty retreat. When we dressed, were dirtier after the plunge
than before. Our coaches had all blinds down, wherever our train stopped, we
gave the natives money to buy us candy and after the train had started, the officers
would come around and take our sweets.[12]

Henderson left Camp Travis on June 9 and arrived at Camp Mills five
days later. He sailed for Liverpool on June 20.

Whiskey was also on the mind of some soldiers aboard the troop trains.
In late January 1918, Hale Hunt, a musician with the 127th Infantry
Regiment, 32nd Division, left Fort MacArthur, Texas, for Camp
Merritt, New Jersey, another embarkation camp. Despite efforts by the
authorities, he recalled that "boot legging" took place at every large train
station at which his train stopped.[13]

Arriving at Camp Merritt, Hunt's unit was quarantined because many
soldiers were sick with either the flu or pneumonia. In Hunt's words,
"We are a sick feeling outfit and blue." It would be two weeks before his
regiment departed for Europe. Quarantining troops about to be sent
abroad during the unusually severe winter of 1917–18 and during the
height of the influenza epidemic in September–October 1918 was not
unusual at both the embarkation camps and the cantonments. Herbert
L. McHenry, a private who was being sent as a replacement to serve in a
"shot-up regiment," had a similar experience before boarding one of the
packed troop transports. His officers had been told to "keep these men
isolated; keep them clean; keep them healthy. We must get them to
Europe and when they embark they must be physically fit – one hundred
per cent fit."[14]

As the transatlantic shipment of troops dramatically expanded from May onward the available transport tonnage began to outstrip the supply of trained men.[15] Divisions had to be brought up to strength at the embarkation camps by cannibalizing men who had recently been drafted and were still undergoing training in the cantonments. A goodly number of these men were thus raw recruits like McHenry and Henderson, who received only a few weeks of training before being shipped to France.

Getting men to the embarkation ports in a timely fashion did not present the same problems as securing the required ship tonnage to get them to France. Without warning and with no prior preparation the War and Navy Departments were charged with transporting, protecting, and supplying an expeditionary force in Europe. At the signing of the Armistice on November 11, 1918 the Cruiser and Transport Force of the United States Fleet had forty-two troop transports and 453 cargo ships under its direction. The latter carried approximately 95 percent of the AEF's war materials, including clothing, food, ordnance, engineering supplies, horses, mules and trucks, and 1,791 locomotives and 26,994 standard-gage freight cars.[16]

In April 1917, however, the Army Transport Service had no troop carriers ready or suitable for the transatlantic passage. Its ships were slow and had limited bunker capacity; for its part, the Navy had only one transport, the slow and unseaworthy *Hancock*, and the *Henderson*, which was under construction.[17] America also possessed a quite small deep-water merchant marine when compared to other great industrial countries such as Great Britain and Germany.

Ironically, Germany unwittingly provided crucial assistance in transporting troops to Europe and supplying them. The outbreak of the European war in 1914 stranded many German vessels, including ocean liners, in US ports. After America entered the war, US Customs Officers commandeered these interned ships, which included the *Vaterland* (later renamed the *Leviathan*), which had been launched in Hamburg in 1913. This passenger ship, the largest in the world, transported more than 150,000 Doughboys to France prior to the Armistice.[18]

Anticipating that the American government might seize their ships German crews attempted to disable them by taking chisels and sledge hammers to the main engines. American workers, laboring day and night, seven days a week, however, soon had many of these ships in working order. Rather than manufacture new cylinders, which would have taken up to a year, they used electro welding to weld cast steel pieces or patches to the parts of the cylinders that remained intact. Meanwhile, crews refitted ships as troop carriers by adding thousands of bunks (frequently just hammocks), enlarging galleys, and expanding toilet and bathing facilities.[19] Even with commandeered and refitted German ships, however, the United States still did not possess nearly enough passenger tonnage to meet Pershing's expanding demands for men.

Boarding had not gone well initially as many soldiers embarked on their first sea voyages, with chaos prevailing on the piers and troops being haphazardly loaded.[20] But a system soon emerged. The Embarkation Service banned loved ones and the curious from the docks. Before departing upon what Theodore Roosevelt had proclaimed the "Great Adventure," a soldier signed a form to enable authorities to notify next of kin in case of death. He then joined the long lines of soldiers that crowded the gangways. Once aboard he was directed to his berthing compartment and instructed to remain in his bunk to avoid congestion. Initially soldiers were also told to stay below deck until their ships reached the open sea in a misguided attempt to mask troop shipments from the prying eyes of potential German agents. The authorities, however, later relaxed these precautions and bands played and soldiers packed the decks as troop transports cleared port. Emotions ranged from excitement to foreboding. As he sailed from Hoboken, Private Henry Henderson wanted "to see what I could as we didn't know then whether we would ever see it again."[21]

The War Department had been on edge in June as the first troops sailed for Europe in four convoys. The oceans had become a shooting gallery for U-boats since the resumption of unrestricted U-boat warfare. As recently as April German torpedoes had sent 169 British ships and 204 of other nationalities to the bottom.[22] Some departing soldiers had been put at risk because of the hasty arrangements that characterized their departure. For example, the men of the Sixth Field Artillery (1st Division) once aboard ship discovered that there were not nearly enough life jackets or life boats to go around.[23]

Baker subsequently spent anxious days before the first contingent of US troops landed safely in Europe. "My own feeling at the time," he later noted,

was that if the submarines had managed to sink two or three ships in that convoy, with the loss of seven or eight thousand men, the country would have been disposed to regard the task of transporting American troops to Europe under the circumstances as impossible. There would certainly have been enormous pressure brought to bear to limit American participation to financial, economic, and purely naval operations.[24]

Some army leaders expressed similar concern. As Harbord noted at the time: "Our American people are not, in my judgment, very keen for the war. They do not realize its perils. Losses in battle that also cost German lives they could understand, but if a troopship or two is torpedoed and a thousand or two American boys are drowned like rats, I wonder if the President could hold them in line."[25]

To counter the U-boat threat, most American soldiers crossed the Atlantic in convoys. The protection given his convoy certainly impressed Lieutenant Hugh W. Ogden, a member of the 42nd Division's headquarters staff, when he emerged from below deck in October 1917. "I wish I could put on paper the picture," he later wrote, "when I came on deck in the morning, – gray troop ships all around, looking like liners except that they were all war paint; great battleships wallowing along in the trough of the sea, their funnels spouting black smoke, – and further off on the horizon torpedo boat destroyers, skimming along like gulls."[26]

In the end Germany's undersea threat to America's "bridge of ships" proved much exaggerated. The British steamer *Tuscania*, converted to transporting soldiers, became the first and only troop carrier to Europe to be torpedoed and sunk. Having sailed from Hoboken on January 24, 1918 with 2,013 American soldiers aboard, the *Tuscania* on February 5 at 5:40 p.m. suffered a direct hit by a German torpedo fired by submarine U-77. Fortunately, the *Tuscania* did not sink for another four hours. By 7 p.m. all of its life boats had been launched although some men remained aboard. Only 200 Americans lost their lives. The Germans enjoyed slightly more success against homeward-bound US troop transports. U-boats sank the *Antilles, President Lincoln,* and *Covington.* An armored cruiser, the *San Diego*, also sank after striking a mine laid by a German submarine.[27]

The question must be asked. Why didn't the German Admiralty concentrate on US troop ships in 1917–18? Ludendorff's forceful support of unlimited U-boat warfare had been based on the belief that American reinforcements could not reach the European battlefields in 1918. When Germany made its fateful decision to resume unrestricted U-boat warfare, on January 9, 1917, Admiral von Holtzendorff, Chief of Naval General Staff, had assured the generals: "I guarantee on my word as a naval officer that no American will set foot on the Continent!"[28]

When Ludendorff later urged the German Admiralty to focus its attention on ships bearing troops from the United States, von Holtzendorff was quick to remind him that the U-boat campaign had dual targets: US troop ships and the Entente's merchant fleet. The latter, the submarine campaign's original object, remained the Navy's highest priority, a reflection of Germany's underestimation of the consequences of American belligerency. Another consideration for the German Admiralty according to von Holtzendorff was that troop ships could

Fig. 12 Embarked for France. Western Newspaper Union, 1917

approach the coasts of Europe anywhere between the north of England and
Gibraltar, a front of some fourteen hundred nautical miles. It was impossible
effectively to close this area by means of submarines. One could have
concentrated them only on certain routes; but whether the troop-ships would
choose the same routes at the same time was the question. As soon as the enemy
heard of submarines anywhere, he could always send the ships new orders by
wireless and unload at another port.[29]

Despite the lack of success by U-boats, many Doughboys remained on
edge as their troop ships steamed across the Atlantic (Fig. 12). Often the
first thing a soldier received when he embarked was a life jacket. Anxious
soldiers and crew members spotted real and imagined submarines.
"We had a real submarine scare," recalls Sergeant Major Mervyn Burke,
who was attached to Headquarters, 1st Division.

The siren blew, a gun went off on one of the ships, and we took off like a scared
jackrabbit ... Before many minutes all four guns aboard were fired – almost
simultaneously! In addition, we had an army machine gun mounted atop the
rear bunk house, and it started pop-popping. I doubt if any gunner ever saw a sub
in his sights.[30]

Occasionally ships collided when they took evasive zigzag routes to
avoid potential torpedoes.

Lookouts with binoculars constituted the ship's first line of defense against undersea assault. Soldiers formed a circle, twenty-four men strong, and scanned the horizon for submarines or their torpedoes. Each man was assigned to cover fifteen degrees. To keep lookouts alert, officers changed watches frequently, usually at thirty-minute intervals. Additional lookouts took their positions aloft.[31] The duty of a lookout was not always easy. Marine Private Aitken describes being lashed to the prow "so as not to [be] wash[ed] away by the waves ... Try and see anything," he lamented, "when it is pitch dark and your eye [is] full of sea water; battered and buffeted by the waves, being warned time and again by the bridge to note objects. It's a great life, I'm going to be a farmer in the next war. I'd rather have the dust than all the sea water."[32]

Troops conducted fire drills, inspections, and, most importantly, abandon-ship drills (or "drowning drills" as some sarcastically called them) in both daylight and darkness. Since many submarine attacks occurred at twilight, reveille was sounded an hour before daybreak while sailing through the "danger" zones. As a further precaution against submarines, lights were extinguished during the entire voyage. "No matches, no electric torches, no open port holes, nothing," reported Lieutenant Hugh Ogden, the Assistant Judge, Advocate, 42nd Division Headquarters. "You sit in absolute darkness from sun down till bed time, and then go to bed in a ship that is sealed up tight."[33]

Despite efforts to keep troops busy, the men had little to see or do during their crossing except an endless ocean and shooting craps or playing poker. Corporal Paul Murphy, 309th Infantry Regiment, 78th Division, arrived in Britain via Halifax in a British convoy. His voyage of seventeen days "completely cut [him] off from the world, no news, no wireless nor any contact with any one. We were lost in a vacuum with nothing but sea and sky to the horizon ... It was a very monotonous trip with nothing to do but put in time; we were so crowded that there was scarcely room to move." He sailed on the *Kaiora*, a converted British cattle ship which had been transporting cattle from Argentina prior to boarding American soldiers at Hoboken. "I don't think the cattle had been out very long," Murphy writes,

before they moved us in. However, the cargo hold had been renovated, tables set up for dining and hooks installed from which to hang hammocks, which were the most uncomfortable sleeping devices ever known. The sides would come up, wrap around you and you would sink to the bottom and they were strung up every which way and so close together that every time you moved you bumped into someone in the next hammock.[34]

Murphy ate twice a day, the norm for transatlantic troop carriers. On large troop ships, men typically stood in long lines and received their food cafeteria style. The largest troop carrier, the *Leviathan*, had twenty "feeding stations." Cooks rapidly filled outstretched field mess kits with grub, dishing it out of ten-gallon aluminum containers placed on serving tables at the rate of seven seconds a man. Soldiers then shoveled down their food while standing before narrow mess tables. When finished they exited by another door where they washed their mess kits in hot water in washing-troughs. If anyone wanted "seconds," they returned to the back of the line.[35]

Gabriel Bentson, a medic with the 47th Infantry Regiment, 4th Division, who sailed on another converted cattle boat, the *Caserta*, had no appetite for "seconds." "They have been feeding us cold storage Hares for dinner a number of days," he noted,

but my appetite went the first day we had them. I found out they had been in cold storage since 1914. That year they were supposed to have been shot in Scotland. I also happened to see them skin them and when I saw they only put them in one cleansing water and at once put them in a boiler to make stew out of them I had enough dinner already.[36]

On May 12, 1918 Marine Private Aitken penned a letter to his mother. It was Mother's Day and he obviously wanted to keep his parents from worrying about him. He also had to be concerned about his lieutenant who censored his letters home. He thus wrote his mother two letters. The first, censored, read as follows: "We had a beautiful trip across, really it was, only a few days of rough weather and nearly everyone stood up for their meals and we were hollering for more so you see we were a bunch of sea goers." A second, uncensored appreciation by Aitken told another story: "Chow is almost impossibility unless you are possessed of a very strong stomach, for sea sick people are not conducive to an appetite. We eat below decks and the odors are rather upsetting. I cant write about the conditions, its too revolting."[37]

American soldiers arriving in Liverpool had to face one more boat trip as they crossed the Channel to France. On March 27, 1918 Hale Hunt, a musician in the 127th Infantry Regiment, 32nd Division, who had made the transatlantic voyage on the *Leviathan*, boarded "an old cattle boat at South Hampton ... a horrible ship." Sharing the boat with several hundred mules aboard left Hunt and his comrades little room. Six hundred men were crowded together in one large hole in the boat. Soldiers slept "standing up, lying on the floor and in every available warm spot."[38]

Before the war's end the United States had its own substantial fleet of small wood and steel vessels to ferry men and supplies across the Channel. These vessels had been leased from Sweden or Norway (25 percent), taken from America's inland waterways, or manufactured by the Emergency Fleet Corporation. When Hunt arrived on French soil he experienced another form of transportation endured by almost every Doughboy. He climbed aboard what he described as a "toy" freight car upon which the following French words had been written: "40 Hommes, 8 Chevaux" (forty men, eight horses). "We were jammed in like sardines. Joked a lot at first, but soon got crabby,"[39] he writes.

The Cruiser and Transport Force of the United States enjoyed great success in safely shipping Doughboys to Europe. But could enough of them arrive in time? In October 1917 Major Georg Wetzell, head of operations of the *Oberste Heeresleitung* (*OHL*) (Supreme Army Command), had stated clearly the dilemma facing Ludendorff and Hindenburg in 1918: "If we do not wish to succumb to false illusions, then we must count on the fact that the Entente will survive the winter . . . and that the Americans will have added significant forces to the western war theatre in the spring of 1918 (10 to 15 divisions)." A German peace consequently depended upon delivering "an annihilating blow to the British before American aid can become effective."[40]

On April 7 Haig sent Lord Derby, the Secretary of State for War, a note tinged with panic. Since March 21 the BEF's losses, excluding the sick, had been 115,868. His casualties, including the sick, would rise to 221,000 by April 15, or approximately 50,000 men a week since the beginning of the German offensives. "In the absence of reinforcements, which I understand do not exist," the British commander-in-chief informed Derby, the situation will "become critical unless American troops fit for immediate incorporation in my Divisions arrive in France in the mean time."[41]

Pressure on Pershing and the Wilson administration to contribute more to the ground war effort was now enormous. After one full year of war the United States had only one division, the 1st, ready for offensive action, and had suffered only 163 combat deaths.[42] "We expected to see two million cowboys throw themselves upon the Boches," the French complained, "and we see only a few thousand workers building warehouses."[43]

As late as February 1918 Wilson had hoped that peace elements in the Central Powers might still triumph over the militarists. His interest in peace initiatives by war-weary Austria–Hungary had turned to fury when the Allied Supreme War Council showed no interest in general peace discussions that included Germany as well as Austria–Hungary. The British and French only sought to detach Vienna while isolating an unhumbled Berlin.[44] "There is infinite stupidity in action of this sort. It stiffens every element of hatred and belligerency in the Central Powers and plays directly into the hands of the military parties," the President had written Secretary of State Lansing on February 4.[45]

The ferocity of the German attacks, which ended all hope of a negotiated settlement, clearly startled Wilson and made him question his views
on "peace without victory" and the moral equivalency of the Entente and
Central Powers. He told the British intelligence officer William Wiseman
that if

the Allies became exhausted, what should we do? He supposed we should have to
make a compromise peace, but we could not deceive ourselves – it would be a
German peace, and mean in effect a German victory. The Germans would no
doubt be prepared to deal generously with France and Belgium, and other
questions, providing she was allowed practically a free-hand in Russia ... He
could not help being aware (he said) of the position of America. She was now
supplying a large part of the material support of the war, and she was also the
potential military factor. It meant, he said, that the decision as to whether the war
should continue would rest in his hands. It was a terrible responsibility, and a
question which he certainly would not regard from solely an American point of
view: he must consider it also from the point of view of the Allies and indeed the
whole world.[46]

Wilson's comments to Wiseman mirrored the American public's
growing alarm over German expansionism. Among other considerations,
Wilson had been shaken by the annexationist treaty that the Central
Powers forced upon the Bolsheviks. Earlier, in his Fourteen Points
address to a joint session of Congress on January 8, he had demanded
that Germany evacuate all of its occupied Russian territory. The Treaty
of Brest-Litovsk, signed on March 3, 1918, however, deprived Russia of
44 percent of its people (62 million) and 25 percent (roughly 1,267,000
square miles) of its territory. Economically, the former Romanov state
lost 73 percent of its iron ore, 75 percent of its coal, and 33 percent of its
farm land.[47] This rapacious treaty, which reflected the influence of the
all-powerful *OHL*, extended Germany's control of Eastern Europe to
the Arctic Ocean and the Black Sea, and gave Berlin more control of the
former Russian empire than Hitler achieved at the height of his invasion,
1941–42.

Some Americans now spoke in alarmist terms of Germany's threat to
US security. If Germany were not defeated, the Brooklyn *Eagle* proclaimed, "the specter of Prussian Imperialism will spread in time to all
of Asia as well as over Europe, and thus entrenched, this hemisphere will
be the next to fall under the Prussian yoke." "German plans for the
spoliation of Eastern Europe have taken shape with spectacular sudden-
ness," warned the *New York Tribune*. "We now see the Teuton plans,
however, in all its nakedness. They translate into reality the wildest
dreams of the wildest Pan-Germans. Gorged with her eastern booty,
Germany is now the most formidable Power bestriding the world."[48]

On the anniversary of American entry into the war, Wilson gave expression to the public's emerging fear of Germany's potential threat to their country. Before an enthusiastic audience, the President painted a vivid portrait of Germany's evolving global threat.

Their purpose is undoubtedly to make all the Slavic peoples, all the free and ambitious nations of the Baltic peninsula, all the lands that Turkey has dominated and misruled, subject to their will and ambition and build upon that dominion an empire of force upon which they fancy that they can then erect an empire of gain and commercial supremacy – an empire as hostile to the Americas as to the Europe which it will overawe – an empire which will ultimately master Persia, India, and the peoples of the Far East.[49]

Prior to March 21, 1918 Pershing had successfully thwarted British attempts to get the United States to ship battalions rather than divisions. But it took five times the tonnage to ship whole divisions with their artillery and transport. With Germany on the ascendancy on both the Western Front and in the East, the British believed that Wilson might acquiesce to the shipping of surplus battalions of infantry and machine gunners, a first step toward amalgamating US units with British divisions. Lord Reading, who had succeeded the ailing Spring Rice as ambassador, cabled London that the United States now understood that Britain was "standing between her and German militarism" and now "realized as it were in a flash their own military shortcomings and the time they have lost since they entered the war. This has already produced an outburst in the Press and Congress which naturally enough takes the form of an attack on the Administration."[50]

On the same day that he cabled London, Lord Reading spoke at the Lotos Club in New York, and delivered a direct appeal from Lloyd George to the American public for support. His words echoed an earlier appeal from officials in London to the American military attaché attached to the War Office: "For God's sake, get your men over!"[51]

The American commander-in-chief was now prepared to have American soldiers train with British troops but he held firm against integrating American soldiers into British divisions to keep them up to strength. It is difficult to argue with the position that he took. "There was nothing vainglorious in our attitude, but no people with a grain of national pride would consent to furnish men to build up the army of another nation," Pershing later wrote. "Misunderstandings and recriminations would inevitably follow any reverse by such a mixed force."[52]

Although Wilson and Pershing rebuffed Allied attempts to keep their divisions up to strength with Americans, the British still agreed to reallocate 200,000 tons of shipping from their merchant marine to speed up the transport of American troops to Europe. Long food lines had become commonplace in Britain during the last months of 1917 as a result of Germany's resumption of unrestricted U-boat war. It was not unusual for someone to wait six or more hours only to discover that no butter, tea, or bacon remained on the shelves. The adoption of compulsory rationing and the convoy system, however, soon ameliorated this food crisis. By May food lines had virtually disappeared.[53]

Several weeks before Ludendorff launched the first of his offensives to achieve a victor's peace, Peyton March had entered the Chief of Staff's office in Washington. March was impersonal, demanding, and frequently tactless. The expression, "didn't suffer fools gladly," applied to him in spades. He once famously commented, "One is proud to be hated, if it is a consequence of doing one's work well."[54]

Before departing for his new position in the War Department, March conferred with the Army's two four-star generals in Europe, Bliss and Pershing. Both men impressed upon him the need to speed up the transport of men to Europe. Bliss suggested two divisions a month. When a division's support troops were included this amounted to approximately 90,000 men. March promised to do better than that. The War Department had a history of making pronouncements which it did not carry through. But March meant what he said. "He took the War Department like a dog takes a cat by the neck, and he shook it,"[55] commented one General Staff officer.

During the three months prior to March's arrival at the War Department, approximately 50,000 troops had been shipped to France each month. In April March more than doubled that figure to almost 118,642 men, and in May the flow of troops across the Atlantic took off, with more than 10,000 men a day disembarking in European ports during many weeks during the summer. March utilized every British ship made available by cramming it with recruits, whether they had completed their prescribed basic training or not. Under-strength divisions arriving at the embarkation ports were brought up to full strength by drafts of men from other camps, most of whom had not completed their scheduled program of training. Many of their officers, especially the second lieutenants who had completed only three months of training in the officer training camps before being commissioned, were as inexperienced as the men they were expected to lead. March's dramatic increase in the flow of troops across the Atlantic thus came at a heavy price for the AEF's combat effectiveness during the last half of 1918.

On April 24 Pershing sent an urgent cable to the War Department, expressing concern to both March and Baker about untrained men being sent across the Atlantic. Given the "urgency of the situation here,"

Pershing warned that his schedule of overseas training before committing soldiers to combat was no longer feasible.

To send them into the trenches or into battle without requisite training would mean useless and unwarranted loss of life. Therefore urgently recommend that no men be sent over who have not had at least four months intensive training and who have not also had full and thorough instruction in target practice and that a limited number of divisions be broken up to accomplish this if necessary.[56]

Pershing's request, of course, was inconsistent with his urgent demands for reinforcements, and the War Department continued to send him untrained or partially trained recruits, including some who had yet to fire their rifles.

March also made a dramatic change in the manner in which men were shipped across the Atlantic. "I had determined to use the transport service as a ferry, and not as passenger transatlantic service," he notes in his *Nation at War.*[57] The transatlantic voyage was a relatively short one, so March did not concern himself with the comfort of passengers. "This was war-time, and any discomfort suffered was slight. This increased the carrying capacity of the ships we had by over 40 per cent," he later wrote. March also shipped men without taking into consideration whether or not he could provide them with sufficient supplies once they arrived in France. In his words, "I had put my men on half rations many times when campaigning in earlier days in the Philippines and kept on going."[58]

To increase capacity, workers ripped out passage and cabin walls. On the fastest ships, they created additional sleeping space by placing berths in tiers. Bunks were never unoccupied, with men sleeping in shifts. The commandeered *Leviathan* had its troop capacity increased by 100 percent (from 7,000 to 14,000 men). Never before had so many people sailed aboard one ship. Its speed (along with the *Great Northern* and *Northern Pacific*) represented another advantage for the *Leviathan*. It did not have to sail in slow-moving convoys and could make the round trip to Europe in less than twenty-seven days. (The average "turnaround" for all troop transports had been reduced to thirty-five days.)

Ludendorff was both surprised and dismayed when he discovered that American soldiers, packed in their transports like sardines, were crossing the Atlantic in ever increasing numbers. Naval experts continued to assure him that the United States could not possibly obtain the required tonnage space, even with the assistance of her allies, to transport as many as 1 million Americans and their required supplies across the Atlantic.[59]

By the end of 1918 some 2,079,980 members of the AEF had been transported to Europe in 1,142 troop ship sailings. American ships carried 952,581 men or 46.25 percent of the total (one-half sailing in commandeered German ships).[60] The British, however, provided the additional tonnage that made this transportation miracle possible. At the beginning of 1918, the British had made available four large ocean liners and four small transports. Following Germany's bid for victory, London dramatically increased its contributions, resulting in 49 percent of the AEF's personnel being carried in British holds; Italian (3 percent), French (2 percent), Russian (1 percent), and one Brazilian ship made up the difference. With the exception of the single "loaned" Brazilian ship, the government chartered these foreign carriers and Americans aboard sailed as "paid passengers." Initially the British attempted to charge a flat rate of $150 a man, but the War Department negotiated a more reasonable rate of $81.75.[61]

As the AEF rapidly expanded its manpower with soldiers who had received progressively less stateside training, the Army Transport Service struggled to keep up. In the summer of 1917 Pershing required 16,000 tons a month to supply his small force. By the fall of 1918 his requirements had risen to an astonishing and unsustainable 700,000 tons a month.[62] If the war continued as expected into 1919 or even 1920 and the War Department succeeded in its goal of having 80 divisions in Europe by the spring of 1919, Army planners both at home and abroad faced a monumental task not only in ferrying supplies to Europe but in transporting those supplies to the battle front. As it has been noted elsewhere, "everything *weighed more* than it does today: plastics had yet to supplant iron and wood."[63]

11 Neck of the bottle

Pershing's leadership of the AEF suggested that no objective was more important to him than the formation of an independent American force in France capable of delivering a decisive blow against the German Army. The United States, however, had never created an army of such size and complexity, and it attempted to do so thousands of miles from its factories, raw materials, and farm land. During the prewar years, equipping, supplying, and transporting thousand-man regiments did not present the almost insurmountable difficulties associated with the super-sized AEF division of some 28,000 men. According to Johnson and Hillman, "it demanded twenty-eight times that effort – and General Pershing was asking for a hundred divisions!"[1] Establishing effective lines of communication for an expeditionary force that would grow to some 2 million men by the Armistice was the foundation of everything that would follow. In Harbord's words, the AEF's lines of communication were "the neck of the bottle through which all men and supplies must pass."[2]

In selecting the region of Lorraine as the area in which to establish an all-American army, Pershing could not have selected a theater of operations more difficult for the War Department and Pershing's staff to sustain. Great Britain, the other great power assisting the French to liberate their homeland, had established its battle front just across the Channel. Difficult lines of communication for the AEF with its own ship berths, warehouses, and in some cases railways, however, was the price that Pershing was prepared to pay to establish an independent army. By war's end the War Department had shipped 1,500 locomotives, 20,000 railway cars, and 30,410 railway personnel. Even then the AEF failed to establish its own infrastructure that could possibly keep up with the escalating Allied demands for ever more American soldiers. Pershing consequently continued to depend upon the French for vital logistical support, including most of his motorized and animal transport for men and supplies. The United States had horses and mules (although many had been shipped to Europe prior to American intervention) and the industrial base to mass produce trucks, but it did not have the required shipping to get them to Europe. Consequently only 40,000 of the AEF's 200,000 horses came from the United States and most Doughboys traveled in French trucks driven by Vietnamese.[3]

When the famous British military correspondent, Colonel Repington, visited Chaumont in October he found Pershing's staff grappling with the multiple problems involved in building a great army on foreign soil. Confusion often reigned in the War Department with Chaumont and the General Staff in Washington not always on the same page. The first contingents of the recently arrived 26th Division, for example, had reached Neufchâteau without its commanding general or staff, "with only their personal effects, and without anything else, not even doctors or rations or bedding or cooking utensils." As General Alfred E. Bradley told Repington: it was "worse than in 1898" – the Spanish–American War.[4]

As early as July 11, 1917 Pershing began to reveal to the War Department the magnitude of his expeditionary force's needs when he asked for the expansion of French docks, the repair of French railways, and additional rolling stock to handle the increased flow of troops and their required supplies. Ominously he noted: "The French have practically no material available so that both material and labor must come from the United States."[5] He requested, among other items, timber for fuel, railroads, telegraph poles, and building projects such as barracks and warehouses.

Repington found Pershing's staff to be first rate but he feared that French bureaucracy and inexperience might sabotage its effort to create the necessities for an independent force. "If they want to build a hospital the indent for the ground has to go to Compiègne, and then the engineers have long discussions with the French Mission and French public departments [on] how the building material is to be obtained, where the wood is to be cut, and how it is to be brought up. All of this takes time," Repington noted in his diary. "Besides, each American Department scheme has to be argued like a legal case with the other sixteen departments before Pershing can settle it, and, in fact, the peace system of an out-of-date Army is being subjected to the terrific strain of a great war. The men even bring their kit boxes and beds from America, but this can hardly continue."[6]

When the French government reluctantly gave its permission to timber some of its protected forests, yet another cable from headquarters arrived at the War Department. Pershing wanted to organize a forestry service in France composed of sawmill units and experienced lumbermen along with from eight thousand to ten thousand unskilled laborers.[7]

Officials in the War Department, who had struggled mightily to supply Pershing's needs during his limited campaign in Mexico in 1916, certainly did not anticipate that Germany's defeat might depend in part on shipping lumbermen to Europe. Nor could the War Department have imagined that Pershing's supply and transportation organization, in his own words,

would have to become a great army in itself ... organized simply as a great business enterprise to receive and transport not only the combatant troops but every conceivable requirement shipped from home or obtained abroad for their maintenance. Concisely stated, the establishment behind the Zone of Operations would practically require the organization in France on an unprecedented scale of another War Department, and this is precisely what it became.[8]

Time was of the essence, especially after Ludendorff sought to achieve a German peace in 1918 with a series of powerful offensives. Pershing began escalating his demands for additional support troops. The number of troops being ferried across the Atlantic dramatically increased from May 1918 onward but out of necessity many of these men were infantry-men rather than support troops. When the fighting ended on November 11, 1918 the personnel of the SOS totaled some 670,000 men. This number was more than five times the size of the Regular Army in April 1, 1917.[9] Many of these support troops, however, had only arrived in France during the last weeks of the war.[10] Harbord, who became the Chief of Staff of the SOS on July 27, believed that the efficient running of the AEF's supply system required a manpower ratio of one to three; yet eleven weeks before the Armistice he commanded fewer than 300,000 men. "We were long on bayonets," he later wrote in his memoirs, "and short on stevedores, railroad operating men, engineers and the like."[11]

In February 1918 Pershing relocated his Line of Communications (LOC) from his headquarters at Chaumont to the old French regimental barracks at Tours, a city approximately halfway between the southwestern French ports and Chaumont and at the crossroads of major railways. The LOC's supply and transportation system also included Great Britain, but its primary responsibilities were in France, which the LOC leadership divided into three zones for transporting troops, and, more importantly, supplying them: a Base Section, an Intermediate Section, and an Advance Section.

The Base Section, subdivided into seven parts,[12] included new docks, extensive railway yards, and camps for black stevedores. Adjacent to these ports, American workers built warehouses to store supplies which could be sorted and either immediately transported forward or held in reserve. To disembark its supplies, the AEF initially utilized the ports of Saint-Nazaire, La Pallice, and Bordeaux. Soldiers shipped directly to

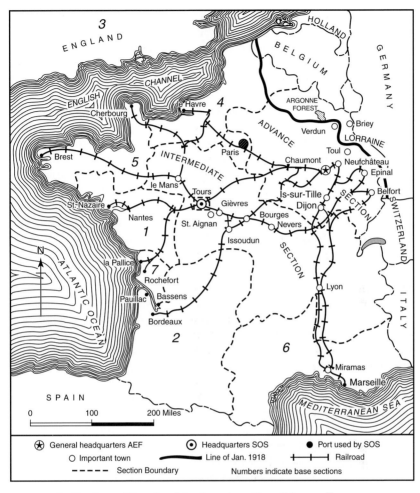

3. Services of Supply of the American Expeditionary Forces

France landed at Brest; those who arrived in France by way of Liverpool disembarked at Le Havre. Workers constructed rest camps in these ports to house incoming soldiers prior to their being dispatched inland.

The LOC also had to make dramatic improvements in French docking facilities. In November 1917, for example, stevedores at Bordeaux at best could unload only two cargo ships a day. A year later additional stevedores and docks, the latest electric gantry cranes, and new railway tracks made it possible for fifteen steamships a day to be unloaded (Map 3).

The monthly total, 26,056 tons of cargo unloaded in November 1917, improved by November 1918 to 236,563 tons of supplies along with 6,933 animals and 2,027 troops.[13]

What was being unloaded from the cargo ships, however, did not always seem essential to the AEF's performance. Pershing cabled the War Office that no "further shipments be made of bath bricks, bookcases, bathtubs, cabinets for blanks, cuspidors, office desks, floor wax, hose except fire hose, stepladders, lawn mowers, refrigerators, safes except iron field safes, settees, sickles, stools, window shades – and added that further stop orders would follow soon." As Harbord acidly notes in his memoirs: "Whether engaged in trench or open warfare, the General did not feel the need of any lawn mowers, cuspidors or stepladders."[14]

Tours, the nerve center of the AEF's lines of communication, was located in the Intermediate Section, which served as a central storage area for accumulated supplies both to keep the advance depots filled and to retain a reserve. The AEF's hospitals and new hospital trains were also concentrated in the Intermediate Section. Initially Pershing wanted a ninety-day reserve of food, clothing, and other essential items: forty-five days at the base ports, thirty days at the intermediate depots, and fifteen days at the advance depots. The AEF's rapid increase in size during the last six months of the war, however, quickly put paid to these ambitious targets, which initially had been calculated at fifty pounds per man per day.

During the last six months of the war, according to Ayres, Doughboys received on average the following clothing: "Slicker and overcoat, every 5 months. Blanket, flannel shirt, and breeches, every 2 months. Coat, every 79 days. Shoes and puttees, every 51 days. Drawers and undershirt, every 34 days. Woolen socks, every 23 days."[15] This may have been the average, but the reality was that many soldiers in heavy combat went hungry and were poorly clothed and shod.

The Greve depot, located near Tours and situated on the main railway line of the Paris–Orléans railroad between Saint-Nazaire and Saincaize, became the largest of the Intermediate Section's depots. When chosen as a site in August 1917 it was little more than fields and pine woods. By November 1918, served by over 20,000 men, it had become a twelve-mile square depot of 2,600 acres of warehouses, track, and turnouts. An average warehouse, 50 feet by 400 feet, held enough ration items to supply the requirements of a division for six days. Greve had forty-five miles of track in its receiving, classification, and departure yards and on average handled 2,300 cars a day.

Fig. 13 US Army soldier eating

This depot also had a cold storage plant, the largest in the world at that time, with a capacity of 10 million pounds of frozen meat. American soldiers never developed a taste for canned beef, or even French meat butchered near the battlefield (Fig. 13). To provide quality meat for its soldiers, the War Department shipped American beef to Europe along with refrigerator railway cars to transport it to the front. "There probably has never been an army which had continuously had such excellent beef even at the very front under combat conditions and with the longest line of communications in all history," proudly claims the US Army's official history.[16]

As American supplies were transported closer to the battlefield they entered the third and last section: the Advance Section, which included the critical regulating stations and regulating officers which American officials adopted from the French model. American engineers built two massive regulating stations, one at Is-sur-Tille, which by August supplied 1 million men, and another at Liffol-le-Grand, which was still under construction when the Armistice went into effect. With US soldiers operating all along the front, French facilities also had to be utilized. Saint-Dizier, for example, served as the regulating station for the Meuse-Argonne offensive. These large regulating stations had railway yards with enormous storage facilities attached to them. Regulating officers supervised loading the correct number of trains and sending them forward in a timely fashion to smaller regulating stations at railheads from which daily rations and other supplies were then loaded on a division's transport (trucks and horse-drawn wagons) and taken to their division, whether it was resting, in the line, or on the march.[17] With success or failure depending upon these regulating officers, "the main trouble for the Americans was in deciding who should regulate the regulating officer," notes the military historian Huston.[18] As it turned out, regulating officers were attached to the G-4 Section at GHQ; at the same time they continued to belong to the headquarters of the army in which they served.[19] "Information from the front was telegraphed or telephoned to the Regulating Officer at the Station each evening, as to the needs of the next twenty-four hours," writes Harbord. "Each day a train went forward to the end of the railroad, known as the Rail-Head, with load based on the information received the evening before."[20]

Daily rations had to be automatically transported as well as men and material to fulfill special needs, such as massive amounts of shells prior to an offensive and replacements during or after an offensive when troops were on the move. As the AEF rapidly expanded and became involved in heavy fighting during the last months of the war the SOS experienced serious shortages in both truck and animal transportation. Bad weather and roads clogged with trucks and wagons drawn by mules and horses, many returning to the dump after delivering their vital supplies to the front, created monumental traffic jams which undermined the AEF's operational mobility.

This logistical infrastructure on foreign soil, of course, proved enormously expensive, costing almost twice the amount spent building the Panama Canal. French citizens looked on in astonishment as American soldiers cut trees, laid track, strung telegraph and telephone wire, and engaged in extraordinary building projects with their huge machines. They were involved, Harbord asserts, in "the most stupendous industrial enterprise ever undertaken by the army; one of the most gigantic ever undertaken by any one."[21]

Not surprisingly some French citizens questioned the magnitude of this effort. "These Americans were cutting down French forests to make structures which were of no use to the French, or even to the Americans themselves if they were not going to remain in France," notes Major Frederick Palmer, the Chief of the AEF's Press Division.

"Did the French army, in order to fight the Germans, need ice to store its meat? All these acres of wooden buildings? A candy factory? Chewing-gum as well as cigarettes? And such extensive apparatus in order to unload ships? So many new telephone wires? So many typewriters clicking out such quantities of orders and memoranda?"[22]

Since most French workmen were in uniform or involved in war-related work the Americans received some assistance from German prisoners of war (POWs) as well as from Chinese coolies, but "Yanks," including combat soldiers, had to provide most of the labor. Hugh A. Drum, a member of Pershing's staff and later Chief of Staff of the 1st Army, noted in his diary in April 1918 that the AEF now had "half a million men in France. But we are building so many installations that 3/5 of them are involved in service of rear work. I am afraid that there is great waste in this."[23]

Many young Americans soon became disillusioned with their non-combatant roles abroad. In early 1918, the Army had briefly changed the name of the Line of Communications to Services of the Rear, a renaming quite demeaning to noncombatants who performed essential, strenuous, and sometimes dangerous war work whatever their proximity to the front lines. Not surprisingly, the Army quickly dropped Services of the Rear for Services of Supply. Nonetheless, as the social historian Keene suggests, "noncombatants were becoming an increasingly alien-ated faction within the wartime army. Even those who chose an assign-ment in the rear had anticipated that going to France would be an exciting, dangerous adventure, and the actual monotony of life in the rear thus took these troops by surprise."[24]

The Army also seemed to go out of its way to emphasize that SOS personnel were not true soldiers by giving them little or no training in the use of the rifle and bayonet. A popular song sung by soldiers was "Mother, take down your service flag, your son's in the SOS."[25] This was equally true for many divisional support troops such as engineers, signalmen, and drivers. When he responded to the *World War I Survey* about the weapons he saw or used in the service, Charles Mechura, Company A, 101st Engineer Regiment, 26th Division, simply noted that "he used carpenter tools and common shovels." Corporal Carroll T. Horton, 310th Field Signal Battalion, 85th Division, responded to the same question as follows: "I never saw a weapon until after the armistice and then we were issued side arms consisting of colt automatics." It is also true that many men rushed by the War Depart-ment to Europe during the last half of 1918 had not been trained for the task to which they were assigned, combat or otherwise. His superiors gave Wagoner George A. Fiske, Company B, Ammunition Train,

26th Division, an ammunition truck to drive. As he ruefully admits, "we were supposed to be expert auto drivers. I'd never even driven an auto."[26]

Black men performed a disproportionate amount of the hard labor. By assigning the great majority of black soldiers to stevedore units, assorted labor battalions at depots, pioneer infantry units, and salvage companies the Army sent the following message to blacks: you are conscript workers and not warriors. The War Department's views on race were in part a reaction to heightened racial tension stateside in 1917–18. On August 23, 1917, responding to Jim Crow laws and an assault by the police on two black soldiers who were protesting the police department's treatment of black women, black Regulars in the 24th Infantry's 3rd Battalion rioted in Houston, Texas. Armed black soldiers, most of them northerners, went on a rampage, randomly killing Hispanics and whites. When arrested, the Army held these black soldiers on a blanket charge of murder; nineteen were later hanged. The Houston riots reinforced the racist view that blacks in uniform represented a threat to America's segregationist policies. James K. Vardaman, a racist senator from Mississippi, had earlier warned segregationists of the dangers implicit in drafting blacks. He feared that this would fill the streets of every community with "arrogant strutting representatives of the black soldiery."[27]

In November 1917 Baker outlined the War Department's position on uniformed blacks when he wrote Scott that his policy was "to discourage discrimination against any person by reason of their race . . . At the same time there is no intention on the part of the War Department to undertake at this time to settle the so-called race question."[28] Subsequently, Baker and Scott attempted to mollify the black community by falsely claiming that black draftees were going to be employed in combat in the same proportion as whites.[29] To the contrary, the settled Army policy became one of deploying most blacks as workers rather than fighters and to maintain a large white majority in all training camps.[30] Most of the 368,000 black draftees consequently received little if any serious combat training although approximately 180,000 of them later served with the AEF. The War Department in fact created only one fully organized black combat division (commanded by white officers), the 92nd or "Buffalo" Division. The 93rd Division, an incomplete or "provisional" black division, without supporting or service troops, had its regiments integrated with French divisions, the only American soldiers to be permanently amalgamated with an Allied force on the Western Front (Fig. 14).

One of the regiments in the 93rd Division, the First Provisional Infantry Regiment (Colored), later designated 371st Infantry, received its training at Camp Jackson in Columbia, South Carolina. White soldiers

Fig. 14 US Army Infantry troops, African American unit, marching northwest of Verdun, France, in World War I

initially mocked black draftees as they marched into camp in October 1917. Their arrival had been delayed by the War Department so that South Carolina's cotton crop could be picked. Having been told by local draft boards that they would be given new clothing, these black draftees chose not to wear their Sunday best. "It was a sight never to be forgotten," recalls one of their white officers, Captain Chester D. Heywood.

There were big ones and little ones; fat ones and skinny ones; black ones and tan ones; some in rags and in tatters; others in overalls and every sort of clothing imaginable. They came with suit cases and sacks; with bundles and bandanna handkerchiefs full of food, clothing and knick-knacks. Many were barefoot. Some came with guitars or banjos hanging from their backs by strings or ropes.

Given a chance, however, these rural blacks excelled. "No longer was the regiment the laughing stock of the camp," writes Heywood. "The marching and the close order drill were excellent; the manual of arms unbelievably perfect. The men took the greatest pride in their uniforms and in their equipment."[31]

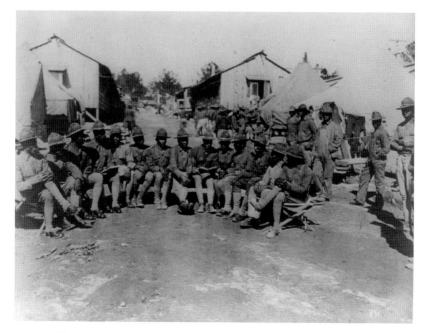

Fig. 15 Black soldier reading to boys who can't read. Camp Gordon, Ga., 1917–18

Although these young black men looked like soldiers their instructors had not given them live ammunition. They could aim but not fire their weapons because the War Department planned to employ them as support troops. When the Commander of Camp Jackson protested, however, the War Department relented and assigned the 371st to the newly created 93rd Division, made up of black draftees from Connecticut, the District of Columbia, Illinois, Maryland, Massachusetts, New York, Ohio, Tennessee, and South Carolina (Fig. 15). The 371st Regiment now received combat training which included "actual shooting on the range," along with bayonet and grenade drills under foreign instructors.[32]

Freddie Stowers, a farm worker from Shady Springs, South Carolina, was one of these black draftees. The grandson of a slave, Corporal Stowers was later killed on September 28, 1918, his regiment fighting alongside French soldiers of the 157th Division in the Champagne Marne sector. He died leading his company in an attack against a German machine gun position. Seventy-three years after his death

President George H. W. Bush posthumously awarded him the nation's highest honor for valor, the Medal of Honor. America's only black recipient of the Medal of Honor during the Great War is today interred in the Meuse-Argonne Cemetery, the country's largest overseas military cemetery.

There were, of course, few if any opportunities for support troops serving behind the front to receive recognition for their service. The Army viewed their work as essential but certainly not heroic. When the United States entered the war the Army recognized only one decoration, the Medal of Honor, which Congress had adopted in 1861. In January 1918 President Wilson authorized two new decorations, the Distinguished Service Cross and the Distinguished Service Medal. Later, in July, Congress established another decoration, the Silver Star. The Medal of Honor, Silver Star, and Distinguished Service Cross were designed to recognize men for extraordinary service in armed combat. Support troops only qualified for the Distinguished Service Medal which was awarded to "any person while serving in any capacity with the Army of the United States" who distinguished himself or herself "in especially meritorious service to the Government in a position of great responsibility." The last four words, "position of great responsibility," virtually eliminated enlisted men and junior officers in the SOS from consideration.

The Army's use of medals emphasized the divide between combat and support troops. The only recognition available to SOS enlisted men and junior officers was a gold chevron given to all who served overseas. As Harbord reminds us, "veterans in their reminiscences deal with blood and thunder rather than with handling freight and manipulating gantry cranes. The heroes suppose themselves to have been exclusively employed at the front."[33] There was, of course, an element of truth in this, especially when officers were involved. Harbord called his SOS command a "human salvage plant" for officers where "misfits" came after they had "tried out and failed at the front."[34] Conversely, many SOS officers, although they might be engineers or serving with forestry or railway troops, requested transfers to the front even though they had little or no training for combat.[35] Many enlisted men as well were disappointed with their role as support troops in the SOS.

Divisional support troops such as engineers and signalmen, who were commonly classified as noncombatants, were more likely to become casualties because of their presence near or on the battle front. Private Ermine Sordillo, F. Company, 2nd Battalion, 101st Engineer Regiment, 26th Division, had first attempted to enlist in the Italian Army at the outbreak of World War I, but he had been rejected by the Italian

Consulate. Still eager to join the fight, he volunteered for the First Corps of Cadets (thinking it was a machine gun "outfit") a few weeks after America's entry into the war, only to discover to his chagrin that he had joined an engineer regiment. To add insult to injury he found himself assigned to the kitchen as a cook. After persuading his top sergeant to transfer him from the kitchen, he later discovered that engineer work could be quite dangerous. The Germans shelled and gassed his company as he dug trenches and strung wire.[36] As a matter of fact, the first Americans to go into combat following Ludendorff's March 21 offensive were the 6th Engineers who were employed doing railway work near the British battle front on the Somme. They found themselves in the path of the rapidly advancing Germans. Issued rifles and under heavy bombardment and rifle and machine gun fire they fought back. Two companies, fifteen officers, and about 530 men held their position for four days before being relieved. Seventy-eight were killed, wounded, or captured.[37]

Those classified as noncombatants were obviously less likely to be killed by German shells and bullets, but the Spanish influenza pandemic during the last months of the war made no distinction between uniformed men, whether they were frontline soldiers or working behind the trenches, or even if they remained at home. Between September 1 and November 11, 1918 influenza killed 32,000 members of the AEF (23,000 stateside and 9,000 abroad), almost the same number who died from combat wounds.[38]

Support troops as well as advancing Doughboys with fixed bayonets deserved recognition. In a letter home, dated June 9, 1919, Marine Private Aitken, of the 67th Company, 5th Regiment, who saw action, argued that members of the SOS should be recognized for their part in

winning the War as well as those that were more lucky than they, and had the privilege of Banging away at the Hinies. You and any other broad minded people know that the troops that were fighting couldn't have possibly gotten along without the SOS at all, and that it wasn't the fault of those that were in the SOS that they were in that organization, in fact it wasn't the fault of any of us that we were picked for the fighting job.[39]

In future American conflicts, as the ratio of support troops to combat forces expanded dramatically, the Army increasingly recognized the service of noncombatants, so much so that eventually "medals recognizing heroic combat service were often lost among the multiple rows of ribbons worn by virtually every career member of the armed forces, the vast majority of whom had never been subjected to enemy fire."[40]

All had not gone well initially as the AEF's leadership struggled to build an effective supply system in Europe. The clogged arteries of the supply chain began at the ports where it took an average of fifteen days between the arrival and departure of cargo ships. Ports became congested and delivered supplies piled up on the docks, especially as the flow of men and supplies increased dramatically from May onward, with an average of some 9,500 men disembarking each day. If this did not change, and soon, an American army in Europe would be stillborn.

By granting Pershing powers never before held by an American field commander Wilson and Baker had unwittingly encouraged him to create a rival war department in Europe – a state of affairs that he readily admits in his war memoirs. Although the raising and equipping of an army intertwined with its effective deployment overseas, the General Staff in the War Department had been pushed into the background. Pershing took the position that the War Department "simply and without cavil" should support his "efforts to the fullest extent by promptly forwarding men and supplies as requested. The Secretary of War was completely in accord with this conception, but it was evident that the staff departments had not grasped it or else the disorganization and confusion were such that it could not be carried out."[41] In short, Pershing wanted his relationship with the General Staff to be that of a master to a servant. Prior to Peyton March's arrival in the War Department, Pershing had clearly occupied that position without protest from presiding chiefs of staff.

The Chief of Staff's role had evolved since the position had been created in 1903 but his precise role in the chain of command between the President and Secretary of War in Washington and Pershing in France remained murky. The President exercised his constitutional role as commander-in-chief through his Secretary of War. That much was clear. In fact Wilson gained an enormous increase in his wartime authority when he signed the Overman Bill in May 1918, giving him the authority to reorganize executive agencies such as the War Industries Board, National Labor Board, and Committee of Public Safety without consulting Congress. "Few statutes have in so few words surrendered so much; and none has vested more discretion in the President than was done by the Overman Act," suggests Paxson.[42]

But exactly what was the Chief of Staff's role in the chain of command? Was he just to act as a conduit for the exercise of civilian primacy (Wilson and Baker) or was he rightfully the supreme authority within the military realm? For example, did he have superior authority over field commanders in the command structure? Peyton March's relationship with Pershing was complicated by the instability that initially characterized the General Staff's wartime leadership with three men: Scott, Biddle, and Bliss, rotating as either Chief or Acting Chief of Staff until March made his presence felt.

Differing philosophies also played a role. When Scott stepped down as Chief of Staff and was replaced by Bliss he recommended in his last final report that (acting on behalf of the Secretary of War) "in all that concerns discipline, recruiting, instruction, intelligence, training, arming, equipping, mobilization, promotion, detail and selection of officers, the Chief of Staff should be the medium of recommendation to the Secretary and of execution for his orders. He should have ample authority for ... coordination of all activities of the military establishment."[43]

When Bliss subsequently became the US military representative on the Supreme War Council, he viewed himself as the "Assistant Chief of Staff to the Chief of Staff of the [American Expeditionary Forces]."[44] Bliss clearly recognized his awkward position. He and Pershing were America's ranking generals in Europe (both had four stars); and he was anxious to avoid any division with Pershing that the Allies might exploit, especially on such delicate issues as amalgamation. The officer recommended by Pershing to keep Bliss's chair warm while the latter was in Europe had been Major John Biddle, a friend of the AEF's commander-in-chief. When Biddle, as Acting Chief of Staff, quickly proved that he was not up to the task, Baker chose Major General March to replace him.

The son of a distinguished college professor, March excelled as both an athlete and student when he attended and graduated from Lafayette College in Pennsylvania where his father taught. As a senior, March told his classmates that his future plans included "Fighting Injuns." After completing class work he entered West Point and later served in the Spanish–American war where he demonstrated his courage under fire. Armed with a pistol he led a successful attack against an enemy blockhouse. While at West Point he had been a lance corporal in Pershing's Company A during the summer of 1885 and later shared an office with him when they served together on the General Staff in Washington.[45] Prior to leaving France for Washington, March paid a courtesy visit to General Headquarters. Following his visit, a member of Pershing's staff told his commander-in-chief that March was "going to cause you trouble." Pershing agreed but also acknowledged that March was "a capable officer."[46]

Both statements proved to be correct in spades. It would not be long before Pershing and March, two of America's strongest and most stubborn senior officers, were at sixes and sevens. Some of the issues, Sam Browne belts and promotions, were clearly not essential to the AEF's success. Named after the British officer who had designed it, the Sam Browne belt was a diagonal over-the-shoulder leather strap attached to a British officer's belt. Always immaculately attired, Pershing liked its look and ordered all AEF officers to purchase one (Fig. 16). Clearly not

Fig. 16 General Pershing; General March

needed to hold one's pants up, this belt became a symbol that separated AEF officers from their men, and, more importantly, from officers serving at home who were forbidden by regulations to wear this belt. Many stateside officers, holding responsible positions in the War Department or training troops for combat, consequently grew to detest this belt which many viewed as demeaning to their home service. Because of a growing leather shortage, March suggested that Pershing get rid of this superfluous belt but he refused to do so.[47]

March and Pershing's clash over promotions was more serious because of the bad blood that it created between them. Soon after arriving in the War Department, March asked Pershing for his recommendations for new brigadier and major generals. Pershing, who previously enjoyed a free hand over promotions, submitted a list of twenty-seven names, the exact number which had been requested. Pershing's criteria emphasized "strong and robust" officers, and he did not trust the War Department's judgment, which he suggests was "to appoint officers to the higher grades according to seniority with the intention of weeding out the inefficient later on."[48] This, he writes in his memoirs, resulted in many stateside officers being promoted "ahead of others in France whose experience and abilities had shown them especially qualified for promotion."[49] This was surely an oversimplification of the differences which emerged between General Headquarters and the General Staff. If Pershing continued to exercise total control over promotions and selected only those who served in France, it would effectively make him "the arbiter over the career of every officer in the army."[50] March took the position that he must view the army as a whole, and believed it essential to reward capable officers who performed critical war work on the domestic front.

Later, when the President appointed twenty-five brigadier generals, of which only seventeen were currently serving with the AEF, Pershing was shocked. He immediately fired off a cable (April 19, 1918) that requested that "confirmations be suspended until an additional list of deserving officers on duty here . . . can be submitted."[51] It was now March's turn to be offended. "The assumption by General Pershing that he could dictate to the President what nominations he should send to the Senate, and demand their withdrawal after the President had acted in the matter, passed the limit of forbearance."[52]

March chose not to show the President Pershing's intemperate cable. Instead he lectured the AEF's commander-in-chief: "The American Expeditionary Force is only a part of the American Army and whatever promotions to the grade of Major General and Brigadier General are necessary will be made by him [Secretary of War] from the entire Army."[53]

To Pershing's chagrin, March followed this prescription with the next promotion list issued in July which once again included recommendations from March as well as Pershing to the Secretary of War. March had asked Pershing to recommend six major generals and thirty-three brigadier generals. Once again some officers such as Dennis E. Nolan and Fox Conner recommended by Pershing had been denied promotion while others not recommended by him, Douglas MacArthur for example, had been elevated in rank. "The question of promotion," Pershing noted in his diary, "involves some transactions on the part of the Chief of Staff in Washington which I am afraid would not look well in the light of an honest investigation."[54]

Harbord, Pershing's staunch ally, especially felt that March's motives were suspect, accusing him of holding grudges from his days on the AEF's staff. In his view March had exceeded his authority as Chief of Staff. "All you wish from America is such Staff Service there as will insure you a steady flow of troops and supplies. You do not want there a Staff dealing with any phase of your business here." He also suggested that March's assumption that he was the senior officer in the army because he was Chief of Staff was "hallucination."[55]

Pershing actually needed little encouragement from Harbord to suspect that his command in Europe was being undermined by March and the War Department. In July he received an unwelcome proposal from the Secretary of War to send General George W. Goethals, the builder of the Panama Canal and a skilled administrator currently doing outstanding work as Director of the Purchase, Storage and Traffic Division, to France to assume control of the AEF's supply system. "The idea was that he would have coordinate authority with me and be in control of supplies from the source at home, thence across the Atlantic and up to the Zone of the Armies, and be directly under orders from Washington," Pershing notes in his memoirs.[56]

The origins of this proposal dated back to early June 1918 when Colonel House, concerned that Pershing's myriad responsibilities as commander-in-chief hampered his effectiveness, suggested to Wilson that Pershing should focus on being a fighting general. "What I have in mind to suggest to you is that Pershing be relieved from all responsibility except the training and fighting of our troops. All his requirements for equipping and maintaining these troops should be on other shoulders."[57]

When consulted by the President, Baker agreed that they had conferred heavy responsibilities, both military and political, upon Pershing when he had been chosen to lead the AEF. It seemed reasonable that he could be more effective if he focused exclusively on military operations.

Pershing, however, saw it differently, especially after Baker informed him that Goethals would not be his subordinate. He understandably did not want to give up direct control of his logistical support.

Wilson and Baker were not the only ones concerned about America's limited contribution to the Allied cause thus far. Jan Christian Smuts, the South African leader and member of the British War Cabinet, made an extraordinary suggestion to diminish Pershing's authority to Lloyd George on June 8. Smuts had an inflated view of his abilities as a general. The recent campaign he led in German East Africa in 1917 against von Lettow-Vorbeck had not lived up to its contemporary press clippings. Yet he suggested in a letter to the Prime Minister that he be appointed the "fighting commander" of American forces in Europe with Pershing being relegated to "all organizations in the rear." Smuts' argument was that although the AEF would become "a first class instrument of action" by late autumn it would be "without a reliable Higher Command. Pershing is very commonplace, without real war experience, and already overwhelmed by the initial difficulties of a job too big for him. It is also doubtful whether he will loyally co-operate with the Allied Higher Commands. He could not get together a first-class Staff either." If Pershing were not replaced, Smuts warned that "the American Army will not be used to the best advantage; and victory for us depends on squeezing the last ounce of proper use out of the American Army."[58] A more outrageous suggestion would be hard to imagine. Pershing and Wilson opposed integrating American soldiers into British divisions to keep them up to strength. One can easily guess their reaction if they had been aware of the suggestion that the AEF should be turned over to one of the British Empire's most avid and influential imperialists. Lloyd George wisely kept Smuts' proposal to himself.

American suspicions of British motives would also have been raised by discussions of future strategy by the British Empire's statesmen in London. On June 18 Sir Henry Wilson, who had replaced Sir William Robertson as CIGS, discussed future imperial strategy at a meeting of the Committee of Prime Ministers (which included the Dominion prime ministers). Pointer in hand, he stood before a large map of Europe and Asia. Concerned about the developing Turko-German threat in Asia, he told the imperial statesmen that

no military decision, as far as I can see, that we can get *here* now will settle the east. It is for that reason that I think that between the days when all anxiety is past, this autumn, and the time when we throw down the glove *here* for a final clinch, we ought to exploit the outside theaters as much as we can, so that at the Peace Conference we, the British anyhow, will not be so badly off.[59]

In sum, the British hoped to shift the burden of killing Germans on the Western Front to the Americans while they protected and expanded their eastern possessions.

In June Pershing was more convinced than ever that Germany would ultimately be defeated by the Americans. The Germans had recently concluded their fourth offensive of the year, during which American forces had joined the battle, first in an attack against the village of Cantigny and then at Château-Thierry where they assisted the French in blunting the German drive toward Paris. Germany's recent offensives had inflicted heavy losses on the Allied armies and Pershing believed, as he wrote House on June 19, that "the Allies are done for, and the only thing that will hold them (especially France) in the war will be the assurance that we have force enough to assume the initiative."[60] On this day Pershing asked the War Department to send him sixty-six divisions to increase the AEF's strength to 3 million men by May 1919 compared to the some 900,000 that he presently commanded.

A few days later, however, he dramatically upped the ante. On June 23 he met with Clemenceau and Foch at Chaumont. Having gained the understanding that his divisions fighting alongside the Allies would sooner rather than later be gathered under his command to create an independent army, he readily agreed to their request for 100 American divisions by July 1919, or more infantry divisions than the United States organized in World War II. One hundred US divisions equaled at least 200 European divisions, even more in 1918 with Allied and German divisions woefully under strength after months of hard fighting.

Pershing's request speaks volumes about the breakdown in communications between General Headquarters and the General Staff. Pershing made this commitment without referring to the General Staff whose responsibilities included training, supplying, and transporting the reinforcements he requested. To achieve his goal Pershing wanted the War Department to begin drafting 400,000 men per month. Additional men could be found – and Congress passed the necessary legislation in August – by extending the draft age limits from eighteen to forty-five. But existing training camps could not possibly accommodate this many men, so Pershing made the extraordinary suggestion that draftees be billeted in American homes.[61] Pershing clearly made his request for 100 divisions with little forethought. As he explains in his memoirs, "I did not think it possible, from our experience, that we could accomplish so much," and even 80 divisions "would probably overtax our facilities of transportation and supply ... I was willing to ask for the greater numbers, feeling, however, that the War Department would do wonders if it could carry out even the 66-division plan."[62]

Among many unresolved questions between the General Staff in the War Department and the AEF General Staff was the required number of men to fulfill Pershing's request for 100 divisions. A figure could not be arrived at by simply multiplying 28,000 (the approximate size of a US division) by 100. Replacements, SOS personnel, corps, and army troops also had to be included. Clemenceau thought that 100 divisions equaled 4,160,000 men, which was close to the General Staff's estimates, while Bliss at the Supreme War Council thought in terms of only 3,375,000 men. Pershing, on the other hand, apparently assumed that his request was for around 5 million men, which would have dwarfed the existing Allied forces on the Western Front.[63]

Whatever their number Pershing's reinforcements had to be equipped and fed. Even the eighty-division program, which the War Department eventually embraced, placed the US economy under enormous strain. The War Industries Board (WIB), established in July 1917, had not come close to matching the AEF's escalating military requirements with what US industry could actually provide. In fact, the WIB had spent its first nine months fighting for its political survival. Finally, in March 1918, the White House placed the WIB on a firmer footing with a new leader, Bernard Baruch, who reported directly to the President. Responsible for the production of some 30,000 different items, however, the WIB failed to meet the AEF's requirements. As Geoffrey Perret rightly notes: "Under the most favorable circumstances it would have taken about two years to convert the economy to full war production."[64]

The War Department had discovered, in the words of Chief of Staff March, that "an army fights and moves on steel, not on its stomach." In late July Wilson sent a letter to all of the agencies involved in war production that emphasized that the nation's steel requirements for the next six months would be at least 3.5 million tons more than US mills were capable of producing. Consumer products from baby carriages to automobiles had to be drastically reduced from 1917 levels. Tin toys for children, metal caskets for the dead, and steel stiffening for corsets were forbidden. Even the production of farm implements had to be cut. The Quartermaster Corps purchased 17 million woolen trousers and breeches, 22,198,000 flannel shirts, and 26,423,000 shoes prior to the Armistice. The boots furnished to Doughboys were of such poor quality that they lasted only a few weeks in combat. To clothe the force contemplated by the War Department, the entire wool production in 1918 and 1919 would be required. To save wool the War Department removed some pockets from army coats and limited chevrons to indicate rank to the right arm.[65] An exasperated March wrote Bliss that the problem alone of getting wool for woolen uniforms for such a command in Europe is practically prohibitive. We have commandeered the entire wool supply of the United States and civilians will have to wear shoddy during the coming winter in order to put woolen clothing on the backs of the men in the trenches even if we go through with a lesser program.[66]

With sacrifice the United States might eventually produce the supplies necessary to support additional divisions. But it would not have the required cargo tonnage in 1918 to sustain eighty, much less 100, divisions in Europe. On July 12, Goethals furnished March with figures which suggested that the available cargo tonnage could sustain sixty divisions but that a 100-division program would exceed America's shipping capacity by over 15 million tons.[67] Tonnage requirements could be cut by reducing supply from fifty pounds a man to thirty pounds, and indeed they were, but this was not sustainable. Moreover, there were not nearly enough ships' berths in France available for US cargo ships to provide for a 100-division program.[68]

March informed Pershing on July 5 that he could not commit to a fixed number of divisions until the General Staff had made a careful study. "I intend to raise a certain number of divisions each month based upon the program determined upon for the year and regardless of the number which will finally be determined upon as what is physically possible to do."[69] Having completed its study the General Staff told March they could assuredly ship sixty and perhaps even eighty divisions in the required time. March then recommended that the eighty-division program be attempted and Wilson gave his approval. March's goal of raising eighty divisions which included all supply, auxiliary, and depot units, however, still did not put him on the same page with Pershing. When Pershing's staff referred to the eighty-division program it thought in terms of eighty *combat* divisions plus sixteen *depot* divisions, or some 1,255,000 men above the General Staff's estimates.[70]

Differences over promotions, the size of the AEF, and the effective management of the SOS reflected a dysfunctional command structure. In August 1918, Pershing sought to gain the upper hand when he wrote Baker suggesting that March be replaced by someone from his staff to improve the working relationship between the War Department and the AEF. After the war when March learned of Pershing's machination he accused him of wanting "a rubber stamp for Chief of Staff at home, so he could be entirely independent of any supervision or control."[71]

Unrelated to Pershing's letter, March also attempted to assert his authority over Pershing by issuing General Orders No. 80 which asserted: "The Chief of the General Staff is the immediate advisor of the Secretary of War on all matters relating to the Military Establishment, and is charged by the Secretary of War with the planning development, and execution of the Army program."[72] Without Baker's support, however, this General Order did not as he wished establish him as the senior uniformed officer in the Army. The feud between March and Pershing continued.

Pressure from the War Department in the form of attempting to appoint Goethals to run the SOS did lead to improvements in the AEF's supply system. Determined to protect his supply lines from outside interference, Pershing turned to one of his closest and most loyal friends. On July 27, 1918 he appointed Harbord to Commanding General, SOS. "I am his man," Harbord once remarked; "he can send me to Hell if he wants to."[73] Harbord replaced Major General Francis J. Kernan, who had been preceded in turn by two other officers, Mason B. Patrick and Robert M. Blatchford.

On the day that he appointed Harbord, Pershing made it clear to Baker in a confidential cable that he was determined to retain control of his lines of communication. He argued that his supply system included

transportation up to the trenches and is intimately interwoven with our whole organization. The whole must remain absolutely under one head. Any division of responsibility or coordinate control in any sense would be fatal. The man who fights the armies must control their supply through subordinates responsible to him alone. The responsibility is then fixed and the possibility of conflicting authority avoided. This military principle is vital and cannot be violated without inviting failure.[74]

In contrast to his predecessor Kernan, who was inclined to administer the supply system from his desk and seldom ventured beyond Tours in an auto, Harbord took a hands-on approach. He and Pershing immediately departed on a tour of ports, railroads, and storehouses in Pershing's special and well-equipped train with its own kitchen and dining room manned by black soldiers with Pullman experience. At Bordeaux they found the main storage plant half completed and supplies stacked on the docks: so much so that engineers feared that their weight might cause the wharves to side-slip into the river. Elsewhere, however, Pershing and Harbord observed American organization at its best, especially at the great US supply depot at Greve. During their inspection of this enormous supply depot in the Intermediate Zone, a telegram arrived at 8:15 a.m. with an order for

exactly 4,596 tons of supplies, including 1,250,000 cans of tomatoes, 1 million pounds of sugar, 600,000 cans of corned beef, 750,000 pounds of tinned hash, and 159,000 pounds of dry beans. At 6:15 o'clock in the evening or just ten hours later, this colossal requisition which required 457 cars for transports, was loaded and on its way to the advance depot.[75]

Unlike Kernan, Harbord did not view the administration of his far-flung organization as a desk job. As he bluntly put it, "Well-written orders and concise endorsements will not do it."[76] He asked for and got a train from the French railway authorities, equipping it with dining and sleeping quarters (the better to travel at night), a communications car with telegraph and telephone which could be connected at any station, and a box car for two automobiles. During his first 100 days of command Harbord spent fifty-five nights aboard his special train.

On his inspection tour with Harbord, Pershing attempted to inspire members of the SOS to work harder. He had concluded that many members of the SOS were unenthusiastic because they had been given the impression that "they were not exactly doing the work of soldiers."[77] This proved especially true for black stevedores who unloaded vital supplies from cargo ships arriving from America. Pershing's solution was to suggest that especially productive stevedores be rewarded by being sent to the front lines. This apparently did not always resonate with some members of his audience. Following one of his impromptu speeches, Pershing's aid, Colonel Carl Boyd, asked one of the stevedores what he thought of Pershing's suggestion. After some hesitation, the stevedore responded that "he hoped the Colonel would please tell the General that he was very well satisfied where he was."[78]

This particular stevedore might not have been excited by Pershing's reward system, but he almost certainly responded in a positive way to Harbord's quite different approach. The new head of the SOS started a competition: "The Race to Berlin." He promised that the winning company would be the first to embark for Hoboken at the war's end. Moreover, the winning company would be given a leave of absence and a vacation on the Mediterranean as soon as the competition was over. Army bands played ragtime music as stevedores engaged in inter-squad and inter-company competition unloading cargo. Harbord claims that the tonnage offloaded during this competition increased by 20 percent.[79] But what if supplies being shipped could not keep up with the rapidly expanding AEF?

Although Pershing retained control of his supply lines and Harbord made improvements, only the unexpected end of the fighting in November prevented a major breakdown in both shipping and the transport of essential supplies from the United States to the battlefield. GHQ provided figures in its final report that underlined the widening gap between AEF requirement and supplies arriving at the French ports (Table 5). After Pershing launched his Meuse-Argonne offensive on September 26, his frontline logistics immediately floundered. "Whether because of incompetence or inexperience or both," Smythe graphically

Table 5 *American Expeditionary Force orders and US supplies arriving at French ports*

Month	Tons cabled for by AEF	Tons unloaded in France from United States
August 1918	700,527	511,261
September 1918	869,438	530,018
October 1918	1,022,135	623,689

Source: "Chronological review of important activities of G-1," Department of the Army, Historical Division, *United States Army in the World War, 1917–1918*, 17 vols. (Washington, DC: Government Printing Office, 1948), pt. 1, vol. 12, p. 117.

suggests, "the First Army was wallowing in an unbelievable logistical snarl. It was as if someone had taken the army's intestines out and dumped them all over the table."[80] On October 3, Pershing sent an alarmist cable to the War Department: "Unless supplies are furnished when and as called for, our armies will cease to operate."[81]

No one was more aware of the near collapse of the flow of supplies from the ports to the battlefield than Harbord, who was inclined to blame SOS manpower shortages rather than inexperience magnified by the AEF's super-sized divisions which were difficult to transport and sustain, especially during the inevitable chaos of a major battle.[82] Harbord and Pershing blamed the War Department for deficiencies in the AEF's supply chain. The reality was that there was not enough tonnage available to the War Department to ship hundreds of thousands of soldiers to France and sustain them with all of the paraphernalia required for modern industrialized warfare, which ranged from sandbags for trench warfare to Sam Browne belts for officers to ambulances for the wounded. On October 27, Goethals noted in his diary: "We based our program of 80 divisions overseas by July next on certain estimates of the shipping Board, but this body has fallen down most woefully and there seems no chance of gaining enough impetus to make their monthly output, let alone the existing deficiency. I shouldn't be surprised to see the whole shipping situation collapse."[83] Goethals' gloomy assessment is yet another example of how the acceptance of the eighty-division program undercut all previous planning and made an orderly military expansion difficult if not impossible.

The War Department and AEF General Staff continued to bicker over the eighty-division program which the War Department insisted include both combat and base divisions. By including an additional sixteen-depot division, however, Pershing's staff inflated the War Department's eighty-division program by 1,130,000 men and sixteen divisions, making a total of ninety-six divisions.[84] Pershing believed that his supply system was on the verge of collapse; yet he expected the War Department to ship and supply over 3 million soldiers during the next nine months to provide him with a force of 4,766,944 men by July 1, 1919.[85]

On October 10 March attempted to bring Pershing down to earth by firmly telling him that he was asking for the impossible: The "maximum number of Class A men made available by the changes in the draft law is estimated at 2,300,000, which will permit us to have on July 1, 1919 an army of 4,850,000 men, of which 3,360,000 men will be in France and the remainder in America or insular possessions and Siberia."[86] The War Department to its surprise had discovered, according to March, "that the number of men who were qualified physically and in every other way to fight for their country was, relatively, surprisingly small." If the war had lasted into 1919 it would have been necessary to recruit men who had been previously deferred because of essential work. And outfitting them would have placed considerable strain as well on the economy. In 1918, for example, the Army had had to purchase twice as many blankets and more woolen socks and stockings for its use than the country usually produced in a year.[87]

By failing to establish a definite chain of command the President and his Secretary of War must bear much of the responsibility for the misunderstandings that arose between March and Pershing. Once again Wilson, abetted by Baker, demonstrated his flaws as the constitutional commander-in-chief. Both Baker and Wilson encouraged Pershing to develop what amounted to a separate war department in France and then failed to establish a clear chain of command between the War Department and GHQ which greatly complicated orderly planning. In a devastating critique of Wilson and Baker's role during the March–Pershing feud, Brian Neumann notes: "Civilian control over the military is a core American principle, and a definite chain of command is a military axiom. Both were betrayed by officials at the highest levels of American government during the First World War, and a victorious outcome cannot be allowed to countermand the seriousness of the offense."[88]

The "seriousness" of their "offense" would have been plain for all to see if the war, as almost everyone expected, had continued into 1919. Brigadier General Hugh Johnson, the Director of Purchase and Supply, later claimed that "it is my firm conviction, supported by accurate information and by the opinions of other men, that had the war continued two months longer there would have been a serious disaster in the supply of our Army. I think it was the finger of God that saved this government from the most terrible cataclysm that ever overtook the nation."[89]

Harbord expressed very similar views when he too later wrote his account of the war.

With twenty-five per cent of the necessary transportation in France, with a prospect of increasing troop arrivals and double the cargo to be discharged within thirty days – General Pershing, in what proved to be the final struggle of the World War, played our whole military fortune on khaki to win, before the supply crisis that was imminent should have left his Armies stranded for lack of a thousand things necessary to any further movement. He won – but at what risk.[90]

12   Uncertain times

No previous offensive since the beginning of trench warfare on the Western Front had achieved the initial success of Operation "Michael." In a single day the Germans along a broad front ruptured British defenses and advanced across open countryside, killing 7,000 British soldiers and capturing another 20,000. Many British units took flight without putting up much of a fight. In two days, German "mobile" and "attack" divisions advanced an incredible forty miles behind the Somme. William II congratulated the troops and ordered schools closed to celebrate a great victory. He also told his entourage as they drank champagne that "if an English delegation came to sue for peace it must kneel before the German standard for it was a question here of a victory of the monarchy over democracy."[1]

On March 25 Major General Oliver Nugent, commander of the Ulster division, drew a vivid picture of the collapse of his front for his wife:

> It is all a ghastly nightmare. I cannot credit that it is only 5 days ago that we were holding the trenches just in front of St Quentin ... My men have had no food, some of them for 2 and 3 days. They have had no sleep for 5 nights. They are absolutely beat ... This is truly Armageddon. Unless we can finally stop the German attack soon, I fear it will be the end ... I had to go up to the front and it was a horrible scene of confusion. French and British retiring, guns, wagons, horses and men in most inexplicable confusion, a roar of shelling and machine guns and the very heaviest kind of German shells bursting all round us.[2]

Pershing concluded that the German breakthrough vindicated his views on open warfare. "In this sort of warfare the British were seriously handicapped on account of their long adherence to stabilized warfare," he writes in his memoirs. "Their officers said that when the men had to leave the trenches they acted as though something were radically wrong in that there was not another trench somewhere for them to get into." It was not that simple. Trench warfare indeed played a role in the demoralization of the British Fifth Army, but it was not what Pershing imagined. British infantry had suffered heavy losses in often atrocious conditions at Passchendaele during Haig's dogged but unsuccessful

199

attempt to reach the Belgian coast during the fall of 1917. Consequently, British morale was low. In truth, as Harris contends, "it is doubtful whether any troops in the world could have stood their ground for long under the weight of fire against the weight of numbers on an imperfectly fortified front, supported by an inadequate infrastructure."[3]

Momentarily it appeared that Ludendorff's offensive would drive a wedge between the French and British forces, with the British falling back to defend the Channel ports while the French defended their capital. German long-range guns shelled Paris to general panic. Pershing witnessed what he described as "terror-stricken crowds" in Parisian train stations fleeing from villages being threatened by the German advance.[4] The French commander-in-chief Pétain attempted to put up a brave front and sent his armies the following message: "Hold your ground! Stand firm! Our (American) comrades are arriving. All together you will throw yourselves upon the invader ... The fate of France hangs in the balance."[5]

The same might be true for the United States. A dispatch published in the *New York Tribune* by Ralph Block put the American people on notice of the global consequences of a German victory:

Victory for Germany in France, a drive to Paris and the Channel ports would put France out of the war. It would lead dangerously close to British submission to German terms, and would put up to America the sudden question of fighting alone or making peace in order to prepare for Germany's attack on the Monroe Doctrine in South America.[6]

American soldiers, however, seemed destined to be onlookers during what appeared to be the decisive moment of the war. In private, Pétain told Clemenceau on March 25: "The Germans will defeat the English in open country; after that they will defeat us."[7] If his prophecy became reality American units scattered throughout France were destined to become German POWs.

The 1st Division had been the first US division to arrive in France. This was one of several "firsts." It was the first to complete its training schedule abroad with a French division, the first to take its place in the trenches, and the first to kill Germans. Although Regular Army, the Big Red One had been brought up to strength with many recruits who had just joined the army. They had difficulty remembering to salute their officers, much less use their weapons. When its commander, Major General William Sibert, reviewed the advanced training schedule given him by the commander of the crack French 47th Infantry Division, he responded with the following admission:

Over fifty percent of the soldiers in the division are recruits almost entirely without training. Practically all of the officers below the grade of captain have been appointed less than six months ... it is essential that the training of the troops shall be limited for the next four weeks, at least, to elementary work and the development of a proper military disciplinary spirit.[8]

Fortunately the upper ranks of the 1st Division were dominated by professional soldiers.

An especially severe winter had hampered the division's training. Major General Bullard provides a vivid description of five days of trench maneuvers by brigade and division in early January. "They began with rain, which changed into sleet and snow and slush, and lasted the entire five days without break," he writes. "Men stood in the trenches and out in the open over shoe-tops in mud and snow and water; with the snow four or five inches deep upon the open ground; and from start to finish were never clear of these hardships. Ears, fingers, and noses were frozen; horses fell from cold and exhaustion, some dying upon the field." In Bullard's view these five days constituted "the fiercest strain to which I ever saw troops subjected outside of the hardest battles."[9]

It would be over three months before the 1st Division received training sufficient to allow it to occupy a quiet sector of the front lines near Sommerville under the instruction of the French 18th Infantry. On October 23, 1917 American artillerymen fired their first shot of the war at 6:10 a.m. (This French artillery piece was subsequently shipped to the United States and used in patriotic parades.) Two days later Lieutenant De Vere H. Harden of the Signal Corps became the first American officer to be wounded when a German shell struck his dugout. On November 2–3, a German raid by soldiers from the 7th Bavarian Landwehr regiment killed three and wounded five Americans. Twelve were taken prisoner. In late November the 1st Division left its trenches for additional training that emphasized both trench and open warfare. It returned to the trenches near Seicheprey in mid-January.[10]

The 2nd Division, another Regular Army division, similarly included many men who were soldiers in name only. As many as 90 percent of the men in some units had served less than a year. Most of its superior officers, however, were professional soldiers. This division had been created in France and had the distinction of including a Marine Brigade. Its training overseas had been interrupted by pick and shovel work on lines of communication and the progressive arrival of units from the United States. Serious training under French tutelage did not really begin until mid-January and was similarly hampered by one of the worst winters in French history. In mid-March it had joined French units in the trenches.[11]

The War Department had created the 26th Division from National Guard units throughout New England in August 1917. Called the

"Yankee" Division it was the first National Guard Division to be sent to Europe. A goodly number of its members had served on the Mexican border in 1916. It arrived in France in November 1917 to begin training under French direction.

The War Department assigned some regular officers to the division but most of its officers were Guardsmen. These former part-time soldiers were sometimes dismissed by Regulars as "Boy Scouts," although many of them could trace their warrior lineage back to the American Revolution. Their commander, Major General Clarence R. Edwards, came in for severe criticism from Pershing and his staff for his perceived leadership failures. To his credit, however, Edwards emphasized artillery and machine guns over the rifle and bayonet. "Although Edwards may have struggled to adequately train his unit to employ all its firepower," notes Grotelueschen, "he certainly understood its importance."[12] In early February his division entered a quiet sector of the trenches in the Chemin des Dames area near Soissons.

This sector may have been "quiet" but conditions in these trenches differed little from other sectors of the front. Soldiers had to combat lice, flooded trenches when it rained and freezing temperatures in the winter, and rats the size of kittens. Trench raids, gas attacks, and sniper fire constantly kept soldiers on edge. And then there were the smells that many soldiers never forgot: decaying flesh, unwashed soldiers, and human excrement and urine from the trench latrines.

Lieutenant Kenneth E. Walser, 101st Field Artillery, 26th Division, served for a few weeks as a liaison officer with the infantry. From a forward observation post, on February 27, he wrote his family from "an old Boche 'pillbox' with a meter of very good concrete around, except in one place where a French shell cracked the roof and the rain is dripping on my bed." His family had recently suggested that they mail him a copy of a popular potboiler by an English soldier, Coningsby Dawson, which romanticized trench warfare. Walser was not interested, commenting that he laughed until he

cried when you said you were going to send me *The Glory of the Trenches*, for I was standing up to my knees in the stickiest mud that ever existed, watching a bombardment to our left and reading your letter at the same time. Before me, the ground was a mass of shell holes and debris of battle and beside me were the remains of a Boche ... stuck out of the side of the trench. *The Glory of the Trenches* – it is not a martial glory that is evident here.[13]

Walser, as did many other soldiers, found life in the trenches quite depressing. As he wrote in his diary:

Such desolation I have never seen. Everything that is used in war, strewn over the landscape, piles of shells[,] hand grenades, overcoats, lots of pitiful helmets with

Fig. 17 American soldiers in trenches, France, 1918: USASC #23056 (near Verdun)

great jagged holes through the top-wire ... there are dugouts here which have never been cleared out, and I shudder to think what it will be next spring. It is bad enough to walk out now after lunch, and run across a skull with the flesh and hair still on it.[14]

In reality, however, with many American divisions arriving in Europe during the last months of the war, most American soldiers were introduced into combat without spending much if any time occupying trenches (Fig. 17). And then only in quiet sectors. Walser's observation post was actually on one of these relatively quiet French fronts where the exchange of artillery shells constituted the most serious military activity. This "live and let live system" on sectors of the French front, which was not uncommon on quiet sectors, initially puzzled the American soldiers when they occupied trenches. These unofficial truces, for example, frequently included "breakfast truces" when the guns fell silent on both sides of the front. With German and Allied troops experiencing common discomforts, it was perhaps not surprising that mutual empathy inevitably arose.[15]

Many officers, eager to instill aggressive behavior in their men, encouraged trench raids to counteract these tacit truces. For example, Bullard issued the following instructions to his men on February 5, 1918:

1. There are no orders which require us to wait for the enemy to fire on us before we fire on him; do not wait for him to fire first. Be active all over no-man's-land; do not leave its control to the enemy.

2. Front line commanders will immediately locate and report all places where there is a favorable opportunity for strong ambushes and for raids on the enemy's line and advance posts.[16]

Other commanders followed Bullard's lead. Despite his efforts, Bullard eventually concluded that more than a few weeks in the trenches inevitably robbed his men of their "offensive spirit."[17]

On February 23 soldiers from the 101st Infantry, 26th Division, undertook what many consider the first successful American trench raid, capturing twenty-four men, including two officers. Scheduled to begin a month of open-warfare training, the last elements of this division left the trenches on March 21. By April 3, however, the 26th Division was back at the front, occupying trenches on the southern face of the Saint-Mihiel salient which had previously been held by the US 1st Division as well as the French 10th Colonial Division.[18] In this sector the Germans held the high ground and the Americans occupied poorly drained trenches with mud three feet deep in places. The French had also organized their defenses on the principle of "defense in depth," which involved vulnerable outposts in front of the main line of defense. On April 10 and 12 the Germans welcomed the 26th Division to their front by launching two raids against the 104th Infantry which acquitted itself quite well, taking forty prisoners and losing only one of its own.[19]

During the following days the Germans brought up assault troops called *Stosstruppen* or "stormtroopers." Armed with flame throwers, grenades, and automatic weapons, these specially trained soldiers had been instructed to bypass strong points and move forward rapidly. At approximately 5 a.m. on April 20, following a "box-barrage" of high-explosive shells designed to prevent defenders from retreating and support troops from coming to their assistance,[20] almost 3,000 enemy troops emerged from the fog and fell upon Companies C and D, 1st Battalion of the 102nd Infantry, in the vicinity of the town of Seicheprey. As bitter and often hand-to-hand combat continued throughout the day, US reinforcement joined the fray. The next day the Germans withdrew to their former trenches. Losses had been heavy on both sides, with American casualties numbering 81 killed, 187 wounded, 214 gassed, and 187 missing or prisoners, or a total of 669 casualties, by far the most costly battle yet fought by the Americans.[21]

Ludendorff was generally dismissive of the Americans after their first serious encounter with the German Army, writing in his memoirs that "the individual American fought well, but our success had, nevertheless, been easy."[22] Although the Guardsmen had fought bravely at Seicheprey (as this melee became known), Pershing seems to have agreed with Ludendorff's analysis. His concern was no doubt magnified by his acute sensitivity to any performance by his inexperienced troops that might be used to justify amalgamation with the veteran French and British armies. Apparently not understanding the current French (and German) practice of defense in depth, he criticized the disposition of US troops around Seicheprey in a strongly worded memorandum dated April 30, 1918. He also expressed dismay that American troops sat "quietly in trenches during a heavy fog" and allowed "a surprise attack to be sprung" upon them. This "inexcusable" conduct, he emphasized, was not going to be "tolerated."[23]

Pershing's position was quite unfair to both the men and officers of the 26th Division. The 102nd Infantry had indeed suffered heavy losses, but two of its companies had fought valiantly against a force six times its size that included the units of the feared *Stosstruppen*. The American press trumpeted Seicheprey as an American success. "For the first time the Germans have met the Americans in serious fighting," reported one American war correspondent, "and, as the French say, 'they have broken their noses.'"[24] As Michael Shay suggests, "Pershing should have touted it as a victory and moved on."[25]

The fourth "pioneer" division was a composite division made up of Guardsmen from twenty-six states, the 42nd Division. Activated on November 1, 1917 at Camp Mills, New York, the Rainbow Division shipped off to France in October and November, its last units arriving on December 3, 1917. The division (less its artillery) began its training under French tutelage in the Vaucouleurs Area.

In a letter home dated November 23, 1917 Private Sam Ross, a member of a machine gun company, 165th Infantry Regiment, described his new environment. His "place" was a town located near the front where he could "hear the big guns all the time." He and twenty-three other "Yanks" were billeted in a house which at first "looked rotten but after a little work it was fine, a fireplace and everything and it looks better every hour." He quickly became acquainted with the locals and their customs. "Each French town has a place for washing, a building especially for that purpose, and you only wash there, so now you see fourteen or fifteen soldiers and a few

French women washing and borrowing soap, the men trying to speak French and the women English."[26]

American emphasis on hygiene surprised many French civilians, especially when it came to their manure piles scattered throughout a village. Trouble quickly arose when the Americans attempted to remove them. "They are damned touchy about their manure," Major Leland Beekman Garretson, 314th, later 315th, Machine Gun Battalion, 80th Division, noted in his diary. "You know you can engineer a fairly active 'affaire' with a Frenchman's wife with very little risk, and if you can beat him in a bargain, he is not a bad sport, but if you cut down one of his trees, or fuss with his manure pile he takes on something awful."[27]

Having completed its training the 42nd Division on February 21 was attached to the French 7th Army Corps at the front in the Luneville sector. Similar to the other "pioneer" divisions it received little open-warfare training in division or even brigade maneuvers and was handicapped by equipment shortages. Lieutenant Colonel Pierpont L. Stackpole, the aide to Major General (later Lieutenant General) Hunter Liggett, noted in his diary on January 30: The 42nd Division "is short of transportation and has only fifty trucks against the three hundred which it should have. Major General [Charles T.] Menoher, the division's commander[,] has converted about fifty medical department Ford trucks into supply trucks by cutting off the back of the bodies, which leaves them with a carrying capacity of eight hundred pounds without straining the springs." Stackpole also took note of soldiers' footwear. "Some had on the old issue light shoe, and the new issue shoes seemed run down at the heels or over on the side or to be too light in the sole."[28]

Accompanying Major General Menoher, Stackpole observed Alabamians (168th Infantry) in the Rainbow Division undergoing French training to combat chemical warfare:

Practice in gas discipline was conducted by lining up one-half a company thirty-five yards away from the other half and at a signal one side would run to the other, mimicking rolling gas and estimated to reach the waiting side in six seconds. The journey took about eight seconds, and those whose masks were not adjusted in this time were "gassed." The Alabamians were a rather seedy looking crowd, though alert in the drill.[29]

When it is recalled that the War Department had no organized divisions when the country went to war, or modern weapons with which to equip them or ships to transport them to Europe in a timely fashion, it represented a considerable achievement to have four divisions in Europe in various stages of readiness when Ludendorff launched Operation

"Michael." This powerful German offensive in March now threatened to split the Anglo-French armies and appeared to make irrelevant future AEF plans. If the United States did not provide all possible assistance to their allies in 1918 there might not be a 1919 campaign.

With the Anglo-French military alliance in jeopardy the political leaders, Raymond Poincaré, the French President, Clemenceau, and Milner, held an emergency session at Doullens on March 26 with Foch, Pétain, Haig, and Sir Henry Wilson, who had replaced Robertson as CIGS. Determined to keep British communications from falling to the Germans, Milner proposed that Foch coordinate operations in the Amiens sector to preserve the vital link between the British and French armies.

At Doullens Haig wanted to go even further and gained approval for Foch being given coordinating authority for British and French forces on the Western Front, which would make him in some respects the de facto commander-in-chief.[30] No US forces had yet joined the battle and with an independent US force in the distant future no reference was made of American forces; nor was Pershing consulted.

On the following day, March 27, the American liaison officer at Pétain's headquarters cabled Pershing that "the British and French flanks joined."[31] It now seemed likely that the Allies would survive this mighty German offensive. But this might only be a respite, and the Permanent Military Representatives at Versailles, which included Bliss, issued Joint Note No. 18, which stated: "It is highly desirable that the American Government should assist the Allied Armies as soon as possible by permitting in principle the temporary service of American units in Allied Army corps and divisions." The important qualification was added that "such reinforcements must however be obtained from other units than those American divisions which are now operating with the French, and the units so temporarily employed must eventually be returned to the American army." Both Bliss and Baker, who was in Europe at the time, also made it clear that this was a temporary measure and must not interfere with the creation of an independent American force. Both were determined, as Bliss emphasized, that the United States would not become "a recruiting ground to fill up the ranks of the British and French armies."[32] Some British and French leaders, however, dared to hope that they had finally won over the American government to amalgamation. As one British newspaper proclaimed: "In plain English the Americans will be available as drafts to fill up the gaps in French and British units."[33]

On March 28, Pershing visited a small farm house at Clermont-sur-Oise where he found Clemenceau, Foch, and Pétain anxiously studying a map. After the others left the room to allow Foch and Pershing to meet privately, the American commander-in-chief became quite emotional. In French, he proclaimed:

I have come to tell you that the American people would consider it a great honor for our troops to be engaged in the present battle. I ask you for this in their name and my own.

At this moment there are no other questions but of fighting.

Infantry, artillery, aviation, all that we have are yours; use them as you wish. More will come, in numbers equal to requirements.

I have come especially to tell you that the American people will be proud to take part in the greatest battle of history.[34]

An emotional Foch took Pershing by the arm and escorted him outside where the others were waiting, asking him to repeat his declarations. He did and the next day his words of support appeared in newspapers across France.

Pershing's encouraging words meant little for the present. Pétain questioned the combat readiness of the American divisions but he welcomed the chance to substitute American divisions in quiet sectors for veteran French divisions which could be deployed north of the Oise River to contest the German advance. Subsequently, the 26th Division on April 3 relieved the 1st Division on a relatively quiet front near Seicheprey. The 1st Division then engaged in additional training before returning to the front near the village of Cantigny. The 2nd Division, which had begun its second phase of trench training with French units in mid-March, just north of Saint-Mihiel, relieved a French division deployed to stop the German advance. On March 31 the 42nd Division arrived in the Baccarat sector to relieve the French 123rd Division which was being dispatched elsewhere to stem the tide of the German offensive.[35]

The AEF's strength, which included a great many support troops, now totaled approximately 300,000 men, with three divisions occupying quiet sectors of the front. Consequently, none of these divisions played any role in contesting the German drive.[36] In his memoirs Pershing expresses disappointment that Pétain did not immediately "put into battle" his available US divisions.[37] Given their state of readiness, however, it would have been premature.

On April 3 Pershing and Bliss attended a meeting of the Supreme War Council at Beauvais. The crisis atmosphere that pervaded the Doullens meeting had abated. On March 28 the British had repulsed the second phase of Operation "Michael," forcing this great German offensive to grind to a halt. The French and especially the British, however, had suffered heavy casualties in blunting this German drive.[38] Haig had committed forty-eight of his fifty-six divisions and Pétain had eventually sent forty divisions north and extended his front some ninety kilometers which included the south bank of the Oise.[39]

The Beauvais meeting enhanced Foch's position by granting him control of the "strategical direction of military operations." Although not consulted earlier when Foch had been granted "coordinating authority," Bliss and Pershing enthusiastically supported enhancing the French general's powers. Pershing even read a short memorandum that proposed elevating him to supreme commander.

The French and British later agreed to confer upon Foch the official title of "General-in-Chief of the Allied Armies in France" and extended his powers of coordination to the Italian front.[40] Lloyd George's government insisted on this precise wording because it had earlier assured Parliament that General Foch would not be appointed commander-in-chief or Generalissimo of the Allied forces.[41] Whatever his formal title, the differences between general-in-chief and commander-in-chief were soon blurred. Foch's powers, however, should not be exaggerated. The Frenchman had no Allied Joint Chiefs of Staff as General Dwight Eisenhower did during World War II. Instead he relied on his own small staff. Each national commander-in-chief also retained tactical control of his troops and reserved the right to appeal to his government if he disagreed with any of Foch's directives. Foch consequently often assumed the role of a coordinator or persuader-in-chief rather than that of a true commander-in-chief. It has been suggested that his "role was to inspire and to encourage, just as a school principal imparts an ethos on a school or college and a CEO imparts an ethos to a company."[42]

When the original draft establishing Foch's authority neglected to mention the US Army, Pershing raised objections. When Pétain pointed out the obvious – no US Army existed to be coordinated – Pershing responded: "There may not be an American army in force functioning now but there soon will be, and I want this resolution to apply to it when it becomes a fact."[43] Pershing, of course, wanted recognition given to the independent American army he would soon create. What he did not realize at the time was that the creation of an Allied general-in-chief in combination with the recently created Supreme War Council gave the Allies a mechanism through which to pressure both him and President Wilson on such questions as military intervention in Russia and amalgamation.

If Allied leaders had their way, the creation of an independent US force in Europe would occur, if at all, in the distant future. American reinforcements never seemed more urgent when the Germans launched a second major offensive in April on the river Lys. Originally called "St. George" it was renamed "Georgette" when Ludendorff was forced to use both "trench" divisions as well as "attack" divisions. This time Ludendorff focused on a twenty-mile section of the British front in Flanders.

Once again the *OHL* had no fixed objectives once a breakthrough was achieved. As Ludendorff informed the Chief of Crown Prince Rupprecht's Army Group in April: "We shall simply tear open a hole, and the rest will follow. That is the way we did it in Russia."[44] Haig's greatest fear was that the Germans might overrun his vital supply lines: the communications center at Hazebrouck, with its juncture of five railway lines, and perhaps even the Channel ports.

On April 9, following a four-and-a-half-hour bombardment of overwhelming power, fourteen divisions from the German Sixth Army advanced along a twelve-mile front running north from the La Bassée Canal to Armentières. The brunt of the attack fell on a Portuguese division which quickly gave up the fight and fled the battlefield. Some Portuguese soldiers appropriated signalers' bicycles only to be killed by mistake miles behind the front by British reinforcements who believed that they were advancing Germans.[45]

On the following day, the German Fourth Army, thirty-three divisions strong, attacked north of Armentières. Operation "Georgette" provoked panic at both General Headquarters and the British War Office. Haig had "an agitated frame of mind" and became "desperately anxious."[46] In London, an assessment by the head of intelligence on the British General Staff drew an ominous conclusion. More than the defense of Hazebrouck and the Channel ports was at stake. "Germany is endeavoring to destroy the British Army and decide the war by concentrating all her available reserve against the British front," an alarmed Lieutenant General George M. W. Macdonogh warned. Unless France and the United States sent substantial reinforcements and most of Britain's troops were withdrawn from the periphery, Britain faced "decisive defeat."[47]

The British, who in April extended conscription to men between the ages of eighteen and fifty (and even up to fifty-six if required),[48] intensified their pressure on Pershing and Washington to brigade American soldiers with their depleted divisions. After receiving some veteran soldiers from the British campaign in Palestine, Haig had only raw recruits to fill the depleted ranks of his combat soldiers. As Rawlinson, the commander of the British Fourth Army, lamented to Sir Henry Wilson at the time: the reinforcements he had been receiving were "composed of young boys who were under fire for the first time. I fear that the heavy bombardment which he put on before the attack for 4 hours with a certain amount of gas shell must have shaken these children."[49]

Once the first German offensive ground to a halt, President Wilson had begun to qualify his already tentative support of brigading US units with British divisions which had been implied in Joint Note No. 18 agreed upon by the Permanent Military Representatives (which included Bliss) at Versailles. He had March cable Bliss on April 6 that he had only agreed to "send troops over as fast we could make them ready and find transportation for them. That was all."[50]

Lloyd George, however, believed that he had gotten an American commitment to keep the BEF up to strength, and on April 8 asked the Wilson administration to ship 480,000 infantry and machine gun troops, or 120,000 men a month.[51] He subsequently cabled Washington: "We can do no more than we have done. It rests with America to win or lose the decisive battle of the war."[52]

On April 19 President Wilson canceled a Cabinet meeting to confer with his Secretary of War who had just returned from his inspection tour of American forces in Europe. Both the President and Baker were now under enormous pressure to commit to a program of transporting just combat troops to France which would delay if not make impossible the creation of an independent American army. The outcome of their discussions has rightly been characterized as a "masterpiece of studied ambiguity."[53]

Their response was handed to Reading on the evening of April 19 and received in London on April 21. Washington followed its official response with a stern warning from Colonel House to the War Cabinet through Reading: America's position "should be accepted, not only without raising any objection, but also without having any in mind."[54] Although the qualified US response seemed to support brigading, Baker reassured Pershing that its purpose was to avoid a "definite and obligatory promise as will permit representatives of the British government to feel that they have a right to watch what we do and sit in judgment on our action."[55]

At this juncture discussions between London and Washington took another twist. Pershing had been conducting his own discussions with Lord Milner, who had just replaced Derby as Secretary of State for War. These discussions led to the so-called London Agreement which basically represented a return to Pershing's six-division plan, the major differences being that only the infantry and machine gun units of six divisions were to be shipped in May. If necessary these soldiers could be introduced to combat but the reality was that these mostly raw recruits would have to be trained first.

Pershing probably clinched the deal when he suggested on April 22 that the war would ultimately be won with "an American army fighting side by side with the British" on the Flanders front.[56] Pershing even gave the British the impression that he agreed with them on the merits of foreign tutelage for his men. After leaving London he visited Haig at British GHQ on April 21 where he encountered Lord Derby, who was on his way to Paris to head a special mission to the French government. In a private chat, he gave the former Secretary of State for War the impression that he saw "very clearly how bad his generals and their various staffs are, and therefore he will be anxious to leave them under our people." According to Lord Derby, "he was very frank about this." Derby apparently read into Pershing's comments what he wanted to hear, for the American commander-in-chief also made it quite clear that he alone would decide when Americans training with British units were ready to be included in the formation of an American Army. As Derby wrote Henry Wilson, he was "very firm as to his having this power."[57]

Two understandings concerning the deployment of newly arriving US troops now existed, the London Agreement of April 24 and the so-called Baker–Reading Agreement of April 21. Pershing naturally preferred his arrangement with Milner and Sir Henry Wilson, which impinged less on the creation of an independent army. The former also limited the War Department's commitment to shipping combat soldiers to May (or six divisions, the equivalent of 120,000 combat soldiers instead of the 480,000 as mentioned in the so-called Baker–Reading Agreement of April 21).

Matters came to a head during the Supreme War Council's meeting at Abbeville on May 1. The military situation no longer appeared as grim as it had been a few days earlier. Having failed to capture Hazebrouck, and with his offensive losing its momentum, Ludendorff called off Operation "Georgette" on April 29. Once again Ludendorff had failed to deliver a crushing blow against the BEF. Foch's comments during the dark days of mid-April to Frederick Maurice, the Director of Military Operations at the War Office, had proven prophetic. "If he," Foch had proclaimed, "had to choose between playing his own hand or that of Ludendorff, if he had to get to Berlin he would prefer Ludendorff's hand, but as his mission was to check Ludendorff he preferred his own."[58]

Although not recognized at the time and future crises lay ahead, the war now began to turn in the Entente's favor. The failure of operations "Michael" and "Georgette" to deliver a knockout blow against the British, according to Gerhard Ritter, constituted a "crushing disappointment" to frontline German troops.

Once again war's end had receded into the distant future, once again hecatombs had done no more than haplessly lengthen the front; and how could what had not been achieved in the first great blow, struck with every resource, full surprise, and tremendous artillery barrages, now be won with far weaker forces, consisting largely of decimated and exhausted divisions?[59]

German soldiers were "being ground to pieces in one useless, pointless and hopeless offensive action after another."[60] Only four US divisions occupied trenches at the front, but 429,375 "Yanks" had now arrived in France and that number was destined to grow dramatically as US troops flowed across the Atlantic.

The British had suffered over 300,000 casualties during "Michael" and "Georgette" while the French had lost fewer than 100,000 men assisting them.[61] Although the French had previously enjoyed a virtual monopoly over US troops, Clemenceau discovered that the British by unilateral negotiations had gained an apparent monopoly over future US soldiers arriving in France. His anger was exacerbated by his belief that the British had heretofore not made the same commitment as his country to the killing fields of France. The French Premier believed that they had not conscripted enough available men into their armies and that they retained far too many soldiers in Britain for home defense.[62] The French had called up 91.9 percent of the 1904–15 classes for its conscript armies while the British had taken for military service only 48.7 percent of men aged between nineteen and forty-one.[63]

This French comparison was not quite fair because victory depended equally on British maritime contributions and its industry and mining. A British industrial and maritime collapse could be just as fatal to the Entente's hopes as a German victory in France. In World War II, Russian manpower played an essential part in Nazi Germany's defeat, but American industrial might and maritime supremacy were equally important. Elizabeth Greenhalgh rightly points out that among allies "strict equity is simply not possible in a modern industrial war." Nonetheless there were many more grieving French than British mothers over lost sons at the war's end. As Hankey suggested in July 1918, he would rather have British men "alive in our dockyards and factories than dead in some stricken battlefield, however glorious and fateful for the history of the world."[64]

Clemenceau was in high dudgeon when the Allied military and political leaders assembled at Abbeville, May 1–2. The French Premier stressed that Foch's command was not "a mere decoration." If the British got 120,000 "Yanks" in May, the French must get their 120,000 in June. "There is no agreement between my Government and anybody else," Pershing emphasized. Somewhat ingenuously he argued that he had only made a private arrangement with British leaders to acquire shipping to bring over six US divisions for training with the British. Taking a different tack, Foch then suggested that the current military situation demanded that the United States ship just infantry and machine gun units.

Pershing had heard enough. Surely his comrades-in-arms were not saying that "the American Army is to be entirely at the disposal of the French and British commands," he indignantly noted. He then attempted to turn the discussion to the future. "We must look forward to the time when we shall have our own army," he emphasized. "We must insist on its being recognized." Refusing to extend preferential shipping of infantry and machine gun units beyond May, he stressed that he did "not wish to commit the American army so long in advance. If need be, I shall recommend the extension into June. I can see no reason for it now."

Lloyd George's rejoinder to this was that "at the present time, we are engaged in what is perhaps the decisive battle of the war. If we lose this battle, we shall need tonnage to take home what there is left of the British and American armies." The British Prime Minister also denied that the British wanted "to treat American troops as drafts for the British Army." These intense discussions continued as Foch, Milner, and Pershing closeted themselves in a separate room. Despite their entreaties Pershing stood his ground. Foch asked him, "You are willing to risk our being driven back to the Loire?" "Yes, I am willing to take the risk," the American calmly replied. "Moreover, the time may come when the American Army will have to stand the brunt of this war, and it is not wise to fritter away our resources in this manner." The heated discussions continued when the politicians rejoined the discussion. "Can't you see that the war will be lost unless we get this support?" pleaded Lloyd George. The meeting abruptly concluded when Pershing struck the table with his fist, announced that he would "not be coerced," and walked out of the meeting.[65]

Pershing understood that his insistence for an independent US force might delay America's contribution to the war effort and even increase AEF casualties as US troops learned to fight by fighting. But he continued to resist any real integration of US units in Allied divisions. When his liaison officer at Foch's headquarters relayed the general-in-chief's concerns to him, he emphasized that

he was going to create American Divs & Corps, that our gen'ls could soon learn – learn by fighting & my saying that this was expensive in men he said then it could not be helped, that if it cost 20% more in losses for our men to be in American divs. & Corps commanded by American gen'ls, he would cold-bloodedly accept this loss rather than put in our rgts singly in the French & British Divs.[66]

When the Supreme War Council reassembled the following day, Pershing stood absolutely alone. Even Bliss did not agree with him. With the outcome of the war apparently still in doubt, his inflexibility of the previous day seemed indefensible. Lloyd George was especially blunt when he pointedly suggested that "if Great Britain and France had to go under, it would be an honourable defeat, because each had put their every last man into the army, whereas the United States would go under after putting in only as many men as had the Belgians." In sum the United States had only put its "little finger in the struggle." With Foch, the Allied commander-in-chief, going over his head and sending Wilson "a statement pointing out the gravity of the situation," Pershing agreed to extend the London Agreement into June. In return he got a resolution that stated that "the American army should be formed as early as possible under its own commander and under its own flag."[67]

Rather than placing the Allies in a precarious position by rejecting amalgamation Pershing believed that his position saved the Allies. As he noted in a postwar review of relations with the Allies:

I believe that it is not too much to say that the Allied cause would have been lost had we neglected the influence of national psychology and despised the pride of a people in the accomplishments of its soldiers by accepting any proposal to employ our man power in such a way that the results of their heroic efforts would have served to enhance the glory of any flag but their own.[68]

Pershing's tough stand at Abbeville dismayed the British War Cabinet. Two weeks earlier its members had considered using American soldiers to restore their shattered British divisions, and perhaps then exchanging these divisions for British divisions in Italy. By their calculations the Abbeville arrangement might make available at most only 72,000 combat troops.[69]

Baker and Wilson, however, favorably received the Abbeville agreement. Encouraged by Pershing to believe that the Abbeville solution represented a true meeting of the minds rather than capitulation to his intransigence, they expressed delight over an agreement "which relieves us from any possible embarrassment due to a misunderstanding of our execution of the resolution [Joint Note No. 18] of the Permanent Military Representatives at Versailles."[70]

As they gained a clearer impression of Pershing's conduct at Abbeville from French and British sources, however, they both had second thoughts. Haig's comments in his diary captured what many Entente leaders now thought of the American commander-in-chief after Abbeville. "I thought Pershing was very obstinate, and stupid. He did not seem to realise the urgency of the situation." Haig, as was the case with most Allied generals, thought Pershing's determination to create "*a great self contained American Army*'" was unrealistic. "Seeing that he has neither Commanders of divisions, nor of Corps, nor of Armies, nor Staffs for same," he noted in his diary, "it is ridiculous to think such an Army could function alone in less than 2 years time!"[71]

On May 11, Baker cabled Pershing: "It has been suggested to the President that General Foch may reopen this subject with you and the President hopes you will approach any such interviews as sympathetically as possible, particularly if the situation as to replacements which has been presented to him is as critical as it seems."[72] Pershing's response was disingenuous and uncompromising to say the least. He expressed surprise that his position at Abbeville had been criticized and insisted that he would give "every early assistance possible to meet an emergency." At the same time he remained "strongly of the opinion that we must form our own divisions and corps as rapidly as possible and use them as such for the additional moral effect such an army would have."[73] And there the matter stood until the next German offensive.

As Pershing looked to the future and the creation of an independent army, an increasing number of American soldiers, organized in divisions, began arriving behind the British front for training. General Henry S. Rawlinson, the British commander of the Fourth Army, found them "green and untrained" but "magnificent material" for soldiering.[74]

To administer these divisions (less their artillery) being billeted with the BEF, Pershing formed the American Second Army Corps on February 24, 1917, choosing Lieutenant Colonel (later brigadier general) George S. Simonds as its Chief of Staff. Pershing and his Chief of Staff Harbord made it clear that they expected Simonds to ensure that British training conformed to the AEF doctrine of open warfare.[75] Simonds subsequently told the British that their training facilities must be suitable for long-range rifle practice and space for maneuvers by large units. He also sent a stern memorandum to US division commanders informing them that their officers were to retain "absolute control of, and responsibility for, the training" of US soldiers. The British, although not without reluctance, sought to comply with Pershing's instructions. They made special arrangements along the coast for long-range musketry at 600 yards but open tracts of land suitable for maneuvers for units as large as a brigade were difficult to secure.

Veteran British officers found AEF doctrine especially wanting. Major Walter Guinness, a staff officer with the 66th Division, thought the AEF's training schedule much too rigid and criticized the absence of any provision for route marching. He concluded that Pershing was "the stupidest man in France, showing quite remarkable narrow-mindedness and obstinacy."[76] When two additional US Divisions, the 27th (formed at Camp Wadsworth, South Carolina, in July 1917) and the 33rd (concentration of this division began at Camp Logan, Texas, in August 1917), both National Guard divisions, began to deploy behind his front for training in May, Rawlinson, although impressed with their quality, expressed alarm about their combat readiness. On May 24, he wrote Sir Henry Wilson: "They can[']t move or feed themselves and they know nothing even of the rudiments of tactics. Pershing 'Schedule of Training' is shocking. Nothing in it."[77]

The British agreed to supply the American troops with rations, weapons, transportation, and all essential equipment except distinctive items of American army dress. Arriving US soldiers kept their original uniforms, shirts, underclothing, socks, shoes, and so forth. But the British provided them with replacement clothing, including, among other articles of clothing, field shoes, tunics, trousers, overcoats, and undergarments. British field boots tended to be popular, coarse British underwear not so much. Since Doughboys tended to be bigger than Tommies, exchanges did not usually go well when bulk issues of clothing took place. A soldier in the 27th Division had this to say: "Clothes didn't fit. Equipment was English which made it unfamiliar ... We cussed the Huns and sometimes the English."[78]

Many "Yanks" reluctantly exchanged their superior American Springfield rifles for the British Lee-Enfield. The British also provided them with trench mortars, steel helmets, gas masks, automatic rifles, and machine guns. An unfortunate consequence of being trained with British weaponry was that when American units later fought alongside the French they were equipped with French weaponry. For example, machine gunners who had trained with British Vickers machine guns were issued French Hotchkiss machine guns when they were deployed along the French front.[79]

Doughboys had difficulty adjusting to British rations, which included tea rather than coffee and a canned stew, used as a substitute for meat and vegetables. This stew, sometimes mixed with onions, caused especially foul flatulence. British rations were also not as substantial as Americans expected and had to be adjusted. But it all worked out in the end, and many Americans grew to admire the efficiency of the British system which delivered routine supplies promptly and efficiently. These supplies and associated costs were not free. After involved negotiations British and American authorities eventually agreed that the average cost amounted to $30.24 per soldier per day.[80]

Ten US divisions eventually trained with the BEF, but only two of them, the 27th and 30th divisions, actually fought under Haig's command. Despite friction between Pershing's staff and the British over training, the Yanks who trained for a time in the British sector almost certainly benefited from their association with veteran British officers assigned to each regiment. "To the British the division was indebted for the practical training. Which was of untold benefit to us and we left them with a feeling of appreciation for their courtesy and their fighting ability," recalls Corporal Paul Murphy, Company H, 309th Infantry Regiment, 78th Division.[81]

With the Germans maintaining the offensive initiative in June, Lloyd George's government continued to link the British Empire's survival with the integration of the American military role with their own. At a meeting of the SWC in early June, Foch suggested that five US divisions training in the British zone be moved to inactive sectors in Alsace to relieve French divisions for action elsewhere. Pershing, who was actively making arrangements to create an independent army in Alsace, immediately fell in with this arrangement. A miffed Haig noted in his diary: "In 3 weeks' time these Americans will be fit for battle. I doubt if the French Divisions they relieve will ever fight!"[82] But he made no formal objection to Foch.

The British government, suspecting sinister motives in Foch's actions, concluded that he sought to exploit his position as generalissimo to force the British to find replacements from their own manpower resources to maintain their front. On June 7, Milner and Sir Henry Wilson confronted Foch at the French Ministry of War about the transfer of five US divisions from their zone. Foch assured them that he did not plan to take any more US divisions from Haig and that he assigned equal weight to the defense of the Channel ports and Paris.[83] But British anxiety grew when it became apparent that Pershing had no intention of replacing the five divisions taken from the British zone and positioned along the French front.

Faced with Pershing's granite-like determination to achieve an independent US force, the British tried another tack. On June 14, Colonel Lloyd C. Griscom, Pershing's liaison officer with the British War Office, dined at Haig's General Headquarters. Griscom subsequently reported to Pershing that Haig believed that

the sooner we had American Corps and Armies operating the better he would be pleased and he had told General Foch that it was folly to send two of our good divisions to the Vosges to relieve second-rate French Divisions. He said he would do anything he could to help get an American Army together, and that geographically he thought the place for our concentration now was in or opposite Belgium in view of the immediate crisis.[84]

Believing that the war would last at least until 1919, Lloyd George and many other British leaders took the long view on America's role in the war. There was common agreement that the British Empire did not have the required manpower to survive future battles of the magnitude of the Somme and Passchendaele. If Lloyd George had his way the bloody burden of taking on the German Army would be passed to the Americans. During discussions of the "Plan of Operations for 1919" he argued that "if the Americans concentrated a great Army on the Western Front next year, it might be possible for our Army to follow its traditional *rôle* of operations on the outskirts of the war area."[85]

Of course, before the British transferred men to the outer theaters to expand or protect their empire, they needed Americans to man the trenches that they abandoned. But Foch rather than Haig controlled the positioning of US forces. In mid-June he repositioned two of the American divisions withdrawn from the British sector. The 4th and 28th were halted on their move southward and established on the west side of the Marne salient not far from Château-Thierry. They joined the US 2nd, 3rd, 26th, and 42nd divisions, which were already in the area, giving Pershing the nucleus for an independent army and strengthening the defense of Paris at the same time.[86]

The Prime Minister, convinced that Foch with Pershing's cooperation had, "intentionally or unintentionally, 'done' us in [in] the matter,"[87] filed a protest with the War Department. Wilson was not pleased when brought into the discussion. "If the English continue to maneuver around and about, this way and that, to have their own way," Wilson wrote Baker, "I shall speak very plainly."[88] On July 7, Baker wrote Pershing a confidential and personal note stressing two points. "(1) I want the Germans beaten, hard and thoroughly – a military victory. (2) I want you to have the honor of doing it."[89]

Three days earlier, on July 4, American forces had participated in a successful but largely forgotten joint offensive with British imperial forces. Companies C and E, 131st Infantry, and Companies A and G, 132nd Infantry, 33rd Division, joined elements of the Australian Army Corps commanded by Lieutenant General John Monash, in an attack against the small village of Hamel.

Monash was an unusual commander in the BEF to say the least. Of Prussian Jewish origin, he had been a civil engineer in civilian life. Initially viewed with some disdain by professional British officers because they thought him a "Saturday-afternoon soldier" because of his service in the Australian militia, he became known for his meticulously planned "set-piece" offensives which emphasized firepower over the role of the infantry.

I had formed the theory that the true rôle of the infantry was not to expend itself upon heroic physical effort, nor to wither away under merciless machine gun fire, nor to impale itself on hostile bayonets, nor to tear itself to pieces in hostile entanglements ... but, on the contrary, to advance under the maximum possible array of mechanical resources in the form of guns, machine guns, tanks, mortars and aeroplanes; to advance with as little impediment as possible.[90]

Monash and Brigadier General A. Courage, the commander of the tanks attached to the British Fourth Army, largely based their plans on the earlier Cambrai offensive in November 1917 spearheaded by tanks. Courage had at his disposal sixty new Mark V tanks, which were faster and more reliable than their predecessors, the Mark I and the Mark IV, and could be driven by one man rather than four. Monash and Courage emphasized surprise and massive firepower, concentrating more than 600 guns along a 7,000-yard front against approximately 2,500 Germans who manned a single line of trenches and some shell holes. To gain the element of surprise, Monash planned no extended preliminary bombard-ment, with British heavy guns being silently registered. Monash also emphasized counter-battery fire to neutralize the enemy's artillery.[91]

Following an opening bombardment with high explosive shells and gas, which some Americans described as better than "any previous Fourth of July demonstration they had ever heard," Australian and American troops rose and began to advance behind a rolling barrage that proceeded at the studied pace of one hundred yards every three minutes, so slow in fact that some men stopped to light cigarettes.[92] This well-coordinated advance across no-man's-land spearheaded by tanks captured 41 German officers, 1,431 other ranks, several big guns, 171 machine guns, and 26 trench mortars. The Australians lost 51 offi-cers and 724 ranks; the Americans, 6 officers and 128 other ranks, killed, wounded, or missing.

The untested Americans performed extremely well. Corporal Thomas A. Pope won the Medal of Honor by singlehandedly capturing an enemy machine gun nest, killing several Germans with his bayonet. An Austra-lian company commander reported to his superiors: "United States troops are now classified as 'Diggers.'" The British government attempted to exploit the date of the operation, July 4, for their own purposes. The next day Milner and Lloyd George visited the 33rd Division. After reviewing US troops and saluting the American flag, the Prime Minister stood in an automobile and spoke of the common struggle of the two English-speaking Atlantic powers against German militarism.[93]

Despite the success of this joint offensive Pershing seethed. In his view the joint attack represented yet another example of Americans attempting to gain their independence from the British. He previously had made it clear that American troops were in the British zone for training purposes only and could only be introduced into combat in an extreme emergency. When he first caught wind of Monash's operation he personally told Haig and Major General Read, the Commander of the American Second Corps, that he refused to allow US troops to participate in a joint attack.[94] When Haig passed on Pershing's instructions to Rawlinson, the commander of the Fourth Army dutifully informed Monash. Receiving his orders at 4:00 p.m. on July 3, Monash was aghast: if he withdrew the American companies, the resulting gaps in his orchestrated attack would force cancellation. When he protested, Rawlinson gave him permission to proceed. "It was too late to withdraw them," Rawlinson later explained, "so I am afraid I had to disobey the order. All went well and the Yankees did not have many casualties but if things had gone wrong I suppose I should have been sent home in disgrace!!" Furious with Pershing, Rawlinson thought the American general "a tiresome[,] ignorant and very obstinate man as we shall find later on when he begins to try conclusions with the Boche on his own."[95] Pershing was equally put out with the British. In his view, this incident "showed clearly the disposition of the British to assume control of our units, the very thing which I had made such strong efforts and had imposed so many conditions to prevent. Its immediate effect was to cause me to make the instructions so positive that nothing of the kind could occur again."[96] And it did not. Yet the success enjoyed by American soldiers fighting alongside imperial troops in this minor set-piece battle demonstrated the superiority of British methods over Pershing's emphasis on courageous and self-reliant foot soldiers. Monash's meticulous planning along with superior firepower and enhanced weaponry had resulted in the capture of Hamel with modest losses. That this was the way forward in stalemated trench warfare had earlier been illustrated by the first American offensive of the war at Cantigny in late May.

13   Cantigny

By the previous standards of trench warfare on the Western Front Ludendorff's offensives in March and April had been great successes. His armies twice broke through the British front and rapidly advanced across open terrain. But the semi-mobility achieved by the rupture of the British front could not be maintained, and these break-ins could not be converted to a break-out. Slow-moving and often unreliable tanks (of which the Germans had few) could not maintain the momentum of the drive. Nor could mounted soldiers who were extremely vulnerable to machine guns. Cratered battlefields made the forward movement of big guns difficult, and infantry proved helpless once it got beyond the range of its own artillery. Logistics also played a central role as German troops marched well beyond their railheads. As infantry outdistanced its artillery and supplies these offensives lost their momentum and inevitably ground to a halt. The will of the British remained unbroken.

As his casualties mounted, Ludendorff's position began to appear untenable. "He had become a typical chair-borne general who conducted operations from an office desk," concluded Walter Goerlitz. "Clausewitz had designated strategy as the art of applying available means. Ludendorff could no longer distinguish between what was possible and what was not. Everything was possible if you barked out the order for it in a loud, gruff tone of voice."[1] His offensives created bulges in the enemy's front but they also created vulnerable salients his own troops had to defend. Occupying makeshift defenses along an expanded front with precarious flanks, his armies were now much more vulnerable than previously when they occupied the strongest defensive positions on the Western Front.

During the last stages of the 1916 Battle of the Somme, during which British artillery came to dominate the battlefield, the *OHL* had decided to build sophisticated defenses in depth as opposed to massing troops in a series of linear frontline trenches. Ludendorff envisioned an elastic system, arguing that "the whole system of defense had to be made broader and looser ... Forward infantry positions with a wide field of fire were easily seen by the enemy. They could be destroyed by the artillery of the enemy, and were very difficult to protect by our own artillery."[2] In sum the Germans sought to limit their own casualties while maximizing the losses of the attackers.

In late 1916 and early 1917 tens of thousands of Russian POWs and German workers built a series of linked fortified positions (or "Stellungs") from the North Sea to the area around Verdun. Running from north to south they were: the "Wotan Stellung," the "Siegfried Stellung," the "Albrecht Stellung," the "Brunhild Stellung," and the "Kriemhilde Stellung." The "Siegfried Stellung," built in the Cambrai–Saint-Quentin sector, was the first built and most strongly fortified.[3] The British called this defensive system the "Hindenburg Line."

The *OHL*'s imaginative defensive strategy emphasized firepower over manpower. The first lines of defense consisted of a series of outposts, camouflaged pillboxes manned by machine gunners arranged in a checkerboard pattern to create mutually supporting strongholds. German troops in this outpost zone were not expected to fight to the last man; rather their officers instructed them to fall back before being overwhelmed. The Germans also left extended gaps, or "killing zones," between these outposts and their primary defenses, a network of linear trenches some fifteen feet deep and twelve feet wide strengthened by concrete dugouts reinforced by steel which could withstand 15 cm shells. Rows and rows, sometimes hundreds of yards deep, of coiled concertina wire, stacked as high as eight feet in places, also served as a serious obstacle for Allied troops who advanced beyond the range of their supporting artillery. When possible the Germans also sought to establish these main defenses on a reverse slope for protection against the enemy's artillery.[4]

Although the brunt of the German offensives in March and May 1918 had fallen on the BEF, the French had been forced to extend their front some ninety-two kilometers and transfer forty-seven divisions to the north. They now held two-thirds of a front once manned by the British. As Foch suspected, the British remained Ludendorff's primary target. But, as Americans in increasing numbers flowed across the Atlantic, Ludendorff was running out of time. Having suffered heavy losses his soldiers lost heart and were becoming undisciplined. "Our troops had fought well; but the fact that certain divisions had obviously failed to show any inclination to attack in the plain of the Lys provided food for thought . . . the way in which the troops stopped round captured supplies, while individuals stayed behind to search houses and farms for food, were serious matters," he writes in his memoirs. "This impaired success and showed poor discipline."[5]

As Ludendorff made preparations for his third offensive of 1918, the French gave American troops their first opportunity to fight as a unit in an offensive operation. Previously the Americans had only come to grips with the Germans in trench raids launched by either side. On April 1, 1918 Pershing ordered the 1st Division, commanded by the Alabamian Robert Lee Bullard, to an assembly area north of Paris prior to joining the French First Army on the southern end of the salient created by Operation "Michael." After being relieved by the 26th Division near Seicheprey, the Big Red One on April 8 arrived near Gisors, northwest of Paris and about forty-three miles southwest of Montdidier.[6] Pershing wanted a final exercise in open warfare before releasing the division for service on an active front. In reality, although the division did put on a demonstration for Pershing and a French military delegation, it did not actually conduct full-scale maneuvers in open warfare as intended.[7]

Prior to the Big Red One's departure for the front, Pershing gave its officers an impromptu pep talk. Although not known for his oratory, Pershing made up for any absence of eloquence by speaking from the heart

I have every confidence in the 1st Division. You are about to enter this great battle of the greatest war in history, and in that battle you will represent the mightiest nation engaged ... Centuries of military tradition and of military and civil history are now looking toward this first contingent of the American Army as it enters this great battle. You have behind you your own national traditions that should make you the finest soldiers in Europe to-day. We come from a young and aggressive nation. We come from a nation that for one hundred and fifty years has stood before the world as the champion of the sacred principles of human liberty. We now return to Europe, the home of our ancestors, to help defend those same principles upon European soil.[8]

His words, according to George C. Marshall, then serving as the 1st Division's G-3 (or Chief of Operations), "made a profound impression on all those present."[9]

On April 17 the men of the 1st Division began their advance to the front, first by train and then on foot. Corporal Jesse Evans and his comrades in Company L, 18th Infantry, 1st Division, marched "with packs of seventy to one-hundred pounds on our backs," covering as many as fifteen miles a day.[10] The pleasant countryside of Beauvais with its quaint villages and farmland across which they marched had been spared the ravages of warfare. Their eventual destination was the sector around Cantigny, a small village roughly five miles northwest of German-held Montdidier.

The German Eighteenth Army, in a supporting role to the main attack delivered in the north by the Seventeenth and Second Armies during

"Michael," had overrun the British Fifth Army's trenches and advanced across open countryside to Montdidier. The battlefield remained fluid as the German Eighteenth Army fought to defend or capture terrain vital to Montdidier's defense. Neither side had had the opportunity to prepare strong defensive positions and the fighting resembled semi-open warfare rather than the static siege warfare which was the norm on the Western Front.

Around Cantigny troops sought protection in shell holes, the ruins of the town, or shallow trenches and fox holes. Primitive and incomplete communication trenches being dug made the resupply of frontline troops dangerous for both sides. Artillery battles waged almost continuously and continued in darkness as the French, anticipating that the Germans might launch another offensive, maintained artillery fire from 11 p.m. until dawn to discourage assault divisions from being brought forward under cover of darkness.[11] The Germans responded in kind.

Americans began to relieve French units during the evening of April 24 (Fig. 18). Sandwiched between the French 45th and 162nd divisions, they found themselves in a precarious position. Fighting from primitive defensives both the Americans and Germans were vulnerable to high explosive shells and chemical warfare. Renowned for their prewar chemical industry, the Germans monopolized the use of poison gas, releasing 52,000 tons during the war, more than the combined total of the British, French, and Americans. Mustard gas shells, which only the Germans produced in great quantities, served as their chemical weapon of choice in 1918. Gas masks offered limited security against this blistering agent which attacked the skin, contaminated the ground, and frequently lingered on the battlefield for days.[12]

The Americans first experienced mustard gas shells, which George C. Marshall called a "particularly hideous phase of warfare,"[13] at Cantigny. Major Ray Austin, 6th Field Artillery Regiment, provided his mother with a vivid description of the horrors of this particular poison gas. "Two men of the Infantry foolishly washed their faces in water from a shell hole which happened to contain 'mustard' and six hours later they were scarred and burned terribly as with a hot iron. I have seen a Frenchman who was burned from sitting in the grass where a mustard shell had burst."[14]

Tactically the division was a part of the Tenth Corps, commanded by General Charles Vandenberg, and the French First Army, commanded by General Marie Eugène Debeney. Eager to get into action, Bullard lobbied Vandenberg and Debeney for an American offensive. In early May they gave him permission to prepare an offensive in conjunction with the French.

4680

Fig. 18 Equipped for the trenches

Initially Debeney and Vandenberg planned an attack by three divisions
to bring German-held Montdidier under Allied artillery. The 1st Division, given extensive technical support by the French in the form of
artillery, tanks, aircraft, and a flamethrower section, was one of these
divisions but its objective was not originally Cantigny's capture. This
changed when the French, anticipating a German offensive north of the

Oise, called off the joint offensive. Bullard then modified his original plans to a limited attack to capture Cantigny by one US regiment, the 28th Infantry, commanded by Colonel Hanson E. Ely, a tough former football player at West Point.[15] Vandenberg approved this independent US operation which he viewed as being "analogous to a powerful raid." With the technical support provided by the French, the commander of the Tenth Army Corps expressed confidence that the Americans would win "a complete and easy success, susceptible to having great moral effect."[16]

Situated on a ridge, the largely destroyed village of Cantigny occupied a bulge in the front about 1,000 meters deep and 1,500 meters wide. Its German defenders, the 82nd Reserve Corps, composed of healed veterans, raw recruits, dismounted cavalrymen, railway guards, and over-age members of the *Landwehr* (or militia), was by no definition a first-line division, and had previously been inactive on the Russian front for many months before being retrained and sent to the west.[17]

After gaining approval for a limited attack, Bullard left little to chance. Although he gave lip service to the official American doctrine of open warfare he found much to admire in the tactics which the French had learned through trial and error in four years of coming to grips with the German Army, arguably the best armed force in the world. Viewing the rifle and bayonet as secondary weapons, Bullard thought that artillery, machine guns, and tanks were the key to success. He even went so far as to suggest that veteran foreign officers be utilized as small-unit commanders in American offensive operations.[18] He displeased GHQ when he reduced his rifle company's platoons from fifty to forty men in an attempt to create a reserve battalion for each regiment which could be held back to replenish a regiment's losses. Although GHQ allowed his downsizing of rifle platoons it insisted that the men thus provided be organized as supply parties.[19]

Bullard chose two exceptional officers, his operations officer, Lieutenant Colonel George C. Marshall, and the AEF's artillery commander, Brigadier General Summerall, to plan the attack. They subsequently devised a set-piece battle that emphasized surprise and artillery superiority. During a two-day dress rehearsal all units down to the level of platoons were drilled in their specific roles and taught to coordinate their advance with tanks and flamethrowers. To emulate the exploding wall of shells of the rolling barrage Ely trained his infantry to follow men carrying tree branches at the pace of one hundred yards every four minutes.[20]

The Americans achieved overwhelming artillery superiority by massing US and especially French artillery. On a front of only 2,200 meters,

Summerall concentrated 234 pieces which included 75-mm guns, 155-mm howitzers, 220-mm and 280-mm long heavy howitzers, and trench mortars. Summerall planned a violent preliminary bombardment of one hour, with some guns shifting to smoke shells during the final minutes to obscure the advancing tanks and men as they moved forward behind a rolling barrage. French and American gunners gave particular attention to counter-battery work to neutralize the enemy's return fire. Three sections of machine gunners also provided a fire barrage during the advance.

After completing their training for the assault, the 28th Infantry Regiment returned to the front on the nights of May 26 and 27. Equipped for action, each man carried 220 rounds, small arms ammunition, two hand grenades, one rifle grenade, one Bengal flare, four sand bags, two days' reserve rations, two canteens of water, marking panel, and either a heavy pick or a heavy shovel. Each company also advanced with Stokes mortars, 37-mm guns, and a machine gun company.[21]

On May 28, at 4:45 a.m., the big guns opened up, some concentrating on the village and others on suspected enemy artillery positions and counterattack assembly areas. "It was a remarkable sight – great clouds of smoke rolling up from the shelled districts, against which the flashes of bursting shells stood out," noted one observer.[22] After an hour of tremendous shelling, the men of the 28th Infantry Regiment, with bayonets fixed, rose to begin their advance. Major Ray Austin, 6th Field Artillery, describes its progress:

At the same time as the barrage left the line of departure (our front line trenches) the infantry suddenly appeared on the slope of the ridge close behind our barrage – a long brown line with bayonets glistening in the sun. They seemed to have sprung from the earth, as in reality they had when they went over the top. They walked steadily along behind our barrage accompanied by the tanks which buzzed along with smoke coming out from their exhausts and their guns.[23]

The advance started at 6:45 a.m. with the Second Battalion, 28th Infantry, entering Cantigny fifteen minutes later. As men of the 28th rapidly swept through the village, they found many Germans packed into deep cellars and dugouts in a desperate attempt to survive the violent bombardment. German dead soon littered the village. Flushed from their hiding places, often with flamethrowers, many Germans had been quickly dispatched rather than taken prisoner. (The Addendum to the "Report on Capture of Cantigny" admits: "Practically no prisoners were taken.")[24] Advancing to the east of the village the Doughboys began furiously digging with picks and shovels to prepare a defensive position. The resulting trenches, many only three feet deep and dug on open slopes, however, offered little protection when German artillery and machine guns came into play as the Germans launched counterattacks to recapture Cantigny.

In securing the town the 28th Infantry suffered few casualties. "How easy it had been!," noted 1st Lieutenant Daniel Sargent, Battery F, 5th Artillery, who had been assigned to the French artillery batteries as a liaison officer. Confident of success, Bullard later wrote: "I know that it was so carefully prepared that it could not have failed, but it is a fact also that the execution by the troops was very good."[25] Pershing observed the village's capture along with Bullard at the Post of Command. "Like me, however, he did not as long as he was with me, seem to be impressed with the wonder of the performance. He seemed to take the capture, as I took it, as a simple affair."[26] But this soon changed. The French previously had occupied the village twice but had been forced to retreat when the Germans counterattacked.

A determined Pershing insisted that this would not happen to the Americans. "Within a few hours there came back a letter from him," writes Bullard, "impressing upon me in most earnest, emphatic terms his order to hold the position that we had taken, and under no conditions, under no pressure, to quit it."[27] Bullard surmised that his commander-in-chief had encountered some Allied officers who had expressed doubt that the Americans could retain their position. Just recently Pershing had angrily told him of how some Allied officers assumed superior airs in his presence:

"Do they patronize you?" he asked, looking at me keenly. "Do they assume superior airs with you?"

"No, sir," I answered, "they do not. I have been with them too long and know them too well."

"By—! They have been trying it with me, and I don't intend to stand a bit of it," he said, vehemently. He meant it.[28]

The rapid occupation of the village with few casualties quickly proved misleading. At 7:24 a.m. Ely had telephoned Brigadier General Beaumont B. Buck, his brigade commander: "Nearly all of objectives reached. Everything going fine according to schedule. All objectives taken. Very little loss."[29] As the 2nd Battalion finished off the shell-shocked Germans defending the village, however, the 1st Battalion on the southern flank and the 3rd Battalion on the northern flank encountered stiff resistance. Company K of the 3rd Battalion, for example, had been driven back and sought safety in shell holes in no-man's-land. With its flanks not keeping up, the 28th Infantry's advance through Cantigny "created a salient within a salient."[30]

Meanwhile, the Germans brought up reinforcements and launched a series of counterattacks. Easily observed in their exposed position on open slopes and in the ruins of what had once been a village, the Americans presented German gunners an inviting target as they opened up with their 210-mm guns. Marshall describes the effect of these heavy guns: "A 3-inch shell will temporarily scare or deter a man; a 6-inch shell will shock him; but an 8-inch shell, such as these 210-mm ones, rips up the nervous system of everyone within a hundred yards of the explosion."[31] "I never endured such heavy shell-fire as here," Corporal Jesse O. Evans, Company L, 18th Infantry, later observed. His company, one of three companies of the 18th Infantry, reinforced the 28th Infantry during the evening of the 28th. "The Germans had all their heavy guns at Montdidier, a few miles away, and they turned them all loose on us. Cantigny had not a wall left standing when we went through. Two of our men went insane from the intense fire."[32]

At 5:45 p.m. Ely's report to brigade headquarters reflected the deterioration of his position: "1st and 3d Bns., 28th Inf. reported falling back under heavy fire artillery and M.G. [machine guns] . . . Unless heavy artillery can give us support it will [be] necessary to withdraw for entire front line is battered to pieces with artillery."[33]

On the following day the fighting reached a new level of intensity as the Germans sought to recapture the village. "The battle," writes Allan Millett, "lost its last vestiges of tactical sophistication and became a contest between the wills of the opposing commanders and troops and the weight of their supporting artillery."[34] At 8:55 p.m. Ely telephoned brigade headquarters: "Front line pounded to hell and gone, and entire front line must be relieved tomorrow night [or] he would not be responsible."[35]

The 28th Regiment's initial artillery supremacy had been lost. On the eve of the American attack against Cantigny, Germany had unleashed a powerful offensive on the Chemin des Dames. Pétain urgently required elsewhere the critical French artillery assistance and air support provided to the 28th Regiment and which had been essential to the capture of Cantigny and the suppression of German artillery. During the evening of May 28–29 the Americans lost two full regiments of French artillery leaving them with mostly short-range 75s which proved unsuitable for counter-battery fire.[36]

On May 30 the fighting began to die down although shelling continued and German aircraft, unmolested by French planes, bombed and strafed American positions. Three days of hellish combat had reduced the 28th to a spent force. Roughly a quarter of its men, thirty-eight officers and 903 men, had been either killed or wounded, most of them by German artillery and machine gunners.[37] Casualty rates this high were by no means unusual for offensives on the Western Front, but Ely was clearly justified in requesting relief for his depleted and now shell-shocked regiment. When someone on the division staff dared suggest that his men could continue to stand their ground, he erupted: "Let me tell you one thing and you put it down in your notebook. These men have been fighting three days and three nights and have been successful, but five of them are *not worth now what* one of them was when he came in . . . It is an injustice not to relieve the men who have been fighting so long."[38] During the night the 16th Infantry arrived to relieve the 28th. The stench of death hung in the air. "It's not a pleasant subject, but when the wind is right you can smell Cantigny two miles away," Major Austin wrote his mother.[39]

It has been argued that the Americans, once they lost their French air and artillery support, should have proclaimed success and quickly withdrawn from Cantigny. The village had little tactical value and was of no strategical significance. By insisting that the Americans hold their ground, Pershing wasted American lives by furnishing "German gunners with three days of target practice,"[40] or so it has been argued. The Germans, however, suffered almost twice as many casualties as the Americans. And a cancellation of the offensive once under way would not have dramatically reduced US casualties on this front. The "Big Red One" occupied this section for another seventy-three days, and as a consequence suffered an additional 5,000 casualties.[41]

With the threat of amalgamation hanging over his head, Pershing also needed to show Allied leaders as well as his political leadership that he and his staff were capable of putting an effective force in the field. "This was our first offensive," Marshall later wrote, "which had been ordered primarily for the purpose of its effects on the morale of the English and French armies. For the First Division to lose its first objective was unthinkable."[42] Encouraging the British and French was surely a consideration for Pershing. But, much more importantly, he believed that he had made the case for creating an independent American army. He cabled the War Department: "This action illustrates the facility with which our officers and men learn, and emphasizes the importance of organizing our own divisions and higher units as soon as circumstances permit. It is my firm conviction that our troops are the best in Europe and our staffs are the equals of any."[43]

Pershing may have been caught up in the moment but there was truth in what he said about the fighting qualities that Americans displayed at Cantigny. As Hunter Liggett, who later commanded the First Army, notes: "It was the first cold foreboding to the German that this was not, as he had hoped, a rabble of amateurs approaching."[44]

What Pershing could not reasonably argue was that the capture of Cantigny vindicated his doctrine of open warfare. Bullard and his staff had overwhelmed German defenders by conducting a carefully rehearsed set-piece battle backed by overwhelming firepower. They succeeded by following the French playbook rather than the American one which emphasized open warfare and undervalued the dramatic technical advances which de-emphasized nineteenth-century weapons such as the rifle and bayonet. Combat conditions at Cantigny had been a product of the fluid nature of the fighting in Picardy after the German March 21 breakthrough. It is correct that the subsequent makeshift defenses as new fronts formed were more representative of the conditions of open warfare envisioned by the AEF's staff than the siege warfare which previously existed on stabilized fronts with mature and increasingly sophisticated defenses such as the Hindenburg Line. Yet French methods that emphasized firepower, combined arms, and meticulous planning proved superior to American doctrine that continued to stress self-reliant infantrymen whose primary weapons were the rifle and bayonet.

As one French lecturer warned American officers at the AEF's General Staff:

Never venture Infantry in an attack against organized positions without having carefully prepared this attack. And when I say organized positions I do not only mean trenches and wire entanglements. I also mean strong points, hastily organized as they may be; every possible strong point which has to be attacked or outflanked must be taken under strong artillery fire. It is the only way for preventing tremendous and useless losses.[45]

Cantigny, as Millett bluntly asserts, demonstrated "once again that infantry of the Western Front could not fight – they could only die – without massive, accurate, properly timed artillery support."[46]

The realities of the battlefield, however, continued to make little impression on many members of Pershing's staff. Colonel Harold B. Fiske, who would soon be placed in charge of the AEF training section, had this to say on July 4, 1918: "In many respects, the tactics and technique of our Allies are not suited to American characteristics or the American mission in this war. The French do not like the rifle, do not know how to use it, and their infantry is consequently too entirely dependent upon a powerful artillery support."[47]

14 Into the breach

After the German failure to capture Hazebrouck in April, the unanswered and critical question for Allied leaders was: where would Ludendorff strike next? The responsibility for coming up with the correct answer now rested on the shoulders of General-in-Chief Foch. Believing that Ludendorff would once again strike on the British front, he ordered Pétain to send most of his reserves north to assist Haig. On May 7, 1918 the French commander-in-chief met with him to express his growing concern about concentrating his reserves between the Channel and the Oise River. But Foch did not share his fears and lectured his French comrade: "On the front between the Lys [south of Hazebrouck] and the Oise a German attack of great energy can come at any moment and achieve results that will have the gravest consequences because of the proximity of important objectives."[1]

The Germans had only to advance eighty kilometers along the Somme to reach the Channel. If the BEF clung to the French Army and retreated south of the Somme it would cut itself off from its key rail centers of Amiens and Hazebrouck and its essential Channel ports of Calais and Dunkirk. Faced with such a bleak prospect London might choose to evacuate its armies to Britain rather than maintain contact with the French Army.

Foch also insisted that Pétain resume the offensive as soon as possible north of the Oise River. "Only the offensive will permit the allies to terminate the battle victoriously and regain, along with the initiative in operations, moral ascendancy," he firmly proclaimed.[2] With Foch positioning most of his reserves between the Channel and the Oise and talking of future offensives, a disheartened Pétain considered resignation. He now had only one-third of his reserves to defend against a German offensive from the Oise River to Switzerland.[3]

Like Pétain, Sir Henry Wilson had become disenchanted with Foch. The British had suffered three casualties for every one French casualty since March 21. Holding his reserves for a counterattack, Foch refused to relieve frontline British troops while a battle was in progress. Although

Foch's personal friend, Wilson began to express serious reservations about his leadership. On April 24, he sent a memorandum to Secretary of War Milner protesting Foch's policy of "allowing British divisions to continue to be punished to such an extent as to necessitate their transfer to different parts of the Western Front in relief of French divisions." If this continued the British Army might disappear into "scattered fragments impossible [to] control by our General Headquarters."[4]

Following Sir Henry Wilson's April 24 letter, Foch, asserting his authority as general-in-chief, shifted four battered British divisions from the IX Corps to replace French troops in the supposedly quite French sector of Chemin des Dames. He then positioned French divisions thus relieved as reserves for the BEF. Other British divisions were scheduled to go to the Argonne, and the II British Corps had been interposed between the Belgians and the French *DAN* (*Détachement d'Armée du nord* – Northern Army Detachment) in Flanders.

On May 9 Sir Henry Wilson spoke in alarming terms with Lord Milner. The French are "absorbing us, our Army, our bases, our Merchant Marine, our Food, Italy, Salonica, etc.," he told the Secretary of State for War.[5] In Wilson's view, Foch's deployment of British divisions was "not only tactically and strategically unsound from every point of view but it also presents most serious administrative difficulties especially as regards medical and supply arrangement."

Foch's solution, enthusiastically supported by Pershing, was pooling Allied resources. If Foch succeeded Pershing believed that it would hasten the creation of an independent US force and eliminate any leverage that the British had over his troops now training with and being supplied by the British. As Wilson told Lloyd George and Milner,

Pershing was abetting the French in their aims by his scheme for a pooling of all resources. The reason for this was that the number of troops he could feed by the French southern ports was limited, and consequently he wished to get a part use of the Northern ports for the American Army, in order that he might thereby avoid putting American troops in the British Army and increase the strength of the American Army.[6]

The British would have been even more exercised if they had known that Pershing was in the process of striking a secret deal with Pétain to reclaim his divisions training with the British "as soon as their instruction is completed and the present crisis has reached its termination."[7]

Not surprisingly, the British strongly resisted pooling Allied resources. "We have assisted and are prepared to assist our Allies in every possible way and we do so daily," Wilson wrote Milner, "but I consider that any idea of pooling all resources and placing them under the orders of one authority would be fatal." General Wilson also gained the backing of Milner and the British Army Council against further dissemination of the British Army which would make it "dependent on a common pool."[8] Milner forwarded Wilson's and the Army Council's recommendations to Lloyd George, noting that "when we agreed gladly to strategic unity of control, we never contemplated the administrative unification of the French and British Armies, & that it is quite impossible for us to agree to it."[9] For the moment, however, Lloyd George favored a conciliatory approach toward Foch. In his view, "the first consideration was to win the battle; nothing must be done which handicapped General Foch in this respect."[10]

On May 15 the X-Committee, a new War Cabinet subcommittee, composed of Lloyd George, Milner, Wilson, Hankey, and Leo Amery, held its first meeting. Amery, who took notes, and especially Hankey, were secretaries but they enjoyed influence on military and geopolitical questions far beyond their official status. American reinforcements dominated its first and many of its future meetings. Major General R. Hutchinson, the Director of Organization in the War Office, attended the meeting. Having recently returned from Washington where he had assisted the War Department in accelerating its transportation of troops to embarkation ports, he painted a bleak picture of US mobilization. He had learned from General Enoch H. Crowder, who administrated selective service as Provost Marshal, that the War Department had drafted only 250,000 in May although it could have brought in 400,000. (Incredibly, the War Department prior to May had been drafting only around 116,000 men a month.)[11] Hutchinson had learned from other services "that the shortage of clothing and equipment was the limiting factor. The Administration was reluctant to call up men until they could be equipped and clothed, lest the inadequacy of their arrangements should be discovered." Hutchinson also discovered divided opinion over the number of men who had actually completed their scheduled training. He concluded that part of the problem was the General Staff's decision to train men in battalions and divisions before training them as individuals. Hutchinson's criticisms of American mobilization had validity but he was proved dead wrong when he characterized Chief of Staff March as "inadequate."[12]

Two days later, during a meeting of the X-Committee, Lloyd George launched into a tirade against the AEF's leadership, especially its training program and deployment of forces. "During the present year the Staff work of the Americans was so inferior as to prevent them from achieving any considerable results," he grumbled, and that unless a drastic change of method were made they would not be materially better next year. After President Wilson had agreed that American troops should be brigaded with British and French troops, General Pershing had stepped in and overruled him. The result was that an amateur army was fighting a professional army. General Pershing had refused to brigade his troops with British and French; he had refused to interlard American Divisions with British and French divisions; he had refused General Weygand's plan of using French Staff Officers to correct the American inexperience, and, unless a change was made, the same thing would happen next year. The result would be that great numbers of brave men would die like flies without achieving any considerable results.[13]

With what he described as a "first-class military" crisis threatening, he wanted "Marshal Foch to talk straight to Colonel House about the American Army."[14]

It was not unusual for Lloyd George to find fault with generals and the volatile Welshman soon turned his attention from Pershing to the general-in-chief and began anxiously questioning Foch's reaction to Ludendorff's third offensive of 1918, codenamed "Blücher," which he launched on May 27.

The German Army had suffered 326,000 casualties from March 21 to April 29,[15] which included many of its best infantry. Ludendorff began to resemble a tired boxer behind on points, swinging wildly as he desperately sought to connect with a knockout punch before American reinforcements overwhelmed his forces. He still believed that the shortest route to victory was through British trenches and desired to continue his attacks north of the Oise. Bolstered by French reinforcements, however, that front now seemed too strongly defended for a successful offensive. To draw some of these French reserves south of the Oise, Ludendorff decided to threaten Paris with an attack on the Chemin des Dames before resuming his offensive against the British.

In preparing for its third offensive of 1918, the *OHL* as usual took great care to mask its preparations. German troops above the strength of a battalion marched at night. Divisions initially involved in the offensive hid in the large wooded areas close to the front. As they drew nearer the French front they bound the tires of their vehicles with bags of sawdust and wrapped cloth round the axles to deaden noise.[16]

Oblivious of the storm about to break on the Chemin des Dames, French intelligence remained confident that Ludendorff's next offensive would focus again on separating the French and British armies north of the Oise.[17] Warnings from the American Intelligence Section at Chaumont that the Germans were preparing to strike next along the Aisne were brushed aside.[18] Not until the eve of the attack did *Grand Quartier Général* (*GQG*) learn the truth. A captured German officer, under the threat of being executed as a spy if he offered false information, broke down and revealed German plans on May 26.[19] At 4:20 p.m. the Sixth Army notified its corps commanders of the impending offensive by Crown Prince Wilhelm's Army Group scheduled to begin at 1 a.m. the following morning.

Although the Germans failed to achieve complete surprise there was little that the French Sixth Army could do to cushion the hammer blow about to be delivered by Crown Prince Wilhelm, the eldest son of the Kaiser. The French commander Denis Duchêne had fatally compromised French defenses. Pétain, in Directive No. 4, of December 1917, had ordered his commanders south of the Oise, where they had more room to maneuver, to establish defensive systems in depth with the majority of the troops stationed in a second line where troops would be less vulnerable to a German bombardment. General Duchêne, however, ignored these instructions and concentrated the British and French soldiers he commanded along the Chemin des Dames ridge. He defended his actions by arguing that a strong defense in well-prepared positions atop the Chemin des Dames was preferable to one along the Aisne which was almost immediately behind his front lines. Although Pétain protested this decision, he did not relieve Duchêne of his command.[20] Thus when Crown Prince Wilhelm's artillery opened up on May 27 the Sixth Army heavily defended a narrow strip of territory on the German side of the Aisne.

General Duchêne had eleven divisions with four divisions in reserve to defend his front of ninety kilometers. The Germans attacked along a section of his front, approximately fifty kilometers, mostly defended by six divisions, which included three battle-weary British divisions, the 8th, 21st, and 50th, which Foch had recently sent to recuperate in a "quiet" sector.[21] British soldiers found little to disabuse themselves of this comforting thought when they arrived. In some places they discovered arbors in trenches covered with rambling roses. One British officer actually told members of the 8th Division as they departed for the Chemin des Dames that they were being transferred to trenches that rather resembled "the Savoy Hotel removed underground."[22]

For his offensive Crown Prince Wilhelm massed 5,263 guns and 1,233 trench mortars against only 1,422 British and French artillery pieces. Some 2 million shells, both gas and high explosive, crashed into the French and British defenses to a depth of twelve kilometers. With an advantage of 3.7 to 1 in gun tubes on a shorter front than "Michael," it represented the most intense German bombardment yet. The conductor of this orchestra of death was the famous artillery commander Georg Bruchmüller, called "*Durchbruchmüller*" ("Breakthrough Müller") by an admiring German public. Colonel Bruchmüller had made his reputation on the Russian front before becoming the army's chief artillery adviser in 1918.[23] His bombardment during the early morning hours of May 27 proved so effective that many German troops had only to advance across no-man's-land to take possession of the British and French trenches from the dead, wounded, or shell-shocked defenders. By 9 a.m. the Germans had crossed the heights of Chemin des Dames and were marching toward the Aisne.

The Germans advanced so rapidly that by mid-morning they had secured the bridges across the Aisne before the French could destroy them. French reserves ordered forward from secondary defenses were quickly pushed aside. Pétain later explained what happened:

The General commanding XI Corps gave the order to send north of the Aisne four battalions of the 157th Division that were holding the second position south of the Aisne. This order came at an inopportune moment, for it was executed just as the mass of enemy infantry descended the Chemin des Dames toward the river. The four battalions of the 157th, plus a fifth battalion that also moved forward because of an error, were thrown head over heels without ever being deployed.[24]

Throughout the day German troops advanced as if they were participating in a route march during a training exercise. By the end of the day Prince Wilhelm's Army Group had created a salient twenty-five miles wide at its base and up to twelve miles deep in places, reaching the Vesle River at Fismes.[25] With reinforcements arriving piecemeal, Pétain had no chance of immediately plugging this gap. On the following day the Germans continued their advance against weak opposition. Ludendorff originally had hoped to advance as far as Fismes and Soissons. But by the third day his original objectives in Ludendorff's own words "had in places been left far behind." On May 31, the Germans reached the Marne and Château-Thierry. During the previous seventy-two hours German troops had advanced some thirty miles and the front existed wherever they chose to halt for the day. A flood of civilians and retreating soldiers clogged the roads ahead of them. Some 60,000 French and British soldiers had been taken prisoner, along with 650 guns and 2,000 machine guns.[26]

Operation Blücher had in fact proven so successful that Ludendorff, falling into a trap of his own making, no longer regarded it as a diversionary tactic to draw French reserves away from the British front. His breakin had in fact created a deep salient poorly served by railways, and his rapidly advancing troops quickly outdistanced their supplies and artillery. Despite Ludendorff's developing difficulties, which became more apparent in retrospect, his advance in the direction of Paris sowed panic within the French and British leadership. On May 30 Pershing dined with General Foch and his staff at Sarcus, a tiny village between Beauvais and the Channel. Although its headquarters was located far from the thunder of guns Pershing found Foch's staff much affected. "It would be difficult to imagine a more depressed group of officers," he later recalled. "They sat through the meal scarcely speaking a word as they contemplated what was probably the most serious situation of the war."[27]

GQG began considering desperate plans. Its so-called "big plan" included withdrawing French troops from Verdun to Switzerland to form two large forces, one southeast of Reims and another southwest of Montdidier, as a prelude to launching a massive counterstroke. It is Doughty's view that this resembled a Kamikaze attack: "little more than a desperate counteroffensive before almost certain defeat." As a step toward implementing this plan, Pétain had his northern and eastern army-groups begin planning for a possible reconfiguration of their forces. An officer in the French Operations Bureau bluntly informed an American liaison officer: "The war will be over in about two weeks."[28]

From his office in London, Sir Henry Wilson also contemplated Armageddon. He scribbled in his diary: "I find it difficult to realize that there is a possibility, perhaps a probability, of the French Army being beaten. What could this mean? The destruction of our Army in France? In Italy? In Salonica? What of Palestine and Mesopotamia, India, Siberia & the Sea? What of Archangel & America?" In the following days, the British government considered plans to evacuate the BEF. Subsequently, the Admiralty reported that shipping was available to embark from 300,000 to 400,000 men daily.[29]

On June 1–2 the Supreme War Council reassembled at Versailles in a crisis atmosphere. Pétain suggested that Clemenceau should move his government to Bordeaux with the capital under bombardment by long-range German guns and attacked by Gotha bombers. Although the French government stayed in Paris, many Parisians fled the capital in panic. With Allied leaders equally on edge the anti-German coalition momentarily teetered on the brink of disintegration. French leaders accused the British of undermining their country's survival by not making commensurate manpower sacrifices to sustain their divisions in the field. For their part the British, who indeed were considering limiting their manpower obligations on the Western Front in 1918–19 and concentrating additional manpower in the outer theaters, suspected Foch of using his position to favor French over British security concerns.

On one question, however, the British and French leadership agreed: Pershing must be coerced into dropping his granite-like opposition to shipping only American combatants and feed them into the existing

French and British armies. In effect they wanted him to postpone indefinitely his plan to create an independent US Army. In a classic understatement Pershing writes in his memoirs: "Every one realized the gravity of the Allied situation, but there was a decided difference of opinion as to the best way to meet it."[30]

Pershing, who a month earlier had been put through the ringer by Allied leaders at Abbeville, suggested that the Supreme War Council had no right to decide either the composition or the disposition of US troops being shipped to Europe. He insisted that these questions should properly be dealt with outside the Council. Consequently, on the afternoon on June 1, he met with Lord Milner, General Foch, and his loyal subordinate, General Maxime Weygand, in Clemenceau's office. They were later joined by Sir Henry Wilson, Graeme Thomson, a British expert on transportation and supply, and Lloyd George, among others.

Pershing emphasized that his earlier concessions on shipping infantrymen and machine gunners had seriously affected his logistical ability to maintain his divisions. He also stressed that America had depleted its supply of trained soldiers at home by shipping them abroad. Surely the French did not want him to ship untrained soldiers. Why not, he suggested, use the shipping available to ship stevedores and other noncombatants to build up his SOS organization which could then better serve American combatants after they had completed their training and been shipped to France? Foch remained unmoved by talk of future American assistance when the Germans were at the gates of Paris. He repeatedly waved his arms and emotionally exclaimed: "*La bataille, la bataille, il n'y a que ça qui compte*" ("The battle, the battle, there is nothing else that matters"). With the participants at loggerheads Pershing suggested that they adjourn for the day.[31]

The following day Pershing felt the full wrath of the Allied political and military leadership which demonstrated by its comments that it had little confidence in his leadership of the AEF. Lloyd George even dared suggest that he defer to the British military in deciding when American troops training with the British should be committed to combat.[32] Foch also repeated the provocative question he had earlier put to Pershing at Abbeville.

"You are willing to risk our being driven back to the Loire?" he asked.

"Yes," Pershing shot back, "I am willing to take the risk."

"Well, we will refer this to your President," Lloyd George threatened.

"Refer it to the President and be damned," Pershing angrily shot back. "I know what the President will do. He will simply refer it back to me for recommendation and I will make to him the same recommendation as I have made here today."[33]

Pershing's tough stance put the coalition at risk. But not as much as one might think. Other than feeding his available divisions piecemeal into battle (which he was already doing) there was nothing he could do differently in the short term. Postponing the creation of an independent American army by shipping only infantrymen during the next two months would have zero effect on the battle waging in front of Paris. Moreover (as the British already understood), there existed a depressingly small number of trained riflemen in US training camps. This was also true of the AEF, for Pershing's total rifle strength on June 1 was only 215,000 out of the 601,243 men who had been shipped to Europe.[34] Foch demanded that 500,000 infantrymen be shipped in June and July but the War Department would not have nearly that many trained infantry available during the next two months.

Milner, Foch, and Pershing eventually hammered out an agreement as follows. If the shipping were available Pershing agreed to ship 170,000 combat troops in June and another 140,000 in July. Assuming the availability of sufficient tonnage for 250,000 men a month, the space not taken by combat troops would be filled with support and supply troops (making a total of 190,000 noncombatants for the two months). The War Department actually did better than this. Some 585,000 men were shipped in June and July, but the emphasis on infantrymen still left the SOS short of manpower.[35] Also, the desperate need for riflemen meant that many American soldiers were destined to be sent into battle during the following months with insufficient or even no battlefield training. As noted in the Pershing–Milner–Foch agreement: "We recognize that the combatant troops to be dispatched in July may have to include troops which have had insufficient training but we consider that the present emergency is such as to justify a temporary departure by the United States from sound principle of training especially as a similar course is being followed by France and Great Britain."[36]

With the Germans reoccupying territory along the Marne that they had held in September 1914, Pétain visited Pershing on May 30 and urgently requested that he put American troops in the line in the region of Château-Thierry. Pershing had two regular army divisions within easy reach of Château-Thierry, the 3rd Division commanded by Major General Joseph T. Dickman and the 2nd Division commanded by Major General Omar Bundy.

The 3rd Division had been organized at Camp Greene, North Carolina, in November 1917, with its last units arriving in France on May 12. It was currently training south of Verdun at Chaumont. Pershing on May 30 placed the division (less its artillery and engineers) at the disposal of the Groupe d'Armées du Nord which immediately assigned it to the defense of the Marne crossings. The chief adviser of the French Military Mission with the 3rd Division also embedded French officers in the division, one for every commanding colonel and at least one for every battalion.[37] Many American officers did not think this a happy arrangement, and Dickman was soon complaining that his division was "rapidly passing to the control of the French commanders, and the brigade and regimental commanders have practically ceased to function as such."[38]

The first unit of the 3rd Division to go into action was the motorized 7th Machine Gun Battalion. The French sent the battalion speeding down the road in its light Ford trucks to defend the bridges across the Marne at Château-Thierry, the first squads arriving at about 6 p.m. on May 31. The French then positioned American machine gunners on both sides of the Marne and by 4 a.m. seventeen guns were in position and firing although the men manning the guns had not slept for thirty-six hours. Under continuous artillery and machine gun fire the 7th Machine Gun Battalion was finally relieved in the early hours of June 4.[39] Meanwhile, infantry regiments of the 3rd Division, under the command of the French XXXVIII Army Corps, had been deploying east of Château-Thierry south of the Marne River for some ten miles. Dickman reported: "Health of men: Good. Morale: excellent. Tired and weary but intensely earnest, and anxious to participate in the actual fight."[40] Given its limited training Pershing did not want the division involved in offensive operations. (The 7th Infantry did, however, relieve the Marine Brigade for about a week in Belleau Wood.) For the rest of the month the 3rd Division defended a relatively quiet front which allowed Dickman to focus his attention on preparing a defensive system in depth.

While the 3rd Division prepared for a possible resumption of the German offensive on its front, the 2nd Division was involved in heavy combat for most of June. Although Regular Army, the 2nd Division included the 4th Marine Brigade, composed of the 5th and 6th Regiments. Following America's entry into the war, the Marine Corps Commander Major General George Barnett quickly moved to establish training camps at Quantico, Virginia, and at San Diego, California. When the decision was made to send an expeditionary force to France, he successfully lobbied to include a Marine presence. On May 29, 1917 Secretary of the Navy Daniels instructed him to organize a force, known as the 5th Regiment of Marines. The result was the creation of a regiment composed of Regulars with prewar experience. Later, another regiment, the 6th Regiment of Marines, composed of fresh volunteers and a few experienced officers, was organized and dispatched to France to join the 5th Regiment, forming the 4th Marine Brigade.

Determined to maintain the highest possible standards, Barnett demanded that to be accepted all volunteers had to be literate, have good eyesight and hearing, and possess "at least twenty teeth." An astonishing 60 percent of the new recruits for the 6th Marine regiment had previously attended college, many of them completing their degrees. Former football players were especially prized recruits. Marine instructors emphasized toughness and marksmanship, with 65 percent of the Marines qualifying as marksmen.[41]

Billeted in villages in the area of Chaumont-en-Vexin the 2nd Division was undergoing training in terrain exercises when Pershing placed it under French command on May 30. Within hours the commander of the French Group Reserve Armies at Noailles ordered the division to begin a two-day march on the following day to the Beauvais area. These orders were quickly countermanded and the division ordered to assemble in the area of Meaux, a town some forty kilometers west of Château-Thierry. The French provided trucks to carry the infantry and trains for artillery and animal transportation. Staff officers frantically worked throughout the night preparing orders and schedules for the transport of 28,000 men and their equipment.[42]

At 3 a.m. on May 31 buglers awoke the men of the 2nd Division. They ate a hurried breakfast from their rolling kitchens, and marched to awaiting French trucks. At 5 a.m., twelve hours after the division had received its instructions, men began climbing aboard trucks with canvas tops (called *camions*). Asians from Hue, Danang, Vinh, Hanoi, Saigon, and other areas in French Indochina drove these trucks. Soldiers holding their rifles sat across from each other on narrow wooden bench seats along the sides, back packs piled between them, with as many as thirty men to a truck. The hard-rubber wheels guaranteed a bumpy ride. As the fourteen-mile convoy neared the Marne Valley the distant sounds of cannonading could be heard.

Staff officers preceded the trucks by motor car. Harbord drove through Paris and on another twenty miles to Meaux. He found the town, recently bombed by German aircraft, "in a state of wild confusion, not to say terror."[43] Leaving the ancient town he witnessed a rout in progress as the narrow highway he traveled was clogged with retreating soldiers and civilians.

Men, women, children hurrying to the rear; tired and worn, with stark terror in their faces. Artillery caissons and trucks were carrying some. Many were walking, an occasional woman wheeled a perambulator with the baby in it. Sick people were lying exhausted beside the road. Some were driving carts piled high with their worldly goods. I saw one poor woman driving a pair of goats while she plodded along. Little flocks of sheep, a led cow, crates of chickens on carts. We passed many French officers and soldiers all coming *from the front*.[44]

Confusion also reigned about the positioning of the 2nd Division. After climbing out of their trucks near Meaux where the Ourcq River joined the Marne, the Doughboys took up a position between Gandelu and Montigny northeast of Meaux. After marching to this location they received new French orders that positioned the division astride the Château-Thierry to Paris road. This required the infantry to march throughout the night. By 9 a.m. on June 1 the 2nd Division had approximately 13,000 men blocking the Château-Thierry to Paris road. By evening most of the rest of the division's infantrymen had arrived. They carried only 100 rounds each and their artillery and machine gunners lagged behind.[45] Having taken up two different positions during the night the men were exhausted.

Some of the division's machine gun companies had no available trucks to transport them to their original assembly point at Meaux so they hiked. "At eight o'clock in the morning of June 1st we had covered 48 kilometers," writes Sergeant Bernard J. McCrossen, Machine Gun Company, 23rd Infantry,

and marched for almost twelve hours straight with occasionally the usual ten minutes halt. At 8:30 we halted ... The feet of the men were bandaged up and at 10:30 we were again in the road and did not halt until 4 o'clock ... We had covered over 84 kilometers since we began our march 17 hours before, with only two hours rest. Translated into English this means that we had with practically uninterrupted marching covered about fifty miles.[46]

And they had yet to catch up with the infantry.

That morning Bundy and his Chief of Staff, Colonel Preston Brown, conferred with General Jean-Marie Degoutte, the commander of the XXI Corps, at his headquarters at the town of Coupru. The Germans were now only a few miles away having seized the high ground west of Château-Thierry (Hill 204), occupied the town of Vaux, and entered Château-Thierry. A desperate Degoutte proposed feeding US infantry piecemeal into battle as they arrived. All too aware that their exhausted and inadequately armed infantrymen were in no condition to confront the advancing Germans, Bundy and Brown offered a counter proposal. The French would continue to maintain the front while the newly arrived and arriving Doughboys constituted a secondary defensive position. Once the 2nd Division was fully constituted the frontline French soldiers could withdraw through the American lines.[47]

Bundy and Brown's proposal made sense to Degoutte and he accepted it, later defending the American officers from charges that they had been reluctant to enter "the battle line." "Arriving on the field after an extremely hard night march and sent to a part of the front which was being heavily attacked," he wrote to the commander of the French Sixth Army,

the American troops advanced without stopping, in spite of their fatigue, and arrived in time, a short distance back of our front. Their unexpected arrival and the way in which they entered the zone of fire created a decidedly favorable impression on our troops. The bringing into action of machine guns, here and there, at long range, made it possible to inflict heavy losses on the enemy.[48]

On June 2 at 10:30 a.m. Degoutte formally instructed Bundy that his regiments were "to hold in place and that French elements driven back by hostile attack are to be allowed to pass through the American lines, in order that they may be reorganized under the protection of their American comrades."[49] On June 4 the French troops remaining in front of the 2nd Division were formally relieved and they retreated through the US lines. "There was no beating of drums and no flags flew," Harbord later wrote. "They were tired and demoralized. They came back not in company formations, but in small, dragging, half-dazed groups of three or four men together."[50]

Flanked by the French 167th Division and the French 10th Colonial Division and assisted by French aircraft and artillery, the 2nd Division now awaited the anticipated onslaught by the German IV Reserve corps (7th Army) commanded by von Conta. But Ludendorff's third powerful offensive of 1918, like the previous two, had by now run its course. German troops had advanced forty miles and established a foothold along the Marne, but without resupply, rest, and the arrival of additional supporting arms the offensive began to lose its momentum as early as June 2. On June 4, von Conta ordered his forces to assume a defensive position.[51]

His Chief of Staff von Unruh later wrote: "Though we told ourselves and our men, 'On to Paris,' we knew this was not to be ... Our casualties were increasingly alarming; ammunition was running short and the problem of supply, in view of the large demands, became more and more difficult ... In truth the brilliant offensive had petered out."[52]

Ludendorff's priorities had already shifted before June 4. His primary objective continued to be the defeat of the British but the initial success of Operation Blücher had encouraged him to continue his offensive. This resulted in considerable tactical success but also drew down his forces and created a huge salient which was both difficult to defend and supply. With his flanks threatened from Reims and from the wooded hills of Villers-Cotterêts on the south face of the salient, he ordered another

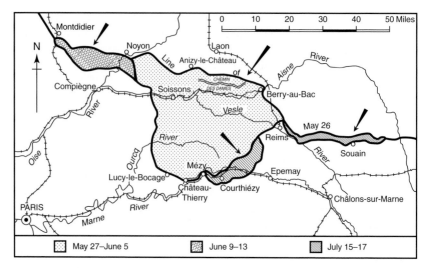

4. Ground gained by German offensives of May, June, and July, 1918

offensive to broaden the shoulders of the salient and improve his communications. But his Noyon–Montdidier Offensive, launched on June 9 and suspended on June 13, did not surprise the French and failed to achieve anything close to his previous 1918 offensives (Map 4).

Although Paris was no longer threatened, the arrival of the Americans on the battlefront encouraged the French to continue the war. According to Pétain, seventeen of his thirty-seven French divisions "had been completely used up." The Germans had lost 105,370 killed, wounded, or captured during their offensive and Ludendorff could not replace his losses, but the Allies could with the increasing flow of Americans across the Atlantic. By June 26, there would be 820,000 American soldiers in Europe, an increase of almost 400,000 since May 1.[53] Clemenceau spoke for many Allied leaders when he remarked: "I am gambling the war on American intervention which will bring us such resources that we cannot fail to finish the Germans off."[54]

As American troops replaced French units along a section of the front Clemenceau defended his government and generals against violent defeatist attacks. In an emergency session of the Chamber of Deputies on June 4 he stressed the growing number of American soldiers in France and issued these fighting words: "I will fight in front of Paris, I will fight in Paris, I will fight behind Paris."[55]

Hence the arrival of American forces to defend the Marne crossings and the road from Château-Thierry to Paris should not be underestimated. The new world seemed to be replacing the old on the battlefields of France. "The spectacle of this magnificent youth from across the sea, these youngsters of twenty years with smooth faces, radiating strength and health in their new uniforms, had an immense effect," noted one French officer. "They offered a striking contrast with our regiments in soiled uniforms, worn by the years of war, with our emaciated soldiers and their somber eyes who were nothing more than bundles of nerves held together by an heroic, sacrificial will. The general impression was that a magical transfusion of blood was taking place."[56]

On the same day that the Tiger spoke to the Chamber of Deputies, American soldiers went on the offensive near Château-Thierry. Believing that the Germans planned to continue their attacks, General Degoutte on June 5 ordered the 2nd Division and the French 167th Division to push forward to straighten their front and improve their defensive position. Harbord subsequently ordered the Marine Brigade to occupy at least part of the Bois de Belleau (Belleau Wood), the neighboring village of Bouresches, and a small knoll just to the west of Belleau Wood designated as Hill 142.

A frontal assault by the 2nd Division did not seem reckless to the inexperienced Americans, especially since the rapidly advancing Germans had not had time to prepare anything resembling their usually sophisticated defensive systems. And with the noted exception of Belleau Wood the rolling countryside of a few groves of light timber and pastures and wheat fields dotted with homes and farm buildings appeared to offer little natural protection to the Germans. In sum it seemed the perfect environment for the Americans to test their open warfare doctrine.

An overconfident Harbord, the commander of the 4th Marine Brigade, did not think that prevailing conditions necessitated significant artillery support. In the only previous American offensive of the war at Cantigny some five weeks earlier, the 1st Division had succeeded against makeshift German defenses because of meticulous planning and technical support from tanks, aircraft, flamethrowers, and especially artillery. Yet Harbord's staff provided little artillery support – some "raking fire" the previous evening and "violent annihilating fire" five minutes before the advance began, both by light guns. Rolling barrages which had preceded the infantry into Cantigny were not called for and perhaps were not possible given the hasty arrangements for the attack.[57]

In conjunction with an advance by the French 167th Division to their left and Major Maurice Berry's 3rd Battalion on its left, the 1st Battalion, 5th Marines, led by Major Julius S. Turrill, advanced at 03:45 against Hill 142 along a front of some 800 meters. The assault began badly when only two, the 67th and 49th, of the battalion's four rifle companies arrived in time. At half-strength the battalion advanced in dressed lines. (General Bundy had earlier stressed that this would "insure the highest degree of control by subordinate commanders.") "A beautiful deployment, lines all dressed up and guiding true," was the way that Lieutenant John Thomason remembers the advance of his assault platoon. The results were all too predictable, especially when German artillery held up the supporting attacks on Turrill's flanks. German water-cooled Maxim machine guns tore through the ranks of the advancing Marines armed only with rifles and bayonets. With indomitable courage the Marines seized the crest of Hill 142 but at a cost of ten officers and about 400 men.[58] Captain George Hamilton's message reached Turrill at about 10 o'clock: "Our casualties are very heavy. We need medical aid badly ... We need artillery assistance to hold this line tonight. Ammunitions of all kinds is needed ... All my officers are gone."[59]

One of the bloodiest chapters in Marine history, however, was just beginning and would last for another three weeks. That afternoon the Marines focused on Belleau Wood, which had once been a hunting preserve for the Château of Belleau. Harbord provides a vivid retrospective account of what lay ahead for his Marines. "The timber was what in this country would be called second growth, but it had never been underbrushed and there was a dense tangle of undergrowth, with here and there a wood road through it," he writes in his account of the war. "The topography of the greater part of the wood, especially in the eastern and southern portions, represented an obstacle course for any attacking force."[60] It has been described as "a wilderness of trees, brush and limestone caves, amid great jutting rocks, on a terrain more fitting for encounters between savage tribes armed with bolos and spears where every advantage was with the defense."[61] None of this was shown in any maps available at the time. The German defenders of these woods, the 461st Infantry Regiment of the 237th Division, which numbered twenty-eight officers and 1,141 men plus a few attachments, would have been hard pressed to find a more advantageous position.

Prior to the assault the French, according to Harbord, assured him that the woods were lightly defended when in fact the Germans strongly manned this former hunting preserve with three lines of trenches which included barbed wire, rifle pits, and machine gun nests. Unfortunately, the Americans accepted this promising French intelligence and conducted no reconnaissance of their own, which Harbord later blamed on "inexperience."[62]

Conceived of as a surprise attack, Harbord and his staff assigned even less supporting artillery for the infantry than it had during the morning assault against Hill 142. Self-reliant American infantry, armed with rifles and bayonets, were pretty much on their own as three companies of the 3rd Battalion (5th Marines) under Major Benjamin S. Berry and the 3rd Battalion (6th Marines) and elements of Major Thomas Holcomb's 2nd Battalion (6th Marines) under Major Berton W. Sibley prepared to advance across waist-high wheat fields toward the woods. "To attempt to storm it except after the most thorough artillery preparations seemed suicidal," Van Every later wrote in his popular account of the war. "The bare fields around it were like the bottomless moats of a medieval castle. They made approach all but impossible since any attack would be in the open and subjected to a terrific machine gun fire."[63]

At 5 o'clock, following a thirty-minute perfunctory bombardment, officers blew their whistles and Marine assault battalions moved forward at a steady pace in four skirmish lines, the men placed five yards apart. As one officer observed, "the Marines were seen advancing in splendid order. The spectacle was inspiring."[64] A French or British survivor of earlier linear advances with insufficient artillery support, however, could have predicted the results. Soon the chat-chat-chat of German machine guns and the crack of rifles could be heard and men began to fall. Sensing hesitation in the ranks, a sergeant (thought to be Sergeant Dan Daily, who wore two Medals of Honor won at Peking, 1900, and Haiti, 1915) could be heard above the clamor. "Come on, you sons of bitches! Do you want to live forever?"[65]

The skirmish lines faltered in places, with men throwing themselves to the ground to avoid the hail of bullets from German machine guns and rifles. Some Marines adopted tactics more suited to the modern battle-field. They continued to advance into the teeth of enemy fire with short rushes before dropping to the ground and then rising again and moving forward. Some Marines had the satisfaction of entering the woods and dispatching their tormentors with bayonets or rifles. But by nightfall thirty-one officers and 1,056 men had been killed, wounded, or were missing, the deadliest single day in Marine history until Tarawa, twenty-five years later.[66] The Marines had seized the village of Bouresches and occupied sections of the woods including the southern portion. As night fell, according to Second Lieutenant Laurence T. Stallings, a platoon commander in the 47th Company, elements of the Marine Brigade "lay shattered and exhausted in the confused tangle of the Bois de Belleau."[67] The battle had just begun.

Ironically the US press celebrated this Marine assault on June 6 as a great victory. The *Chicago Daily Tribune*'s headline trumpeted: "US MARINES SMASH HUNS, GAIN GLORY IN BRISK FIGHT ON THE MARNE, CAPTURE MACHINE GUNS, KILL BOCHES, TAKE PRISONERS." The

New York Times blazoned: "OUR MARINES ATTACK, GAIN MILE AT
VEUILLY, RESUME DRIVE AT NIGHT, FOE LOSING HEAVILY."
What explains these misleading headlines, which suggested that the
Marines were singlehandedly pushing the Germans back along the
Marne, not just at Belleau Wood but at Château-Thierry as well? Floyd
Gibbons, a well-known American war correspondent attached to the 4th
Marine Brigade, had filed a preliminary dispatch with the Army censor
following the morning assault which he planned to complete after what
he assumed was going to be a successful assault later that day. Advancing
with the Marines attacking Bouresches and the southern end of the
wood, he was shot through the eye and badly wounded. Assuming that
he had been killed the army censor in Paris, a long-time friend of
Gibbons, "laid aside his blue pencil and said, 'This is dear old Floyd's
last press dispatch. I will pass it just as he wrote it.'"[68] Harbord char-
acterizes this misleading dispatch which highlighted Marine achievement
at the expense of other units as "unforgivable publicity for the Marines"
and suggests that "the wounds inflicted by publicity received by someone
else do not rate a wound stripe but they are a long time healing."[69]

    Harbord also later referred to the June 6 assault as "a costly failure
bravely attempted."[70] The younger son of Dwight Eisenhower is much
more direct in his description, referring to the assault as "a tragedy, a
useless slaughter of valiant, dedicated men for minimal gain."[71]
Unfortunately this costly failure did not at first encourage the 4th
Brigade's leadership to adopt new approaches. After a pause on the
7th, the Marines resumed their attacks, once again with inadequate
artillery support. Major General John A. Lejeune, who in late July
succeeded Harbord as commander of the 2nd Division, later evaluated
these attacks which devalued artillery support. "Each time little progress
was made," he writes, "and it became apparent that the reckless courage
of the foot soldier with his rifle and bayonet could not overcome machine
guns well-protected in rocky nests."[72]

    This changed on the 10th when "thorough artillery preparation" pre-
ceded a set-piece Marine assault (Map 5). An observer reported from the
front that the artillery had "blown the Bois de Belleau to mince-meat."[73]
On the following day a rolling barrage accompanied troops into enemy
lines following another heavy shelling of German positions. Although the
Germans clung to the northwest corner of the wood, the Marines captured some 400 prisoners and a large amount of equipment with its
coordinated and firepower-based attack. "Strikingly obvious is the great
need for artillery in attack, when one contrasts the little progress made
without it and the advances of the last two days,"[74] Lejeune later

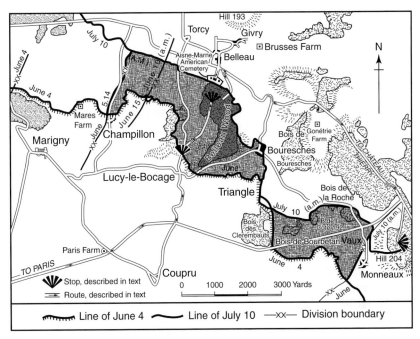

5. 2nd Division operations, June 4–July 10, 1918

concluded. Harbord apparently did not see it this way initially because between June 13 and 24 he continued to order assaults with insufficient or even no artillery support.[75]

Given the natural cover and limited visibility in the densely overgrown woods Marines had to be constantly vigilant. Marine Private Aitken had joined 67th Company, 5th Regiment in early May 1918 after receiving four months' stateside training interrupted by a case of mumps. He later recalled his duty as a sentry in Belleau Wood:

This post was some 200 yds in front of each platoon and consisted of two men in daytime and three at night. The two men in the day were never relieved until dusk, unless an emergency arose; the three men at night were relieved hourly, and sometimes oftener. It consisted of an overgrown foxhole with a place for the sleeper or sleepers ... we reported by sending the third man as messenger at night; in daytime by firing a shot. In the daytime the post was used only to prevent a surprise attack. Several times we went out in the early morning to relieve the post for the day, and they had all been killed. Several times during the nights I was on duty, we repelled boarders. No shooting, knives and rough and tumble ... "C'est le Guerre."[76]

In mid-June headquarters detached the 7th Infantry, 3rd Division, from the Château-Thierry sector where it had been in reserve and sent it to relieve the exhausted Marine Brigade after it had been subjected to an especially heavy mustard gas bombardment.[77] Although this was the 7th Infantry's baptism of fire, Harbord wanted the Doughboys to be aggressive and criticized Lieutenant Colonel John P. Adams, the veteran Regular Army 1st Battalion's commander, when he attempted to put up wire to defend his position. The 7th Infantry's mission, Harbord insisted, was to exert pressure "until those people are killed or driven out." Adams dutifully attacked but he bluntly told Harbord that any advance unsupported by artillery would fail. "The woods is almost a thicket," he told Harbord, "and the throwing of troops into the woods is filtering away men with nothing gained."[78] After a second failed assault, the Marine Brigade, reinforced by 2,800 replacements, re-entered the woods on three consecutive nights, June 21–23, to replace the 7th Infantry.

On June 25 Harbord returned to the formula described by Grote-lueschen as a "firepower-based set-piece" assault.[79] Prior to their advance, the infantry withdrew from their forward positions and light and heavy artillery from all three regiments shelled the enemy positions for hours. Troops then advanced behind a rolling barrage, 100 meters every three minutes. With most of the German machine guns neutralized the Marines began to clear the northern fringe of Belleau Wood of Germans. Suffering only 123 casualties the Marines inflicted upon the Germans 423 casualties, including 260 captured.[80] After mopping up a few diehard Germans on June 26, Major Maurice E. Shearer, 3rd Battalion, triumphantly informed Harbord: "Woods now US Marine Corps entirely." On June 30 the French Army honored the Marines by renaming Belleau Wood "Les Bois de la brigade de Marine" (Fig. 19).

Two battalions of the 3rd Brigade followed up the Marine success at Belleau Wood by overrunning the village of Vaux on July 1. Unlike the 4th (Marine) Brigade the 3rd Brigade did not have to launch a hastily planned attack. Similar to Cantigny preparations, the division's staff spent days coordinating the artillery and rehearsing assault units. Particular attention was paid to the dwellings in Vaux. French refugees, especially stone masons, were interviewed. "Few doomed villages were ever so thoroughly reconnoitered before being reduced to rock piles," writes Stallings. "All soldiers of the 23rd Infantry, and those of the 9th Infantry who had sought and been given a piece of the action, knew the nature and location of every machine gun pit ringing the town, every house in it, and some even knew the names of the occupants, long since fled."[81]

Fig. 19 German prisoners captured by Americans at Belleau Woods

The presence of five French flying squadrons guaranteed air supremacy and three balloons placed German artillery and troop movements
under observation. Platoons of machine gunners, 3-inch Stokes mortars,
which fired an 11-pound high-explosive shell and had a range of some
800 meters, and 37-mm guns (called "one pounders"), which fired a flat-
trajectory 1.2-pound high-explosive shell with an effective range of up to
1,500 meters, provided additional firepower for the infantry.[82] For
twelve hours prior to the attack at 6 p.m. sixty-six light guns, thirty-six
heavy howitzers, and some large trench mortars blasted an area only
2 kilometers deep and 2 kilometers wide. Chemical warfare also made
its appearance on this American battlefield. Private John A. Hughes, "C"
Battery, 15th Field Artillery, describes his initial response to firing gas
shells. "It was some kind of liquid gas[;] when you shook a shell the gas
would make a noise as though it was full of water . . . All of us had to wear
oilskin pants and coats, also hot rubber gloves and our gas mask at alert.
We looked more like fishermen than soldiers."[83] Following this intense
bombardment, the infantry easily overran Vaux, suffering only 328 casualties, approximately one-third of the German losses.[84]

When the American infantry first began appearing on the battlefield at
Château-Thierry, Ludendorff put up a brave front. "Americans who had
been a long time in France had bravely attacked our thinly held fronts,"
he writes in his account of the war, "but they were unskillfully led,
attacked in dense masses, and failed. Here, too, our men felt themselves
superior. Our tactics had proved sound in every way, our losses, compared with those of the enemy and the large number of prisoners, though
in themselves distressing, had been very slight."[85]

The capture of Vaux, however, proved that the 2nd Division could
learn from its disastrous assault on June 6. As Grotelueschen notes, the
2nd Division's staff now "dismissed any notion of self-reliant infantry

and open warfare" and embraced "the much-maligned Allied doctrine so closely associated with trench warfare."[86] Nonetheless, it had been a costly learning experience and little of strategic value had been gained by the capture of Belleau Wood besides strengthening the American front. By June 6, the German offensive had lost its momentum and Paris was no longer threatened.

The 2nd Division when relieved by the 26th Division on July 9 badly needed rest and refitting. From June 1 to July 10, the division had suffered losses of 217 officers and 9,560 men. The Marine Brigade had suffered almost 5,000 casualties at Belleau Wood alone, or over half of the original strength of the brigade. Replacements, however, meant a net reduction in effective strength of 101 officers and 2,339 men.[87] Pershing himself had been much affected by these heavy losses. Dining with fellow officers at Chaumont "his voice broke and he showed deep emotion" in discussing the casualties of the first days.[88]

An army's success is not always measured in territory gained. Despite its heavy losses the 2nd Division had given a dramatic lift to French morale by its presence on the battlefield. It had convincingly demonstrated to the rank and file of the four German divisions that battled them at different times at Belleau Wood that Americans were not afraid to die. "It was a contest of skill against skill, will against will, endurance against endurance, valor against valor, and esprit de corps against esprit de corps,"[89] writes Lejeune, the future commander of the 2nd Division. Captured prisoners from the crack 28th German Division readily admitted to their captors that it had been "decided to use picked men against the Americans" to prevent them from achieving "a moral success." The opposite had occurred, and a German intelligence officer produced an assessment that made alarming reading at the *OHL*. "The 2nd American Division may be classified as a very good division, perhaps even as assault troops," he wrote. "The individual soldiers are very good. They are healthy, vigorous and physically well developed ... The troops are fresh and full of straightforward confidence. A remark of one of the prisoners is indicative of their spirit: 'We kill or get killed.'"[90]

Time was now running out for Ludendorff. One question German prisoners always seemed to ask when captured was "How many Americans were in France?"; and "Didn't the submarines torpedo [y]our ships?"[91] The United States now had twenty-one divisions in France, with one division, the 41st Division, designated as a depot division. Many more were now in the pipeline.

On July 4 Pershing took an incremental step toward creating an independent army when the American First Corps took over a section held by the French Sixth Army now commanded by General Degoutte. The staff of the First Corps had been organized at Neufchâteau, France, as early as mid-January 1918. But American divisions had been scattered throughout France, and its commander, Major General Hunter Liggett, did not have a corps to command until the American First Corps took over the tactical command of a seven-kilometer front previously defended by the French Third Army Corps.

The First Corps consisted of three divisions: the US 2nd and 26th divisions and the French 167th Division. The 26th and 167th manned the front line while the 2nd remained in close support. Some 70,000 American and French troops and 200 guns now blocked the Château-Thierry–Paris road. "It was the first time French troops had served under American tactical command since the American Revolution," Liggett notes, "and the beginning of the first tactical operation of an American army corps since the Civil War."[92]

15 American soldiers in north Russia and Siberia

On May 14, 1918 a trainload of Hungarian soldiers drew up alongside a train packed with Czecho-Slovak soldiers at the railway station at Chelyabinsk, Russia. Called the doorstep to Siberia, Chelyabinsk stood in the southern part of European Russia where Europe borders with Asia. The Hungarians, formerly POWs being held in Siberia, were being repatriated to Austria–Hungary. Czecho-Slovak soldiers were headed in the opposite direction, to Russia's primary port on the Pacific Ocean, Vladivostok, a six-day or 8,300-kilometer train ride along the famous Trans-Siberian Railway.

Following the outbreak of war the Russian Army created a small detachment composed of Czechs and Slovaks then dwelling in the Russian Empire. The democratic Provisional Government that followed the demise of the Romanovs expanded considerably this detachment by including Czech and Slovak POWs. Now the size of an army corps, and fighting for the creation of an independent Czecho-Slovak state, the so-called Czech Legion accepted the general direction of the French Supreme Command which originally viewed this disciplined military force, numbering some 60,000 men, as reinforcements for the Western Front. The British War Office, however, hoped to use this force as a nucleus around which a pro-Allied force might be organized in Siberia. With their future in limbo, the Czechs at Chelyabinsk and elsewhere were aboard trains heading east, perhaps to be transported to France if shipping were available at Vladivostok, or perhaps to be used by the Allies to control the strategic Trans-Siberian Railway.[1]

The close proximity of Czech and Magyar soldiers – historical enemies – created an explosive situation. A Hungarian hurled a chunk of scrap iron, killing a Czech soldier. The inflamed Czechs then seized the offender and lynched him. When an investigation by Soviet authorities led to the arrest of several Czechs, their comrades freed them. Lev Trotsky, the Commissar for War, responded by ordering Soviet authorities to disarm the Czech Legion. He followed up this order with the threat that all Czechs found with arms would be shot on the spot, a declaration that amounted to a declaration of war, and the Czechs responded in kind.[2] On June 30 they seized control of Vladivostok. Within the next few weeks they overthrew the Soviet regime from the Urals to the Pacific Ocean. Through control of the Trans-Siberian Railway they in effect held sway over a territory as large as North America.

This chunk of iron hurled by a Magyar sparked a chain of events that eventually led to US military intervention in both north Russia and Siberia and the beginning of what has been called "the first cold war."[3] American soldiers killed in combat with the Bolsheviks in north Russia and in Siberia remain the first and only American ground forces killed in direct combat with Russians. In 1959 the Soviet leader Nikita Khrushchev reminded Americans of their undeclared war with Russia in 1918–19: "We remember the grim days when American soldiers went to our soil headed by their generals ... Never have any of our soldiers been on American soil, but your soldiers were on Russian soil."[4]

The democratic Russian Provisional Government had been undermined by, among other factors, political infighting, peasant and worker unrest, and the refusal of the new government to quit an unsuccessful war. Its destruction in November 1917 by the Bolsheviks, however, plunged Russia into even greater chaos. The Bolsheviks were soon at odds with their socialist rivals, the Mensheviks (whose leaders generally believed that Russia was not yet ready for a full-bloodied Marxist regime) and the Social Revolutionaries (the party of peasant socialism). When rightist supporters of the former Tsarist regime, liberal elements such as the Cadets, and the independent-minded Cossacks were added to this mix, the result was political anarchy.

The Allies viewed the triumph of Lenin's party as a disaster of the first magnitude, especially after the Bolsheviks in early December murdered the commander-in-chief of the remnants of the Russian Army, General N. N. Dukhonin, and began peace negotiations with the Central Powers at the fortress town of Brest-Litovsk in German-occupied Poland. With the collapse of the Eastern Front from the Baltic to the Black and Caspian Seas, Germany and perhaps Austria–Hungary might concentrate their armies on the Western Front and circumvent the Allied blockade by extracting food and raw materials from the lands of the former Tsarist Empire. This desperate situation led to desperate Allied measures.

The new Bolshevik government, both politically and militarily, appeared quite fragile. Following the successful Bolshevik *coup d'état* on November 7 that overthrew the Provisional Government, Lieutenant General Sir Charles Barter, the head of the British military mission at

Russian military headquarters, advised the British War Office that the "mere announcement of the landing of foreign troops ... would bring about the total collapse of the Bolsheviks."[5] Discipline had indeed collapsed in the Russian armed forces. A disastrous offensive against the Germans in July 1917 served as the catalyst for the greatest army mutiny in history. "The great tide of deserters that flowed away from the front that summer now swelled into a human flood so vast that none could count its numbers," writes W. Bruce Lincoln.[6]

The ruling Bolsheviks, initially dependent for military support from their ragtag detachments of Red Guards (factory workers given guns and turned into soldiers) and mutinous soldiers and sailors, however, were quite vulnerable. The armed opposition that materialized immediately after the Bolshevik seizure of power, however, was even weaker. In southern Russia, the Don Cossacks in early November elected General A. M. Kaledin as their ataman. As the head of the Cossack *Voisko* (army or host), Kaledin condemned the Bolshevik *coup d'état* and expressed his support for the Allies.[7]

The emergence of Kaledin encouraged Lieutenant General Sir George Macdonogh, the normally level-headed Chief of Intelligence on the British General Staff, to submit a truly extraordinary proposal. At this time the Romanian Army still remained in the war despite the demise of the pro-Allied Russian Provisional Government. To keep that country as an ally and to block a German advance into the Ukraine, Macdonogh suggested that military intervention might result in the creation of a sizable pro-Ally force. When he finally put down his pen he had conjured up an impressive force of 500,000 Poles, 400,000 Cossacks, 80,000 Czechs and Slovaks, 300,000 Romanians, 15,000 Serbians, 105,000 Armenians, and 25,000 Georgians. In a final flight of fancy, he suggested that 575,000 Knights of St. George, storm battalions, volunteers, and loyal elements from the Russian Army could also be collected, making an army of an even 2 million men. How this sizable force could be provided weapons and supplies he did not venture. He did, however, suggest that his proposed polyglot army required glue in the form of "say two American divisions" to hold it together.[8]

One can only imagine what the War Department and Pershing would have made of his suggestion had it been forwarded to Washington. In November Pershing commanded only three under-strength divisions in France, the 1st, 2nd, and 26th; and his staff was considering cannibalizing the recently arrived 42nd Division to make up some of the deficiencies in the other three divisions.[9]

During the following months British and French military representatives at the Supreme War Council lobbied for military intervention in

Russia to support anti-Bolshevik elements. In Joint Note No. 5, dated December 24, 1917, they advocated the establishment of direct communications with Kaledin either along the Trans-Siberian Railway or through military operations against Turkey.[10] Confronted in the west by a German Army reinforced by troops from the declining Eastern Front, the Allies had few if any troops of their own to spare for intervention in Russia. The British War Cabinet agreed to finance Kaledin's movement but it and the French government looked to the United States and Japan for the necessary manpower.[11]

Wilson's speech at the Fifth Regiment Armory in Baltimore on the anniversary of America's entry into the war, quoted in Chapter 10, could be interpreted as a rationale for intervention in Russia to block Germany's expansionism. He accused Berlin of wanting to erect an empire of gain and commercial supremacy, "an empire as hostile to the Americas as to the Europe which it will overawe – an empire which will undoubtedly master Persia, India, and the peoples of the Far East."[12]

Although President Wilson loathed the Bolshevik regime he favored economic means over any military action. In his and the War Department's view Germany's drive for world empire could be thwarted by victory on the Western Front rather than by trying to revive the moribund Eastern Front. Hence he continued to oppose military intervention in Russia that would divert military resources from the Western Front. In April, when the military representatives of the SWC in April voted to approve Joint Note No. 20, "The Situation in the Eastern Theater," which called for military intervention to reconstitute the Eastern Front, Bliss, aware of the President's adamant opposition, withheld his signature, thus blocking a discussion by the Allied political leadership at the next meeting of the SWC.[13] Faced with a perilous military situation on the Western Front, however, the French and British continued to support armed intervention in Russia.

Wilson, whose initial and primary focus had been on diplomatic questions during the first months of American belligerency, had effectively abdicated his responsibilities as commander-in-chief as the United States prepared to fight a great land war overseas. He seemed largely uninterested in important military and strategic questions and was loath to discuss the actual fighting with either his Cabinet or new War Cabinet, allowing Pershing extraordinary control of the army's deployment in Europe. Although he often conferred with Baker the reality was that he essentially left him alone to run the War Department. On December 22, 1917 Colonel P. D. Lockridge, the Acting Chief of the War College Division, had sent the Chief of Staff a memorandum that stated the obvious: "In no other belligerent country is the Chief Executive and his immediate council so insulated against the military viewpoint." To remedy this deficiency Lockridge suggested that the Chief of Staff be invited to attend Cabinet meetings.[14]

Wilson, who certainly was not privy to this memorandum, almost certainly would not have gone that far. Questions dealing with amalgamation and military intervention in Russia, however, which involved questions with serious political ramifications, increasingly forced him to seek military advice. When Baker left Washington for an extended tour of American forces in Europe, he had sought the professional advice of the new Chief of Staff Peyton March. March continued in this role after Baker returned from Europe, usually accompanying him when the Secretary of War visited the White House to confer with the President.[15]

March, who describes himself as a "pronounced Western Fronter," had decided views about involving American soldiers in Russia. On June 24, 1918 he dictated a long memorandum for the President that did not mince words.

I do not believe that any man, or men, or combination of men representing the Allied Nations will ever be able to reconstitute Russia into a military machine ... The situation in Russia, while superficially hopeless and impossible of solution, will in reality be solved by our concentrating the entire energies of the nation on putting such a number of men on the Western front as will permit us to drive through to Berlin, where the terms of peace which we would dictate should include a just and satisfactory solution of the internal troubles of Russia.[16]

Continued pressure from Britain and France, in combination with the dire military situation in France, however, forced the President to consider armed intervention in Russia. On March 6, 1918 130 Royal Marines from the British battleship *Glory* landed at Murmansk, the only northern Russian port opened year round. Prison labor had completed a railway from St. Petersburg across thick forest and swamp in the spring of 1917. The completion of this 900-mile railway made Murmansk, the recently constructed town of log cabins, wooden barracks, and warehouses, a vital port for war supplies being shipped to Russia by the Allies. Because of the deterioration of Russia's overused railway system, however, many of these supplies remained in Murmansk after they had been unloaded.

The landing of the British Royal Marines, ironically on the invitation of the Murmansk Soviet, did not really constitute a hostile act by the British. Once ashore, the Royal Marines simply bedded down in barracks for the night. There was no reaction from the Soviet leadership which apparently did not even know of the landing of foreign troops at Murmansk. Nonetheless this incident is often viewed as the beginning of armed intervention in Russia.[17]

In early April Wilson took a baby step toward armed intervention in north Russia when he agreed to send an American warship to join British and French warships already at Murmansk. He apparently did this in part "to allay suspicions held by some" that Britain was "acting for her own selfish interests."[18] The Navy Department subsequently selected the cruiser USS *Olympia*, Admiral Dewey's flagship at the Battle of Manila during the Spanish–American War, to show the American flag at Murmansk.

Wilson also apparently took this action because he believed that Germany – especially after Berlin in early April dispatched General von der Glotz's Baltic Division to Finland – might seize the large store of war materials remaining at Murmansk. Wilson thus associated military action in this area as being directly related to the American effort on the Western Front. Deeply suspicious of Japanese intentions, however, he continued to oppose armed intervention in Asiatic Russia. Hence the British in late April focused on the deployment of American troops in north Russia which they claimed was now being threatened by Germany. On May 28 British Foreign Secretary Balfour instructed Reading to ask Wilson to dispatch a brigade, including artillery, to north Russia. Balfour assured the Americans that it was "not necessary that the troops should be completely trained, as we anticipated that military operations in this region will only be of irregular character."[19]

On June 1, Bliss informed the SWC military representatives that Wilson was willing to support "any practical military efforts which can be made at and from Murmansk and Archangel" if they were not designed to restore "the ancient regime or any other interference with the political liberty of the Russian people." The SWC on June 3 then approved Joint Note No. 31, "Allied Intervention at Russian Allied Ports," which advocated the occupation of Archangel as well as Murmansk by an Allied force under the command of a British officer.[20]

Pershing followed suit on June 14 with a dispatch to Baker and March recommending "prompt favorable action." Wilson and Pershing thus supported this limited military intervention over the War Department's opposition. Baker and Chief of Staff March rightly feared that pressure to expand the operation would begin almost as soon as an American soldier set foot in north Russia. Baker's position, as he wrote Wilson, was that "if I had my own way about Russia and had the power to have my own way, I would like to take everybody out of Russia except the Russians . . . and let the Russians settle down and settle their own affairs."[21]

March's concern about "mission creep" seemed confirmed when the British, even before the landing of an American force in north Russia, sought to enlarge this force to three battalions of infantry and machine guns, two batteries of field artillery, three companies of engineers, and the necessary administrative staff and medical services, about 4,600 men altogether. Against the opposition of the War Department Wilson accepted this larger figure with the exception of the artillery units. As he told Baker, "he felt obliged to do it anyhow because the British and French were pressing it upon his attention so hard and he had refused so many of their requests that they were beginning to feel that he was not a good associate, much less a good ally."[22]

Members of the 339th Regiment, most of whom were from Michigan (about 500 Wisconsin draftees had been added to fill vacancies), had been drafted in June 1918, the month that Wilson acquiesced to sending American soldiers to north Russia. After completing a month's training at Camp Custer, its members boarded troop transports and crossed the Atlantic to take on the German army, or so they thought. After landing in Liverpool on August 3, 1918 Pershing assigned them a new mission.

On the day before the troop ships carrying the regiment docked at Liverpool, a small force of about 1,200 Scots, Canadians, French, and Serbians, commanded by the British Major General Frederick K. Poole, landed at the northern Russian port of Archangel. This motley force also included fifty-one American sailors and three officers from the USS *Olympia*.[23] Having easily secured the town, Poole dispatched troops into the interior along the railway line toward Vologda and south on the Dvina River. The Allied armed invasion of Russia had begun, and the US 339th Regiment and its support troops were destined to join this invasion.

Before being transported to frigid north Russia (Murmansk was within the Arctic Circle and Archangel was just below it), British authorities replaced their US-made Enfield rifles with the Russian Moisin-Nagant 7.62-mm rifle which had been manufactured in the United States for the Russian Army, in large part because a plentiful supply of ammunition for this rifle had already been shipped to Murmansk. Bayonets had to be attached to these rifles because they had been manufactured without scabbards. More seriously the Moisin-Nagant rifle frequently jammed and was so inaccurate that some soldiers suggested that it had been designed to shoot around corners.

Members of the 339th also exchanged their regular olive drab winter uniforms after arriving in north Russia for British winter uniforms designed by the arctic explorer, Sir Ernest Shackleton. A typical American soldier in the line wore

two sleeveless sweaters under an olive drab blouse, a sleeveless leather tunic, felt lined, over a blouse; a heavy overcoat made of waterproofed material giving a general effect of leather . . . two pair of knit mittens, knit so as to leave thumb and trigger finger free; a pair of huge waterproofed mittens hung around the neck ... a very heavy Balaclava cap with the smallest possible opening for the face; over that a cap of white duck lined with black fur having flaps that could be brought down over the ears and tapes tied under the chin, or pulled up and secured by the tapes over the top; a pair of woolen socks; knit leggings that reached the knee; and a pair of Shackletons, canvas boots leather-soled reached half way to the knee and confined by tapes that bind them around the leg.[24]

One American officer sarcastically inquired if the British planned to complete their "Britishizing" process by supplying 5,000 monocles.[25] On a more positive note this winter clothing prevented Americans from freezing to death during the extreme Russian winter.

Although many Americans appreciated their warm British clothing the same could not be said of British field rations. Soldiers welcomed the rum ration but not the food, especially the biscuits, four inches wide and two inches long, which seemed designed to break one's teeth, bully beef, corned beef from Argentina, and tea rather than coffee.[26] "To Hell with British rations!," Paul H. Totten, Company F, 339th Infantry Regiment, noted in his diary on February 20, 1919. "Everybody is familiar with hardtack, but this M and V–! The letters stand for meat and vegetables. It was an un-Godly Limy [British soldier] concoction. Putrid is the only description, so let your mind wonder."[27] Many Americans concluded that they were slowly being starved to death. "There was never sufficient [rations] for any group of troops and the balance to actually keep us alive was stolen from the British and scrounged and traded with the Russians,"[28] wrote Harold Weimeister, a member of the 337th Ambulance Company.

Packed aboard three British transports, the 339th Regiment arrived at Archangel on September 4 with many soldiers aboard suffering from influenza. "Congestion was so bad," remembered one soldier, "that men with a temperature of only 101 or 102 were not put into the hospital but lay in their hammocks or the deck."[29] Private Floyd L. Lewis, HQ Company, later recalled that "many soldiers had to be helped down the gang plank. Others were carried on stretchers. Many died. For a while there were funerals every afternoon with caskets stacked four and five to a covered wagon and our regimental band following and playing a funeral dirge."[30] The American Russian Expeditionary force had gotten off to an ominous start.

Although March opposed placing American units under foreign command, the administration had agreed to put the regiment's commander, Lieutenant Colonel George E. Stewart, under Major General Poole, the leader of the north Russian expeditionary force. Stewart, an immigrant from Australia, had joined the US Army as a private in 1896. Awarded the Congressional Medal of Honor during the Philippine Insurrection War, he later commanded a small post in Alaska prior to World War I. Promoted to colonel when the wartime army expanded, he quickly proved that he was out of his depth in dealing with the confused political/military situation in north Russia. And the absence of clear directions from Washington only made his job more difficult. His only precise instructions had been to report to General Poole.[31]

Almost as soon as Stewart's regiment disembarked at Archangel, the British divided his force and dispatched his men into the interior (Map 6). Packing half of Stewart's force into boxcars Major General Poole sent them south along the railway toward Vologda. He then loaded four other companies on coal barges towed by a tugboat and sent them some 140 miles upstream on the Dvina. British officers now commanded most of Stewart's regiment while he remained remote from his men in Archangel.

The primary military rationale accepted by Wilson for sending US troops to Russia had been to keep the stockpile of war supplies in Russia's northern ports from falling into German hands. A secondary concern had been the anticipated arrival of members of the Czech Legion at the northern ports, where in theory they could be transported to the Western Front. These arguments enabled the President to connect armed intervention in Russia, especially after Foch gave his approval, with the war on the Western Front. But by August, after military intervention had been set in motion, the Germans were pulling out of Finland and been thrown back on the defensive on the Western Front. Ludendorff now needed all available manpower to defend the extended front he had created with his five offensives from March into July.[32] If the multinational force being established in north Russia engaged in combat, it would be against Bolsheviks and not Germans. Moreover, no Czechs ever arrived at either Archangel or Murmansk.

A danger for Washington was that once US troops engaged in combat Allied pressure would mount to send in more soldiers. As Bliss warned an already wary March on the day before Stewart's regiment landed at Archangel: "I have no reason to suppose that the United States would engage in this venture any further than it has done . . . the Allies think that having made a beginning in Russia and having put the foot in the crack of the door the whole body must follow."[33] Bliss need not have worried. On September 26 Washington informed the Allies that "no more American troops will be sent to Northern ports." And they were not, except for 720 noncombatants to work on the railways; all of the men in these railway companies volunteered and served under American command.

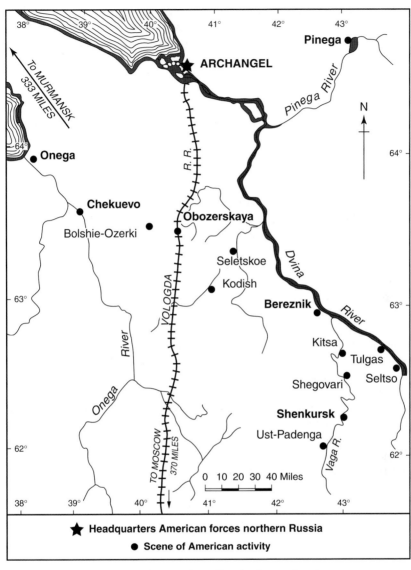

6. American troops in northern Russia, September 4,
1918–August 5, 1919

Including these reinforcements, the American North Russian Expeditionary Force now consisted of 189 officers and 4,718 men.[34]

That the geography around the Russian northern ports, with its extreme winter and thick forests and bogs, seemed similar to the northern regions of Michigan and Wisconsin proved small comfort to the 339th Regiment ("Detroit's Own"), many of whose members were actually city boys. Indifferently trained they were commanded by British officers who they came to detest. Unlike American soldiers in Siberia, they found themselves involved as frontline troops, stationed either on the Dvina and its tributary the Vaga or some 100 miles south on the railway front, combating swarms of mosquitoes in the summer and extreme cold and snow in the winter, as well as Bolsheviks. Paul H. Totten, Company F, 339th Regiment, recorded the following in his diary on February 18, 1919 after emerging briefly from his blockhouse: "Between 50 and 60 degrees below zero reported this morning. Couldn't endure more than a few minutes outside. The sensation of exposure to weather in this temperature is really an experience. The minute you step out in it you feel it grip you all over. Just like a frigid shawl, under pressure being suddenly applied to a warm body."[35]

Ironically the most intense American combat in north Russia occurred following the Armistice. In fact on the very day that the Armistice was signed 300 Americans of Companies B and D fought for their lives on the lower Dvina River, some 200 miles removed from Archangel.[36] The men of the 339th Regiment found themselves fighting an undeclared war that they had not expected and did not understand. Letters home reflected this attitude: so much so, that the War Department intervened. Colonel Stewart's staff had to issue the following directive: "The War Department invites the attention of this Headquarters to lack of proper censorship by officers, by allowing soldiers to forward letters most unsoldierly in tone and anti-British in sentiment."[37]

With no end in sight in this undeclared war, morale continued to plummet. Four members of Company B circulated a resolution demanding relief from the front lines on the lower Dvina River no later than March 15.

After this date we positively refuse to advance on the Bolo lines including patrols and in view of the fact that our object in Russia has been accomplished & having duly acquitted ourselves by doing every thing that was in our power to win – and asked of us, we after six months of dilligent [sic] and uncomplaining sacrifice after serious debate arrive at this conclusion and it is not considered unpatriotic to the US.

They stressed that Germany had been defeated and yet they continued fighting "people with whom we have no quarrel."[38] The American public

Table 6 *North Russian campaign casualties*

Killed in battle	109
Died of wounds received in action	35
Died of disease, drowning, etc.	100
TOTAL DEATHS	244
Wounded, not mortally	305

Source: Peyton March, *The Nation at War* (Garden City, NY: Doubleday, Doran & Co., Inc., 1932), p. 150.

now recognized this as well. As soon as the ice melted at Archangel in June 1919, troop transports, the *Menominee* and *Porto*, arrived to evacuate the American North Russian Expeditionary Force.

American armed intervention in Russia represented a true test of the contentious issue of amalgamation. Colonel Stewart's Regiment had been divided, sent to the front lines, and placed under British officers. The superior attitude assumed by these officers infuriated most members of the 339th Regiment. Even when they attempted to ingratiate themselves by handing out medals wholesale the British often got it wrong. The spit and polish Brigadier General W. P. Richardson, who replaced Stewart, felt that these decorations were "done apparently in much the same manner as the distribution of gifts by masters to their slaves in the South."[39]

A vivid demonstration of the bad blood between British and American soldiers occurred during the American evacuation in June 1919. During a brief stopover at Murmansk the troopship *Menominee* moored alongside the British troopship *Steigerwald* filled with incoming British troops. "They were not very happy, with their lot to replace us and resented stepping into our shoes. They started to throw anything loose at us – coal, mud balls, fruit, bolts and nuts," concluded Paul Totten of Company F. A full-scale battle erupted, especially after British soldiers "displayed an American flag and proceeded to stomp on it ... How lucky there was a strip of water between us. There never was too much unity between our GI's and the British authority under whom we had been forced to serve during our expedition."[40] On this unhappy note the 339th left Russia, sailing for France and then home. Casualties for the entire campaign were 244 dead and 305 wounded (Table 6). An additional 577 sick men were sent to Britain for enhanced observance or permanent disability.[41]

Following Wilson's decision to send troops to north Russia, the Allies through the Supreme War Council intensified pressure on him to intervene in Siberia as well, especially after the Czechs established their control of the strategic Trans-Siberian railway.[42] The French and British might talk of rescuing the supposedly beleaguered Czech Legion, but their primary motive was to revive the Eastern Front, an objective that both Wilson and the War Department deemed impossible. And the Americans were right. To transport and sustain large armies between the Pacific and the Urals was simply not feasible. Moreover, the Japanese, who represented the largest Allied force in Siberia, never had any intention of advancing into western Siberia.

With Wilson prepared to send a small expeditionary force to Vladivostok, Baker and March attended a critical meeting with him in the upper room of the White House. Lansing, Daniels, and Admiral William S. Benson, Chief of Naval Operations, also attended. After they took their seats Wilson entered the room and stood before them. As he talked he referred to notes he held in his hand. March felt that he was once again in a classroom as the President outlined his Siberian policy which would later be expressed formally in what became known as his *aide mémoire*, which served as General William S. Graves's marching orders after he was chosen to command US troops in Siberia.

After the President finished his lecture, Lansing, Daniels, and then Baker gave their approval. When Wilson turned to March, however, he discovered his Chief of Staff vigorously shaking his head in disapproval. Somewhat taken aback, Wilson asked, "Why are you shaking your head, General?" As Wilson already knew, March, deeply suspicious of Japan's ulterior motives, did not believe that Tokyo would limit its military role as promised. "Just that, and for other military reasons which I have already told you," March told Wilson. "Well, we will have to take that chance," the President curtly responded.

It has been suggested by Norman Saul that Wilson received confirmation for his belief that his well-intentioned military intervention would be welcomed by most Russians when he met with Colonel Maria Bochkareva, the former commander of the Russian Army's Women's Battalion of Death. After giving an emotional appeal for US assistance, "she threw herself on the floor and clasped her arms about the President's knees begging him for help, for food, for troops to intervene against the Bolsheviks. The President sat with tears streaming down his cheeks, and assured her of his sympathy."[43]

If ordered to send troops to Siberia, March already had in mind the officer he wanted to lead any expeditionary force: William S. Graves, who had had extensive experience on the General Staff in the War Department as its secretary. After March returned from France to head the General Staff, he told Graves, "If anyone has to go to Russia, you're it."[44] Graves, however, eager for service in France, had recently gained the command of the 8th Division, which was in training at Camp

Fremont, California. On August 2, shortly after his arrival at Camp Fremont, Graves received a coded message from the War Department instructing him "to take the first and fastest train out of San Francisco and proceed to Kansas City, go to the Baltimore Hotel, and ask for the Secretary of War, and if he was not there, for me to wait until he arrived."[45] When March's train pulled into the station at Kansas City later that day, Baker awaited him on the platform. Their meeting was short. According to March, Baker succinctly explained the expeditionary force's mission as follows:

(a) To guard military stores at Vladivostok which may subsequently be needed by the Russian forces;

(b) To render such aid as may be practicable to the Russians in the organization of their own defense;

(c) To help the Czecho-Slovaks consolidate their forces and to get into successful cooperation with their Slavic kinsmen;

(d) To steady any efforts at self-government or self-defense in which the Russians themselves may be willing to accept assistance.[46]

Baker also handed Graves a sealed envelope, telling him that "this contains the policy of the United States in Russia which you are to follow. Watch your step; you will be walking on eggs loaded with dynamite. God bless and good-bye." When Graves later opened this mysterious envelope in the privacy of his hotel room, he found a Department of State document of seven pages, dated July 17, 1918, and simply titled *"aide mémoire."* Graves read the document, which had been written by the President himself, several times. When he put it down, he believed that he had gotten the "meaning of each and every sentence" and did not feel that he needed to ask "for elucidation of any point."[47]

The seasoned diplomat/scholar George F. Kennan expresses amazement at the clarity and relevance that Graves perceived in this document, especially given the extraordinarily complicated situation confronting him in Siberia. "It was," Kennan writes,

even at the time it was presented to him, utterly inadequate to its purpose, that it was still out of date by the time he arrived in Siberia, and that within two months after his arrival it had lost all conceivable relevance, seems never to have occurred to him. He accepted it with that unquestioning and religious reverence which sterling soldiers normally bear for directives from supreme authority.[48]

Graves believed that his instructions showed "an absolute determination on the part of President Wilson that the United States would not take part in military intervention in Russia ... It would have been difficult to have used language that would have made plainer the intent of the

270 The American Army and the First World War

United States in so far as the use of the United States troops in Siberia is concerned."[49] A public statement released to the press a few days later on "American–Japanese action in Siberia" seemed to confirm March's belief that his charge had been to deploy military force, not to fight a war, but to maintain peace while coming to the rescue of the Czechs. "Military intervention in Russia would be more likely to add to the present sad confusion there than to cure it and would injure Russia rather than help her out of her distresses," noted this press release, which also stressed that any effort to revive the Eastern Front was "likely to turn out to be merely a method of making use of Russia than to be a method of serving her."[50]

Carol W. Melton contends that the AEF in Siberia was the forerunner of future peacekeeping missions by the US Army.[51] Given the chaotic conditions that Graves discovered when he arrived at Vladivostok it would be hard to imagine a more difficult assignment for any American officer, even when compared to later "peacekeeping" American military missions in Somalia and Kosovo.

Wilson thought in terms of a small force of 7,000 men. Initially the War Department believed that available manpower, equipment, and shipping might make it difficult to find even that many men and arrange their necessary logistical support. As the President moved toward armed intervention, March suggested that the two under-strength infantry regiments in the Philippines, the 27th and 31st, exchange their tropical clothing for winter clothing and be shipped to Vladivostok. After selecting Graves as commander of the Siberian expeditionary force, the War Department ordered him to form a staff and select 5,000 men from the 8th Division to reinforce the American Philippine regiments being deployed in Siberia.

The men selected from 8th Division had not completed their training at Camp Fremont and were not scheduled to embark for Europe until late October. Most of the division's units in fact never made it overseas.[52] Many of the reinforcements selected from the division to bring the 31st and 27th Regiments up to strength consequently received insufficient training. Private Joseph P. Ahearn, Company F, 31st Infantry Regiment, arrived in Vladivostok without ever having shouldered a rifle. "The first time I was handed a rifle was when our troop train stopped going from Vladivostok to join 'F' Co., of the 31st Infantry. Found the rifle was loaded, but wasn't even shown how to fire it."[53]

On August 16 American troops dispatched from the Philippines disembarked at Vladivostok: fifty-three officers and 1,537 men of the 27th Regiment (Fig. 20). (They were not the first US troops on Siberian soil. The American cruiser *Brooklyn* had earlier disembarked a handful of

Fig. 20 American troops in Vladivostok parading before the
building occupied by the staff of the Czecho-Slovaks

Marines on June 29, 1918 to protect the American consulate in
Vladivostok.)[54] The 31st Regiment, with its forty-six officers and 1,375
men, soon followed. Prior to the arrival of these American troops,
French, British, and Japanese units had disembarked. This international
force discovered a city recently cleared of armed Bolsheviks in street-
to-street fighting by Czecho-Slovaks who had reached the city via the
Trans-Siberian Railway. "The air reeked from ruin and neglect," writes
an American soldier.

Beneath bullet-riddled fronts along broad Svetlandskaya, piles of chipped stone
and splintered glass still lay unswept from the streets. Meanwhile, White Russians
[anti-Bolsheviks] by the trainloads had begun pouring back into the relieved city.
Everywhere new leaders were proclaiming themselves. A dozen new White
governments to replace the recently collapsed Kerensky regime were being
talked up and shouted down.[55]

On September 1 General Graves arrived with the first reinforcements
from the United States. When these reinforcements from California were
combined with troops from the Philippines, the Siberian Expeditionary
Force eventually totaled 296 officers and 9,058 men, roughly twice
the size of the American North Russian Expeditionary Force and

considerably more than Wilson's original limit of 7,000 men.[56] Some 60,000 Czech and 70,000 Japanese soldiers, however, greatly outnumbered this US force. Allied intervention eventually included additional Canadian (more than 4,000) and British (some 2,000) troops along with smaller contingents from France, Italy, and Poland.[57]

Graves's first challenge was to maintain the independence of his forces. On September 2, he visited General Kikuzo Otani of the Japanese Army. Otani, the senior Allied officer in Siberia, who commanded the largest national contingent of troops, shocked Graves when he asked him if he understood that he commanded all foreign troops in Siberia. At least that is what he had been told by the US State Department. For the first and certainly not the last time Graves discovered that he was at odds with State Department officials including the consul generals at Irkutsk and Vladivostok, many of whom took a hard line against Bolshevism. Graves, with the War Department's support, however succeeded in maintaining the independence of his command.

Because of his understanding of Wilson's *aide mémoire*, Graves assumed the role of peacekeeper. But he had absolutely no understanding of the complex political and military situation confronting him or the bewildering cast of characters with whom he had to deal. "I have often thought it was unfortunate I did not know more of the conditions in Siberia than I did when I was pitch-forked into the melée at Vladivostok," he later reminisced. "At other times I have thought that ignorance was not only bliss in such situation, but was advisable ... I landed in Vladivostok without any preconceived ideas as to what should or should not be done. I had no prejudice against any Russian faction and anticipated I would be able to work harmoniously and in a cooperative spirit with all the Allies."[58]

Working "harmoniously and in a cooperative spirit with all the Allies," however, proved impossible. Great Britain, France, and Japan had different agendas and intrigue dominated their relations with each other and with the Americans. Japanese military elements, for example, equipped and financed two war lords: Grigori Semenov, a young Trans-Baikal Cossack officer who commanded a "volunteer army" of Mongols, Cossacks, and former German and Turkish prisoners, as well as a Serbian company and some Chinese; and Ivan Kalmykov, who had become the ataman of the Ussuri Cossacks by killing his legitimate rival. According to Graves, Kalmykov "was the worst scoundrel I ever saw or ever heard of and I seriously doubt, if one should go entirely through the standard dictionary, looking for words descriptive of crime, if a crime could be found that Kalmikoff [Kalmykov] had not committed ... Kalmikoff [Kalmykov] murdered with his own hands, where Semenoff

[Semenov] ordered others to kill."[59] Japanese troops also burned villages and committed atrocities against civilians. The Japanese military fomented turmoil to justify its occupation of Eastern Siberia and the Chinese Eastern Railway, a 1,073-mile link in the Trans-Siberian railway that ran across Manchuria and shortened the Asian route to Vladivostok by some 350 miles. Central Manchuria, which included the city of Harbin, had in effect become a semi-Russian colony.[60]

In addition to these two unscrupulous war lords, Siberia included a kaleidoscope of political factions: liberals who favored a democratic government, rightists who hoped to revive the Tsarist regime, and socialists, some who supported the Bolshevik *coup d'état* in November 1917 and others who did not. To add to the confusion several competing anti-Bolshevik governments existed. Siberian peasants found themselves caught in the middle between these warring political factions. Former Tsarist officers, Admiral Aleksandr V. Kolchak, who had commanded the Black Sea Fleet during the war, and General Dimitri L. Horvat, the Director of the Chinese Railway, emerged as possible political leaders. Several days after the November 11 Armistice that ended the fighting in France, Kolchak seized control of the All-Russian Provisional Government, dominated by moderates and Social Revolutionaries and located at Omsk, and conferred upon himself the portentous title of "Supreme Ruler of All Russia and Chief Commander of All Russian forces of the Land and the Sea."[61]

Located in and around Vladivostok, American soldiers largely became bystanders during this political turmoil. In contrast with some members of the American diplomatic corps and even some members of the expeditionary force who had "heard and let themselves believe that the American army had been sent to Siberia to crusade against Bolshevism,"[62] Graves refused to take sides. His strict neutrality included the Bolsheviks. "The word 'Bolshevik,' as used in Siberia, covered most of the Russian people and to use troops to fight Bolsheviks or to arm, equip, feed, clothe or pay white Russians to fight them was utterly inconsistent with 'non-interference with the internal affairs of Russia,'" he emphasizes in his account of his Siberian command.[63] The result, according to one soldier, was that while Americans were fighting the Germans in France "here in remote Siberia were ten thousand American soldiers sitting about, as idle as hoboes, asking each other what their part of the war was supposed to be."[64] The danger, of course, was that these American troops might become involved in serious combat with the Bolsheviks or perhaps even the Japanese. In October 1919 Baker actually asked the Secretary of Navy if the United States could win a naval engagement with Japan in the Pacific.[65]

Table 7 *Siberian intervention casualties*

Killed	27
Died of wounds	8
Died of disease and other causes	135
TOTAL DEATHS	170
Wounded (not mortally)	52
Deserted	50

Source: Peyton March, *The Nation at War* (Garden City, NY: Doubleday, Doran & Co., Inc., 1932), p. 132.

Fortunately, American soldiers saw little combat and spent most of their active duty protecting war materials, not from the Central Powers but from corrupt Russian officials and thieves, standing guard over German and Austrian POWs and guarding bridges and culverts on sections of the Trans-Siberian Railway. Fortunately for them winters in Vladivostok were relatively mild when compared to the ports of north Russia which were within or on the fringes of the Arctic Circle. Graves actually compared Vladivostok's climate to North Dakota's.[66]

Following the collapse of the Kolchak regime and his execution by a firing squad in early February 1920 the US government withdrew its troops from Siberia, the last soldiers leaving on March 31, 1920. For many it was not soon enough. Following the war's end in Europe, American soldiers in Siberia, largely forgotten by the American public and no longer commanding the close attention of Wilson, had endured two long Siberian winters and confronted innumerable political and military complications that had little if any connection to their country's involvement in the world war. Dispatched to Siberia on what the President and his commander of the Siberian Expeditionary Force defined as a peacekeeping mission, American soldiers, frequently at odds with the British and especially the Japanese, failed utterly in bringing either peace or stability to Siberia. Their government had sent them on an ill-defined mission impossible (Table 7). It would not be the last time that US soldiers were misused by misguided political leaders. Colonel Fred W. Bugbee, the Commander of the 31st Infantry Regiment, wrote his wife on December 6, 1919: "If I could see where we are doing any good I might feel different. It seems to me that our country should take us out of here immediately. I can't help but feel that any lives we may lose over here will be lost in vain."[67]

March could not have agreed more with Colonel Bugbee. Wilson rejected his and Baker's advice on the wisdom of military intervention, and it proved to be one of the President's worst decisions of the war as he attempted to micro-manage armed intervention in Russia while expressing his good faith toward the Russian people. Viewing Siberian intervention as "a military crime," March never forgave the President for bowing to Allied requests for intervention and for leaving troops in Siberia for almost fifteen months after the Armistice. In his words, "the usual formula given despairing relatives inquiring about such matters – 'important diplomatic considerations not understood by you' – was a poor sop to mothers whose sons were killed in that far-away land after the Armistice with no one in the United States knowing why they were there."[68]

16 The beginning of the end

Time was running out for the Germans. The trickle of American reinforcements had turned into a torrent. Ludendorff's four previous offensives in 1918 had cost him some 500,000 casualties; meanwhile the youth of America poured across the Atlantic, infusing hope and energy into the war-weary Allied forces. Prior to Germany's last offensive of the war in July, the German Chief of the General Staff of the Field Army, Foreign Armies, submitted the following assessment: "Considering its small experience of war and defective training the combat value of the American division can in general be described as good. In defense even the most recently arrived troops represent an opponent worthy of respect. The American soldier shows himself to be brave, strong, and skillful. Losses are not avoided. However their leadership is not yet all that good."[1]

In the Marne salient, the French commander-in-chief, Henri-Philippe Pétain, had in mid-July three US divisions on the western flank of the Marne salient, two at the base and one supporting General Henri Gouraud's Fourth Army. Elsewhere unbloodied US divisions occupied quiet sectors in Alsace-Lorraine or trained with the French and British. Many more divisions apparently were on the way, for Pershing had made a commitment to the British and French in June (unrealistic as it turned out) to ship 100 divisions to France by July 1919.

Although delighted at the prospect of even more American troops America's allies continued to argue that these fresh troops could best be deployed to strengthen their depleted divisions. On June 17 Pershing had been visited by Foch and Weygand who asked him to deploy newly arrived US regiments "in the most fatigued French divisions." Foch emphasized that "the effect of young, vigorous American soldiers on the worn-out French divisions would be most advantageous; that the Americans might in the meantime learn something and that they would certainly have a very strong tendency to put the tired French divisions on their feet." Not surprisingly the Frenchman's entreaties did not impress Pershing, especially when Foch made the preposterous suggestion that

"these regiments would be needed for only a few weeks." Pershing
knew that once amalgamated he would have great difficulty retrieving
these men, so he talked of uniting US soldiers "into one American
fighting army."[2]

Despite his recent concentration on the French front Ludendorff still
believed that the shortest route to a German victory was through the
British Army in Flanders. His previous attacks against the French had
been designed to draw Allied reserves down from Flanders prior to
delivering a decisive blow against the British. But the initial success of
these diversionary offensives had encouraged him to continue them. His
fifth and as it turned out final offensive was similarly designed while at
the same time securing Germany's precarious logistical situation in the
Marne salient. It has been suggested that he may have momentarily
convinced himself that another dramatic breakthrough on their front
might force the French to seek a negotiated peace favorable to German
interests.[3] There is, however, no evidence that the German high command expected to capture Paris in July. The key railway center of
Reims, the capture of which would go a long way toward resolving
Germany's logistical snarl in the Marne salient, remained Ludendorff's
focus.[4]

Desperation mixed with a strong dose of unreality now characterized
the German high command. Many of its best trained and highly motivated troops had been used up during the four previous offensives in 1918,
reducing the army to a force of tired and in many cases demoralized
troops. The effect on morale of another failed offensive might be catastrophic, especially after Ludendorff chose the code name of *Friedensturm*
(or "Peace Offensive"), which suggested to German soldiers that the
approaching offensive would be an all or nothing effort.

In retrospect it is clear that the war was now unwinnable for Germany
as the American presence rapidly grew in Europe. As grim as Germany's
prospects appeared prior to *Friedensturm*, however, no key Allied leader
anticipated a German collapse in 1918. Some even expected the war to
last into 1920. Although the French Army had experienced both a
serious mutiny in 1917 and the Chemin des Dames disaster in May
1918, many French officers were actually more optimistic about the
future than the British. As early as May 30, staff officers at *GQG* had
begun preliminary studies for a surprise counter-thrust on the western
end of the Marne salient. A proposal to launch a major attack against
Soissons on July 5 by General Charles Mangin, who had assumed
command of the 10th Army in mid-June, gained Pétain's enthusiastic
support. "Beyond a doubt," he noted, "this operation presents not only
the best chance of success but also the opportunity for a fruitful

exploitation; additionally, it constitutes the most effective parry to the imminent German offensive."[5] Foch concurred and suggested that the Sixth Army commanded by General Jean-Marie Degoutte, positioned to the right of the 10th Army, also join in the attack.

Excellent intelligence gathered from air reconnaissance and from German prisoners provided the French with an exceptional picture of German intentions to launch a new offensive in July east and west of Reims along an extended front. General Marie-Émile Fayolle, the commander of the Army Group Reserve, wrote in his diary on July 12: "The Germans are going to attack between Château-Thierry and Reims. This is more and more certain."[6] The French actually knew not only the day but also the precise time when German artillery preparation for an offensive was scheduled to begin: ten minutes past midnight French time on July 15.[7]

As Foch asserted his authority to shift troops to meet this German threat, the British military and political leadership reacted with growing alarm. On July 8 General Wilson warned the War Cabinet that "the Germans could now put in a bigger attack [against the British] than they did on the 21st March." Although the British had improved their defenses he argued that they were "weaker in the respect that we [are] not in a position to give ground as was possible on that occasion."[8]

Lloyd George and other ministers now questioned Foch's motives, believing that his deployment of American troops was designed to force the British to deploy every available soldier on the killing fields of France. By the end of July the infantry and machine gun units of thirty US divisions would be in France, yet the BEF would apparently have only five US divisions on its front. On July 11 the War Cabinet instructed Lloyd George to remind Clemenceau that Foch was "an *Allied* and not merely a French commander-in-chief, and that he must treat the Allied interests as a whole, making his dispositions on this basis and not mainly from the point of view of French interests."[9] In his subsequent letter to Clemenceau (copy to Foch), Lloyd George did not mince words in his conclusion. "Should the British forces be overwhelmed by superior numbers," he warned, the responsibility would lie with the general-in-chief's deployment of British divisions and "would undoubtedly be fatal to the continuance" of unity of command. In sum Foch must not give the Imperial statesmen the view that "their armies have been let down by the united command."[10]

Confident that the Germans were going to continue their attacks in Champagne, however, Foch continued to shift troops southward. He ordered Haig to send four divisions from British reserves south of the Somme to an area southeast of Chalons and to be prepared to dispatch an additional four divisions. Previously Foch had shifted the last six French divisions of the Detachment de L'Armée du Nord, the French army group in Flanders, south to Beauvais, where they could reinforce either the French or British sector.

Curiously Haig seems not to have been privy to French intelligence concerning German intentions, noting in his diary: "And all this when there is nothing definite to show that the enemy means to attack in Champagne. Indeed Prince Rupprecht still retains 25 divisions in reserve on the British front."[11]

Fearing that the BEF might be "overwhelmed," Lloyd George convened an emergency council of war and suggested that the British veto Foch's transfer of British divisions unless Haig could guarantee that the British front would not be attacked by the Germans, a commitment that no commander-in-chief could honestly give. Fortunately, Lloyd George's colleagues persuaded him to rely on Haig's judgment and Smuts was dispatched to GHQ to ascertain whether Haig "was satisfied with the evidence on which General Foch was acting."[12]

As Lloyd George panicked, the French military leadership remained generally confident. Many French officers had learned from the Chemin des Dames disaster that French soldiers, packed in the front lines, became easy targets for Bruchmüller's sophisticated artillery preparation. General Henri Gouraud, the commander of the Fourth Army on the eastern side of the Marne salient, consequently devised an elastic defense in depth. Gouraud, who had lost an arm and been wounded in both legs at Gallipoli, sought to neutralize German artillery by creating a false front, thinly manned and aptly named the "sacrificial line" by the *poilus*, many of whom faced certain death or capture if they remained in their outposts. German troops, after passing through this first line, had to advance across open fields designed as "killing zones" for French artillery before they confronted a second or intermediate line of trenches built about a mile and a half beyond the sacrificial trenches. If the Germans penetrated this second line (and they did not) they would still be confronted by a third and final line of defense.

One US division, the 42nd or Rainbow Division, commanded by Major General Charles T. Menoher with Colonel Douglas MacArthur as his Chief of Staff, formed part of the French Fourth Army's imaginative defenses east of Reims. To the west, defending the south bank of the Marne in the Château-Thierry region, were two more US divisions, the 3rd and parts of the 28th Division, whose first units had only arrived in France in mid-May. With the exception of the 7th Infantry Regiment, 3rd Division, which had briefly fought under difficult conditions at Belleau Wood, none of the soldiers in these two divisions had experienced hard combat.

These two American divisions were part of General Joseph Degoutte's Sixth French Army, which also included two Italian divisions and the French 125th Division. Unfortunately for the untested Americans, Degoutte did not believe in Gouraud's elastic defensive system, instead ordering the south bank of the Marne to be defended in strength, which placed the Americans within easy range of German artillery.

Flanked by the French 125th Division on its right, the 3rd Division manned outposts on the river bank. Some 350 yards behind these makeshift defenses, the division positioned itself along a railway embankment and beyond that in the hills of the Surmelin Valley. In an especially vulnerable position were four companies of the Pennsylvania National Guard (28th Division), which had been integrated with French units and placed just to the right of the 3rd Division. Each of these companies had two platoons dug in on the river bank.

The Germans chose July 15 for the launching of their offensive because the previous day was Bastille Day, a holiday celebrating French independence, with festivities throughout the country, on the assumption that many French soldiers would not be at their fighting best during the early hours of the 15th.

That Crown Prince Wilhelm's offensive would not surprise the French was demonstrated when the French artillery began interdicting and harassing fire on German infantry assembling for the attack minutes before the big German guns began their scheduled preparation for the infantry assault. German tube superiority of 2 to 1 was actually less than in previous 1918 offensives but German guns still fired an astonishing 4.5 million shells on the first day. This German cannonading knocked pictures off the walls in some Parisian districts, but much of the bombardment east of Reims was wasted on unoccupied or thinly occupied trenches in the new French system of elastic defense in depth.[13]

The most violent German artillery preparation (three hours and forty minutes) occurred along the Marne where German soldiers faced the difficult task of crossing the narrow but deep river on collapsible canvas boats (twenty men to a boat) and by erecting floating footbridges or pontoon bridges for heavier equipment. Under constant shelling and rifle and machine gun fire from the Doughboys many Germans never made it across the river but enough did to place the Americans defending the river bank in dire peril. Many had already been killed, wounded, or become shell-shocked by the German big guns. As Lieutenant Hervey Allen, 111th Infantry, 28th Division, recalls:

I was so frightened myself, I could scarcely get the men together ... There were three or four maniacs from shell shock whom we had to overpower. We dug some of the poor devils out and started them up the hill. The faint sounds and stirrings in the caved-in-banks were terrible. Some we could not reach in time and one of these was smothered. We had one party of wounded all together and started up the hill at once, when a big shell fell right in their midst. I saw men blown into the air. Awful confusion again ... The state of a wounded man, wounded again, and still under fire, is beyond description.[14]

The four rifle companies of the 28th Division were cut off when their French allies fell back, and few Americans made it to their own lines.

The withdrawal of the French 125th Division because of the ferocity of the shell fire also imperiled the 38th Regiment, 3rd Division, commanded by Colonel Ulysses Grant McAlexander, by exposing its flank. Along with the 30th Regiment it endured the heaviest fighting and suffered the most severe casualties while generally holding its ground.

Along a fourteen-kilometer front the Germans crossed the Marne and advanced in places from five to six kilometers.[15] But they succeeded only in bending rather than breaking the front, earning the 3rd Division the proud nickname of the "Rock of the Marne." By the afternoon of the 16th Major General Joseph T. Dickman, the commander of the 3rd Division, reported: "There were no Germans in the foreground of the Third Division sector except the dead."[16] At midnight on July 17 *OHL* issued orders to begin withdrawing across the Marne.

Five battalions and the artillery of the Rainbow Division on Gouraud's sector east of Reims also played a role in stemming the German tide. The waves of gray infantry who survived the advance beyond the sacrificial trenches through exploding artillery shells and deadly gas were repeatedly repulsed by defenders of the intermediate or secondary line of defense. "In all the war," General Liggett later wrote, "no attack on such a scale accomplished so little."[17] Bloody hand-to-hand combat characterized some of the fighting in the American sector. Private Martin J. Hogan of Brooklyn, New York, vividly recalls the ferocious combat:

They broke furiously upon our line and the line of the Sixty-ninth became a dizzy whirl of hand-to-hand combats ... Clubbed rifles were splintered against skulls and shoulder bone; bayonets were plunged home, withdrawn and plunged home again; automatics spit here and there in the line; grenades exploded; while a man occasionally shot his dripping bayonet from his enemies body. Our front line became a gruesome mess.[18]

The Rainbow Division lost 450 killed and 1,300 wounded.

But the line held and by nightfall it was obvious that the German offensive had been a disaster, especially east of Reims. The only real advantage that the Germans had enjoyed throughout the day had been air superiority. Rudolf Binding, a German staff officer, summed up this fateful day for the German Army. "I have lived through the most disheartening day of the whole war." The French had "deliberately lured" the Germans to attack a false front. "They put up no resistance in front; they had neither infantry nor artillery in this forward battle-zone ... Our guns bombarded empty trenches; our gas-shells gassed empty artillery positions; only in little hidden folds of the ground, sparsely distributed, lay machine gun posts, like lice in the seams and folds of a garment, to give the attacking force a warm reception."[19] On July 16 the German high command suspended operations against the French Fourth Army although intense fighting continued south of the Marne as French counterattacks drove the Germans back.

As the Germans floundered, Foch and Pétain turned their attention to the offensive. Anticipating the most recent German offensive Foch had concentrated his reserves, which now included four British and five American divisions, in Champagne. From the Argonne to Switzerland he had only a single French division behind the front to call upon if the Germans chose to attack in that area. But this gamble paid off. Pétain had thirty-eight infantry and six cavalry divisions in reserve to call upon when on July 17 he issued his final order for a powerful counteroffensive against the vulnerable German salient.[20]

The French planned to attack with the French Fifth, Sixth, Ninth, and Tenth Armies along both the base and flanks of the German salient (Map 7). *GQG* scheduled its major attack by Charles Mangin's Tenth Army on July

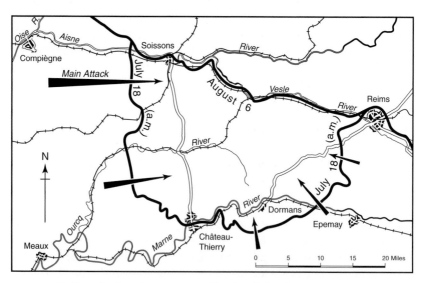

7. French–American counteroffensive, July 18, 1918

18 against the German right flank. Supported by tanks, aircraft, and massed artillery, this force, largely concealed in the thickly wooded forests of the Marne sector, included two US divisions (First and Second) which had been assigned to General Pierre E. Berdoulat's XX Corps. The Tenth Army, with its five corps and twenty-two infantry divisions and three cavalry (really mounted infantry) divisions, constituted a formidable strike force.[21]

Similar to September 1914 and in the very same locality, an overconfident German high command had created an exposed right flank on the Marne vulnerable to counterattack. The Germans simply could not believe that Foch and Pétain could assemble a force capable of launching a serious attack against their right flank, especially after the Germans launched their assaults on both sides of Reims. "Not only could he furnish a sufficient number of units for his defensive front, but he was able to place full strength divisions in readiness for his main offensive drive," incredulous German staff officers subsequently concluded.[22]

Berdoulat assigned the 1st and 2nd American divisions a key objective, a drive toward Soissons to interdict vital German rail and road connections essential to the supply of German forces in the salient. Pershing had just appointed new commanders to both of these divisions, Harbord, who was on leave in Paris, and Major General Charles Pelot Summerall, who had recently replaced Bullard, the newly appointed commander of the American Third Corps. Of the two men Harbord faced the most difficult situation. The French had made arrangements for the approaching counteroffensive in great secrecy, and Harbord was surprised to learn that his 2nd Division had been attached to the XX Corps (which included the 1st Moroccan Division) in Charles Mangin's Tenth Army. Mangin, called the "butcher" by some of his men, was known for his blunt but realistic comments. As his losses had mounted during the costly fighting over Verdun in 1916, he had remarked: "Whatever you do, you lose a lot of men."[23] He was, however, no "chateau" general commanding from afar. Staying close to the action, he had twice been wounded.

Few if any American generals have been promoted to then confront a position as confused as Harbord's. His division had been placed within the French supply and transportation system and committed to an offensive at some undisclosed location. Moreover, his artillery train had been separated from his infantry. Harbord's hands were also tied because he had been placed under the tactical control of the experienced but youthful General Berdoulat.

On Tuesday evening, July 16, Harbord finally caught up with the commander of the XX Corps at his headquarters at Rétheuil. Over a hurried meal Berdoulat informed him that his division then scattered through the Aisne Department and entirely out of my hands, would be in the attack on Thursday at daybreak ... but I knew nothing of where they were to go, and was powerless to hurry or change conditions. A division of twenty-eight thousand men, the size of a British or French Army Corps, had been completely removed from the knowledge and control of its responsible Commander, and deflected by truck and by marching through France to a destination uncommunicated to any authority responsible for its supply, its safety or its efficiency in an attack but thirty hours away.

When a discombobulated Harbord raised questions, French officers sitting around the table shrugged their shoulders, some remarking "*c'est la guerre*."[24]

In his account of his meeting with Berdoulat, Harbord notes that French staff officers provided him the battle plan of the XX Corps and some maps. He also mentions that French officers offered to help him prepare his division's battle or attack order. "I declined with thanks and perhaps a little ice in my voice," he later wrote.[25] Later, on July 17, General Albert Daugan, the commander of the 1st Moroccan Division, provided him with battle orders written by his chief of staff. Having fought in this area, General Daugan's staff knew both the enemy and the ground over which the Americans would advance. Harbord, however, turned down this offer as well. He later argued that "to draw Battle Orders requires not only professional knowledge and tactical judgment but an estimate of the morale and efficiency of the commanders and units affected. It also involved in this case knowledge of the American temperament and character. No French officer had these special qualifications."[26]

Harbord's parochialism perhaps worked to the detriment of the men he commanded. His "Plan of Attack," which he and his Chief of Staff Colonel Preston Brown completed at 4:30 a.m. on July 17, omitted any mention of supporting fire by machine gun barrages or the deployment of light 37-mm guns. Instead it mirrored the official AEF doctrine that emphasized self-reliant infantrymen. Each soldier received two days of rations and 220 rounds of ammunition.[27]

Even if Harbord had been otherwise inclined, the conditions he inherited were surely partly responsible for the 2nd Division's lack of firepower. His division had literally been picked up by the French and hurled into battle, many of its soldiers arriving on the battlefield with only minutes to spare and without adequate supporting arms. Emerging from the woods and advancing across waist-high wheat fields the men of the 2nd Division were without grenades, mortars, or machine guns. Masses of French tanks supported the attack but the 2nd Division had never trained with tanks.

The usual rolling barrage also supported the infantry but extensive artillery preparation had been prohibited to ensure surprise. Fortunately, the Germans thinly held their front and fought from makeshift defenses. German artillery initially caught off balance by the surprise attack and nests of Maxim machine guns posed the greatest danger to advancing Americans. Unlike the First Moroccan's attack order, which provided for a measured advance with pauses to regroup, emphasize Johnson and Hillman, the Americans attacked "with a uniform rate of advance irrespective of terrain or enemy, and without consideration for pauses to consolidate and reorganize, much less pass fresh units through so as to maintain the momentum."[28]

As Harbord and his Chief of Staff Brown put the finishing touches on their "Plan of Attack" in the early morning hours of July 17, US troops began arriving in the region of Rétheuil. Although they had marched throughout the night and had been given no hot food, many of these troops had another fifteen or so miles to cover before reaching their assault positions.

On the previous day Major Ray Austin, 6th Field Artillery, 1st Division, began to understand fully the magnitude of the approaching offensive. "Truck trains in endless numbers moved along every road," he wrote at the time,

batteries of light artillery, immense tractor-drawn 6, 8 and 12 inch guns, staff cars hastening in all directions, blue snake-like columns of French infantry, regiments of Senegalese troops (big negroes whose blackness makes the blackest negroes I have ever seen appear pale in comparison), brown-skinned Moroccans in olive drab uniforms similar to ours, groups of Indo-Chinese laborers, strangely camouflaged tanks, military police at all turns and cross roads directing traffic, like policemen in a big city.[29]

The route to their assault position took Harbord's troops through the forest of Villers-Cotterêts. Twelve miles square, this former royal hunting ground was thickly forested with towering oak and beech trees in full bloom. A national road ran diagonally to Soissons but many smaller roads, with numerous intersections, crisscrossed the forest, constituting a veritable maze for the marching troops. "Occasionally," Private Fitch L. McCord, 82nd Company, 6th Marines, recalls, "a heavy gun or caisson slips into the ditch somewhere ahead, and the diversified column jams up, remaining in a solid, almost motionless pack, and amid a jamborees of sounds, squawks, horns, whistles and shouts, sways back and forth a few times and moves on."[30]

Sleepy and exhausted men plodded along these narrow roads now deep in mud because of a violent rainstorm accompanied by thunder and lightning. When darkness came, men slipped into ditches, sometimes breaking arms and legs. Many held hands or put a hand on the shoulder of the man in front of him to guide their way. "They had no maps, no guides," writes Harbord. "They were not told where to go, and could only follow the instinct of the American soldier and march to the sound of the cannon, seldom silent on that front."[31]

According to one Marine, "no battle tried them half as hard as the night road to Soissons."[32] Some units had to double time (a lead battalion in the 2nd Division actually ran the last ten minutes) to get to their assigned assault positions in order to advance behind the rolling barrage scheduled to begin precisely at 4:35 a.m. The necessity to meet this deadline frequently meant that communication equipment and machine gun companies did not make it to the front in time.

From his vantage point with the 6th Field Artillery, 1st Division, Major Austin described the effect of the moving wall of exploding shells behind which the infantry advanced at the rate of one hundred yards every three minutes:

Our Infantry, following close at a walk, were upon the Germans almost before they had recovered from the shock of the barrage passing over them, and the smoke shells which we fired every fourth shot made a smoke screen which helped conceal our Infantry from the observation of enemy machine gunners. All watches had been synchronized, of course, and when the artillery "cut loose" it made the ground tremble and every hill and valley was just a mass of flashes in the dim light of early morning. I never realized that there was that much artillery in the world. The guns of my three American batteries (I also had three French, but saw little of them as they did only barrage works) were set almost hub to hub and there were many batteries above and below them on the same hillside. The Infantry went forward in a long line extending as far as could be seen to either side, the successive waves following each other at even intervals, and the lines which I saw were a small part of a similar line some forty kilometers long that was moving forward in the same way at the same time, supported by artillery the whole distance.[33]

Further south in this lengthy wave of advancing infantry was the American 26th Division and battalions of the 4th Division, interspersed with veteran French troops from the II and VII French Army Corps. Approximately one-half of the advancing soldiers along the German right flank were American.[34]

Berdoulat placed the 1st and 2nd US Divisions and the 1st Moroccan Division in the first line for the offensive and the two French divisions, the 58th and 59th, in the second line (Map 8). The Moroccans, sandwiched between the American 1st and 2nd Divisions, were some of the fiercest warriors in the French Army. Originally composed of French Legionnaires, this division was now largely made up of Senegalese,

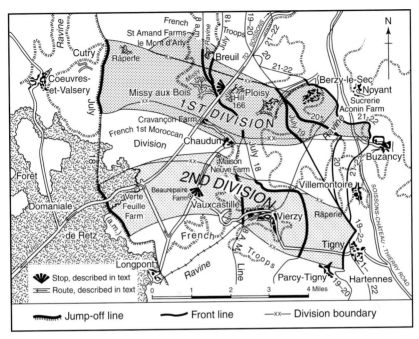

8. French–American attack south of Soissons, July 18–22, 1918

Muslim blacks from West Africa, clothed in mustard-colored uniforms with helmets bearing a crescent emblem. In close combat, they preferred bayonets and broad-bladed knives over rifles. In Liggett's words, "they were more at home with sharp steel than with lead."[35]

They seemed to have impressed almost every American soldier with whom they came in contact. "The looks on those Moroccans were enough to make the enemy drop his guns and run," remembered Private Charles M. Engel, 119th Field Artillery Regiment, 32nd Division.[36] Fighting alongside them at Soissons, Lieutenant John Thomason, 49th Company, 5th Marine Brigade, later wrote:

Kill, which is at best an acquired taste with the civilized races, was only too palpably their mission in life ... Each platoon swept its front like a hunting-pack, moving swiftly and surely together ... the hidden guns that fired on them were located with uncanny skill; they worked their automatic rifles forward on each flank until the doomed emplacement was under a scissors fire; then they took up the matter with the bayonet, and slew with lion-like leaps and lunges and a shrill barbaric yapping ... They carried also a broad-bladed knife, razor-sharp, which disemboweled a man at a stroke.

During a lull in the fighting a Senegalese sergeant approached Thomason and offered him "a brace of human ears, nicely fresh, and strung upon a thong. 'Bo'jour, Américain! Voilà! Beaucoup souvenir ici bon!'"[37]

Thomason may have been unsettled by the Senegalese sergeant's offer of German ears, but he and other Americans learned from the tactics of the First Moroccans who flanked German machine gun nests or took them from the rear rather than taking them head on. An officer in the 1st Division, Edward S. Johnston, later suggested that

it was by observation of the Moroccans in this action that the regiment learned the method of advance ordinarily utilized by European veterans, whereby the assault line, having lost the barrage, progressed steadily forward, individuals, under the eye of their squad leaders, moving at a run from shell-hole to shell-hole. When stopped by resistance – usually a machine gun – the squad, section, or platoon engaged it by fire from the front, while flankers immediately worked around with rifles and grenades to take it from the flank. It was a common saying in the 1st Division that the Moroccans taught them how to fight.[38]

Initially the offensive went extremely well, with easy and rapid advances made by the infantry supported by artillery, tanks, and aircraft. The 26th Regiment, 1st Division, for example, advanced two kilometers and achieved their first objectives with little loss or resistance.[39] By late afternoon, however, German resistance stiffened and losses mounted. "On the first day the enemy was able to gain a great success, as figured in ground gained and men and matériel captured," a German assessment concluded, "but did not know how to exploit it to the limit on the same day ... his advance already began to waver on the next day and he was unable to gain the objective doubtlessly planned." Nonetheless, this German assessment characterized July 18 as "a turning point in the history of the World War."[40]

On July 19 the butcher's bill became even greater as higher officers lost touch and control of smaller units while the Germans fed in fresh divisions. "Communications really existed only when the commander went forward in person, and only when the troops had halted long enough for someone from the rear to find them," suggest Johnson and Hillman.[41] In their haste to get forward, American infantry courage-ously, although recklessly, attacked in dense and rigid formations with-out adequate fire support. By pushing ahead of French troops on their flanks they also exposed themselves to flanking fire. Through no fault of their own, the 6th Marines provided an especially egregious example of how not to assault German positions. Believing that the enemy was about to crack on July 19 the XX Corps ordered Harbord to interdict the strategically important Soissons–Château-Thierry Road. Upon receiving these orders Harbord decided to commit his division's reserve, the 6th Marines. Although on the previous day two regiments had failed to achieve this objective, the 6th Marines alone attempted to overrun a position now held by fresh German troops brought up overnight.[42]

After advancing to the jump-off line through heavy enemy shelling, the Marines began their assault around 8:30 a.m. across flat, cultivated fields with no cover and without supporting artillery fire. Ominously, the Marines had seen this before at Belleau Wood. Without supporting arms, which included Stokes mortars and French-made 37-mm guns still to the rear in their regimental train, Marine mortar teams and gunners were given rifles and employed as infantry. An opening barrage had been fired prematurely at 7:00 a.m.[43] Hence no supporting fire shepherded them across the open field. A few French tanks offered assistance but German artillery quickly knocked out most of them. Advancing in two waves separated by about fifty yards, Marines "were falling torn and mangled beyond description. The shells seemed to come in one solid, screaming, rushing stream," one Marine recalled. "The ground seemed alive with bursting geysers of smoke and dust."[44]

As they came under fire many Marines instinctively leaned forward as if they were advancing against a strong wind. "I would see a man walking across the fields with his rifle at his hip[,] suddenly he would take another step and there wouldn't be no step there and he would go down," recalls Corporal Joseph E. Rendinell of the 6th Marines. "Some fell flat. Some grabbed at their wounds and sort of crumpled down. And some would sit down slow like they were sitting down in a chair. I don't remember ever seeing a man throw up his arms and fall back."[45]

By nightfall 1,300 of the 2,450 Marines involved in the attack were dead or wounded. The Marines had advanced some two kilometers and were within rifle range of the Château-Thierry highway, but they could go no further. Although its men had been hungry and exhausted, short of vital equipment, and unfamiliar with the terrain, the 2nd Division had advanced almost eleven kilometers and fought three distinct battles, all in a little over twenty-four hours.[46] But it could do no more. Harbord sent the following message to General Berdoulat: "I desire to insist most strongly that [my division] should not be called on for further offensive effort . . . the troops in the fighting line of the division have many of them been without water or food for over twenty-four hours."[47]

As Harbord's battered and exhausted division, which had suffered 4,319 casualties, was being relieved during the night by the French 58th Colonial Division, XX Corps ordered the 1st Division to take the hilltop town of Berzy-le-Sec which overlooked the Soissons–Château-Thierry road and the Soissons–Villers-Cotterêts railway. At 5:30 a.m. on July 22 the 1st and 2nd Battalions of the 28th Infantry and elements of the 18th Infantry joined the 26th Infantry, which began the attack with its 2nd and 3rd Battalions in assault waves and ended with all survivors advancing in "one thin line";[48] they succeeded in driving the Germans out of Berzy-le-Sec.

In five days of combat German artillery and machine guns had inflicted staggering losses on the 1st Division. All of the 26th Infantry's field officers, for example, had either been killed or wounded. On July 23, the day Haig's 15th (Scottish) Division relieved the 1st Division, Lieutenant Shipley Thomas, the 26th Regiment's intelligence officer, attempted to contact the division's adjutant. Major General Summerall answered the phone and the following conversation ensued:

"Hello," the commander of the 1st Division said, "this is General Summerall. Who is this?"

"Lieutenant Thomas, sir, 26th Infantry."

"Well, how are things?"

"I have to report that we have broken through as far as we can. Our colonel is dead, our lieutenant colonel is dead, and all the majors are dead or wounded. And God knows how many captains and lieutenants are down. And the situation with the men is just as bad."

"Dear God, Mr. Thomas! Who is commanding the regiment?"

"Captain Barney Legge."

"How is he doing?"

"Fine, sir, with what he has left."

"Well, who is his executive officer?"

"I guess I am."[49]

Shipley Thomas's regiment had begun the offensive on July 18 with 3,100 men and 96 officers. The Germans had killed or wounded 62 officers and 1,560 enlisted men.[50] Other regiments in the division suffered even greater casualties. The 28th Infantry, for example, suffered its heaviest losses of the war at Soissons: 56 officers and 1,760 men killed or wounded. Casualties for the entire division amounted to 234 officers and 7,083 men.

Tragically, the secrecy and haste which had characterized the launching of the offensive toward Soissons had militated against providing adequate hospital facilities. One field hospital, with only 200 beds, had to care for over 3,000 men before the 1st and 2nd Divisions were relieved. Inevitably some soldiers who would have survived died from neglect.[51]

It was painful for the Scottish soldiers who relieved the 1st Division to see so many dead young Americans in and around Berzy-le-Sec. According to the British historian John Terraine it reminded them of their young and eager comrades who had not survived their initial introduction to industrialized warfare at the Battle of the Somme in 1916 where they had waged war with similar enthusiasm and raw courage.[52]

American soldiers had not been wounded or killed in vain. The Allies had at long last regained the initiative and the Germans were in full retreat from their vulnerable salient. The counteroffensive launched after the Second Battle of the Marne represented the beginning of the end for German hopes of becoming the hegemonic power on the European continent. General Liggett recounts the story of General Albert Daugan, the commander of the 1st Moroccan Division, who was observed with tears in his eyes during the Battle of Soissons. "Does not the day go well, my general?" someone asked him. "Mais oui!" he responded. "I weep for the families and sweethearts of these Americans. See how they go into battle as we did in 1914! My division, the flower of the French Army, no longer can keep up with them."[53] Liggett goes on to add: "Courage sometimes is the only substitute for the skill that comes of experience. It is a fearful price to pay, and we always have paid it in our wars."[54]

Other American divisions also participated in the Allied counteroffensive, officially called the Aisne-Marne Counteroffensive (July 18–August 6). Foch's plan initially involved six American divisions, the 1st, 2nd, 3rd, 4th, 26th, and 28th. By the time the counteroffensive officially concluded on the Vesle River on August 6 an additional three divisions, the 32nd, 42nd, and 77th, had also participated.

Although heavy fighting characterized the staged German withdrawal, sufficient Allied forces had not been available for the Allied wings advancing eastward from Soissons and westward from Reims to trap the German divisions within the salient.

The 26th ("Yankee") Division and 4th Division, fighting in the center of the salient, also participated in the July 18 counterstroke. The 4th Division, whose last elements had only disembarked a few weeks earlier, included many thinly trained recruits, some of whom had only recently learned to load and fire their rifles. According to Van Every they actually received their first rifle practice training north of Meaux within "sound of the hammering guns at the front."

Baker sought to justify the War Department's policy of sending untrained soldiers across the Atlantic with a most questionable rationale. "We have learned," he wrote Pershing in July, "that to keep men too long in training camps in this country makes them grow stale and probably does as much harm by the spirit of impatience and restlessness aroused as it does good by the longer drills. The men in our training camps are champing at the bit, and this applies not only to the officers, who naturally want their professional opportunity, but to the men as well."[55] It, of course, goes without saying that the type of training proved much more important than the length of training.

Because of its inexperience, the 4th Division when it entered the line was broken up and its battalions intermingled with French troops in the II and VII French Army Corps.[56] The more experienced 26th ("Yankee") Division, commanded by the verbose Major General Clarence R. Edwards, a West Pointer (1883) who was considered by his superiors to be something of a loose cannon, remained intact, and along with the French 167th Division constituted Liggett's First Corps which was attached to General Degoutte's Sixth Army. When Edwards visited Liggett and asked him for advice prior to his advance ordered by Degoutte, he was told "not to crowd men too much in front line to take shell fire and not to let the attack run away beyond the objective." Liggett also emphasized to Edwards that he must keep "in touch with the movement and preserve liaison."[57]

On July 18 the 52nd Brigade of the 26th Division launched an early morning assault in the Belleau Wood region. Although the German front was not strongly manned the Americans faced well-placed and well-concealed machine gun nests. To his credit Edwards supported his advancing troops with heavy machine gun fire. Losses mounted as the advance continued. An officer told Pierpont Stackpole, Liggett's aide, that "confusion in the 52nd Brigade was hopeless" with "stragglers and trophy hunters all over the place." After four days of fighting and an advance of ten kilometers the 52nd Brigade showed signs of disintegration. Degoutte, however, issued new orders for "push, push, push" the next day, July 22.[58]

Liggett subsequently ordered the 52nd Brigade to shift to its left and take the place of the spent French 167th Division whose ration strength was less than an American brigade. The division's 51st Brigade then occupied the place being vacated in the line. Confusion reigned, with units becoming intermingled. Meanwhile, officers had difficulty controlling their men. Advancing across a wheat field, Captain Daniel W. Strickland, 102nd Infantry, 51st Infantry Brigade, saw his men seek cover without orders. This checked the rush of the advance and it became necessary for squad leaders to drive their men forward in some cases by force. Greenhorns in the rear tried to fire through the ranks ahead and increased the casualties. It developed that morning that the last batch of replacements sent up could not even load a rifle, much less fire it.[59]

These replacements had landed in France only sixteen days earlier. Now some of them were about to be killed.

On July 23 Colonel Frank Parker, the commander of the 102nd Infantry, 51st Brigade, reported to Liggett that "the First Battalion had 175 men; Second Battalion 250, Third Battalion 500; all the rest dead." Liggett, however, believed that "a large portion of the missing were asleep in the woods or straggling." Stackpole described the atmosphere at Edwards's headquarters as similar to "a morgue – everybody dead or dying or in a state of collapse of crying for relief."[60] On the night of July 25/26 the fresh 42nd Division took over the front of the First Corps, a relief that did not go well. Units of the 101st, 102nd, 111th, and 112th Regiments had become intermingled in the advance and their removal from the line in darkness proved difficult. During the advance the 26th Division had suffered 4,857 casualties and another 1,200 men had been evacuated because of exhaustion or illness.[61]

The Rainbow Division found itself facing a prepared line of defense, the *Caesar* Line, one of four German withdrawal positions between the Marne and the Aisne. On July 26 the Rainbow Division assaulted the La Croix Rouge Farm whose numerous stone buildings and stone walls had been converted into a formidable machine gun nest. Alabamians of the 167th and Iowans of the 168th Regiments approached the farm through woods and then advanced in waves across a cleared field into the teeth of German artillery and machine guns (Map 9). The results were as horrific as they were predictable. In their bayonet assault Iowans and Alabamians overran the German position but lost over 1,000 men, either killed or wounded. Survivors spent a miserable night without food (the men had not been fed all day) on muddy ground in pouring rain.[62]

The Rainbow Division next confronted a strong German defensive position just ahead on the other side of the nearby Ourcq River, really more a creek than river and only some five yards across in the American sector. The heights and deep woods on the north bank, thick with German machine guns, however, ensured that any attack would be costly. The advance across the Ourcq River by three US divisions, the 3rd, 28th, and 42nd, constituted the largest all-American offensive thus far in the war.[63]

To the 42nd fell the greatest challenge, storming the heights on both sides of the village Sergy. For five days and nights the 42nd Division,

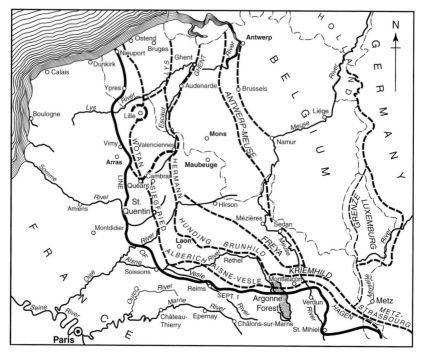

9. German defensive positions behind the Western Front,
September 1918

supported by two battalions from the 4th Division, battled a crack
German division, the 4th Guard Division. Sergy changed hands seven
times during the battle with the hard-charging 42nd Division taking
heavy losses as it repeatedly assaulted the slopes.

On August 1 Pétain cautioned Liggett "against too much eagerness on
part of Americans and attempts to take tons of machine gun nests by
direct attack." He told Liggett and his staff that "the French had learned
this lesson with cost and we must learn ours as quickly as possible."
Liggett agreed, noting that "he had been continually impressing this on
the divisions, brigade and other commanders."[64] That evening the
Germans broke contact and retreated to a new defensive position along
the Vesle. On August 3 the 4th Division, which entered the line for the
first time as a complete division, relieved the 42nd Division, which had
lost 8,000 men killed or wounded since July 14.[65]

Many US divisions received their baptism in battle during the advance
from the Marne to the Vesle. Losses had been heavy for these inexperienced divisions and not every American soldier displayed the heart of a

lion. "Far back of our lines and camps my provost marshal now began to gather large numbers of American soldiers that had straggled from these various divisions. The French villages were full of them," recalls General Robert Lee Bullard, who rose to General Officer Commanding (GOC) of the Second Army by the end of the war.

Relatively to the number of American soldiers that had been here, the stragglers were few, but actually their numbers were great ... When to-day after the war, I read in their histories the bragging of some of our divisions of the fierce warrior bravery and high sense of duty of all their men, all, without any exception mentioned, I cannot help remembering the great number of their dead-beats that we herded up.[66]

Although fighting continued, the Aisne-Marne Offensive officially ended on August 6 with the opposing forces facing each other across the Vesle and Aisne rivers along a generally straight line running from Soissons to Reims. Some 132,000 Doughboys had assisted the French in repulsing Ludendorff's last offensive, and 200,000 participated in the counterattacks that cleared the Marne salient.[67]

Ludendorff's gamble for victory had proven to be a disaster. As he later wrote: "The attempt to make the Entente peoples ready for peace by defeating them before the arrival of the American reinforcements had failed. The impetus of the army had been insufficient to deal the enemy a decisive blow ... I realised clearly that this made our general situation very serious."[68]

Germany's military position was about to become even more precarious. On August 8 German defenders on the British front at Amiens were stunned as a heavy early morning mist began to dissipate. "The sight of a mass of 400 tanks trundling towards them was plainly too imposing a sight for numbers of German troops ... A great many of them fled or surrendered."[69] The British Fourth Army's heavy artillery suppressed the enemy's artillery while a combined arms attack by infantry with tanks, Lewis guns, trench mortars, and rifle grenades neutralized German machine guns. The Allies now possessed a widening technological superiority over Germany. For its offensive at Amiens, the BEF had at its disposal 1,386 field guns and howitzers in addition to 684 heavy guns. British and Imperial troops also had 1,900 aircraft available along with 342 heavy tanks, 72 light Whippet tanks, and 120 supply tanks. By nightfall, with the Canadians and Australians especially distinguishing themselves, the Germans had been pushed back some eight miles on a 15,000-yard front. French divisions also participated in this offensive which rather than the Battle of Amiens should properly be called the Battle of Amiens-Montdidier. The main attack had been delivered by the

Australian and Canadian Corps but Debeney's First Army also advanced southwards beyond Montdidier.

A delighted Haig recorded in his diary: "Enemy blowing up dumps in all directions and streaming eastwards. Their transport and limbers offer splendid targets for our aeroplanes." In four days this Anglo-French offensive had overrun more enemy front than they had taken during four and a half months during the 1916 Battle of the Somme. This Allied success at Amiens-Montdidier dramatically emphasized how the face of battle had changed by the summer of 1918. As Haig wrote his wife, "Who would have believed this possible even 2 months ago?"[70]

In contrast to the AEF's official doctrine which continued to associate successful operations with self-reliant infantry armed with rifles and bayonets, many Doughboy officers began adapting to the realities of the modern battlefield. This included General Edwards, who had certainly not distinguished himself during the just-concluded Aisne-Marne Offensive and had become increasingly unpopular with both Pershing and Liggett. But Edwards's official report on the 26th Division's recent operations reflected an understanding of the challenges presented by the modern battlefield and offered solutions. Edwards suggested that when possible an attack in strength should be preceded by reconnaissance squads to identify machine gun nests and to neutralize them by employing greater firepower (artillery mortars, heavy machine guns). He also said that "it goes without saying" that when possible machine gun nests should be outflanked rather than attacked head on. He also advocated greater firepower to assist advancing infantry, especially rolling barrages with a mixture of exploding shells and gas, and better communication between infantry and divisional artillery. Aware of the superior Browning automatic weapons now being produced in American factories, he asked that his division be furnished with them as soon as possible. His recent advances had not been assisted by tanks and he requested them (four for every infantry battalion), as well as air support. He made no mention of rifles and bayonets.[71]

Edwards's discussions of tactics would have very much displeased his commander-in-chief who at this time was busily torpedoing a War Department plan to have experienced French and British officers conduct advanced courses in the United States for higher commanders. America's allies do not make use of the rifle's "great power," he argued, and their doctrine "was based upon the cautious advance of infantry with prescribed objectives, where obstacles had been destroyed and resistance largely broken by artillery."[72]

Although the offensive initiative on the Western Front now passed to the coalition against Germany Ludendorff refused to accept defeat. On August 14 Germany's political and military leadership assembled at the Spa Crown Council presided over by the Emperor. Germany's leaders appeared to recognize that their nation had reached its limits of endurance. Yet Ludendorff stubbornly argued that the German Army could yet paralyze the enemy's "will to fight by a strategic defensive" and "force him to accept peace."[73]

Although Amiens and the Aisne-Marne Offensive lifted Allied spirits, no one in London, Paris, or Washington anticipated that the killing would be over in another three months. On the same day that Ludendorff talked of imposing German will on the enemy through defensive warfare, Bliss, reflecting the mood of the Allied military representatives at the SWC, dispatched a message to Baker and March at the War Department: "Everything now points to favorable conditions for launching a conclusive campaign on the Western Front next year, and if enemy's resistance is crushed on this front it will cease everywhere."[74]

With Americans appearing on the battlefield in ever increasing numbers, Pershing now focused on collecting his scattered divisions and forming an independent army with its own strategical objectives, a goal which soon put him at sixes and sevens with Haig and Foch, and even more so with the British Prime Minister Lloyd George.

17 Establishment of the American First Army and Saint-Mihiel

On July 10, 1918 General Foch issued a statement from his headquarters at Bombon that could have been written by Pershing. "The day when there are one million Americans in France, America cuts a figure in the war," he proclaimed. "America has a right to an American army; the American army must be. The Allied cause moreover will be better served by having an American army under the orders of its one leader, than by an American army scattered all about."[1]

Pershing and his staff enthusiastically received Foch's statement but they wanted more than an independent army. Operational objectives were equally important, and they sought Foch's approval of an advance toward Metz which had been percolating within Pershing's staff since September 1917. Foch, however, favored Allied attacks from the Argonne Forest to Arras rather than in Lorraine. Fox Conner, chief of operations at GHQ, spoke for Pershing's staff on July 14 when he wrote the following: "A campaign limited to the front planned by General Foch carries with it no reasonable prospect of final victory during 1919. This final victory can only be had by reaching the vitals of Germany and by destroying her armed forces. Since her vitals are in Lorraine the simplest method is to take the most direct road to that region."[2]

On the morning of July 21 Pershing met with Pétain and made clear his intention of collecting his divisions into an American army. Although he insisted that as commander-in-chief he expected to direct "plans and the conduct of operations," he dared not cut the material umbilical cord that existed between US and French forces. "It seemed best in the beginning," he writes in his memoirs, "to place our army on the same footing as the French armies in order to secure their full cooperation."[3] In sum, although he commanded the First Army, Pershing agreed to serve under Pétain.[4] In return he expected the French to continue policing civilians behind his front and supplying his soldiers with essential military support that included artillery, tanks, aircraft, and transport.

Although Congress had voted the enormous sum of $640 million to build at least 4,500 aircraft by June 1918, Doughboys remained almost totally dependent upon their war partners for aircraft and other modern weapons. Pershing and his staff bore some of the responsibility for the failure of US industry to meet AEF needs for industrialized warfare. They had not a clue when it came to understanding the problems faced by American manufacturers of tanks, aircraft, and artillery. For example, as explained by Beaver, "they ordered fighters, bombers, and observation planes in certain quantities one month only to cancel the order the next month. A month later the same planes would be reordered in completely different numbers."[5]

Initially it had been thought that the dynamic American auto industry could manufacture combat aircraft almost as quickly as cars and trucks rolled off its assembly lines. The close tolerances required and a general ignorance of aircraft design, however, contributed to colossal failures. Automobile engineers, believing that aircraft could be assembly-line produced like autos, designed the Liberty as an all-purpose engine for aircraft. The result was an engine that did not provide the required power for fighter aircraft. Consequently, not a single fighter plane built in the United States flew in support of the AEF as the war ended.[6] The only American-built aircraft being used in combat was the British-designed Dehaviland (or DH-4). American industrialists, however, lessened the value of this bomber/observation aircraft by substituting the Liberty for the superior but more expensive British Rolls Royce engine. Another complaint made by some American pilots was that the large gas tank situated between the pilot and the gunner made the DH-4 a "Flaming Coffin." Only in November 1918 did American aircraft industry finally hit its stride, with 500 aircraft being produced per week. By April 1919 American manufacturers expected to have the capacity to turn out 40,000 flying machines a year.[7]

In May 1918 President Wilson by executive order replaced the Aviation Section, US Signal Corps, with the US Army Air Service. Pershing subsequently appointed Major General Mason Patrick, an engineer and former West Point classmate of his, as Chief of Air Service, AEF. Upon assuming command Patrick asked Liggett what he should do with two of his most ambitious officers, William ("Billy") Mitchell and Benjamin Foulois, who seemed to detest the ground the other walked on. Foulois was an experienced pilot. Mitchell had only learned to fly in 1916, with mixed results. Some called him the "master of the controlled crash."[8] In Patrick's view they were both "absurdly ambitious and selfish." Liggett's advice was that Mitchell could "deliver the goods on the line and has behind him loyal and well disciplined squadrons." On the other hand, he told Patrick that he should tell Mitchell "that he was not indispensable and would be promptly relieved if he failed to stick to

Fig. 21 Tank plowing its way through a trench and starting toward the
German line, during World War I, near Saint-Michel, France

his own business."[9] By the opening of the Battle of Saint-Mihiel, Patrick
had established the following chain of command. Foulois served as his
Assistant Chief, Air Service, AEF, while Mitchell served as Chief of Air
Service, First Army, and controlled all combat units.[10] By the war's end
the US Air Service, flying mostly French-made aircraft, had had 235 aviators killed in action and had conducted 150 bombing raids.[11]

American industry disappointed the American Tank Corps as well as
the Air Service. The War Department signed a contract with Ford to
build 15,000 two- and three-man tanks. When several of these Ford
tanks finally made it to Europe, in October 1918, the AEF Tank Corps
and ordnance authorities deemed them "death traps." A handful of
American-built Renault tanks shipped to Europe before the Armistice
received a similar reception. Because they were constructed of mild steel
soldiers discovered that they could be penetrated by a 30-caliber round
(Fig. 21). In fact the great majority of the tanks on order in the United
States in 1918 were deemed useless by Pershing's staff.[12]

Throughout the war the Allies provided the American Tank Corps
with its tanks. In September 1918 Colonel George Patton, who organized the first US tank school at Langres, led the 1st Provisional Tank

Brigade, accompanied by French tanks, in the first American tank assault of the war at Saint-Mihiel. All of Patton's tanks were of the light Renault variety. If the war had continued into the spring of 1919, the "Liberty" heavy tank (a successor to the Mark V), being manufactured at the Anglo-American plant at Châteauroux, France, would have been available and the Americans were scheduled to receive the first 600 of these "Liberty" tanks coming off the assembly line.[13]

The AEF also depended upon its allies for most of its firepower in 1917–18, including its artillery. Initially the Allies furnished the AEF with artillery in exchange for raw materials, steel billets, rough forgings, and steel castings. Dissatisfied with the number of big guns furnished from Allied stocks, Pershing asked the War Department in November 1917 to launch a full-scale artillery production program.[14] According to Beaver, despite the government's efforts, "field and heavy-artillery production could not surmount inexperience, overconfidence, faulty shop practices, and the escalating demands of the AEF." The only artillery successfully produced by private industry was the model 1917 75-mm gun and the 8-inch howitzer.[15] Few if any of these guns, however, ever made it to the front lines. US Army Chief of Artillery, Major General William J. Snow, freely admitted that "it may be said, then, that we could not and did not equip our Army with artillery during the War."[16]

One finds it difficult not to agree with Lloyd George's harsh assessment of America's war industry. "It is one of the inexplicable paradoxes of history," he writes in his frequently polemical style, "that the greatest machine-producing nation on earth failed to turn out the mechanism of war after 18 months of sweating and toiling and hustling. The men placed in charge of the organisation of the resources of the country for this purpose all seemed to hustle each other – but never the job."[17]

It has been suggested that Pétain "wholeheartedly" supported Pershing and believed that AEF officers had the "capability to form an autonomous army."[18] It is more likely that the Frenchman bowed to the inevitable. He later explained his acquiescence to Pershing's demands in a conversation with the well-connected British war correspondent Charles à Court Repington. Pétain told him that he agreed that from the Allied perspective it was not the best solution, but given Pershing's "will of iron" there "was nothing more to be said." Pétain expressed admiration for the "great dash" of Doughboys, but worried that their inexperienced staff officers might limit the AEF's operational mobility, especially given its rapid expansion and its supply and transportation problems.

Pétain thus pinpointed the AEF's Achilles' heel, operational mobility. When Pershing's staff later made its first attempt to move on its own a single division (the 89th Division to Toul), trucks had to be collected from all over the AEF. Repington noted in his diary that his country's political and military leadership agreed with Pétain about the AEF's limitations, "but I thought, with him, that we should do well to make the best of things as they were."[19]

Following their conversation Pétain accompanied Pershing to meet with Foch at Bombon. Pershing told Foch that he wanted to collect his divisions, then scattered across the Western Front, and place them in two sectors, one which was active and another which was quiet (Saint-Mihiel–Toul–Nancy), which he described as the "American front proper." In the active sector (north of the Marne) he planned to establish two army corps, each with two divisions in the first line and one in reserve. Placed "side by side" these two corps would form a part of the American First Army. Sugarcoating his request Pershing added that his proposal did not preclude (his choice of words was "it was quite possible") US divisions fighting in other sectors as well. Foch made no commitment but promised a prompt response. On the following day he gave his assent.[20]

Two days later Foch convened a council of war with his national commanders at Bombon. With the failure of Ludendorff's fifth offensive of the year the offensive initiative now passed from his hands to Foch's. Ludendorff could not replace his losses while Foch could, with American reinforcements. "The moment has come," stressed Foch, "to abandon the general defensive attitude imposed upon us until now by [our] numerical inferiority and to pass to the offensive." Foch did not expect a war-winning offensive in 1918. Nor was he contemplating prolonged battles of attrition such as Verdun or Passchendaele. To keep the initiative and further demoralize the enemy he proposed a series of sharp but limited blows against the salients created by German offensives. His strategical objectives focused on railway lines and raw materials.[21]

To Pershing's immense satisfaction Foch included the reduction of a salient that the German invasion had created during the first weeks of the war, the Saint-Mihiel salient. Pershing viewed its elimination as a prelude to his war-winning advance on Metz. On August 9, the day before the First American Army became operational, Foch instructed Pershing to form "with the utmost haste" what he referred to as the "American Army of the Woëvre."[22]

With the First American Army's headquarters established at Neufchâteau on August 10, with Pershing serving as field commander as well as commanding general of the AEF, staff officers began building the largest American army in history, even larger than the Grand Army which had passed in review on Pennsylvania Avenue in 1865 before being disbanded. One of Pershing's staff officers, Colonel Hugh Drum ("Drummie"), took the lead in gathering American divisions from the English Channel to Switzerland and concentrating them in the Saint-Mihiel sector. Drum, who served as Chief of Staff of the First Army, performed brilliantly and by all accounts practically ran the show during the formative period of the First Army.[23]

The rapid expansion of the First Army led to many officers being advanced in rank without adequate preparation, either through schooling or experience. One day an American officer might lead a regiment, the next month a brigade, and several months later a division. Many officers like Drum rose to the occasion but others did not.

It now appeared certain that the plans made by Pershing's operations staff in September 1917, which had decisively shaped his approach to coalition warfare, were about to be realized. The British, however, refused to allow the contentious issue of amalgamation to die. Lloyd George, anxious over Britain's worsening manpower situation, continued to suspect Clemenceau of manipulating Foch to take unfair advantage of the British and force them to exhaust their manpower. He exploded when Foch cabled London of his decision to create two independent American forces, placing both of them on French fronts. Foch also suggested that Pershing might "ask for the divisions now in the British zone to go to the American zone when fully trained, if they are left holding back lines, but that if it is proposed to use them in active operations General Pershing will probably not ask for them."[24]

On July 26 Lloyd George launched into a tirade at a meeting of the "X" Committee. "It was intolerable that the French should attempt to put the screw upon us in that way and he was determined that if this continued he would ask the authority of the Cabinet to refuse the French any ships for the conveyance of American troops to France ... He was determined to call a halt to this process of putting the screw on us." The Prime Minister followed up his angry words with decisive action, asking for and receiving the War Cabinet's approval to use British shipping "as a lever to secure a fair redistribution of Allied forces in the line on the introduction therein of the American divisions."[25]

In the initial draft of a letter to Clemenceau Lloyd George spoke bluntly about France's monopolization of US troops.[26] But his communication sent on August 2 was less direct. With the War Department now planning to send eighty rather than 100 US divisions to Europe by the summer of 1919, Lloyd George informed Clemenceau that he had just been informed by his Minister of Shipping, Sir Joseph

Maclay, that Britain would "be unable to render further assistance in cargo tonnage, and will probably have to reduce our troop transport tonnage."[27]

Representatives of the British Empire, as members of the Imperial War Cabinet, were currently in London conferring with Lloyd George's government. To facilitate the formulation of future war strategy Lloyd George initiated and chaired a new and smaller body, the Committee of Prime Ministers, which included the political leaders of Canada, New Zealand, Australia, and Newfoundland, and Smuts, who represented general Louis Botha, the Prime Minister of South Africa. Milner, as Secretary of State for War, and Sir Henry Wilson, as CIGS, also occupied a place around the table.

In discussing future strategy, Lloyd George insisted that the British must limit its "strategy to our income." In 1916 the British nation had provided 1,200,000 recruits. In 1918 the government estimated that it might find 700,000; and in 1919 a projected 300,000 (of these, 90,000 would go to the air force and 40,000 to the navy, leaving only 170,000 for the army). In short, the army could expect for all of 1919 a little more than half the number of men that the United States now shipped to Europe in a single month.[28]

The military situation appeared much brighter to the Americans and French than it did to the leaders of the British Empire. To men like Smuts, Milner, and Lloyd George, now the dominant members in the British government, the diminished British Army meant that the Western front must be a secondary theater until a vast American force asserted itself in 1919. Witness the following comments made in the Committee of Prime Ministers on July 31.

MILNER: "In his view the Western front was a candle that burned all the moths that entered it."

SMUTS: "He did not question that the Western front was the decisive front, but from the beginning of the War it has always proved the fatal front."[29]

Sir Henry Wilson (who unlike the civilians surely knew of the decision by Foch and the national commanders on July 25 at Bombon to return to the offensive) now found himself at odds with his superiors. Earlier he had pleased them by talking about peripheral campaigns; now he submitted a memorandum, "British Military Policy in 1918–1919," in which he recommended limited military operations on the Western Front as a prelude to a war-winning offensive in 1919.

Wilson found little support. In Milner's view it was "out of the question" that Britain could ever again "play the great *rôle* on the Western

front." Lloyd George gave a graphic example of the political consequences of following Sir Henry Wilson's advice:

We might batter the enemy, and possibly they might have to sue for peace. What
would be the conditions when that occurred? America would have an Army
equivalent to 120 divisions, France perhaps 40, and the British Empire perhaps
23. When Australia said she wanted the Pacific Islands, or Palestine, President
Wilson would look down his nose and say: That he had entered the War with
quite different ideas in view, he would say he had his 120 divisions ready to
continue the war, and he would ask what assistance we could give.

Before deciding "to put our Army on the table next year and get it
smashed to pieces," said Lloyd George, "this consideration ought to be
very carefully weighed."[30]

Lloyd George and many other imperial-minded leaders wanted to
focus on military operations away from the Western Front. If the Prime
Minister's views were accepted, Hankey recorded in his diary, the British
Empire would halve its commitment to the Western Front in 1919 and
focus on Italy, the Balkans, or the Ottoman Empire. "This of course will
get us into great difficulties with our allies," he readily admitted.[31]

Haig's brilliant success at Amiens in early August, however, made it
difficult for the British leadership not to support Foch's efforts to maintain pressure on Ludendorff in 1918. Utilizing American manpower on
the British front now appeared to Lloyd George the only way of winning
a decent peace without destroying the BEF in the process. Hence he
continued to press the Americans over amalgamation. Troop ships
packed with Americans steaming across the Atlantic were not accompanied with nearly enough cargo ships to sustain them. Why not, Lloyd
George asked the Imperial War Cabinet, "fit them into our organization"? He had in mind an independent American force of between fifty
and sixty divisions. The surplus, from twenty to thirty divisions, could
fight within the British and French armies and be fed, equipped, and
transported by the existing Anglo-French supply and transportation
systems. The Welshman's machinations now found little sympathy in
the British War Office. When brought into the discussion, Sir Percy de
B. Radcliffe, the General Staff's Director of Military Operations, told the
civilians that "it would be wrong to give the Americans the impression
that we were trying to tie them to our apron strings."[32]

Lloyd George pressed on nonetheless. On August 21 he ordered the
War, Shipping, and Foreign Offices to make no new pledges on
American troop and cargo transport. He also emphasized that existing
arrangements to ship American troops lasted only through December
1918.[33] It is perhaps just as well that Haig had not yet informed his
government about a visit from Pershing on August 12. "He stated that he

might have to withdraw the 5 American Divisions now with British," the Scotsman scribbled in his diary. "I pointed out to him that I had done everything to equip and help the American Army, and to provide them with horses. So far, I have had no help from these troops (except the 3 battalions which were used in the battle near Chipilly [Le Hamel] in error)."[34]

In Washington cabinet members now examined the promising war maps displayed in the War Department with mounting excitement and confidence. Bliss reported from the Supreme War Council that "everything now points to favorable conditions for launching a conclusive campaign on the western front next year, and if the enemy's resistance is crushed on this front it will cease everywhere."[35] As confidence blossomed in Washington and at Pershing's headquarters, German alarm grew, especially over the growing number of American soldiers now on their side of the Atlantic. General Max von Gallwitz, who commanded a German Army Group, scribbled in his diary in August: "I never expected such speedy developments. The Americans are becoming dangerous."[36]

The darkest cloud on the horizon for the AEF seemed to be Lloyd George's threats to limit British sea transport. In the wake of continued setbacks in American merchant ship construction, this threat could not be ignored. If the British withdrew or reduced its shipping, America's military effort in Europe would be plunged into uncertainty. "There must be a show-down on this subject," Baker wrote the President, who accepted his Secretary of War's suggestion that he sail to Europe to confront the British.[37] On August 31, he departed for France on an American troop ship.

Across the Atlantic another "show-down" occurred, this time between Pershing and America's allies. After Amiens the British and French kept up the pressure on the war-weary Germans. On August 20 Mangin's Tenth Army launched an attack between the Oise River and Soissons and in two days drove forward twelve kilometers. On the following day the British Third Army opened the Battle of Albert and rapidly advanced across the cratered battlefield of the Somme, the graveyard of tens of thousands of British soldiers in 1916.

On August 27 Haig wrote Sir Henry Wilson that he had suggested to Foch that he distribute

American Divisions amongst British and French to enable a concentric movement being begun without delay on Cambrai, on St Quentin, & from the south on Mézières. The attack on St. Mihiel will lead to nothing (a) because it is eccentric, and (b) Germans have already taken steps to make a new line across the salient. A *small* attack in this salient would educate the American Higher Command and might be allowed for purposes of camouflage! The main attack should be launched between Rheims and Verdun in direction of Mézières etc. under French direction.[38]

In sum Haig suggested that the bulging German front from the English Channel to the Meuse be treated as a single giant salient and attacked along its shoulders.

Two days later when the two men met at Mouchy le Château the British commander-in-chief discovered that Foch's mind was moving in the same direction. Recently Foch had told President Poincaré that he planned to "light fires everywhere, widen the battle and continue without letup."[39] The specifics of this wide-ranging offensive decided upon by Foch and Haig were as follows: the British were to advance in the direction of Cambrai while the French and Americans pushed forward between the Meuse and Aisne rivers toward the vital railway center of Mézières. This town, with three railway lines running from Germany to France, represented the primary strategical prize of these converging attacks.[40]

On August 29 Pershing established an advanced headquarters closer to the town of Saint-Mihiel at Ligny-en-Barrois. On the following day, with his staff just getting settled in, Foch arrived with a proposal that turned his world upside down. Foch asked him to limit his forthcoming offensive by attacking only the southern face of the Saint-Mihiel salient and then placing most of his divisions under French command for two separate offensives in the direction of Mézières.

Having moved heaven and earth to create an independent army with its own operational objectives, Pershing could not believe what he was hearing as Foch outlined his plan. "This arrangement," he sputtered, "would cause a separation of the American forces, leaving some Americans in the Woëvre, then the French Second Army with some Americans on its left; then some French; then some Americans on the Aisne and then the French. That this destroys the thing we have been trying so long to form – that is, an American Army."

As Pershing continued to raise objections, Foch became persistent, with the following exchange taking place:

Marshal Foch asked very plainly: "Do you wish to take part in the battle?" ("Voulez-vous aller à bataille?")

General Pershing replied: "Most assuredly, but as an American Army."

Marshal Foch replied, that means it will take a month.

General Pershing proposed that Marshal Foch immediately give him a sector, that he will take it at once.[41]

Although not recorded in the official record quoted above, Pershing recounts the following conversation in his memoirs. As Foch continued to insist that Pershing accept these new and startling arrangements, Pershing held his ground. "You have no authority," he declared, "as Allied commander-in-chief to call upon me to yield up my command of the American Army and have it scattered among the Allied forces where it will not be an American army at all." When Foch fired back "I must insist upon the arrangement," both men rose from their chairs. Pershing later admitted that he thought of striking the Frenchman. Instead he responded verbally: "Marshal Foch, you may insist all you please, but I decline absolutely to agree to your plan. While our army will fight wherever you may decide, it will not fight except as an independent army." After telling Pershing that he might change his mind after reflecting upon his proposal a pale and exhausted Foch collected his maps and papers and left the room.[42]

In retrospect it is difficult to believe that Pershing surprised Foch with his violent reaction to a directive to divide the American First Army and place many of its divisions under French command. It has been suggested in a recent and richly researched study of Foch's command that Clemenceau ordered him to pick a fight with Pershing to get the stubborn American general replaced. Earlier, Lord Derby, the British ambassador in Paris, encouraged the French Premier to believe that President Wilson "accepted Foch as being in supreme command and they might rely on him supporting Foch even against Pershing."[43] Such a supposition is most unlikely. Wilson linked success by an independent American army on the battlefield with the furthering of his liberal diplomacy. He could not have found a stronger advocate of this policy than Pershing. As Pershing told Foch, "the American people, the American Government, Secretary of War from the President, insisted that the American Army shall fight as such."[44]

On August 31 Pershing conferred with Pétain before submitting his reply to Foch. The French commander-in-chief was and remained Pershing's favorite foreign general. In an attempt to mollify Pershing, Pétain suggested that he stick to his plan of eliminating the entire Saint-Mihiel salient. But he also pointed out that before the Americans could advance on Metz they would need to protect their flank by driving the Germans from the Meuse-Argonne sector. To keep his divisions together the French commander-in-chief also suggested that the Americans take over the entire sector between the Moselle River and the Argonne Forest (although the French would continue to defend Verdun). Pétain also questioned whether Pershing had enough time to prepare two distinct operations.[45]

Late that evening Foch received Pershing's response which concluded with the words: "If you decide to utilize American forces in attacking in the direction of Mézières, I accept that decision, even though it complicates my supply system and the care of my sick and wounded, but I do insist that the American Army must be employed as a whole, either east of the Argonne or west of the Argonne, not four or five divisions here and six or seven there."[46]

Among other points addressed by Pershing in his response to Foch were Allied criticisms of the formation of the American First Army while it still remained a "beggar" army without its own modern weapons and adequate infrastructure. Pershing readily admitted these deficiencies but he blamed it on Allied demands that the War Department ship only infantrymen and machine gunners during the military crisis that began with Germany's powerful offensive in March. Pershing had a point when he emphasized manpower shortages in his Services of Supply caused by emphasis on combat soldiers. But March had shipped men over as fast as he could and soon ran out of men adequately trained for combat so he began shipping men really suitable only for the services and auxiliaries. Yet many of these men were rushed into combat. No matter how much shipping tonnage was available, however, the reality is that American industry still could not furnish the AEF with tanks, aircraft, or artillery; nor would the superior Browning automatic weapons be readily available until the last weeks of the war.

With tempers somewhat cooled Pershing and Pétain met with Foch on September 2 which resulted in the approval of a united campaign that ultimately destroyed the Second Reich. In its revised form the campaign plan called for the following. Supported by the French on their right the British would continue their advance toward Cambrai–Saint-Quentin. In the center the French attacked between Soissons and Reims with the purpose of driving the Germans beyond the Aisne and Ailette. To pacify Pershing, Foch directed the new American First Army to execute two offensives. First, the clearing of the Saint-Mihiel salient in order to secure the Paris–Avricourt Railway and create a "satisfactory base of departure for later operations," and following this operation Pershing would shift the bulk of his forces west of the Meuse and in cooperation with the French left advance in the "general direction of Mézières." This latter offensive, which Foch insisted must be "prepared with the greatest speed," had to be launched no later than September 20–25, or less than two weeks after Saint-Mihiel.[47]

This extraordinary timetable placed enormous pressure on the First Army's headquarters. The brilliant young staff officer Colonel George Marshall, who would later serve his country as Chief of Staff, Secretary of State, and Secretary of Defense, succinctly describes the dilemma he and other operations officers faced. "Here we were – a brand-new staff of a brand-new army, three times the size of a normal army, just entering the line for the first time and approaching its first operation, and already immersed in the preparations for a much larger operation, quickly to follow on another front."[48] Among other problems, the First Army's artillery and its ammunition would have to be transferred to a new front across a limited network of substandard roads. A single division's artillery, a complement of seventy-two guns, took up ten miles of road space.[49] When first given the primary responsibility for making the arrangements, Marshall was dumfounded. In his view, "there seemed no precedent for such a course, and, therefore, no established method for carrying it out."[50]

Nonetheless, Marshall and other operations officers immediately set to work, setting in motion convoys of troop-laden trucks and long columns of infantry moving toward the salient, approximately 200 miles square and named after the town of Saint-Mihiel which lay close to its apex. Speed was of the essence, not only because of a second offensive in the Meuse-Argonne area, but because the approaching rainy season made any campaign in the Woëvre plain, with its lakes, rivers, and marshes, extremely difficult.

Lieutenant Herbert Snyder, 9th Infantry, 2nd Division, recorded the following in his diary.

Sept 1st (Sunday). At 5:00 o'clock got orders for our move by truck – and that means a battle, sure. I hope I am alive at the end of it; of victory I am certain. Sept 2d: We fell in at 10:00 o'clock and at 1:30 trucks arrived . . . We piled into trucks and set off for an unknown place. Passed through Toul while most of the time I was asleep . . . At daybreak we arrived in a big woods and ordered out. Everyone slept all day. There was no rain but we had nothing to eat.[51]

Some soldiers had experienced combat but most had not. Private Herbert L. McHenry, a replacement soldier, was one of these soldiers. After receiving his draft notice on May 28, 1918 he had reported to Camp Lee in Virginia. After a few weeks of instruction in trench warfare the War Department shipped him to France. Arriving on July 29 the authorities placed him, as he put it, in "a shot-up regiment." After additional training, which in his case consisted of a single day's bayonet drill, he was on his way to the front. Although he had never trained with machine guns the authorities assigned him to a machine gun company in the 16th Infantry Regiment, 1st Division.

A machine gun company consisted of three platoons, each of which had four squads, making a total of twelve machine guns. Commanded by a corporal, a squad consisted of seven other men: five ammunition carriers (who hauled the twenty-five-round metal strips), one gunner who carried the Hotchkiss heavy machine gun (maximum rate of fire of 400 rounds a minute), and a loader who carried the tripod (together the machine gun and tripod weighed 109 pounds). Recent fighting had reduced McHenry's new company from ninety-six to thirty-five men and the squad he joined had been "shot down from eight to four men."[52] He entered combat as an ammunition carrier and finished the war as a gunner.

McHenry held distinct memories of his advance to Saint-Mihiel. "Each side of the road was heavily crowded with moving vehicles. As this transportation of munitions of war was done only in the black darkness of the night and not a spark of light was allowed to exist, there were accidents," he later recalled. "There were head-on collisions and tele-scope collisions and there was the side-swipe variety of accident ... As accidents constantly occurred throughout the night, and soldier language was hurled from one soldier to another, there was a constant roar of profanity from that highway." Just before dawn the men and their trans-port were hidden in forests and villages while the wrecked vehicles and horse carcasses, dead from exhaustion or lack of forage and water, were removed from the roads. "When night again fell over the land, as if by magic, that silent highway became a turbulent, noisy and highly profane channel of travel."[53]

As suggested in McHenry's account, the First Army's leadership made extensive efforts to mask preparations, including night marches, for its forthcoming offensive. Pershing also appointed an unsuspecting Major General Omar Bundy as commander of the Sixth Corps, which existed on paper only, and created a dummy headquarters at Belfort to mislead the Germans into thinking that the Americans planned an invasion of Alsace in the southeast. American officers increased their wire messages (usually a sure sign of approaching military activity) and aircraft flights while registering American artillery pieces. Intelligence officers prepared fake attack orders for an offensive in Alsace. Colonel A. L. Conger later told an American reporter that after examining a carbon copy of this bogus attack order "to see that it was perfectly legible," he "crumpled [it] up and dropped [it] in the wastebasket. I left the room for five minutes to walk around the corridor of the principal hotel in Belfort and upon my return found it gone as I hoped it would."[54]

The so-called "Alsace Ruse" did indeed keep the Germans guessing, but their intelligence services were soon aware of American preparations around the Saint-Mihiel salient. On September 10 the Germans correctly concluded that the Americans planned an attack against the south side of the salient, accompanied by a weaker diversionary or secondary assault on the west side. Believing that this offensive would not start until

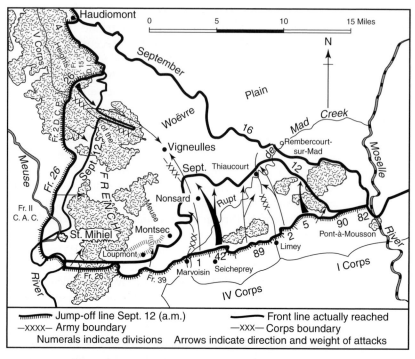

10. Plan of attack of First Army, September 12, 1918

September 15, an anxious Lieutenant General Georg Fuchs, the German commander of Army Detachment C at Saint-Mihiel, gave orders to destroy bridges, roads, and water supplies as the first step toward a staged withdrawal called the Loki movement, to the recently constructed Michel line at the base of the salient. The first German troop movements, including its heavy artillery and some infantry, were scheduled to take place during the night of September 11–12.[55]

Along with tanks and aircraft, Pershing as usual depended heavily upon the Allies, especially the French, for additional artillery support, including gun crews and artillery staffs. The French responded handsomely, providing Pershing from their armies and artillery reserve an additional ninety-nine batteries of French 75s and fifty batteries of heavy howitzers.[56] On September 12 the First Army had at its disposal 667 batteries for a total of 3,010 guns, many of them of a heavy caliber. The French and British also assured the First Army of having an almost five to one advantage in aircraft (Map 10).

Pershing's staff considered three plans dealing with artillery preparation: eighteen hours of artillery fire, about five hours, or no prior bombardment. Initially Pershing and his staff favored the third option, but Colonel Marshall argued that this approach violated previous practice in assaulting "elaborately fortified positions." He also had another motive. He writes in his memoir that he feared excessive losses in the First Army's first offensive might cost Pershing his job, especially given the hostility toward him by many Allied political and military leaders.[57]

To assure success Pershing committed his battle-tested divisions, the 1st, 2nd, 4th, 26th, and 42nd, placing them alongside inexperienced divisions with little combat or only sector training. Liggett's I Corps (2nd, 5th, 82nd, and 90th Divisions) and Dickman's Fourth Corps (1st, 42nd, and 89th Divisions) led the assault, advancing from the southern face of the salient across the Rupt de Mad, a small stream emptying into the Moselle River. Major General George H. Cameron's Fifth Corps (French 15th Colonial Division, 26th Division, and a brigade from the 4th Division) delivered a secondary assault across the hilly, wooded western face of the salient. Meanwhile, three divisions of the French II Colonial Corps were to launch a holding operation with strong trench raids against the apex or nose of the salient.

If everything went according to plan, American forces advancing from the west and south would join hands in the vicinity of Vigneulles in the center of the salient, thereby trapping German soldiers retreating from the salient's apex. In reserve, Pershing had three additional divisions, the 35th, 80th, and 91st. This massive force of 550,000 Americans and 110,000 Frenchmen confronted a German force of eight war-weary and under-strength divisions and one brigade. Estimates differ widely on how "under-strength" these divisions actually were. Estimates of the Germans facing this onslaught range from a low of 23,000 to a high of 100,000. The correct number is probably somewhere in between.[58]

During the night of September 11–12, US troops in miserable weather moved into the front trenches for an early morning assault. "We left on time for the assembly trench in a heavy rain, passed through woods where it was so dark we held each other's hand. Finally breaking from the woods we could see little lights everywhere. At first we were nervous because that might attract the Boche artillery," Lieutenant Snyder recorded in his diary. But German guns remained strangely silent. Unknown to Snyder and his mates the Germans had begun a staged withdrawal of their artillery. Snyder passed through the town of Limey and dropped down into "the communicating trench for the assembly line. It was full of men passing up and down, so we were delayed. The trench was thigh-deep in water. We had to keep in it for over a mile. It continued to rain."[59]

Soldiers had earlier discarded their full packs. Private McHenry's battle pack included the following: a razor, a comb, a tooth brush, a towel, and soap, together with mess kit and rations for forty-eight hours, along with a two-quart canteen. Shovels, picks, and heavy wire pliers also made up part of some soldiers' battle gear along with gas masks, ammunition, and grenades. As a member of a machine gun squad McHenry carried two boxes of ammunition, each weighing about thirty pounds. His company had been assigned to protect infantrymen if they were forced to fall back and reform. (Machine guns were also now being used in some divisions to provide fire support for assaults.)

At precisely 1 o'clock on the morning of September 12 artillery preparation heralded the primary attack along the southern face of the salient where over 60 percent of the artillery had been massed. "The very earth seemed to belch forth the flame that shimmered over all that the eye could see," recalls the history of the 1st Division. "With a steadiness that was appalling in its volume, the convulsion continued. Above the crashing roar could be heard the deeper boom of the great railroad guns that were sending their tons of steel to the enemy's back area and tearing up his rest camps and communications."[60]

This artillery preparation created chaos behind the front because it caught German infantry as well as artillery in the process of withdrawing from the salient. Columns of marching enemy troops, especially at the crossroad junctions and towns along the roads leading out of the salient, disintegrated under a shower of exploding shells. Many Germans fled in panic to find shelter and never rejoined their units, surrendering to the first Americans they encountered.[61]

McHenry's description of his division's advance demonstrates that officers in the veteran 1st Division understood the human cost of men bunching up in battle. The division had been trained to conduct a detailed set-piece battle, undergoing exercises in the Vaucouleurs training area for ten days which began at the squad level and concluded with the entire division conducting a dress rehearsal, advancing several kilometers across terrain similar to what they would encounter at Saint-Mihiel.[62] On September 12 McHenry writes that our "first wave consisted of Infantry in very wide open order. The soldiers on the first line are some thirty feet apart, back of them is another line of soldiers about thirty feet apart. There are many, many lines in each wave."[63]

Tanks, manned partly by Americans and partly by Frenchmen, accompanied the advancing infantry while bombers and fighter aircraft, piloted by men of both nations, flew above. The French had provided "Billy" Mitchell, who directed air operations, with the most powerful

Fig. 22 Germans fixing barbed-wire tangle

air cover yet in the war, 1,400 aircraft, none of them American made.[64] Driving rain throughout the night followed by an early morning fog, however, initially hampered the role of the American Air Service. Balloonists in particular experienced difficulties fulfilling their observation mission because of strong winds. Although every balloon ascended at dawn as scheduled, many had to be retrieved because of the weather. Balloon companies also struggled to keep up with the rapidly advancing infantry although a bright sun emerged once the heavy fog lifted, allowing one American aviator to report to headquarters that an "entire [enemy] company was waiting in a trench at a certain point to surrender."[65]

The greatest difficulty encountered proved not to be German resistance or the thick barbed wire entanglements so feared by the planners of the offensive but the muddy ground and German trenches which "were of different depths and different widths, but were mostly too wide to jump over, and we were compelled to sort of tumble into one side and crawl out of the other."[66] Tanks, Bangalore torpedoes, and wire cutters sometimes cleared paths through the barbed wire but in many cases American soldiers simply walked through rusty and poorly maintained wire (Fig. 22). One French officer, sent with a team to investigate this remarkable feat, concluded that Americans had been able to walk across the wire because their feet were so large.[67]

Along many parts of the southern front German resistance quickly crumbled. By 11 a.m. the 2nd Division had achieved its first-day objectives, reaching the town of Thiaucourt. When they entered this town that had been under German occupation since late September 1914 they were greeted by a population "frantic with joy. They hugged the doughboys, offered them chow and literally jumped on their necks, showering them with blessings and kisses." Sergeant Bernard J. McCrossen, MG Co., 28th Infantry, and his comrades especially appreciated the "very pretty mademoiselles."[68] This was a scene to be repeated many times in World War II when Americans liberated French towns following D-Day. Unfortunately, many other towns in the salient, such as Heudicourt, Vigneulles, Hattonville, and Hattonchâtel, were heavily shelled during the fighting or set fire to by retreating Germans.

Even cavalrymen participated in the rapid American advance. Major General James T. Dickman, a former cavalryman, had four troops from the 2nd Cavalry, commanded by Lieutenant Colonel O. P. M. "Happy" Hazard, in his Fourth Corps. Three of these troops (D, F, and H) were attached to the 1st Division. Dickman sent them in the direction of Vigneulles to cut the Heudicourt–Vigneulles railway. Hazard's men, however, were inexperienced, and their horses, convalescents from veterinary hospitals, had never been trained as cavalry mounts. When these cavalrymen came under heavy machine gun fire, notes Hallas, "the nags from the veterinary hospitals laid back their ears and bolted for the rear. Sawing frantically at the reins, most of the inexperienced recruits were carried away in the debacle." At dawn the next day mounted soldiers had better luck, capturing an enemy battery and seventy-three Germans.[69] Despite this success, mounted soldiers, although they promised to provide speed and mobility for an advancing army, had in reality become obsolescent on battlefields dominated by artillery, rapid-fire weapons, and barbed wire.

At 7:30 p.m. Edwards on the western face of the salient received an order to advance immediately on Vigneulles, which lay some five miles from his front lines. "This is your chance, old man, Go do it . . . Try to beat the 1st Division in the race and clean up," George H. Cameron urged Edwards.[70] The race to Vigneulles was now on between Regulars and National Guardsmen. The 102nd Regiment, 51st Brigade, spearheaded the 26th Division's advance. Given a head start, and rapidly advancing, sometimes on the double quick and without its artillery, elements of the 26th Division reached Vigneulles before 3 a.m. The 1st Division began its advance shortly after midnight and by 6 a.m. its advance elements made contact with outposts of the 26th Division at Vigneulles, cutting the main escape road out of the salient. Mopping up continued and by nightfall on the 13th the Saint-Mihiel salient had been eliminated, with Germans repositioning themselves in a straight line along their Michel defensive system. Some 16,000 Germans had surrendered to the advancing Americans, a goodly number of them without a fight. Although the fighting flickered on as local operations continued until September 16, the Americans had effectively cleared the salient in thirty-six hours.[71]

Pershing and Secretary of War Baker, who at midday came to First Army headquarters to view maps showing the progress of the battle, watched the artillery preparation and the early stages of the battle from different vantage points.[72] Even though it had taken seventeen months, they both felt vindicated in their determination to create an independent US army on European soil. "This striking victory completely demonstrated the wisdom of building up a distinct American army," Pershing later wrote. Some Allied leaders might sneer that this was the battle where "the Americans relieved the Germans." But Pershing believed that "no form of propaganda could overcome the depressing effect on the enemy's morale of the fact that a new adversary had been able to put a formidable army in the field against him which, in its first offensive, could win such an important engagement."[73]

An elated Pershing also viewed the Saint-Mihiel victory in chauvinistic terms. He told his chief intelligence officer, Brigadier General Dennis Nolan, that the United States, a nation of immigrants, had produced "a type of manhood superior in initiative to that existing abroad, which given approximately equal training and discipline, developed a superior soldier to that existing abroad." Pershing even toyed with the idea that when the AEF, which now had twenty-nine divisions in France, surpassed the combined Anglo-French armies in manpower, an American (himself no doubt) should replace Foch as generalissimo.[74]

Pershing was right about the effect of the American success on German leaders, including Ludendorff, who spoke of the "severe defeat of Composite Army C." A stunned Ludendorff could "only hope that the Group of Armies employing the forces which I am allotting to it will hold the position. The Group of Armies will bear the complete responsibility for this. I am not willing to admit that one American division is worth 2 German."[75]

During September the American public's attention focused on the First Army's reduction of the Saint-Mihiel salient and the beginning of its great offensive in the Meuse-Argonne. Elsewhere on the Western Front, however, some Americans still fought under either French or

British command. After training with the British 39th Division, the 77th Division had relieved the US 4th Division in the Vesle sector on August 13. Originally composed of draftees from New York City and its suburbs, the members of this division are said to have spoken forty-three languages and dialects. Major General Robert Alexander, who became its new commander in late August, believed that "probably every race on the globe was represented except the Negro,"[76] a statement that unintentionally emphasized the prevailing segregation in the US Army.

As other US divisions in the Vesle sector were transferred eastward Alexander's division on September 9 had been attached to the French XVI Corps, commanded by General Deville. On the morning of September 14, as the Battle of Saint-Mihiel died down, the 77th Division joined the French in an attack in echelon, a method not approved of by Alexander. "If a successful outcome is to be anticipated, the most exact cooperation is demanded. If one of the major units fails of the given time or place the advance of the others is greatly impeded," he writes in his memoirs.[77] Sure enough, when the French 62nd Division failed to advance, uncovering the 77th Division's right to flanking fire, the Americans had to fall back. This ended the month-long campaign of the 77th during which it had pushed north of the Vesle to the Aisne, the only US division to do so. Its dead and wounded numbered more than 7,000.[78]

Further north Pershing had withdrawn three of the five US divisions training in the British sector. The two that remained, the 27th and 30th, Second American Corps, had been attached to Rawlinson's Fourth Army, which also included Australian and Canadian divisions. On September 24–25 the American divisions entered the line, the 27th replacing the British 18th and 74th Divisions and the 30th the 1st Australian Division, to participate in the Somme Offensive against the central defenses that the British called the Hindenburg Line and which included the Saint-Quentin Canal. In the American sector, a tunnel section of this canal went underground. Monash, the architect of the earlier successful set-piece battle of Le Hamel in which the Americans had participated, drew up the plan for this offensive. Convinced that the formidable German defenses could not be breached without lengthy artillery preparation he proposed that British artillery fire a preliminary bombardment followed by a creeping barrage.[79]

Since Monash's plans included a jump-off position still in German hands in the tunnel line section, he assigned the Americans a preliminary operation to secure this area. On September 26 the 118th Infantry, 59th Brigade, 30th Division, advanced some 500 yards beyond the jump-off point on its front. On the following day it did not go so well for the 53rd

Brigade, 27th Division, as it attempted to secure its jump-off point along a ridge line. Advancing through an early morning fog, the Americans failed to detect some German machine gun nests and bypassed them. When the fog lifted they came under a cross-fire, many soldiers being pinned down. Forced to withdraw, the 53rd Brigade left behind wounded soldiers and isolated pockets of men in front of the ridge line.[80]

The presence of these Americans in no-man's-land presented Monash and Rawlinson with a terrible dilemma. John F. O'Ryan, the commander of the 27th, asked Monash if the main offensive, scheduled for the 29th, could be delayed until these marooned soldiers were retrieved. Monash forwarded this request to Rawlinson who insisted that the attack go on as scheduled. When Haig visited Monash on September 28 he found the Australian in "a state of despair." But the Scotsman clearly agreed with Rawlinson's decision, commenting in his diary that "it was not a serious matter and he [Monash] should attack tomorrow morning in force as arranged."[81]

O'Ryan, the only National Guardsman to retain command of a division throughout the war, clearly disagreed with Haig's contention that it was not "a serious matter." But he accepted Rawlinson's decision to send the 27th over the top without British artillery shelling the ridge line or protecting the advancing New Yorkers with a creeping barrage. "The 53rd Brigade, which was gallantly holding its gains, was entitled to every consideration, even though some sacrifice was involved," he later wrote. "To voluntarily assume the risk of destroying those because of a decision to increase the security of the 54th Brigade, no matter how logical it might be in the tactical sense, would be repulsive to the mass of the officers and men of the division, and destructive of morale."[82]

On September 29, assisted by the crossing of the Saint-Quentin Canal by the British 46th Division on its right – one of the great achievements of the entire war – the US 30th Division occupied Bellicourt and took most of the tunnel defenses. Meanwhile, the US 27th Division without artillery support could not make progress against German machine guns and artillery (the latter had been moved during the night and consequently had not been subjected to the last phase of British counterbattery fire). British tanks, driven by men of the 301st American Tank Battalion, which was attached to the British 4th Tank Brigade, supported the advance. The Americans, fresh from the British tank training center at Bovington, England, however, had never trained with infantry. Many tanks were put out of action by artillery and some were destroyed when they drove through a British minefield.[83] The 3rd Australian Division suffered the same fate as the 27th when it followed on the heels of the Americans at 11 a.m. Believing that the German defenders were about to crack, Monash ordered a resumption of the attack that afternoon. By nightfall the Americans and Australians occupied the ridge line, or the anticipated jump-off position for the main offensive, but the Germans remained firmly in control of their strong tunnel defenses some 2,000 yards distant.[84]

Rawlinson delivered the following harsh verdict on the failure of the 27th to achieve its objectives: "The Americans appear to be in a state of hopeless confusion and will not I fear be able to function as a Corps so I am contemplating replacing them with the XIII Corps ... I fear [their] casualties have been heavy but it is their own fault."[85] Not so. Rawlinson had ordered this American division to advance without artillery support, an almost certain prescription for failure and excessive losses.

To give the Americans a much needed rest Rawlinson withdrew the Second Corps from the line. Meanwhile, the British Fourth Army (September 30–October 5) secured control of the Hindenburg Line and pushed forward through a secondary German defensive position, the Beaurevoir Line. After its brief respite the Second Corps returned to the line, replacing the exhausted Australian Corps. The 30th Division took its place on the front line while the 27th Division remained in reserve.

With the German defensive system breached the Americans advanced across open countryside against stubborn German resistance offered by German machine gun nests. During the evening of October 11, the New Yorkers of the 27th Division relieved the 30th. The "Old Hickory" Division, composed of troops from Tennessee, North Carolina, and South Carolina, had distinguished itself, its men winning twelve Medals of Honor, the most awarded to any division during the war. On October 17, with the 30th Division back in the line, both divisions crossed the Selle, a river eighteen feet wide with a depth of from three to four feet.[86]

Following this successful drive by the Fourth Army Rawlinson passed the torch to the British Third and First Armies on his left although his troops continued to support the advance of the Third Army. Rawlinson also relieved the American Second Corps which had received no replacements to keep it up to strength, replacing it with the British IV Corps. Withdrawn from British control, the Second Corps retired to the rear for additional training. The war was over for this corps. The 27th Division (thirty-two days in combat) and the 30th Division (thirty-five days in combat) had experienced a high casualty rate: 3,470 men killed and 13,279 wounded for a total of 16,749 men.[87]

Prior to its participation in the British Somme Offensive, Lloyd George had feared that Haig would misuse the American Second Corps as he believed he had the Canadians during the lengthy Battle of Arras in the spring of 1917. The BEF's casualty rate at Arras had been approximately 4,076 per day during this wearing-out battle by three British Armies.[88] The Prime Minister told members of the "X" Committee that "some indication should be given that the War Cabinet did not want a repetition of last year's experience. If the Americans got badly smashed up it would be as bad as in the case of the Canadians, since in that case General Pershing would never send any more men to the British line."[89]

Fighting under foreign officers, of course, proved just as unattractive to American officers then as it would today. Rubs and tensions were inevitable whether it was French or British command. Rawlinson and Deville's direction of US divisions had certainly not been without controversy and did not bode well for joint operations with US soldiers under foreign command.

Meanwhile, Baker had a showdown with Lloyd George over shipping. The Secretary for War had not sailed to Europe to observe the baptism of fire by an independent US force (although with significant French support) at Saint-Mihiel. His mission was to confront Lloyd George, who remained determined that the British would get what he deemed as their fair share of Americans on the British front.

Lloyd George knew that it would be March 1919 at the earliest before the United States built enough ships to support the War Department's eighty divisions program.[90] On August 26 he outlined his strategy to Lord Reading, who was involved in negotiations with Baker in London: "Clemenceau and Foch mean to compel us to keep up our numbers on the British front by refusing to take over the line. This policy would be fatal to the British Empire as we have no reserve of men here which would enable us to keep up anything approximating to the number of divisions we now maintain in the field." In Lloyd George's view this would leave Britain in 1919 "with no army at all for the rest of the war." The volatile Welshman promised to employ "every available resource" to get a fair share of Americans on the British front, including not giving "any further assistance in the matter of shipping."[91]

Obsessed with the question, Lloyd George on September 28 pressed Sir Joseph Maclay, the British Shipping Controller, "relentlessly" to pursue the placement of more Americans with the BEF during discussions with the Inter-Allied Maritime Council, reminding the Shipping Controller he had the backing of the War Cabinet and was acting as the "trustee of the interests of the British soldier." Lloyd George also wrote Secretary of War Milner that "the American Army is not to be used merely for the relief of the French line whilst our men are left in an exhausted and depleted condition to hold the mud through the winter."[92]

On September 30 Baker at the invitation of Lloyd George visited the Prime Minister, who was recovering from what was almost a fatal case of influenza, at Danny Park. The account by Colonel Lloyd C. Griscom, Pershing's personal representative in the British War Office, is the only record of their conversation, but in its essentials it has the ring of truth. The British Army had just broken through the Hindenburg Line while the American drive in the Meuse-Argonne had stalled. As far as the British war effort was concerned, Lloyd George angrily proclaimed, Pershing's force was "perfectly useless, and the shipping devoted to bringing it over utterly wasted." Baker, who had personally witnessed the US success at Saint-Mihiel, remained calm, denying that the US Army was "useless." He also stressed that US forces presently fighting at Meuse-Argonne were opposed by a considerable part of the German Army. He then called Lloyd George's bluff. "I shall cable immediately to Washington to cease sending troops on British ships, which may then be released at once."[93]

On the drive back to London, Reading casually told Baker: "Oh, by the way, Mr. Secretary, the Prime Minister sent for me before we started and asked me to excuse his not saying good-by. Incidentally, he also asked me to say to you that you should think no more about the matter which he raised for discussion after lunch."[94]

Subsequently, the Allied Maritime Transport meeting at Lancaster House, October 1–2, recommended that no reduction be made in US troop transportation for the rest of the year. In fact, an additional 500,000 tons (which included 200,000 tons that had already been arranged for in discussion between Baker and Reading) was diverted from imports to the American program.[95] On October 6, a triumphant Baker sent the following message to the White House: "Tonnage situation favorably cleared up."[96] Baker's optimism proved premature and he was soon complaining about the British not fulfilling their tonnage commitments.

Meanwhile, the Germans initiated peace negotiations which they hoped would not represent total defeat. A peace based on Wilson's Fourteen Points appeared to be their best hope. Consequently, they sent the following message to Wilson by way of Berne during the night of October 3–4: "The German Government requests the President of the United States of America to take steps for the restoration of peace, to notify all belligerents of this request, and to invite them to delegate plenipotentiaries for the purpose of taking up negotiations." Upon receiving this message Wilson told his secretary Joseph P. Tumulty and Colonel House, "This means the end of the war."[97] But did it? There had been false starts before and the AEF's Meuse-Argonne offensive was stalled.

At the beginning of September, Pétain, agreeing with most Allied political and military leaders, thought that Germany had the capacity to continue the war into 1919 even if the Allies breached the Hindenburg Line. French intelligence identified a series of new German defensive positions still to be overrun. And the arrival of winter might give the exhausted German Army a respite to rest and reinforce its spent divisions. On September 8, the French commander-in-chief wrote the following: "When the battle commences again in 1919 our adversary undoubtedly will be established behind a strongly fortified front, abundantly supplied with means of defending against tanks and covered by a deep zone of advance posts or by lines of water." American manpower made Pétain confident of ultimate victory but he placed even greater emphasis on the growing material disparity between the opposing armies. "The battle of 1919," he predicted, "will be a battle of aviation and tanks."[1]

With Allied forces maintaining the offensive initiative, however, September turned out to be a calamitous month for Germany's military fortunes. Berlin had begun the month with more than 2.5 million men in uniform and all of its allies still in the war. Gray-clad infantry occupied more French and Russian territory than they had during the previous September and possessed the strongest defensive system on the Western Front, which remained intact. But setback followed setback, and Ludendorff's darkening mood mirrored the bleak prospects facing German soldiers by the end of the month.

Germany's leading general had lost touch with reality. His tactical victories during the first half of 1918 had not led to strategical success, and he no longer could distinguish between what was possible and what was not. Ludendorff's response to any reverse had been to raise the ante by ordering further offensives to break the spirit of the enemy. Meanwhile, young Americans flowed across the Atlantic providing the French and British with both the will and the manpower to continue the war. In September Ludendorff consequently lost his nerve. His resulting crying spells and erratic behavior alarmed members of his staff who called in Dr. Hochheimer, a retired military physician, for consultation. Dr. Hochheimer prescribed a regimen of rest and relaxation at Spa, a thermal spring resort in eastern Belgium, which included singing German folk songs and admiring roses in the villa gardens.[2]

An improved military situation would have been better therapy. On September 19, General Allenby's imperial forces launched an attack against the Turks in Palestine, annihilating the Turkish 7th and 8th Armies. On September 22, Allenby wired the British War Office: "The two Turkish armies west of the JORDAN have practically ceased to exist. Captures up to date are estimated at least 25,000 prisoners and 260 guns, with the whole of the transport of the armies."[3] With the Turks on their last legs, even more dire news arrived at Spa from southeastern Europe. Allied forces on September 15 had launched a powerful offensive that soon led to the collapse of morale in the Bulgarian army. With Bulgaria on the verge of making a separate peace, the *OHL* initiated arrangements to dispatch reinforcements, but it proved too late to stop the Bulgarians from signing an armistice on September 29. Subsequently, the German Eleventh Army was disarmed and its soldiers became POWs. Bulgaria's withdrawal from the war also seemed to guarantee the collapse of the Ottoman Empire along with the loss of the vital oil fields of Rumania if that country, as Berlin feared, reentered the war. In his memoirs Ludendorff characterized Germany's dire situation as follows: "There was the utmost doubt as to whether we could succeed in establishing in Serbia and Rumania a new flank protection for Austria–Hungary and our Western Front, and keeping up communications with the Rumanian oil-fields. In Italy an attack was sure to come, and it was quite uncertain how the Austro-Hungarian troops there would fight."[4]

According to some accounts Ludendorff suffered a nervous collapse, foaming at the mouth and rolling about on the floor.[5] What is clear is that he understood Germany's precarious position because of its faltering allies and now exposed southeastern flank. "We can't stand up against that; we can't fight the whole world," he lamented to Hermann von Kuhl, Chief of Staff to Crown Prince Rupprecht's Army Group.[6]

In the view of many AEF leaders, including Pershing, Germany's situation by the end of September would have been even more precarious if the American First Army had been allowed to exploit its success by marching on Metz after eliminating the Saint-Mihiel salient. "Had not the operation been definitely limited in order to permit troops participating in it to be withdrawn immediately and marched to the Meuse-Argonne in time for that battle," writes Colonel Marshall, "there is no doubt in my mind but that we could have reached the outskirts of Metz by the late afternoon of the 13th, and quite probably could have captured the city on the 14th, as the enemy was incapable of bringing up reserves in sufficient number and formation to offer an adequate resistance."[7] Brigadier General Fox Conner, the head of G-3 (Operations at GHQ), is equally positive. "Viewed after the event, there is no reasonable doubt but that the continuation of the Saint-Mihiel offensive would have broken the Hindenburg Line. Whether or not even greater successes might have been attained is an interesting subject for speculation."[8] James Hallas, who has written the only account of Saint-Mihiel, *Squandered Victory*, also suggests that "the situation after the first day of the attack clearly offered the possibility of a strategic coup of enormous magnitude."[9]

On the other hand, the First Army's operational mobility at Saint-Mihiel was suspect, as demonstrated by the traffic snarl that began immediately after the Americans went "over the top." The artillery officer Major Austin provides a graphic example of logistical failures as inexperienced American officers struggled to provide artillery support for advancing American units during the first day's action. In a letter to his mother, he described the chaos that ensued when the Rainbow Division "moved some of its artillery and wagon trains over onto that road which had been exclusively reserved for our use by Corps order, thus blocking up everyone including themselves." Some of Austin's inexperienced young officers also "seemed almost helpless to pull themselves out of bad places," he noted.

They know all about figuring firing data on a map, but they haven't had any experience in field soldiering. For example, I had one of my guns detached for accompanying gun with infantry. It was supposed to follow up close onto the infantry to knock out machine gun nests, etc. I found it on a road a couple of miles back, moving along behind a slowly moving damaged tank.

Austin immediately asked the tank commander to move to the side. "In thirty seconds we had done something which the Lieutenant in charge should have done an hour before, instead of sitting there on his horse like a dummy."[10]

The incident mentioned by Austin was multiplied many times over across the expanding battlefield as the AEF's logistical system faltered, and it is quite likely that the First Army would have quickly found itself mired in the autumn mud of the Woëvre Plain if it continued its drive during the rainy season. Moreover, as Pétain had earlier emphasized to Pershing, a drive towards Metz left the First Army's left flank exposed to the big German guns on the Meuse heights.

Liggett is almost certainly correct when he later noted: "The possibility of taking Metz and the rest of it, had the battle been fought on the original plan, existed, in my opinion, only on the supposition that our army was a well-oiled, fully coordinated machine, which it was not as yet." He than gratuitously added: "We may lay the blame, if such exists, for all these wasted chances at the door of our perpetual unpreparedness for war."[11]

Whatever conclusion is drawn about the First Army's possible missed opportunities at Saint-Mihiel, one point is clear: Pershing's decision to launch this offensive had serious consequences for his subsequent Meuse-Argonne offensive. Untested as a field commander Pershing in rushed conditions was now about to direct an offensive by the largest American Army in history and the largest single army on the Western Front. Fifteen of his twenty-nine divisions had been involved at Saint-Mihiel; another five were occupying quiet sectors, including two with the BEF; four were in training areas; and three were coming out of the line on the Vesle.[12]

Pershing had enjoyed his greatest successes at Allied conference tables resisting attempts to integrate his forces into existing British and French armies. Once again he had succeeded by frustrating attempts to divide his forces and deploy them under foreign command in different sectors. But his divisions were about to pay a terrible price for the bargain that he had struck with Foch.

Foch's war-winning strategy did not include prolonged Anglo-French attacks to achieve a breakthrough and a distant advance. Instead, the generalissimo envisaged a series of powerful attacks, more lateral than forward, which exploited the Allied advantage in material without creating deep salients with vulnerable flanks. When German resistance stiffened in one sector he shifted to another front.[13] The cumulative effect of these attacks served to exhaust and demoralize the German Army.

Foch assigned Pershing a lengthy front of some ninety-four miles, running eastwardly from the Argonne Forest to the Moselle River (although the XVII French Army Corps continued to man the defenses of Verdun). But Pershing limited his offensive or moving front to the area between the Meuse River and the western edge of the Argonne Forest at the juncture where his forces joined General Henri Gouraud's French Fourth Army (positioned between the Argonne Forest and the Suippe River).

On this relatively narrow front of approximately eighteen miles,[14] the American First Army had to advance straight ahead across a series of formidable defenses, strengthened by German ingenuity and the rugged terrain which featured a hogback down the middle, the Barrois Plateau, with defiles on both sides. "It was probably the most comprehensive system of leisurely prepared field defense known to history," asserts Harbord. "Old, rusty, new, twisted, straight, netted, crossed and over-lapping barbed wire was strung in endless miles with fortified strong points, dugouts, concrete machine gun emplacements, skillfully selected natural machine gun emplacements, and many lines of trenches flanking and in parallel depth."[15]

The Argonne Forest, six miles wide and twenty-two miles deep, represented another obstacle, really another Belleau Wood, only larger. "It was a dense forest gashed by steep ridges and deep ravines, littered by the debris of many storms, natural and man-made. It was a region forgotten when level ground was being created," notes Harbord. "Guns could not be driven through it. No man's horizon was more than a few yards away."[16] In this "almost impenetrable undergrowth," according to Alexander, the commander of the 77th Division that fought in the forest, "only a few passages existed and every path, wood-road and trail was covered by numerous groups of enemy machine-gun nests."[17]

As the First Army advanced on this relatively narrow front, its flanks became exposed to German artillery from the heights of the Meuse and from German-occupied sections of the Argonne Forest. Unlike French and British commanders, Pershing did not have the option of shifting to another front if German resistance stiffened and his offensive stalled. "There was no elbow room," Drum, one of the AEF's most able officers, has written. "We had to drive straight through."[18] If the First Army failed to advance quickly across the multilayered German defensive system before enemy reinforcements arrived its offensive might mirror the pro-longed and costly Allied and German offensives of 1915–17, with the Americans having no choice but to plow straight ahead if they were to interdict Germany's only railway running laterally east to west from Lille to Switzerland. The fact that the Americans had the shortest distance to cut this vital railway which serviced the German Army on fully one-half of the Western Front made it imperative that the Germans stand their ground.[19]

George Marshall later made the dubious argument that the ensuing prolonged and costly Meuse-Argonne offensive was in line with Ameri-can national characteristics. "Our men gave better results when employed in a 'steamroller' operation," he argues,

that is, when launched in any attack with distant objectives and held continuously to their task without rest or reorganization until unfit for further fighting. Their morale suffered from delays under fire, their spirits were best maintained by continued aggressive action, even though the men themselves were approaching the point of complete exhaustion. They bitterly resented casualties suffered while being held in position, without doing any damage to the enemy.[20]

In agreeing to two distinct operations at Saint-Mihiel and Meuse-Argonne, Pershing accepted an extraordinary timetable, especially for a neophyte force with inadequate logistics. George Marshall and other staff members had only ten days after breaking off the offensive at Saint-Mihiel to move American forces over poor roads to the Meuse-Argonne sector. Furthermore, this massive movement of men and equipment to replace the French forces on this front had to take place in darkness in an attempt to mask the approaching offensive from prying German eyes.

The few and inadequate roads between the two battlefields became "a solid mass of transportation, mostly motor-drawn. There was no light of any kind, except occasionally from the exhaust flames of the large tractors hauling heavy guns," recalls Marshall. With French and American troops and equipment moving in opposite directions as Americans assumed control of a front previously manned by the French, confusion abounded. As recalled by Marshall, "two Americans could stir up a pretty violent argument over interference between their respective columns in the darkness, and the addition of a Frenchman to the discussion made it highly explosive."[21] Yet, according to Marshall,

it was surprising how few collisions occurred, though the roadside was fairly well littered with broken trucks, automobiles – particularly Dodge cars – and motorcycles ... Near Void there was a jam, resulting from one busload of soldiers being driven into the river and the following truck wedged on the bridge. At the same point the following night another busload of soldiers crashed through the railroad gate and was struck by an engine, several of the men being killed and a number injured.[22]

Despite the many obstacles, Marshall and his staff successfully replaced the some 220,000 French soldiers at the front with 600,000 Americans, an extraordinary achievement. Nonetheless, German intelligence anticipated the offensive just prior to its being launched and enemy reinforcements began to enter the line as early as September 26.

Another problem, unrelated to logistics, was that Pershing had earlier deployed most of his battle-tested divisions, the 1st, 2nd, 26th, and 42nd, in the Saint-Mihiel salient to ensure success. Consequently, of the nine divisions, the equivalent of some twenty-seven under-strength 1918 German divisions, initially deployed on the Meuse-Argonne front, only one of them, the 33rd, could be considered a veteran division.[23] Two of the National Guard Divisions, the 79th and 91st, had been in France for only two months. When the 79th departed for Europe, for example, it included many draftees who had been in uniform for only a few days or weeks. Yet Pershing assigned this division the most difficult and critical objective of the first day, the capture of Montfaucon Hill (or Falcon Mountain), some four miles beyond the first line of German defenses, which dominated the entire front because of its elevation.[24]

From left to right, approximately 100,000 Doughboys lined up as follows against Germany Army Group "von Gallwitz." On the left, the First Corps (77th, 28th, and 35th Divisions) advanced, commanded by Major General Liggett. Liggett's First Corps had the following assignment: assisted by the French Fourth Army on its left, the 77th (New Yorkers, supplemented by 4,000 replacements drawn mostly from California) was to make a frontal assault on the Argonne Forest to pin down German defenders. Meanwhile, a pincer movement by the French Fourth Army on Alexander's left and the 28th (Pennsylvania, National Guard) on his right, between the left bank of the Aire River and the fringes of the Argonne Forest, assisted by the 35th (Missouri, Kansas, National Guard) on the opposite side of the Aire, caved in the enemy's flanks, to force the Germans out of this heavily forested and mountainous region.

Elsewhere on the moving front, Major General George H. Cameron's Fifth Corps, composed of the 91st (Pacific Coast, National Army), 37th ("Buckeye," the Ohio National Guard), and 79th (Middle States, National Guard), drove straight ahead to seize the commanding heights of Montfaucon.

Finally, Major General Robert L. Bullard's Third Corps, consisting of the 4th (Regular Army), 80th (National Army, mostly draftees from Virginia), and 33rd (Illinois, National Guard), attacked between Montfaucon and the Meuse. The 4th advanced straight ahead while the 80th and 33rd pivoted on the Meuse.

AEF planners developed an extraordinarily optimistic offensive plan which called for a rapid advance of some sixteen kilometers. They expected the First Army's inexperienced divisions to capture Montfaucon on the first day, advance through the German multilayered defensive system, and no later than the second day penetrate Germany's third and key defensive position, the Kriemhilde Stellung, before this section of the German defensive system could be reinforced. Having established a new front running from Grandpré to Romagne, the First Army would then be poised to interdict Germany's vital railway communications.[25] Rather than the key German railway center at Mézières, whose seizure had now been assigned to Gouraud's Fourth Army, Pershing shifted the First Army's ultimate objective to interdicting the lateral German rail link between Carignan and Sedan, which with some justification he characterized as "the most sensitive part of the German front being attacked."[26]

On the eve of the greatest battle yet fought by any American force, Pershing visited the headquarters of his division and corps commanders, noting that "they were all alert and confident and I returned feeling that all would go as planned."[27] Pershing apparently had no hesitation in deploying raw troops to achieve these ambitious objectives because of his belief of almost religious fervor that Americans possessed a fighting spirit no longer prominent in either Allied or German units. Training, experience, and doctrine be damned. "In my opinion," he wrote in his final report, "no other Allied troops had the morale or the offensive spirit to overcome successfully the difficulties to be met in the Meuse-Argonne sector."[28]

As usual, however, the artillery's success in suppressing enemy resistance rather than the raw courage of attacking forces determined the success or failure of offensives on the Western Front. The French furnished the guns (with the exception of some US naval guns) and ammunition and approximately one-half of the artillerymen, including the chiefs of artillery for the First and Fifth Corps. On the battle front there were 2,711 guns or 96.9 guns per kilometer; an additional 1,291 guns were positioned on the defensive front from the Meuse to the Moselle, giving Pershing "the largest assembly of artillery that had ever been under control of one American commander in battle."[29] In 1918 the French and British and especially the Germans had given chemical warfare an essential role in their offensives. The American bombardment, however, did not include poison gas due to both a shortage of gas shells and American inexperience in utilizing this formidable weapon. The distant objectives given the US divisions also meant that they would if successful inevitably advance beyond the supporting fire of their artillery.[30]

Artillery preparation for the offensive began at 11:30 p.m. on September 25. Among the American artillerymen was a future US President, Harry S. Truman, the commander of Battery D, 129th Field Artillery, 60th Brigade, 35th Division. To the rear 14-inch naval guns mounted on railway carriages, commanded by an American admiral, lobbed enormous 1,400-pound high-explosive shells against long-range targets such as Montfaucon and German rear communications. During this fierce bombardment Allied artillery expended more ammunition than both sides had used during the entire American Civil War.[31]

Most of this storm of shells, however, fell harmlessly on Germany's frontline defenses which the Germans thinly held and used primarily for either outposts, manned by machine gunners, or observation positions. The main defensive position, manned by some 24,000 infantrymen and situated along ridges, was some six kilometers beyond these frontline defenses.

At 5:30 a.m. US infantry, preceded by the now standard creeping barrage, advanced in extended order through a thick morning fog (Map 11). Light tanks, most of them commanded by Lieutenant Colonel

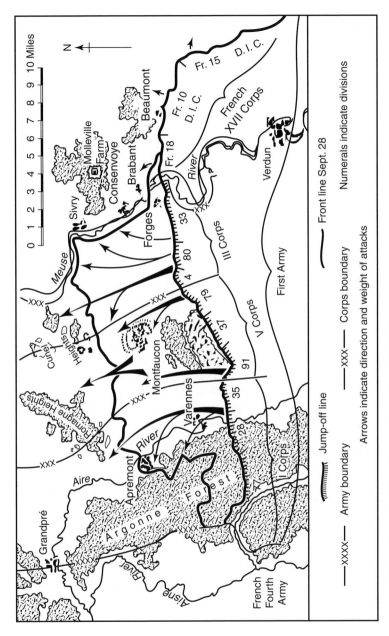

11. Plan of attack of First Army, September 26, 1918

331

George S. Patton, spearheaded the attack in the sector of the First Corps. These tanks, although a great advance in military technology, failed to live up to expectations. Many broke down, became bogged down in mud or trench works, or were knocked out by German guns. Patton's tank brigade lost forty-three of its 140 tanks on September 26, and Patton himself was wounded in the upper thigh and buttocks and had to be evacuated to a hospital.[32]

Isolated machine gun nests (Bullard later suggested that Germany's "first defense seemed to be almost wholly machine guns"),[33] massive barbed wire entanglements, and torn-up terrain initially offered the greatest impediment to rapid movement. Bullard's Third Corps achieved the greatest success. He later recalled that his Third Corps advanced "almost as far as we had anticipated. I was feeling good. We crossed the awful wire entanglements of No Man's Land and beyond ... the enemy's reaction in our front had not been violent and my corps that day had suffered no great losses. Yet we had had no walk-over."[34] On the far left of the moving front Alexander's 77th Division found the "deep belts of wire and intricate trenches" to be "formidable obstacles to rapid progress. Those immobile defenses had been churned by our preparatory fire into the most amazing tangle imaginable, and our men had much difficulty in getting through and over them."[35] The forest itself with its thick undergrowth offered an even greater obstacle for the advancing 77th. According to Alexander, the Germans had suspended "wire netting ('chicken wire') on the trunks of the trees and bushes. The undergrowth was so thick that this was not observable until the troops were in contact with it, and the wire was always backed up by groups of cleverly placed machine guns." Casualties were heavy, and Alexander later estimated that his New Yorkers suffered ten casualties during the campaign for every one inflicted upon the enemy.[36]

Although the First Army's green divisions had breached the thinly defended German front in several places, in Marshall's estimation they "were not yet qualified to exploit this tremendous advantage, which would have required great celerity and careful coordination of movement. There was an abundance of courage available but too little technique to secure its most advantageous employment."[37] The lack of experienced staff officers had actually been exacerbated by Pershing who insisted that some of the best and brightest officers in the assaulting divisions attend the fourth class of the General Staff College at Langres scheduled to begin on October 1.[38]

Nowhere did the Americans pay a greater price for their inexperience at the command level as well as in the ranks than the failure of the 79th

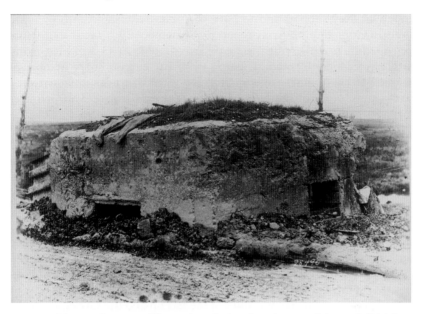

Fig. 23 German pillbox taken during the advance of the 79th Division, Haucourt, Meuse, France

Division to capture the key German defensive position, Montfaucon Hill, on the first day (Fig. 23). As Professor Ferrell suggests, "sometimes a single failure is enough to cause a great enterprise to lose its momentum, stumble, and if not fall then at least come to a standstill. In the opening days of the Meuse-Argonne, this may have been the failure to take Montfaucon on the first day of the attack (the First Army took it at noon on the second day)."[39]

Enemy resistance stiffened as German reserves reached the battlefield, some reinforcements having arrived as early as September 26. By September 29 the equivalent of nine German divisions blocked the American advance. Although the First Army still held an overwhelming numerical superiority, its inexperience at all levels and the enemy's strong defenses and superior firepower largely neutralized this advantage.

Most German soldiers were equipped with automatic rifles or machine guns, the latter often manned by a single soldier. German artillery also dominated the battlefield following the opening American bombardment which had concentrated upon thinly occupied German frontline positions. "The American infantry is reported to have attacked without

much artillery support and to have been generally shot down by fire,"
noted a German Fifth Army report on September 29.[40] German aviators
provided their artillerymen, according to the former G-3 of First Army
artillery, Colonel Conrad H. Lanza, with an "extraordinary number of
targets, artillery, tanks, rolling kitchens, wagons, trucks, infantry, etc.,
with almost complete absence of camouflage on our part. The Germany
artillery had some wonderful shoots."[41] In addition to intelligence
furnished by aviators, German artillerymen relied on balloonists and
observation posts, some of the latter being located in tree tops and
camouflaged towers in the Argonne Forest. In addition to the high
ground of the Argonne Forest, Americans also came under enfilading
fire from German guns positioned on the heights of the Meuse. This
artillery fire focused on American troops and supplies being brought
forward as well as the advancing infantry. According to Pershing, German
guns "had almost full play on the more exposed elements of the advance
and its cross-fire caused us many casualties."[42]

American assaults also proved less effective than they might have been
because of tactical deficiencies by inexperienced troops led by half-trained
junior officers. "The complexities of the terrain and the German defense
required that junior leaders have a 'master's degree' in tactics," Faulkner
notes, "while most of the American junior officers were barely out of the
grade school of the profession."[43] Doughboys made no attempt to outflank machine gun nests and pushed straight forward in tightly packed
formations. The following quotations from reports from the German
Fifth Army are representative of German analysis of US infantry assaults:

"The American Infantry is very unskillful in the attack. It attacks in thick
columns, in numerous waves echeloned in depth, and preceded by tanks. This
kind of attack offers excellent targets for the fire of our artillery, infantry and
machine guns."

"Provided the infantry does not allow itself to be intimidated by the advancing
masses but remains calm, it can make excellent use of its weapons, and the
American attacks fail, with the heaviest losses."

"The troops must be impressed with the hollowness of the American attacks. The
denser the advanced masses, the more they are hampered in an advance, and
the greater the losses caused by the fire of the defenders. Single machine guns,
on several occasions, have compelled entire attacking companies to flee in
disorder."[44]

Serious logistical problems also plagued the First Army. A vast wasteland
existed on the Meuse-Argonne front after four years of war. A map might
show a handful of prewar roads running across no-man's-land toward the

German lines. But these roads had now been replaced by shell craters and scattered stones. At best there were only three usable roads into the Meuse-Argonne sector. Private Herbert McHenry, 16th Infantry, 1st Division, noted the following as his division marched toward the sound of battle.

The road on which we would have traveled had been mined and blown up. Great holes were in it, in which a country school house could easily have been dropped, and none of it would have appeared above the surface. It was evident from all about us that there had been severe fighting there as the whole surface was torn by shell holes. The surface showed such a torn and tossed up condition, that it resembled the turbulent waves of a stormy ocean with the waves standing stationary, if such a thing could be.[45]

Add to this the spongy nature of the soil which could not sustain heavy traffic, especially under the wet conditions that prevailed.

The problems associated with repairing, really rebuilding, these roads were exacerbated by the AEF's failure to prepare for such an eventuality. Neither the War Department nor Pershing's staff had given much attention to rebuilding or repairing war-damaged roads. Ship berths and railways had been given a higher priority, with only a small number of engineering troops initially assigned to road building. The engineers and pioneers who had the experience did not arrive at the Meuse-Argonne front until the day before the offensive began, only to discover that most of their trucks had already been claimed by the SOS.[46]

With the means they had, engineers frantically worked to rebuild roads while out of necessity they remained in use. Confusion prevailed with an inevitable logjam occurring while traffic moved both toward and away from the front. According to Bullard it took two or three days for a vehicle to make a round trip and "drivers and chauffeurs were frequently found sitting bolt upright sound asleep, their vehicles at a standstill."[47]

Conditions apparently did not improve much over the next three weeks. A French report (shared with the British War Office) probably accurately captures the chaotic logistics of the First Army from September 26 to October 18. It will be quoted at length.

The American idea of road control appeared to be that someone on the spot would rise to the occasion and straighten things out. In actual practice this led to one unit's transport trying to jockey that of every other unit. The result was great congestion on the roads on which transport was often double-banked, effectively blocking them for hours at a time. Small bodies of American troops were scattered everywhere, not apparently under any control. Where work was being carried out three men appeared to be trying to do one man's job; lorries were seen covered with soldiers who ought to have been walking, and supplies were being looted from supply columns as they went forward. The result was that the soldiers in the front line were unable to get either food or ammunition. Requests for reinforcements coming in from the front, which were usually granted, still further added to the congestion, and when supplies did not arrive parties began to drift to the rear, and effectives melted. Liaison from rear to front appeared to be unsatisfactory, and panicky reports kept coming in, such as might be expected in the case of raw troops, as indeed there were ... Headquarters were making frenzied endeavours to get the troops forward, but the knowledge and grip of the situation necessary to organise attacks in these conditions were not possessed by the staff.[48]

Artillery support for advancing infantry following the opening offensive on September 26 also proved inadequate. When the guns eventually caught up with the advancing infantry inexperienced officers frequently misused their guns, often because of poor liaison. Examples of miscues and tactical mistakes provided by Colonel Lanza included the following:

A regiment of field artillery was ordered to advance. It did so. While marching it was ordered to fire a barrage immediately.

An artillery brigade commander was ordered to detail four batteries to fire on as many targets, with a particular kind of gas, at a specified rate of fire, and for a specified length of time. The targets varied in nature and in range, and in no case was the fire ordered correctly.

One brigade of artillery delivered all its fire in the form of a barrage, regardless of the nature of the target.

Rolling barrages were ordered for excessive lengths of time. In one case the barrage was ordered to roll at a constant speed for 9 hours without a stop, instead of being regulated on the progress of the battle.[49]

Broken wires, wayward carrier pigeons, mist or fog, and runners who lost their way or became disorientated on the battlefield contributed to these breakdowns in liaison. Outright incompetence on the part of some officers also at times played a role in the failure of artillery to coordinate its fire with advancing infantry. The 35th Division was especially poorly served in this regard. The division's artillery commander, Brigadier General Lucien G. Berry, for example, did not believe in airplane spotting. Nor did he sanction rapid fire. In a misguided attempt to spare his guns he limited his 75-mm guns to firing one or two shells a minute. The 35th Division's communication also suffered from the ineptitude of one of its signal officers, Lieutenant Colonel George A. Wieczorek, who according to Ferrell destroyed "the division's ability to use signals of any sort."[50]

Yet another reason for the breakdown in liaison between artillery and infantry should not be ignored. Few accurate maps of the combat zone existed and artillerymen and their signal officers had not been given an opportunity to familiarize themselves with their new theater of operations when the First Army abruptly shifted from one battlefield to another in mid-September. The artillerymen, who struggled to keep up with the advancing infantry after the initial bombardment on September 26, found themselves in an almost hopeless situation. When the guns finally caught up with the infantry, it was not unusual for gunners to find that the infantry, keeping to a prescribed schedule, had already begun their attack and would be subjected to "friendly" fire if they fired their guns. Unfamiliar with the wild terrain of trees, ravines, and hills over which the infantry advanced, artillery officers, even under the best of circumstances, also had little idea of their target's coordinates.

Under the circumstances it is not surprising that many US divisions failed to achieve their objectives. On September 29, after four days of heavy fighting and some 45,000 casualties, the entire First Army's offensive had clearly stalled. Its inability to penetrate or even reach the Kriemhilde Stellung actually seemed an even greater failure when compared with the success of Allied attacks during this period that ruptured the Hindenburg Line and pushed the Germans back in Flanders.

On September 30 Pershing removed the battered 79th Division which had initially failed to take Montfaucon and replaced it with the more experienced 3rd Division. Inexperience as well as poorly trained soldiers had contributed to the 79th Division's failures. Inspector General Major General André Brewster brutally suggested that the 79th Division now had only two choices: change its number or have its men reassigned to other divisions.[51] Changing the commander of the 79th Division, Major General Joseph E. Kuhn, would perhaps have been a better place to start. Kuhn, first in his class at West Point and former president of the War College, appeared on paper to be an obvious choice to command a division. But when his time came he had not risen to the occasion, which was equally true of some of the other untested division commanders.[52]

Brigadier General Peter E. Traub, who had been a classmate of Pershing's at West Point, fought in the Philippine Insurrection, and taught Spanish at West Point where he had written a book on verbs, provides an even more egregious example of poor leadership. Recently appointed commander of the 35th Division he played a role in his division's disintegration at Meuse-Argonne. Just prior to the battle he abruptly and, to many, inexplicably removed his senior line officers. In the case of Brigadier General Charles I. Martin, a popular National Guardsman who commanded the 70th Brigade, some perceived a prejudice against the National Guard.[53]

Once the battle was joined Traub's division floundered and began to go to pieces as it encountered strong resistance pushing along the Aire. By September 29, the 35th Division was retreating in some disarray. The War Diary of the German Third Army reported: "For a while, the entire American front between the Aire and the left wing of the army was moving back. Concentrated artillery fire struck enemy masses streaming to the rear with annihilating effect."[54]

Brigadier General Traub assumed the role of a battlefield adventurer/tourist during his division's four days of combat, losing contact with his command post and thereby compromising his ability to provide leadership. After his broken division was withdrawn from the line, with many of his men still unaccounted for, he boasted to fellow officers at First Corps headquarters of his attempts to make personal contact with his brigade commanders. He "had lived without sleep for four days and nights, subsisted exclusively on coffee and cigarettes, was the pet target of every German battery, was frequently bracketed in the open with an expenditure of three hundred or more shells in the process, almost walked into the German lines, was gassed, in short had a hell of a time." "'You bet your life,'"[55] he excitedly exclaimed over dinner with Liggett and his staff.

During the first phase of the Meuse-Argonne offensive, it became obvious to a disappointed Pershing that his offensive had failed despite his vigorous efforts to spur his troops on. During the second day of the offensive he had instructed Drum to send the following message to his battle commanders: "All officers will push their units forward with all possible energy. Corps and division commanders will not hesitate to relieve on the spot any officer of whatever rank who fails to show in this emergency those qualities of leadership required to accomplish the task that confronts us."[56] On September 28 he visited Liggett and talked emotionally of "the enormous importance of our operations and the possibility of ending the war right here if they were successful and the imperative need of drive and push."[57]

Pershing's enemy counterpart, Von der Marwitz, also believed in the vital importance of the Meuse-Argonne front, and was just as determined to defend his front as Pershing was to break it. On October 1, with the American advance resisted to a standstill, he issued his version of Haig's famous "Backs to the Wall" Special Order of the Day in which the British commander attempted to encourage his troops during Germany's spring offensive. "According to available information the enemy intends to attack the Fifth Army east of the Meuse and attempt to drive on Longuyon," Von der Marwitz correctly noted.

The purpose of this attack is to cut us off from the Longuyon–Sedan Railroad, the most vital artery of the Western Front. Moreover, the enemy intends to deny us the use of the Briey iron mines on which our shell production depends substantially. Consequently, during the coming weeks the main burden of the fighting and the security of the fatherland may again become the responsibility of the Fifth Army. The fate of a great part of the Western front, and perhaps the very fate of our people, depends on maintaining our unshaken hold of the Verdun Front.[58]

Pershing's generals clearly felt the pressure as their commander-in-chief kept his foot on the throttle. When Major General Adelbert Cronkhite, the commander of the 80th Division (composed of draftees from West Virginia, Virginia, and Pennsylvania), asked permission from Bullard (Third Corps) to suspend his attempt to occupy the strongly defended woods called the Bois des Ogons after two failed attempts, he was bluntly told: "Give it up and you are a goner; you'll lose your command in twenty-four hours."[59] Cronkhite subsequently attacked and took the woods. Alexander, for his part, if anything, superseded his commander's orders to spur his 77th Division on in the Argonne Forest. In Stackpole's view, he was "acting very hastily" in relieving officers who were experiencing combat for the first time.[60]

Liggett (First Corps) sought to temper his commander-in-chief's zeal for unrelenting offensive action without pauses to regroup and reconnoiter the positions to be attacked. Apparently concerned that some attacking divisions might be pushed to the breaking point, Liggett emphasized to Pershing the difficult terrain, "the insidious character of the opposition, and the handicap all the divisions suffered from by reason of inexperience, lack of training, new officers, losses of officers, and poor ones."[61]

Foch did not necessarily believe that an American military success would be the deciding factor in ending the war, but he increasingly became concerned about the inability of both the American First Army and the French Fourth Army, commanded by General Henri Gouraud, to get a move on in contrast to the successful Allied advances on other fronts (Map 12).

If anything, Clemenceau expressed more concern than Foch about the US effort. The volatile premier (for good reason his countrymen called him the Tiger) had been appalled by the colossal traffic jam he had been caught up in on September 28/29 when he attempted to celebrate his 77th birthday by visiting the American front at Montfaucon. Instead of a heroic effort to supply soldiers at the front he saw only chaos. He responded by pressing Foch to remove Pershing from command.

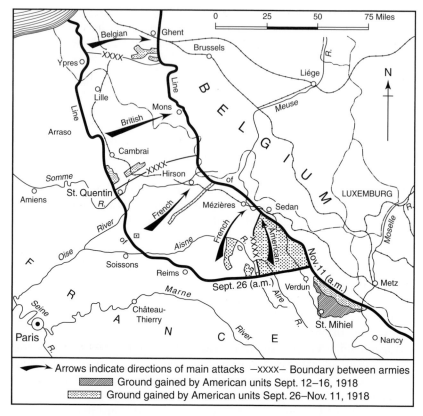

12. American and Allied attacks on the Western Front, September 26–
November 11, 1918

Foch initially reacted by sending a staff officer to explore the First
Army's logistical problems. This officer's subsequent eight-page report
emphasized failings by both Pershing and his staff.[62] Haig was equally
perturbed by the collapse of US logistics. "What very valuable days are
being lost! All this is the result of inexperience and ignorance on the part
of the Belgian and American staffs of the needs of a modern attacking
force," he wrote in his diary.[63]

In retrospect, although inexperienced staff work clearly played a role, it
can be argued that even more important reasons for the congestion were
the deplorable conditions of the few roads leading to the battlefield, the
haste in which the offensive had been prepared, and an undermanned

and poorly equipped American Services of Supply, already struggling to secure the means, especially when it came to horses, mules, and trucks, to maintain the rapidly expanding American presence in Europe.

On October 1, having conferred with Pétain, Foch sent his chief assistant General Maxime Weygand to Pershing's headquarters with an explosive suggestion. Rather than continue to advance along his narrow front, Foch wanted Pershing to broaden his front by placing US divisions west of the Argonne with the French XXXVIII Corps and east of the Meuse with the XVII Corps, thus advancing on both sides of that river. Foch's proposal placed Pershing in command of Franco-American troops fighting on both sides of the Meuse while a French general, Hirschauer, commanded French and American forces on both sides of the Argonne Forest, an arrangement that Foch apparently believed would alleviate some of the logistical snarl behind Pershing's front because of improved staff work by more experienced French officers. A consequence of this rearrangement, however, would be the dismemberment of the US First Army with American divisions being placed directly under a French commander.

Not surprisingly Foch's suggestion of placing American divisions under French command on what had been an all-American front did not appeal to Pershing. Perhaps just as importantly, if he accepted Foch's proposal, it might be viewed in Washington as an admission that his offensive had failed. He had just played down its limited success in a letter to Baker, noting that "operations here have gone very well, but, due to rains and the condition of the roads have not gone forward as rapidly nor as far as I had hoped."[64]

Faced with Pershing's objections, Foch agreed to allow him to retain command on the Meuse-Argonne front but only on the condition that he immediately resume his offensive and continue without pause.[65] Foch's position, which was bound to be interpreted as an insult by both Pershing and his staff, was akin to lighting a match in a gas-filled room and the Frenchman got the reaction that he must have expected. On October 3 Pershing told his liaison officer at Foch's headquarters, Colonel T. Bentley Mott, that Foch's response suggested that the generalissimo questioned the courage of his men and believed that the pause in his operations was unjustified. If Foch did not repudiate these words he would "refuse to have anything to do with him personally hereafter & I will not obey any of his orders that do not fall strictly within his mandate as laid down in the Versailles agreement."[66]

Foch, however, initially showed no inclination to retreat from his position. In his view the pressure on the Germans along an active front that now stretched some 250 miles from the Meuse to Dixmude must be maintained. As he told Mott: "Everyone must march, and march to the end. I am the conductor of the orchestra. Here is the American tenor, the French baritone and the British brass. I make them play together. The bass says that he is out of breath, I say no, you are going to play to the end of the piece." Foch took the position that he had acquiesced to Pershing's desire to keep his forces together and attack at Meuse-Argonne when he himself believed that greater success would be gained by deploying American forces west of the Argonne at Champagne. Although he had been granted "strategic direction of military operations," he had allowed Pershing to have his way. But he also had admonished him at the time: "You want to do it your way? Right, but on condition that you begin and do not stop."[67]

Both men had a point, but Pershing, who had pushed some of his divisions up to and, in the case of the 35th with half of its infantry either killed or wounded, beyond the limits of its endurance, justifiably called a pause in his operations to allow his exhausted divisions to be replaced by fresh ones. Despite his bluster, Foch may in his heart have understood this. For his part Pershing may have concluded if he pushed matters too far with Foch he might be replaced, especially since his offensive thus far had fallen considerably short of his own expectations.

If Clemenceau and Lloyd George had had their way Foch would have replaced Pershing. On October 21 Clemenceau sent Foch an intemperate letter that stressed Pershing's "invincible obstinacy" and accused the AEF commander of prolonging the war, thereby increasing French casualties. Pershing's troops were not "unusable," he emphasized, "they are merely being unused." Clemenceau demanded that Foch tell President Wilson "the truth, the whole truth concerning the situation of the American troops."[68] For his part Lloyd George wanted Foch to tell House (who had just returned to Europe) that the British and French armies would be discouraged if changes were not made "to enable the American Army to pull its own weight."[69]

Baker had been in Europe during the launching of the American offensive. In conversation with Allied leaders the Secretary of War almost certainly detected a strong undercurrent of concern about Pershing's leadership, and it is possible that he considered the possibility of finding a replacement. What is recorded is that Baker during this period asked Pershing directly about a possible successor in the event of the latter's death, certainly a diplomatic way of posing the question of a possible successor. Pershing said that he had never considered such a prospect but promised to provide Baker his choice. When no answer was forthcoming Baker asked him once again before returning to the

United States. Pershing, perhaps not wanting to load a potential executioner's gun, said that he had been unable to make a selection. Baker then prepared his own list: Liggett, Harbord, and Summerall.[70] But Baker apparently remained firmly in Pershing's camp because he defended the AEF's commander-in-chief against these Allied criticisms, writing Wilson that "the slow progress made by the American first army is to be expected under the circumstances."[71]

After reorganizing, the First Army resumed its offensive (sometimes called the Champagne offensive) on October 4. Liggett's First Corps now included the elite 1st Division which had replaced the broken 35th Division. The 82nd Division (All-American), which included America's most celebrated combat soldier, Sergeant Alvin G. York, was later added to Liggett's Corps on October 7 to assist in a sideways movement by the First Corps to force a German evacuation of the Argonne Forest. In the center, Cameron's Fifth Corps had all of its original three divisions withdrawn and replaced with the 32nd and 3rd Divisions. John L. Hines's Third Corps to the east, which had enjoyed the greatest relative success during the first phase of the offensive, remained unchanged (4th, 80th, and 33rd Divisions). These eight divisions hoped to overrun the Kriemhilde Stellung (which Pershing had originally expected to penetrate no later than two days after his offensive had been launched on September 26) and establish themselves along the line Grandpré–Romagne–Brieulles.

To force its way through the most formidable section of the German multilayered defenses, the First Army needed to silence German artillery located in the wooded heights of Romagne-Cunel on the hogback running through the middle of the battlefield and neutralize the deadly enfilading fire directed from the heights of the Meuse and from the hogback in the Argonne Forest.

The initial results of the resumption of the First Army's offensive were disappointing, with the following being noted in the German War Diary, Group of Armies Gallwitz, on October 4:

At 5:30 a.m. heavy artillery fire opened suddenly on the entire fronts of Meuse Group-West [XX Army Corps] and of Meuse Group-East [V Res. Corps]. This was the opening phase of the large-scale attacks which had been expected by this Group of Armies for days. These attacks started on 6:30 a.m. simultaneously with heavy attacks against the left wing of the Third Army; they continued throughout the day, with great tenacity and a reckless commitment of men and material. The main effort was made against the right wing of the Fifth Army. The attacks collapsed, in general, under the brave and obstinate resistance of our infantry and the performance of our artillery. Wherever the enemy succeeded in effecting local penetrations, they were eliminated by powerfully executed counterattacks ... The enemy suffered heavy losses in killed and wounded.[72]

Losses continued to mount as the Americans fought with what the Germans described as "great tenacity and a reckless commitment of men and material." (Aircraft and French Renault tanks, however, did not play a significant role in these assaults. The Germans easily knocked out the small French tanks and German aircraft continued their domination of the skies.)

The 2nd Division's success in capturing the Blanc Mont Ridge, a key German defensive position in Champagne on the left flank of the US front at Meuse-Argonne, was one bright spot for American arms in early October. On September 16 Pétain had asked Pershing to reinforce Henri Gouraud's French Fourth Army with three US divisions. Pershing responded by offering two: Lejeune's veteran 2nd Division and the newly arrived 36th Division, which had yet to receive its artillery, engineers, and logistical support. Fearful that his division might be parceled out in brigades to various French divisions, Lejeune told Gouraud "that if the 2nd Division is kept together as a unit and is allowed to attack on a narrow front, I am confident that it can take Blanc Mont Ridge in a single assault."[73] Blanc Mont (or White Mountain), which had remained in German hands since September 1914, represented a formidable defensive position for the 2nd Division to overrun.

Marine Private Aitken, of the 67th Company, 5th Regiment, has left us with a vivid image of this range of hills of white limestone.

It was water-soluble and stuck to you like your debts. It attacked the membranes of the entire body and got into the armpits and into your soup. A shell or a bullet would strike near you and you would look like a piece of plaster; just covered with the fine smoke-like powder ... Champagne was as near HELL as I want to get.[74]

Believing that his depleted and tired French divisions would be unable to capture this important German position, Gouraud readily agreed, assigning the 2nd Division to General Andre Naulin's XXI Corps.[75] Although Naulin wanted Lejeune to attack on October 2, Lejeune asked for and got a delay of one day in order to reconnoiter the battlefield and get all of his artillery into position.[76]

The ensuing attack by the 2nd Division proved a brilliant success. It is Grotelueschen's view that the 2nd Division's assault "resembled just the kind of limited-objective, firepower-based, set-piece attacks Pershing so derided ... The infantry relied heavily on the fire of automatic rifles, machine guns, mortars, and 37mm guns. Lejeune knew, if Pershing did not, that the concept of 'self-reliant infantry' was meaningless in nearly all offensive operations."[77]

Foch rewarded Lejeune for his success by insisting that the capture of the Blanc Mont Ridge be "exploited to the limit. All must press forward at once, without hesitation. The breach is made, the enemy must not be given time to repair it."[78] With the French on his flank unable to make progress, Lejeune resisted a large-scale assault to rupture the German front and initially agreed only to minor operations. The French, however, persisted, and Lejeune agreed to resume his offensive but with limited objectives. With the French still unable to make progress, and with his division's losses mounting, Lejeune wanted the fighting to die down. But Naulin reinforced his division with the untested 71st Brigade from the American 36th Division and insisted that he use these raw troops in a general offensive scheduled for October 8.[79] Over Lejeune's protests the men of the 71st Brigade went over the top and suffered more than 1,000 casualties, in part because they lost contact with their creeping barrage. During the night of October 9–10 the remaining brigades of the 36th moved into the forward trenches to relieve the 2nd Division.[80]

As the Meuse-Argonne offensive continued and losses mounted fresh divisions were brought forward. On October 15, after two or three days of forced marching, the 78th Division, composed of draftees from New York, New Jersey, and Illinois, entered the line in darkness and pouring rain to relieve Alexander's 77th Division. Immediately they were ordered to attack. (The US First Army and the French Fourth Army were attempting to clear the Bois des Loges and the southern part of the Bois de Bourgogne on the left of the American front.)

At 5 a.m. Paul Murphy's platoon found itself in an "open field on the edge of the Argonne, with no cover of any kind as far as you see and with no idea of where the Germans were or how many were there, but as soon as we showed up shells began to explode all around us." Murphy continues:

We started out in what was called the first and second assault waves, advancing as "skirmishers," with the first wave about 100 yards ahead of the second and with an interval of about 50 feet between the men in line, so that we were spread out over a large section of the terrain, this to avoid the mass killing that would occur when a shell bursts in a closely packed group ... We kept advancing alternately falling down in the mud, dodging shells, then getting up and running to the next row of trenches.

Soon Murphy's platoon was confronted with a band of barbed wire about twenty feet in depth. While carefully navigating his way across this wire laid out in a zigzag pattern, Murphy heard "a swishing noise, like wires in the wind or a whip lash[,] and had no idea of what was causing this sound until I looked down and saw dirt being kicked up and holes being drilled in the ground by bullets landing right between my feet and all around our vicinity." Somehow Murphy survived this "murderous" machine gun fire although he didn't even know where it was coming from. Pinned down, Murphy and his comrades sought safety in some abandoned trenches. With darkness they fell back to their own lines.[81]

The maiming and death of many young Americans clearly took its toll on the commander-in-chief. As Pershing later admitted in his memoirs, the first days of October "involved the heaviest strain on the army and on me."[82] Driving toward the front with his aide Colonel John G. Quekemeyer, Pershing broke down. He buried his face in his hands, spoke the name of his wife, who had tragically died in a fire prior to US entry into the war, and cried, "Frankie . . . Frankie . . . my god, sometimes I don't know how I can go on."[83]

The First Army now numbered over 1 million men along a front of 130 kilometers. Pershing responded by splitting his forces on October 10. On October 12 the new Second Army, with Bullard as its commander, began to function along a front of forty-one kilometers at the base of what had been the Saint-Mihiel salient.[84] Pershing also relieved himself as field commander, selecting Liggett as commander of the First Army, although the latter delayed resuming command until October 16. As an army-group commander, Pershing now enjoyed the same status as the French and British commanders-in-chief. He established his advance headquarters at Ligny-en-Barrois, but he obviously found it difficult to give up his field command and spent considerable time in his special train on a spur near the First Army's headquarters at Souilly. "An extraordinary spectacle is presented by Pershing, who has directed General Liggett to assume command of the First Army," Stackpole wrote in his diary, "hanging around and worrying everybody with endless talk, rather than giving his orders and leaving the First Army to carry them out."[85]

Pressed by Foch, Pershing wanted Liggett to keep the pressure on the Germans. The new commander of the First Army, however, insisted that his exhausted forces needed time to rest and regroup before launching "any aggressive attack except in a limited way in local operations."[86]

A critical issue for the AEF leadership in October was maintaining the strength of divisions depleted by heavy combat. Private McHenry, a machine gunner in the 16th Infantry Regiment, 1st Division, provides a vivid illustration of the AEF's casualties in the Meuse-Argonne. After fresh troops relieved his company he related what he remembers as

one of the saddest events that occurs in the life of a soldier – roll call immediately after a battle. The first name called was Elden S. Betts, First Lieutenant, Company Commander, and someone answers, "killed in action." The next name called was Sidney U. Swartz, Second Lieutenant, and someone answered "killed in action." The third man called was Reginald S. Young, Second

Lieutenant, and the answer was "killed in action." The third name called was A. B. Helsley, Second Lieutenant, and the answer came, "seriously wounded in action." Those four officers were all the officers of the company and they were either killed or wounded. The roll call ran over the whole company and fully three-fourths of the enlisted men were reported either "killed or wounded in action."[87]

Fox Conner viewed the manpower situation as being "desperate" with the only solution being the cannibalization of newly arriving divisions. GHQ broke up seven divisions, including the 34th, 38th, 84th, and 86th. Although it proved impossible to replace all of the losses of the "fighting" divisions, and the size of companies had to be reduced from 250 to 185,[88] these replacement troops allowed Pershing to maintain a "reasonable" strength in his frontline divisions, which, according to Conner, "contributed in a large degree to concluding the war in 1918."[89] On October 23 the combat strength of the AEF was as follows: 1,256,478, of which 592,300 were in the First Army.[90]

Inadequately trained replacement troops it must be once again emphasized did not all just come from cannibalized divisions in France. It was common practice for the War Department to complete new divisions just prior to their disembarkation for Europe. The much maligned 79th Division, for example, had been brought up to strength before sailing by the addition of 15,000 men, all of whom had been inducted after May 9.[91]

In addition to replenishing and resting his divisions, Liggett needed time to bury the First Army's dead. Hale Hunt, a musician in the 127th Regiment, 32nd Division, had been assigned to one of these grisly burial details. "Many times, on burial detail," he recorded in his diary,

we dug a big pit maybe twenty by twenty feet and several feet deep. Then we scout through the woods or trenches and hillsides and valleys for bodies. In the Argonne they were not hard to find. We carried the bodies to the grave, laid them side by side, removed the tag, and covered them with army GI blankets. After the grave was full the chaplain invoked a prayer and made a short sermon.

Hunt found "this gruesome and sad job" especially difficult when he had to pull "maggot covered bodies out of a fox hole."[92]

Liggett initially rearranged the First Army as follows: the First Corps (77th and 82nd Divisions) under Joseph T. Dickman who had succeeded Liggett; the Fifth Corps (42nd and 32nd Divisions) under Charles P. Summerall; and the Third Corps (5th, 3rd, and 4th Divisions) under John L. Hines. East of the Meuse the 33rd and 29th Divisions were attached to the XVII French Corps.[93]

As the fighting continued a serious straggler crisis emerged. Soldiers separating from their units and gravitating to the rear did not represent a recent phenomenon in American military history. Liggett reminds us that the Union Army in the Civil War "lost nearly four times as many men by desertion from 1861 to 1865 as were killed on the field." In Liggett's view, however, the draft had created a more disciplined US armed force than previous ones because "the equal liability of all males of military age to defend their country brought into the army a more representative body of citizens and fostered a much higher average of self-discipline."[94]

It is true that the American straggler crisis never approached the level of insubordination experienced by the European armies where mutinies involving entire divisions or even armies occurred in 1917–18. Nonetheless, General Bullard later admitted that "the hardest work that I did or saw done by others in France was the holding of men to duty in service and battle. In the early days some of our military theorists who had been little at the front desired to reduce the military police used for this purpose." As the fighting intensified, however, divisional military police had to be tripled and "an unbroken line of them now followed our attacks."[95]

Despite the increased presence of military police, Liggett discovered when he took command of the First Army in mid-October that there might be as many as 100,000 stragglers or roughly one out of every ten Doughboys at or near the front. The Inspector General of the AEF, for example, concluded that "one division reported that it had only 1600 men in the front line including an engineer battalion that had been sent forward ... This division was taken out of the line and upon arriving in its rest area it found that the infantry regiments alone had in them 8418 men not counting the Engineer battalion." If these numbers were correct it meant that more than 6,000 of these men had been stragglers.[96]

"I am under no patriotic illusion that one good American can whip any ten foreigners," Liggett later wrote. "I know, on the contrary, that one well-trained, well-led foreigner is much more likely to whip ten good but untrained Americans."[97] Thus any list of reasons for the extraordinary number of American stragglers would begin with inadequate training and inexperienced leadership. Men who resembled soldiers only because they wore uniforms cannot be expected to perform like veterans. Recently drafted replacements had been rushed into battle, in some cases even before they had been taught to load and fire their weapons. Many of the NCOs and junior officers were also almost as inexperienced as the men they led. "In many of the AEF's small units, it was simply the case of the unwilling being led by the unready into the unknown," Faulkner has astutely observed. "As soldiers weighed their chances of survival in combat and opted to 'vote with their feet,' the quality of their leaders was undoubtedly one of the factors that influenced their decision."[98]

"In any aggregation of individuals," General Alexander later wrote, "there is always to be found an appreciable number who, at the crucial moment, find their heart action too feeble to permit them to keep step with their more hardy comrades."[99] And indeed some soldiers took extreme measures to avoid battle. Sergeant Joseph Shapiro, Company C, 39th Infantry, 4th Division, was later to recall:

Many soldiers wore the army band with S.I.W. on it. This meant self inflicted wound. Here is an example ... One day I heard a shot fired by one of our soldiers, and when I went to see what had happened, he had taken a shot at his foot and missed ... then there was another soldier that shot two fingers off and he had to wear the Self Inflicted Wound band on his sleeve.[100]

It seems likely, however, that many American soldiers on the Meuse-Argonne battlefield who absented themselves from the sound of battle were not physical cowards. The musician Hale Hunt, who served in the 127th Infantry, 32nd Division, later recalled how he and his buddies went AWOL. He had been withdrawn from the front lines for a few days of rest where he received entertainment, decent food, clean underwear, and new blankets. At night he found refuge from German bombs in a deep dugout formally occupied by the Germans. At 2:30 a.m. on November 1 he and four other soldiers were awakened when they heard troops moving out. Ignoring a sergeant's command, they stayed put. "If anyone thought of being AWOL, he kept it to himself," he later wrote. After a good night's sleep, however, he and his buddies attempted to catch up with their unit, easily finding food along the way "without any questions at field kitchens." When they finally joined their company on November 3 Hunt records that they were "bawled out on showing up but no other reprimand. Lucky!"[101]

As the stalemated American offensive continued, many frontline soldiers also suffered serious privations from the miserable weather and also because army authorities had been unable to provide them with many of the basic requirements for a modern army. "There was more mud and rain and drizzle and fog and wet weather etc., than in Oregon and Washington combined ... During the thirty days I doubt if the sun rose or set; it was daylight then dark," Aitken recalls.[102] Many soldiers, still clothed in their summer uniforms, shivered at night, slept in shell holes, and did not have access to rolling field kitchens. As a soldier in the 42nd Division noted, "The condition of the roads is wretched. The orders are, 'guns up first, then ammunition for the guns, coffee and food later.'"[103] Some soldiers resorted to searching dead comrades and enemy soldiers for rations. According to Private McHenry, his 16th Infantry's one meal a day came from tin cans and water tanks which had been scattered in darkness just behind his front. "It was always safe to eat that food, as the tins prevented the poisoned gasses from getting to the food. But it was impossible for that detail to scatter enough food and water along back of the lines to fully supply the men," he later recalled.[104] The spreading influenza epidemic, with almost 70,000 men being treated in hospitals,[105] also took its toll on morale.

When relieved, the condition of McHenry's company shocked replacements moving forward to the front. As McHenry noted,

There was not a man among us who had full and complete equipment ... Parts of our clothing were missing, and what was left was badly torn. Physically, we were wrecks. Many of our men could not speak above a whisper, owing to the action of gas on the vocal cords. We were weak, but were not sick. We were just worn out.

One of the replacements, a soldier from Kentucky, shared his impressions with McHenry, telling him it appeared that he and his comrades had "been through hell, and have had a miraculous escape."[106]

The same could be said of many other units. Following Saint-Mihiel, for example, the 26th Division had remained at the front for three weeks while many men became sick and officers remained in short supply. A lieutenant actually commanded one battalion. Poorly clothed and fed, infested with lice, the men lived in tents or at the front in shell holes. It is surely not surprising that this division was on the verge of a physical and moral collapse when it was sent into combat once again east of the Meuse in mid-October.[107]

Soldiers being withdrawn from the fighting at Meuse-Argonne were in even worse shape than members of the 26th Division. On October 20 Hunt's regiment was finally relieved after seventeen days of active fighting. "They were muddy, unshaven and tired, and their ranks had been thinned badly ... I never saw infantry men look so completely fatigued as our men coming out of the fighting." Hunt had previously observed numerous shell-shocked Doughboys. "The thing is not to let your nerves crack up and become what we call – 'shell shocked.' The strongest guys sometimes are the first to crack."[108]

Between April 6, 1917 and November 31, 1918 just 5,584 men (both home and abroad) were actually charged with desertion, with only 2,657 being found guilty. Wilson recognized that a majority of Americans wore the uniform because he had embraced the draft. Because of his strong opposition to imposing the death penalty the AEF's leadership did not officially execute a single soldier for being AWOL. "Everyone insists that shooting is the only remedy," Stackpole scribbled in his diary after a visit to Hines's headquarters, Third Corps, but "that can't be done under President Wilson's policy." In an attempt to get around the President's opposition, Pershing sent a letter to corps and division commanders in late October that included the following command. "When men run away in front of the enemy, officers should take summary action to stop it, even to the point of shooting men down who are caught in such disgraceful conduct. No orders need be published on the subject, but it should be made known to younger officers that they must do whatever is required to prevent it."[109]

During the general lull in the fighting during the last half of October, Liggett vigorously dealt with the straggler crisis. His command established straggler posts on all roads, and patrols searched dugouts and the neighboring woods. Some of Liggett's commanders took extreme steps. General George B. Duncan, 82nd Division, had signs painted in white: "STRAGGLERS FROM THE FRONT LINES," which were pinned to the backs of repeat offenders before they were sent back to the front.[110]

Some officers actually argued that inspectors who reported incidents of the inability of the AEF's leadership to provide basic needs for frontline troops were themselves responsible for lowering morale. On October 20 Brigadier General Hugh Drum, the Chief of Staff of First Army, suggested the following in a memorandum: "Public investigations of this nature have a tendency to create in the minds of the troops, not only a desire but a feeling that they should be relieved and that replacements should be sent to them."[111]

General Hines, Third Corps commander, was soon reporting to Liggett that he was "getting some hold on the straggler situation and both Brown and Ely are succeeding in rounding up some of them."[112] In his account Liggett takes the high road, writing: "My staff and I traveled constantly among the troops, making every effort to profit by past mistakes and to encourage the fighting spirit of the army for the impending attack on the enemy's main positions, and never was response more immediate or effective." But was it? Two days before the Armistice went into effect, the Second Army Provost told his subordinates that "straggling has been allowed to become a menace to the success of operations," and MPs continued to round up stragglers.[113]

In contrast to some of the stragglers, when their time came, many American soldiers demonstrated extraordinary courage and tenacity at Meuse-Argonne. This was certainly true of the several companies and two machine gun sections of Major General Robert Alexander's 77th Division. On October 2 six companies of the 308th Infantry and one from the 307th aggressively advanced down the Charlevaux valley in the Argonne Forest. As night fell the men of these companies, commanded by Major Charles Whittlesey, who in civil life had practiced law in New York City, found themselves surrounded and cut off from their division. They dug in on the north side of a steep ravine. Over the next five days they were shelled, once by "friendly" artillery, and fought off repeated attacks by superior German forces. They quickly exhausted their rations and had to depend upon the tiny Charlevaux brook for drinking water. They had no shelter, not even blankets or raincoats, and carrier pigeons served as their only means of communication. On October 4 Whittlesey sent the following desperate message: "Cover bad if we advance up the hill. Very difficult to move the wounded if we re-change our position. Situation is cutting into our strength rapidly. Men are suffering from hunger and exposure and the wounded are in very bad condition. Cannot support be sent at once?"[114]

An enterprising American reporter gained national attention when he referred to these isolated companies as the "lost" battalion. Their plight in fact became the biggest American newspaper story of the entire war. The division's leadership, of course, knew about the location of its beleaguered companies but was initially unable to rescue them.

On October 7 the Germans dispatched a captured US soldier with an ultimatum for Whittlesey which in effect said surrender or be annihilated. Whittlesey responded: "Go to hell." Twenty-six years later, General Anthony McAuliffe, the acting commander of the 101st Airborne Division, was to give a similar and equally memorable response, "nuts," when asked by a German officer to accept the inevitable and surrender his forces at Bastogne. Later that same day, October 7, the Germans were forced to abandon their position because they were being outflanked, especially by the advance of the 82nd Division. Whittlesey waited until the following day to withdraw from his position. Of the 554 men who had advanced on October 2 only 194 walked out. Ambulances carried out another 202.[115]

Other US soldiers during this period made their nation proud, none more so than Corporal Alvin C. York, a member of the 328th Regiment, 82nd Division. On the day that the survivors of the "lost battalion" withdrew from the Charlevaux Valley this Tennessee mountaineer singlehandedly destroyed a German machine gun battalion in the Argonne Forest. An expert marksman, he "jes teched off" one enemy soldier after another, encouraging a large number of Germans to surrender without a fight. When Brigadier General Julian Lindsey later remarked, "Well York, I hear you have captured the whole damned German army," he modestly responded that he had "only" captured 132.[116]

Another less-known but remarkable Doughboy was John Lewis Barkley, a farm boy from Holden in west-central Missouri, who like York was awarded the Congressional Medal of Honor. Barkley, a member of the 4th Infantry Regiment, 3rd Division, killed hundreds of enemy soldiers on October 7, 1918. Finding refuge in an abandoned French tank he singlehandedly held up a German advance. Having commandeered a maxim machine gun and more than 4,000 rounds he opened fire on German infantrymen as they emerged from a neighboring woods. "I took a long breath," he later wrote, "worked the barrel of my gun out through the port, picked the direction of fire that promised the greatest results all the way across to the farther flank, let out a little breath, laid the gun waist-high on the man who was closest to me, and eased down on the trigger."[117] He spent the rest of the afternoon killing Germans until advancing American soldiers relieved him. Barkley's exploits clearly made an impression on his commander-in-chief. Pershing, inclined to emphasize the raw courage of American soldiers, armed with rifles and bayonets, defeating the German Army, mentions Barkley in his memoirs, noting that "the effectiveness of the machine guns was well demonstrated by the exploit of one of our men near Cunel."[118]

Yet another American soldier recognized for his bravery during this phase of the war was a member of the Choctaw Nation in Oklahoma, Joseph Oklahombi (Choctaw for "man-killer" or "people-killer"). Private Oklahombi was among the some 10,000 Indians, many of whom unlike Blacks were integrated into units, who served during the war. Congress later recognized their sacrifices by granting all Native Americans US citizenship in 1924. Oklahombi fought alongside members of Company D, 1st Battalion, 141st Regiment, 36th Division, and was one of the original "code talkers," who confused the Germans by sending messages over field telephones in Choctaw to be decoded into English. On occasion translation problems developed. For example, Choctaw had no modern equivalent for "machine gun" or "casualties" so these words were rendered as "little gun shoot fast" and "scalp."

On October 8 Oklahombi's National Guard division composed of men from Oklahoma and Texas advanced as part of the French Fourth Army between Saint-Étienne and Médéah Farm. Oklahombi and twenty-three members of his company attacked a German machine gun position, killing as many as seventy-nine of the enemy and capturing another 171. Called "Oklahoma's Greatest Hero," Oklahombi received the Silver Star in recognition of his heroism.[119]

By October 14, the First Army had eliminated the deadly enfilading fire from the big German guns on its flanks by forcing the Germans to withdraw from the northern extremity of the Argonne Forest and the heights east of the Meuse. The Kriemhilde Stellung, which Pershing had expected to reach no later than the first day of his offensive, however, remained in German hands. Smythe's succinct summary of the military fortunes of the First Army is as follows: "On the first day of the offensive, September 26, the First Army had advanced eleven kilometers with relatively light losses, but since then, during the next three weeks, it had advanced only five kilometers with heavy losses."[120]

Following the resumption of the offensive on October 14 the results proved somewhat more promising despite heavy losses. The 32nd Division occupied the Côte Dame Marie ridge on that day. Two days later the 42nd Division captured the Côte de Chatillon. On October 14 the hard-driving Summerall, the commander of the First Army Corps, told MacArthur that his brigade must capture Côte de Chatillon "or report a list of five thousand casualties." MacArthur's flamboyant response was: "All right, General. We'll take it, or my name will head the list."[121] Fortunately, MacArthur was dissuaded from ordering a suicidal bayonet charge that night with "no firing" allowed.[122] Two days later, supported by a tremendous machine gun barrage, the 84th Brigade of the 42nd Division secured the ridge. With the capture of these two important German defensive positions the First Army secured control of the Romagne heights and finally cracked the defenses of the Kriemhilde Stellung. But the exhausted First Army was now in no condition immediately to exploit this success.[123]

Despite the First Army's limited advance in the Meuse-Argonne, Allied advances elsewhere created a hopeless military situation for Berlin, and discussions in the warring capitals, especially between Berlin and Washington, portended an early and unexpected end to the fighting.

19 Breakout, November 1–11

At the beginning of October Ludendorff bombarded his government with repeated appeals for an immediate armistice, which he viewed as a *temporary* cessation of the fighting to allow the German Army time to recover from its recent setbacks. The result had been the first German peace note, transmitted through the Swiss *chargé d'affaires*, that reached Washington on October 6.

Wilson cautiously responded on October 8. Bliss had warned him that more was required than a withdrawal of German forces from occupied territory on the Western Front. The German Army (as indeed Ludendorff desired) might use an armistice to improve its position by retiring to "strong positions behind the Rhine with their armies and armaments and supplies intact" while retaining troops in the former Tsarist Empire. This might give Berlin leverage to retain some of its eastern conquests. On October 12 Prince Max of Baden, who had replaced Count Georg von Hertling as Chancellor, accepted Wilson's Fourteen Points in principle as a basis for peace negotiations. Wilson then responded with a demand that the Germans withdraw from all conquered territory.[1]

Pershing had furthered the president's political objectives by maintaining an independent army in the European theater, in the process making London and Paris more dependent upon the United States for ultimate victory. Following the failure of Germany's final offensive on the Western Front, however, the march of military events now increasingly favored the Allies, making them less reliant upon American support, especially if the war ended now. In a memorandum circulated to the King and the War Cabinet, Jan Christiaan Smuts, the South African military leader and Imperial statesman, argued that peace now would be a "British peace." Conversely, if the war were prolonged Wilson would become the "diplomatic dictator of the world." Lord Reading agreed with Smuts, telling the War Cabinet on October 26: "At present it [is] in the main America and the British Empire that [are] dominating the situation and we [are] in a position to hold our own ... by continuing the War it might become more difficult for us to hold our own."[2] Wilson, however, seemed oblivious to these *realpolitik* considerations, conducting unilateral armistice talks with Berlin as if he still held Britain's and France's fate as well as Germany's in his hands.

After delivering to Lloyd George news of Germany's response to Wilson's first note, Philip Kerr, the Prime Minister's private secretary, reported: "There is awful language going on upstairs, I can tell you! He thinks that the Allies are now in a devil of a mess. Wilson has promised them an armistice." The French were equally aggravated. As one French officer warned an American liaison officer: "Doesn't your President realize with what swine he is dealing? They'll fool him if he is not very, very canny."[3]

Meanwhile, at a joint meeting the Allied Naval Council and the Permanent Military Representatives of the SWC drew up tough terms for any armistice. General Bliss, without any instructions from President Wilson, withheld his signature. "Judging from the spirit which seems more and more to actuate our European allies," he noted, "I am beginning to despair that the war will accomplish more than the abolition of German militarism while leaving *European* militarism as rampant as ever."[4]

The Republicans, who were about to capture control of both the Senate and the House of Representatives on November 5, were also up in arms. The resulting Republican majority in the Senate elevated Henry Cabot Lodge, arguably the president's strongest congressional critic, to the chairmanship of the Foreign Relations Committee. Lodge believed that US military power should be deployed to protect American security as opposed to Wilson's idealistic crusade to "make the world safe for democracy."

The some 2 million Doughboys in Europe, incidentally, were not allowed to vote because neither Pershing nor the War Department thought it feasible for an army in combat to cast a vote, even if arrangements were made to allow soldiers to vote by mail. A soldier's ballot, of course, could not be kept secret, for every letter sent from France was subject to inspection by military censors.[5]

Lodge and Roosevelt, among others, now clamored for total victory and the disarmament of Germany. With America's deadliest battle now underway at Meuse-Argonne, many Democrats joined the Republicans in fearing that the President might be inclined to be too lenient with the Germans. The War Department chimed in when General March advised the president that "military opinion was to carry on the war."[6]

On October 14 the Democratic Senator, Henry Ashurst of Arizona, visited the White House and warned Wilson that if he failed to reflect the

"American spirit" in his negotiations he would be "destroyed." Wilson
stood his ground, telling Ashurst that, "So far as my being destroyed,
I am willing if I can serve the country to go into a cellar and read poetry
the remainder of my life." Ashurst fired back that if he did not demand
"unconditional surrender" he would indeed have to read poetry in a
cellar "to escape the cyclone of the people's wrath."[7]

Despite political opposition at home and the obvious concern of the
British and French, Wilson continued his independent pursuit of an
armistice. Germany appeared to be giving him the opportunity to achieve
what he had failed to accomplish in 1916: serve as the mediator of a
liberal political settlement that did not represent a harsh "victor's peace."
Earlier, on September 27, at a Liberty Loan drive in New York City, he
had spoken of a "permanent" peace that could only be made without
"any kind of compromise or abatement" of his liberal principles. He
invited the Allies to join him in making a peace that would reflect
the "final triumph of justice and fair dealing."[8] In sum, Wilson was not
waging war to maintain the balance of power in Europe, expand the
British Empire, or even strengthen French security. He put his faith in
a liberal peace settlement that guaranteed national security for future
American generations by ending "wars for all time."[9]

On October 14 Wilson and House discussed the American response to
the latest German note. House had never seen him

more disturbed. He said he did not know where to make the entrance in order to
reach the heart of the thing. He wanted to make his reply final so there would be
no exchange of notes. It reminded him, he said, of a maze. If one went in at the
right entrance, he reached the center, but if one took the wrong turning, it was
necessary to go out again and do it over.[10]

The greatest pressure came from America's allies. There could be no
armistice unless the French and British agreed to silence their guns.
Wilson understood that essential to gaining British and French support
were naval and military restrictions that made it impossible for Germany
to resume the war if peace negotiations collapsed. Consequently, Wilson
told his cabinet that the terms of any armistice "would be left to their
military men, and they would practically decide the outcome of the war
by the terms of the armistice, which might include leaving all heavy guns
behind, and putting Metz, Strasburg, etc., in the hands of the Allies, until
peace was declared."[11]

Prince Max's government received Wilson's response of October
14 with some dismay. Ludendorff, who along with Hindenburg had been
serving as de facto military dictators of Germany since mid-1916,
rejected Wilson's terms. Ludendorff it must be emphasized only wanted

a cessation of hostilities that might allow the *OHL* to withdraw its forces to a new defensive position along the Meuse or the German frontier, regroup, and then if necessary continue fighting to gain a decent peace settlement. At a meeting with the War Cabinet on October 17, Ludendorff consequently opposed an armistice, arguing that an Allied breakthrough was "possible" but not "probable." He admitted that the military situation might "grow worse at any moment" but "recent fighting had brought no surprises. The front had held neither better nor worse than before. Our troops had done what we expected of them. The enemy's strength in attack seemed to be falling off."[12]

Over the opposition of Ludendorff and naval leaders, the German government responded to Wilson on October 20. Although this third German note insisted that any armistice should maintain the existing balance of power there was no hope of this with British and French officers determined to set the military and naval terms of the armistice. Meanwhile, momentum for peace began to build in Germany with both the soldiers and public avidly following the exchange of notes between Berlin and Wilson.[13] As some Germans put it, "Max equals Pax." On October 23 Wilson informed Prince Max that he would turn over the German–American correspondence to the Allies. On October 27 the Germans accepted this note and agreed to await Allied proposals for an armistice. Meanwhile, following an angry confrontation with the Kaiser, Ludendorff resigned. His successor, William Groener, after the American breakthrough at Meuse-Argonne, decided on November 4 to retreat to a new and not particularly well-defined "Antwerp-Meuse line."[14]

On October 23, Foch and Pershing over lunch had discussed possible armistice terms. At this meeting Foch discovered that Pershing's tough approach paralleled his own. Two days later Foch convened a meeting with the Allied commanders-in-chief at Senlis, which now served as his headquarters. With the First Army preparing to resume its Meuse-Argonne offensive, Pershing clearly supported the Generalissimo's position that "when one hunts a wild beast and finally comes upon him at bay, one then faces greater danger, but it is not the time to stop, it is time to redouble one's blows, without paying any attention to those he, himself, receives."[15] Pershing had already instructed his corps and division commanders to fight vigorously and suggested that the American offensive had played a key role in Berlin's peace efforts (Fig. 24). "Our strong blows are telling, and continuous pressure by us has compelled the enemy to meet us, enabling our Allies to gain on other parts of the line. There can be no conclusion to this war until Germany is brought to her knees."[16] At Senlis, as Foch no doubt anticipated,

Fig. 24 American soldiers in trenches, France, 1918: USASC #22343
(foliage atop trench)

Pershing supported armistice terms that guaranteed that the German
Army would not have either the means or a defensible position to resume
fighting with any hope of success.[17]

Five days later, however, Pershing spoke of continuing the war rather
than the armistice Wilson sought. The President had forwarded his views
on the armistice on October 28 to House, who had just arrived in France
to represent him, suggesting that he wanted an armistice that made it
impossible for Germany to resume fighting but at the same time was
"as moderate and reasonable as possible within those limits, because it
is certain that too much success or security on the part of the Allies
will make a genuine peace settlement exceedingly difficult if not
impossible."[18]

Meanwhile, without consulting House, Pershing submitted a letter to
the Supreme War Council that argued that a "complete victory can only
be obtained by continuing the war until we force unconditional surrender
from Germany, but if the Allied Governments decided to grant an
armistice, the terms should be so rigid that under no circumstances could

Germany again take up arms." Lowry, who has written the most comprehensive account of the Armistice, concludes that the catalyst for
Pershing's extraordinary intervention were President Wilson's communications that seemed to suggest softer armistice terms than he thought
prudent. According to Lowry, "Pershing believed that his own terms, or
ones of the same order, would ratify military victory, and that Wilson's
terms would serve as little more than an inconvenience to Germany."[19]
This really was not the case, for Wilson had clearly signaled that he was
prepared to leave armistice arrangements in the hands of the military
professionals.[20]

A stunned House telegraphed Wilson:

Urgent. Secret. For the President. Five minutes before I entered into conference
this afternoon of Prime Ministers and foreign Secretaries and without previous
notification General Pershing handed me a copy of the communication I quote
herewith, the original thereof having already been sent to the Supreme War
Council at Versailles ... No allied general has ever submitted a document of
this character to the Supreme War Council without a previous request having
been made by the civilian authorities.[21]

Was Pershing about to become President Wilson's General George
B. McClellan, who had challenged Lincoln's authority during the
Civil War?

Not surprisingly, both the War Department and the White House reacted
angrily at Pershing's effrontery. March expressed "amazement and frank
expressions of distress" that Pershing had submitted an appreciation to
the SWC that was "at variance" with the President's instructions. Baker
agreed, writing Wilson that Pershing "is obviously on record one way
with you and another way with the Supreme War Council! It is really
tragic." Baker responded by sending Pershing a stern message (approved
by Wilson) that made clear that in future the administration's views on
the armistice would be represented in the SWC by either his civilian
(House) or military (Bliss) representatives.[22] Not wanting to let the
matter rest Baker drafted a letter to Pershing that did not mince words.
He pointed out that no Allied general had submitted "a document of this
character" without being asked to by his civilian authorities. "Independent expressions of opinion by you," he went on to write, "on questions
involving both military and political considerations might at some time
produce the deep embarrassment of a variance of opinion between you
and your commander-in-chief. Obviously, the views of the United States
upon any question of national policy could be expressed only by the
President."[23]

Although Pershing's actions constituted a serious breach of his authority, Baker never sent this reprimand. After Pershing went out of his way

to apologize to House, Wilson decided to let the matter drop. After all, any differences between his position and the one taken by Foch and Pershing on the military clauses of an armistice were minimal. Wilson also apparently did not take seriously the farfetched rumors now circulating that Pershing was mixing politics with questions of national security. Colonel House, for example, had scribbled in his diary: "I cannot understand General Pershing's extraordinary communication ... Everyone believes it is a political document and a clear announcement of his intention to become a candidate for the Presidency in 1920."[24]

In any event Pershing's support for continuing the war until Germany surrendered unconditionally became a reality in every thing but name because of the way in which Allied military and naval leaders approached the armistice. If the Germans came to him seeking an armistice, Foch privately told Pershing, he was not prepared to announce that any ceasefire would be based on their unconditional surrender. But the terms demanded would "approximate to that."[25] That is certainly the way that many German generals received the armistice terms. As General Max von Gallwitz, who commanded German troops in the Meuse-Argonne triangle, noted when he first learned of the Allied terms: "I never expected conditions so humiliating! This was not armistice but rather an unconditional surrender!"[26]

Wilson, of course, sought to impose his Fourteen Points on his allies as well as the enemy. As he telegraphed House: the United States was "pledged to fight not only to do away with Prussian militarism but with militarism everywhere. Neither could I participate in a settlement which did not include league of nations because peace would be without any guarantee except universal armament which would be intolerable."[27] On the other hand, by allowing Foch and the soldiers to impose conditions on Berlin that amounted to unconditional surrender the President undermined the liberal peace conditions he had enunciated in his Fourteen Points and provided German nationalists with plenty of ammunition to later argue that Berlin had been duped by the Allies and "stabbed in the back" by their own politicians.

It is unlikely that Pershing was thinking of a future political career in demanding conditions that might prolong the war. But his and the AEF's role in defeating Germany remained very much on his mind. Thus far his offensive in Meuse-Argonne had fallen considerably short of his own expectations, and he was aware of and increasingly sensitive to unfavorable comparisons being made between US and Anglo-French military contributions to defeating Germany.

With some justification, Pershing saw a political motive, believing that Clemenceau's criticism of the progress of the First Army in October represented an attempt "to discredit our accomplishments" to "minimize America's prestige at the peace conference."[28] Pershing would have been even more offended if he had been aware of what Haig was telling the British leadership on October 19. The British commander-in-chief told members of the "X" Committee that the First Army "is disorganised, ill-equipped and ill-trained with very few N.C.O.'s and officers of experience." The AEF leadership's "ignorance of modern war" meant that it would be "at *least a year* before it became a serious fighting force."[29]

The First Army's resumption of the offensive on November 1 put paid to these foreign criticisms of the AEF's combat effectiveness. Previously, American forces had been rushed into combat with little or no time for either preparation or reconnoitering the ground over which they advanced. "For the first time we were about to engage in a grand operation on a front which we already occupied," Marshall later emphasized. "It was a great contrast to the opening of the battle when both staffs and troops all arrived on the scene for deployment at the eleventh hour."[30]

The First Army had begun its Meuse-Argonne offensive on September 26 with many untested men and officers and without an effective logistical system or the essential specialized corps and army units. It had taken nineteen months but in November America now had an army with its own communications, telegraph lines, water supply, ammunition, and supply dumps. In sum, as Liggett writes, "we had an American Army in the full sense of the word for the first time in the war."[31]

The words of the First Army's commander, however, do not ring true when it came to modern weaponry. The War Department now provided American soldiers with a limited number of superb firearms designed by John Moses Browning, the M1917 Browning water-cooled heavy machine gun, which could fire 450 rounds a minute, and the Browning Automatic Rifle (or B-A-R), a gas-operated, magazine-fed, air-cooled weapon. But the French (with the exception of 1,427 trench mortars supplied by the British) continued to supply the AEF with most of its essential weaponry, including tanks, aircraft, and artillery.[32]

In an attempt to force the Germans to withdraw to the east of the Meuse River, Liggett assigned the Fifth Corps (Summerall), 89th and 2nd Divisions, the primary task of advancing nine kilometers in the center to secure the critical wooded heights of the Barricourt Ridge. Meanwhile, the First Corps (Dickman), 78th, 77th, and 80th Divisions, on the left assisted Gouraud's French Army by pressuring the Germans in the Bois de Loges while the Third Corps (Hines), 90th and 5th Divisions, sought to widen the front on the right along the Meuse River.

Initially the resumption of the First Army's offensive at Meuse-Argonne had been scheduled for October 28. But on the afternoon of October 25, when at Pétain's suggestion Liggett and Drum met with Gouraud, the Americans discovered that the French Fourth Army could not be ready to attack as early as October 28. As Liggett notes of this meeting with the badly wounded French general, who had had one arm amputated, Gouraud "threw up his hand – the General had only one hand – despairingly, exclaiming, 'I cannot possibly move before November 2. The Army simply can't be made ready an hour earlier.'" "Secretly delighted" by the extra three days to prepare for his offensive, Liggett readily agreed to move back D-day to November 1, the day before Gouraud said his men could leave their trenches (Map 13).[33]

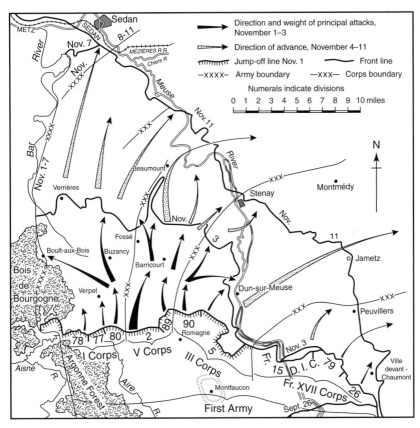

13. Operations of First Army, November 1–11, 1918

Liggett had already given the divisions involved in the forthcoming offensive a much-needed respite. The 77th Division, for example, had been withdrawn from the line in the early morning hours of the 16th. One of the first orders of business for division commanders had been to give their soldiers, filthy from unrelenting combat, a bath. Engineers had constructed large bathing establishments, with plenty of hot water. It took three days but every soldier eventually got a bath. Supply departments also provided the men with new uniforms, including underwear and shoes.[34]

Liggett's plan (an offensive thrust in the center) and terrain (woods on the left and river on the right) resembled the First Army's initial offensive on September 26. But there were many differences between September 26 and November 1. First, Liggett had realistic objectives, expecting the Fifth Corps to advance only nine kilometers in securing the area around Buzancy and the high ground of Barricourt Ridge. He assigned his two corps on the left and right of the Fifth Corps a limited, supporting role.

Secondly, and more importantly, the First Army's "set-piece" offensive on November 1 reflected a serious evolution of tactics that differed from the AEF GHQ's open warfare doctrine. Heavy combat at Belleau Wood, the Aisne-Marne counteroffensive, July 18–August 6, and the first stages of Meuse-Argonne, had served as a costly but effective laboratory for many AEF officers and their men. American divisions had learned to fight by fighting. GHQ's original doctrine based on self-reliant infantry had been severely tested and found wanting.

The three officers most responsible for capturing Barricourt Ridge, Lejeune, Liggett, and Summerall, emphasized artillery and planned a "set-piece" offensive with realistic objectives. Lejeune, whose 2nd Division spearheaded the drive in the center, had earlier during the capture of Blanc Mont and elsewhere taken extreme measures to limit his casualties. For his part, Liggett took care to select objectives for the First Army that remained within the range of his artillery and prudently employed his infantry on the flanks of the main attack.[35]

Summerall deserved the reputation of being one of Pershing's most aggressive and bombastic generals. To prepare his Fifth Corps for its forthcoming offensive he daily visited units in his divisions, attempting to inspire his men as if he were their football coach, resorting to phrases such as "There is no excuse for failure." "No man is ever so tired that he cannot take one step forward." "The best way to go take machine guns is to go and take 'em! Press forward."[36] But, as an artillerist, Summerall did not expect his men to win the day by smothering German machine gun nests with their corpses. Much more important than his pep talks was Summerall's belief that a successful advance had to be based on "fire superiority, rather than sheer man power." This resulted in the development of what has been described as "the most powerful and comprehensive American attack plan of the war."[37]

Unlike September 26, the First Army now had a plentiful supply of poison gas and the confidence in utilizing it. Prior to the attack US artillerymen sought to neutralize known batteries, dumps, crossroads, and other vital areas with deadly mustard gas and high-explosive shells. They paid particular attention to German artillery on the flanks of the advancing Fifth Corps, especially the Bois de Bourgogne, essentially an extension of the Argonne Forest, which received 41.4 tons of yperite, mustard gas, to avoid the deadly enfilading fire which had hampered the American advance during the initial phases of the Meuse-Argonne offensive. Summerall also arranged a continuous and powerful rolling barrage some 1,000 meters ahead of his advancing troops. This curtain of coordinated firepower was further enhanced by employing batteries of mortars, machine guns, and 37-mm guns.[38]

Aircraft from the Allied Air Force supporting the First Army had seen its numbers decreased by 50 percent since the Saint-Mihiel campaign.[39] Squadrons of the AEF Air Service, however, gave valuable support to the infantry's advance after November 1. An advanced weapon that Liggett did not have at his disposal were masses of tanks which figured prominently in British and French offensives in 1918. The War Department had placed orders for 23,405 tanks, but the greatest steel producer in the world had not been able to design, manufacture, and deliver battleworthy tanks to the AEF by November 1918.[40]

Unable to sleep, Lejeune was awake and watching the opening bombardment from a high ridge soon after it began at 2 a.m. "It was, if anything," he later wrote, "more terrific than at Saint-Mihiel, and seemed as if it were an elemental cataclysm closely approximating the simultaneous eruption of many volcanoes, combined with the continuous lightning and the innumerable reverberations which characterize a thunderstorm in a mountain county."[41]

As expected, the continuous rolling barrage played an important role as US infantry steadily advanced behind a wall of exploding shells. Carrier pigeons arriving at First Army headquarters soon carried reports of success as the battle progressed – with one exception: the First Corps in the Bois des Loges, especially Alexander's 77th Division. Alexander, who was prone to fault others for any setbacks his divisions suffered, blamed one of his brigade commanders, General Smedberg, for launching a frontal rather than flanking attack from the east against the strongly defended village of Champigneulle.[42]

Curiously, neither Dickman nor Alexander understood Liggett's plan of forcing the Germans to withdraw from the Loges and Bourgogne woods by collapsing the center of their front. According to Liggett, he expected Dickman's First Corps to

threaten furiously, but not to fight the first day, except to protect the Fifth Corps' left flank, but our men were so eager that part of the corps got out of hand and the demonstration developed into a real attack on Champigneulle. It was magnificent but it was not war, for it played into the enemy's hands and led to deplorable waste of life.[43]

Pershing also did not comprehend Liggett's plan and complained to him about the failure of Dickman's First Corps to get a move on. A confident Liggett assured him that Summerall's breakthrough in the center would force the Germans to evacuate the Loges and Bourgogne woods. On the following day the Germans did exactly what Liggett had predicted.

Machine gun nests, which constituted the Fifth Army's principal defenses, could not stop the advancing Americans. The Fifth Army's *War Diary* on November 2 included the following battlefield report: "All the frontline commanders report that the Americans as attacking in mass formations in the general direction of Stenay, that the [German] troops are fighting courageously but just cannot do anything. Therefore it has become imperative that the Army be withdrawn in rear of the Meuse and that said withdrawal be effected immediately."[44]

The Doughboy newspaper *Stars and Stripes* triumphantly reported: "The thick wall of the German resistance in Argonne against which the First Army has been hammering since the last week in September gave way with a crash on November 1, and the Yankee troops who had gone stubbornly through more than a month of murderous, inch-by-inch, hammer-and-tongs fighting came at last into their reward."[45]

To keep the retreating Germans on their heels, the 2nd Division resorted to a new tactic, infiltration of the enemy's front through night marches to neutralize rearguard actions by his inevitable and deadly machine gun nests. When daylight broke and the American advance slowed, two regiments of the 2nd Brigade had advanced some six kilometers, with light casualties. On the following night elements of the 2nd Division once again caught German troops off guard and advanced another four kilometers in darkness. The 89th Division also rapidly advanced as the German front disintegrated in the center.[46]

Elsewhere, on Fifth Corps' flanks, the First and Third Corps joined the pursuit. Too weak to launch a counterattack, Von der Gallwitz's battered forces fell back all along their front, with German infantry throwing away their packs to speed their retreat. Only rearguard machine guns and the poor mobility of the advancing Americans saved the Fifth

Army from annihilation. Gallwitz's situation appeared so dire that Liggett later argued that if he had had two divisions of cavalry the Germans would never have escaped across the Meuse.[47]

American aviators flying mostly foreign aircraft harassed the German Fifth Army as it retreated (Fig. 25). Previously the bombing squadrons of the Army Air Service had focused on German communications and

Fig. 25 Pilot standing in front of US army airplane during World War I

dumps rather than direct support for the advancing infantry.[48] At Buzancy on November 3 General Alexander observed a massive battle formation of 182 aircraft piloted by Americans attack the German-occupied village of La Bézace. "The whole air seemed crowded with them and, passing over the town, their bombs came down upon the enemy's line in plain view from our position."[49]

This bombing attack in close support of the infantry was at variance with William Mitchell's approach to the air war. As Pershing's operational air commander, Mitchell proved to be a visionary, once attempting to convince Pershing that the Army Air Service could parachute an American division behind German lines. He especially championed attention-gaining bombing raids that foreshadowed the massive air raids that leveled German cities in World War II. Incredibly, one bombing mission on October 9 dropped 39 of the 139 tons dropped by the American Air Service during all of 1918. These mass bombing attacks, however, were not particularly accurate and proved for the most part ineffective.[50]

Mitchell's position that bombing rear areas distracted the enemy from his front lines overlooked the most important assistance that aircraft could give the infantry in 1918: serving as their eyes. French and German authorities, for example, assigned over one-half of their aircraft to reconnaissance.[51] Artillery shells, often directed by aerial spotting, proved far and above a greater threat to the infantry than bombs. At Meuse-Argonne, despite often miserable weather, German airmen and balloonists had provided extensive aerial spotting for their artillery. Meanwhile, the skies over the Meuse-Argonne battle front remained thinly populated by the Army Air Service. Liaison between US aviators and infantry and artillerymen was lacking, sometimes because of faulty communication and lack of experience, but even more so because of indifference on the part of the Army Air Service's leadership.[52]

Orders emanating from Liggett's headquarters on November 4 reflected the rout under way: "The enemy is apparently unable to recover from the shock of our surprise attack. His main line of resistance has been ruptured and his forces are retiring in disorder; his troops are disorganized; his reserves have been absorbed and some of his divisions are retiring on their own initiative without orders."[53]

Elsewhere on the Western Front the British Fourth and Third Armies, with the assistance of the French Fourth Army on its right and the British First Army on its left, delivered another mortal blow to the Germans by breaching their defenses in the north on the Sambre River and opening the way for an advance to the Meuse.

On the following day, November 5, Pershing issued orders that reflected the disappearance of any recognizable German front before his First Army. He instructed AEF drivers to "use lights on all motor transport" and ordered his commanders to "push troops forward wherever resistance is broken, without regard for fixed objectives and without fear for their flanks."[54]

The fluid nature of the battlefield contributed to one of the AEF's most controversial incidents, the 1st Division's hell-for-leather advance on Sedan. Although this French town, vital to Germany's railway communications, was in the French Fourth Army's sector, Pershing apparently believed that he had the approval of General Paul Maistre, who commanded the four French armies of Army Group Center, to occupy Sedan if Americans reached it first.[55]

In reality, the Americans could cut this lateral railway line without occupying the town. According to Marshall, American heavy guns by November 4 were positioned to "fire on the sole line of rail communication which supplied all of the German Army from Picardy to Carignan, southeast of Sedan."[56] But the symbolic value of Sedan seemed greater than its military worth. In Liggett's view, many American officers, through their extensive prewar studies of the Franco-Prussian War battlefields, developed a "fascination with Sedan," where Prussians had surrounded and captured Napoleon III and his army. In the AEF, Liggett writes, "'On to Sedan' replaced 'On to Berlin' as a shibboleth and even the cooks talked knowingly of Sedan."[57]

If anything this town served as an even more powerful symbol for French officers because its capture might gain them a measure of revenge for the French Army's humiliation at Sedan in 1870. Harbord suggests that Pershing's request that the Americans might occupy Sedan was akin to Rochambeau asking "to be permitted to elbow Washington out of the reviewing stand at Yorktown."[58]

The so-called "race" to Sedan between the 1st Division (Fifth Corps) and 42nd Division (First Corps) began on the afternoon of November 6 and ended three days later. It appears that Pershing instigated this competition when he instructed Fox Conner, his Chief of Operations, to have Colonel Marshall, the G-3 for First Army, make the necessary arrangements. According to Marshall, Conner showed up at his headquarters at four o'clock and told him: "It is General Pershing's desire that the troops of the First Army should capture Sedan, and he directs that orders be issued accordingly." Marshall then prepared orders instructing the First Corps, assisted by the Fifth Corps, advancing without any pause during the night, to march on Sedan. With both Liggett and his Chief of Staff Hugh Drum absent from GHQ, Marshall hesitated to transmit this order without one of their signatures. Drum eventually showed up and signed the order, adding the following sentence because the marching orders required the First Corps to intrude upon the zone of the Fourth French Army: "Boundaries will not be considered binding."[59]

Dickman (First Army), after receiving these orders, read correctly into Drum's words that he should send one of his divisions, the 42nd Division, which was now next to the French, straight on for Sedan. Meanwhile, Summerall (Fifth Army) issued direct orders that one of his divisions, the 1st Division, commanded by General Frank Parker, reach Sedan ahead of the 42nd Division. Parker subsequently interpreted the instructions that boundaries should not "be considered binding" as permission to violate the advance zone of the 42nd Division, not to mention other areas occupied by the 77th Division. In doing so Summerall and Parker invited a rebuke from any soldier with a rudimentary knowledge of tactics. As General Alexander succinctly notes, "a unit as large as a division, once committed to a line of advance, can only move straight to the front or straight to the rear, on its own roads; it cannot move laterally through territory already occupied by other troops."[60] But Parker marched his men behind the 77th Division and in front of the 42nd Division!

When Liggett discovered that Parker, who was supposed to be in the rear of the Fifth Corps, had marched his "division in seven columns – handling 25,000 men like a battalion – right through the First Army Corps upon Sedan," he blew up. His disposition did not improve when he learned that American soldiers in the confusion had fired upon each other and that elements of the 1st Division had mistaken Douglas MacArthur, the new commander of the 42nd Division, for a German spy and taken him prisoner. (In their defense, MacArthur, wielding a swagger stick and clothed in a scarf and mashed-down hat, certainly did not look like an American general.) When the 26th Infantry, commanded by Colonel Theodore Roosevelt Jr., violated the French zone of operations, he was told in no uncertain terms that he must withdraw his men within the hour or be fired upon.[61]

More seriously, according to Liggett, the 1st Division's ill-advised movement "had thrown the first corps front and the adjoining French front into such confusion that had the enemy chosen to counter attack in force at the moment a catastrophe might have resulted." Fortunately the enemy had no reserves. In his account of the incident, Harbord's comments are just as damning as Liggett's. "As an illustration of lack of team work, and an example of undisciplined inexperience," he writes, "it justified much that our Associates thought and said of us."[62]

"This was the only occasion in the war when I lost my temper completely," Liggett later admitted,[63] and if the war had not come to a conclusion on November 11 he says that he would have had one or both of the men (Summerall and Parker) he held most responsible court-martialed. Significantly, he also blamed Pershing, who appeared "much amused at the rivalry between the First and Forty-second."[64]

Elements of both the 42nd Division and the 1st Division occupied the heights dominating Sedan on November 7 but neither division was allowed to displace French forces that liberated the town. Although the so-called "race" to Sedan, really a clash of warrior egos, came to naught it had serious physical consequences for the soldiers involved. The history of the 18th Regiment vividly depicts the unnecessary hardships imposed by gloryseeking generals who ordered their men to march through darkness and rain along muddy and inadequate roads to no good purpose.

Through the entire night the men literally forced themselves onward. Loss of sleep and fatigue had numbed their senses. Time became a matter of halts and marches. Each march represented so much effort in going forward, each halt meant so much rest allotted to stretch weary legs. Little else was thought of . . . The regiment had been marching and fighting two days and nights without resting or sleeping.[65]

The other three regiments of the 1st Division faced similar circumstances. According to one history of the 1st Division, "between 4:30 P.M., November 5th, and midnight, November 7th, the Division marched and fought without sleep or rest. The 16th Infantry covered fifty-four kilometers, the 18th Infantry, fifty-three kilometers, the 26th Infantry seventy-one kilometers, and the 28th Infantry fifty-two kilometers."[66] Marshall suggests that some soldiers actually died from exhaustion during this unnecessary march although he argues that these senseless deaths represented "examples of self-sacrifice and utter devotion to duty."[67]

In his account of the march, Private McHenry, 16th Infantry Regiment, 1st Division, suggests that members of his machine gun company were not motivated by such lofty thoughts.

During the last two or three days a look of pallor had come over every face; eyes seemed to be set in sockets, and men mostly looked straight ahead, giving one the impression that dead men had been galvanized into action, and from their ghostly habitations had come to put the finishing touches on the war . . . we were out of food, and hunger was not as inconvenient as our thirst. Along this march we did not dare to drink the water, as we feared the Germans had poisoned it.

A lasting memory for Herbert McHenry concerned the wounded that his unit left behind. "We were under constant fire from our right. That fire was both machine-gun fire and shell fire . . . The hardest thing about that march was the cry of the wounded as they plead[ed] with us to not leave them there, but the pressing needs of war compelled us to move on."[68]

As the men of the 1st and 42nd Divisions trudged towards Sedan on November 6, a peace delegation charged with negotiating an armistice departed Berlin for France. They left a country in the throes of revolution. Following a naval mutiny at Kiel revolutionary sentiment spread to other German cities, including Berlin. Revolutionaries in Munich overthrew the Wittelsbach monarchy, established a Workers', Soldiers', and Peasants' Council, and demanded peace. On November 8, the German peace delegation led by Matthias Erzberger, the Center Party leader, met with the Allied delegation headed by Foch in a railway car in the forest of Compiègne. No Americans were present.

When Erzberger told Foch that the Germans were prepared to listen to the Allied proposals, Foch surprised him by saying, "I have no proposals to make." After several false starts Erzberger came to understand that the Allies expected him to initiate discussion by formally requesting an armistice. After doing so he and the other members of the German delegation were stunned by Allied terms that left no doubt that they were expected to sign an agreement that spoke the language of unconditional surrender. Foch rejected Erzberger's request for a ceasefire while talks continued, giving him seventy-two hours to accept or refuse the terms.[69] To keep the pressure on the Germans, Foch also issued an order that day that included the following instructions to British, French, and American troops: "Our advance should be kept going and speeded up."[70]

Pershing welcomed these instructions because he planned another offensive to achieve the objectives outlined some thirteen months earlier by his Operations Section on September 25, 1917: the capture of Metz and the coal and iron deposits of the Saar Basin. To the consternation of British and French war leaders, Pershing had allowed these objectives drawn up by Fox Conner and his staff to shape critical aspects of the AEF's participation in the war. Three days before he received Foch's instructions he in fact had issued marching orders to elements of the First Army and to the recently created Second Army to advance in the Woëvre. Foch, in a personal note, gave his approval on November 8.[71]

On the following day the six divisions of Bullard's Second Army in conjunction with Mangin's French Tenth Army began preliminary operations on the Woëvre for a major offensive scheduled for November 14 designed to envelop Metz and occupy the Briey-Longwy iron ore basin. Meanwhile, elements of the First Army, having fought their way across the Meuse, positioned themselves to protect the Second Army's flank with a drive east of the Meuse toward Longwy.

To Pershing's dismay this offensive, which he saw as the AEF's crowning achievement of the war, never took place. At 5:10 a.m. the

British and French signed the final draft of the armistice agreement. Foch then sent the following message by telephone and radio, including a transmission from the Eiffel Tower: "Hostilities will cease on the entire front beginning at 11:00 a.m. November 11, 1918." At 5:45 a.m. Pershing and his staff knew that fighting would cease in a little over six hours.

Sixteen US divisions were in the line and nine of them fought until the armistice went into effect. Following Foch's instructions to the letter, Major General Joseph E. Kuhn ordered his 79th Division to advance up the west slope of the Côte de Romagne. Until the armistice officially went into effect Kuhn insisted that "operations ordered will be pressed with vigor. At 11 hours our line will halt in place, and no man will move one step backward or forward."[72]

A few less hours of combat would have been welcomed by many Doughboys. Their orders, however, were to fight until the last minute. "It seemed that each side tried itself to see which could do the more damage in the short time that was left. Consequently, a few of our men were wounded and killed just before 11 a.m.," remembers Corporal Samuel M. Kent, Company K, 128th Infantry, 32nd Division.[73]

At 11:59 a.m. Private Henry Nicholson Gunter, Company A, 313th Regiment, from Kuhn's division, a draftee from Baltimore whose parents were German immigrants, advanced against a German machine gun position. Although the Germans attempted to wave him off, he continued his headlong charge and was shot dead at 11:59 a.m. He is thought to be the last US soldier killed in action.[74]

Many other war-weary soldiers naturally were determined not to emulate Gunter and be killed a few hours or even minutes before the armistice went into effect. Second Lieutenant Lawrence Bertram, Battery D, Field Artillery Regiment, 92nd or "Buffalo" Division, Second Army, found himself on the heights of the Moselle River with his division advancing towards Metz on November 11. "I was in a brick building basement at Bn C.P. Shells fell in the street and one struck the building. I thought 'to be killed the last day of the war. Never!' Fear was in my mind for the first time. I would not leave the shelter of that basement until noon next day."[75]

A surprisingly large number of soldiers were either not as fortunate or cautious as Lieutenant Bertram as the guns fell silent after some 1,566 days of death and destruction (Fig. 26). Persico contends that the opposing sides on the Western Front suffered 10,944 casualties, including 2,738 who died, on the last day of the war, or more casualties than on D-Day, June 6, 1944, when Allied soldiers stormed the Normandy beaches. As he notes: "The men storming the beaches were

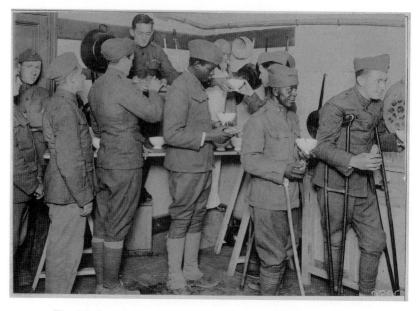

Fig. 26 American soldiers getting their bowls of chocolate and
rolls in the American Red Cross canteen at Toulouse, France

fighting for victory. Men dying on Armistice Day were fighting in a war
already decided."[76]

On November 11 Colonel Lloyd C. Griscom, Pershing's personal
representative in the British War Office, found a curiously deflated
commander-in-chief at Chaumont examining a large war map in his
office. With his Woëvre offensive about to be launched in three days,
he lamented: "What an enormous difference a few days more would have
made!"[77]

But could Pershing have ended the war in November with his offensive
planned for November 14? Harbord, who was in a position to know,
suggests that

if the armistice had not come when it did, there would have had to be a
suspension of hostilities and movement until the supply and troop program
could be brought back into balance. A very great proportion of the transport
fleet would have had to bring personnel and supply material for the impoverished
S.O.S., and the further shipment of combatant troops would have had to wait.[78]

For his part, Marshall contends that the AEF "would have gone straight
through the enemy's line" on November 14. But he argues that this

would not have ended the war. The disintegration of the German Army would have been a mixed blessing. Independent German units would have initiated guerilla warfare while the country plunged into anarchy leaving no organized government with which to negotiate. The victorious coalition would then have had to take over "practically all of Germany, which would have been a very difficult and lengthy task."[79]

The United States had only begun to play a significant role in the fighting in July 1918 but the sense of relief as the clock struck eleven was no less great for AEF members. "The last day was one I'll never forget," recalls private Antonio Flamino, Company A, 109th Infantry, 28th Division, whose company had been cutting German barbed wire in preparation for an advance.

There was a thick fog all morning. For miles word came by word of mouth from one soldier to another that no one should shoot after 11:00 o'clock in the morning. The Germans were on a hill & and a barbed wire between us. Many died. I was on the front and I prayed ... At 11:00 o'clock the sun came out & all firing ceased. The German soldiers & American boys exchanged friendly greetings & shared cigarettes.

Another member of the 28th Division, corporal Edward J. Banner, Company B, 109th Regiment, had a similar experience on his section of the front. He and other soldiers climbed out of their trenches and "went up and shook hands with the German soldiers who were very friendly with us. We hadn't had a hot meal for a long time and they then sent hot soup & tea to us and also the Germans."[80]

The guns may have been silenced but peace had yet to be made. Consequently, fifteen minutes after the Armistice went into effect, Liggett sought to prevent any fraternization with the enemy. "All communication with the enemy is forbidden pending further instructions," his Chief of Staff Drum wrote. "The cessation of hostilities is an armistice only, and not a peace, and there must be no relaxation of a vigilance. The troops must be prepared at any time for a rapid forward movement."[81] As usual, Summerall went over the top when he translated this order for his Corps: "Intercourse with the enemy is an act of treason and is punishable by death."[82]

Nonetheless, the atmosphere at the front quickly and dramatically changed for the soldiers. One could actually emerge from beneath the earth's surface and stand erect. With a sense of awe, Marine Private Aitken wrote the following to his mother: "As far as one could see on each side were large bonfires[,] fellows standing around the fires in groups smoking and laughing[,] something that never has been done before unless way back in the S.O.S. and then we had to be careful of aeroplanes. It all seems like a dream to me and I am surely glad it is a true dream."[83]

As victory over Germany appeared imminent, both the French and the British attempted to play down America's role in the war for political purposes. Lloyd George, referring to the AEF as an "amateur army," told members of the X-Committee that the American press was sending out "the most absurd accounts of the prowess of their Army," and that Wilson was "probably being misled." In his last note, the President had spoken of the "supremacy of the troops of the United States of America and their Allies, or some such phrase." If the Germans signed an armistice, the Welshman insisted, it would be because of the "splendid" Grand Fleet that had "provided the essential foundation of victory," and the victories of the BEF, which was now "the finest fighting force in the field."[84]

In sum London and Paris did not want Wilson to believe that US military accomplishments placed him in a position to dominate the peace settlement. Harbord got it wrong when he later commented that the armistice "ended two wars for us – the one with our friends, the other with our enemies."[85] At the Paris Peace Conference Wilson found himself at odds with the German people as well as with the victorious allies in his campaign to reshape the world along the lines of his Fourteen Points.

It can be argued that had the war continued into 1919, with the exhausted Allied armies now wholly dependent upon fresh American soldiers to deliver the knockout punch, Wilson would have been in a stronger negotiating position to achieve his liberal objectives. This raises an important question. How important in the final analysis was America's contribution to Germany's defeat? It goes without saying that US credit in 1917–18 staved off financial disaster for the Entente. And in total expenditure only Germany and Great Britain spent more of their treasure than the United States on the war.[86]

But what about the military side of the equation? Numbers provide a crude perspective. Table 8 shows the strengths of the Allied forces on the Western Front at the beginning of November 1918. Table 9 shows the number of prisoners and armaments taken by Allies during the war-winning offensives from July 18 to November 11.

War-weary and depleted French forces manned the longest front at the war's end. The French, of course, throughout the war defended more of their homeland and committed more manpower to the trenches. With a population of fewer than 38 million France mobilized 8.5 million men and suffered 5.3 million casualties (1.5 million killed, 800,000 mutilated, and 3 million wounded).[87] Twenty percent of these casualties had come during the last year of the war.

Table 8 *Allied forces on the Western Front at the beginning of November 1918*

	Combatant strength	Ration strength
British	1,202,000	1,794,000
French	1,554,000	2,562,000
American	1,175,000	1,876,000
Belgian	115,000	145,000
Italian	23,000	55,000

Source: John Terraine, *To Win a War: 1918, the Year of Victory* (Garden City, NY: Doubleday, 1981), p. 236 n. 26.

Table 9 *Prisoners and armaments taken by Allies, July 18–November 11, 1918*

	Prisoners	Guns
British	188,700	2,840
French	139,000	1,880
Americans	43,000	1,421
Belgians	14,500	474

Source: John Terraine, *To Win a War: 1918, the Year of Victory* (Garden City, NY: Doubleday, 1981), p. 234.

Creating a European force of some 2 million represented a remarkable achievement for the War Department. It is usually not recognized that the US Army fought its largest and most costly battle in its history at Meuse-Argonne, with twice as many soldiers being killed than at Okinawa.[88] In forty-seven days of heavy combat the First Army suffered 117,000 casualties while inflicting an estimated 100,000 casualties upon the enemy.[89]

Because of the relatively brief period the United States engaged in intense fighting its casualties, however, were relatively small when compared with other powers that waged war for years rather than months. Two of every 100 Americans who took part in the war were either killed or died from other causes, mostly disease. The United States suffered 50,300 battle deaths, most of which occurred during the last six weeks of the war. Only Greece (7,000) and Portugal (2,000) suffered fewer battlefield deaths. More US servicemen – over 63,000 – died from other causes. Estimates of total battle deaths for the chief combatants range from 7,485,000 to as many as 8.5 million.[90]

Pershing, confident of American exceptionalism, preached a doctrine of "open warfare" that stressed self-reliant infantry armed with rifles and bayonets to overcome sophisticated German defenses. "Ultimately, we had the satisfaction of hearing the French admit that we were right, both in emphasizing training for open warfare and insisting upon proficiency in the use of the rifle," he triumphantly proclaims in his war memoirs. No such admission by any French officers, however, could be located by a research assistant assigned to the task.[91]

With American divisions having to learn to fight by fighting on battle-fields dominated by machine guns and artillery, the cost of victory was arguably unnecessarily high. Yet Pershing's reputation remained intact long after the war ended. This was largely due to the war's abrupt end with the AEF finally achieving dramatic success on the battlefield.

Victory in 1918 also tended to obscure the performance of America's war industry and the near collapse of the AEF's logistical infrastructure. Pershing commanded a beggar army in 1917–18, dependent upon his allies for much of his transportation (troop ships, horses, mules, and trucks)[92] and modern weaponry, including tanks, artillery, and aircraft. America provided its war partners with vital steel and oil but, with the exception of rifles, her allies, most notably the French, provided the AEF with its firepower. Without this critical material support, an essentially nineteenth-century American army would have been forced to fight a twentieth-century war. This stood in stark contrast to World War II when the United States literally overwhelmed its enemies with its advanced technology and astonishing war production. American manu-facturers provided two-thirds of all Allied military equipment, including 297,000 aircraft, 86,000 tanks, and 2 million trucks, and furnished vital transportation for the Red Army as it advanced on Berlin.[93] In 1941–45 the US Army also mastered its formidable logistical challenges and waged successful campaigns in both Europe and the Pacific, in part because of the work of newly created Construction Battalions (CBs or "Seabees").[94] On November 11, 1918, when the Armistice went into effect, however, the AEF's logistical infrastructure was on the verge of collapse. "It is certain that if the Armistice had not come when it did, there would have had to be a suspension of hostilities and movement until the supply and troops program be brought back into balance," Harbord later admitted.[95] And manpower was only one of many problems plaguing the SOS.

Any evaluation of the US military role in the war should also include psychological consequences of American participation. The prospect of future American help in 1917 encouraged the French and the British to fight on and caused Ludendorff to take desperate steps in 1918 to achieve a victor's peace before US forces dramatically tipped the military balance in the Entente's favor. His five offensives, which began in March and continued into July 1918, placed his armies in vulnerable salients beyond the formidable Hindenburg Line and depleted and demoralized his troops, making an Allied victory possible in 1918.

Finally, and most importantly, the American offensive at Meuse-Argonne played a significant, arguably decisive, role in abruptly and unexpectedly ending the war in November 1918. Although critical of the tactical effectiveness of the AEF, General Max von Gallwitz, who commanded German troops defending the Meuse-Argonne triangle, emphasizes the "vastness and vigour of America's military expansion" and concludes that this "astonishing display of American strength ... definitely decided the war against us."[96]

Hindenburg agreed and said as much in a remarkable interview with four American journalists immediately following the Armistice. Violating military regulations, George Seldes joined three other journalists who commandeered two Cadillac sedans and drove into Germany where they were granted an interview with the German commander-in-chief.

When asked directly by Seldes what event finally ended the stalemate, Hindenburg responded as follows:

The American infantry in the Argonne won the war. I say this as a soldier, and soldiers will understand me best ... The Argonne Battle was slow and difficult. But it was strategic ... From a military point of view the Argonne Battle as conceived and carried out by the American command was the climax of the war and its deciding factor. The American attack continued from day to day with increasing power but when two opposing divisions had broken each other, yours were replaced with ten thousand eager men, ours with decimated, ill-equipped, ill-fed men suffering from contact with a gloomy and despairing civilian population. I do not mean to discredit your fighting power. I repeat: without the American blow in the Argonne we could have made a satisfactory peace at the end of a long stalemate, or at least held our last positions on our own frontier indefinitely – undefeated. The American attack won the war.[97]

Unfortunately, Hindenburg's words have been generally lost to history because Army censors refused to allow this interview to be published.

The AEF's critical contributions to Germany's defeat allowed Wilson to play a prominent role in peacemaking and he subsequently praised American soldiers for their role in a "war of redemption" and suggested that they had waged war as "crusaders" to bring "salvation" to the European people.[98] The creation of the League of Nations he championed (but which his countrymen rejected) failed to establish a new world stability based on collective security.

The US military effort may have momentarily thwarted Germany's attempt to dominate the European Continent but the Second Reich's defeat did not prove to be "the war to end all wars." Not surprisingly, many US veterans, initially proud of their service, became disillusioned about their overseas experience and came to believe that their government had dispatched them to wage a pointless war. And many civilians agreed. Consequently, in later years American participation in the Great War received much less public attention than either the American Civil War or the Second World War. This occurred despite the AEF's role in France becoming the tipping point for the role that the United States subsequently played in global politics. The dominant isolationist mood that developed in the wake of World War I proved to be both a temporary and an unworkable doctrine for the United States to embrace as the United States emerged in the 1940s as the world's greatest military power.

20   Epilogue

On November 17 the 28th Infantry, 1st Division, after its exhausting and helter-skelter march toward Sedan, was on the move again as part of the new Third Army, commanded by Major General Joseph T. Dickman, which had been organized at Ligny-en-Barrois between November 7 and November 15 to serve as the American Army of Occupation in Germany. At 8:00 a.m. the 28th Infantry crossed the old "no-man's-land" near the town of Abancourt. Once past the "armistice line" the regiment marched through land scarred by war, ruined villages, and abandoned trenches. Soon soldiers encountered masses of French, Russian, and Italian POWs, released by the Germans, moving in the opposite direction. By the second day, the regiment began passing through pleasant French towns which had escaped the war's destruction where joyous French civilians welcomed the Americans with open arms.[1]

The Third Army's destination was the Rhine and many soldiers wondered how they would be received on enemy soil. Under the terms of the Armistice the Allies gave the German Army thirty-one days to make a staged withdrawal to and just beyond the Rhine. It would not be the first and certainly not the last time that Washington deployed US troops to govern and police potentially hostile territory. Prior to becoming a belligerent in World War I the United States had deployed its soldiers on similar missions in Cuba, Puerto Rico, the Philippine Islands, Panama, Nicaragua, Mexico, Haiti, and the Dominican Republic, but never in the territory of a great power or on such a scale.[2] It would be January 1923 before Washington brought the last American soldier home from their watch on the Rhine.

After a lengthy advance, the first American infantrymen (39th Infantry, 4th Division) on December 8 reached the city of Coblenz where the Moselle River joins the Rhine. Behind them approximately 250,000 Doughboys of the American Army of Occupation (eight divisions in all, the 1st, 2nd, 3rd, 4th, 32nd, 42nd, 89th, and 90th) were on their way to occupy more than 2,500 square miles of German territory.[3] Three days later elements from all of these divisions reached the Rhine, quickly establishing footholds on the eastern bank of the river.

Initially American authorities sought to rule with a firm hand with wide-ranging regulations that banned public meetings, censored the press, and even monitored the use of carrier pigeons. Although it would not be until September that army authorities no longer discouraged troops from fraternizing with the German population,[4] it seems that Doughboys generally ignored their officers in this regard with many soldiers obviously getting along with German civilians, especially young women, from the very first. Erika Kuhlman suggests that "American soldiers treated the antifraternization ban with contempt and repeated disobedience."[5]

"It is a unique experience to be advancing through a conquered country and to see no evidence of hatred," Captain William D. Hasselton, 1st Division Headquarters, wrote his family.

We are everywhere received (or accepted) with courtesy and respect. Our orders and wishes are carried out exactly to the letter. I have not seen a single act of discourtesy ... It is not at all an uncommon sight to see a doughboy passing the time of day with the villagers even with discharged Boche soldiers who only a couple of weeks ago they were in a death struggle within the Argonne sector. It is almost unbelievable but nevertheless true.[6]

John Lewis Barkley, Company K, 4th Infantry Regiment, 3rd Division, had been eager to "see what the German people were really like. We'd heard so much that it didn't seem possible they could be like the rest of the world. But when we marched through the little German towns, and they crowded out in the streets to watch us go by, they didn't seem much different from the people I'd always known. Not as different as the French."[7] A truly extraordinary experience occurred as the 4th Division marched through the town of Hayingen. Suddenly a man and woman began "excitedly calling" to a duty sergeant named Schultz as he marched past. When questioned by a superior officer if he knew the couple, Schultz responded, "Yes sir, my parents."[8]

As this personal account illustrates, many US soldiers had German rather than French roots. Hale Hunt served with the 32nd Division, largely made up of men from Michigan and Wisconsin, many of whom spoke German. Not surprisingly, his company found a warm welcome in Butzweiler, where the "natives opened their kitchens to many of our soldiers who enjoyed the warmth of a stove. It is surprising how willing the German people are to cook a little feed of potatoes for the American soldiers, especially the women."[9] Barkley relates how a friend in his company discovered that he had German relatives living near

Meisenheim where his unit was stationed. "There were several German soldiers in the family," Barkley relates, "but just the same they staged a big celebration for their American cousin. He came back to camp so full of liquor and food that it took him two or three days to get over it."[10]

The growing rapport between natives and occupiers began to concern the higher ups. In January Pershing wrote in his diary that "a good proportion of our men, if not the majority of them, who have been in the Army of Occupation, will go home with a feeling of more respect for the Germans than for the French."[11] Pershing had reason to be worried, for peace had yet to be made. On the anniversary of the sinking of the *Lusitania*, May 7, 1919, Allied peacemakers presented their terms to the German delegation that had journeyed to Versailles. Stunned by the severity of these terms the German delegation refused to sign. Foch and other Allied generals then formulated plans to advance on Berlin in two stages with thirty-nine divisions. The initial invasion involved an advance to the Weser River. "The forward march does not frighten me but if this does not immediately bring us the desired result," Sir Henry Wilson on June 15, 1919 wrote Lloyd George, "the straggling occupation of an enormous country where our troops can nowhere be strong, and in which we shall probably have to rule by martial law fills me with apprehension."[12]

Earlier, Bliss, who now served as the military representative on the American Commission to Negotiate Peace, had voiced concern that many Americans in the Army of Occupation, who seemed to have much in common with the Germans, might refuse to take up arms against the fatherland if Berlin rejected Allied peace terms. US intelligence officers wrongly believed that German agents were involved in a clever campaign to enlist support from American soldiers against the harsh peace settlement.[13]

Black soldiers, who did not participate in the occupation of Germany, apparently had a much higher opinion of the French people than many of their white comrades in arms. Only in death had blacks been fully integrated in the AEF. If anyone visits the beautifully maintained American cemeteries at Meuse-Argonne and elsewhere in France he/ she will discover no distinction between officers and men or between blacks and whites. French society was hardly without racial tension, but many blacks concluded that French society was more color-blind than their homeland, which made the existing Jim Crow laws in the United States seem even more intolerable. "You know now that the mean contemptible spirit of race prejudice that curses this land is not the spirit of other lands," the Reverend F. J. Grimké told a group of returning black servicemen.[14]

On June 23, ninety minutes before the Armistice was scheduled to expire, the Germans announced that they were prepared to sign what they described as a "dishonorable peace." Five days later German delegates formally signed the Treaty of Versailles in the Hall of Mirrors of Louis XIV's palace. The War Department subsequently changed the name of American occupation forces along the Rhine to American Forces in Germany (AFG). By July 1919 American forces in Germany had been reduced to approximately 6,800 men.[15]

Following the official end of the war the Army Transport Service intensified its efforts to transport troops home, a task made more difficult because most of the British ships that had transported approximately one-half of the US forces to Europe were no longer available. Among other responsibilities, Britain had to return tens of thousands of its colonial troops to their homelands. To meet demands the Army Transport Service refitted fifty-eight cargo ships as troop ships. In June 1919 as many as 350,000 Doughboys made the Atlantic crossing. By the end of August only the rapidly diminishing force on the Rhine and 40,000 logistical troops remained.[16] Of those who remained in the AFG a large number married or attempted to marry German women. By January 1921, 10 percent of the Doughboys in the Rhineland had taken German brides and an equal number had applied but been turned down, mostly because army authorities deemed the Fräuleins' character "questionable" (i.e., they were prostitutes).[17]

Most soldiers in the AEF naturally wanted to shed their uniforms and return to civilian life as soon as possible. Corporal Floyd H. Invester, Company C, 4th Infantry Regiment, 4th Division, spoke for many of them. "I'll be lucky if I ever get home," he wrote in a letter on June 2, 1919. "No one can blame the boy – for becoming discouraged and disgusted. A dose like this would take the heart out of the best man in the world. Imagine yourself being a slave in a country where your language is not spoken and where you couldn't escape if you tried and you'll have the situation in a nut shell, of our sentiments."[18] Rumors ran rampant. "One day we are on our way home[,] the next day we are to stay longer here until 'hell won't have us,'" a disgruntled Aitken wrote his father on March 9, 1919.[19]

Initially, the army leadership emphasized training exercises and "spit and polish" inspections to keep soldiers busy and in line. Raymond Fosdick, the progressive reformer who chaired the CTCA, while touring AEF units after the Armistice, suggested a different approach toward soldiers soon destined to return to civilian life. "To see a battery that has fired 70,000 rounds in the Argonne fight going listlessly through the movements of ramming an empty shell into a gun for hours at a stretch," he observed, "or training the sights on an enemy that does not exist, is depressing enough to watch, and its effect on the spirits of the men is apparent. They seem to wilt under it."[20] Pershing supported Fosdick and told his division commanders to limit their training schedules.

To provide these young and restless men with healthy outlets while they waited to be shipped home the military authorities also began organizing entertainment for the troops as well as wide-ranging athletic events, with Americans competing against their allies in sports and games. In June and July 1919 the Inter-Allied Games took place in Paris in the Pershing Stadium which had been largely constructed by Dough-boy engineers. Many units also organized theatrical troupes that traveled throughout the AEF giving performances.[21]

The military authorities also established a multifaceted system of education to develop the mind as well as the body. In addition to secondary and high school courses the army created numerous technical schools offering a wide range of instruction from horseshoeing to tele-phone wiring to automobile repair. Soldiers who attended these schools had their daily military obligations reduced. In the Côte d'Or section of France the military established the AEF's University at Beaune with open admissions apparently for everyone except blacks. Some 9,000 soldiers engaged in advanced studies with officers often being lectured and graded by privates from the ranks who had previously been employed as teachers before becoming soldiers in 1917–18.

Army authorities also encouraged Doughboys to study at British and French universities.[22] Private Gordon N. Christopher, Company C, 101st Machine Gun Battalion, 26th Division, attended the University of Rennes in Brittany. He remembers his studies as a "tremendous experi-ence."[23] Before the war he had worked as a tire finisher. Following the war he became a French teacher in Connecticut. As many as 230,000 soldiers took advantage of these educational programs.[24]

The army also supported the broadening experiences of travel. Dough-boys found themselves in the position of involuntary tourists in Europe. Why not make their extended deployment abroad as enjoyable and as enlightening an experience as possible? On January 6, 1918 AEF head-quarters issued General Order No. 6, which provided leave time "if mili-tary conditions permitted" every four months. Military authorities initially provided transportation and soldiers had to pay for their room and board. This changed when traveling soldiers were placed on "duty status," which allowed the military to pay for their room and board. Between 400,000 and 600,000 soldiers took advantage of this generous leave program.[25]

In February 1919 an excited Corporal Murphy, Company H, 309th Infantry, 78th Division, learned that he was eligible for a leave on the

French Riviera. He traveled first class by train (later a special train, the "American Express," transported soldiers from Paris to the Riviera) and stayed in a first-class hotel. "We had the best of everything in French food," he later recalled, "and slept in beds with sheets for the first time since being in the Army." He also took conducted tours to places such as Monaco and Monte Carlo.[26]

Team sports, excursions to beautiful and interesting places, and extensive educational opportunities proved a welcome relief from regimented military life. But the best moment for most Doughboys, especially for those whose demobilization had been long delayed, was when they finally arrived at the demobilization centers in the United States to pick up their discharge papers.[27] A few soldiers decided to make the army a career but most eagerly returned to civilian life. On November 11 the total strength of the US Army had been 3,703,273. By June 1919, 2,608,218 enlisted men and 128,436 officers had picked up their discharge papers.[28]

The last marches for many soldiers after returning to the United States were victory parades demanded by a patriotic public. During the first six months of 1919 as many as 500 parades took place throughout the United States with entire divisions marching through the streets of New York and Washington. The War Department welcomed this public support but drew the line when one New York politician wanted to require all citizens to give the military salute to returning servicemen.[29]

During their demobilization process the government strongly encouraged soldiers to continue paying premiums for their government-subsidized life insurance policies. A letter from the Treasury Department informed them that they held "a form of insurance which marks the highest point ever reached by a Government in the protection of those in the service ... The wealth of the nation stands behind every policy."[30] Many soldiers followed this advice.

A soldier also received his uniform, shoes, either a raincoat or overcoat, and other articles of military dress. If he had served overseas the authorities allowed him keep his helmet and gas mask as souvenirs. The War Department also gave him his discharge pay, a $60 bonus, and an allowance to pay for transportation home from his demobilization center. To ensure that unemployed soldiers did not congregate in urban areas or spend their travel allowances for other purposes, officers often escorted them directly to train stations. "All personnel, morale, and other officers cooperated," March writes, "to impress on the men the importance of immediately purchasing railroad transportation, rather than run the risk of losing or squandering their money and thus becoming a burden upon some near-by community."[31]

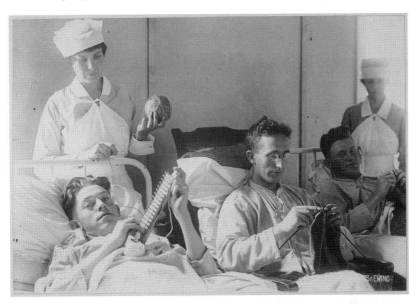

Fig. 27 Bed-ridden wounded, knitting. Walter Reed Hospital,
Washington, DC, Harris & Ewing, *c.*1918–*c.*1919

With the exception of a few females attached to the US Marines, however,
women who had served in the capacity of nurses and telephone operators
were not allowed to retain their insurance or receive the $60 bonus.[32] That
women could occupy official non-nurse status in the military had its beginning during the war. The Marine Corps had used Marine-F[emale] personnel to handle clerical and administrative tasks. For his part, Pershing had
requested female telephone operators who could speak French for service in
France. The War Department responded by sending uniformed female
telephone operators across the Atlantic as civilian contract employees.[33]

Veterans demobilized in 1919 discovered a deteriorating economy and
a weak job market. When the guns fell silent on the Western Front the
government began canceling military contracts and war-related industries began shedding jobs. Farmers as well as factory workers faced hard
times. During the war American farms had fed Europe. To meet growing
demand farmers had abandoned crop rotation and plowed from fence
row to fence row. Following the war, however, demand declined and a
surplus of produce drove down prices.

In addition to life insurance policies the government also created the
Veterans Bureau and established hospitals to treat injured or sick soldiers
(Fig. 27). But the Wilson administration, having spent billions of dollars

on the war effort, attempted to discourage veterans from expecting the sort of financial and medical benefits that Union soldiers and their dependents had been given by the federal government after the Civil War. In 1891 one out of every three dollars spent by the federal government had gone for Civil War military pensions. By 1902, 999,446 individuals (when widows and dependents were included) were on the pension rolls.[34]

The War Department's Employment Service, however, found it impossible to fulfill its promise to find many demobilized soldiers a job. The $60 bonuses now seemed inadequate compensation to a growing number of veterans, especially to those who had been forced to leave good jobs to serve their country. The American Legion (created in Paris in 1919) began pressing the Coolidge administration to provide a more generous bonus. President Coolidge responded by proclaiming that "patriotism … bought and paid for is not patriotism." Congress subsequently overrode Coolidge's veto and granted 3,662,374 veterans $1.00 for each day of service at home and $1.25 for each day of service abroad. The catch was that the budget-conscious Congress gave veterans bond certificates that matured in 1945 rather than the cash payments that many veterans originally demanded.[35]

With the arrival of the Great Depression many veterans, especially those without jobs, began to have second thoughts about these bond certificates and organized demonstrations in the capital. The catalyst for the so-called Bonus Expeditionary Force was a twenty-day trek in May 1932 by some 200 Oregonian veterans from Portland to Washington, DC. With the press giving extensive coverage to this pilgrimage, veterans from all over the country began descending on the capital. By July there were as many as 20,000 veterans, many accompanied by their wives and children, established at a camp on the Anacostia flats some two miles southeast of the Capitol. President Hoover, however, refused to meet with the Bonus Marchers, and the Senate overwhelmingly (62–18) defeated a bill passed by the House to pay the veterans a bonus by simply printing more money. When many of the veterans refused to return home, Hoover deployed federal troops, backed by tanks but using bayonets rather than bullets or shells, to disperse the Bonus Marchers.[36]

Roosevelt's election did not initially lead to increased government support for veterans. To the contrary, a key feature of Roosevelt's campaign had been a balanced budget and, among other money-saving measures, he struck nearly 100,000 veterans from the disabled rolls and reduced by one-half the compensation that war-injured veterans had been receiving. Vigorous lobbying by the American Legion along with further marches on Washington, however, convinced Congress to restore most of these lost benefits. Meanwhile, the government offered places for unemployed veterans in the newly created Civilian Conservation Corps. Eventually 213,000 veterans found work in this semi-military work program which included penalties for going AWOL from the camps. Although the US Army, first with Regulars and then largely with reservists, initially ran this program the government forbade military instruction in any of the camps. One irony is that the government paid army privates $17.85 a month while the CCC men received $30.[37] Meanwhile, Roosevelt continued to oppose attempts by Congress to give veterans cash bonuses.

By 1936, however, as the economy gradually improved, Congress had the necessary votes to override the president's veto and the veterans finally received their cash bonus. These bonuses did not come cheaply, amounting to almost one-half of the federal budget that year ($3.9 billion out of $8.4 billion).[38] More importantly, these cash bonuses set the stage for the passage of the Servicemen's Readjustment Act in 1944 (better known as the G.I. Bill), which provided substantial educational, housing, and unemployment benefits to World War II veterans.[39]

That the United States needed a large and well-equipped army and might become involved in another world war even more destructive than the one now being called the Great War did not seem remotely possible to most Americans. Wilson and many of his supporters argued that acceptance of the League of Nations would provide security for the United States and make unnecessary a large US Army. Those who opposed the League generally fell into the isolationist camp and opposed the United States developing the ability to play a global military role or become involved in collective security arrangements.

President Wilson had been laid low by a stroke and a serious urinary blockage in October 1919. Several months later, on March 19, 1920, the Senate refused to ratify the Treaty of Versailles. Article X, which implied that member powers might be required to use force, proved to be an especially controversial article. Lodge posed a key question: "Are you willing to put your soldiers and your sailors at the disposition of other nations?"[40] Wilson took the position that if you omitted Article X the League would be little more than a "debating society." At the same time he argued that the article "imposed a moral not a legal obligation" and did not impinge upon Congress's power to declare war.[41]

The prevailing political atmosphere, with most Americans opposed to the United States accepting a global military role in harmony with its great power status, played a crucial role in determining the US Army's immediate future.[42] Immediately after the Armistice, March writes, "I took up at once the preparation of a bill for the reorganization of the permanent military establishment, so as to take advantage of the lessons of the war."[43] In doing so the Chief of Staff reignited the debate over whether the nation should be defended by a professional or a largely citizen force. March wanted an army of 500,000 men based on the Uptonian concept of an expandable professional army. To create the necessary manpower reserves for rapid expansion of the standing army, March suggested that all nineteen-year-old males be given three months of rudimentary military training by professional soldiers. Because of the brevity of this training March refused to equate his scheme with compulsory service.

The War Plans Division, assigned by March the responsibility of fleshing out the details, disappointed him with the direction of its inquiry. "The Division had gone far beyond the principles outlined to them and produced a reorganization founded on universal military service with eleven months of training," he later noted in his account of his days as Chief of Staff. March's version is that he opposed a lengthy compulsory training period because he believed that it would lead to the militarization of society in much the same way that the mass conscript armies of the European powers had done prior to 1914.[44] It is more likely, however, that March advocated a short training period to make universal service more palatable to Congress.[45]

Unhappy with the direction of the War Plans Division's deliberations, March then turned over the reorganization of the army to Frank McIntyre, the Assistant Chief of Staff, and Henry Jervey, his Chief of Operations. These two officers subsequently produced a plan mirroring their chief's views: a peacetime army of one field army of five corps, a skeletal force of about 50 percent of its paper strength designed to provide sufficient manpower for extensive training of the specialists and their branches associated with modern warfare. Universal service for nineteen-year-olds provided the necessary manpower to expand this force in the event of war. This plan provided young recruits with their transportation, clothing, shelter, food, and five dollars a month during their three-month training period. March argued that this plan represented a terrific bargain for taxpayers. "We had the camps and cantonments, we had a large reserve of uniforms; we had guns and ammunition."[46]

This reorganization plan, known as the Baker–March Bill, however, relegated the National Guard to third rank after the Regulars and conscripted reservists, a decision certain to inflame the National Guard's numerous advocates in Congress. Many Americans also no longer saw the need for a large army whatever its makeup. As Hiram Johnson of California noted at the time, "I can not quite fathom why at this particular time, when we are facing an era of universal peace, we should have an Army many times larger than we had had in our history before."[47] Johnson was joined in his skepticism about spending money on soldiers by another Republican Senator from California, Julius Kahn, who chaired the Senate Military Committee. If Kahn had his way the peacetime Army would be reduced to 100,000 men, approximately the same number that the victors of World War I imposed on Germany in the Treaty of Versailles to make that country militarily impotent.[48]

Soldiers as well as civilians found much they disliked in the Baker–March Bill. One of them was an army intellectual, Colonel John McAuley Palmer, who had served five years as a chemistry professor at West Point, and now advised the Senate Military Affairs Committee on military questions. An important point of departure with the Baker–March Bill concerned the Regular Army's size. In testimony before the Senate Military Affairs Committee Palmer suggested that citizen rather than professional soldiers should serve as the foundation of the nation's defense. To achieve this goal he advocated a slimmed-down Regular Army, supported by a National Guard organized into large tactical units. The Officers' Reserve Corps and the Enlisted Reserve Corps provided additional manpower.

With Pershing's support Palmer played a leading role in shaping the National Defense Act of June 4, 1920, which emphasized citizen rather than professional soldiers. In a devastating critique of March's plan, Palmer told Congress that "the War Department bill proposes incomplete preparedness at excessive cost, and under forms that are not in harmony with the genius of American institutions."[49]

A missing and critical element in the subsequent National Defense Act of 1920, however, was Palmer's proposal for an organized reserve based on universal military training. Congress, steadfastly opposed to universal military training in any form, denied the War Department the necessary trained reservists to expand the army rapidly. Moreover, despite authorizing a standing army of some 280,000 men and 18,000 officers, Congress provided funds for only 200,000 men.

The budget-conscious Congress, innately suspicious of professional soldiers, also provided meager funding for the army throughout the 1920s and 1930s. Appropriations ranged from a low of $255,542,147 (1935) to a high of $460,201,254 (1939).[50] In the 1920s a soldier's daily ration of toilet paper might be limited to three sheets and even light bulbs remained in short supply. Cuts ranged from ammunition for training purposes to travel allowances for officers.[51] The army also had its manpower cut to the bone. Regular Army personnel strength ranged from a low of 118,348 enlisted men and 12,906 officers (1923) to a high of

174,079 enlisted men and 13,814 officers (1939). For eleven years, from 1925 to 1935, Regular Army personnel never surpassed 140,000 men.[52]

Scattered throughout the country in small military posts, the War Department, with approximately one-fourth of the Regular Army stationed abroad, could not collect enough combat soldiers in the continental United States to fill Soldiers' Field in Chicago to capacity. Denied adequate funding by a parsimonious Congress, the National Guard also fell considerably short of the 435,000 force contemplated in the 1920 National Defense Act.[53] Weigley is probably correct when he concludes that "the Army during the 1920s and early 1930s may have been less ready to function as a fighting force than at any time in its history."[54] On the other hand, with no apparent foreign threat to the continental United States and with no collective security obligations, it is not surprising that many Americans opposed spending money on soldiers or armaments between the wars. Coffman reminds us that "from 1921 to 1939 the army was more at peace than ever before in its history. There were no conflicts: no fighting Indians as before 1898 nor, as later, fighting Filipinos, Moros, and Mexicans."[55]

This was a time in which many Americans took seriously the Kellogg–Briand Pact. In 1927 the French Premier Aristide Briand asked the United States to sign a pact outlawing war between the two nations. Coolidge's Secretary of State Frank Kellogg responded by suggesting a joint statement opposing war that any nation might sign. The resulting Kellogg–Briand Pact (1928), signed by virtually all the great powers, including Germany, Japan, and Italy, with the signatories promising to settle their differences peacefully, was approved by the US Senate with only one dissenting vote. Some Americans dared hope that a new era in international politics had arrived when nations no longer used war as an instrument of national policy. On the eve of the Great Depression in 1929 President Herbert Hoover announced: "There is the most profound outlook for peace today that we have had at any time in the last half century."[56]

Pershing, America's leading soldier, clearly did not agree with the American isolationists who actually thought that war had been "outlawed" but he believed that the United States was unlikely to become involved in a European theater where armies in the millions might once again be locked in stalemated and immobile warfare. "Our army is most likely to operate on the American Continent," he argued, "and mobility is especially necessary under all probable conditions of warfare in this theater." To improve the army's operational mobility America's most prominent soldier wanted to replace the large four-regiment or square division of some 28,000 men and officers with the triangular or three-regiment division of approximately 17,000 men. He also suggested a dramatic reduction in artillery support.[57]

Pershing expressed these views in 1920 in response to a report prepared by the AEF Superior Board on Organization and Tactics, which had been charged with divining the "lessons learned" from the Great War. Its finished report suggested that the AEF's campaign in France in 1918, where armies had little opportunity to maneuver and firepower and machines dominated the battlefield, should serve as the model for future US campaigns. In some respects, however, the Superior Board delivered a mixed message, apparently a reflection of the tension between prewar American doctrine and the battlefield realities of France. Its report emphasized both "self-reliant" infantry and the critical importance of providing infantry with every form of firepower, from automatic rifles and machine guns to artillery and tanks. Its report also suggested that power rather than mobility was the key to victory, much in the same way that Grant had ultimately triumphed over Lee during the American Civil War.[58]

The new edition of the *Field Service Regulations* reflected this ambivalence as it attempted to elucidate the lessons of World War I and establish the army's tactical doctrine for the future. Completed in 1923, the General Staff published this new manual in 1924. As reflected in the quotes below this doctrinal review represented a compromise between advocates of firepower and Pershing's emphasis on what he believed set the US Army apart from the armies of other nations: its offensive spirit and the aggressiveness of its infantry.

Infantry is essentially the arm of close combat. This role rather than the nature of its armament distinguishes the infantry as a combatant arm ... Infantry fighting power rests upon the basis of morale ... It is the special duty of the higher command to stimulate and cultivate the fighting spirit, aggressiveness, and initiative of the infantry soldier.[59]

Infantry alone thus possesses the power to close with the enemy and enforce the decision of battle. Its forward movement is the indispensable condition of victory.[60]

Infantry is equipped with an armament which enables it to discharge the various missions which fall to it in combat. Its principal offensive weapon is the rifle and bayonet. Its automatic weapons reinforce the firepower of its rifles and contribute to the attainment of the fire superiority upon which the ability of the infantry to advance depends.[61]

And then the advocates of mass firepower had their say. As Grotelueschen suggests, the new edition of the *Field Service Regulations* actually "contained more concepts of a firepower-based doctrine than anything before in American military history."[62]

No one arm wins battles. The combined employment of all arms is essential to success ... It is the task of higher commanders to coordinate and direct the action of each army with a view to the most efficient exploitation of its powers and their adoption to the ends sought ... The special mission of other arms are derived from the powers to contribute to the execution of the infantry mission.[63]

Superior fire constitutes the best protection against loss as well as the most effective means of destruction. Fire superiority rests chiefly upon the coordination of the action of the infantry and the artillery and the mutual support of infantry units ... Artillery is charged with the general fire support of the infantry; machine guns and infantry cannon take over the close support of rifle companies ... [after infantry closes with the enemy]. The loss of the direct fire support of the artillery is compensated for by the action of tanks and attack airplanes which intervene at this stage of the attack. Artillery, tanks and attack airplanes support the penetration through the depth of the hostile position.[64]

Artillery fire of pursuit and aerial attack constitute the most effective means of defeating the enemy's attempts to reorganize his forces for their movement in retreat.[65]

Brainstorming by the US Army's leadership included more than doctrine and the army's role in future conflicts: army reformers also paid attention to mobilizing the country's industry for war. It is sometimes overlooked that the National Defense Act provided for an Assistant Secretary of War whose responsibility was to prepare "for the mobilization of material and industrial organizations essential to wartime needs."[66] Subsequently, the Assistant Secretary of War, who created his own Planning Branch, developed a series of mobilization plans in the 1920s and 1930s. Harbord, the former director of the AEF's Services of Supply, chaired a board which considered ways in which the Assistant Secretary of War might work with the General Staff to effect the orderly industrial and business mobilization. Another step in this direction was the creation of the Army and Navy Munitions Board in 1922.[67]

This industrial mobilization planning implied that future wars might be won in the same way that the Allies triumphed in World War I. The German Army in 1918 had not been defeated by brilliant generalship that outmaneuvered Ludendorff or turned his flanks but by an increasing material superiority in such areas as aircraft, tanks, and artillery and the massive addition of US manpower.

As the 1930s ended ominous storm clouds gathered over Europe and Asia, forcing the American public to come to grips with world affairs again. As President Roosevelt observed, "The rest of the world – Ah! There is the rub."[68] On July 7, 1937 Chinese and Japanese troops clashed at Marco Polo Bridge and fighting quickly erupted throughout China. In December the Japanese Army shocked the world with its "rape of Nanjing" which resulted in the rape or death of tens of thousands of Chinese civilians by Japanese soldiers. In Europe, Hitler, after making a pact with Stalin, overran Poland in September 1939. The following year Hitler defeated France and began making preparations for a cross-Channel invasion of Britain, raising the frightening possibility that Germany might gain control of both the British and French navies. In 1941 Hitler unleashed his legions against the Soviet Union, initiating the most destructive military campaign in history. America's moral diplomacy, as reflected by the Kellogg–Briand Treaty, was clearly bankrupt as fighting spread across the globe.

In mid-1940 Congress responded to the widening war by initiating the first peacetime draft in American history and passing a joint resolution that authorized Roosevelt to call National Guardsmen and Reservists, which included many officers trained by college ROTC programs, to active duty. This resulted in nearly 1,650,000 men under arms when the Japanese attacked Pearl Harbor in 1941. With supplemental appropriations Congress also increased the War Department's budget to almost $3 billion in 1940 (it had been $460,201,254 in 1939).[69] Much had yet to be done but the US Army in December 1941 was a far different one from the essentially constabulary force, more designed to wage war with Indians than Germans, that had marched off to war in 1917.

Notes

NOTES TO CHAPTER I

1 *Literary Digest* (February 26, 1898), vol. 16, p. 242.

2 Allan Millett, "The American Military as an Instrument of Power," in John Jessup and Louise Ketz (eds.), *Encyclopedia of the American Military* (New York: Charles Scribner's Sons, 1994), vol. 1, p. 183.

3 Russell Weigley, *History of the United States Army* (New York: Macmillan Publishing Co., Inc., 1967), pp. 296–98.

4 Daniel Beaver, *Modernizing the American War Department* (Kent, Ohio: Kent State University Press, 2006), p. 28.

5 Robert Doughty and Ira Gruber, *American Military History and the Evolution of Western Warfare* (Lexington, Mass., D. C. Heath and Co., 1996), p. 244; Frederick Palmer, *Newton D. Baker: America at War* (New York: Dodd, Mead, 1931), vol. 1, p. 31.

6 Weigley, *History of the United States Army*, p. 304.

7 Quoted in Foster Rhea Dulles, *America's Rise to World Power, 1898–1954* (New York: HarperCollins, 1955), p. 43.

8 *Ibid.*, p. 58.

9 Precise figures cannot be calculated. See Ian Beckett, *The Great War, 1914–1918* (Harlow: Pearson Education Limited, 2001), p. 204.

10 See Walter Goerlitz, *History of the German General Staff, 1657–1945* (New York: Frederick A. Praeger, 1953), pp. 69–142.

11 Philip Jessup, *Elihu Root* (New York: Dodd, Mead & Co., 1938), vol. 1, p. 215.

12 Palmer, *Newton D. Baker: America at War*, vol. 1, p. 33.

13 Frederic Paxson, *American Democracy and the World War* (New York: Cooper Square Publishers, Inc., 1966), vol. 1, pp. 112–13.

14 Timothy Nenninger, "The Army Enters the Twentieth Century," in Kenneth J. Hagan and William R. Roberts (eds.), *Against All Enemies: Interpretations of American Military History from Colonial Time to the Present* (Westport, Conn.: Greenwood Press, 1986), p. 223.

15 Weigley, *History of the United States Army*, p. 317.

16 On this point, see William R. Roberts, "Reform and Revitalization, 1890–1902," in Kenneth J. Hagan and William R. Roberts (eds.), *Against All Enemies: Interpretations of American Military from Colonial Times to the Present* (Westport, Conn.: Greenwood Press, 1986), p. 213.

17 *Ibid.*, p. 322; see also Jessup, *Root*, vol. 1, pp. 256–63 and Beaver, *Modernizing the American War Department*, pp. 30–31.

18 Edward Coffman, *The War to End All Wars* (Madison: University of Wisconsin Press, 1986), p. 12.

19 Edward Coffman, *The Regulars: The American Army, 1898–1941* (Cambridge, Mass.: Harvard University Press, 2007), p. 185.

20 See Timothy Nenninger, "American Military Effectiveness in the First World War," in Allan Millett and Williamson Murray (eds.), *Military Effectiveness*, vol. 1, *The First World War* (Boston, Mass.: Unwin Hyman, 1989), pp. 135–36.

21 Coffman, *The Regulars*, p. 188.

22 Weigley, *History of the United States Army*, p. 323.

23 Jessup, *Root*, vol. 1, p. 265.

24 Quoted *ibid.*, p. 268.

25 See Beaver, *Modernizing the American War Department*, pp. 31–32 and Weigley, *History of the United States Army*, pp. 320–22.

26 Nenninger, "The Army Enters the Twentieth Century," p. 220.

27 Coffman, *The Regulars*, p. 97.

28 *Ibid.*, p. 127.

29 *Ibid.*, pp. 129–31.

30 Jack Lane, *Armed Progressive: General Leonard Wood* (San Rafael, Calif.: Presidio Press, 1978), p. 149.

31 Coffman, *The Regulars*, p. 187.

32 Beaver, *Modernizing the American War Department*, p. 35.

33 *Ibid.*, p. 34.

34 See Lane, *Armed Progressive*, pp. 161–67 and Weigley, *History of the United States Army*, pp. 330–32.

35 Palmer, *Newton D. Baker: America at War*, vol. 1, p. 69.

36 Weigley, *History of the United States Army*, p. 332.

37 John Finnegan, *Against the Specter of a Dragon: The Campaign for American Military Preparedness, 1914–1917* (Westport, Conn.: Greenwood Press, 1975), p. 18.

38 *Ibid.*, pp. 17–19; see also Weigley, *History of the United States Army*, pp. 335–40 and Lane, *Armed Progressive*, p. 177.

39 Robert Alexander, *Memories of the World War, 1917–1918* (New York: The Macmillan Co., 1931), p. 103.

40 Nenninger, "The Army Enters the Twentieth Century," pp. 223–24.

41 John Lejeune, *The Reminiscences of a Marine* (Philadelphia, Pa.: Dorrance, 1930), pp. 188–89.

42 Edward Coffman, "The AEF Leaders' Education for War," in R. J. Q. Adams (ed.), *The Great War, 1914–1918: Essays on the Military, Political and Social History of the First World War, 1914–1918* (College Station: Texas A&M University Press, 1990), p. 149.

43 Hunter Liggett, *AEF Ten Years Ago in France* (New York: Dodd, Mead, 1928), pp. 289–90.

44 Paxson, *American Democracy and the World War*, vol. 1, p. 114; Lee Kennett, *The First Air War, 1914–1918* (New York: Free Press, 1991), p. 7.

NOTES TO CHAPTER 2

1 Quoted in Arthur Link, *Wilson the Diplomatist: A Look at His Major Foreign Policies* (Baltimore, Md.: Johns Hopkins University Press, 1957), p. 5.
2 House to Wilson, May 29, 1914, *PWW*, vol. 30, p. 109.
3 See Harry DeWeerd, *President Wilson Fights His War: World War I and the American Intervention* (New York: Macmillan, 1968), p. 5.
4 Letters of July 29 and August 2, 1914, *PWW*, vol. 30, pp. 316, 330.
5 "An Appeal to the American People," August 18, 1914, *PWW*, vol. 30, pp. 393–94.
6 *PWW*, vol. 30, p. 352. See also Arthur Link, *The Struggle for Neutrality, 1914–1915* (Princeton, NJ: Princeton University Press, 1960), p. 66.
7 Arthur Link, *The New Freedom* (Princeton, NJ: Princeton University Press, 1956), vol. 2, p. 77.
8 Quoted in Robert Ferrell, *Woodrow Wilson and World War I, 1917–1921* (New York: Harper & Row Publishers, 1985), p. 50.
9 Gerard to Wilson, June 8, 1915, *PWW*, vol. 33, p. 371.
10 Palmer, *Newton D. Baker: America at War*, vol. 1, pp. 40–41.
11 *Ibid.*, p. 57.
12 Weigley, *History of the United States Army*, p. 568.
13 Allan Millett, "Cantigny, 28–31 May 1918," in Charles Heller and William Stofft (eds.), *America's First Battles, 1776–1965* (Lawrence: University Press of Kansas, 1986), p. 151.
14 See Beaver, *Modernizing the American War Department*, pp. 89–93; Coffman, *War to End All Wars*, pp. 17–18; Leonard Ayres, *The War with Germany: A Statistical Summary* (Washington, DC: Government Printing Office, 1919), pp. 63–68, 73–77; John Chambers, *To Raise an Army: The Draft Comes to Modern America* (New York: Free Press, 1987), p. 75; DeWeerd, *President Wilson Fights His War*, pp. 206–07.
15 Quoted in Robert Zieger, *America's Great War: World War I and the American Experience* (Lanham, Md.: Roman & Littlefield Publishers, 2001), p. 66.
16 Wilson to Garrison, June 21, 1915; Garrison to Wilson, August 12, 1915; Wilson to Garrison, August 19, 1915, *PWW*, vol. 34, pp. 4, 173–74, 248.
17 *Statement of a Proper Military Policy for the United States* (Washington, DC: Government Printing Office, 1916), p. iii.
18 *Ibid.*
19 *Ibid.* p. 4.
20 Emory Upton, *The Military Policy of the United States from 1775* (Washington, DC: Government Printing Office, 1904), pp. vii, xi, xiii–xiv.
21 Weigley, *History of the United States Army*, pp. 280–81.
22 David Fitzpatrick, "Emory Upton and the Army of a Democracy," *Journal of Military History* 77 (2013): 465.
23 Garrison to Wilson, September 17, 1915, *PWW*, vol. 34, p. 483.
24 "Study of the Cost of the Army of the United States as Compared with the Cost of the Armies of Other Nations," November 1915. War College Division 9053-120 (Washington, DC: Government Printing Office, 1916), p. 5.

25 Figures taken from the American Institute for Economic Research.

26 This included increased expenditures for coastal defense.

27 Wilson to Edith Bolling Galt, August 31, 1915, *PWW*, vol. 34, p. 392.

28 Quoted in Link, *New Freedom*, vol. 2, p. 68.

29 Notes of March 29, 1935, Box 2, Nolan MSS, AHEC.

30 Letter of August 31, 1915, *PWW*, vol. 34, p. 392.

31 Arthur Link, *Confusion and Crises, 1915–1916* (Princeton, NJ: Princeton University Press, 1964), pp. 15–17.

32 Beaver, *Modernizing the American War Department*, p. 70.

33 Chambers, *To Raise an Army*, p. 105.

34 *PWW*, vol. 35, p. 169.

35 Quoted in Link, *Confusion and Crises*, p. 31.

36 Palmer, *Newton D. Baker: America at War*, vol. 1, p. 58.

37 Link, *Confusion and Crises*, p. 24.

38 Committee on Military Affairs, January 10, 1916, quoted in "Report of the Chief of Staff," in *War Department Annual Report*, 1916, vol. 1, p. 160.

39 Scott to Editor of *Philadelphia Bulletin*, January 4, 1931, Box 181, Pershing MSS, LOC Manuscript Division.

40 Link, *Confusion and Crises*, p. 51.

41 Garrison to Wilson, *PWW*, vol. 35, p. 469.

42 *PWW*, vol. 36, p. 36.

43 *Literary Digest* (February 5, 1916), vol. 52, p. 269.

44 *Literary Digest* (March 18, 1916), vol. 52, p. 701.

45 Palmer, *Newton D. Baker: America at War*, vol. 1, p. 8.

46 Thomas Knock, *To End All Wars: Woodrow Wilson and the Quest for a New World Order* (New York: Oxford University Press, 1992), p. 82.

47 Paxson, *American Democracy and the World War*, vol. 1, pp. 295–96.

48 Weigley, *History of the United States Army*, p. 346.

49 Quoted in Link, *Confusion and Crises*, p. 329.

50 *Ibid.*, p. 330.

51 Weigley, *History of the United States Army*, p. 568.

52 *Literary Digest* (May 27, 1916), vol. 52, p. 1520.

53 *US Statutes at Large*, vol. 39, pt. 2, p. 185.

54 *Ibid.*, pp. 197–98.

55 *Literary Digest* (May 27, 1916), vol. 52, p. 1571.

56 *Ibid.*, p. 207.

57 *US Statutes at Large*, vol. 39, pt. 2, p. 198.

58 *Literary Digest* (March 4, 1916), vol. 52, p. 548.

59 See Coffman, *War to End All Wars*, p. 17 and Link, *Confusion and Crises*, p. 332.

60 *US Statutes at Large*, vol. 39, pt. 2, p. 213.

61 Paxson, *American Democracy and the World War*, vol. 1, pp. 304–05, 403 and David Kennedy, *Over Here: The First World War and American Society* (New York: Oxford University Press, 1980), pp. 114–17.

62 Weigley, *History of the United States Army*, p. 350.

63 Link, *Confusion and Crises*, p. 332.

64 Peyton March, *The Nation at War* (Garden City, NY: Doubleday, Doran & Co., Inc., 1932), p. 241.

65 Palmer, *Newton D. Baker: America at War*, vol. 1, p. 145.
66 *Literary Digest* (May 27, 1916), vol. 52, p. 1521.
67 John Pershing, *My Experiences in the World War* (New York: Frederick A. Stokes Co., 1931), vol. 1, pp. 8–9.
68 *Statutes at Large*, vol. 49, pt. 2, pp. 167–69.
69 "Comments on Pershing's Book," Box 3, Nolan MSS, AHEC; March, *Nation at War*, p. 19.
70 Finnegan, *Specter of the Dragon*, pp. 33–34.
71 Liggett, *AEF Ten Years Ago in France*, pp. 21–22.
72 Robert Ferrell, *America's Deadliest Battle: Meuse-Argonne, 1918* (Lawrence: University Press of Kansas, 2007), p. 12.

NOTES TO CHAPTER 3

1 Link, *Confusion and Crises*, p. 111.
2 See Fritz Fischer, *Germany's Aims in the First World War* (New York: W. W. Norton & Co., 1967), pp. 103–04.
3 Charles Seymour (ed.), *The Intimate Papers of Colonel House* (Boston, Mass.: Houghton Mifflin, 1926–28), vol. 2, pp. 201–02.
4 Memoranda by Grey to Bertie, February 17 and 22, 1916, FO 800/181, NA.
5 War Committee, February 22, 1916, CAB 42/9/3.
6 *Literary Digest* (April 1, 1916), vol. 52, pp. 884–85.
7 *PWW*, vol. 36, p. 321.
8 Squier, "Memorandum for the Ambassador, Subject: Interview with Field Marshal Earl Kitchener, Secretary of State for War, London, April 27, 1916," Baker Papers.
9 "A Colloquy with a Group of Antipreparedness Leaders," May 8, 1916, *PWW*, vol. 36, p. 644.
10 *PWW*, vol. 37, p. 116.
11 "A Colloquy with a Group of Antipreparedness Leaders," May 8, 1916, *PWW*, vol. 36, p. 646.
12 Spring Rice to Balfour, January 19, 1917, Balfour MSS, BL Add. 49740.
13 *PWW*, vol. 37, p. 126.
14 Quoted in Arthur Link, *Wilson: Campaigns for Progressivism and Peace, 1916–1917* (Princeton, NJ: Princeton University Press, 1965), p. 24.
15 Justus Doenecke, *Nothing Less Than War: A New History of America's Entry into World War I* (Lexington: University Press of Kentucky, 2011), p. 205.
16 See Fischer, *Germany's Aims in the First World War*.
17 Holger Herwig, *The First World War: Germany and Austria–Hungary, 1914–1918* (New York: St. Martin's Press, 1997), p. 229.
18 See *ibid.*, pp. 312–15 and David Woodward, *World War I Almanac* (New York: Facts on File, 2009), p. 165.
19 Quoted in Lane, *Armed Progressive*, p. 210.
20 Chambers, *To Raise an Army*, p. 129.
21 *PWW*, vol. 41, p. 87; Link, *Wilson: Campaigns for Progressivism and Peace*, p. 398.
22 *PWW*, vol. 41, pp. 111–12.

23 Chambers, *To Raise an Army*, p. 130.
24 Link, *Wilson: Campaigns for Progressivism and Peace*, p. 309; Lane, *Armed Progressive*, p. 211.
25 Nenninger, "American Military Effectiveness," p. 118.
26 *PWW*, vol. 40, pp. 67–70.
27 *PWW*, vol. 31, pp. 227–28; Daniel Beaver, *Baker and the American War Effort* (Lincoln: University of Nebraska Press, 1966), pp. 25–26.
28 Quoted in Link, *Campaigns for Progressivism and Peace*, vol. 5, p. 414.
29 Barbara Tuchman, *The Zimmermann Telegram* (New York: Macmillan, 1966), p. 183.
30 *PWW*, vol. 41, pp. 436–44.
31 Ferrell, *Woodrow Wilson and World War I*, p. 14.
32 David Woodward (ed.), *Military Correspondence of Field Marshal Sir William Robertson: Chief of the Imperial General Staff, December 1915–February 1918* (London: Bodley Head, 1989), p. 149.
33 Quoted in James Rainey, "The Questionable Training of the AEF in World War I," *Parameters: Journal of the US Army War College* 22 (1992–93): 89.
34 See Kathleen Burk, *Britain, America and the Sinews of War, 1914–1918* (Boston, Mass.: Allen & Unwin, 1985); *PWW*, vol. 41, p. 442; Ferrell, *Woodrow Wilson and World War I*, p. 87.
35 *PWW*, vol. 41, p. 522.
36 *Ibid.*, p. 525.
37 *Ibid.*, pp. 557–58.
38 Doenecke, *Nothing Less than War*, p. 297.
39 *Ibid.*, p. 294.
40 *Literary Digest* (April 14, 1917), vol. 54, pp. 1046–47.
41 March, *Nation at War*, p. 1.
42 Quoted in Mark Sullivan, *Our Times: The United States, 1900–1925*, vol. 5, *Over Here, 1914–1918* (New York: Charles Scribner's Sons, 1933), p. 497.
43 Quoted *ibid.*, p. 496.
44 Chambers, *To Raise an Army*, pp. 134–44.
45 *Literary Digest* (April 21, 1917), vol. 54, p. 1147.
46 Congressional Record, 65th Cong., 1st Sess. (April 27, 1917), pp. 1354–58, 1360.
47 Jerry Cooper, "The National Guard Mobilizations of 1916 and 1917," in Steven Weingartner (ed.), *Cantigny at Seventy-Five* (Chicago, Ill.: Robert R. McCormick Tribune Foundation, 1994), p. 50.
48 The age limit for the first registration drive was between the ages of 21 and 30 (later raised to 31 in the second registration drive). Ayres, *War with Germany*, p. 19.

NOTES TO CHAPTER 4

1 Ronald Schaffer, *America in the Great War: The Rise of the War Welfare State* (New York: Oxford University Press, 1991), pp. 3–10.
2 Sullivan, *Our Times*, vol. 5, p. 298.
3 See Chambers, *To Raise an Army*, p. 184 and Woodward, *Almanac*, p. 200.

4 Schaffer, *America in the Great War*, pp. 10–12.

5 *Literary Digest* (June 16, 1917), vol. 54, p. 1831.

6 *Second Report of the Provost Marshal General to the Secretary of War on the Operations of the Selective Service System to December 20, 1918* (Washington, DC: Government Printing Office, 1919), p. 199.

7 Meirion Harries and Susie Harries, *Last Days of Innocence: America at War, 1917–1918* (New York: Vintage Books, 1998), p. 97.

8 *Second Report of the Provost Marshal*, pp. 199–203.

9 [Editorial staff of *Review of Reviews*], *Two Thousand Questions and Answers about the War* (New York: The Review of Reviews Co., 1918), p. 233.

10 See Chambers, *To Raise an Army*, p. 186 n. 15. See also Jennifer Keene, *Doughboys, the Great War, and the Remaking of America* (Baltimore, Md.: Johns Hopkins University Press, 2001), pp. 18–19.

11 Coffman, *War to End All Wars*, pp. 62–63.

12 Weigley, *History of the United States Army*, p. 358.

13 Mark Meigs, *Optimism at Armageddon: Voices of American Participants in the First World War* (New York: New York University Press, 1997), p. 14. Edward A. Gutierrez offers a quite different interpretation. He focuses on soldiers' attitudes immediately after they returned from Europe and concludes that "as a whole, the men of the AEF whether they belonged to the Regular Army, enlisted or waited to be drafted, were ready to serve the United States to attain their manhood": "'Sherman Was Right': The Experience of AEF Soldiers in the Great War," Ph.D. diss. Ohio State University, 2008, p. 64.

14 Meigs, *Optimism at Armageddon*, p. 232.

15 Chambers, *To Raise an Army*, pp. 185–86.

16 Palmer, *Newton D. Baker: America at War*, vol. 1, p. 255; Coffman, *War to End All Wars*, p. 31.

17 "An Account of my Personal Experiences in World War I," April 1, 1963, *WWIS*.

18 March, *Nation at War*, p. 8.

19 Henderson Diary, *WWIS*.

20 "An Account of my Personal Experience in World War I," April 1, 1963, *WWIS*.

21 *WWIS*.

22 *WWIS*.

23 Blaser to brother, April 2, 1918, *WWIS*.

24 Quoted in Keene, *Doughboys*, p. 12.

25 *WWIS*.

26 *Infantry Drill Regulations, US Army, 1911, with text corrections to February 1917. Changes No. 18* (New York: Military Publishing Co., 1917).

27 "An Account of my Personal Experience in World War I," April 1, 1963, *WWIS*.

28 Sullivan, *Our Times*, vol. 5, p. 322.

29 Beaver, *Modernizing the American War Department*, p. 90.

30 *WWIS*.

31 Aitken to mother, April 16, 1918, *WWIS*.

32 *WWIS*.

33 Weigley, *History of the United States Army*, p. 371.
34 Ayres, *War with Germany*, p. 25.
35 Dennis Gordon (ed.), *Quartered in Hell: The Story of American North Russian Expeditionary Force, 1918–1919* (Missoula, Mont.: Doughboy Historical Society and GOS, Inc., 1982), p. 36.
36 *WWIS*.
37 *WWIS*.
38 Weigley, *History of the United States Army*, p. 357.
39 Keene, *Doughboys*, p. 2.
40 Quoted in Schaffer, *America in the Great War*, p. 178.
41 Nancy Ford, *Americans All: Foreign-Born Soldiers in World War I* (College Station: Texas A&M University Press, 2001), p. 9.
42 *Ibid.*, p. 10.
43 *Ibid.*, p. 138.
44 *Ibid.*, p. 109.
45 Entry of May 20, 1918, in C. Callwell (ed.), *Field-Marshal Sir Henry Wilson: His Life and Diaries* (London: Cassell & Co. Ltd., 1927), vol. 2, p. 101.
46 Quoted in Ford, *Americans All*, p. 3.
47 Mark Stout, "World War I and the Invention of American Intelligence," Ph.D. diss., University of Leeds, 2010, p. 123.
48 *Ibid.*, pp. 122–55.
49 *WWIS*.
50 Meigs, *Optimism at Armageddon*, pp. 13–15.
51 Woodward, *Almanac*, p. 313.
52 "Study of the Cost of the Army of the United States as Compared with the Cost of the Armies of Other Nations," WCD 9053–120, p. 15.
53 K. Walter Hickel, "War, Region and Social Welfare: Federal Aid to Servicemen's Dependants in the South, 1917–1921," *Journal of American History* 87 (March 2001): 1370.
54 See also Ferrell, *Woodrow Wilson and World War I*, p. 19.
55 Paxson, *American Democracy and the World War*, vol. 2, p. 208.
56 Kennedy, *Over Here*, p. 188.
57 Coffman, *War to End All Wars*, p. 61.
58 Jennifer Keene, *World War I: The American Soldier Experience* (Lincoln: University of Nebraska Press, 2011), pp. 46–47.
59 Howard Anderson, Company A, 34th Infantry Regiment, 4th Division, *WWIS*.
60 See Baker to Wilson, April 2, 1917, *PWW*, vol. 41, p. 527.
61 Quoted in Coffman, *The Regulars*, p. 80.
62 Quoted in Palmer, *Newton D. Baker: America at War*, vol. 1, p. 311.
63 *Literary Digest* (June 16, 1917), vol. 54, p. 1852.
64 Schaffer, *America in the Great War*, p. 101.
65 March, *Nation at War*, p. 236.
66 Donald Smythe, *Pershing: General of the Armies* (Bloomington: Indiana University Press, 1986), p. 251; see also Alexander, *Memories*, p. 305.
67 March, *Nation at War*, pp. 214–15.
68 *WWIS*.

69 George C. Marshall, *Memoirs of My Services in the World War, 1917–1918* (Boston, Mass.: Houghton Mifflin, 1976), p. 64.

70 Douglas Johnson, "A Few Squads Left and Off to France: Training the American Army in the United States for World War I," Ph.D. diss., Temple University, 1992, p. 246.

71 Thomas Lonergan, *It Might Have Been Lost: A Chronicle From Alien Sources of the Struggle to Preserve the National Identity of the AEF* (New York: G. P. Putnam's Sons, 1929), Appendix No. 7, p. 281.

NOTES TO CHAPTER 5

1 For the inadequate instruction in these officer training camps for modern warfare, see Richard S. Faulkner, *The School of Hard Knocks: Combat Leadership in the American Expeditionary Forces* (College Station: Texas A&M University Press, 2012), pp. 99–139.

2 Ayres, *War with Germany*, p. 31.

3 IWM 77/132/1.

4 Mark Grotelueschen, *AEF Way of War: The American Army and Combat in World War I* (Cambridge: Cambridge University Press, 2007), p. 284.

5 *WWIS*.

6 Alexander, *Memories*, p. 2.

7 David Herrmann, *The Arming of Europe and the Making of the First World War* (Princeton, NJ: Princeton University Press, 1996), p. 22.

8 Quoted in Robert Doughty, *Pyrrhic Victory: French Strategy and Operations in the Great War* (Cambridge, Mass.: The Belknap Press of Harvard University Press, 2005), p. 26.

9 *Ibid.*, pp. 27–28 and John Terraine, *White Heat: The New Warfare, 1914–1918* (London: Sidgwick & Jackson, 1982), pp. 70–71.

10 Paddy Griffith, *Battle Tactics of the Western Front: The British Army's Art of Attack, 1916–1918* (New Haven, Conn.: Yale University Press, 1994), p. 49.

11 *Ibid.* See also John English and Bruce Gudmundsson, *On Infantry*, rev. edn. (Westport, Conn.: Praeger, 1994), pp. 1–13.

12 See Beckett, *Great War*, p. 165.

13 US War Department, *1914 Field Service Regulations, with text corrections to December 1916* (Washington, DC: Government Printing Office, 1917), p. 68.

14 US War Department, *1911 Infantry Drill Regulations, with text corrections to February 1917* (Washington, DC: Government Printing Office, 1917), miscellaneous note 575.

15 Mark Grotelueschen, *Doctrine Under Trial: American Artillery Employment in World War I* (Westport, Conn.: Greenwood Press, 2001), p. 5.

16 See Beckett, *Great War*, p. 165.

17 Grotelueschen, *Doctrine Under Trial*, p. 138.

18 Beaver, *Modernizing the American War Department*, pp. 64–65.

19 Grotelueschen, *AEF Way of War*, p. 13.

20 *Ibid.*, pp. 10–25.

21 US War Department, *1914 Field Service Regulations* (Washington, DC: Government Printing Office, 1914), pp. 68, 75.

22 Terraine, *White Heat*, p. 90.

23 Griffith, *Battle Tactics*, pp. 29–30.

24 Quoted in Woodward, *Almanac*, pp. 86–87; English and Gudmundson, *On Infantry*, p. 2; Robin Neillands, *The Death of Glory: The Western Front 1915* (London: John Murray, 2006), pp. 250–54.

25 See especially Tim Travers, *How the War was Won: Command and Technology in the British Army on the Western Front, 1917–1918* (New York: Routledge, 1992).

26 Doughty, *Pyrrhic Victory*, pp. 250–51.

27 Tim Travers, *The Killing Ground: The British Army, the Western Front, and the Emergence of Modern Warfare, 1900–1918* (Boston, Mass.: Allen & Unwin, 1987), pp. 132–46.

28 "Notes as to the Battle West of Serre on the morning of 1st July 1916, by Brigadier General H. C. Rees, DSO, temporarily Commanding 94th Infantry Brigade, 31st Division," LHCMA, Robertson MSS, 1/35/65.

29 John Keegan, *The Face of Battle: A Study of Agincourt, Waterloo and the Somme* (New York: Vintage Books, 1977), pp. 277–78.

30 See Travers, *Killing Ground*, pp. 152–66 and Robin Prior and Trevor Wilson, *Command on the Western Front* (Oxford: Blackwell Publishers, 1992), pp. 154–70.

31 Doughty, *Pyrrhic Victory*, pp. 293–94.

32 See R. Foley, "Learning War's Lessons: The German Army and the Battle of the Somme 1916," *Journal of Military History* 75 (2011): 498.

33 Griffith, *Battle Tactics*, p. 33.

34 March, *Nation at War*, p. 269.

35 Douglas Johnson and Rolfe Hillman, *Soissons 1918* (College Station: Texas A&M University Press, 1999), p. 23.

NOTES TO CHAPTER 6

1 Palmer, *Newton D. Baker: America at War*, vol. 2, p. 120.

2 Reports by Davis of November 17, 18, 27, and December 18, 1916, RG 165/9910-1, 2, 3.

3 See *ibid*. See also Ronald Spector, "You're Not Going to Send Soldiers Over There Are You!" *Military Affairs* 36 (1972): 1–4.

4 Kuhn to Davis, February 5, 1917, RG 165/9910-6.

5 Memorandum by Kuhn, February 3, 1917, RG 165/9433-4.

6 See "A Study of Conditions Affecting Possible Operations in the Macedonian Theater in Case of War with Germany," and "Study of the Possibility of Holland becoming involved in the Present European War, through the Sinking of Her Ships in the North Sea, and Permitting the Invasion of France in rear of the Western German Army," and covering memorandum by Kuhn, March 29, 1917, RG 165/10050-6.

7 Quoted in Doughty, *Pyrrhic Victory*, p. 339.

8 J. Harris, *Douglas Haig and the First World War* (Cambridge: Cambridge University Press, 2008), p. 326.

9 War Cabinet (103), March 23, 1917, CAB 23/2.
10 General Staff Memorandum, February 5, 1917, WO 106/467.
11 Balfour MSS, FO 800/208.
12 Quoted in Robert Bruce, *A Fraternity of Arms: America and France in the Great War* (Lawrence: University Press of Kansas, 2003), p. 38.
13 Repington to Robertson, April 10, 1917, in A. Morris (ed.), *Letters of Lieutenant-Colonel Charles à Court Repington: Military Correspondent of The Times, 1903–1918* (Stroud: Sutton Publishing Limited, 1999), pp. 265–66.
14 Box 121, House MSS, fol. 4274.
15 Spring Rice to Balfour Mission, April 13, 1917, Balfour MSS, FO 800/208.
16 General Sir William Robertson to Field-Marshal Sir Douglas Haig, April 10, 1917, NLS Acc. 3155, no. 112, Haig MSS.
17 Bridges to Scott, April 30, 1917, WO 106/467.
18 Robertson to Haig, April 10, 1917, NLS Acc. 3155, no. 112, Haig MSS.
19 Bridges to Scott, April 30, 1917, WO 106/467.
20 Bridges to Robertson, April 29, 1917, Balfour MSS, FO 800/208.
21 Robertson to Hankey, May 18, 1917, WO 106/311.
22 Bridges to Robertson, April 29, 1917, Balfour MSS, FO 800/208.
23 Memorandum by Percy, April 4, 1917, Balfour MSS, FO 800/208.
24 Charles Repington, *The First World War, 1914–1918* (London: Constable and Co., 1920), vol. 1, p. 31; Tom Bridges, *Alarms & Excursions: Reminiscences of a Soldier* (London: Longmans, Green, 1938), p. 175.
25 Bruce, *Fraternity of Arms*, pp. 43–44.
26 Quoted *ibid.*, p. 39.
27 Notes by Bliss relating to Roosevelt–Baker correspondence, n.d., but apparently April 1917. Baker MSS.
28 See War College Division memoranda of May 10 and 11, 1917. RG 165/10050-8.
29 Minutes of conference with Baker, May 14, 1917, transmitted to French Ministry of War, Department of the Army (Historical Division), *United States Army in the World War, 1917–1919*, vol. 2, p. 5.
30 Bridges to Robertson, May 3, 1917, WO 106/467.
31 Bruce, *Fraternity of Arms*, pp. 58–59.
32 Baker to Wilson, May 8, 1917 and Wilson to Baker, May 10, 1917, Baker MSS.
33 Moore to House, May 17, 1917 and Wilson to Baker, May 23, 1917, *PWW*, vol. 52, pp. 373–74, 377.
34 Baker MSS.
35 *PWW*, vol. 52, pp. 498–504.
36 Memorandum by Kuhn, June 7, 1917, RG 165/10050-30.
37 Bliss to Baker, May 25, 1917, confidential copy for Pershing, Box 123, Pershing MSS, LOC Manuscript Division.
38 B. Liddell Hart, *Reputation: Ten Years After* (London: John Murray, 1928), p. 289.
39 James Harbord, *American Army in France, 1917–1918* (Boston, Mass.: Little, Brown, 1936), p. 46.

40 Quoted in Richard Goldhurst, *Pipe and Clay and Drill: John J. Pershing. The Classic American Soldier* (New York: Reader's Digest Press, 1977), p. 133. See also Smythe, *Pershing: General of the Armies*, p. 2.

41 Robert Bullard, *Personalities and Reminiscences of the War* (Garden City, NY: Doubleday, 1925), p. 46.

42 James Harbord, *American Army in France*, p. 35.

43 Frank Vandiver, *Black Jack: The Life and Times of John J. Pershing* (College Station: Texas A&M University Press, 1977), vol. 2, p. 673.

44 Pershing to Mrs. Dickens, April 29, 1917, Box 64, Pershing MSS, LOC Manuscript Division.

45 Vandiver, *Black Jack*, vol. 2, p. 676.

46 Quoted in March, *Nation at War*, p. 68.

47 Pershing, *My Experiences*, vol. 1, p. 37.

48 Baker to Pershing, May 26, *PWW*, vol. 52, pp. 404–05; Palmer, *Newton D. Baker: America at War*, vol. 1, p. 170; Pershing, *My Experiences*, vol. 1, pp. 38–40.

49 Frederick Palmer, *Pershing: General of the Armies. A Biography* (Harrisburg, Pa.: Military Service Publishing, 1948), p. 84.

50 Palmer, *Newton D. Baker: America at War*, vol. 1, p. 180.

51 *Ibid.*, p. 159.

52 J. Cooke, *Pershing and his Generals: Command and Staff in the AEF* (Westport, Conn.: Praeger, 1977), p. 6. Pershing's initial headquarters consisted of 59 General Staff officers and other officers, 56 clerks, 67 guards and orderlies, and 4 interpreters, a total of 186 men. By the end of the war GHQ had grown to 4,271 men. "General Staff at General Headquarters," June 30, 1919, *USAWW*, pt. 1, vol. 12, pp. 90–93.

53 James Harbord, *Leaves from a War Diary* (New York: Dodd, Mead, 1925), p. 18.

54 Quoted in Millett, "Cantigny, 28–31 May 1918," p. 155.

55 Memorandum by Kuhn, April 13, 1917, RG 165/9433-24.

56 Memorandum by Bridges, June 14, 1917, War Policy Committee (5), CAB 27/7.

57 Smythe, *Pershing: General of the Armies*, p. 14; Pershing, *My Experiences*, vol. 1, p. 83.

58 Slocum to War Department, April 27, 1917, RG 165/10050-9.

59 Quoted in Repington, *First World War*, vol. 1, p. 584. See also translation of telegram from Major James A. Logan (US military attaché in Paris), May 17, 1917, RG 165/10050-19; Bridges to Scott, April 30, 1917, WO 106/467.

60 Quoted in Smythe, *Pershing: General of the Armies*, p. 239.

61 Allan Millett, "Over Where? The AEF and the American Strategy for Victory, 1917–1918," in Kenneth J. Hagan and William R. Roberts (eds.), *Against All Enemies: Interpretations of American Military History from Colonial Times to the Present* (Westport, Conn.: Greenwood Press, 1986), p. 238.

62 Memorandum by Pershing, dated September 3, 1917 on reverse, G-3, GHQ, AEF, Secret General Correspondence, File 1003, No. 681, Pt. 2, Box 3112, RG 120.

63 "A Strategical Study on Employment of the AEF against the Imperial German Government, September 25, 1917," p. 1, Box 15, Drum MSS, AHEC.

64 Prepared by Fox Conner, LeRoy Eltinge, and Hugh Drum, G-3, GHQ, AEF, Secret General Correspondence, File 1003, No. 681, Pt. 2, Box 3112, RG 120.

65 *Ibid.* and "A Strategical Study on Employment of the AEF against the Imperial German Government, September 25, 1917, pp. 1–2, Box 15, Drum MSS, AHEC.

66 "A Strategical Study on Employment of the AEF against the Imperial German Government, September 25, 1917," p. 1, Box 15, Drum MSS, AHEC.

67 Millett, "Over Where?," p. 227.

68 The first American soldiers to reach Europe, a group composed of medical staff and orderlies, had arrived in England on May 18, 1917. Martin Gilbert, *First World War: A Complete History* (New York: Henry Holt and Co., Inc., 1994), p. 333.

69 Frederick Palmer, *America in France: The Story of the Making of an Army* (New York: Dodd, Mead, 1918), pp. 26–27.

70 See William L. Sibert, Commanding General, 1st Division, to Commanding General, 47th Division, French Army, July 18, 1917, *USAWW*, vol. 21, p. 426.

71 Marshall, *Memoirs of My Services*, p. 12.

72 Smythe, *Pershing: General of the Armies*, p. 30.

73 Pershing, *My Experiences*, vol. 1, p. 92.

74 "A Strategical Study on Employment of the AEF against the Imperial German Government, September 25, 1917, p. 20, Box 15, Drum MSS, AHEC.

75 Harbord, *American Army in France*, p. 82.

NOTES TO CHAPTER 7

1 Pershing, *My Experiences*, p. 78. See also Harbord, *American Army in France*, pp. 90–91.

2 See Bruce, *Fraternity of Arms*, pp. 108–09.

3 Robert Dalessandro and Michael Knapp, *Organization and Insignia of the American Expeditionary Force, 1917–1923* (Atglen, Pa.: Schiffer Publishing Ltd., 2008), p. 10.

4 Keene, *Doughboys*, p. 39.

5 Pershing's cable, July 6, 1917, *USAWW*, vol. 2, p. 17 and "Report on Organization," July 10, 1917, *USAWW*, vol. 1, p. 93.

6 Harbord, *American Army in France*, p. 101.

7 Smythe, *Pershing: General of the Armies*, p. 36.

8 See Baker Report, received by the War Department on July 26, 1917, *USAWW*, vol. 1, pp. 55–89.

9 See "Memorandum of a Conference on Organization and Equipment," July 11, 1917, *USAWW*, vol. 1, pp. 107–14.

10 Australian and Canadian Divisions, fighting with the BEF, had a total strength of some 21,000 men. See Grotelueschen, *AEF Way of War*, p. 27 n. 42.

11 March, *Nation at War*, p. 250.

12 Nenninger, "American Military Effectiveness in the First World War," p. 150.

13 John Votaw, *The American Expeditionary Forces in World War I* (Oxford: Osprey Publishing Ltd., 2005), p. 32.

14 Harbord, *American Army in France*, p. 103.

15 Johnson and Hillman, *Soissons 1918*, p. 26.

16 Faulkner, *School of Hard Knocks*, p. 167.

17 Alexander said he reduced his companies to 185 men but other commanders reduced their companies to 175. *Memories*, p. 263.

18 Griffith, *Battle Tactics*, p. 43.

19 Alexander, *Memories*, p. 45.

20 Quoted in Harbord, *American Army in France*, p. 101.

21 *USAWW*, vol. 1, p. 68.

22 *Ibid.*, pp. 112–13.

23 Grotelueschen, *AEF Way of War*, p. 38. See also his *Doctrine Under Fire*, p. 10.

24 March, *Nation at War*, p. 3.

25 Beaver, *Modernizing the American War Department*, pp. 83–86.

26 Edward Lengel, *To Conquer Hell: The Meuse-Argonne, 1918. The Epic Battle that Ended the First World War* (New York: Henry Holt and Co., 2008), p. 35.

27 "The General Principles Governing the Training of Units of the American Expeditionary Force," General Headquarters, AEF, April 9, 1918, *USAWW*, vol. 2, p. 296.

28 Quoted in Smythe, "John J. Pershing: A Study in Paradox," *Military Review* 49 (1969): 66.

29 Sibert to Commanding General of the French 47th Infantry Division, July 18, 1917, *USAWW*, vol. 21, p. 426.

30 Keene, *Doughboys*, p. 68.

31 "The General Principles Governing the Training of Units of the American Expeditionary Forces," April 9, 1918, *USAWW*, vol. 2, p. 296.

32 *WWIS*.

33 Gerard Oram, *Military Executions during World War I* (New York: Palgrave, 2004), p. 3.

34 Pershing, *My Experiences*, vol. 1, p. 150.

35 Diary entry, February 8, 1918, Walser MSS, IWM 80/25/1.

36 Letter home, November 1, 1917, *ibid.*

37 Frampton Diary, Special Collections, Marshall University Library; Faulkner, *School of Hard Knocks*, pp. 9, 67.

38 Entries of October 2–3, 1917, Frampton Diary, Special Collections, Marshall University Library.

39 R. Bullard, *Personalities and Reminiscences*, p. 59.

40 Entries of October 6–November 8, 1917, Frampton Diary, Special Collections, Marshall University Library.

41 Entries of November 13, 1917–March 12, 1918, *ibid.*

42 Ragueneau to commander-in-chief of the armies of the north and northeast (Cabinet), March 6, 1918, Box 15, Drum MSS, AHEC.

43 *USAWW*, vol. 2, p. 296.
44 Extract of a memorandum by Pétain, May 1, 1918, *USAWW*, vol. 21, p. 292.
45 Memorandum for [AEF] Chief of Staff from Colonel Harold B. Fiske, July 4, 1918, *ibid.*, pp. 330–31.
46 *WWIS.*
47 Extract of a memorandum by Pétain, May 1, 1918, *USAWW*, vol. 21, p. 294.
48 Harbord, *American Army in France*, pp. 149–50.
49 War Cabinet (300), December 1917, CAB 23/4.
50 Harbord, *American Army in France*, p. 150.
51 Quoted in Johnson, "A Few Squads Left," pp. 169–70. See also Paul Braim, *The Test of Battle*, 2nd edn. (Shippensburg, Pa.: White Mane Books, 1998), p. 31.
52 See Griffith, *Battle Tactics*, p. 62.
53 Herwig, *First World War: Germany and Austria–Hungary*, pp. 399–400.
54 Erich von Ludendorff, *Ludendorff's Own Story: August 1914–November 1918*, 2 vols. (New York: Harper Brothers Publishers, 1919), vol. 2, p. 201. See also Hubert Johnson, *Breakthrough Tactics, Technology and the Search for Victory on the Western Front in World War I* (Novato, Calif.: Presidio Press, 1994), pp. 217–23.
55 Grotelueschen, *AEF Way of War*, pp. 53–55.
56 Johnson, "A Few Squads Left," p. 247.
57 "Training," July 4, 1918, *USAWW*, vol. 21, pp. 330–31.
58 Baker to House, July 18, 1917, Baker MSS.

NOTES TO CHAPTER 8

1 Cabinet Paper GT 1549 of July 29, 1917, CAB 24/21.
2 W. Bruce Lincoln, *Passage through Armageddon: The Russians in War and Revolution* (Oxford: Oxford University Press, 1986), p. 411.
3 Doughty, *Pyrrhic Victory*, pp. 361–66.
4 Quoted *ibid.*, p. 366.
5 Pershing, *My Experiences*, vol. 1, p. 233.
6 Military Conference of July 26 (attended by Cadorna, Robertson, Pershing, Pétain, and Foch) and "Addendum to the Military Conference of July 26th," Cabinet Paper GT 1533 of July 26, CAB 24/21.
7 Robertson, "Policy to Adopt Should Russia Be Forced Out of the War," Report of Military Conference on July 26, covering note by CIGS, July 26, *ibid.*
8 Steven Roskill (ed.), *Hankey: Man of Secrets*, vol. 1, *1877–1918* (London: Collins, 1970), p. 418.
9 Lloyd George to President Wilson, September 3, 1917, Lloyd George MSS, F/60/1/1.
10 Maurice (DMO) to Colonel Edward Spiers, French War Ministry, Paris, October 3, 1917, and Brigadier General James Douglas McLachlan (military attaché in Washington) to War Office, October 5, 1917, WO 106/468.
11 Memorandum enclosed in Wilson to Baker, September 22, 1917, Baker MSS.
12 Entry of September 16, 1917, House Diary, *PWW*, vol. 44, p. 203.

13 Baker to Wilson, September 22, 1917, *PWW*, vol. 44, p. 239; Colonel P. D. Lochridge (Acting Chief of the War College Division), "Memorandum for Committee Consisting of the Chairman of the War College Division Committee," September 22, 1917, RG 165/10050-111.

14 "Possible line of action from the head of the Persian Gulf," September 25, 1917, App. III. This appreciation was included in Lochridge, "Strategy of the present war," n.d., along with "Possible lines of action in the Eastern Mediterranean," September 28, 1917, App. I, and "Possible line of action through Russia," n.d., App. II, RG 165/10050-111.

15 Colonel F. S. Young, "Strategy of the present war. Line of advance through Russia," September 28, 1917, RG 165/10050-111.

16 Russell Weigley, *The American Way of War: A History of United States Military Strategy and Policy* (New York: Macmillan Publishing Co., Inc., 1973), p. xxi.

17 Wilson to Baker, October 4, 1917, Baker MSS.

18 Wilson to Baker, November 20, 1917, Baker MSS.

19 Bliss to War Department, sent December 4, received December 5, 1917, Baker MSS; Pershing, *My Experiences*, vol. 2, p. 105.

20 Smythe, *Pershing: General of the Armies*, p. 63; Conner to Harbord, November 6, 1917, *USAWW*, vol. 2, p. 68.

21 Wilson to Baker, n.d., Baker MSS.

22 WP 62, October 26, 1917, CAB 27/8.

23 Haig, "Memorandum on the Question of an Extension of the British Front," Manpower Committee (21), December 15, 1917, CAB 27/14.

24 War Cabinet (282), November 26, 1917, CAB 23/4.

25 Hankey, "Future Military Policy," November 24, 1917, Hankey MSS, CAB 63/23.

26 Wilson to House, November 16, 1917, *PWW*, vol. 45, p. 69.

27 WO 106/407.

28 Bliss to Mrs. Bliss, November 8, 1917, Box 244, Bliss MSS.

29 Cabinet Paper GT 2755 of November 23, 1917, CAB 24/33; War College Division, "Statement of the General Staff Plan for the Organization and Dispatch of Troops to Europe," October 1917, RG 165/100050-119.

30 Beaver, *Modernizing the American War Department*, p. 145.

31 Major Fulton Q. C. Gardner, "Memorandum for Colonel Lochridge. Subject: General Bliss Cablegram of December 4th," December 21, 1917, RG 165/6576-23.

32 Bliss to Baker, December 23, 1917, RG 165/6291-60.

33 Bliss, "Report of the Representative of the War Department," December 14, 1917, Department of State, *Papers Relating to the Foreign Relations of the United States, 1917*, supplement 2, vol. 1, p. 388.

34 *Ibid.*, pp. 390–91.

35 Benson, "Report of the Representative of the Navy Department," December 14, 1917, *ibid.*, p. 386.

36 House, "Report of the Special Representative of the United States Government," December 15, 1917, *ibid.*, pp. 356–57.

37 Baker to Wilson, note to Pershing enclosed, December 18, 1917, *PWW*, vol. 45, p. 328.

38 Fox Conner, "Strategical Study Directed by the Chief of Staff," January 7, 1918, G-3, GHQ, AEF, Secret General Correspondence, No. 681, Pt. 4, Box 3112, RG 120.

NOTES TO CHAPTER 9

1 Doughty, *Pyrrhic Victory*, p. 394.
2 WC (302), December 19, 1917, CAB 23/4.
3 See Doughty, *Pyrrhic Victory*, p. 406; Harris, *Douglas Haig*, p. 418.
4 Lloyd George's minute on "Extracts from Sir W. Robertson's Memo," November 19, 1917, Lloyd George MSS, F/162/3.
5 Note by Lord Milner, June 7, 1917, WC (159A), June 8, 1917, CAB 23/16.
6 Milner to Lloyd George, November 3, 1917, Lloyd George MSS, F/38/2/20.
7 War Cabinet (351A), February 21, 1918, CAB 23/13; see also David French, *The Strategy of the Lloyd George Coalition, 1916–1918* (Oxford: Clarendon Press, 1995), pp. 187–92 and David Woodward, *Trial by Friendship: Anglo-American Relations, 1917–1918* (Lexington: University Press of Kentucky, 1993), pp. 130–48.
8 French, *Strategy of Lloyd George Coalition*, p. 184.
9 *Ibid.*, p. 190.
10 Doughty, *Pyrrhic Victory*, p. 404.
11 *Ibid.*, p. 423.
12 Baker to Wilson, note to Pershing enclosed, December 18, 1918, *PWW*, vol. 45, p. 328.
13 Pershing, *My Experiences*, vol. 1, p. 272.
14 Note from Baker, January 3, 1918, *PWW*, vol. 45, p. 438.
15 Palmer, *Newton D. Baker: America at War*, vol. 1, p. 398.
16 Manpower Committee (3), December 11, 1917, CAB 27/14.
17 See Trevor Wilson, *The Myriad Faces of War* (Cambridge: Polity Press, 1986), p. 633.
18 W. Kirke (for CIGS) to Hankey (War Cabinet), January 27, 1918, with enclosure, "Note by the French General Staff on American Military Assistance in 1918," WO 107/467.
19 French, *Strategy of Lloyd George Coalition*, p. 236.
20 Sir William Robertson, *Soldiers and Statesmen, 1914–1918* (New York: Charles Scribner's Sons, 1926), vol. 1, p. 326.
21 David Woodward, *Field Marshal Sir William Robertson: Chief of the Imperial General Staff in the Great War* (Westwood, Conn.: Praeger, 1998), pp. 158–68.
22 Robertson, *Soldiers and Statesmen*, vol. 1, pp. 329–30.
23 Account of a meeting between General Pershing, Robertson, and Maclay, shipping controller, on January 9, 1918, WO 106/466.
24 Robertson, "American Battalions for British Divisions," January 12, 1918, Lloyd George Papers, F/163/4/1.
25 Robertson to Haig, January 12, 1918, quoted in Woodward, *Military Correspondence of Robertson*, p. 270.
26 *The Times*, October 8, 1917.

27 Bullard, *Personalities and Reminiscences*, p. 83.
28 David Stevenson, *With Our Backs to the Wall: Victory and Defeat in 1918* (Cambridge, Mass.: The Belknap Press of Harvard University Press, 2011), p. 368.
29 *Literary Digest* (December 22, 1917), vol. 55, p. 4.
30 *New York Times*, December 14, 1917.
31 *Ibid.*, December 19, 1917.
32 *Ibid.*, December 22, 1917.
33 *Literary Digest* (January 12, 1918), vol. 56, p. 10.
34 Coffman, *The Regulars*, p. 97.
35 *Literary Digest* (January 12, 1918), vol. 56, p. 10.
36 *New York Times*, January 11, 1917.
37 Smythe, *Pershing: General of the Armies*, p. 233.
38 See Beaver, *Modernizing the American War Department*, pp. 162–65.
39 *New York Times*, January 20, 1918.
40 *Ibid.*, January 19, 1918.
41 Quoted from Daniels' diary, *PWW*, vol. 46, p. 41.
42 *PWW*, vol. 46, p. 55.
43 Pershing, *My Experiences*, vol. 1, p. 334.
44 Quoted in Doughty, *Pyrrhic Victory*, p. 423.
45 *Ibid.*, p. 295.
46 Quoted in John Keegan, *The First World War* (New York: Alfred A. Knopf, 1999), pp. 393–94.
47 Pershing, *My Experiences*, vol. 1, p. 308.
48 David Trask, *The AEF and Coalition Warmaking, 1917–1918* (Lawrence: University Press of Kansas, 1993), pp. 40–41.
49 Entry of January 29, 1918, Haig Diary, Acc. 3155, No. 123.
50 Wiseman to Drummond (for Balfour), February 3, 1918, Balfour MSS, BL Add. 49741.
51 Wilson to Baker, February 4, 1918, Baker MSS.
52 Pershing, *My Experiences*, vol. 1, p. 291.
53 Quoted in Bruce, *Fraternity of Arms*, p. 164.
54 Quoted in Smythe, *Pershing: General of the Armies*, p. 85.
55 Quoted in Beaver, *Baker and the American War Effort*, pp. 154–55.
56 Quoted *ibid.*, pp. 155–56.
57 Quoted in Palmer, *Newton D. Baker: America at War*, vol. 2, p. 61.
58 *Literary Digest* (January 19, 1918), vol. 56, p. 17.
59 *Ibid.* (January 26, 1918), vol. 56, p. 11.
60 For a defense of Wilson's war leadership, see Arthur Link and John Chambers, "Woodrow Wilson as Commander in Chief," in Reichard Kohn (ed.), *The United States Military under the Constitution of the United States, 1789–1989* (New York: New York University Press, 1991), pp. 317–45.
61 Quoted in Beaver, *Modernizing the American War Department*, p. 172.
62 In his biography of Baker, Palmer notes that "Baker was in full control of the War Department. Nothing is so clear as this on the evidence of the Baker files." Palmer, *Newton D. Baker: America at War*, vol. 1, pp. 370–71. See also David Woodward, "'Black Jack' Pershing: The American Pro Consul in

Europe," in Matthew Hughes and Matthew Seligman (eds.), *First World War: Personalities in Conflict* (London: Leo Cooper, 2000), pp. 141–57.
63 Beaver, *Modernizing the American War Department*, p. 78.
64 Palmer, *Newton D. Baker: America at War*, vol. 1, pp. 370–71.
65 The only record of the war cabinet's discussions is the skimpy published diary of Secretary of Navy Daniels. See Edmund Cronon (ed.), *The Cabinet Diaries of Josephus Daniels, 1913–1921* (Lincoln: University of Nebraska Press, 1963), p. 294.
66 Kendrick Clements, *The Presidency of Woodrow Wilson* (Lawrence: University Press of Kansas, 1992), p. 186.
67 Quoted in Bullard, *Personalities and Reminiscences*, pp. 23, 26, 28.
68 March, *Nation at War*, pp. 39–40.
69 Coffman, *Hilt of the Sword*, p. 54.
70 Quoted in Beaver, *Baker and the American War Effort*, p. 94.
71 Smythe, *Pershing: General of the Armies*, p. 89.
72 Beaver, *Modernizing the American War Department*, p. 101.
73 March, *Nation at War*, p. 196.
74 Beaver, *Modernizing the American War Department*, p. 103.
75 Stevenson, *Backs to the Wall*, p. 223.
76 War Cabinet (362 and 364), March 11 and 12, 1918, CAB 23/5; Doughty, *Pyrrhic Victory*, p. 429.
77 Holger Herwig, "Dynamics of Necessity: German Military Policy during the First World War," p. 102; Harris, *Douglas Haig*, p. 447. The number of British and German divisions is taken from Harris.
78 See David T. Zabecki, *Steel Wind: Colonel Georg Bruchmüller and the Birth of Modern Artillery* (Westport, Conn.: Praeger, 1995), p. 68 and Harris, *Douglas Haig*, p. 447.
79 Nicholas Perry (ed.), *Major General Oliver Nugent and the Ulster Division, 1915–1918* (Stroud: Sutton Publishing Limited for Army Records Society, 2007), p. 210.
80 Donald Goodspeed, *Ludendorff: Genius of World War I* (Boston, Mass.: Houghton Mifflin, 1966), p. 244.

NOTES TO CHAPTER 10

1 David Lloyd George, *War Memoirs of David Lloyd George* (London: Odhams Press Limited, 1938), vol. 2, p. 1820; see also figures provided by Colonel Cyril H. Wagstaff, a British liaison officer attached to Pershing's staff, in Lonergan, *It Might Have Been Lost*, p. 237.
2 WC (397), April 23, 1918, CAB 23/6.
3 French, *Strategy of Lloyd George Coalition*, p. 180.
4 WC (449), July 19, 1918, CAB 23/7.
5 Doughty, *Pyrrhic Victory*, p. 1.
6 Ayres, *War with Germany*, pp. 17–18.
7 SOS Hist. Dup.: File 9-1, *USAWW*, vol. 14, pp. 260–61.
8 *Ibid.*, p. 263.

9 See "Study of Tonnage Requirements," May 21, 1918, 1st Section, General Staff, *USAWW*, vol. 14, pp. 271–77.

10 Paxson, *American Democracy and the World War*, vol. 2, p. 96.

11 March, *Nation at War*, p. 192.

12 *WWIS.*

13 *WWIS.*

14 *WWIS.*

15 See Coffman, *Hilt of the Sword*, p. 74.

16 Ayres, *War with Germany*, pp. 44–46.

17 Albert Gleaves, *A History of the Transport Service: Adventures and Experiences of United States Transport and Cruisers in the World War* (New York: George H. Doran, 1921), pp. 28–30, 81.

18 *Ibid.*, p. 189.

19 *Ibid.*, pp. 68–72.

20 Thomas Frothingham, *The American Reinforcements in the World War* (New York: Doubleday/Page, 1927), p. 101.

21 *WWIS.*

22 Wilson, *Myriad Faces of War*, p. 429.

23 John Fye (ed.), *History of the Sixth Field Artillery, 1798–1932* (Harrisburg, Pa.: Published under direction of Headquarters, Sixth Field Artillery, 1933), p. 154.

24 Quoted in Frothingham, *American Reinforcements*, p. 95.

25 Harbord, *Leaves from a War Diary*, p. 50.

26 *WWIS.*

27 Gleaves, *History of the Transport Service*, p. 30.

28 Quoted in Tuchman, *Zimmermann Telegram*, p. 141.

29 Ludendorff, *Ludendorff's Own Story*, vol. 2, p. 244.

30 *WWIS.*

31 Gleaves, *History of the Transport Service*, pp. 78–79.

32 *WWIS.*

33 *WWIS.*

34 *WWIS.*

35 Gleaves, *History of the Transport Service*, p. 186.

36 *WWIS.*

37 *WWIS.*

38 *WWIS.*

39 *WWIS.*

40 Herwig, *First World War: Germany and Austria–Hungary, 1914–1918*, p. 394.

41 See War Cabinet, April 10, 1918, CAB 23/14.

42 Smythe, *Pershing: General of the Armies*, p. 111.

43 *Ibid.*, p. 69.

44 V. Rothwell, *British War Aims and Peace Diplomacy, 1914–1918* (Oxford: Clarendon Press, 1971), pp. 158–71.

45 Box 121, House MSS, fol. 4282.

46 Wiseman, "Notes on Interview with the President," April 1, 1918, Balfour MSS, BL Add. 49741.

47 Lincoln, *Passage through Armageddon*, p. 508.

48 *Literary Digest* (March 23, 1918), vol. 56, p. 13; (April 20, 1918), vol. 57, p. 13.

49 *PWW*, vol. 47, p. 269.

50 Reading to Balfour, March 27, 1918, Box 1, Wiseman MSS, fol. 7.

51 Quoted in W. Robertson, *Soldiers and Statesmen, 1914–1918*, vol. 2, p. 331; William Fowler, *British–American Relations, 1917–1918* (Princeton, NJ: Princeton University Press, 1969), p. 139.

52 Pershing, *My Experiences*, vol. 2, pp. 254–55.

53 George Cassar, *Lloyd George at War, 1916–1918* (London: Anthem Press, 2009), pp. 72–74.

54 Coffman, *Hilt of the Sword*, p. 147.

55 *Ibid.*, p. 64.

56 In Bliss to March and Baker, April 24, 1918, Box 226, Bliss MSS.

57 March, *Nation at War*, pp. 69–70.

58 *Ibid.*, p. 70.

59 Ludendorff, *Ludendorff's Own Story*, vol. 1, p. 374.

60 Gleaves, *History of the Transport Service*, pp. 91–92; Frothingham, *American Reinforcements*, p. 108.

61 March, *Nation at War*, p. 89; Frothingham, *American Reinforcements*, pp. 263–64.

62 Frothingham, *American Reinforcements*, pp. 207–08.

63 Stevenson, *Backs to the Wall*, p. 223.

NOTES TO CHAPTER 11

1 Johnson and Hillman, *Soissons 1918*, p. 27.

2 Harbord, *Leaves from a War Diary*, p. 347.

3 Stevenson, *Backs to the Wall*, pp. 241–43.

4 Repington, *First World War*, vol. 2, p. 88.

5 Pershing, *My Experiences*, vol. 1, p. 102.

6 Repington, *First World War*, vol. 2, p. 89.

7 "Report on Operations," n.d., *USAWW*, vol. 14, p. 105.

8 *Ibid.*, p. 110.

9 Coffman, *War to End All Wars*, pp. 18, 129; "Report on Operations," n.d., *USAWW*, vol. 14, p. 5. A different set of figures is given by James Huston for an earlier date, October 31, 1918: "81,800 officers and 1,037,000 men in zone of armies, 855,600 in rear (including combat replacements as well as service troops)," *The Sinews of War: Army Logistics, 1775–1953* (Washington, DC: US Army Office of the Chief of Military History, 1966), p. 385.

10 "Report on Operations," n.d., *USAWW*, vol. 14, p. 5.

11 Harbord, *American Army in France*, p. 400.

12 Later two more sections were added, one in Italy and another on the Rhine, the latter to supply American occupation forces in Germany.

13 "Quartermaster Aspect of Strategic Supply," n.d., *USAWW*, vol. 14, p. 167.

14 Harbord, *American Army in France*, p. 183.

15 Ayres, *War with Germany*, p. 61.

16 "Final Report of Assistant Chief of Staff, G-4," *USAWW*, vol. 14, p. 170.

17 Ayres, *War with Germany*, pp. 66–70.
18 Huston, *Sinews of War*, pp. 374–75.
19 *Ibid.*, p. 376.
20 Harbord, *American Army in France*, pp. 365–66.
21 Harbord, *Leaves from a War Diary*, p. 349.
22 Palmer, *Newton D. Baker: America at War*, p. 92.
23 Drum Diary, April 1–31, 1918, Box 15, Drum MSS, AHEC.
24 Keene, *Doughboys*, p. 53.
25 Huston, *Sinews of War*, p. 366.
26 *WWIS*.
27 Quoted in Kennedy, *Over Here*, p. 159.
28 Beaver, *Baker and the American War Effort*, p. 228.
29 *Ibid.*
30 Keene, *Doughboys*, pp. 83–85.
31 Chester Heywood, *Negro Combat Troops in the World War: The Story of the
    371st Infantry* (New York: Negro Universities Press, 1969), pp. 3–4, 10.
32 *Ibid.*, p. 14.
33 Harbord, *American Army in France*, pp. 162–63.
34 Harbord, *Leaves from a War Diary*, p. 364.
35 *Ibid.*, p. 346.
36 *WWIS*.
37 "Employment of American Troops during Period of German Offensives"
    (March 21–July 18), *USAWW*, vol. 14, p. 19; "Combat Activities of 6th
    Engineers," n.d., *USAWW*, vol. 4, p. 38; Smythe, *Pershing: General of the
    Armies*, p. 102.
38 Keene, *Doughboys*, p. 54.
39 *WWIS*.
40 Donald Baucom, "Awards, Decorations and Honors," in John Chambers II
    (ed.), *The Oxford Companion to American Military History* (Oxford: Oxford
    University Press, 1999), p. 68.
41 Pershing, *My Experiences*, vol. 1, pp. 319–20.
42 Paxson, *American Democracy and the World War*, vol. 2, pp. 224–25.
43 Quoted in Beaver, *Baker and the American War Effort*, p. 94.
44 Brian Neumann, "A Question of Authority: Reassessing the March–Pershing
    'Feud' in the First World War," *Journal of Military History* 73 (2009): 1119.
45 See Coffman, *Hilt of the Sword*, prologue and pp. 4–7.
46 Quoted in Smythe, *Pershing: General of the Armies*, p. 88.
47 Coffman, *Hilt of the Sword*, p. 162.
48 Pershing, *My Experiences*, vol. 1, p. 124.
49 *Ibid.*, p. 350.
50 Neumann, "Reassessing the March–Pershing 'Feud,'" p. 1126.
51 Quoted *ibid.*, p. 1126; March, *Nation at War*, p. 264.
52 Quoted in March, *Nation at War*, pp. 264–65.
53 Quoted *ibid.*, pp. 265–66.
54 Quoted in Smythe, *Pershing: General of the Armies*, p. 167.
55 Quoted in Neumann, "Reassessing the March–Pershing 'Feud,'" p. 1129.
56 Pershing, *My Experiences*, vol. 2, p. 180.

57 House to Wilson, June 3, 1918, *PWW*, vol. 48, pp. 231–32.
58 Smuts to Lloyd George, June 8, 1918, Lloyd George Papers, F/45/9/18.
59 Quoted in David Woodward, *Lloyd George and the Generals* (London and New York: Frank Cass, 2004), p. 317.
60 Pershing to House, June 19, 1918, Box 89, House MSS, fol. 3073.
61 Pershing to Baker, June 18, 1918, in Pershing, *My Experiences*, vol. 2, pp. 110–13.
62 *Ibid.*, p. 121.
63 *Ibid.*, pp. 121–22; Smythe, *Pershing: General of the Armies*, pp. 146–47; Coffman, *War to End All Wars*, p. 179.
64 *A Country Made by War* (New York: Random House, 1989), p. 321.
65 Woodward, *Almanac*, p. 356; Beaver, *Modernizing the American War Department*, p. 127; Coffman, *War to End All Wars*, p. 35; March, *Nation at War*, pp. 174–75; Perret, *A Country Made by War*, pp. 322–23.
66 Quoted in Cooke, *Pershing and his Generals*, p. 110.
67 Coffman, *Hilt of the Sword*, p. 87.
68 Smythe, *Pershing: General of the Armies*, p. 147.
69 Quoted in Neumann, "Reassessing the March–Pershing 'Feud,'" p. 1137.
70 *Ibid.*, p. 1139; Coffman, *War to End All Wars*, p. 181.
71 March, *Nation at War*, p. 266.
72 Quoted *ibid.*, pp. 49–50.
73 Smythe, *Pershing: General of the Armies*, p. 163.
74 *Ibid.* See also Harbord, *American Army in France*, pp. 349–52.
75 Pershing, *My Experiences*, vol. 2, p. 346; Harbord, *American Army in France*, p. 377.
76 Harbord, *American Army in France*, p. 380.
77 Pershing, *My Experiences*, vol. 2, p. 194.
78 *Ibid.*, p. 197.
79 Harbord, *American Army in France*, pp. 391–92.
80 Smythe, *Pershing: General of the Armies*, p. 200. See also Cooke, *Pershing and his Generals*, p. 146.
81 Pershing, *My Experiences*, vol. 2, p. 310.
82 Nenninger, "American Military Effectiveness," pp. 150–51.
83 Quoted in Harries and Harries, *Last Days of Innocence*, p. 410.
84 Baker to Chief of Staff, September 23, 1918, *USAWW*, vol. 2, p. 610; March to Pershing, September 25, 1918, *ibid.*, p. 613.
85 Fox Conner to March, September 29, 1918, *ibid.*, p. 614. See also Pershing to March, October 2, 1918, *ibid.*, p. 618.
86 March to Pershing, October 10, 1918, *ibid.*, p. 625.
87 March, *Nation at War*, pp. 168, 235.
88 Neumann, "Reassessing the March–Pershing 'Feud,'" p. 1142.
89 Quoted in Beaver, *Modernizing the American War Department*, p. 195.
90 Harbord, *American Army in France*, pp. 443–44.

NOTES TO CHAPTER 12

1 Herwig, *First World War: Germany and Austria–Hungary*, p. 406.
2 Perry, *Major General Oliver Nugent*, pp. 14–15.

3 Keegan, *First World War*, p. 400; Pershing, *My Experiences*, vol. 1, pp. 354–55; Harris, *Douglas Haig*, pp. 447–48.

4 Pershing, *My Experiences*, vol. 1, p. 359.

5 Quoted *ibid.*, p. 356.

6 *Literary Digest* (April 6, 1918), vol. 17, p. 14.

7 Doughty, *Pyrrhic Victory*, p. 437.

8 *USAWW*, vol. 21, p. 426.

9 Bullard, *Personalities and Reminiscences*, p. 124.

10 Grotelueschen, *AEF Way of War*, pp. 62–67.

11 *Ibid.*, pp. 200–04; Coffman, *War to End All Wars*, p. 147.

12 Grotelueschen, *AEF Way of War*, p. 149.

13 Letter dated February 22, 1918, IWM 80/25/1. See also Malcolm Brown, *The Imperial War Museum Book of 1918: Year of Victory* (London: Sidgwick & Jackson, in association with Imperial War Museum, 1998), p. 150.

14 Walser diary entry, February 19, 1918, IWM 80/25/1.

15 David Woodward, "Christmas Truce of 1914: Empathy under Fire," *Phi Kappa Phi Forum* (2011): 18–19; see also Tony Ashworth, *Trench Warfare, 1914–1918: The Live and Let Live System* (New York: Holmes & Meier Publishers, 1980).

16 Quoted in John Eisenhower, *Yanks: The Epic Story of the American Army in World War I* (New York: Touchstone, 2001), p. 88.

17 Bullard, *Personalities and Reminiscences*, p. 167.

18 Grotelueschen, *AEF Way of War*, pp. 154–56; Coffman, *War to End All Wars*, p. 148.

19 Coffman, *War to End All Wars*, p. 148.

20 Society of the First Division, *History of the First Division during the World War, 1917–1919* (Philadelphia, Pa.: John C. Winston, 1922), p. 55.

21 Smythe, *Pershing: General of the Armies*, p. 107.

22 Ludendorff, *Ludendorff's Own Story*, vol. 2, p. 243.

23 Michael Shay, *The Yankee Division in the First World War* (College Station: Texas A&M University Press, 2008), pp. 88–89.

24 *Literary Digest* (May 4, 1918), vol. 17, p. 13.

25 Shay, *Yankee Division*, p. 89.

26 IWM 81/14/1.

27 Diary entry, September 10, 1918, IWM 95/6/1.

28 Entry of January 31, 1918, in Robert Ferrell (ed.), *In the Company of Generals: The World War I Diary of Pierpont L. Stackpole* (Columbia: University of Missouri Press, 2009), p. 21.

29 *Ibid.*

30 French, *Strategy of Lloyd George Coalition*, pp. 224–27. See also Elizabeth Greenhalgh, *Foch in Command: The Forging of a First World War General* (Cambridge: Cambridge University Press, 2011), pp. 300–07 and Doughty, *Pyrrhic Victory*, pp. 435–38.

31 Quoted in Doughty, *Pyrrhic Victory*, p. 439.

32 *USAWW*, vol. 2, pp. 257–58; Trask, *AEF and Coalition Warmaking*, pp. 53–54.

33 *Literary Digest* (April 20, 1918), vol. 57, p. 13.

34 Pershing, *My Experiences*, vol. 1, pp. 364–65.
35 Dalessandro and Knapp, *Organization and Insignia of the American Expeditionary Force*, pp. 200–01.
36 Trask, *AEF and Coalition Warmaking*, p. 53.
37 Pershing, *My Experiences*, vol. 1, p. 365.
38 Trask, *AEF and Coalition Warmaking*, p. 52.
39 David Stevenson, *Cataclysm: The First World War as Political Strategy* (New York: Basic Books, 2004), p. 336; Doughty, *Pyrrhic Victory*, p. 441.
40 See WC (391 and 405), April 15 and May 6, 1918, CAB 23/6.
41 See WC (389A), April 11, 1918, CAB 23/14.
42 Greenhalgh, *Foch in Command*, p. 337.
43 Pershing, *My Experiences*, vol. 1, p. 376.
44 Gerhard Ritter, *The Sword and Scepter*, vol. 4, *The Reign of German Militarism and the Disaster of 1918* (Coral Gables, Fla.: University of Miami Press, 1973), p. 230.
45 C. Cruttwell, *A History of the Great War, 1914–1918* (Oxford: Clarendon Press, 1964), pp. 516–17.
46 Harris, *Douglas Haig*, pp. 468–69.
47 Memoranda by Macdonogh, April 10, 1918, WO 106/982.
48 Beckett, *Great War*, p. 214.
49 Rawlinson to Wilson, April 24, 1918, in Keith Jeffery (ed.), *Military Correspondence of Field Marshal Sir Henry Wilson, 1918–1922* (London: Bodley Head, 1985), p. 39.
50 March to Bliss, April 6, 1918, *PWW*, vol. 461, p. 271.
51 Beaver, *Baker and the American War Effort*, p. 137.
52 Lloyd George to Reading, April 14, 1918, *PWW*, vol. 461, p. 338.
53 Beaver, *Baker and the American War Effort*, p. 140.
54 WC (397), April 23, 1918, CAB 23/6.
55 Quoted in Beaver, *Baker and the American War Effort*, p. 141.
56 See "Memorandum of General Pershing's Visit to the British War Office, and Interview with General Sir Henry Wilson, and Lord Milner," April 22, 1918 and "London Agreement," April 24, 1918, *USAWW*, vol. 2, pp. 340–44.
57 Lord Derby to Wilson, April 21, 1918, in Jeffery, *Military Correspondence of Sir Henry Wilson*, pp. 38–39.
58 War Cabinet (393), April 17, 1918, CAB 23/6.
59 Ritter, *Sword and Scepter*, vol. 4, p. 232.
60 *Ibid.*
61 Elizabeth Greenhalgh, "David Lloyd George, Georges Clemenceau, and the 1918 Manpower Crisis," *Historical Journal* 50 (2007): 402.
62 See, for example, Pershing's letter to Baker, in Pershing, *My Experiences*, vol. 1, pp. 386–87.
63 Greenhalgh, "David Lloyd George, Georges Clemenceau, and the 1918 Manpower Crisis," p. 403.
64 Quoted *ibid.*, p. 420.
65 SWC, May 1, 1918, CAB 28/3/IC-57; Smythe, *Pershing: General of the Armies*, pp. 113–15; *USAWW*, vol. 2, pp. 361–65.

66 Mott's diary, April 27, 1918, quoted in Greenhalgh, *Foch in Command*, p. 324.
67 *USAWW*, vol. 2, pp. 367–71.
68 *Ibid.*, pt. 1, vol. 12, pp. 72–73.
69 WC (393 and 404), April 17 and May 3, 1918, CAB 23/6.
70 Baker to Wilson, May 4, 1918 and Wilson to Baker, May 6, 1918, *PWW*, vol. 461, pp. 517, 535.
71 Entry of May 1, 1918, Gary Sheffield and John Bourne (eds.), *Douglas Haig: War Diaries and Letters, 1914–1918* (London: Weidenfeld & Nicolson, 2005), p. 409.
72 Quoted in Beaver, *Baker and the American War Effort*, p. 144.
73 Quoted in Trask, *AEF and Coalition Warmaking*, p. 34. See also Beaver, *Baker and the American War Effort*, p. 146.
74 Rawlinson to Allenby, June 24, 1918, Letter Book, vol. 4, Versailles & 1918, Rawlinson MSS, IWM.
75 Mitchell Yockelson, *Borrowed Soldiers: Americans under British Command, 1918* (Norman: University of Oklahoma Press, 2008), p. 34.
76 Quoted *ibid.*, p. 65.
77 Letter Book, vol. 4, Versailles & 1918, Rawlinson MSS, IWM.
78 Quoted in Charles Shrader, "'Maconochie's Stew': Logistical Support of American Forces with the BEF, 1917–18," in Adams, *The Great War, 1914–1918*, p. 116.
79 Faulkner, *School of Hard Knocks*, p. 152.
80 *Ibid.*, pp. 116–21.
81 *WWIS*.
82 Entry of June 3, 1918, Sheffield and Bourne, *Haig: War Diaries and Letters*, p. 418.
83 Entry of June 7, 1918, *ibid.*, pp. 419–20.
84 Griscom to Pershing, June 14, 1918, Box 85, Pershing MSS, LOC Manuscript Division.
85 "X" Committee (19), July 1, 1918, CAB 23/17.
86 Smythe, *Pershing: General of the Armies*, p. 143.
87 "X" Committee (14), June 17, 1918, CAB 23/17.
88 Wilson to Baker, June 19, 1918, Baker Papers.
89 Quoted in Beaver, *Baker and the American War Effort*, p. 183.
90 Quoted in John Terraine, *To Win a War: 1918, the Year of Victory* (Garden City, NY: Doubleday, 1981), p. 68.
91 Prior and Wilson, *Command on the Western Front*, pp. 295–300.
92 Dale Van Every, *The AEF in Battle* (New York: D. Appleton, 1928), pp. 85–86.
93 Coffman, *War to End All Wars*, pp. 287–89; *The Times*, July 5–6, 1918; Pershing, *My Experiences*, vol. 2, pp. 137–38; Arthur Page, *Our 110 Days' Fighting* (Garden City, NY: Doubleday/Page, 1920), pp. 204–05; Terraine, *To Win a War*, pp. 67–72; M. Yockelson, "'We Have Found Each Other at Last': Americans and Australians at the Battle of Hamel in July 1918," *Army History* 65 (2007): 17–25.
94 Pershing, *My Experiences*, vol. 2, p. 137.

95 Rawlinson to Clive Wigram, July 7, 1918, Letter Book, vol. 4, Rawlinson MSS.
96 Pershing, *My Experiences*, vol. 2, p. 138.

NOTES TO CHAPTER 13

1 Goerlitz, *German General Staff*, p. 194.
2 Ludendorff, *Ludendorff's Own Story*, vol. 1, pp. 323–24. See also Martin Samuels, *Command or Control? Command, Training and Tactics in the British and German Armies, 1888–1918* (Portland, Oreg.: Martin Cass, 1995), pp. 158–97.
3 Terraine, *White Heat*, p. 231.
4 See www.westernfrontassociation.com/great-war-on-land/65-germany-allies; Rod Paschall, *The Defeat of Imperial Germany, 1917–1918* (New York: Da Capo Press, 1994), p. 36; Herwig, *First World War: Germany and Austria–Hungary*, pp. 247–48; Prior and Wilson, *Command on the Western Front*, pp. 346–48.
5 Ludendorff, *Ludendorff's Own Story*, vol. 2, p. 245.
6 "Cantigny, May 28–31, 1918," *USAWW*, vol. 1, pp. 19–20.
7 Grotelueschen, *AEF Way of War*, p. 70.
8 Pershing, *My Experiences*, vol. 1, p. 394.
9 Marshall, *Memoirs of My Services*, p. 78.
10 Article by Evans, n.d., p. 2, 2007.65.5.1, McCormick Research Center, Cantigny; Millett, "Cantigny, 28–31 May 1918," p. 164.
11 Marshall, *Memoirs of My Services*, pp. 82–83.
12 Stevenson, *Backs to the Wall*, pp. 200–02.
13 Marshall, *Memoirs of My Services*, p. 85.
14 *WWIS*.
15 Millett, "Cantigny, 28–31 May 1918," p. 168.
16 Vandenberg to Debeney, May 12, 1918, *USAWW*, vol. 4, p. 270.
17 Millett, "Cantigny, 28–31 May 1918," p. 167.
18 Grotelueschen, *AEF Way of War*, p. 71.
19 Millett, "Cantigny, 28–31 May 1918," p. 170.
20 Society of the First Division, *History of the First Division*, pp. 78–79; Eisenhower, *Yanks*, p. 126.
21 H. E. Ely, "Report on Capture of Cantigny and Consolidation of Position," June 2, 1918, *USAWW*, vol. 4, p. 329; Grotelueschen, *AEF Way of War*, p. 74.
22 W. S. Grant, "Account by an Eye-Witness of the Attack on Cantigny," May 29, 1918, *USAWW*, vol. 4, p. 321.
23 R. Austin's account, *WWIS*.
24 "Report on Capture of Cantigny," June 2, 1918, *USAWW*, vol. 4, p. 331.
25 Bullard, *Personalities and Reminiscences*, p. 197.
26 *Ibid.*
27 *Ibid.*, p. 198.
28 *Ibid.*
29 *USAWW*, vol. 4, p. 300.

30 Millett, "Cantigny, 28–31 May 1918," p. 173.
31 Marshall, *Memoirs of My Services*, p. 96.
32 Article by Evans, n.d., 2007.65.5.1, McCormick Research Center, Cantigny.
33 *USAWW*, vol. 4, p. 307.
34 Millett, "Cantigny, 28–31 May 1918," p. 177.
35 *USAWW*, vol. 4, p. 319.
36 Smythe, *Pershing: General of the Armies*, p. 127.
37 These are the casualty figures used by Millett, "Cantigny, 28–31 May 1918," p. 179. One of the regiment's histories notes that one-third of its men and more than half of its officers "were missing from its ranks" when relieved. See *The Story of the Twenty-Eighth Infantry in the Great War: American Expeditionary Forces*. Foreword by C. P. Summerall (n.p., 1919).
38 Quoted in Smythe, *Pershing: General of the Armies*, p. 128.
39 Letter of May 1918, *WWIS*.
40 Harries and Harries, *Last Days of Innocence*, p. 245.
41 Trask, *AEF and Coalition Warmaking*, p. 67.
42 Marshall, *Memoirs of My Services*, p. 97.
43 Pershing to Adjutant General, June 1, 1918, *USAWW*, vol. 2, p. 434.
44 Liggett, *AEF Ten Years Ago in France*, p. 70.
45 Quoted in Grotelueschen, *Doctrine Under Trial*, pp. 23–24.
46 Millett, "Cantigny, 28–31 May 1918," p. 185.
47 Memorandum for [AEF] Chief of Staff from Colonel Harold B. Fiske, July 4, 1918, *USAWW*, vol. 21, pp. 380–81.

NOTES TO CHAPTER 14

1 Quoted in Doughty, *Pyrrhic Victory*, p. 446.
2 Quoted *ibid.*, p. 447.
3 *Ibid.*
4 Memorandum of April 24 mentioned and quoted in Wilson to Milner, May 15, 1918, Lloyd George MSS, F/38/3/32.
5 Entry of May 9, 1918, Wilson Diary, IWM.
6 "X" Committee (2), May 16, 1918, CAB 23/17.
7 See Pershing, *My Experiences*, vol. 2, p. 37; "X" Committee (2), May 16, 1918, CAB 23/17; Pershing to Lloyd George, April 28, 1918, Box 89, House MSS, fol. 3072; "Interview on Occupation of American Sector," May 19, 1918, *USAWW*, vol. 2, pp. 413–14.
8 Wilson to Milner, May 15, 1918, Lloyd George MSS, F/38/3/32.
9 *Ibid.*
10 "X" Committee (2), May 16, 1918, CAB 23/17.
11 Smythe, *Pershing: General of the Armies*, p. 135.
12 "X" Committee (1), May 15, 1918, CAB 23/17.
13 "X" Committee (3), May 17, 1918, CAB 23/17.
14 *Ibid.*
15 Stevenson, *Backs to the Wall*, p. 78.
16 Cruttwell, *Great War*, p. 525.
17 Doughty, *Pyrrhic Victory*, p. 448.

18 Harbord, *American Army in France*, p. 269.
19 Cruttwell, *Great War*, p. 526.
20 Doughty, *Pyrrhic Victory*, pp. 449–50; Stevenson, *Backs to the Wall*, p. 81.
21 Doughty, *Pyrrhic Victory*, p. 450.
22 Quoted in Brown, *1918: Year of Victory*, p. 117.
23 Doughty, *Pyrrhic Victory*, p. 450; John Bourne, *Who's Who in World War One* (London: Routledge, 2001), p. 41. Stevenson suggests that the French had six rather than five divisions in reserve. See his *Backs to the Wall*, pp. 82–83.
24 Quoted in Doughty, *Pyrrhic Victory*, pp. 451–52.
25 These numbers are provided by Stevenson, *Backs to the Wall*, p. 83. Ten miles or less is often used as the maximum penetration on May 27 in other accounts.
26 Ludendorff, *Ludendorff's Own Story*, vol. 2, p. 268; Pershing, *My Experiences*, vol. 2, p. 61.
27 Pershing, *My Experiences*, vol. 2, p. 65.
28 Doughty, *Pyrrhic Victory*, p. 453.
29 Stevenson, *Backs to the Wall*, p. 85; "X" Committee (7 and 8), June 5, 1918, CAB 23/17; Fourth Sea Lord, "Arrangements for Evacuation from France," June 25, 1918, Milner MSS, dep. 374; entry of June 1, 1918, Callwell, *Field-Marshal Sir Henry Wilson*, vol. 2, p. 103.
30 Pershing, *My Experiences*, vol. 2, p. 71.
31 *Ibid.*, pp. 70–73; Smythe, *Pershing: General of the Armies*, pp. 133–34.
32 "Conference on Transportation of American Troops," June 2, 1918, *USAWW*, vol. 2, p. 439.
33 Quoted in Smythe, *Pershing: General of the Armies*, p. 134.
34 "Monthly Summary of the AEF," July 26, 1918, Lonergan, *It Might Have Been Lost*, p. 237.
35 Ayres, *War with Germany*, p. 36; Smythe, *Pershing: General of the Armies*, p. 136.
36 Quoted in Trask, *AEF and Coalition Warmaking, 1917–1918*, p. 75.
37 "Attachment of French Officers to 3rd Division," May 29, 1918, *USAWW*, vol. 4, p. 171.
38 "Operations Report," June 2, 1918, *ibid.*, p. 195.
39 Lieutenant Colonel F. L. Davidson, "Special Operations Report," June 12, 1918, *ibid.*, pp. 211–13.
40 "3rd Division Activities," May 30/31–June 1, 1918, *ibid.*, p. 187.
41 Harries and Harries, *Last Days of Innocence*, p. 248; Harbord, *American Army in France*, p. 280; Edwin Howard Simmons and Joseph Alexander, *Through the Wheat: The US Marines in World War I* (Annapolis, Md.: Naval Institute Press, 2008), pp. 13, 18–28.
42 "Journal of Operations," May 30, 1918, *USAWW*, vol. 4, pp. 70–71.
43 Harbord, *American Army in France*, p. 271.
44 *Ibid.*, p. 272.
45 Bundy, "Operations Report," June 6, 1918, *USAWW*, vol. 4, pp. 151–54.
46 McCrossen's Diary, in Oliver Spaulding and John Wright, *The Second Division: American Expeditionary Force in France, 1917–1918* (New York: Hillman Press, 1937), pp. 247–48.

47 Eisenhower, *Yanks*, p. 140.
48 Degoutte, "Contradiction of Rumor," June 3, 1918, *USAWW*, vol. 4, p. 136.
49 Degoutte, "Withdrawal of French Front Line Troops," June 2, 1918, *ibid.*, pp. 96–97.
50 Harbord, *American Army in France*, p. 287.
51 "Assumption of the Defensive," June 4, 1918, *USAWW*, vol. 4, p. 161; Paschall, *Defeat of Imperial Germany*, p. 156.
52 Quoted in Robert Asprey, *The German High Command at War: Hindenburg and Ludendorff Conduct World War I* (New York: HarperCollins Publishers, 1993), p. 424.
53 Stevenson, *Backs to the Wall*, p. 87; Lonergan, *It Might Have Been Lost*, p. 237.
54 Quoted in Stevenson, *Backs to the Wall*, p. 87.
55 Quoted in Bruce, *Fraternity of Arms*, p. 205.
56 Quoted in Doughty, *Pyrrhic Victory*, pp. 454–55.
57 Grotelueschen, *AEF Way of War*, p. 211.
58 *Ibid.*, pp. 211–12; Harries and Harries, *Last Days of Innocence*, pp. 254–55; Simmons and Alexander, *Through the Wheat*, pp. 101–02; Bruce, *Fraternity of Arms*, pp. 210–11.
59 Quoted in Simmons and Alexander, *Through the Wheat*, p. 102.
60 Harbord, *American Army in France*, p. 289.
61 Spaulding and Wright, *The Second Division*, p. 84.
62 Harbord, *American Army in France*, p. 289.
63 Van Every, *The AEF in Battle*, p. 65.
64 P. Malone, Colonel, 23rd Infantry, "Operations Report," *USAWW*, vol. 4, p. 379.
65 Simmons and Alexander, *Through the Wheat*, p. 107.
66 It should be noted that two battalions of Doughboys from the 23rd Infantry were also involved in an afternoon assault in support of the 4th Brigade just south of Bouresches, suffering 27 killed and 225 wounded or missing. Grotelueschen, *AEF Way of War*, p. 214; Simmons and Alexander, *Through the Wheat*, p. 111.
67 Larry Stallings, *The Doughboys: The Story of the AEF, 1917–1918* (New York: Harper & Row, 1963), p. 97.
68 Lejeune, *Reminiscences of a Marine*, p. 294.
69 Harbord, *American Army in France*, p. 291.
70 *Ibid.*, p. 290.
71 Eisenhower, *Yanks*, p. 144.
72 "Operations Report," December 31, 1918, *USAWW*, vol. 4, p. 237.
73 Spaulding and Wright, *The Second Division*, p. 57.
74 *Ibid.*
75 Grotelueschen, *AEF Way of War*, p. 219.
76 *WWIS.*
77 "Report on Critical Condition of 4th Brigade," USMC, June 15, 1918, *USAWW*, vol. 4, p. 485.
78 Harries and Harries, *Last Days of Innocence*, p. 268; Stallings, *Doughboys*, pp. 102–3.

79 Grotelueschen, *AEF Way of War*, p. 221.
80 *Ibid.*, pp. 220–21; Simmons and Alexander, *Through the Wheat*, p. 123; "Operations Report," December 19, 1918, by Major W. E. Burr, Field Artillery Adjutant, 2nd Field Artillery Brigade, 2nd Division, *USAWW*, vol. 4, p. 228.
81 Stallings, *Doughboys*, p. 111; Spaulding and Wright, *The Second Division*, p. 72.
82 Faulkner, *School of Hard Knocks*, pp. 247–48.
83 "Impressions of Attack on Vaux," in Spaulding and Wright, *The Second Division*, p. 255.
84 Grotelueschen, *AEF Way of War*, pp. 221–23.
85 Ludendorff, *Ludendorff's Own Story*, vol. 2, p. 269.
86 Grotelueschen, *AEF Way of War*, p. 225.
87 Spaulding and Wright, *The Second Division*, p. 83.
88 Lejeune, *Reminiscences of a Marine*, p. 258.
89 *Ibid.*, p. 294.
90 Spaulding and Wright, *The Second Division*, p. 86; Smythe, *Pershing: General of the Armies*, p. 140.
91 Extract from the diary of John A. Hughes, Battery, Company C, 15th Field Artillery, in Spaulding and Wright, *The Second Division*, p. 276.
92 Liggett, *AEF Ten Years Ago in France*, pp. 85–86.

NOTES TO CHAPTER 15

 1 Richard Ullman, *Anglo-Soviet Relations, 1917–1921*, vol. 1, *Intervention and the War* (Princeton, NJ: Princeton University Press, 1961), pp. 151–56.
 2 Robert Jackson, *At War with the Bolsheviks: The Allied Intervention into Russia, 1917–1920* (London: Tom Stacy Ltd., 1972), pp. 48–49.
 3 See Donald Davis and Eugene Trani, *The First Cold War: The Legacy of Woodrow Wilson in US–Soviet Relations* (Columbia: University of Missouri Press, 1992).
 4 Quoted in Benjamin Rhodes, *The Anglo-American Winter War with Russia, 1918–1919: A Diplomatic and Military Tragicomedy* (Westport, Conn.: Greenwood Press, 1988), p. 123.
 5 Barter to War Office, sent November 27, received November 29, 1917, Cabinet Paper GT 2817, CAB 24/34. See also Rhodes, *Anglo-American Winter War with Russia*, p. 26.
 6 W. Bruce Lincoln, *Red Victory: A History of the Russian Civil War* (New York: Touchstone, 1989), p. 42.
 7 See Woodward, *Almanac*, p. 251; and Ullman, *Anglo-Soviet Relations*, vol. 1, pp. 40–42.
 8 Memorandum by Macdonogh, November 20, 1917, FO 371/3018.
 9 Smythe, *Pershing: General of the Armies*, pp. 61–62.
10 Lloyd George, *War Memoirs*, vol. 2, pp. 1895–96.
11 For British financial support of Kaledin, see Ullman, *Anglo-Soviet Relations*, vol. 1, pp. 51–52.
12 *PWW*, vol. 47, p. 269, quoted in Woodward, *Almanac*, p. 315.

13 David Trask, *United States in the Supreme War Council: American War Aims and Allied Strategy, 1917–1918* (Middleton, Conn.: Wesleyan University Press, 1961), pp. 113–15.

14 Beaver, *Baker and the American War Effort*, p. 180.

15 *Ibid.*, pp. 180–81.

16 March, *Nation at War*, p. 118.

17 See George Kennan, *Soviet–American Relations, 1917–1918*, vol. 2, *The Decision to Intervene* (New York: Atheneum, 1967), pp. 13–57.

18 Quoted *ibid.*, p. 55.

19 Balfour to Reading, May 28, 1918; paraphrase sent to Lansing, printed in Department of State, *Papers Relating to the Foreign Relations of the United States, 1918, Russia*, vol. 2, p. 476.

20 See Trask, *United States in the Supreme War Council*, pp. 118–19.

21 Quoted in Beaver, *Baker and the American War Effort*, p. 182.

22 Quoted in Kennan, *Decision to Intervene*, p. 378.

23 Norman Saul, *War and Revolution: The United States and Russia, 1914–1921* (Lawrence: University Press of Kansas, 2001), p. 313.

24 Dorothea York, *The Romance of Company "A,"* quoted in Gordon, *Quartered in Hell*, p. 50.

25 *Ibid.*, pp. 49–50; Rhodes, *Anglo-American Winter War with Russia*, p. 33.

26 Rhodes, *Anglo-American Winter War with Russia*, pp. 51–52.

27 *WWIS*.

28 Letter of September 27, 1925, *WWIS*.

29 Quoted in Rhodes, *Anglo-American Winter War*, pp. 34–35.

30 Newspaper article, *Examiner*, November 17, 1981, *WWIS*.

31 Lansing to Wilson, September 11, 1918, with enclosure dated September 10, *PWW*, vol. 49, p. 516.

32 See Ullman, *Anglo-Soviet Relations*, vol. 1, p. 240.

33 Bliss to March, September 3, 1918, *PWW*, vol. 49, p. 531.

34 March, *Nation at War*, pp. 147–50.

35 *WWIS*.

36 Gordon, *Quartered in Hell*, p. 241.

37 "General Orders, No. 6, January 28, 1919," quoted *ibid.*, p. 141.

38 "Resolution #1," *ibid.*, p. 216.

39 Richardson to Adjutant General of the Army, July 23, 1919, *ibid.* See also E. Halliday, *The Ignorant Armies* (New York: Harper & Brothers, 1960), pp. 194–95.

40 Diary entry of June 14, 1919, *WWIS*.

41 March, *Nation at War*, p. 150.

42 See Henry Baerlein, *The March of the Seventy Thousand* (London: Leonard Parsons, 1926), pp. 159–81.

43 Interview with President, July 10, 1918, quoted in Saul, *War and Revolution: The United States and Russia*, p. 292.

44 William Graves, *America's Siberian Adventure* (New York: Peter Smith, 1941), p. 2.

45 *Ibid.*, p. 3.

46 March, *Nation at War*, pp. 127–28.

47 Graves, *America's Siberian Adventure*, p. 4.
48 Kennan, *Decision to Intervene*, p. 414.
49 Graves, *America's Siberian Adventure*, p. 51.
50 "Statement to the Press *re* American–Japanese Action in Siberia," August 5, 1918, *PWW*, vol. 49, p. 170.
51 See Carol W. Melton, *Between War and Peace: Woodrow Wilson and the American Expeditionary Force in Siberia, 1918–1919* (Macon, Ga.: Mercer University Press, 2001).
52 Dalessandro and Knapp, *Organization and Insignia of the American Expeditionary Force*, p. 117.
53 *WWIS*.
54 Simmons and Alexander, *Through the Wheat*, p. 136.
55 Sylvian Kindall, *American Soldiers in Siberia* (New York: R. R. Smith, 1945), p. 16.
56 Coffman, *Hilt of the Sword*, p. 101.
57 Richard Ullman, *Anglo-Soviet Relations, 1917–1921*, vol. 2, *Britain and the Russian Civil War, November 1918–February 1920* (Princeton, NJ: Princeton University Press, 1968), p. 28.
58 Graves, *America's Siberian Adventure*, pp. 55–56.
59 *Ibid.*, pp. 90–91.
60 Betty Unterberger, *America's Siberian Expedition, 1918–1920* (Durham, NC: Duke University Press, 1956), p. 231; Kindall, *American Soldiers in Siberia*, p. 245.
61 Ullman, *Anglo-Soviet Relations*, vol. 2, p. 33.
62 Kindall, *American Soldiers in Siberia*, p. 17.
63 Graves, *America's Siberian Adventure*, pp. 75–76.
64 Kindall, *American Soldiers in Siberia*, p. 19.
65 Coffman, *Hilt of the Sword*, p. 218.
66 Graves, *America's Siberian Adventure*, p. 138.
67 *WWIS*.
68 March, *Nation at War*, pp. 131–32.

NOTES TO CHAPTER 16

1 Robert Walton, *Over There: European Reaction to Americans in World War I* (Itasca, Ill.: F. E. Peacock Publishers, Inc., 1971), p. 163.
2 "Notes on Conversation with General Foch at Chaumont," June 17, 1918, *USAWW*, vol. 2, pp. 468–70.
3 Zabecki, *Steel Wind*, p. 87; Michael Neiberg, *The Second Battle of the Marne* (Bloomington and Indianapolis: Indiana University Press, 2008), p. 88.
4 Neiberg, *Second Battle of the Marne*, pp. 86–89.
5 Quoted in Doughty, *Pyrrhic Victory*, p. 467; see also Greenhalgh, *Foch in Command*, p. 397.
6 Quoted in Neiberg, *Second Battle of Marne*, p. 93.
7 *Ibid.*, p. 99.
8 WC (442), July 8, 1918, CAB 23/7.
9 See "X" Committee (20), July 12, 1918, CAB 23/17 and WC (444A), July 11, 1918, CAB 23/14.

10 Lloyd George to Clemenceau, July 13, 1918, Lloyd George MSS, F/50/3/7.

11 Sheffield and Bourne, *Haig: War Diaries and Letters*, p. 429.

12 Entry of July 14, 1918, Henry Wilson Diary, IWM; IWC (24A), July 15, 1918, CAB 23/44.

13 Zabecki, *Steel Wind*, pp. 89–90.

14 Quoted in James Hallas, *Doughboy War: The American Expeditionary Force in World War I* (Boulder, Colo.: Lynne Rienner, 2000), p. 102.

15 Greenhalgh, *Foch in Command*, p. 399.

16 For the fighting along the Marne, see Eisenhower, *Yanks*, pp. 151–61; Neiberg, *Second Battle of the Marne*, pp. 112–13; Zabecki, *Steel Wind*, pp. 90–91; Coffman, *War to End All Wars*, pp. 224–27; Liggett, *AEF Ten Years Ago in France*, pp. 98–102.

17 Liggett, *AEF Ten Years Ago in France*, p. 98.

18 Quoted in James Cooke, *The Rainbow Division in the Great War, 1917–1919* (Westport, Conn.: Praeger, 1994), p. 108.

19 Rudolf Binding, *A Fatalist at War* (London: Allen & Unwin, 1928), p. 234.

20 Doughty, *Pyrrhic Victory*, p. 468.

21 Neiberg, *Second Battle of Marne*, p. 121.

22 War Diary, July 18[?], 1918, Group of Armies German Crown Prince, *USAWW*, vol. 5, p. 678.

23 Quoted in Bourne, *Who's Who in World War One*, p. 193.

24 Harbord, *American Army in France*, p. 317.

25 Quoted in Spaulding and Wright, *The Second Division*, p. 109.

26 Harbord, *American Army in France*, pp. 321–22.

27 *USAWW*, vol. 5, pp. 328–29; Liggett, *AEF Ten Years Ago in France*, p. 118.

28 Johnson and Hillman, *Soissons 1918*, p. 59.

29 Austin to his mother, July 31, 1918, *WWIS*.

30 Spaulding and Wright, *The Second Division*, p. 257.

31 Harbord, *American Army in France*, p. 324.

32 John W. Thomason, *Fix Bayonets!* (New York: Charles Scribner's Sons, 1926), p. 91.

33 Austin to his mother, July 31, 1918, *WWIS*.

34 Van Every, *The AEF in Battle*, p. 140.

35 Liggett, *AEF Ten Years Ago in France*, p. 115.

36 *WWIS*.

37 Thomason, *Fix Bayonets!*, pp. 104–05.

38 Quoted in Grotelueschen, *AEF Way of War*, pp. 101–02.

39 C. B. Fullerton, *Twenty-Sixth Infantry in France* (Frankfurt: Martin Flock & Co., 1919), p. 37.

40 War Diary, July 18[?], 1918, Group of Armies German Crown Prince, *USAWW*, vol. 5, p. 679.

41 Johnson and Hillman, *Soissons 1918*, p. 91.

42 *Ibid.*, p. 105.

43 *Ibid.*, p. 112.

44 Quoted in Simmons and Alexander, *Through the Wheat*, p. 166.

45 Quoted in Hallas, *Doughboy War*, p. 111.

46 Grotelueschen, *AEF Way of War*, p. 233.

47 Quoted in Eisenhower, *Yanks*, p. 168.
48 Society of the First Division, *History of the First Division*, p. 135.
49 Quoted in Johnson and Hillman, *Soissons 1918*, p. 137.
50 Fullerton, *Twenty-Sixth Infantry*, p. 40.
51 Smythe, *Pershing: General of the Armies*, p. 156.
52 Terraine, *To Win a War*, p. 80.
53 Liggett, *AEF Ten Years Ago in France*, p. 131.
54 *Ibid.*
55 Quoted in March, *Nation at War*, p. 259.
56 Van Every, *The AEF in Battle*, p. 138.
57 Entry of July 17, 1918, Ferrell, *Company of Generals*, p. 101.
58 Entry of July 21, 1918, *ibid.*, p. 108. See also Coffman, *War to End All Wars*, pp. 251–52 and Grotelueschen, *AEF Way of War*, pp. 160–67.
59 Quoted in Hallas, *Doughboy War*, p. 122.
60 Entry of July 23, 1918, Ferrell, *Company of Generals*, pp. 109–10.
61 Van Every, *The AEF in Battle*, p. 151; Grotelueschen, *AEF Way of War*, pp. 171–72.
62 J. Cooke, *Rainbow Division*, p. 122.
63 Van Every, *The AEF in Battle*, p. 155.
64 Entry of August 1, 1918, Ferrell, *Company of Generals*, p. 117.
65 Hunter Liggett, *Commanding an American Army: Recollections of the World War* (Boston, Mass.: Houghton Mifflin, 1925), pp. 41–43; Coffman, *War to End All Wars*, pp. 253–54; Cooke, *Rainbow Division*, pp. 124–35; Neiberg, *Second Battle of Marne*, pp. 171–73.
66 Bullard, *Personalities and Reminiscences*, p. 251.
67 Liggett, *AEF Ten Years Ago in France*, p. 96.
68 Quoted in Fischer, *Germany's Aims in the First World War*, p. 625.
69 Prior and Wilson, *Command on the Western Front*, p. 322.
70 Sheffield and Bourne, *Haig: War Diaries and Letters*, p. 440; Stevenson, *Backs to the Wall*, p. 121; William Philpott, *Bloody Victory: The Sacrifice on the Somme and the Making of the Twentieth Century* (London: Little, Brown, 2009), pp. 522–26.
71 See Grotelueschen, *AEF Way of War*, pp. 173–75.
72 Pershing, *My Experiences*, vol. 2, p. 237.
73 Fischer, *Germany's Aims in the First World War*, pp. 627–28.
74 Quoted in Woodward, *Almanac*, p. 364.

NOTES TO CHAPTER 17

1 *USAWW*, vol. 2, pp. 520–21.
2 Conner, Memorandum for Chief of Staff on Foch–Pershing Conversations, July 10 at Bombon, July 14, 1918, G-3, GHQ, AEF, Secret General Correspondence, File 1003, No. 681, Pt. 4, Box 3112, RG 120.
3 Pershing, *My Experiences*, vol. 2, p. 168.
4 This relationship continued until October 16, 1918. See Coffman, *War to End All Wars*, p. 269.
5 Beaver, *Modernizing the American War Department*, p. 185.

6 *Ibid.*, pp. 186–87.
7 Kennett, *The First Air War*, pp. 215–16.
8 Ferrell, *Deadliest Battle*, p. 124.
9 Entry of May 21, 1918, Ferrell, *Company of Generals*, p. 57.
10 James Cooke, *The US Air Service in the Great War, 1917–1919* (Westwood, Conn.: Praeger, 1996), p. 135.
11 Stevenson, *Backs to the Wall*, p. 199.
12 Beaver, *Modernizing the American War Department*, p. 182.
13 Stevenson, *Backs to the Wall*, p. 219.
14 *Ibid.*, p. 92.
15 Beaver, *Modernizing the American War Department*, pp. 161–62; "Final Report of General Pershing," September 1, 1919, *USAWW*, vol. 12, p. 76.
16 Quoted in Bruce, *Fraternity of Arms*, p. 101.
17 Lloyd George, *War Memoirs*, vol. 2, pp. 1831–32.
18 Bruce, *Fraternity of Arms*, p. 252.
19 Entry of September 4, 1918, Repington, *First World War*, vol. 2, p. 261; Nenninger, "American Military Effectiveness," p. 137.
20 *USAWW*, vol. 8, pp. 4–5.
21 Doughty, *Pyrrhic Victory*, p. 474; Greenhalgh, *Foch in Command*, pp. 408–09; Pershing, *My Experiences*, vol. 2, pp. 171–72.
22 "American First Army to Attack on the Woëvre," August 9, 1918, *USAWW*, vol. 8, p. 8.
23 See Coffman, *War to End All Wars*, pp. 267–68.
24 General Sir John P. Du Cane (British liaison officer with Foch) to Sir Henry Wilson, July 25, 1918, WO 106/522.
25 Entry of July 26, 1918, Wilson Diary; "X" Committee (25), July 26, 1918, CAB 23/17; and WC (452), July 26, 1918, CAB 23/7.
26 See his rough draft enclosed in Hankey to Lloyd George, July 27, 1918, Lloyd George MSS, F/23/3/7.
27 Cipher telegram to Lord Derby (Paris), August 2, 1918 (following for Clemenceau from Lloyd George), Lloyd George MSS, F/50/3/9.
28 Lloyd George made this statement during the meeting when these figures were given. See IWC (27B), August 1, 1918, CAB 23/44.
29 IWC (27A), July 31, 1918, CAB 23/44.
30 *Ibid.*
31 Entry of August 1, 1918, Hankey Diary.
32 IWC (27C), August 6, 1918, CAB 23/44; IWC (32B), August 16, 1918, CAB 23/44.
33 Note ("American Troops") to J. T. Davies (Lloyd George's private secretary), August 21, 1918, Lloyd George MSS, F/47/7/40.
34 Entry of August 12, 1918, Sheffield and Bourne, *Haig: War Diaries and Letters*, p. 443.
35 Bliss to Baker and March, August 14, 1918, *PWW*, vol. 49, pp. 258–61.
36 George Viereck, *As They Saw Us: Foch, Ludendorff and Other Leaders Write Our War History* (Garden City, NY: Doubleday, Doran and Co., 1929), p. 231.
37 Baker to Wilson, August 17, 1918, *ibid.*, p. 277.

38 Haig to Wilson, August 27, 1918, in Sheffield and Bourne, *Haig: War Diaries and Letters*, p. 450.
39 Quoted in Greenhalgh, *Foch in Command*, p. 430.
40 Doughty, *Pyrrhic Victory*, p. 481; entry of August 29, 1918, in Sheffield and Bourne, *Haig: War Diaries and Letters*, p. 451.
41 "Notes on Conversation between General Pershing and Marshal Foch at Ligny-en-Barrois," August 30, 1918, *USAWW*, vol. 8, pp. 38–39.
42 Pershing, *My Experiences*, vol. 2, pp. 246–47; Smythe, *Pershing: General of the Armies*, p. 176.
43 Greenhalgh, *Foch in Command*, p. 433.
44 "Notes on Conversation between General Pershing and Marshal Foch at Ligny-en-Barrois," August 30, 1918, *USAWW*, vol. 8, p. 40.
45 Greenhalgh, *Foch in Command*, p. 436; Doughty, *Pyrrhic Victory*, pp. 483–84.
46 Pershing to Foch, August 31, 1918, *USAWW*, vol. 8, p. 44.
47 "Plan for Converging Attack by Combined Allied Force on the Western Front," September 3, 1918, *USAWW*, vol. 8, p. 50.
48 Marshall, *Memoirs of My Services*, p. 133.
49 Eisenhower, *Yanks*, p. 198.
50 Marshall, *Memoirs of My Services*, p. 139.
51 Spaulding and Wright, *The Second Division*, p. 270.
52 *WWIS*. See also Faulkner, *School of Hard Knocks*, p. 244.
53 *WWIS*.
54 "Alsace Ruse," November 25, 1918, *USAWW*, vol. 8, p. 63.
55 "Extracts from Articles in *The Field Artillery Journal* by Colonel Conrad H. Lanza," p. 2, Box 15, Drum MSS, AHEC; Harries and Harries, *Last Days of Innocence*, p. 541.
56 Trask, *AEF and Coalition Warmaking*, p. 101.
57 Marshall, *Memoirs of My Services*, p. 136; Grotelueschen, *Doctrine Under Fire*, p. 84.
58 See Trask, *AEF and Coalition Warmaking*, p. 106 for the lower figure and Liggett, *AEF Ten Years Ago in France*, p. 149 for the higher figure. It should be noted that these numbers also include some soldiers from Austria–Hungary and that Trask limits his figure to a division's "combat" strength.
59 Entry of September 11, 1918, Spaulding and Wright, *The Second Division*, p. 271.
60 Society of the First Division, *History of the First Division*, p. 162.
61 Lanza, "Extracts from Articles in *The Field Artillery Journal*," p. 2, Box 15, Drum MSS, AHEC.
62 Society of the First Division, *History of the First Division*, pp. 149–50.
63 *WWIS*.
64 Smythe, *Pershing: General of the Armies*, p. 181.
65 Cooke, *US Air Service*, pp. 149–50; Marshall, *Memoirs of My Services*, p. 144.
66 McHenry, *WWIS*.
67 Marshall, *Memoirs of My Services*, p. 147; Notes on Reduction of the St. Mihiel salient, prepared by Fox Conner, Box 15, Drum MSS, AHEC.
68 Diary, n.d., Spaulding and Wright, *The Second Division*, p. 272.

69 James Hallas, *Squandered Victory: The American First Army at Mihiel* (Westport, Conn.: Praeger, 1995), p. 158; Coffman, *War to End All Wars*, pp. 281–82.
70 Quoted in Grotelueschen, *AEF Way of War*, p. 181.
71 Girard McEntee, *Military History of the World War* (New York: Charles Scribner's Sons, 1937), p. 526.
72 Marshall, *Memoirs of My Services*, p. 145.
73 Pershing, *My Experiences*, vol. 2, pp. 272–73.
74 Smythe, *Pershing: General of the Armies*, p. 186.
75 "Ludendorff to Group of Armies von Gallwitz," September 17, 1918, *USAWW*, vol. 8, p. 312.
76 Alexander, *Memories*, p. 108.
77 *Ibid.*, p. 137.
78 *Ibid.*, pp. 140–42, 149.
79 Prior and Wilson, *Command on the Western Front*, pp. 362–66.
80 *Ibid.*, p. 367; Yockelson, *Borrowed Soldiers*, pp. 162–65; Coffman, *War to End All Wars*, pp. 293–95.
81 Entry of September 28, 1918, Sheffield and Bourne, *Haig: War Diaries and Letters*, p. 466.
82 Quoted in Yockelson, *Borrowed Soldiers*, p. 167.
83 Stevenson, *Backs to the Wall*, p. 213.
84 Prior and Wilson, *Command on the Western Front*, pp. 370–71.
85 Yockelson, *Borrowed Soldiers*, p. 176.
86 Coffman, *War to End All Wars*, p. 297; Yockelson, *Borrowed Soldiers*, pp. 190–208; Prior and Wilson, *Command on the Western Front*, pp. 379–86.
87 See Dalessandro and Knapp, *Organization and Insignia of American Expeditionary Force*, pp. 147, 160.
88 See Harris, *Douglas Haig*, pp. 325–26.
89 "X" Committee (27), August 31, 1918, CAB 23/17.
90 Telegram ("Tonnage for Transport and Supply of American Troops") from British Section, SWC, n.d., but almost certainly in late July 1918, Lloyd George MSS, F/47/7/40.
91 Lloyd George to Reading, August 26, 1918, Lloyd George MSS, F/43/1/15.
92 Lloyd George MSS, F/35/2/82; Lloyd George to Milner, September 29, 1918, Lloyd George MSS, F/38/4/20.
93 Lloyd Griscom, *Diplomatically Speaking* (London: J. Murray, 1943), pp. 434–35.
94 *PWW*, vol. 51, p. 435. This statement was furnished by Baker.
95 See Baker to Wilson, September 23, 1918, Baker MSS; Cabinet Paper GT 5932, n.d., CAB 24/66; WC (487), October 16, 1918, CAB 23/8.
96 Quoted in Beaver, *Baker and the American War Effort*, p. 176.
97 Bullitt Lowry, *Armistice 1918* (Kent, Ohio: Kent State University Press, 1996), p. 11; Joseph Tumulty, *Woodrow Wilson as I Know Him* (New York: Doubleday/Page, 1921), p. 309.

NOTES TO CHAPTER 18

1 Quoted in Doughty, *Pyrrhic Victory*, pp. 486–87.
2 Asprey, *German High Command*, p. 467.

3 Allenby to Wilson, September 22, 1918, quoted in Matthew Hughes, *Allenby and British Strategy in the Middle East, 1917–1918* (London: Frank Cass, 1999), p. 182.

4 Ludendorff, *Ludendorff's Own Story*, vol. 2, pp. 372–73.

5 Asprey, *German High Command*, p. 467; Goerlitz, *German General Staff*, p. 199.

6 Ritter, *Sword and Scepter*, vol. 4, p. 340.

7 Marshall, *Memoirs of My Services*, p. 146. See also Pershing, *My Experiences*, vol. 2, p. 270.

8 Conner, "Final Report of G-3," July 2, 1919, *USAWW*, vol. 14, p. 39.

9 Hallas, *Squandered Victory*, pp. 264–65.

10 Austin, *WWIS*.

11 Liggett, *AEF Ten Years Ago in France*, pp. 159, 161.

12 Spaulding and Wright, *The Second Division*, p. 165.

13 Simon Robbins, *British Generalship on the Western Front* (London: Frank Cass, 2005), p. 131; Philpott, *Bloody Victory*, p. 516.

14 The artilleryman Colonel Conrad H. Lanza suggests that the Germans defended a front of twenty-eight kilometers (or slightly less than eighteen miles) when the Americans attacked on September 26. Box 15, Drum MSS, AHEC.

15 Harbord, *American Army in France*, p. 433.

16 *Ibid.*, p. 437.

17 Alexander, *Memories*, p. 163.

18 Quoted in Coffman, *War to End All Wars*, p. 301.

19 Stevenson, *Backs to the Wall*, p. 132.

20 Marshall, *Memoirs of My Services*, p. 179.

21 *Ibid.*, pp. 149, 151.

22 *Ibid.*, p. 154.

23 Trask, *AEF and Coalition Warmaking*, p. 122; Palmer, *Newton D. Baker: America at War*, vol. 2, pp. 357–59.

24 Palmer, *Newton D. Baker: America at War*, vol. 2, pp. 357–59; Braim, *Test of Battle*, p. 85.

25 Coffman, *War to End All Wars*, p. 301; Grotelueschen, *AEF Way of War*, p. 129.

26 Quoted in Trask, *AEF and Coalition Warmaking*, p. 122.

27 Pershing, *My Experiences*, vol. 2, p. 294.

28 Pershing, "Final Report," *USAWW*, vol. 2, pt. 1, p. 38.

29 Lanza, "Extracts from Articles in *The Field Artillery Journal*," Box 15, Drum MSS, AHEC.

30 Grotelueschen, *Doctrine Under Fire*, pp. 115–16.

31 Alexander, *Memories*, p. 189; Votaw, *American Expeditionary Forces*, p. 81.

32 Ferrell, *Deadliest Battle*, pp. 42–43; Trask, *AEF and Coalition Warmaking*, p. 123; Braim, *Test of Battle*, p. 88; Lengel, *To Conquer Hell*, p. 112.

33 Bullard, *Personalities and Reminiscences*, p. 269.

34 *Ibid.*, pp. 268–69.

35 Alexander, *Memories*, p. 190.

36 *Ibid.*

37 Marshall, *Memoirs of My Services*, p. 161.

38 Cooke, *Pershing and his Generals*, p. 124.

39 Ferrell, *Deadliest Battle*, p. 48.

40 *Ibid.*, p. 8.

41 Lanza, "Extracts from Articles in *The Field Artillery Journal*," p. 7, Box 15, Drum MSS, AHEC.

42 Pershing, *My Experiences*, vol. 2, p. 301.

43 Faulkner, *School of Hard Knocks*, p. 267.

44 Lanza, "Extracts from Articles in *The Field Artillery Journal*," p. 7, Box 15, Drum MSS, AHEC.

45 *WWIS*. See also Pershing, "Final Report," *USAWW*, pt. 1, vol. 12, p. 42.

46 Ferrell, *Deadliest Battle*, pp. 52–53.

47 Bullard, *Personalities and Reminiscences*, p. 272.

48 "Notes on American Offensive Operations (From Information Received from French Sources)," in Walton, *Over There*, p. 194.

49 Lanza, "Extracts from Articles in *The Field Artillery Journal*," p. 11, Box 15, Drum MSS, AHEC.

50 Ferrell, *Deadliest Battle*, pp. 68–69.

51 *Ibid.*, p. 49.

52 *Ibid.*, pp. 50–51.

53 *Ibid.*, p. 68.

54 "Officers to Push Forward Energetically," September 27, 1918, *USAWW*, vol. 9, p. 522.

55 Diary entry of October 2, 1918, in Ferrell, *Company of Generals*, p. 151.

56 "Officers to Push Forward Energetically," September 27, 1918, *USAWW*, vol. 9, p. 140.

57 Diary entry of September 28, 1918, in Ferrell, *Company of Generals*. See also Pershing's general order, September 28, 1918, in which he talked of the "splendid spirit, dash and courage of our army to overcome all opposition," *USAWW*, vol. 9, p. 144.

58 *USAWW*, vol. 9, p. 531.

59 Bullard, *Personalities and Reminiscences*, p. 276.

60 Grotelueschen, *AEF Way of War*, pp. 324–25; Diary entry of October 5, 1918, in Ferrell, *Company of Generals*, p. 158.

61 Diary entry of September 28, 1918, in Ferrell, *Company of Generals*, p. 146.

62 Greenhalgh, *Foch in Command*, p. 447.

63 Diary entry of October 1, 1918, in Sheffield and Bourne, *Haig: War Diaries and Letters*, p. 468.

64 Pershing, *My Experiences*, vol. 2, p. 312.

65 Greenhalgh, *Foch in Command*, pp. 450–51; Trask, *AEF and Coalition Warmaking*, pp. 130–31.

66 Quoted in Greenhalgh, *Foch in Command*, p. 451.

67 Quoted *ibid.*, p. 452.

68 Palmer, *Newton D. Baker: America at War*, vol. 2, pp. 367–68.

69 "X" Committee (31), October 23, 1918, CAB 23/17; House telegram, October 27, 1918, *PWW*, vol. 51, p. 462.

70 Palmer, *Newton D. Baker: America at War*, vol. 2, p. 369.

71 Baker to Wilson, October 19, 1918, *PWW*, vol. 51, p. 386.
72 *USAWW*, vol. 14, p. 536.
73 Simmons and Alexander, *Through the Wheat*, p. 198.
74 *WWIS*.
75 Lejeune, *Reminiscences of a Marine*, p. 342.
76 Simmons and Alexander, *Through the Wheat*, p. 199.
77 Grotelueschen, *AEF Way of War*, p. 258.
78 Quoted in Simmons and Alexander, *Through the Wheat*, p. 209.
79 Lejeune, *Reminiscences of a Marine*, pp. 360–61.
80 Grotelueschen, *AEF Way of War*, p. 265.
81 *WWIS*.
82 Pershing, *My Experiences*, vol. 2, p. 320.
83 Quoted in Beaver, *Baker and the American War Effort*, p. 198.
84 "Activation of Second Army," October 12, 1918, *USAWW*, vol. 9, pp. 257–58.
85 Diary entry of October 16, 1918, Ferrell, *Company of Generals*, p. 171.
86 Diary entry of October 20, 1918, *ibid.*, p. 176.
87 *WWIS*.
88 See Alexander, *Memories*, p. 263.
89 Conner, "Final Report of G-3," July 2, 1919, *USAWW*, vol. 14, p. 53; see also Coffman, *War to End All Wars*, p. 332.
90 Pershing, *My Experiences*, vol. 2, p. 357.
91 Ferrell, *Deadliest Battle*, p. 50.
92 Entries of October 14 and 20, 1918, *WWIS*.
93 See Paxson, *American Democracy and the World War*, vol. 2, p. 407.
94 Liggett, *AEF Ten Years Ago in France*, pp. 209–10.
95 Bullard, *Personalities and Reminiscences*, pp. 266–67; Stevenson, *Backs to the Wall*, p. 252.
96 Richard S. Faulkner, "Disappearing Doughboys: The American Expeditionary Force's Straggler Crisis in the Meuse-Argonne," *Army History* 83 (2012): 8. See also Faulkner's *School of Hard Knocks*, pp. 305–15.
97 Liggett, *AEF Ten Years Ago in France*, p. 211.
98 Faulkner, "Disappearing Doughboys," p. 20; See also Grotelueschen, *AEF Way of War*, pp. 349–50.
99 Alexander, *Memories*, p. 212.
100 *WWIS*.
101 *WWIS*.
102 *WWIS*.
103 Huston, *Sinews of War*, p. 383.
104 *WWIS*.
105 Pershing, *My Experiences*, vol. 2, p. 327.
106 *WWIS*.
107 Grotelueschen, *AEF Way of War*, p. 194.
108 *WWIS*.
109 Quoted in Coffman, *War to End All Wars*, p. 333.
110 Ferrell, *Deadliest Battle*, p. 118.
111 Quoted in Eisenhower, *Yanks*, p. 261.

112 Diary entry of October 20, 1918, Ferrell, *Company of Generals*, p. 177.

113 Faulkner, "Disappearing Doughboys," p. 10.

114 Ferrell, *Deadliest Battle*, pp. 73–77; Gary Mead, *Doughboys: America and the First World War* (Woodstock and New York: Overlook Press, 2000), p. 313.

115 Ferrell, *Deadliest Battle*, p. 78.

116 Lengel, *To Conquer Hell*, pp. 279–82.

117 John Barkley, *Scarlet Fields: The Combat Memoir of a World War I Medal of Honor Hero* (Lawrence: University Press of Kansas, 2012), p. 170.

118 Pershing, *My Experiences*, vol. 2, p. 374.

119 www.worldwar1.com/dbc/j_oklah.htm; Woodward, *Almanac*, pp. 393–94.

120 Smythe, *Pershing: General of the Armies*, p. 206.

121 Eisenhower, *Yanks*, p. 256.

122 Ferrell, *Deadliest Battle*, p. 107.

123 Pershing, *My Experiences*, vol. 2, p. 329; Coffman, *War to End All Wars*, pp. 328–29.

NOTES TO CHAPTER 19

1 See *PWW*, vol. 51, pp. 253, 263–64; Ross Kennedy, *The Will to Believe: Woodrow Wilson, World War I, and America's Strategy for Peace and Security* (Kent, Ohio: Kent State University Press, 2009), p. 149.

2 Smuts, "A Note on the Early Conclusion of Peace," Cabinet Paper GT 6091, October 24, 1918, CAB 24/17; WC (491B), October 26, 1918, CAB 23/14.

3 Entry of October 12, 1918, John McEwen (ed.), *Riddell Diaries, 1908–1923* (London: Athlone Press, 1986), p. 241; Doughty, *Pyrrhic Victory*, p. 496.

4 Trask, *United States in the Supreme War Council*, p. 155.

5 V. C. McCormick to Wilson, October 9, 1918, *PWW*, vol. 51, p. 287.

6 Entry of October 23, 1918, Diary of Josephus Daniels, *ibid.*, p. 416.

7 John Cooper, *Woodrow Wilson: A Biography* (New York: Alfred A. Knopf, 2009), p. 444.

8 "An Address in the Metropolitan Opera House [speaking copy]," September 27, 1918, *PWW*, vol. 51, p. 263.

9 For an informed discussion of Wilson's approach to peace and security, see Kennedy, *Will to Believe*.

10 House Diary, October 15, 1918, *PWW*, vol. 51, p. 340.

11 "Memorandum by Franklin Knight Lane," October 23, 1918, *ibid.*, p. 415. See also Lowry, *Armistice 1918*, p. 35.

12 Ludendorff, *Ludendorff's Own Story*, vol. 2, pp. 413–44.

13 Lowry, *Armistice*, p. 38.

14 Stevenson, *Backs to the Wall*, p. 161.

15 Pershing, *My Experiences*, vol. 2, p. 361.

16 *Ibid.*, p. 351.

17 Lowry, *Armistice*, pp. 67–70.

18 *PWW*, vol. 51, p. 473. See also "Draft of a telegram from Newton Diehl Baker to John Joseph Pershing," October 27, 1918, pp. 470–71.

19 Lowry, *Armistice*, p. 96. See also Trask, *AEF and Coalition Warmaking*, pp. 156–57.

20 Kennedy, *Will to Believe*, p. 154.
21 House to Wilson, October 31, 1918, *PWW*, vol. 51, p. 523.
22 Baker to House, October 31, 1918 and Baker to Pershing, November 1, 1918, *ibid.*, pp. 525–26, 545.
23 Baker to Pershing, November 5, 1918, *ibid.*, p. 597.
24 Quoted in Smythe, *Pershing: General of the Armies*, p. 221.
25 Lowry, *Armistice*, p. 99.
26 Viereck, *As They Saw Us*, p. 284.
27 Wilson to House, October 30, 1918, *PWW*, vol. 51, p. 513.
28 Pershing, *My Experiences*, vol. 2, p. 355.
29 "X" Committee (29), October 19, 1918, CAB 23/17.
30 Marshall, *Memoirs of My Services*, p. 180; see also Pershing, *My Experiences*, vol. 2, p. 371.
31 Liggett, *AEF Ten Years Ago in France*, p. 224.
32 See Doughty, *Pyrrhic Victory*, p. 505; Bruce, *Fraternity of Arms*, p. 105.
33 Liggett, *AEF Ten Years Ago in France*, pp. 217–18; entry of October 25, 1918, Ferrell, *Company of Generals*, p. 182.
34 Alexander, *Memories*, p. 262.
35 Grotelueschen, *AEF Way of War*, p. 267.
36 Coffman, *War to End All Wars*, pp. 344–45.
37 Grotelueschen, *AEF Way of War*, p. 268.
38 *Ibid.*, p. 269; Grotelueschen, *Doctrine Under Fire*, pp. 117–30; "Report of the First Army, the Second Operation," November 1–11, 1918, *USAWW*, vol. 9, p. 367; Ferrell, *Deadliest Battle*, p. 138.
39 "Strength of Allied Air Force," October 31, 1918, *USAWW*, vol. 9, p. 362.
40 Russell Weigley, "The Interwar Army," in Kenneth J. Hagan and William R. Roberts (eds.), *Against All Enemies: Interpretations of American Military History from Colonial Times to the Present* (Westport, Conn.: Greenwood Press, 1986), p. 261.
41 Lejeune, *Reminiscences of a Marine*, pp. 383–84.
42 Alexander, *Memories*, pp. 268–75.
43 Liggett, *AEF Ten Years Ago in France*, p. 222.
44 *USAWW*, vol. 9, p. 576.
45 *Stars and Stripes*, November 8, 1918.
46 Ferrell, *Deadliest Battle*, pp. 132–35.
47 Liggett, *AEF Ten Years Ago in France*, pp. 223–24. See also "Report of the First Army, the Second Operation," November 1–11, 1918, *USAWW*, vol. 9, p. 369.
48 "Report of the First Army, the Second Operation," November 1–11, 1918, *USAWW*, vol. 9, p. 367.
49 Alexander, *Memories*, p. 280.
50 Kennett, *The First Air War*, p. 219; Ferrell, *Deadliest Battle*, p. 125.
51 Kennett, *The First Air War*, p. 222.
52 Ferrell, *Deadliest Battle*, pp. 123–24; Lengel, *To Conquer Hell*, pp. 447–48.
53 H. S. Drum, "First Army to Press Pursuit," November 4, 1918, *USAWW*, vol. 9, p. 381.
54 Pershing, *My Experiences*, vol. 2, pp. 377–78.

55 *Ibid.*, p. 381.

56 Marshall, *Memoirs of My Services*, p. 188.

57 Liggett, *AEF Ten Years Ago in France*, p. 227.

58 Harbord, *American Army in France*, p. 455.

59 See Marshall, *Memoirs of My Services*, pp. 189–90.

60 Alexander, *Memories*, p. 298; see also Coffman, *War to End All Wars*, pp. 349–52.

61 Harbord, *American Army in France*, p. 459.

62 *Ibid.*

63 Liggett, *AEF Ten Years Ago in France*, pp. 229–30.

64 Diary entry of November 9, 1918, Ferrell, *Company of Generals*, p. 191.

65 Ben-Hur Chastaine, *History of the 18th US Infantry First Division, 1812–1919* (New York: Hymans Publishing Co., [1920?]), p. 109.

66 Society of the First Division, *History of the First Division*, p. 235.

67 Marshall, *Memoirs of My Services*, p. 192.

68 *WWIS.*

69 Lowry, *Armistice*, pp. 157–58.

70 Joseph Persico, *Eleventh Month, Eleventh Day, Eleventh Hour* (New York: Random House, 2004), p. 325.

71 Pershing, *My Experiences*, vol. 2, p. 383.

72 Persico, *Eleventh Month*, p. 347.

73 *WWIS.*

74 Stanley Weintraub, *A Stillness Heard Round the World: The End of the Great War, November 1918* (New York: Oxford University Press, 1987), p. 198.

75 *WWIS.*

76 Persico, *Eleventh Month*, pp. 378–79.

77 Quoted in Griscom, *Diplomatically Speaking*, p. 446.

78 Harbord, *American Army in France*, p. 401.

79 Marshall, *Memoirs of My Services*, p. 203.

80 *WWIS.*

81 "Field Order," November 11, 1918, *USAWW*, vol. 9, p. 412.

82 Persico, *Eleventh Month*, p. 354.

83 *WWIS.*

84 See "X" Committee (29 and 31), October 19 and 23, 1918, CAB 23/17; WC (489A), CAB 23/14.

85 Quoted in Smythe, *Pershing: General of the Armies*, p. 233.

86 See Burk, *Britain, America, and the Sinews of War*; Stevenson, *Backs to the Wall*, pp. 351–55; Niall Ferguson, *The Pity of War* (New York: Basic Books, 1999), p. xxv.

87 Doughty, *Pyrrhic Victory*, pp. 1, 509.

88 Ferrell, *Deadliest Battle*, p. 148.

89 Pershing, *My Experiences*, vol. 2, p. 389.

90 Ayres, *War with Germany*, p. 119; Doughty and Gruber, *American Military History and the Evolution of Western Warfare*, p. 367; Eisenhower, *Yanks*, p. 288; Votaw, *American Expeditionary Forces*, p. 88.

91 Smythe, *Pershing: General of the Armies*, p. 235.

92 McEntee, *Military History of the World War*, pp. 413–15.

93 Stevenson, *Backs to the Wall*, p. 363. See also Arthur Herman, *Freedom's Forge: How American Business Produced Victory in World War II* (New York: Random House, 2012).
94 See Paul Kennedy, *Engineers of Victory: The Problem Solvers Who Turned the Tide in the Second World War* (New York: Random House, 2013).
95 Harbord, *American Army in France*, p. 401.
96 Viereck, *As They Saw Us*, pp. 286–87.
97 George Seldes, *Witness to a Century: Encounters with the Noted, the Notorious, and the Three SOBs* (New York: Ballantine Books, 1987), pp. 98–101.
98 Quoted in Lloyd Ambrosius, *Wilsonian Statescraft: Theory and Practice of Liberal Internationalism during World War I* (Wilmington, Del.: SR Books, 1991), pp. 132–33.

NOTES TO CHAPTER 20

1 *The Story of the Twenty-Eighth Infantry in the Great War*, p. 35.
2 See A. F. Barnes, "Representative of a Victorious People: The Doughboy Watch on the Rhine," *Army History* 77 (2010): 7.
3 *Ibid.*
4 *Ibid.*, pp. 11–12, 16.
5 Erika Kuhlman, "American Doughboys and German Fräuleins: Sexuality, Patriarchy, and Privilege in the American-Occupied Rhineland, 1918–23," *Journal of Military History* 71 (2007): 1078.
6 *WWIS.*
7 Barkley, *Scarlet Fields*, p. 217.
8 "Letter from Corporal Robert H. Branchaud, 4th Division Headquarters Troop, to US Military History Institute," March 20, 1980, *WWIS.*
9 *WWIS.*
10 Barkley, *Scarlet Fields*, p. 218.
11 Quoted in Keene, *Doughboys*, p. 124.
12 Entry of June 20, 1919, Callwell, *Field-Marshal Sir Henry Wilson*, vol. 2, p. 199; Jeffery, *Military Correspondence of Sir Henry Wilson*, p. 115.
13 Keene, *Doughboys*, pp. 122, 125.
14 *Ibid.*, p. 126.
15 *American Armies and Battlefields in Europe* (Washington, DC: Government Printing Office, 1938), vol. 21, p. 492.
16 Coffman, *Hilt of the Sword*, pp. 158–59; Ayres, *War with Germany*, pp. 37, 47–48.
17 Kuhlman, "American Doughboys and German Fräuleins," 1093–94.
18 *WWIS.*
19 *Ibid.*
20 Coffman, *War to End All Wars*, p. 358.
21 *American Armies and Battlefields in Europe*, vol. 21, p. 492.
22 *Ibid.*; Meigs, *Optimism at Armageddon*, pp. 190–92.
23 *WWIS.*
24 *American Armies and Battlefields in Europe*, vol. 21, p. 492.
25 Meigs, *Optimism at Armageddon*, pp. 80–81, 89.

26 *WWIS*.
27 For problems and delays in demobilizing soldiers, especially those in the European theater, see Keene, *Doughboys*, pp. 132–43.
28 March, *Nation at War*, pp. 310, 315.
29 Coffman, *Hilt of the Sword*, p. 159.
30 Letter, Private Earl H. Gammons, Company D, 8th Machine Gun Battalion, 3rd Division, *WWIS*.
31 March, *Nation at War*, pp. 322–23.
32 Meigs, *Optimism at Armageddon*, p. 218.
33 *Ibid.*; D. F. Harrison and N. H. Loring, "Socialization of the Armed Services," in Jessup and Ketz, *Encyclopedia of the American Military*, vol. 1, pp. 447–48.
34 S. McConnell, "Veterans: Civil War," in Chambers, *Oxford Companion to American Military History*, p. 752.
35 www.Wikipedia.org/wiki/Bonus_Army; Keene, *Doughboys*, p. 174.
36 Keene, *Doughboys*, pp. 186–94.
37 Coffman, *The Regulars*, p. 243.
38 W. Pencak, "Veterans: World War I," in Chambers, *Oxford Companion to American Military History*, p. 752.
39 Keene, *Doughboys*, pp. 197–204; Coffman, *The Regulars*, pp. 243–44.
40 Lloyd Ambrosius, *Wilson and the American Diplomatic Tradition: The Treaty Fight in Perspective* (New York: Cambridge University Press, 1987), p. 139.
41 Cooper, *Woodrow Wilson: A Biography*, pp. 508, 515.
42 For a discussion of the national debate over future national security, see Kenney, *Will to Believe*, pp. 203–27.
43 March, *Nation at War*, p. 330.
44 *Ibid.*, pp. 336–39.
45 Coffman, *Hilt of the Sword*, p. 201.
46 March, *Nation at War*, p. 340.
47 Coffman, *The Regulars*, p. 228.
48 March, *Nation at War*, p. 341.
49 Coffman, *Hilt of the Sword*, p. 199.
50 William Odom, *After the Trenches: The Transformation of US Army Doctrine, 1918–1939* (College Station: Texas A&M University Press, 1999), p. 82.
51 Coffman, *The Regulars*, p. 234.
52 Odom, *After the Trenches*, p. 84.
53 Coffman, *The Regulars*, pp. 233–34; Weigley, "Interwar Army," p. 259.
54 Weigley, *History of the United States Army*, p. 402.
55 Coffman, *The Regulars*, p. 233.
56 Walter Lafeber, *The American Age: United States Foreign Policy at Home and Abroad since 1750* (New York: W. W. Norton & Co., 1989), p. 337.
57 Weigley, "Interwar Army," p. 257.
58 *Ibid.*, p. 258; Grotelueschen, *AEF Way of War*, pp. 353–55.
59 US War Department Document, *Field Service Regulations, United States Army, 1923* (Washington, DC: Government Printing Office, 1924), p. 11.
60 *Ibid.*, p. 12.
61 *Ibid.*

62 Grotelueschen, *AEF Way of War*, p. 361.
63 *Field Service Regulations, 1923*, p. 11.
64 *Ibid.*, p. 84.
65 *Ibid.*, p. 101.
66 Weigley, "Interwar Army," p. 267.
67 *Ibid.*
68 Dulles, *America's Rise to World Power*, p. 167.
69 Coffman, *The Regulars*, p. 417; Weigley, *History of the United States Army*, pp. 425, 427–28; Odom, *After the Trenches*, p. 82.

Bibliography

OFFICIAL DOCUMENTS

National Archives (formerly Public Record Office), Kew, United Kingdom
    Files of the Cabinet Office, including
        Cabinet Memoranda
        Imperial War Cabinet
        Supreme War Council
        War Cabinet
        War Committee
        "X" Committee
    Files of the Foreign Office
    Files of the War Office
National Archives, Washington, DC
    Record Group 120 (American Expeditionary Force)
    Record Office 165 (Chief of Staff, War Plans, and Army War College files)

MANUSCRIPT COLLECTIONS OF INDIVIDUALS

I Military and political leaders
Asquith, H. H.; Bodleian Library, Oxford
Baker, Newton D.; Library of Congress Manuscript Division, Washington, DC
Balfour, Arthur J.; National Archives, Kew; Manuscript Collections, British
    Library, London
Bliss, Tasker H.; Library of Congress Manuscript Division, Washington, DC
Drum, Hugh A.; US Army Heritage and Education Center (AHEC),
    Carlisle, Pa.
Haig, Sir Douglas; National Library of Scotland, Edinburgh
Hankey, Maurice; Churchill College Archives Centre, Cambridge
House, Edward M.; Manuscripts and Archives Department, Sterling Memorial
    Library, Yale University, New Haven, Conn.
Lloyd George, David; House of Lords Record Office, London
Milner, 1st Viscount; Department of Western Manuscripts, Bodleian Library,
    Oxford
Nolan, Dennis E.; US Army Heritage and Education Center, Carlisle, Pa.
Pershing, John J.; Library of Congress Manuscript Division, Washington, DC
Rawlinson, Sir Henry; National Army Museum, London

Robertson, Sir William; Liddell Hart Centre for Military Archives, King's
    College London
Scott, Hugh L.; Library of Congress Manuscript Division, Washington, DC
Wilson, Sir Henry; Department of Documents, Imperial War Museum, London
Wiseman, Sir William; Manuscripts and Archives Department, Sterling
    Memorial Library, Yale University, New Haven, Conn.

**II Unpublished reminiscences of ordinary soldiers
(manuscripts, letters, and diaries)**
Unless otherwise noted the following collections are in the World War I Survey
Collection, US Army Heritage and Education Center (AHEC), Carlisle, Pa.

Ahearn, Joseph P.; Company F, 31st Infantry Regiment, AEF/Siberia
Aitken, Malcolm; 5th Marine Regiment, 2nd Division
Anderson, Howard; 34th Infantry Regiment, 4th Division
Austin, Ray; 6th Field Artillery, 1st Division
Bentson, Gabriel; 47th Infantry Regiment, 4th Division
Bertrum, Lawrence; 349th Field Artillery, 92nd Division
Blanchard, Robert H.; Headquarters, 4th Division
Blaser, Paul J.; 11th Machine Gun Battalion, 47th Division
Bugbee, Fred W.; 31st Infantry Regiment, AEF/Siberia
Burke, Mervyn; Headquarters, 1st Division
Christopher, Gordon N.; 101st Machine Gun Battalion, 26th Division
Engel, Charles M.; 119th Field Artillery Regiment, 32nd Division
Evans, Jesse O.; 18th Infantry Regiment, 1st Division, Robert H. McCormick
    Research Center, Cantigny, Ill.
Flamino, Antonio; 109th Infantry Regiment, 26th Division
Frampton, Charles Edward; 9th Infantry Regiment, 2nd Division, Special
    Collections, Marshall University Library, Huntington, W.Va.
Gammons, Earl H.; 8th Machine Gun Battalion, 3rd Division
Garretson, Leland Beekman; 314th (later 315th) Machine Gun Battalion, 80th
    Division, Department of Documents, Imperial War Museum, London
Hall, Gilbert; Member of British military mission (machine gun instructor) for 89th
    Infantry Division, Department of Documents, Imperial War Museum, London
Hasselton, William D.; Headquarters, 1st Division
Heig, Oscar C.; 332nd Machine Gun Battalion, 86th Division
Henderson, Henry L.; 358th Infantry Regiment, 90th Division
Hunt, Hale W.; 127th Infantry Regiment, 32nd Division
Invester, Floyd H.; 4th Engineer Regiment, 4th Division
Kent, Samuel M.; 128th Infantry Regiment, 32nd Division
Klaesi, Carl; 4th Ammunition Train, 4th Division
Lewis, Floyd L.; 339th Infantry Regiment, AEF/North Russia
McHenry, Herbert L.; 16th Infantry Regiment, 1st Division
Munder, Howard W.; 109th Infantry Regiment, 28th Division
Murphy, Paul; 309th Infantry Regiment, 78th Division
Ogden, Hugh W.; Headquarters, 42nd Division
Poorbaugh, Earle R.; 26th Infantry Regiment, 1st Division

Ross, Sam; Machine Gun Company, 165th Regiment, 42nd Division,
    Department of Documents, Imperial War Museum, London
Schaffer, Edward A.; 102nd Infantry Regiment, 26th Division
Shaw, Frederick; 18th Infantry Regiment, 1st Division
Totten, Paul H.; 339th Infantry Regiment, AEF/North Russia
Vaux, Harold C.; 360th Infantry Regiment, 90th Division
Walser, Kenneth E.; 101st Field Artillery, 26th Division, Department of
    Documents, Imperial War Museum, London
Weimeister, Harold; 337th Ambulance Company, AEF/North Russia

PUBLISHED SOURCES

SERIAL PUBLICATIONS

Literary Digest
New York Times
Stars and Stripes
The Times

BOOKS, ARTICLES, AND DISSERTATIONS CITED

Alexander, Robert. *Memories of the World War, 1917–1918*. New York: The
    Macmillan Company, 1931.
Ambrosius, Lloyd. *Wilson and the American Diplomatic Tradition: The Treaty Fight
    in Perspective*. New York: Cambridge University Press, 1999.
    *Wilsonian Statescraft: Theory and Practice of Liberal Internationalism during World
    War I*. Wilmington, Del.: SR Books, 1991.
American Armies and Battlefields in Europe. Washington, DC: Government
    Printing Office, originally published in 1938.
Ashworth, Tony. *Trench Warfare, 1914–1918: The Live and Let Live System*. New
    York: Holmes & Meier Publishers, 1980.
Asprey, Robert. *The German High Command at War: Hindenburg and Ludendorff
    Conduct World War I*. New York: HarperCollins Publishers, 1993.
Ayres, Leonard. *The War with Germany: A Statistical Summary*. Washington, DC:
    Government Printing Office, 1919.
Baerlein, Henry. *The March of the Seventy Thousand*. London: Leonard Parsons,
    1926.
Barkley, John. *Scarlet Fields: The Combat Memoir of a World War I Medal of Honor
    Hero*. Lawrence: University Press of Kansas, 2012.
Barnes, A. "Representative of a Victorious People: The Doughboy Watch on the
    Rhine." *Army History* 77 (2010): 6–19.
Baucom, Donald. "Awards, Decorations and Honors" in John Chambers II
    (ed.), *The Oxford Companion to American Military History*. Oxford: Oxford
    University Press, 1999.
Beaver, Daniel. *Modernizing the American War Department*. Kent, Ohio: Kent
    State University Press, 2006.
    Newton D. Baker and the American War Effort. Lincoln: University of Nebraska
    Press, 1966.

Beckett, Ian. *The Great War, 1914–1918.* Harlow: Pearson Education Limited, 2001.

Binding, Rudolf. *A Fatalist at War.* London: Allen & Unwin, 1928.

Bourne, John. *Who's Who in World War One.* London: Routledge, 2001.

Braim, Paul. *The Test of Battle,* 2nd edn. Shippensburg, Pa.: White Mane Books, 1998.

Bridges, Tom. *Alarms & Excursions: Reminiscences of a Soldier.* London: Longmans, Green, 1938.

Brown, Malcolm. *The Imperial War Museum Book of 1918: Year of Victory.* London: Sidgwick & Jackson, in association with Imperial War Museum, 1998.

Bruce, Robert. *A Fraternity of Arms: America and France in the Great War.* Lawrence: University Press of Kansas, 2003.

Bullard, Robert. *Personalities and Reminiscences of the War.* Garden City, NY: Doubleday, 1925.

Burk, Kathleen. *Britain, America and the Sinews of War, 1914–1918.* Boston, Mass.: Allen & Unwin, 1985.

Callwell, C. (ed.). *Field-Marshal Sir Henry Wilson: His Life and Diaries,* 2 vols. London: Cassell & Company Ltd., 1927.

Cassar, George. *Lloyd George at War, 1916–1918.* London: Anthem Press, 2011.

Chambers, John. *To Raise an Army: The Draft Comes to Modern America.* New York: Free Press, 1987.

Chastaine, Ben-Hur. *History of the 18th US Infantry First Division, 1812–1919.* New York: Hymans Publishing Company, [1920?].

Clements, Kendrick. *The Presidency of Woodrow Wilson.* Lawrence: University Press of Kansas, 1992.

Coffman, Edward. "The AEF Leaders' Education for War" in R. J. Q. Adams (ed.), *The Great War, 1914–1918: Essays on the Military, Political and Social History of the First World War, 1914–1918.* College Station: Texas A&M University Press, 1990.

Hilt of the Sword: The Career of Peyton C. March. Madison: University of Wisconsin Press, 1966.

The Regulars: The American Army, 1898–1941. Cambridge, Mass.: Harvard University Press, 2007.

The War to End All Wars. Madison: University of Wisconsin Press, 1986.

Cooke, James. *Pershing and His Generals: Command and Staff in the AEF.* Westport, Conn.: Praeger, 1977.

The Rainbow Division in the Great War, 1917–1919. Westport, Conn.: Praeger, 1994.

The US Air Service in the Great War, 1917–1919. Westport, Conn.: Praeger, 1996.

Cooper, Jerry. "The National Guard Mobilizations of 1916 and 1917" in Steven Weingartner (ed.), *Cantigny at Seventy-Five.* Chicago, Ill.: Robert R. McCormick Tribune Foundation, 1994.

Cooper, John. *Woodrow Wilson: A Biography.* New York: Alfred A. Knopf, 2009.

Cronon, Edmund (ed.). *The Cabinet Diaries of Josephus Daniels, 1913–1921.* Lincoln: University of Nebraska Press, 1963.

Cruttwell, C. *A History of the Great War, 1914–1918.* Oxford: Clarendon Press, 1964.

Dalessandro, Robert, and Michael Knapp. *Organization and Insignia of the American Expeditionary Force, 1917–1923*. Atglen, Pa.: Schiffer Publishing Ltd., 2008.

Davis, Donald, and Eugene Trani. *The First Cold War: The Legacy of Woodrow Wilson in US–Soviet Relations*. Columbia: University of Missouri Press, 1992.

Department of the Army, Historical Division. *United States Army in the World War, 1917–1918*. 17 vols. Washington, DC: Government Printing Office, 1948 [republished, 1988–92, by United States Army].

Department of State. *Papers Relating to the Foreign Relations of the United States, 1917*, supplement 2, *The World War*, 2 vols. Washington, DC: Government Printing Office, 1932.

Papers Relating to the Foreign Relations of the United States, 1918, Russia, 3 vols. Washington, DC: Government Printing Office, 1937.

DeWeerd, Harry. *President Wilson Fights His War: World War I and the American Intervention*. New York: Macmillan, 1968.

Doenecke, Justus. *Nothing Less Than War: A New History of America's Entry into World War I*. Lexington: University Press of Kentucky, 2011.

Doughty, Robert. *Pyrrhic Victory: French Strategy and Operations in the Great War*. Cambridge, Mass.: The Belknap Press of Harvard University Press, 2005.

Doughty, Robert, and Ira Gruber. *American Military History and the Evolution of Western Warfare*. Lexington, Mass.: D. C. Heath and Company, 1996.

Dulles, Foster Rhea. *America's Rise to World Power, 1898–1954*. New York: HarperCollins, 1955.

[Editorial staff of *Review of Reviews*]. *Two Thousand Questions and Answers about the War*. New York: The Review of Reviews Co., 1918.

Eisenhower, John. *Yanks: The Epic Story of the American Army in World War I*. New York: Touchstone, 2001.

English, John, and Bruce Gudmundsson. *On Infantry*, rev. edn. Westport, Conn.: Praeger, 1994.

Faulkner, Richard S. "Disappearing Doughboys: The American Expeditionary Force's Straggler Crisis in the Meuse Argonne." *Army History* 83 (2012): 7–25.

The School of Hard Knocks: Combat Leadership in the American Expeditionary Force. College Station: Texas A&M University Press, 2012.

Ferguson, Niall. *The Pity of War*. New York: Basic Books, 1999.

Ferrell, Robert. *America's Deadliest Battle: Meuse-Argonne, 1918*. Lawrence: University Press of Kansas, 2007.

(ed.). *In the Company of Generals: The World War I Diary of Pierpont L. Stackpole*. Columbia: University of Missouri Press, 2009.

Woodrow Wilson and World War I, 1917–1921. New York: Harper & Row Publishers, 1985.

Finnegan, John. *Against the Specter of a Dragon: The Campaign for American Military Preparedness, 1914–1917*. Westport, Conn.: Greenwood Press, 1975.

Fischer, Fritz. *Germany's Aims in the First World War*. New York: W. W. Norton & Company, 1967.

Fitzpatrick, David. "Emory Upton and the Army of a Democracy." *Journal of Military History* 77 (2013): 463–90.

Foley, Robert. "Learning War's Lessons: The German Army and the Battle of the Somme." *Journal of Military History* 75 (2011): 471–504.

Ford, Nancy. *Americans All: Foreign-Born Soldiers in World War I*. College Station: Texas A&M University Press, 2001.

Fowler, William. *British–American Relations, 1917–1918*. Princeton, NJ: Princeton University Press, 1969.

French, David. *The Strategy of the Lloyd George Coalition, 1916–1918*. Oxford: Clarendon Press, 1995.

Frothingham, Thomas. *The American Reinforcements in the World War*. New York: Doubleday/Page, 1927.

Fullerton, C. *Twenty-Sixth Infantry in France*. Frankfurt: Martin Flock & Company, 1919.

Fye, John (ed.). *History of the Sixth Field Artillery, 1798–1932*. Harrisburg, Pa.: Published under direction of Headquarters, Sixth Field Artillery, 1933.

Gilbert, Martin. *First World War: A Complete History*. New York: Henry Holt and Company, Inc., 1994.

Gleaves, Albert. *A History of the Transport Service: Adventures and Experiences of United States Transport and Cruisers in the World War*. New York: George H. Doran, 1921.

Goerlitz, Walter. *History of the German General Staff, 1657–1945*. New York: Frederick A. Praeger, 1953.

Goldhurst, Richard. *Pipe and Clay and Drill: John J. Pershing. The Classic American Soldier*. New York: Reader's Digest Press, 1977.

Goodspeed, Donald. *Ludendorff: Genius of World War I*. Boston, Mass.: Houghton Mifflin, 1966.

Gordon, Dennis (ed.). *Quartered in Hell: The Story of American North Russian Expeditionary Force, 1918–1919*. Missoula, Mont.: Doughboy Historical Society and GOS, Inc., 1982.

Graves, William. *America's Siberian Adventure*. New York: Peter Smith, 1941.

Greenhalgh, Elizabeth. "David Lloyd George, Georges Clemenceau, and the 1918 Manpower Crisis." *Historical Journal* 50 (2007): 397–421.

    Foch in Command: The Forging of a First World War General. Cambridge: Cambridge University Press, 2011.

Griffith, Paddy. *Battle Tactics of the Western Front: The British Army's Art of Attack*. New Haven, Conn.: Yale University Press, 1994.

Griscom, Lloyd. *Diplomatically Speaking*. London: J. Murray, 1943.

Grotelueschen, Mark. *AEF Way of War: The American Army and Combat in World War I*. Cambridge: Cambridge University Press, 2007.

    Doctrine Under Trial: American Artillery Employment in World War I. Westport, Conn.: Greenwood Press, 2001.

Gutierrez, Edward A. "'Sherman Was Right': The Experience of AEF Soldiers in the Great War." Ph.D. diss. Ohio State University, 2008.

Hallas, James. *Doughboy War: The American Expeditionary Force in World War I*. Boulder, Colo.: Lynne Rienner, 2000.

    Squandered Victory: The American First Army at Mihiel. Westport, Conn.: Praeger, 1995.

Halliday, E. *The Ignorant Armies*. New York: Harper & Brothers, 1960.

Harbord, James. *American Army in France, 1917–1919*. Boston, Mass.: Little, Brown, 1936.

Leaves from a War Diary. New York: Dodd, Mead, 1925.

Harries, Meirion, and Susie Harries. *Last Days of Innocence: America at War, 1917–1918*. New York: Vintage Books, 1998.

Harris, J. *Douglas Haig and the First World War*. Cambridge: Cambridge University Press, 2009.

Harrison, D. F., and N. H. Loring. "Socialization of the Armed Services" in John Jessup and Louise Ketz (eds.), *Encyclopedia of the American Military*. New York: Charles Scribner's Sons, 1994.

Herman, Arthur. *Freedom's Forge: How American Business Produced Victory in World War II*. New York: Random House, 2012.

Herrmann, David. *The Arming of Europe and the Making of the First World War*. Princeton, NJ: Princeton University Press, 1996.

Herwig, Holger. "The Dynamics of Necessity: German Military Policy during the First World War" in Allan Millett and Williamson Murray (eds.), *Military Effectiveness*, vol. 1, *The First World War*. Boston, Mass.: Unwin Hyman, 1989.

The First World War: Germany and Austria–Hungary, 1914–1918. New York: St. Martin's Press, 1997.

Heywood, Chester. *Negro Combat Troops in the World War: The Story of the 371st Infantry*. New York: Negro Universities Press, 1969.

Hickel, K. Walter. "War, Region and Social Welfare: Federal Aid to Servicemen's Dependants in the South, 1917–1921." *Journal of American History* 87 (2001): 1362–91.

Hughes, Matthew. *Allenby and British Strategy in the Middle East, 1917–1918*. London: Frank Cass, 1999.

Huston, James. *The Sinews of War: Army Logistics, 1775–1953*. Washington, DC: US Army, Office of the Chief of Military History, 1966.

Jackson, Robert. *At War with the Bolsheviks: The Allied Intervention in Russia, 1917–1920*. London: Tom Stacy Ltd., 1972.

Jeffery, Keith (ed.). *Military Correspondence of Field Marshal Sir Henry Wilson, 1918–1922*. London: Bodley Head, 1985.

Jessup, Philip. *Elihu Root*. 2 vols. New York: Dodd, Mead & Company, 1938.

Johnson, Douglas. "A Few Squads Left and Off to France: Training the American Army in the United States for World War I." Ph.D. diss. Temple University, 1992.

Johnson, Douglas, and Rolfe Hillman. *Soissons 1918*. College Station: Texas A&M University Press, 1999.

Johnson, Hubert. *Breakthrough Tactics, Technology and the Search for Victory on the Western Front in World War I*. Novato, Calif.: Presidio Press, 1994.

Keegan, John. *The Face of Battle: A Study of Agincourt, Waterloo and the Somme*. New York: Vintage Books, 1977.

The First World War. New York: Alfred A. Knopf, 1999.

Keene, Jennifer. *Doughboys, the Great War, and the Remaking of America*. Baltimore, Md.: Johns Hopkins University Press, 2001.

World War I: The American Soldier Experience. Lincoln: University of Nebraska Press, 2011.

Kennan, George. *Soviet–American Relations, 1917–1918*, vol. 2, *The Decision to Intervene*. New York: Atheneum, 1967.

Kennedy, David. *Over Here: The First World War and American Society*. New York: Oxford University Press, 1980.

Kennedy, Paul. *Engineers of Victory: The Problem Solvers Who Turned the Tide in the Second World War*. New York: Random House, 2013.

Kennedy, Ross. *The Will to Believe: Woodrow Wilson, World War I, and America's Strategy for Peace and Security*. Kent, Ohio: Kent State University Press, 2009.

Kennett, Lee. *The First Air War, 1914–1918*. New York: Free Press, 1991.

Kindall, Sylvian. *American Soldiers in Siberia*. New York: R. R. Smith, 1945.

Knock, Thomas. *To End All Wars: Woodrow Wilson and the Quest for a New World Order*. New York: Oxford University Press, 1992.

Kuhlman, Erika. "American Doughboys and German Fräuleins: Sexuality, Patriarchy, and Privilege in the American-Occupied Rhineland, 1918–23." *Journal of Military History* 71 (2007): 1077–106.

Lafeber, Walter. *The American Age: United States Foreign Policy at Home and Abroad since 1750*. New York: W. W. Norton & Company, 1989.

Lane, Jack. *Armed Progressive: General Leonard Wood*. San Rafael, Calif.: Presidio Press, 1978.

Lejeune, John. *The Reminiscences of a Marine*. Philadelphia, Pa.: Dorrance, 1930.

Lengel, Edward. *To Conquer Hell: The Meuse-Argonne, 1918. The Epic Battle that Ended the First World War*. New York: Henry Holt and Company, 2008.

Liddell Hart, B. *Reputations: Ten Years After*. London: John Murray, 1928.

Liggett, Hunter. *AEF Ten Years Ago in France*. New York: Dodd, Mead, 1928.

Commanding an American Army: Recollections of the World War. Boston, Mass.: Houghton Mifflin, 1925.

Lincoln, W. Bruce. *Passage through Armageddon: The Russians in War and Revolution*. Oxford: Oxford University Press, 1986.

Red Victory: A History of the Russian Civil War. New York: Touchstone, 1989.

Link, Arthur. *Confusion and Crises, 1915–1916*. Princeton, NJ: Princeton University Press, 1964.

The New Freedom. Princeton, NJ: Princeton University Press, 1956.

(ed.). *The Papers of Woodrow Wilson*. 69 vols. Princeton, NJ: Princeton University Press, 1966–94.

The Struggle for Neutrality, 1914–1915. Princeton, NJ: Princeton University Press, 1960.

Wilson: Campaigns for Progressivism and Peace, 1916–1917. Princeton, NJ: Princeton University Press, 1965.

Wilson the Diplomatist: A Look at His Major Foreign Policies. Baltimore, Md.: Johns Hopkins University Press, 1957.

Link, Arthur, and John Chambers, "Woodrow Wilson as Commander in Chief" in Reichard Kohn (ed.), *The United States Military under the Constitution of the United States, 1789–1989*. New York: New York University Press, 1991.

Lloyd George, David. *War Memoirs of David Lloyd George.* 2 vols. London: Odhams Press Limited, 1938.

Lonergan, Thomas. *It Might Have Been Lost: A Chronicle from Alien Sources of the Struggle to Preserve the National Identity of the AEF.* New York: G. P. Putnam's Sons, 1929.

Lowry, Bullitt. *Armistice 1918.* Kent, Ohio: Kent State University Press, 1996.

Ludendorff, Erich von. *Ludendorff's Own Story: August 1914–November 1918.* 2 vols. New York: Harper Brothers Publishers, 1919.

March, Peyton. *The Nation at War.* Garden City, NY: Doubleday, Doran & Company, Inc., 1932.

Marshall, George C. *Memoirs of My Services in the World War, 1917–1918.* Boston, Mass.: Houghton Mifflin, 1976.

McConnell, S. "Veterans: Civil War" in John Chambers II (ed.), *The Oxford Companion to American Military History.* Oxford: Oxford University Press, 1999.

McEntee, Girard. *Military History of the World War.* New York: Charles Scribner's Sons, 1937.

McEwen, John (ed.). *Riddell Diaries, 1908–1923.* London: Athlone Press, 1986.

Mead, Gary. *Doughboys: America and the First World War.* Woodstock and New York: Overlook Press, 2000.

Meigs, Mark. *Optimism at Armageddon: Voices of American Participants in the First World War.* New York: New York University Press.

Melton, Carol W. *Between War and Peace: Woodrow Wilson and the American Expeditionary Force in Siberia, 1918–1919.* Macon, Ga.: Mercer University Press, 2001.

Millett, Allan. "The American Military as an Instrument of Power" in John Jessup and Louise Ketz (eds.), *Encyclopedia of the American Military.* New York: Charles Scribner's Sons, 1994.

"Cantigny, 28–31 May 1918" in Charles Heller and William Stofft (eds.), *America's First Battles, 1776–1965.* Lawrence: University Press of Kansas, 1986.

"Over Where? The AEF and the American Strategy for Victory, 1917–1918" in Kenneth J. Hagan and William R. Roberts (eds.), *Against All Enemies: Interpretations of American Military History from Colonial Times to the Present.* Westport, Conn.: Greenwood Press, 1986.

Morris, A. (ed.). *Letters of Lieutenant-Colonel Charles à Court Repington: Military Correspondent of* The Times, *1903–1918.* Stroud: Sutton Publishing Limited, 1999.

Neiberg, Michael. *The Second Battle of the Marne.* Bloomington and Indianapolis: Indiana University Press, 2008.

Neillands, Robin. *The Death of Glory: The Western Front 1915.* London: John Murray, 2006.

Nenninger, Timothy. "American Military Effectiveness in the First World War" in Allan Millett and Williamson Murray (eds.), *Military Effectiveness,* vol. 1, *The First World War.* Boston, Mass.: Unwin Hyman, 1989.

"The Army Enters the Twentieth Century" in Kenneth J. Hagan and William R. Roberts (eds.), *Against All Enemies: Interpretations of American Military*

History from Colonial Times to the Present. Westport, Conn.: Greenwood Press, 1986.

Neumann, Brian. "A Question of Authority: Reassessing the March–Pershing 'Feud' in the First World War." *Journal of Military History* 73 (2009): 1117–42.

Odom, William. *After the Trenches: The Transformation of US Army Doctrine, 1918–1939*. College Station: Texas A&M University Press, 1999.

Oram, Gerard. *Military Executions during World War I*. New York: Palgrave, 2004.

Page, Arthur. *Our 110 Days' Fighting*. Garden City, NY: Doubleday/Page, 1920.

Palmer, Frederick. *America in France: The Story of the Making of an Army*. New York: Dodd, Mead, 1918.

Newton D. Baker: America at War. 2 vols. New York: Dodd, Mead, 1931.

Pershing: General of the Armies. A Biography. Harrisburg, Pa.: Military Science Publishing, 1948.

Paschall, Rod. *The Defeat of Imperial Germany, 1917–1918*. New York: Da Capo Press, 1994.

Paxson, Frederic. *American Democracy and the World War*. 2 vols. New York: Cooper Square Publishers, Inc., 1966.

Pencak, W. *1918*. New York: Random House, 2004.

"Veterans: World War I" in John Chambers II (ed.), *The Oxford Companion to American Military History*. Oxford: Oxford University Press, 1999.

Perret, Geoffrey. *A Country Made by War*. New York: Random House, 1989.

Perry, Nicholas (ed.). *Major General Oliver Nugent and the Ulster Division, 1915–1918*. Stroud: Sutton Publishing Limited for Army Records Society, 2007.

Pershing, John. *My Experiences in the World War*. 2 vols. New York: Frederick A. Stokes, 1931.

Persico, Joseph. *Eleventh Month, Eleventh Day, Eleventh Hour*. New York: Random House, 2004.

Philpott, William. *Bloody Victory: The Sacrifice on the Somme and the Making of the Twentieth Century*. London: Little, Brown, 2009.

Prior, Robin, and Trevor Wilson. *Command on the Western Front*. Oxford: Blackwell Publishers, 1992.

Rainey, James. "The Questionable Training of the AEF in World War I." *Parameters: Journal of the US Army War College* 22 (1992–93): 89–103.

Repington, Charles. *The First World War, 1914–1918*. 2 vols. London: Constable and Company, 1920.

Rhodes, Benjamin. *The Anglo-American Winter War with Russia, 1918–1919: A Diplomatic and Military Tragicomedy*. Westport, Conn.: Greenwood Press, 1988.

Ritter, Gerhard. *The Sword and Scepter*, vol. 4, *The Reign of German Militarism and the Disaster of 1918*. Coral Gables, Fla.: University of Miami Press, 1973.

Robbins, Simon. *British Generalship on the Western Front*. London: Frank Cass, 2005.

Roberts, William R. "Reform and Revitalization, 1890–1902" in Kenneth J. Hagan and William R. Roberts (eds.), *Against All Enemies: Interpretations of*

American Military from Colonial Times to the Present. Westport, Conn.: Greenwood Press, 1986.

Robertson, Sir William. *Soldiers and Statesmen, 1914–1918.* 2 vols. New York: Charles Scribner's Sons, 1926.

Roskill, Steven (ed.). *Hankey: Man of Secrets,* vol. 1, *1877–1918.* London: Collins, 1970.

Rothwell, V. *British War Aims and Peace Diplomacy, 1914–1918.* Oxford: Clarendon Press, 1971.

Samuels, Martin. *Command or Control? Command, Training and Tactics in the British and German Armies, 1888–1918.* Portland, Oreg.: Frank Cass, 1995.

Saul, Norman. *War and Revolution: The United States and Russia, 1914–1921.* Lawrence: University Press of Kansas, 2001.

Schaffer, Ronald. *America in the Great War: The Rise of the War Welfare State.* New York: Oxford University Press, 1991.

Second Report of the Provost Marshal General to the Secretary of War on the Operations of the Selective Service System to December 20, 1918. Washington, DC: Government Printing Office, 1919.

Seldes, George. *Witness to a Century: Encounters with the Noted, the Notorious, and the Three SOBs.* New York: Ballantine Books, 1987.

Seymour, Charles (ed.). *The Intimate Papers of Colonel House.* 4 vols. Boston, Mass.: Houghton Mifflin, 1926–28.

Shay, Michael. *The Yankee Division in the First World War.* College Station: Texas A&M University Press, 2008.

Sheffield, Gary, and John Bourne (eds.). *Douglas Haig: War Diaries and Letters, 1914–1918.* London: Weidenfeld & Nicolson, 2005.

Shrader, Charles. "'Maconochie's Stew': Logistical Support of American Forces with the BEF, 1917–18" in R. J. Q. Adams (ed.), *The Great War, 1914–1918: Essays on the Military, Political and Social History of the First World War, 1914–1918.* College Station: Texas A&M University Press, 1990.

Simmons, Edwin Howard, and Joseph Alexander. *Through the Wheat: The US Marines in World War I.* Annapolis, Md.: Naval Institute Press, 2008.

Smythe, Donald. "John J. Pershing: A Study in Paradox." *Military Review* 49 (1969): 66.

——— *Pershing: General of the Armies.* Bloomington: Indiana University Press, 1986.

Society of the First Division. *History of the First Division during the World War, 1917–1919.* Philadelphia, Pa.: John C. Winston, 1922.

Spaulding, Oliver, and John Wright. *The Second Division: American Expeditionary Force in France, 1917–1918.* New York: Hillman Press, 1937.

Spector, Ronald. "You're Not Going to Send Soldiers Over There Are You!" *Military Affairs* 36 (1972): 1–4.

Stallings, Laurence. *The Doughboys: The Story of the AEF, 1917–1918.* New York: Harper & Row, 1963.

Statement of a Proper Military Policy for the United States. Washington, DC: Government Printing Office, 1916.

Stevenson, David. *The First World War as Political Strategy.* New York: Basic Books, 2004.

With Our Backs to the Wall: Victory and Defeat in 1918. Cambridge, Mass.: The Belknap Press of Harvard University Press, 2011.

The Story of the Twenty-Eighth Infantry in the Great War: American Expeditionary Forces. Foreword by C. P. Summerall (n.p., 1919).

Stout, Mark. "World War I and the Invention of American Intelligence." Ph.D. diss. University of Leeds, 2010.

"Study of the Cost of the Army of the United States as Compared with the Cost of the Armies of Other Nations," November 1915. War College Division 9053-120. Washington, DC: Government Printing Office, 1916.

Sullivan, Mark. *Our Times: The United States, 1900–1925,* vol. 5, *Over Here, 1914–1918.* New York: Charles Scribner's Sons, 1933.

Terraine, John. *To Win a War: 1918, the Year of Victory.* Garden City, NY: Doubleday, 1981.

White Heat: The New Warfare, 1914–1918. London: Sidgwick & Jackson, 1982.

Thomas, Shipley. *The History of the AEF.* New York: George H. Doran, 1920.

Thomason, John W. *Fix Bayonets!* New York: Charles Scribner's Sons, 1926.

Trask, David. *The AEF and Coalition Warmaking, 1917–1918.* Lawrence: University Press of Kansas, 1993.

United States in the Supreme War Council: American War Aims and Allied Strategy, 1917–1918. Middleton, Conn.: Wesleyan University Press, 1961.

Travers, Tim. *How the War Was Won: Command and Technology in the British Army on the Western Front, 1917–1918.* New York: Routledge, 1992.

The Killing Ground: The British Army, the Western Front, and the Emergence of Modern Warfare, 1900–1918. Boston, Mass.: Allen & Unwin, 1987.

Tuchman, Barbara. *The Zimmermann Telegram.* New York: Macmillan, 1966.

Tumulty, Joseph. *Woodrow Wilson as I Know Him.* New York: Doubleday/Page, 1921.

Ullman, Richard. *Anglo-Soviet Relations, 1917–1921,* vol. 1, *Intervention and the War.* Princeton, NJ: Princeton University Press, 1961.

Anglo-Soviet Relations, 1917–1921, vol. 2, *Britain and the Russian Civil War, November 1918–February 1920.* Princeton, NJ: Princeton University Press, 1968.

United States Statutes at Large, vol. 39, pt. 2. Washington, DC: Government Printing Office, 1917.

Unterberger, Betty. *America's Siberian Expedition, 1918–1920.* Durham, NC: Duke University Press, 1956.

Upton, Emory. *The Military Policy of the United States from 1775.* Washington, DC: Government Printing Office, 1904.

US War Department. *1911 Infantry Drill Regulations, with text corrections to February 1917. Changes No. 18.* Washington, DC: Government Printing Office, 1917.

1914 Field Service Regulations. Washington, DC: Government Printing Office, 1914.

1914 Field Service Regulations, with text corrections to December 1916. Washington, DC: Government Printing Office, 1917.

Field Service Regulations, United States Army, 1923. Washington, DC: Government Printing Office, 1924.

War Department Annual Report, 1916. Washington, DC: Government Printing Office, 1916.

Van Every, Dale. *The AEF in Battle.* New York: D. Appleton, 1928.

Vandiver, Frank. *Black Jack: The Life and Times of John J. Pershing.* College Station: Texas A&M University Press, 1977.

Viereck, George. *As They Saw Us: Foch, Ludendorff and Other Leaders Write Our War History.* Garden City, NY: Doubleday, Doran and Company, 1929.

Votaw, John. *The American Expeditionary Forces in World War I.* Oxford: Osprey Publishing Ltd., 2005.

Walton, Robert. *Over There: European Reaction to Americans in World War I.* Itasca, Ill.: F. E. Peacock Publishers, Inc., 1971.

Weigley, Russell. *The American Way of War: A History of United States Military Strategy and Policy.* New York: Macmillan Publishing Co., Inc., 1973.

History of the United States Army. New York: Macmillan Publishing Co., Inc., 1967.

"The Interwar Army" in Kenneth J. Hagan and William R. Roberts (eds.), *Against All Enemies: Interpretations of American Military History from Colonial Times to the Present.* Westport, Conn.: Greenwood Press, 1986.

Weintraub, Stanley. *A Stillness Heard Round the World: The End of the Great War, November 1918.* New York: Oxford University Press, 1987.

Wilson, Trevor. *The Myriad Faces of War.* Cambridge: Polity Press, 1986.

Woodward, David. "'Black Jack' Pershing: The American Pro Consul in Europe" in Matthew Hughes and Matthew Seligman (eds.), *First World War: Personalities in Conflict.* London: Leo Cooper, 2000.

"Christmas Truce of 1914: Empathy under Fire." *Phi Kappa Phi Forum* (2011): 18–19.

Field Marshal Sir William Robertson: Chief of the Imperial General Staff in the Great War. Westwood, Conn.: Praeger, 1998.

Lloyd George and the Generals. London and New York: Frank Cass, 2004.

(ed.). *Military Correspondence of Field Marshal Sir William Robertson: Chief of the Imperial General Staff, December 1915–February 1918.* London: Bodley Head, 1989.

Trial by Friendship: Anglo-American Relations, 1917–1918. Lexington: University Press of Kentucky, 1993.

World War I Almanac. New York: Facts on File, 2009.

Yockelson, Mitchell. *Borrowed Soldiers: Americans under British Command, 1918.* Norman: University of Oklahoma Press, 2008.

"'We Have Found Each Other at Last': Americans and Australians at the Battle of Hamel in July 1918." *Army History* 65 (2007): 17–25.

Zabecki, David T. *Steel Wind: Colonel Georg Bruchmüller and the Birth of Modern Artillery.* Westport, Conn.: Praeger, 1995.

Zieger, Robert. *America's Great War: World War I and the American Experience.* Lanham, Md.: Roman & Littlefield Publishers, 2001.

Index